Communication Mosaics

An Introduction to the Field of Communication

7e

Lineberger Distinguished Professor of Humanities

Caroline H. and Thomas S. Royster Distinguished Professor of Graduate Education

The University of North Carolina at Chapel Hill

D0207174

WADSWORTH
CENGAGE Learning

Australia • Brazil • Japan • Korea • Mexico • Singapore • Spain • United Kingdom • United States

Communication Mosaics: An Introduction to the Field of Communication, Seventh Edition
Julia T. Wood

Editor in Chief: Lyn Uhl

Publisher: Monica Eckman

Development Editor: Julie Martinez

Editorial Assistant: Colin Solan

Media Editor: Jessica Badiner

Marketing Manager: Jo Confalone

Marketing Coordinator: Brittany Blais

Marketing Communications Manager: Linda Yip

Content Project Manager: Dan Saabye

Art Director: Linda May

Print Buyer: Doug Bertke

Rights Acquisition Specialist: Alex Ricciardi

Production Service: Integra

Text Designer: Ke Design

Cover Designer: Ke Design

Cover Image Student Edition: Erick Davis

Cover Image International Student Edition: Shutterstock

Compositor: Integra

For product information and technology assistance, contact us at
Cengage Learning Customer & Sales Support, 1-800-354-9706
For permission to use material from this text or product, submit all requests online at **www.cengage.com/permissions.**
Further permissions questions can be emailed to
permissionrequest@cengage.com.

Library of Congress Control Number: 2012935927

ISBN-13: 978-0-840-02818-1

ISBN-10: 0-840-02818-0

Wadsworth
20 Channel Center Street
Boston, MA 02210
USA

Cengage Learning is a leading provider of customized learning solutions with office locations around the globe, including Singapore, the United Kingdom, Australia, Mexico, Brazil and Japan. Locate your local office at **international.cengage.com/region**

Cengage Learning products are represented in Canada by Nelson Education, Ltd.

For your course and learning solutions, visit **www.cengage.com.**

Purchase any of our products at your local college store or at our preferred online store **www.cengagebrain.com.**
Instructors: Please visit **login.cengage.com** and log in to access instructor-specific resources.

Printed in Canada
1 2 3 4 5 6 7 16 15 14 13 12

Brief Contents

Contents

Part II: Communication Processes and Skills

3 Perceiving and Understanding   43

7 Creating Communication Climates   133

8 Adapting Communication to Cultures and Social Communities   156

Part III: Contexts of Communication

List of Boxes

SHARPEN YOUR SKILL

FYI CAREER

FYI—ENGAGEMENT

FYI—Diversity

FYI—Technology

Preface

I wrote *Communication Mosaics* to support survey courses that introduce students to the broad and exciting field of communication. Unlike other versions of the introductory course, the survey approach usually doesn't include performance assignments such as giving speeches. Instead, the survey course aims to provide a comprehensive view of the communication field, giving attention to topics beyond those that can be covered in performance oriented introductory classes—such topics include mass communication, organizational communication, and digital communication—and focusing on conceptual understanding of the breadth and importance of communication in many spheres of our lives.

Responses to earlier editions of this book indicate that many faculty appreciate a textbook specifically designed to support a survey approach to the introductory course. Student feedback to previous editions and fifteen years of class testing indicate that students, too, find *Communication Mosaics* useful in giving them an expansive introduction to the communication discipline. In addition to welcoming the approach of this book, faculty and students have been generous in offering suggestions, which I've used to improve this edition.

In the pages that follow, I explain my vision of this book and the features I've woven into it and then call attention to changes I made in preparing the current edition.

Communication as a Mosaic

As the title of the book suggests, communication is an intricate mosaic composed of parts that are distinct yet interrelated. All of the parts work together to create the whole of communication. This book increases students' awareness of the importance of basic communication skills and processes and shows students how those common elements surface in specific forms and contexts of communication.

The book is divided into three parts. Part I introduces students to the discipline of communication, discusses foundations for the study of communication, and describes careers for people who have strong communication backgrounds and skills. Chapter 1 introduces the book, identifies values of studying communication, defines and models communication, and describes careers for people who have strong academic training in communication. Chapter 2 surveys the discipline's evolution and methods of conducting research so that students understand the long and rich intellectual history of the field. This chapter also highlights the discipline's breadth by identifying its primary areas of study and teaching. Part II consists of six chapters, each of which focuses on one of the basic processes and skills that are central to a range of communication situations and goals. These basic communication skills and processes are:

▶ Perceiving and understanding

▶ Engaging in verbal communication

▶ Engaging in nonverbal communication

▶ Listening and responding

▶ Creating communication climates

▶ Adapting communication to cultures and social communities

These basic skills and processes shape the character and effectiveness of communication in a wide range of settings, although how each functions varies from one context to another. For example, we may use different listening skills when trying to understand a close friend and attending to television news.

Part III shows how the basic communication processes and skills covered in Part II function in seven specific contexts:

▶ Communication and personal identity

▶ Communication in personal relationships

▶ Communication in groups and teams

▶ Communication in organizations

▶ Public speaking

▶ Mass communication

▶ Digital media

The CourseMate for *Communication Mosaics* includes a chapter-length discussion of how the processes and skills covered in Part II apply to interviewing.

Features of *Communication Mosaics*

Accenting this book are six features that enhance students' learning and ensure the scholarly integrity of content.

Accessible, Conversational Style

Students who have reviewed this book say that the personal writing style motivated them to read the chapters and made it easier for them to apply ideas in the book to their lives. For this reason, in the current edition I retain the conversational style that encourages students to engage the ideas in this book. I refer to myself as "I" rather than "the author," and I address students as "you" rather than "the student." I also use informal language, such as contractions, just as people do in everyday conversations. In the opening chapter of the book, I introduce myself to students so they know something about my view of communication and my motivations for writing this book.

Another way in which I've personalized my writing style is by including examples from a range of people. At times, I offer reflections from my own life. In addition, I enlarge the conversation beyond just the reader and me by including in all chapters reflective comments from students at my university and other campuses around the country. To protect privacy, I've changed the names of the students who wrote the commentaries.

Learning about communication should be enjoyable. I don't think textbooks have to be dry or burdened with unnecessary jargon. When it's necessary to use specialized terms, I define them so that students understand what they mean, but I've written this book in an accessible, personal style to make it more interesting to read.

Foundation in Research and Theory

A textbook is only as good as the research and theory on which it is built. *Communication Mosaics* draws on the impressive body of research and theory developed by scholars of communication. Although I include important work from scholars in other fields, I draw most heavily on the published research of communication scholars because it is most directly relevant to the topics discussed in this book.

Communication Mosaics reflects my belief that theory and practice go together. Years ago, renowned scholar Kurt Lewin said, "There is nothing so practical as good theory." His words remain true today. In this book, I blend theory and practice so that each draws on and enriches the other. Effective practice is theoretically informed: It is based on knowledge of how and why the communication process works and what is likely to result from different kinds of communication. At the same time, effective theories have pragmatic value: They help us understand experiences in our everyday lives. Each chapter in this book is informed by the impressive theories and research generated by scholars of communication and other fields. To ensure that the perspectives and skills in this book reflect current knowledge of effective communication practices, this edition includes more than 170 new references.

Integrated Attention to Social Diversity

Social diversity is a defining feature of our era. The United States and the world include people of different ages, sexual orientations, gender identities, races and ethnicities, sexes, abilities, spiritual commitments, and economic circumstances.

These differences affect how we communicate. Thus, the idea of universal communication goals and principles must be replaced with understandings of how diverse people use communication to accomplish distinct goals and how they adapt communication to fit a range of social and cultural contexts. *Communication Mosaics* emphasizes social diversity in three specific ways. First, Chapter 8 offers in-depth coverage of the relationships between communication and culture: how cultural factors influence communication style, how communication shapes culture, and how we adapt our ways of communicating to particular people and contexts. Second, I weave research on social diversity into all chapters of the book. For example, Chapter 10 explains differences in how women and men typically communicate in personal relationships. Third, examples in the chapters, as well as photographs, feature a wide range of people and contexts.

Coverage of Digital Media

Online communication, Facebook, texting, tweeting, and other digital media increasingly infuse our lives, and this is reflected throughout this edition of *Communication*

Mosaics. Every chapter includes examples and research related to both mass communication and digital media we use for social, educational, professional, and political purposes. For example, Chapter 4 notes how language has changed in response to digital technologies. We have coined new words (*hypertext, IM*) and developed new meanings for existing words (*mouse, hamster*). Email, IMs and texting have led to abbreviated ways of communicating: brb (be right back), h8 (hate), AYT (are you there?), 2G2BT (too good to be true), 9 (parent in room) 99 (parent is no longer watching or no longer in room) and dropping vowels in words (whl = while, nxt = next, dnt = don't, tmrw or 2mrw = tomorrow). Chapter 10's coverage of personal relationships examines how personal and social media affect the ways in which we meet and get to know friends and romantic partners and the means we have for maintaining long-distance relationships. You will also find a full chapter, Chapter 15, on digital media. In this chapter, I discuss the ways we use digital media and then explore how they affect the ways we think, relate, and act in personal, professional, and social contexts. Finally, I've integrated FYI: Digital Media boxes throughout the book to highlight emerging information about computer-mediated communication.

I've also included technology to extend students' learning online. You and your students have access to the CourseMate for *Communication Mosaics*—for details, see Resources for Students and Instructors, below.

Student Commentaries

Woven into each chapter are commentaries from students' journals and papers. Although students in my classes wrote many of these, students at other universities have also sent me their reflections, many of which are included in this edition. I include student commentaries because in more than 30 years of teaching I've learned that students have much to teach each other and their instructors. The commentaries show how different people relate communication principles and research to their own lives. I encourage students who use this edition to send me their comments and reflections so the next edition can reflect their perspectives and experiences too.

Pedagogical Features

This book includes six features that are specifically designed to maximize learning.

Focus Questions

Opening each chapter are focus questions that orient students to the chapter and help them organize how they read and study the material.

For Your Information (FYI)

Featured in each chapter are "For Your Information" boxes that highlight communication research and the role of communication in everyday life. I use these boxes to call students' attention to particularly interesting and important aspects of communication in a variety of settings. In this edition, some of the FYI boxes specifically focus on communication relevant to careers (FYI: Career), digital media and the online environment (FYI: Digital Media), and diversity (FYI: Diversity), all of which are key themes of communication in our era.

Practical Application

More than previous editions, this edition emphasizes practical application of communication principles and concepts. Every chapter in Parts II and III of this edition provides concrete guidelines for communicating effectively (appearing in a highlighted section under the heading "Guidelines for …"). In addition, each chapter includes selected "Sharpen Your Skill" exercises that invite students to apply skills and principles as they read about them. Some of these exercises encourage students to practice a particular skill, perhaps by engaging in civic life or service learning. Others invite students to observe how communication concepts and principles discussed in the text show up in everyday interactions. Still others ask students to reflect on the ways in which particular skills, theories, or concepts have shaped who they are and how they communicate. Finally, at the end of each chapter, I include questions that invite students to discuss, reflect on, and apply what they've learned in the chapter.

End-of-Chapter Resources

Following each chapter are study resources gathered under the heading Review, Reflect, Extend. These resources include questions that encourage students to reflect on what they have read and to extend and apply the material presented in the chapter, as well as a list of key concepts (with page references), and further recommended resources, including articles, books, films, and Web sites.

Highlighted Key Terms

Within each chapter, I've boldfaced key concepts and terms that students should learn. All boldfaced terms are repeated in a list at the end of each chapter to encourage students to check their retention after they have read the chapter. By each term, I've noted the page on which the term first appears and is defined so that students can easily review concepts. Boldfaced terms are also defined in the glossary at the end of the book.

Experience Communication Case Study

At the end of each chapter, I present a short case study that illustrates how ideas covered in the chapter show up in actual communication. To make the cases engaging and realistic, the CourseMate for *Communication Mosaics* also provides videos in which professional actors perform the scenarios presented in each case study. Questions that encourage students to apply chapter theories and principles accompany the case studies.

Please note that the transcripts at the ends of Chapters 2 and 13, and the online videos available for each are not case studies. Instead, the scenario for Chapter 2 features Tim Muehlhoff, a professor of communication at Biola University, being interviewed by a student about the relevance of ethics to communication, and the video for Chapter 13 is a speech by Elizabeth Lopez, a student in an introductory public speaking class.

Changes in This Edition

Because I teach at a public university, I'm very sensitive to the cost of textbooks. I am not willing to publish new editions of my books with only cosmetic changes. Instead, I insist that a new edition offer substantive changes to justify the expense to students. I believe instructors who are familiar with previous editions of this book will notice significant changes in this edition that are responsive to generous feedback from instructors and students.

As I mentioned, to prepare this edition I read many reviews of the previous editions. Some reviews were written by instructors who teach a basic communication course. Instructors' feedback led me to make the following changes.

Revised Coverage of Digital Media

Faculty who have adopted previous editions of this book will notice that Chapter 15, Digital Media, has been significantly revised in response to reviewers' and students' feedback. I have abbreviated coverage of the history of media technologies, and added new material on how we use digital media to craft identities, connect with others, and participate in education, work, and political and social organizing. I've also enriched the discussion of controversies about digital media.

In addition to revising Chapter 15, this edition further integrates attention to digital media into all chapters by discussing the ways they affect how we live, learn, work, and interact. Throughout the book, I identify related online resources for students that can be accessed via WebLinks provided at the CourseMate for *Communication Mosaics*. Finally, I've also included more FYI boxes (FYI: Digital Media) that focus on digital media that affect communication in our everyday lives.

Increased Intercultural Communication Coverage

In Chapter 8, Adapting Communication to Cultures and Social Communities, I added a new section on cultural values and discussed the five dimensions of culture.

The Latest Knowledge about Human Communication

This edition includes more than 170 new references. This strong infusion of new research ensures that *Communication Mosaics* reflects up-to-date scholarship. For example, Chapter 8 (Cultures and Social Communities) has expanded coverage of cultural values that shape how people communicate. Chapter 11 (Group Communication) includes new material on arbitration and mediation, which are third-party methods of managing conflict, and discusses the nominal group technique as a method of organizing group work. Chapter 14 (Mass Communication) has been revised to include greater attention to the ways we use mass media and are used by it. And, as noted above, I have rewritten Chapter 15 (Computer-Mediated Communication) to reflect the latest knowledge about how personal and social media fit into our lives.

Streamlined Presentation

I've worked to avoid the phenomenon of "page creep," which happens when authors add new material to each new edition of a book without condensing or eliminating any of the material in previous editions. Throughout the book, I've reduced the number of features, tightened prose, and eliminated dated research. This edition is no longer than the previous one, yet it includes new information and the most essential application of concepts and principles.

As part of streamlining the book and reducing production costs, I decided not to include coverage of interviewing. Previous editions included an appendix on interviewing. That appendix is now available online at CourseMate for *Communication Mosaics*.

I hope that this edition of *Communication Mosaics* retains the strengths that instructors and students found in previous editions while also benefiting from their generous suggestions for improvement.

Resources for Students and Instructors

Accompanying this book is an integrated suite of resources to support both students and instructors, many of which are available free of charge when you order them or access to them for your students.

Please note: If you want your students to have access to the online resources for this handbook, please be sure to order them for your course. The content in these resources can be bundled with every new copy of the text or ordered separately. If you do not order them, your students will not have access to these online resources. Please consult your local Wadsworth Cengage Learning sales representative or **www.cengagebrain.com** for more information, user names and passwords, examination copies, or a demonstration of these ancillary products. Available to qualified adopters.

Instructor Resources

Instructors who adopt this book can request a number of resources to support their teaching.

▶ **The Instructor's Resource Manual,** by Ronald Shope of Grace University, offers guidelines for setting up your course, sample syllabi, chapter-by-chapter outlines of content, suggested topics for lectures and discussion, and a wealth of class-tested exercises and assignments. It also includes a test bank with questions marked according to varying levels of difficulty.

▶ **Instructor's Web site.** The password-protected instructor's Web site includes electronic access to the Instructor's Resource Manual and downloadable versions of the book's Microsoft® PowerPoint® slides. To gain access to the Web site, simply request a course key by opening the site's home page.

▶ **PowerLecture.** This one-stop lecture tool makes it easy for you to use using Microsoft PowerPoint to assemble, edit, publish, and present custom lectures for your course. The PowerLecture CD-ROM lets you bring together text-specific lecture outlines and art, along with video and animations from the Web or your own materials—culminating in a powerful, personalized, media-enhanced presentation. Additionally, the CD-ROM offers an electronic version of the Instructor Resource Manual, test bank, ExamView® software, videos, and JoinIn™ on Turning Point® lecture slides.

▶ **ExamView Computerized Testing** enables you to create, deliver, and customize tests and study guides (both print and online) in minutes using the test bank questions from the Instructor's Resource Manual. ExamView offers both a Quick Test Wizard and an Online Test Wizard that guide you step-by-step through the process of creating tests, while its "what you see is what you get" interface allows you to see the test you·are creating on-screen exactly as it will print or display online. You can build tests of up to 250 questions, using up to 12 question types. Using the complete word processing capabilities of ExamView, you can even enter an unlimited number of new questions or edit existing ones.

▶ **JoinIn on TurningPoint.** JoinIn content for Response Systems is tailored to *Communication Mosaics,* allowing you to transform your classroom and assess your students' progress with instant in-class quizzes and polls. TurningPoint software lets you pose book-specific questions and display students' answers seamlessly within the Microsoft PowerPoint slides of your own lecture, in conjunction with the "clicker" hardware of your choice. Enhance how your students interact with you, your lecture, and each other.

▶ **ABC News DVDs for Human Communication, Interpersonal Communication, and Public Speaking.** Launch your lectures with riveting footage from ABC. Footage from *Nightline, World News Tonight,* and *Good Morning America* provides context and real-life examples of communication theories and practices. Footage includes discussion of dozens of communication topics—including family "virtual visitation," cell phone spam, and professional nonverbal communication— as well as significant speeches by public figures.

▶ **Student Speeches for Critique and Analysis on Video and DVD.** These eight volumes offer a variety of sample student speeches that your students can watch, critique, and analyze on their own or in class. All of the speech types are included, as well as speeches featuring nonnative English speakers and the use of visual aids.

▶ **ABC News DVD: Speeches by Barack Obama.** This DVD includes nine famous speeches by President Barack Obama, from 2004 to present day, including his speech at the 2004 Democratic National Convention; his 2008 speech on race, "A More Perfect Union"; and his 2009 inaugural address. Speeches are divided into short video segments for easy, time-efficient viewing. This instructor supplement also features critical thinking questions and answers for each speech, designed to spark class discussion.

▶ **Special-Topic Instructor's Manuals.** Written by Deanna Sellnow, University of Kentucky, these three brief manuals provide instructor resources for teaching public speaking online, with a service-learning approach, and with a problem-based learning approach that focuses on critical thinking and teamwork skills. Each manual includes course syllabi; icebreakers; information about learning cycles and learning styles; and public speaking basics such as coping with anxiety, outlining, and speaking ethically.

▶ *The Teaching Assistant's Guide to the Basic Course* is available to instructors who adopt this textbook. Katherine G. Hendrix, who is on the faculty at the University of Memphis, prepared this resource specifically for new instructors. Based on leading communication teacher training programs, this guide discusses some of the general issues that accompany a teaching role and offers specific strategies for managing the first week of classes, leading productive discussions, managing sensitive topics in the classroom, and grading students' written and oral work.

▶ **TLC Technology Training and Support.** Get trained, get connected, and get the support you need for seamless integration of technology resources into your course with Technology Learning Connected (TLC). This unparalleled technology service and training program provides robust online resources, peer-to-peer instruction, personalized training, and a customizable program you can count on. Visit http://academic.cengage.com/tlc to sign up for online seminars, first days of class services, technical support, or personalized, face-to-face training. Our online or onsite training sessions are frequently led by one of our lead teachers, faculty members who are experts in using Wadsworth Cengage Learning technology and can provide best practices and teaching tips.

▶ **Flex-Text customization program.** Create a text as unique as your course: quickly, simply, and affordably. As part of our flex-text program you can add your personal touch to *Communication Mosaics* with a course-specific cover and up to 32 pages of your own content, at no additional cost. Bonus chapters available now include chapters from *Communication in Our Lives* about public speaking (Planning Public Speaking, Researching and Developing Support for Public Speeches, Organizing and Presenting Public Speeches, Informative Speaking, and/or Persuasive Speaking), as well as discussions of public speaking and civic engagement, advice on conquering speech anxiety, and tips for helping ESL students master the basic course.

Student Resources

Students have the option of utilizing a rich array of resources to enhance and extend their learning while using *Communication Mosaics*.

▶ **CourseMate for *Communication Mosaics*.** This comprehensive site offers a variety of rich learning resources designed to enhance the student experience. These resources include an online appendix on interviewing, an online student companion, interactive video activities, Web Links, self-assessments, Audio Study Tools chapter downloads, InfoTrac College Edition, chapter outlines, flash cards and other resources for mastering glossary terms, and chapter quizzes that help students check their understanding of key concepts. Links to related TED Talks videos from global TED conferences are also provided. All resources are mapped to both key discipline learning concepts as well as specific chapter learn lists.

▶ The **Student Companion** to this edition, which I wrote with L.M. Edmonds of Arizona State University, is available online through the CourseMate and provides students with interactive summaries of chapter content, vocabulary lists, self-tests, and practical activities that help them to develop skills in communicating and apply those skills in their everyday interactions.

▶ The **interactive video activities** feature video of all the Experience Communication Case Studies in the book. These activities let students view the communication scenarios; compare the student speakers with three types of outlines; embed notes on the video; and complete critique and evaluation assignments, which students can check against my suggested answers.

▶ **Audio Study Tools.** This text's mobile content provides a fun and easy way for students to review chapter content whenever and wherever. For each chapter of the text, students will have access to a brief communication scenario example and a five- to seven-minute review consisting of a brief summary of the main points in the text and five to seven review questions. Students can purchase these tools through iChapters (see below) and download files to their computers, iPods, or other MP3 players.

▶ **InfoTrac College Edition™ with InfoMarks™.** This online library provides access to more than 18 million reliable, full-length articles from over 5,000 academic and popular periodicals. Students also have access to InfoMarks—stable URLs that can be linked to articles, journals, and searches to save valuable time when doing research—*and* to the InfoWrite online resource center, where students can access grammar help, critical thinking guidelines, guides to writing research papers, and much more. For more information about InfoTrac College Edition and the InfoMarks linking tool, visit **http://www.infotrac-college.com** and click on "User Demo."

▶ *The Art and Strategy of Service-Learning Presentations*, **Second Edition,** is available bundled with *Communication Mosaics*. Authored by Rick Isaacson and Jeff Saperstein of San Francisco State University, this handbook provides guidelines for connecting service-learning work with classroom concepts and advice for working effectively with agencies and organizations.

▶ *A Guide to the Basic Course for ESL Students* is available bundled with the book. Specifically for communicators whose first language is not English, it features FAQs, helpful URLs, and strategies for managing communication anxiety.

▶ **iChapters.com.** This online store provides students with exactly what they've been asking for: choice, convenience, and savings. A 2005 research study by the National Association of College Stores indicates that as many as 60 percent of students do not purchase all required course material; however, those who do are more likely to succeed. This research also tells us that students want the ability to purchase "á la carte" course material in the format that suits them best. Accordingly, iChapters.com is the only online store that offers eBooks at up to 50 percent off, eChapters for as low as $1.99 each, and new textbooks at up to 25 percent off, plus up to 25 percent off print and digital supplements that can help improve student performance.

Acknowledgments

Although my name is the only one that appears as the author of this book, I could not have written it without the help of many people. I want to take a moment to acknowledge the support and assistance of a number of people who have influenced how I think and write.

I am deeply indebted to the Wadsworth Cengage Learning team. Everyone on that team has been extraordinarily professional and helpful throughout the evolution of this book. Leading the group is Monica Eckman, executive editor for Communication Studies, whose energy, support, and insight seem infinite. In addition to Monica, I am grateful to other key members of the team: Lyn Uhl, senior publisher; and Rebekah Matthews, assistant editor. Also integral to the development of this edition were Joanna Confalone, marketing manager; Colin Solan, editorial assistant; Jessica Badiner, media editor; Heather Preston, copy editor; Dan Saaybe, content production manager; Michelle Dellinger, project manager; Kathleen Shapiro, proofreader; Alex Ricciardi, rights acquisition specialist; Pradeep Kumar, image permissions researcher; and Melissa Tomaselli, text permissions researcher. This book is truly a collaborative effort that involved and reflects the contributions of everyone on the team.

I am particularly grateful to scholars and teachers of communication who contributed helpful comments and suggestions that guided this revision: Emily Anzicek, Bowling Green State University; Tyler Bagwell, College of Coastal Georgia; Farah Chase-Dunn, Utah Valley University; Janet Colvin, Utah Valley University; Jill Hall, Jefferson Community and Technical College; Bruce McKinney, University of North Carolina Wilmington; Greg Rickert, Bluegrass Community & Technical College; Kathleen J. Turner, Davidson College; and Bruce Wickelgren, Suffolk University.

I am also indebted to the reviewers of this book's previous editions: Jess K. Alberts, Arizona State University; Mary Allen, Valencia Community College; Bob Alexander, University of Louisiana at Monroe; Karen Anderson, University of North Texas; Cheryl Bailey, Western Illinois University; Marcia Berry, Azusa Pacific University; Jodi Bromley, Old Dominion University; Peggy Brønn, Norwegian School of Management; Eric Carlson, Collin College; Mary Carpenter, New York University; Diane O. Casagrande, West Chester University; Anita Chirco, Keuka College; Robert A. Cole, State University of New York Oswego; Stephanie J. Coopman, San Jose State University; Janine Crouch, Tidewater Community College; Marcia Dixson, Indiana–Purdue at Fort Wayne; Carol Dostal, Indiana–Purdue at Fort Wayne; Michelle Douglas, University of Arkansas at Little Rock; Wesley Durham, University of Southern Indiana; Tresha Dutton, Whatcom Community College; Belle A. Edson, Arizona State University; Ann Bainbridge Frymier, Miami University; Darin Garard, Santa Barbara City College; Susan Cain Giusto, Augusta State University; Jo Anna Grant, California State University, San Bernardino; Jonathan M. Gray, Southern Illinois University–Carbondale; Jonathan M. Gray, Southern Illinois University Carbondale; Jill Hall, Jefferson Community College; Joy L. Hart, University of Louisville; Javette Hayes, California State University, Fullerton; Patrick Herbert, Northeast Louisiana University; Christine Hirsch, State University of New York at Oswego; Jodee Hobbs,

Northeast Louisiana University; Shannon Hokanson, Monmouth University; Bobbie R. Klopp, Kirkwood Community College; Branislav Kovacic, University of Hartford; Ee Lin Lee, Western Washington University; Krista Longtin, Indiana University–Purdue University Indianapolis; Matt McAllister, Virginia Tech; Shannon McCraw, Southeastern Oklahoma State University; Sandra Metts, Illinois State University; Darrin S. Murray, Loyola Marymount University; Teresa A. Nance, Villanova University; Mark Nelson, University of Alabama; Kim P. Niemczyk, Palm Beach Community College; Shirley Oakley, Coastal Georgia Community College; Marjukka Ollilainen, Virginia Tech; Clark D. Olson, Arizona State University; Lynn Orr, William Paterson University; Rebecca Parker, Western Illinois University; Beth Patrick-Trippel, Olivet Nazarene University; Nan Peck, Northern Virginia County College; Laura Wheeler Poms, George Mason University; Doug Radke, Blue Mountain Community College; Valerie Renegar, San Diego State University; Cynthia A. Ridle, Western Illinois University; Diane Ryan, Tidewater Community College; Mark A. Schlesinger, University of Massachusetts–Boston; Helen M. Sterk, Marquette University; Sharlene R. Thompson, University of Oklahoma; Kyle Tusing, University of Arizona; Scott Vitz, Indiana–Purdue at Fort Wayne; Guy Warner, Augusta State University; John T. Warren, Bowling Green State University; Sue L. Wenzlaff, Austin Peay State University, David W. Worley, Indiana State University; Catherine Wright, George Mason University; and Joseph B. Zubrick, University of Maine–Presque Isle.

The ideas in this book were also influenced by students in my classes and by students at other colleges and universities around the country. They provided insightful feedback and suggestions for ways to improve *Communication Mosaics*. In class discussions, conferences, e-mail notes, and written comments, students push me to do more and tell me which communication issues are prominent in their lives. Invariably, students teach me at least as much as I teach them. Because students are so thoughtful, I include many of their reflections as Student Voices in this book.

Finally, I thank those with whom I am closest. For more than 38 years, Robert (Robbie) Cox has been my partner in love, life, and work. Robbie is my greatest fan and my most rigorous critic, and both his support and his criticism shape all that I write. Special friends, Shelly and Robin, sharpen my thinking and writing by testing my ideas against their experiences communicating with others. My sister Carolyn remains one of the most positive, perceptive, and delightful presences in my life, as do my youngest friends: Michelle, who is 23; Daniel, who is 19; and Harrison, who is 15. These young people continuously remind me of the magic and wonder in human relationships. And of course I must express my appreciation to the four-legged members of our family: our dog, Cassidy, and our kittens, Rowdy and Rigby. When I am having a bad writing day, these three remind me that playing ball and brushing them are important parts of life.

What we do in life is determined by how we communicate.... In the modern world, the quality of life is the quality of communication. Tony Robbins

1

A First Look at Communication

▶ Whenever there is a hint of disagreement between members of your community service team, the leader jumps in and smooths things over. What can you do to ensure that conflict is allowed and managed well so the team can be thorough and critical in its work?

▶ At the end of this term, the person you've been dating will graduate and take a job in a city a thousand miles away. You're concerned about sustaining the relationship when you have to communicate across the distance.

▶ At work, you're on a team that includes people from Mexico and Germany. You've noticed that in some ways they communicate differently from American-born workers. You aren't sure how to interpret their styles of communicating or how to interact effectively with them.

▶ You can't keep up with your e-mail, texts, and voice mail. You don't want to be out of touch with the world, but you sometimes feel overwhelmed by the sheer amount of information that comes in every day.

▶ You volunteer at a literacy center where you teach children as well as adults to read. You believe the program would be more effective if the director did more to build a sense of

FOCUS QUESTIONS

1. What are the benefits of studying communication?

2. How is communication defined?

3. What communication processes and skills are relevant in all contexts?

4. How do different models represent the process of human communication?

5. What careers are open to people with strong backgrounds in communication?

1

community among volunteers. You're wondering how you might encourage her to do that without seeming to criticize her.

▶ A major political figure speaks at your campus, and you attend. You try to listen carefully, but you aren't sure how to evaluate what the speaker says.

From the moment we arise until we go to bed, our days are filled with communication challenges and opportunities. Unlike some subjects you study, communication is relevant to every aspect of your life. We communicate with ourselves when we psych ourselves up for big moments and talk ourselves into or out of various courses of action. We communicate with others to build and sustain personal relationships, perform our jobs, advance in our careers, and participate in social and civic activities. Even when we're not around other people, we are involved in communication as we interact with mass media, personal media, and social media. All facets of our lives involve communication.

Although we communicate continually, we aren't always effective. People who do not have strong communication knowledge and skills are limited in their efforts to achieve personal, professional, civic, and social goals. In contrast, people who communicate well have a strong advantage in personal, social, civic, and professional life. Therefore, learning about communication and developing your skills as a communicator are keys to a successful and fulfilling life.

Communication Mosaics is written for anyone who is interested in human communication. If you are a communication major, this book and the course it accompanies will give you a firm foundation for more-advanced study. If you are majoring in another discipline, you will gain a basic understanding of communication, and you will have opportunities to strengthen your skills as a communicator so that you are effective in your personal and professional life.

This first chapter provides an overview of the book and the discipline of communication. To open the chapter, I first introduce myself and point out the perspective and features of the book. Second, I describe how communication affects our personal, social, civic, and professional life. Third, I define communication and discuss progressively sophisticated models of the communication process. Finally, I identify careers that people with strong backgrounds in communication are qualified to pursue.

An Introduction to the Author

© Julia T. Wood

As an undergraduate, I enrolled in a course much like the one you're taking now. In that course, I became fascinated by the field of communication, and my interest has endured for more than 40 years. Today, I am still captivated by the field—more than ever, in fact. I see communication both as a science that involves skills and knowledge and as an art that reflects human imagination and wisdom. Because communication is central to personal, social, professional, and civic life, it is one of the most dynamic, fastest-growing areas of study in higher education.

When I was a student, I always wondered about the authors of my textbooks. Who were they? Why did they write the books I was assigned to read? Unfortunately, the authors never introduced themselves, so I didn't get answers to my questions about them. I want to start our relationship differently by telling you something about myself. I am a 60-year-old, middle-income, European-American woman who has strong spiritual beliefs and a deep commitment to public education. For 38 years, I have been married to Robbie (Robert) Cox, a professor and a leader of the national Sierra Club.

As is true for all of us, who I am affects what I know and how I think, feel, and communicate. Therefore, some of what you'll read in this book reflects what I have learned in my research, teaching, and life. I grew up in a small rural town in the South. I also grew up in a time marked by movements for civil rights and women's rights, which shaped my values and fueled my commitment to civic engagement. Research by other scholars also informs my perspective. The hundreds of references at the end of this book have shaped both my understanding of human communication and the way I introduce you to the field.

Other facets of my identity also influence what I know and how I write. My thinking is influenced by my roles as a daughter, sister, romantic partner, friend, aunt, teacher, and member of civic groups. On a broader level, I am defined by the categories that Western culture uses to classify people—for instance, race, gender, socioeconomic level, and sexual orientation. Belonging to these culturally created categories has given me certain insights and has limited other insights. As a woman, I understand discrimination based on sex because I've experienced it multiple times. Being middle class has shielded me from personal experience with hunger, poverty, and bias against the poor; and being heterosexual has spared me from being the direct target of homophobia. Because Western culture tends to treat whites as the norm, not as a racial category, I was not socialized to think about my race and its meaning. However, critical race theorists have taught me to interrogate whiteness as fully as any other racial category.

Although I can use cultural categories to describe myself, they aren't as clear or definitive as we sometimes think. For instance, the category "woman" isn't homogeneous. Women differ from one another because of race–ethnicity, sexual orientation, socioeconomic status, ability and disability, and a range of other factors. Likewise, a particular race is not a homogenous category. Members of any race differ greatly as a result of factors such as ethnic background, gender, sexual orientation, socioeconomic status, spiritual and religious values, abilities and disabilities, and so forth. The same is true of people we can place in any category—they are alike in the particular way that defines the category, yet they are also different from one another in many ways.

Like me, your experiences and group memberships have shaped your identity and your perspectives. How are you similar to and different from others who belong to the same culturally defined groups in which you place yourself? If you are a man, for instance, how is your identity as a man influenced by your racial and ethnic background, socioeconomic status, sexual orientation, spiritual commitments, and so forth? What insights does your identity facilitate and hamper?

Although our identities limit what we personally know and experience, they don't completely prevent us from gaining insight into people and situations that are different from our own. As I mentioned before, critical race theorists have taught me to think analytically about whiteness as a racial category. I've also learned from watching others communicate in situations at my workplace and in community groups. Mass media and computer-mediated communication have given me insight into diverse people and situations all over the world. All of these resources allow me—and will allow you, if you choose—to move beyond the limits of personal identity and experiences to appreciate and participate in the larger world. What we learn by studying and interacting with people from different cultures and social communities expands our appreciation of the richness and complexity of humanity. In addition, interacting with people whose lives and communication differ from our own enlarges our repertoires of communication skills.

An Introduction to *Communication Mosaics*

To provide a context for your reading, let me share my vision for this book. Its title reflects the idea that communication is an intricate mosaic composed of basic processes and skills that are relevant to the range of situations in which we interact. Although all of the basic processes and skills affect communication in every situation, the prominence of each one varies according to context. For instance, in public speaking, presentation style stands out, and communication climate is less obvious. Conversely, in team interaction, communication that nurtures a productive climate may be more pronounced than a commanding presentational style.

Communication Mosaics is divided into three parts. The first part comprises two chapters that introduce you to the discipline of communication by explaining its history, research methods, contemporary breadth, and career options. Part II introduces you to six basic communication processes, concepts, and skills:

▶ Perceiving and understanding others

▶ Engaging in verbal communication

▶ Engaging in nonverbal communication

▶ Listening and responding to others

▶ Creating and sustaining communication climates

▶ Adapting communication to cultural contexts

Each of these skills relates to all the others. For example, how we perceive other people is related to the ways we create and interpret verbal and nonverbal communication. The interaction climates we establish in personal and professional relationships are shaped by our listening skills and our verbal and nonverbal communication.

Because communication is a continuous part of life, we need to understand how the basic processes and skills covered in Part II relate to a broad spectrum of communication encounters. Part III explores seven communication contexts that are common in our lives:

▶ Communication with yourself

▶ Interaction with friends and romantic partners

▶ Communicating in groups and on teams

▶ Communication in organizations

▶ Public speaking

▶ Mass communication

▶ Digital media

The Value of Studying Communication

Communication is the seventh most popular field of undergraduate study (McKinney, 2006). One reason for this popularity is the relevance of communication knowledge and skills to career success. In order to advance in professional life, you'll need to know how to build good climates, monitor your perceptions, manage conflicts constructively, present your ideas effectively, and listen carefully. To have healthy, enduring relationships, you'll need to know how to communicate support, deal with conflicts, and understand communication styles that are different from your own. To be an engaged citizen, you'll need critical thinking skills and the verbal ability to express your own points of view. In short, communication skills are vital to personal and professional well-being and to the health of our communities and society.

Because you've been communicating all your life, you might ask why you need to study communication formally. One reason is that formal study can improve skill. Some people have a natural talent for music or athletics. Yet they can become even better musicians or athletes if they take voice lessons or study theories of offensive and defensive play. Likewise, even if you communicate well now, learning about communication can make you more effective. Theories and principles of communication help us make sense of what happens in our everyday lives, and they help us to have the impact we desire.

Personal Life

George Herbert Mead (1934) said that humans are talked into humanity. He meant that we gain our personal identities by interacting with others. In our earliest years, our parents told us who we were: "You're smart," "You're so strong," "You're such a clown." We first see ourselves through the eyes of others, so their messages form the foundations of our self-concepts. Later, we interact with teachers, friends, romantic partners, and co-workers who communicate their views of us. In addition, we learn who we are and how others perceive us as we engage mass communication and computer-mediated communication.

The profound connection between communication and identity is dramatically evident in children who are deprived of human contact. Case studies of children who have been isolated from others for a long time show that they have no concept of themselves as humans, and their mental and psychological development is severely hindered by lack of language. The FYI box on page 6 presents an extreme example of what can happen when human infants are deprived of interaction with other humans.

Substantial research shows that communicating with others promotes health, whereas social isolation is linked to stress, disease, and early death (Crowley, 1995; Fackelmann, 2006; Kupfer, First, & Regier, 2002; McClure, 1997). College students who are in committed relationships have fewer mental health problems and are less likely to be obese (Braithwaite, Delevi, & Fincham, 2010). Heart disease is more common among people who lack strong interpersonal relationships (Ornish, 1998), and cancer patients who are married live longer than single cancer patients ("Cancer," 2009). Clearly, healthy interaction with others is important to our physical and mental well-being.

Personal Relationships

Daniel Goleman, author of *Social Intelligence* (2007), says humans are "wired to connect" (p. 4). And communication—verbal and nonverbal, face to face or mediated—is the primary way that we connect with others. For that reason, effective communication

fyi DIVERSITY

Ghadya Ka Bacha

Ghadya Ka Bacha, or the "wolf boy," was found in 1954 outside a hospital in Balrampur, India. He had callused knees and hands, as if he moved on all fours, and he had scars on his neck, suggesting he had been dragged about by animals.

Ramu, which was the name the hospital staff gave the child, showed no interest in others but became very excited once when he saw wolves on a visit to the zoo. Ramu lapped his milk from a glass instead of drinking as we do, and he tore apart his food.

Most doctors who examined Ramu concluded that he had grown up with wolves and therefore acted like a wolf, not a person (Shattuck, 1980).

© Hulton Archive/Getty Images

In this photo, Ramu is eating raw meat. What do Ramu's behaviors suggest about how we develop self-concepts?

is the heart of personal relationships. We build connections with others by revealing our private identities, asking questions, working out problems, listening, remembering shared history, and making plans for the future. To learn more about Daniel Goleman's work, visit his site and blog by going to the book's online resources for this chapter and clicking WebLink 1.1.

A primary distinction between relationships that endure and those that collapse is the presence of effective communication. Couples who learn how to discuss their thoughts and feelings, adapt to each other, and manage conflict constructively tend to sustain intimacy over time. Friends also rely on good communication to keep in touch, provide support, and listen sensitively. The FYI box on the left demonstrates the centrality of good communication to marriage.

Communication in personal relationships does a lot more than solve problems or allow partners to make personal disclosures. For most of us, everyday talk and nonverbal interaction are the essence of relationships (Schmidt & Uecker, 2007; Wood & Duck, 2006a,b). Although dramatic moments affect relationships, it is our unremarkable, everyday interaction that sustains the daily rhythms of our intimate connections (Duck & McMahon, 2009; Wood & Duck, 2006a, b). Partners weave their lives together through small talk about mutual friends, daily events, and other mundane topics. Couples involved in long-distance romances miss being able to share small talk.

fyi Communication and Marriage

How important is communication to marriage? How much does poor communication contribute to divorce? A national poll conducted in 1998 found answers to these questions. Regardless of age, race, sex, or economic standing, Americans say communication problems are the number one cause of divorce. Fifty-three percent of those polled said lack of effective communication was the principal cause of divorce. Other causes lagged far behind. When asked the primary reason for divorce, 29 percent said money problems, 7 percent said interference from relatives, and 5 percent said sexual problems.

In addition to studying how communication enhances relationships, interpersonal communication scholars investigate the role of communication in destructive relationship patterns such as abuse and violence. Teresa Sabourin and Glen Stamp (1995) have identified strong links between verbal behaviors and reciprocal violence between spouses. Other communication scholars (Lloyd & Emery, 2000; Meyers, 1997; Wood, 2001b, 2004b) have documented a range of social and interpersonal influences on violence between intimates.

Sandy's comment is the first of many student voices you'll encounter in this book. In my classes, students teach me and each other by sharing their insights, experiences, and questions. Because I believe students have much to teach us, I've included reflections written by students at my university and other campuses. As you read these, you will probably identify with some, disagree with others, and be puzzled by still others. Whether you agree, disagree, or are perplexed, I think you will find that the student voices expand the text and spark thought and discussion in your class and elsewhere. I also welcome your comments about issues that strike you as you read this book. You may send them to me in care of Wadsworth Cengage Learning, 20 Channel Center Street, Boston, MA 02210.

 Sandy

When my boyfriend moved away, the hardest part wasn't missing the big moments. It was not talking about little stuff or just being together. It was like we weren't part of each other's life when we didn't talk about all the little things that happened or how we felt or whatever.

Professional Life

Communication skills are critical for success in professional life. The value of communication is clearly apparent in professions such as teaching, law, sales, and counseling, where talking and listening are central to effectiveness.

In other fields, the importance of communication may be less obvious, but it is nonetheless present. Leaders at organizations such as *The New York Times*, FedEx, and GlaxoSmithKline list communication as vital to their organizations' success (O'Hair & Eadie, 2009). Health-care professionals rely on communication skills to talk with patients about medical problems and courses of treatment and to gain cooperation from colleagues, patients, and families for continued care. Doctors who do not listen well are less effective in treating patients, and they're more likely to be sued than doctors who do listen well (Beckman, 2003; Levine, 2004; Milia, 2003). Further, good communication between doctors and patients is related to effective treatment and to patients' mental well-being (Fleishman, Sherbourne, & Crystal, 2000). The pivotal role of communication in health care makes it unsurprising that an increasing number of medical schools base admissions, in part, on applicants' communication skills, especially their ability to work in teams (Harris, 2011).

It's not surprising that 89 percent of employers surveyed in 2010 said colleges should focus on teaching students to communicate effectively to increase job success (Rhodes, 2010). Even highly technical jobs require communication skills. Specialists have to be able to listen carefully to their clients and customers in order to understand their needs. Specialists also need to be skilled in explaining technical ideas to people who lack their expertise. Ann Darling and Deanna Dannels (2003) asked engineers whether communication skills were important to their professional effectiveness. The engineers reported that their success on the job depended on listening well, presenting ideas clearly, and negotiating effectively with others. Fully 75 percent of the engineers said that communication skills had consequences for their career advancement. Sean, an older, returning student, makes this observation about the relevance of communication skills to his professional success:

 Sean

I'm taking this course because I need communication skills to do my job. I didn't think I would when I majored in computer science and went into technology development. But after two years, another guy and I decided to launch our own technical support company. We had trouble getting investors to provide start-up capital, because neither of us knew how to give an effective presentation. We had the tech skills but not the communication ones. Finally, we got our company launched and discovered that we didn't know much about how to supervise and lead either. Neither of us had ever taken courses in how to motivate and support people who work for you. So I'm taking this course as a night student, and I think it will make a major difference in how I do my job and whether our company succeeds.

Civic Life

Communication skills are vital to the health of our society. From painting on the walls of caves to telling stories in village squares to interacting on the Internet, people have found ways to communicate with each other to organize and improve their common social world (Keith, 2009). To be effective, citizens in a democracy must be able to express ideas and evaluate the ethical and logical strength of communication by public figures. To make informed judgments, voters need to listen critically to candidates' arguments and responses to questions. We also need to listen critically to proposals about goals for our communities, the institutions at which we work, and the organizations on which we depend for services.

Civic engagement is more than paying attention to politics and voting. It is also working with others—formally and informally, in small and large groups—to identify needs of communities and society and then to find ways of meeting those needs. John Dewey, a distinguished American philosopher, believed that democracy and communication are intricately connected. He argued that while democracy depends on citizens' voting, it is more basic and important that citizens interact. Dewey insisted that it's vital that citizens talk and listen to each other—they must share ideas, question each other's positions, debate and argue, and collaborate to build communities that are stronger than any individual could build. Without sustained, vigorous communication among citizens, democracy fails. To learn more about John Dewey and his philosophy, go to the book's online resources for this chapter and click WebLink 1.2.

fyi

DIVERSITY
Bowling Together?

When Robert Putnam published *Bowling Alone* in 2000, it caused quite a stir. In it, he claimed that Americans are increasingly disconnected from one another and their communities. Putnam, a professor of public policy at Harvard, amassed evidence showing that Americans at the end of the 20th century were 25 to 50 percent less connected to others than they had been in the late 1960s.

Because he believed that diversity is a strength and that working together makes individuals and the country stronger, Putnam wanted to know what could bring us back together. Working with Lewis Feldstein, who has devoted his life to civic activism, Putnam began searching for examples of people who were connecting with each other to work on community and collective projects.

In *Better Together* (2003) Putnam and Feldstein present 12 stories of diverse people who are working together to build and strengthen their communities. Although the 12 examples are diverse—ranging from Philadelphia's Experience Corps, in which volunteers tutor children from impoverished backgrounds, to UPS: Diversity and Cohesion, which has changed the UPS company from one run almost exclusively by white males to one in which minorities and women have a strong presence in management—they have one thing in common: building and using social capital. The people involved in these efforts realize that they need to build networks of relationships and then draw on those networks to reach goals that are not attainable by individuals working (or bowling) alone.

To promote civic engagement, Putnam, Feldstein, and others established a Better Together initiative at Harvard University's Kennedy School of Government. If you'd like to learn more about building and using social capital, go to the Better Together website by going to the book's online resources for this chapter and clicking on WebLink 1.3.

Communication skills are especially important for effective interaction in our era, which is characterized by social diversity. In pluralistic cultures such as ours, we need to understand people who communicate differently from us. We also need to understand diverse kinds of families and communities and the ways that all of them are sustained. Friendships and workplace relationships between people with different cultural backgrounds enlarge perspective and appreciation of the range of human values and viewpoints. Scott Page (2008), a professor of complex systems, points out that people with greatly different backgrounds and perspectives make for more productive, creative organizations. In much the same way that the health and evolution of a species depends on a rich genetic mixture, the well being of human societies depends on diversity. A recent survey shows that nearly half of first-year students at colleges and universities think that learning about other cultures is essential or very important (Hoover, 2010).

 Luanne

I used to feel it was hard to talk with people who weren't raised in the United States like I was. Sometimes it seems that they have a totally different way of talking than I do, and we don't understand each other naturally. But I've been trying to learn to understand people from other places, and it really is making me realize how many different ways of communicating people have. With so many cultures now part of this country, nobody can get by without learning how to relate to people from other cultures.

David

As an African-American male, I sometimes feel as though I am a dash of pepper on top of a mountain of salt. I have attended many classes where I was the only African American out of 50 or even 100 students. In these classes, the feeling of judgment is cast down upon me for being different. Usually what I learn about is not "people," like the course says, but white people. Until I took a communication course, the only classes that included research and information on African Americans were in the African-American curriculum. This bothered me because white Americans are not the entire world.

Luanne was a student in one of my courses, and David wrote to me after taking a basic communication course at a college in the western United States. Luanne's reflection shows that she is aware of the importance of understanding the communication of people from cultures that differ from her own. David's comment illustrates the importance of weaving diversity into the study of communication. The FYI box on this page further highlights the importance of understanding diverse people in order to communicate effectively in our changing society.

Communication, then, is important for personal, relationship, professional, and civic life. Because communication is a cornerstone of the human experience, your decision to study it will serve you well.

 DIVERSITY

U.S. Demographics in the 21st Century

The United States is home to a wide range of people with diverse ethnic, racial, cultural, and geographic backgrounds. And the proportions of different groups are changing. Currently, one in three U.S. residents is a minority. By 2050 more than one in two U.S. residents will be a minority, and by 2050 non-Hispanic whites will be a minority. The following shifts in the ethnic makeup of the United States are predicted to take place between 2010 and 2050 ("Quick Facts, 2011"; "Demographics," 2009; Roberts, 2008):

	2010	2050
Black	12.6%	13.0%
Asians	4.8%	8.0%
White, non-Hispanic	63.7%	46.0%
Hispanics & Latino/a	16.3%	30.0%
Other	3.0%	5.0%

Numbers do not total 100% because some respondents marked multiple categories.

The Multicultural Pavilion provides an excellent bibliography for those who want to learn more about multiculturalism. To access this site, go to the book's online resources for this chapter and click on WebLink 1.4.

Defining Communication

We've been using the word *communication* for many pages, but we haven't yet defined it clearly. **Communication*** is a systemic process in which people interact with and through symbols to create and interpret meanings. Let's unpack this definition by explaining its four key terms.

Process

Communication is a **process**, which means that it is ongoing and dynamic. It's hard to tell when communication starts and stops, because what happens before we talk with someone may influence

---

*Boldface terms are defined in the glossary at the end of this book.

our interaction, and what occurs in a particular encounter may affect the future. That communication is a process means it is always in motion, moving forward and changing continually.

Systems

Communication takes place within **systems**. A system consists of interrelated parts that affect one another. In family communication, for instance, each family member is part of the system (Galvin, Dickson, & Marrow, 2006). The physical environment and the time of day also are elements of the system. People interact differently in a living room than on a beach, and we may be more alert at certain times of day than at others. The history of a system also affects communication. If a workplace team has a history of listening sensitively and working out problems constructively, then when someone says, "There's something we need to talk about," the others are unlikely to become defensive. Conversely, if the team has a record of nasty conflicts and bickering, the same comment might arouse strong defensiveness.

Because the parts of a system are interdependent and continually interact, a change in any part of a system changes the entire system. When a new person joins a team, he or she brings new perspectives that, in turn, may alter how other team members work. The team develops new patterns of interaction and forms new subgroups; thus, team performance changes. The interrelatedness of a system's parts is particularly evident in intercultural communication. When a corporation moves its operations to a new country, transformations affect everything from daily interaction on the factory floor to corporate culture.

Systems are not collections of random parts, but organized wholes. For this reason, a system operates as a totality of interacting elements. A family is a system, or totality, of interacting elements that include family members, their physical locations, their jobs and schools, and so forth. Before systems theory was developed, therapists who worked with disturbed members of families often tried to "fix" the person who supposedly was causing problems for the family. Thus, alcoholics might be separated from their families and given therapy to reduce the motivation to drink or to increase the desire not to drink. Often, however, the alcoholic resumed drinking shortly after rejoining the family because the behavior of the "problem person" was shaped by the behaviors of other family members and other elements of the family system.

In a similar manner, organizations sometimes send managers to leadership training programs but do not provide training for the manager's subordinates. When the manager returns to the office and uses the new leadership techniques, subordinates are distrustful and resistant. They were accustomed to the manager's former style, and they haven't been taught how to deal with the new style of leadership.

Because systems are organized wholes, they are more than simple combinations of parts. As families, groups, organizations, and societies evolve, they discard old patterns, generate new patterns, lose some members, and gain new members. When new topics are introduced on blogs, new bloggers join, old ones leave, and patterns of communication are reconfigured. Personal relationships grow beyond the two original parts (partners) to include trust or lack of trust, shared experiences, and private vocabularies. Systems include not only their original parts but also changes in those original elements and new elements that are created as a result of interaction.

Systems vary in how open they are. **Openness** is the extent to which a system affects and is affected by outside factors and processes. Some tribal communities are relatively closed systems that have little interaction with the world outside. Yet most cultures are fairly open to interaction with other cultures. This is increasingly true today as more and more people immigrate from one culture to another and as people travel more frequently and to more places. The more open the system, the more factors influence it. Mass media and communication technologies expand the openness of most societies and thus the influences on them and their ways of life.

A final point about systems is that they strive for but cannot sustain equilibrium. Systems seek a state of equilibrium, or **homeostasis**. That's why families create routines, organizations devise policies and procedures, individuals develop habits, groups generate norms, online communities develop conventions and abbreviations, and cultures generate rituals and traditions.

Yet no living system can sustain absolute balance or equilibrium. Change is inevitable and continuous. Sometimes, it's abrupt (a company moves all of its operations to a new country); at other times, it's gradual (a company begins to hire people from different cultures). Sometimes, influences outside a system prompt change (legislation affects importing and exporting in other countries). In other cases, the system generates change internally (an organization decides to alter its marketing targets). To function and survive, members of the system must continually adjust and change.

Communication is also affected by the larger systems within which it takes place. For example, different cultures have distinct understandings of appropriate verbal and nonverbal behaviors. Many Asian cultures place a high value on saving face, so Asians try not to cause personal embarrassment to others by disagreeing overtly. It is inappropriate to perceive people from Asian cultures as passive if they don't assert themselves in the ways that many Westerners do. Arab cultures consider it normal for people to be nearer to one another when talking than most Westerners find comfortable. And in Bulgaria, head nods mean "no" rather than "yes" (Munter, 1993). Different regions of the same country may also have different ways of communicating—Steve makes this point in his commentary. Even within a single culture, there are differences based on region, ethnicity, religion, and other factors. Therefore, to interpret communication, we have to consider the systems in which it takes place. In Chapter 8, we'll discuss different communication practices in diverse cultural contexts.

 Steve

It took me a long time to get used to Southerners. I'm from the Midwest and there we don't chat everybody up like Southerners do. We talk if we have something to say, but we don't talk just to talk. When I first moved here, I thought most of the people I met were real busybodies because people I hardly knew would say things like "you should come to my church" or "mark your calendar for the supper to raise money for schools" like I wanted to go to those. Then I started dating a girl who was born near here and she "decoded" Southern culture for me. She explained that "you should come" is not a command, which is what it sounded like to me, but an invitation because Southerners want to be hospitable and include everyone. She also told me I was being perceived as very standoffish because I didn't chat back like Southerners do.

Symbols

Communication is symbolic. We don't have direct access to one another's thoughts and feelings. Instead, we rely on **symbols**, which are abstract, arbitrary, and ambiguous representations of other things. We might symbolize love by giving a ring, by saying "I love you," or by closely embracing someone. A promotion might be symbolized by a new title and a larger office (and a raise!). Later in this chapter and also in Chapter 4, we'll have more to say about symbols. For now, just remember that human communication involves interaction with and through symbols.

Meanings

Finally, our definition focuses on **meanings**, which are at the heart of communication. Meanings are the significance we bestow on phenomena, or what they signify to us. Meanings are not inherent in experience itself. Instead, we use symbols to assign meanings to experience. We ask others to be sounding boards so we can clarify our thinking, figure out what things mean, enlarge our perspectives, check our perceptions, and label feelings to give them reality. In all these ways, we actively construct meaning by interacting with symbols.

Communication has two levels of meaning (Pinker, 2008; Watzlawick, Beavin, & Jackson, 1967). The **content level of meaning** contains the literal message. If a person knocks on your door and asks, "May I come in?" the content-level meaning is that the person is asking your permission to enter. The **relationship level of meaning** expresses the relationship between communicators. In our example, if the person who asks, "May I come in?" is your friend and is smiling, you would probably conclude that the person is seeking friendly interaction. But if the person is your supervisor and speaks in an angry tone, you might interpret the relationship-level meaning as a signal that your supervisor is not satisfied with your work and is going to call you on the carpet. The content-level meaning is the same in both examples, but the relationship-level meaning differs.

In many cases, the relationship level of meaning is more important than the content level. The relationship level of meaning often expresses a desire to connect with another person (Gottman & DeClaire, 2001). For example, this morning Robbie said to me, "I've got a late meeting today, so I won't be home until six or so." The content-level meaning is obvious—Robbie is informing me of his schedule. The relationship-level meaning, however, is the more important message that Robbie wants to stay connected with me and is aware that we usually have catch-up conversation around 5 p.m. each day. Likewise, the content level of meaning of instant messages (IMs) is often mundane, even trivial: <waz up?> <not much here. U?> On the relationship level of meaning, however, this exchange expresses interest and a desire to stay in touch (Carl, 2006). The Sharpen Your Skill box on the right invites you to pay attention to both levels of communication in your interactions.

SHARPEN YOUR SKILL

Noticing Levels of Meaning in Communication

The next time you talk with a close friend, notice both levels of meaning.

◆ What is the content-level meaning?

◆ To what extent are liking, responsiveness, and power expressed on the relationship level of meaning?

Models of Communication

To complement the definition of communication we have just discussed, we'll now consider models of the human communication process. Over the years, scholars in communication have developed a number of models that reflect increasingly sophisticated understandings of the communication process.

Linear Models

Harold Laswell (1948) advanced an early model that described communication as a linear, or one-way, process in which one person acts on another person. This is also called a *transmission model* because it assumes that communication is transmitted in a straightforward manner from a sender to a receiver. His was a verbal model consisting of five questions that described early views of how communication works:

Who?

Says what?

In what channel?

To whom?

With what effect?

Claude Shannon and Warren Weaver (1949) refined Laswell's model by adding the concept of **noise**. Noise is anything that interferes with the intended meaning of communication. Noises may distort understanding. Figure 1.1 shows Shannon and Weaver's model. Although linear, or transmission, models such as these were useful starting points, they are too simplistic to capture the complexity of human communication.

Interactive Models

The major shortcoming of the early models was that they portrayed communication as flowing in only one direction, from a sender to a receiver (Gronbeck, 1999). The linear model suggests that a person is only a sender or a receiver and that receivers passively absorb senders' messages. Clearly, this isn't how communication occurs.

When communication theorists realized that listeners respond to senders, they added **feedback** to their models. Feedback is a response to a message. It may be verbal or nonverbal, and it may be intentional or unintentional. Wilbur Schramm (1955) depicted feedback as a second kind of message. In addition, Schramm pointed out that communicators create and interpret messages within personal fields of experience. The more communicators' fields of experience overlap, the better they understand each other.

Adding fields of experience to models clarifies why misunderstandings sometimes occur.

Figure 1.1   **The Linear Model of Communication**
Source: From The Mathematical Theory of Communication. Copyright 1949, 1998 by the Board of Trustees of the University of Illinois. Used with permission of the authors and the University of Illinois Press.

You jokingly put down a friend, and he takes it seriously and is hurt. You offer to help someone, and she feels patronized. Adding fields of experience and feedback allowed Schramm and other communication scholars to develop models that portray communication as an interactive process in which both senders and receivers participate actively (Figure 1.2).

Figure 1.2 **The Interactive Model of Communication**
Source: Adapted from Schramm, 1955.

Transactional Models

Although an interactive model was an improvement over the linear one, it still didn't capture the dynamism of human communication. The interactive model portrays communication as a sequential process in which one person communicates to another, who then sends feedback to the first person. Yet people may communicate simultaneously instead of taking turns. Also, the interactive model designates one person as a sender and another person as a receiver. In reality, communicators both send and receive messages. While handing out a press release, a public relations representative watches reporters to gauge their interest. The "speaker" is listening; the "listeners" are sending messages.

A final shortcoming of the interactive model is that it doesn't portray communication as changing over time as a result of what happens between people. For example, new employees are more reserved in conversations with co-workers than they are after months on the job, after getting to know others and learning organizational norms. What they talk about and the way they interact changes over time. To be accurate, a model should include the feature of time and should depict communication as varying, not constant. Figure 1.3 is a transactional model that highlights the features we have discussed.

Consistent with what we've covered in this chapter, our model includes noise that can distort communication. Noise includes sounds, such as a lawn mower or background chatter, as well as interferences within communicators—such as biases and preoccupation—that hinder effective listening. In addition, our model emphasizes that communication is a continually changing process. How people communicate varies over time and in response to their history of relating.

The outer lines on our model emphasize that communication occurs within systems that affect what and how people communicate and what meanings they create. Those systems, or contexts, include the shared systems of the communicators (campus, town, culture) and the personal systems of each communicator (family, religious associations, friends). Also note that our model, unlike previous ones, portrays each person's field of experience and his or her shared fields of experience as changing over time. As we

Figure 1.3 **A Transactional Model of Communication**
Source: Adapted from Wood, 1997, p. 21.

"It's funny how two intelligent people can have such opposite interpretations of the tax code!"

encounter new people and grow personally, we alter how we interact with others.

Finally, our model doesn't label one person a sender and the other a receiver. Instead, both are defined as communicators who participate equally, and often simultaneously, in the communication process. This means that at a given moment in communication, you may be sending a message (speaking or wrinkling your brow), listening to a message, or doing both at the same time (interpreting what someone says while nodding to show you are interested). To understand communication as a transactional process is to recognize that self and others are involved in a shared process: Communication is *we*-oriented (How can we understand each other? How can we work through this conflict?) rather than *me*-oriented (This is what I mean. This is what I want.) (Lafasto & Larson, 2001).

In summary, the most accurate model of communication represents it as a transactional process in which people interact with and through symbols over time to create meaning.

Careers in Communication

Now that you understand what communication is, you may be wondering what kinds of careers are open to people with strong backgrounds in the discipline. As we've seen, communication skills are essential to success in most fields. In addition, people who major in communication are particularly equipped for certain careers.

Research

Communication research is a vital and growing field of work. Many faculty members combine teaching and research. In this book, you'll encounter a good deal of academic research that helps us understand how communication works—or fails to work.

In addition to academic research, communication specialists help organizations by studying processes such as message production and marketing. Companies want to know how people respond to advertisements, logos, and product names. Communication researchers also assist counselors by investigating the ways in which communication helps and harms relationships.

Education

Teaching others about communication is another exciting career path for people with extensive backgrounds in the field. Across the nation, communication teachers at all levels are in demand. Secondary schools, junior colleges, colleges, universities, technical schools, and community colleges offer communication classes.

The level at which people are qualified to teach depends on how extensively they have pursued the study of communication. Generally, a bachelor's degree in communication education and a teaching certificate are required for teaching in elementary, middle, and high schools. A master's degree in communication qualifies a person to teach at community colleges, technical schools, and some junior colleges. The doctoral degree in communication generally is required of university faculty, although some universities offer non-tenured, fixed term positions to people with master's degrees.

Although generalists are preferred for many teaching jobs, college-level faculty members often specialize in certain areas of communication. For instance, my research and teaching focus on interpersonal communication and gender and communication. Other college faculty members specialize in areas such as intercultural communication, family communication, health communication, organizational dynamics, and health communication.

Communication educators are not limited to communication departments. In recent years, more and more people with advanced degrees in communication have taken positions in medical and business schools. Doctors need training in listening sensitively to patients, explaining complex problems and procedures, and providing comfort, reassurance, and motivation. Similarly, good business people know not only their businesses but also how to explain their businesses to others, how to present themselves and their companies or products favorably, and so on.

The Nonprofit Sector

Communication skills and knowledge are vital to careers in the nonprofit sector. Former students of mine who are in nonprofit careers are working with homeless citizens, securing housing for poorer citizens, advancing environmental goals, and teaching literacy. Jobs such as these require strong communication skills. You have to be willing and able to listen and learn from people who are quite different from you in their backgrounds, goals, abilities, and dreams. You must know how to encourage, motivate, and support others and how to build strong teams of staff and volunteers. You must be able to establish a climate of mutual trust and respect with populations that—often for good reason—don't easily trust others. All of these are communication skills.

© Rogelio Solis/AP Photo

Service learning prepares students for careers in nonprofits and for community involvement.

Mass Communication: Journalism, Broadcasting, Public Relations, and Advertising

Strong communication skills are necessary for careers in journalism, public relations, broadcasting, and advertising (Ihlen, Fredrikson, & van Ruler, 2009; Nerone, 2009; Smith, 2009). Good journalists know how to listen carefully and critically when conducting interviews. They also know how to write clearly so that readers are drawn to their stories and speak effectively so viewers understand what their broadcast reports.

Effective public relations depend on understanding actual and potential clients and consumers and adapting messages to their interests, goals, and concerns. Effective advertising professionals help companies brand products so that consumers associate a product with a particular key message or theme. McDonald's advertising team has been effective in branding McDonald's as family-friendly; Porsche is branded as "the ultimate driving experience"; and Nike is identified with the "just do it" attitude.

Training and Consulting

Consulting is another career that welcomes people with backgrounds in communication. Businesses train employees in group communication skills, interview techniques, and interpersonal interaction. Some large corporations have entire departments devoted to training and development. People with communication backgrounds often join these departments and work with the corporation to design and teach courses or workshops that enhance employees' communication skills.

In addition, communication specialists may join or form consulting firms that provide communication training to governments and businesses. One of my colleagues consults with nonprofit organizations to help them develop work teams that interact effectively. Other communication specialists work with politicians to improve their presentational styles and sometimes to assist in writing their speeches. I consult with attorneys as an expert witness and a trial strategist on cases involving charges of sexual harassment and sex discrimination. Other communication consultants work with attorneys on jury selections and advise lawyers about how dress and nonverbal behaviors might affect jurors' perceptions of clients.

Human Relations and Management

Because communication is the foundation of human relations, it's no surprise that many communication specialists build careers in human development or in the human relations departments of corporations. People with solid understandings of communication and good personal communication skills are effective in public relations, personnel management, grievance management, negotiation, customer relations, and development and fund-raising.

Communication degrees also open doors to careers in management. The most important qualifications for management are not technical skills but the abilities to interact with others and to

CAREER

Careers in Communication

Learn more about careers open to people with strong training in communication.

The National Communication Association publishes *Pathways to Careers in Communication*. In addition to discussing careers, this booklet provides useful information on the National Communication Association and its many programs. To learn more about the National Communication Association, go to the book's online resources for this chapter and click on WebLink 1.5.

communicate effectively. Good managers know how to listen, express ideas, build consensus, create supportive climates, and balance tasks and interpersonal concerns in dealing with others. Developing skills such as these gives communication majors a firm foundation for effective management. The FYI box on page 18 shows you how to learn about careers in communication that might appeal to you.

SUMMARY

In this chapter, we've taken a first look at human communication. We noted its importance in our lives, defined communication, and discussed models, the most accurate of which is a transactional model that accurately represents the dynamism of communication.

In the final section of this chapter, we considered career opportunities open to people who specialize in communication. An array of exciting career paths is available for people who enjoy interacting with others and who want the opportunity to be part of a dynamic discipline that evolves constantly to meet changing needs and issues in our world.

REVIEW, REFLECT, EXTEND

The Reflect, Discuss, and Apply Questions that follow will help you review, reflect on, and extend the information and ideas presented in this chapter. These resources, and a diverse selection of additional study tools, are also available online at the CourseMate for *Communication Mosaics.* Your CourseMate includes a student workbook, WebLinks, TED Talks hyperlinks and activities, chapter glossary and flashcards, interactive video activities, Speech Builder Express, and InfoTrac College Edition. For more information or to access this book's online resources, visit **www .cengagebrain.com.**

KEY CONCEPTS

communication, 10
content level of meaning, 13
feedback, 14
homeostasis, 12
meaning, 13
noise, 14

openness, 12
process, 10
relationship level of meaning, 13
symbol, 13
system, 11

Reflect, Discuss, Apply

1. Form groups of five to seven. Have one third of groups use the linear model of communication to describe communication in your class. Have one third of groups use an interactive model to describe communication in your class. The final third of groups should use the transactive model to describe communication in your class. As a class, identify what each model highlights and obscures. Which model best describes and explains communication in your class?

2. Interview a professional in your field of choice. Identify the communication skills that he or she thinks are most important for success. Which of those skills do you already have? Which skills do

you need to develop or improve? How can you use this book and the course it accompanies to develop the skills you need to be effective in your career?

3. Go to the placement office on your campus and examine descriptions of available positions. Record the number of job notices that call for communication skills.

4. Survey the last three editions of your campus newspaper for announcements of opportunities for community service and civic engagement. Can you identify one that interests you? If so, use the contact information provided to pursue this as a possibility for yourself.

Recommended Resources

1. Visit the website of the National Communication Association (NCA), which can be accessed by going to the book's online resources for this chapter and clicking on WebLink 1.6. Click links to learn about the mission, history, and programs that the NCA offers. Click on Educational Resources and then on Communicating Common Ground under the Education tab to learn about NCA's service learning project in which many students are involved.

2. Watch the film *An Unfinished Life*. Analyze the communication among the four main characters, with a focus on the system within which they

operate. What are the elements of the system? Identify two changes in the relationship system, then trace how those affect all parts of the system as the film evolves.

3. Visit the Center for Communication and Civic Engagement, which can be accessed by going to the book's online resources for this chapter and clicking on WebLink 1.7. At this site, you'll find information about Seattle's Student Voices Project, a one-year curriculum focused on civic education. Consider talking with administrators on your campus about a curriculum in civic engagement.

EXPERIENCE COMMUNICATION CASE STUDY

The New Employee

Apply what you've learned in this chapter by analyzing the following case study, using the accompanying questions as a guide. These questions and a video of the case study are also available online through your CourseMate for *Communication Mosaics*.

Your supervisor asks you to mentor a new employee, Toya, and help her learn the ropes of the job. After two weeks, you perceive that Toya is responsible and punctual, and she takes initiative on her own. At the same time, you note that she is careless about details: She doesn't proofread reports, so they contain errors in spelling and grammar, and she doesn't check back to make sure something she did worked. You've also noticed that Toya seems insecure and wants a lot of affirmation and praise. You want to give her honest feedback so she can improve her job performance, yet you are afraid she will react defensively if you bring up her carelessness. You ask Toya to meet with you to discuss her first two weeks on the job. The meeting begins:

You: Well, you've been here for two weeks. How are you liking the job?

Toya: I like it a lot, and I'm trying to do my best every day. Nobody has said anything, so I guess I'm doing okay.

You: Well, I've noticed how responsible you are and how great you are about being a self-starter. Those are real strengths in this job.

Toya: Thanks. So I guess I'm doing okay, right?

You: What would you say if someone suggested that there are ways you can improve your work?

Toya: What do you mean? Have I done something wrong? Nobody's said anything to me. Is someone saying something behind my back?

© Cengage Learning

1. What would you say next to Toya? How would you meet your ethical responsibilities as her mentor and also adapt to her need for reassurance?

2. What responsibilities do you have to Toya, to your supervisor, and to the company? How can you reflect thoughtfully about potential tensions between these responsibilities?

3. How would your communication differ if you acted according to a linear model of communication, as opposed to a transactional one?

There is more than a verbal tie between the words common, community, and communication. John Dewey

2 The Field of Communication from Historical and Contemporary Perspectives

FOCUS QUESTIONS

1. What is the origin of the communication discipline?

2. What methods do communication scholars use to conduct research?

3. What areas of study and teaching compose the discipline of communication today?

4. What themes unify areas of study within the field of communication?

My father loved to tell me stories about my ancestors—his parents, grandparents, and great-grandparents. When I was seven years old and bored with his stories, I asked my father what any of that "ancient history" had to do with me. He responded with a stern lecture—one of many he gave me—in which he told me that the family members who came before me shaped his identity and my own. He went on to tell me that I couldn't understand who I was without understanding the history of my family.

At the time, I didn't fully appreciate my father's wisdom, but I did start listening with more attention to his stories of our family history. In the years that followed, I realized he was right. My father's parents and grandparents had been farmers. Although he became an attorney, my father retained a deep love of animals and land, which he passed on to me and my siblings. I discovered that my impulsive personality was not new in the family; Charles Harrison Wood, my great-grandfather, had been known for being more than a little rash. I also learned that my father's brother Arch had frequently gotten in trouble for his pranks, another tendency I inherited. Later, when it became clear that I had a keen talent for organizing, I felt a kinship with my father's mother, whose organizational skills had been well known in our home county.

Just as you can't fully appreciate who you are without knowing your family's history, you can't understand an academic discipline without learning about its history. This chapter introduces you to how the communication discipline developed over time. We first discuss the long and rich intellectual history of the discipline.

Second, we discuss methods of conducting research that are used by communication scholars. The third section of the chapter surveys the major areas of the contemporary field and highlights themes that unify the different areas.

The History of the Communication Field

As the title of this book suggests, communication is a mosaic, each part of which contributes to the overall character of the field. The mosaic has become richer and more complex since the discipline's birth more than 2,500 years ago.

Classical Roots: Rhetoric and Democratic Life

One theme in the mosaic is that communication plays a vital role in democratic societies. The art of rhetoric was born in the mid-400s b.c. in the Grecian port city of Syracuse on the island of Sicily. At that time, the Sicilians had just overthrown the oppressive political regime led by Thrasybulus, a tyrant who had taken their land and impoverished them. After throwing Thrasybulus out, the citizens began working to establish a democratic society. The first order of business under the new democratic constitution was to regain the property that Thrasybulus had taken from the people. Citizens wanted to do this, but they lacked the skill to present their cases in court. A man named Corax, along with his pupil Tisias, taught citizens how to develop and present persuasive arguments in court. Corax taught the people how to structure speeches, build arguments, and refute the arguments of others. In other words, the communication field came into existence to answer a pressing need of the people of Syracuse.

Rhetoric continued to be central to democratic life in ancient Greece and Rome. Among the most influential philosophers and teachers of rhetoric in this era were Socrates, Aristotle, Isocrates, and Plato. Plato, who was a student of Socrates, lived from 428 to 348 b.c. (Borchers, 2006). In Athens, he founded a school called the Academy. Plato believed that truth is absolute and can be known only in ideal forms and not in concrete reality. Plato was suspicious of rhetoric because he recognized the possibility of misusing rhetoric to manipulate and deceive.

Aristotle, who lived from 384 to 322 b.c. (Borchers, 2006), was a student of Plato. Like many students and teachers today, Aristotle and Plato did not always see eye to eye. A major difference between them was that Aristotle believed truth could be discerned from careful observation of concrete reality. Aristotle also believed it was important to deal with realities, which are often not the ideals Plato so valued. Aristotle's view of truth was related to his belief that rhetoric is central to civic life in a democratic society. He understood that citizens could participate fully only if they were able to speak well and engage in discussion and debate about issues of the day. Building on the teachings of Corax and Tisias, Aristotle taught his students how to analyze audiences, discover ideas and proofs to support claims, organize messages effectively, memorize speeches, and deliver speeches clearly and dynamically.

COMPUTER-MEDIATED COMMUNICATION

Learning from Ancient Theorists

You can study with great ancient rhetorical theorists online. Plato's most famous texts are *Gorgias*, which presents his view that rhetoric is dangerous; and *Phaedrus*, which offers a less critical view of rhetoric. To read *Gorgias*, go to the book's online resources for this chapter and click on WebLink 2.1. To read *Phaedrus*, click on WebLink 2.2. To learn about Aristotle's views of rhetoric, click on WebLink 2.3.

Figure 2.1 The Three Pillars of Persuasion

One of the enduring contributions to our knowledge of rhetoric was Aristotle's thinking about how persuasion occurs. He theorized that there are three ways to persuade, which he called *proofs* (Figure 2.1). **Ethos** is proof based on a speaker's credibility (trustworthiness, expertise, and good will). **Pathos** is proof that appeals to listeners' emotions. **Logos** is based on logic and reasoning. If you think about your experiences in listening to speakers, you're likely to discover that, like people in Aristotle's time, you respond to ethos, pathos, and logos.

Ancient Greece was home to another group of teachers who took quite a different approach to rhetoric. These teachers viewed truth as relative, and they encouraged speakers to adjust their ideas to specific contexts and listeners. Known as *Sophists,* these teachers focused on building the best arguments to move audiences (Borchers, 2006). Today, specious or deceptive reasoning in argumentation is sometimes referred to as *sophistic.*

Liberal Education

The importance of communication to civic life explains why liberal education was regarded as the primary mission of Western higher education. For centuries after Aristotle taught in the *agora* (marketplace) in Athens, rhetoric held a premier spot in liberal education in Europe and the United States. Following Aristotle's view that rhetoric is a practical art, teachers of rhetoric provided pragmatic advice to students who wanted to be effective public speakers.

In the 19th century, many of the most prestigious universities in the United States established chairs of rhetoric, held by distinguished scholars and civic leaders. Among these was president John Quincy Adams, who held the first Boylston Professor of Rhetoric Chair at Harvard University (Foss, Foss, & Trapp, 1991). In the 1800s and early 1900s, rhetoric was taught as a practical art that prepared people for responsible participation in civic life. The emphasis on teaching that marked this period explains why the first national professional organization, founded in 1914, was named the National Association of Teachers of Public Speaking.

In the 1900s, the communication discipline began to broaden beyond public speaking. In the early 20th century, philosopher John Dewey taught at the University of Chicago, which was the intellectual hub of the United States at that time. A pragmatic philosopher, Dewey championed progressive thinking in cultural life. For Dewey, this also meant championing communication in a broad sense. He realized that to have any impact on cultural life, progressive thinking must be communicated. In others words, people must be able to voice their ideas and to listen thoughtfully and critically to the ideas of others; they must talk, interact, debate, and engage in ongoing conversation.

Dewey's interest in progressive thinking and citizen participation grew out of the political context of his time, and that context influenced the field as a whole. After the two world wars, communication professionals felt an urgent need to understand the connections between communication and Hitler's rise to power, the development of prejudice against social groups, willingness to follow authoritarian leaders, the effects of propaganda, and changes in attitudes and beliefs.

In the early 1900s, two major professional communication organizations were formed. The first was the Association for Education in Journalism and Mass Communication (AEJMC), which was founded in 1912. AEJMC promotes both academic and applied journalism, and it sponsors research journals and conferences on journalistic practice, scholarship, and teaching. Today, AEJMC has more than 3,500 members worldwide.

The second organization was founded in 1914. Because its original members were speech teachers, it was called Speech Teachers of America (STA). However, that name did not endure. The organization has changed its name three times, each change signaling evolution in the organization's scope and view of itself. In 1950, the name was changed to Speech Association of America (SAA) to reflect the organization's increasing interest in scholarship as well as teaching. In 1970, the name was changed again to the Speech Communication Association (SCA), a change that emphasized the growing interest in forms of communication other than speech—for instance, nonverbal communication. Finally, in 1997 members voted to change the name to the National Communication Association (NCA), which is still its name today. With more than 7,000 members in 20 countries, NCA's mission is to advance research, teaching, and service relevant to human communication.

Broadening the Field

In the mid-20th century, another part of the mosaic of communication emerged: scientific, empirical research, which gained prominence in almost all of the social sciences. The formation of the International Communication Association (ICA) in 1950 signaled a growing interest in scientific research in the communication field. Today, the ICA has more than 3,000 members.

When the ICA was first formed, it was distinct from NCA in two specific ways. First, NCA (then called the SCA) was steeped in the humanities, which typically are built through qualitative research. Complementing NCA's intellectual and methodological interests, ICA allied itself primarily with the social scientific tradition, which tends to favor quantitative methods of research. Social scientific research continues today as one of several intellectual traditions that contribute to the ever-growing body of knowledge created by communication scholars.

A second difference between the two organizations, in the 1950s and for years after, was membership. As the names suggest, NCA was a national organization that represented the interests of United States scholars of communication and primarily encouraged research in American communication. ICA, however, explicitly sought to attract an international membership and to support research on communication beyond the borders of the United States. ICA's international flavor explains why areas such as cultural studies, which have been influenced by European scholars, are more prominent in ICA than in NCA.

Although NCA and ICA continue to reflect the intellectual and methodological inclinations that were present when they were formed, distinctions between the two organizations are less pronounced than 60 years ago. Today, NCA includes many members whose research is primarily or entirely quantitative, and ICA includes many members who generally favor qualitative research. Also, both organizations now have international memberships, and both promote research on communication in and between a range of cultures and geographic areas.

The 1960s and 1970s saw yet another addition to the communication mosaic. In the United States, this was a time of exceptional social and political upheaval. The Civil Rights Movement and the second wave of the Women's Movement shook up long-standing patterns of personal and social relations. At the same time, youth culture ushered in new ideas about how people should interact and what was important in life. Many college students felt that personal relationships should receive more time and attention than the traditional curriculum provided. Responding to these currents in social life, the communication discipline expanded to include interpersonal communication. Many colleges and universities began to offer classes in family communication and interaction in intimate relationships. Student interest in the expanded communication curriculum was very high and continues to be so today. The interpersonal emphasis also affected group communication courses, adding sensitivity training and human relations to the traditional coverage of group decision making.

The field continues to broaden. In recent years, for instance, health communication has become a major sub-area of the discipline. Scholars and teachers of health communication focus on issues such as doctor–patient interaction, organizational communication in health institutions, and media efforts to promote good health practices. The field today also includes vigorous study and teaching of mediated communication, which has become primary means of communicating.

Communication, Power, and Empowerment

Beginning in the 1960s and continuing to the present day, the relationship between communication and power in cultural life has become increasingly prominent in the communication mosaic. The tumultuous 1960s and 1970s were marked by social and political movements that questioned established power hierarchies. As mentioned above, two of the most notable of these movements were the civil rights movement, which challenged racial discrimination in the United States, and the women's movement, which challenged conventional gender roles in both public and private realms of life. Many scholars and teachers of communication embraced a critical focus on social movements and began to investigate the communicative dynamics that social movements employ and the ways in which social movements affect individuals and society.

The expansion of the field's interests to questions of power reflects the influence of French philosopher Michel Foucault (1970, 1972a, 1972b, 1978), who was deeply concerned with who is and who is not allowed to speak in a society. More specifically, Foucault illuminated the ways in which culturally entrenched rules—often unwritten and unacknowledged—define who gets to speak, to whom we listen, and whose views are counted as important.

Building on Foucault's ideas, a number of communication scholars study the ways in which some people's communication is allowed and other people's communication is disallowed or disrespected. Equally, these scholars seek to empower people whose voices historically have been muted, so that they can participate fully in public and private interactions that shape the character of personal and collective life. Consider one example. Historically, decisions about environmental issues that affect the health and environment of communities have been made almost entirely by privileged citizens: scientists and people in white-collar and technical professions. Left out of these vital discussions have been many blue-collar workers, unemployed or underemployed people, and citizens without formal education (Cox, 2010; Martin, 2007). These citizens often are made voiceless by institutional barriers and administrative practices that define their concerns and their ways of speaking as inappropriate. Pezzullo (2007, 2008) and others (Agyeman, 2007; Norton, 2007; Sandler & Pezzullo, 2007) engage in research that increases our understanding of ways to empower those who suffer environmental problems and who have not had a voice in their communities and the larger society.

Interest in the relationships between communication and power has reshaped many areas of the field. Rhetorical scholars have broadened their focus beyond individual speakers. Many of today's rhetorical scholars study gay rights, pro-life and pro-choice, environmental, and other social movements. They examine coercive tactics, symbolic strategies for defining issues (think of the power of terms such as *pro-life* and *pro-choice* compared with *pro-abortion* and *anti-abortion* or *pro-choice* and *anti-choice*), and how social movements challenge and change broadly held cultural practices and values.

Scholars in other areas of the field share an interest in how communication shapes and is shaped by the historical, social, and political contexts in which it occurs. Today, faculty in interpersonal and organizational communication conduct research and teach about how new technologies affect personal relationships and reshape societies, how organizational cultures and practices affect employees' productivity and job satisfaction, and how national trends such as downsizing and outsourcing affect workers on the job and in their personal lives.

fyi ENGAGEMENT

A Time for Civic Engagement

Speaking in Colorado on July 2, 2008, then-candidate Barack Obama told an audience of supporters, "We need your service, right now, in this moment—our moment—in history." Now, as President, Obama uses persuasion to reinvigorate commitment to public service and civic engagement. He's building on a vital tradition in America. President John F. Kennedy founded the Peace Corps, President George H. W. Bush called on Americans to serve as "points of light" in the world, and President Bill Clinton championed AmeriCorps, which today has 75,000 staff and 1.7 million volunteers who are helping build affordable housing, tutoring children in literacy, and cleaning up the environment (Alter, 2009).

© Michal Czerwonka/Landov

Young people are leading the way in a new era of civic engagement in America.

As this brief historical overview shows, the field of communication responds to the changing character and needs of individuals and society. Perhaps this is why the field has expanded, even during periods of downsizing at many colleges and universities. Just as Aristotle's students found that communication skills allowed them to participate in their society, today's students realize that the modern field of communication offers them effective skills for understanding and participating in the world.

Conducting Research in Communication

Like other scholarly disciplines, communication is based on knowledge gained from rigorous research (Baxter & Bebee, 2004; Carbaugh & Buzzanell, 2009; Reinhard, 2007). So that you can understand how scholars acquire knowledge, we'll discuss four primary approaches to communication research. These approaches are not incompatible; many scholars rely on multiple approaches to study how communication works. Further, even scholars who do not use multiple methods in their own research stay abreast of research that employs a range of methods.

Quantitative Research

Communication scholars use **quantitative research methods,** to gather information in numerical form (Levine, 2009). Descriptive statistics measure human behavior in terms of quantity, frequency, or amount. For example, in the 1998 survey mentioned in Chapter 1 (FYI box, Communication and Marriage), we saw that 53 percent of Americans regard ineffective communication as the principal cause of divorce. Quantitative research tells us that in 2011, 84 percent of undergraduate students in the United States have laptops and 70 percent of students say information technologies make it more convenient to do course activities ("Information Technology," 2011). Quantitative research also tells us that 98.9 percent of American homes have at least one television, and the average American home has more televisions than people—3.3 televisions and fewer than 3 people per household (Media Trends Track, 2010).

A second method of quantitative research is gathering information through surveys, instruments, questionnaires, or interviews that measure how people feel, think, act, and so forth. Surveys are valuable when a researcher wants to discover general trends among a particular group of people—members of an institution, for example, or Americans in general. Surveys often are used in organizations to gain information about employee morale, response to company policies, and relationships between job satisfaction and factors such as leadership style, participation on teams, and quality of communication between co-workers. Once survey data are gathered, they may be analyzed using a variety of statistical methods that help researchers detect patterns in communication and assess their strengths and relationships.

A third method of quantitative research is the experiment, a study in which researchers control the context in order to measure how one variable (called the *independent variable*) that can be manipulated affects other variables (called *dependent variables*). Norman Wong and Joseph Cappella (2009) designed a series of experiments to test the effectiveness of different types of messages designed to persuade people to stop smoking. Some participants received messages that were high in threat and high in efficacy (claiming that smoking is dangerous and quitting is possible) whereas other participants received messages low in threat and efficacy. They found that the higher threat and efficacy message was more effective in motivating participants to seek help to quit smoking.

Qualitative Research

A second approach used by many scholars of communication is **qualitative research methods,** which provide non-numerical knowledge about communication. Qualitative methods are especially valuable when researchers want to study aspects of communication that cannot easily be quantified, such as the meanings of experience, the function of rituals in organizational life, and how we feel about and engage in online communication (Schiebel, 2009). Three methods of qualitative research are most prominent in the communication discipline.

Textual analysis is the interpretation of symbolic activities—for example, how couples manage conflict or how attorneys interrogate witnesses. Texts are not limited to formal written texts or orally presented speeches. Scholars who engage in textual analysis might interpret the meaning of the AIDS quilt, community-building rituals among refugees, tours of toxic waste sites, self-disclosures in chat rooms on the Web, and stories told in families. In each case, communication practices are interpreted, rather than measured, to understand their significance.

Another qualitative method is *ethnography,* in which researchers try to discover what symbolic activities mean by immersing themselves in naturally occurring activities and natural contexts that have not been manipulated by researchers. By spending significant time in these contexts, ethnographic researchers are able to gain insight into the perspectives of those who are native to the context. At the center of ethnographic research is a commitment to understanding what communication means from the perspective of those involved rather than from that of an outside, uninvolved observer. Katy Bodey (2009; Bodey & Wood, 2009) explored how girls in their late teens use social media to develop identities. She visited their blogs and sites, and she talked in-depth with them about what they did online and why. Bodey found that their blogs and pages on social sites are places where they talk about issues such as pressures to be skinny, drink (or not), have sex (or not), and dress particular ways. Bodey noticed that the girls were not just recording what they thought or did related to these pressures, but they were actually working out what they thought and wanted to do in the process of blogging or chatting online. In other words, social media were platforms for them to actively construct identities and get response from others.

A third method of qualitative scholarship is *historical research,* which provides knowledge about significant past events, people, and activities. Scholars rely on historical research to learn about the contexts in which ancient thinkers such as Aristotle and Plato developed their ideas. In addition, scholars study historically significant texts and the conditions that shaped them. The data for historical scholarship include original documents, such as drafts of famous speeches and notes for revision, records that describe events and public reaction to them, and biographical studies of key figures.

Critical Research

A third approach to communication scholarship is **critical research methods,** in which scholars identify and challenge communication practices that oppress, marginalize, or otherwise harm individuals and social groups (Ono, 2009). In other words, critical research aims to challenge oppression and change society.

Critical scholars think that the traditional research goals of understanding, explanation, and prediction are insufficient if academics want the knowledge they generate to have practical consequences. Therefore, critical scholars are passionately committed to using their research to advance social awareness and progress. For this group, specific communication practices are seen as means of reflecting, upholding, and sometimes challenging cultural ideology. For example, the practice of punching a time clock, used in many organizations, upholds the notion that workers must account for their time to those who have the means to own and run businesses. The meaning of punching a time clock is tied to an overall ideology that stipulates who does and who does not have power.

Some critical scholars contribute through original theorizing that helps us understand how certain groups and practices become dominant and how dominant ideologies sometimes are challenged and changed in a society. Other critical scholars engage in empirical work to reveal how particular practices function and whom they benefit and harm. For example, critical scholars have noted that media often represent nonwhite characters as dangerous, irresponsible, or hypersexual (Dubrofsky & Hardy, 2008; Hasinoff, 2008). Black characters are often stereotyped as subordinate, athletic, lazy, criminal or exotic (Dixon, 2006; Ramasubramanian, 2010). Asians, Native Americans, and, with the exception of America Ferrara ("Ugly Betty"), Hispanics are underrepresented on prime-time television (Stroman & Dates, 2008). Critical media scholars also raise questions about how communication technologies shape individual thinking and social relationships (Potter, 2009; Steele, 2009).

Although the quantitative, qualitative, and critical approaches are distinct orientations to conducting research, they are not necessarily inconsistent or incompatible. In fact, scholars often rely on more than one research method in an effort to gain multifaceted understanding of what is being studied. Likewise, scholars often combine different kinds of data or theoretical perspectives to gain a fuller understanding of what is being studied than they would get from any single type of data or theoretical lens.

Studying phenomena in multiple ways is called **triangulation,** a term that shares the same root term as *trigonometry.* Just as trigonometry involves calculating the distance to a particular point by viewing that point in relation to two other points, triangulated research involves studying phenomena from multiple points of view. Communication researchers rely on different types of triangulation. Data triangulation relies on multiple sources of data. For example, to study gender bias in sports reporting, researchers (Eastman & Billings, 2000) used three sources of data: *The New York Times,* CNN's *Sports Tonight,* and ESPN's *SportsCenter.* Researcher triangulation occurs when two or more researchers gather and analyze data so that the data are interpreted through multiple perspectives. Methodological triangulation involves using two or more methodologies to study a phenomenon. To study the relationship between stereotypical media messages about race and ethnicity, and consumers' social judgments of races and ethnicities, Dana Mastro (2003) employed both quantitative and critical methods. Triangulated research allows scholars to study communication from multiple points of view and thus to gain robust understandings of that which is studied.

Rhetorical Criticism

The final mode of research we will discuss, rhetorical criticism, dates back to the earliest teaching and research in the field. Rhetorical criticism is "the process of examining a text to see how it works communicatively" (Renegar & Malkowski, 2009, p. 51).

However, as noted earlier, scholars have a broad view of what counts as a *message* or a *text*. In addition to speeches, texts include any and all symbolic activities—nonverbal actions and artifacts such as the AIDS quilt, verbal but not vocal messages such as written messages and cartoons, films, images, web videos, and everyday performances of identity.

Rhetorical criticism aims to understand how particular texts work. How do they have impact—or fail to have impact—on listeners and viewers? Why do they have the impact they do, or not have the impact their creator intended? To answer such questions, a rhetorical critic first defines the object of criticism—what text is to be studied. Then, because all texts exist within contexts, the critic examines the context (social, economic, political, etc.) in which the text is situated.

Rhetorical critics have deepened our insight into pivotal texts, such as Elizabeth Cady Stanton's speech, "The Declaration of Sentiments," which was the keynote address at the first women's rights convention in 1848 (Campbell, 1989); Martin Luther King, Jr.'s 1963 "I Have a Dream" speech (Cox, 1989); and George W. Bush's on slavery at Gorgee Island (Medhurst, 2010).

In summary, communication scholars rely on quantitative and qualitative research methods, critical research, and rhetorical criticism. Each approach is valuable, and each has contributed to the overall knowledge that makes up communication as a scholarly discipline. Often, researchers combine two or more approaches in triangulated studies. In this book, you'll encounter research reflecting all of the primary approaches we've discussed, so that you can appreciate the range of methods that scholars use to generate knowledge about human communication. Much of this research is woven into the text of chapters, and selected findings from research are highlighted in FYI boxes.

The Breadth of the Communication Field

As we have seen, the communication discipline originally focused almost exclusively on public communication. Although public speaking remains a vital skill, it is no longer the only focus of the communication field. The modern discipline can be classified into eight primary areas and a number of other areas that are part of curricula in some schools.

Intrapersonal Communication

Intrapersonal communication is communication with ourselves, or self-talk. You might wonder whether *intrapersonal communication* is another term for *thinking*. In one sense, yes. Intrapersonal communication does involve thinking because it is a cognitive process that occurs inside us. Yet because thinking relies on language to name and reflect on ideas, it is also communication (Vocate, 1994). Chiquella makes this point in her commentary.

 Chiquella

I figure out a lot of things by thinking them through in my head. It's like having a trial run without risk. Usually, after I think through different ideas or ways of approaching someone, I can see which one would be best.

SHARPEN YOUR SKILL

Analyze Your Self-Talk

Pay attention to the way you talk to yourself for the next day. When something goes wrong, what do you say to yourself? Do you put yourself down with negative messages? Do you generalize beyond the specific event to describe yourself as a loser or as inadequate? The first step in changing negative self-talk is to become aware of it. We'll have more to say about how to change negative self-talk in Chapter 9.

One school of counseling focuses on enhancing self-esteem by changing how we talk to ourselves (Ellis & Harper, 1977; Rusk & Rusk, 1988; Seligman, 1990, 2002). For instance, you might say to yourself, "I blew that test, so I'm really stupid. I'll never graduate, and, nobody will hire me." This kind of talk lowers self-esteem by convincing you that a single event (blowing one test) proves you are worthless. Therapists who realize that what we say to ourselves affects our feelings urge us to challenge negative self-talk by saying, "One test is hardly a measure of my intelligence. I did well on the other test in this course, and I have a decent overall college record. I shouldn't be so hard on myself." What we say to ourselves can enhance or diminish self-esteem. (See the Sharpen Your Skill box on this page.)

We engage in self-talk to plan our lives, to rehearse different ways of acting, and to prompt ourselves to do or not do particular things. Intrapersonal communication is how we remind ourselves to make eye contact when giving a speech, show respect to others ("I need to listen to Grandmother's story"), check impulses that might hurt others ("I'll wait until I'm calmer to say anything"), and impress prospective employers ("I'll research the company before my interview").

Intrapersonal communication also helps us rehearse alternative scenarios and their possible outcomes. To control a disruptive group member, you might consider telling the person to "shut up," suggesting that the group adopt a rule that everyone should participate equally, and taking the person out for coffee and privately asking him or her to be less domineering. You will think through the three options (and perhaps others), weigh the likely consequences of each, and then choose one to put into practice. We engage in internal dialogues continuously as we reflect on experiences, sort through ideas, and test alternative ways of acting.

Interpersonal Communication

A second major emphasis in the field of communication is interpersonal communication, which is communication between people. **Interpersonal communication** is not a single thing but rather a continuum that ranges from quite impersonal (interaction between you and a parking lot attendant) to highly interpersonal (interaction between you and your best friend) (Figure 2.2). The more we interact with a person as a distinct individual, the more interpersonal the communication is.

Scholars of interpersonal communication study how communication creates and sustains relationships and how partners communicate to deal with the normal and extraordinary challenges of maintaining intimacy (Wood & Duck, 2006b). Research shows that intimates who listen sensitively and talk openly have the greatest chance of sustaining a close relationship. Research in this area has also shown that communication is a pivotal influence on how personal relationships develop over time. For example, researchers

Impersonal   Interpersonal

It   You   Thou

© Cengage Learning

Figure 2.2   **The Communication Continuum**

have shown that cross-sex friends engage in everyday talk less frequently than same-sex friends when communicating face-to-face and by phone. However, cross-sex and same-sex friends do not differ in how much they engage in everyday communication online (Ledbetter, Broeckelman-Post, & Krawsczyn, 2011).

Group and Team Communication

A third branch of the field is small-group communication, including communication in decision-making committees and work teams. Small-group research focuses on leadership, member roles, group features, agendas for achieving group goals, and managing conflict. Because groups involve more than one or two people, much teaching and research in this area focuses on how members coordinate their resources to arrive at collective decisions. In Chapter 11, we'll consider how we adapt basic communication processes to be effective when we participate in groups and teams.

A major focus of group communication scholars is team dynamics (Levi, 2010). Some scholars who focus on group communication study issues such as group conflict, group participation, errors in group decision making, and the dynamics of self-managing teams. Interestingly, although self-directed teams are often described as free from the usual hierarchy of power, many such teams become self-governing or self-policing. When this happens, the teams replace the standard power figure with their own enforcement of the hierarchy's values and policies (Ashcraft & Mumby, 2004).

Public Communication

Public speaking remains an important branch of the communication field. Even though many people will not pursue careers that call for extensive formal speaking, many of us will be in situations where speaking up is a responsibility. My editor makes presentations to her sales representatives to explain what her books are about and how to spotlight important features to professors who may want to use them in their courses. I recently coached my doctor, who was asked to address her colleagues on a development in treatment of renal disease. My plumber presents workshops to his staff to inform them of new developments in plumbing products and to teach them how to communicate effectively with customers. My brother-in-law relies on public speaking skills to try cases in court, and my sister gives public speeches to raise money for a center for abused children. My editor, doctor, plumber, brother-in-law, and sister don't consider themselves public speakers, but public speaking is a part of their lives.

Rhetorical critics often take a role in civic life by evaluating how well public figures support their positions and respond to challenges from opponents. Scholars of public communication are also interested in discovering and teaching principles of effective and ethical persuasion (Dillard & Pfau, 2002; Simons, Morreale, & Gronbeck, 2001). Research has also enlightened us about the kinds of argument, methods of organizing ideas, and forms of proof that listeners find ethical and effective.

Within the area of public communication are sub-areas such as argumentation and political communication. Argumentation focuses on how to build effective arguments by using sound reasoning and strong evidence and by developing ideas in ways that respond to listeners' beliefs, concerns, and goals. Skill in argumentation is essential for attorneys and anyone else who aims to persuade others. Political communication has also emerged as a sub-area of public communication. Scholars of political communication are particularly interested in how politicians connect or fail to connect with voters, how political campaigns succeed or falter, how social movements build awareness of issues such as the environment (Cox, 2010), and how rhetorical skills influence the process of policy making (Cox & McCloskey, 1996).

Organizational Communication

Communication in organizations is another growing area of interest. The work of communication scholars has identified communication skills that enhance professional success, and scholars have traced the effects of various kinds of communication on morale, productivity, and commitment to organizations. Scholars of organizational communication study interviewing, listening, leadership, new technologies of communication, and decision making.

In addition, scholars have begun to focus substantial attention on organizational culture and personal relationships in professional settings. **Organizational culture** is the general term for the understandings about an organization's identity and codes of thought and action that members of an organization share. Some organizations think of themselves as families. From this understanding emerge rules for how employees should interact and how fully they should commit to work.

Another area of increasing interest is personal relationships between co-workers. As we increase the number of hours we spend on the job, and as the number of working women increases, opportunities for romantic and sexual relationships in the workplace also increase. Obviously, this adds both interest and complication to life in organizations, as Melbourne notes in her commentary. Co-workers may also be close friends, a relationship that is complicated if one person has higher status than the other. Communication scholar Ted Zorn (1995) analyzed "bosses and buddies," relationships in which one friend is the boss of the other. Zorn discovered a number of ways people cope with the often-contradictory rules for communication between friends and between superiors and subordinates. He identified potential values and hazards of friendships on the job.

Melbourne

It was a real hassle when my supervisor and I started going out. Before, he gave me orders like he did all the other servers, and none of us thought anything about it. But after we started dating, he would sort of ask me, instead of tell me, what to do, like saying, "Mel, would you help out in section seven?" Another thing was that if he gave me a good station where tips run high, the other servers would give me trouble because they thought he was favoring me because we go out. And when he gave me a bad station, I'd feel he was being nasty for personal reasons. It was a mess being his employee and his girlfriend at the same time.

Personal relations on the job also require that people from diverse cultures and social communities learn to understand each other's styles of communicating. For example, women tend to make more "listening noises," such as "um," "uh-huh," and "go on," than men do. If men don't make listening noises when listening to women colleagues, the women may mistakenly think the men aren't interested. Conversely, men may misinterpret women's listening noises as agreement rather than simply interest. Such misunderstandings can strain professional relations.

Mass Media

Mass media is an exciting area in the field of communication. From a substantial body of research, we have learned a great deal about how mass media represent and influence cultural values. For instance, the use of young female models in ads and glamorous young women as reporters and news anchors perpetuates the cultural feminine ideal, which centers on youth and beauty. Films that portray men as daring, brave, and violent perpetuate strength and boldness as masculine ideals.

As noted previously in this chapter, mass media sometimes reinforce cultural stereotypes about race and ethnicity. Communication scholars heighten awareness of how media shape—and sometimes distort—our perceptions of ourselves and society. Franklin's commentary addresses this point.

 Franklin

> *I hate the way television shows African Americans. Most of the time they are criminals or welfare cases or drunks or Uncle Toms. When I watch TV, I understand why so many people think blacks are dumb, uneducated, and criminal. We're not, but you'd never know it from watching television.*

Mediated Communication

We are in the midst of a technological revolution that gives us the means to communicate in more ways at faster speeds with greater numbers of people throughout the world than ever before. How do newer technologies and the accompanying acceleration of the pace of interaction influence how we think and work and how we form, sustain, and end relationships? Some scholars caution that new technologies may undermine human community, whereas others celebrate the ways that mediated communication facilitates building community. Some scholars claim that new communication technologies will fundamentally transform how we think and process information (Steele, 2009). And some technology scholars caution that the abundance of information we can now get on any topic is useless unless we learn how to evaluate it critically and transform raw information into knowledge (Steele, 2009).

Clearly, the verdict on personal and social media will not be in for some time. Meanwhile, we all struggle to keep up with our increasingly technological world.

© Andrew Rich/istockphoto.com

New forms of communication change how we relate to others.

SHARPEN YOUR SKILL

Your Mediated World

How do personal and social media affect your relationships? How are IM and text messages different from face-to-face interactions? Have you made any acquaintances or friends through Facebook, Tumblr, Twitter, LinkedIn, or other social networks? Did those relationships develop differently from ones formed through face-to-face contact? Do you feel differently about people you have never seen and those you see face to face?

Today, students conduct much of their research on the Web or through specialized information services on the Internet, and friends and romantic partners text and instant message to stay in touch throughout the day. Communication scholars will continue to study whether emerging technologies merely alter how we communicate or actually change the kinds of relationships we build.

Intercultural Communication

Although intercultural communication is not a new area of study, its importance has grown in recent years. The United States has always been made up of many peoples, and demographic shifts in the last decade have increased the pluralism of this country. Increasing numbers of Asians, Latinos and Latinas, Eastern Europeans, and people of other ethnic backgrounds immigrate to the United States and make their homes here. They bring with them cultural values and styles of communicating that differ from those of citizens whose ancestors were born in the United States.

Studying intercultural communication increases our insight into different cultures' communication styles and meanings. For example, a Taiwanese woman in one of my graduate classes seldom spoke up and wouldn't enter the heated debates that are typical of graduate classes. One day after class, I encouraged Mei-Ling to argue for her ideas when others challenged them. She replied that doing so would be impolite. Her culture considers it disrespectful to contradict others. In the context of her culture, Mei-Ling's deference did not mean that she lacked confidence.

A particularly important recent trend in the area of intercultural communication is research on different social communities within a single society. Cultural differences are obvious in communication between a Nepali and a Canadian. Less obvious are differences in communication between people who speak the same language. Within the United States are distinct social communities based on race, gender, sexual preference, and other factors. Members of social communities such as these participate both in the overall culture of the United States and in the more specialized norms and practices of their communities. Recognizing and respecting different communication cultures increases personal effectiveness in a pluralistic society. Meikko's commentary reminds us of how cultural values are reflected in language.

Meikko

What I find most odd about Americans is their focus on themselves. Here, everyone wants to be an individual who is so strong and stands out from everyone else. In Japan, it is not like that. We see ourselves as parts of families and communities, not as individuals. Here, I and my are the most common words, but they are not often said in Japan.

Scholars and teachers of intercultural communication do not limit their work to minority cultures and social communities. A good example of this is the growing interest in what is called *whiteness studies*. This area of research and teaching explores what it means to be white. Members of dominant or majority groups often perceive their identities and communication as "standard" or "normal" and perceive the identities and communication of all other groups as different from those of majority groups. Whiteness studies help us realize that white (and other dominant groups) is just as much a race–ethnicity as black or Native American, and that white communication practices are shaped by cultural influences as much as those of other groups are.

Other Curricular Emphases

The eight areas we have discussed are primary ones that are taught at most colleges and universities around the country. In addition to these widely accepted curricular offerings, there are other areas of communication that are emphasized at particular schools. These include ethics, health communication, journalism, performance studies, religious communication, and speech and hearing. Coursework in health communication is often offered at universities that have premier medical schools, and training in religious communication is desired at schools that have religious missions.

Blurring the Lines

The areas of the field that we've just discussed are not as discrete as they may seem. Just as technologies of communication have converged in significant ways, so, too, do areas of the communication discipline converge and interact. For example, my niece Michelle and I instant message (IM) each other several times each day. Our IMs are both social media and interpersonal communication. Similarly, when we Skype with friends, we're simultaneously engaging in interpersonal and computer-mediated communication. Mass communication technology such as television and satellites allow citizens to watch public speeches as they happen. These examples remind us that the areas of communication often overlap and interact.

Unifying Themes in the Communication Field

After reading about the many different areas of study in communication, you might think that the field is a collection of unrelated interests. That isn't accurate. Although there are distinct elements in the communication mosaic, common themes unify the diverse areas of the discipline, just as common colors and designs unify a tile mosaic. Three enduring concerns—symbolic activities, meaning, and ethics—unify the diverse areas of communication.

Symbolic Activities

Symbols are the basis of language, thinking, and nonverbal communication. Symbols are arbitrary, ambiguous, and abstract representations of other phenomena. For instance, a wedding band is a symbol of marriage in Western culture, and a smile is a symbol of friendliness. Symbols allow us to reflect on our experiences and ourselves. Symbols also allow us to share experiences with others, even if they have not had those experiences themselves. We will discuss symbols in greater depth in Chapters 4 and 5, which deal with verbal and nonverbal communication, respectively.

Meaning

Closely related to interest in symbols is the communication field's concern with meaning. The human world is a world of meaning. We don't simply exist, eat, drink, sleep, and behave. Instead, we imbue every aspect of our lives with significance, or meaning. When I feed my cat, Sadie, she eats her food and then returns to her feline adventures. However, we humans layer food and eating with meanings beyond the mere satisfaction of hunger. Food often symbolizes special events or commitments. For example, kosher products reflect commitment to Jewish heritage, and turkey is commonly associated with commemorating the first Thanksgiving in the United States (although vegetarians symbolize their commitment by *not* eating turkey). Eggnog is a Christmas tradition, and mandel brot is a Hanukkah staple. Birthday cakes celebrate an individual, and we may fix special meals to express love to others.

Some families consider meals to be occasions for coming together and sharing lives, whereas in other families meals are battlefields for playing out family tensions. A meal can symbolize status (power lunches), romance (candles, wine), a personal struggle to stick to a diet, or an excuse to spend two hours talking with a friend. Humans imbue eating and other activities with meaning beyond their functional qualities. Our experiences gain significance as a result of the values and meanings we attach to them.

Because we are symbol users, we actively interpret events, situations, experiences, and relationships. We use symbols to name, evaluate, reflect on, and share experiences, ideas, and feelings. In fact, as Benita's commentary points out, when we give names to things, we change how we think about them. Through the process of communicating with others, we define our relationships. Do we have a friendship, or something else? How serious are we? Do we feel the same way about each other? Is this conflict irresolvable, or can we work it out and stay together?

 Benita

It's funny how important a word can be. Nick and I had been going out for a long time, and we really liked each other, but I didn't know if this was going to be long-term. Then we said we loved each other, and that changed how we saw each other and the relationship. Just using the word love *transformed who we are.*

To study communication, then, is to study how we use symbols to create meaning in our lives. As we interact with others, we build the meaning of friendship, team spirit, family, national identity, and organizational culture.

Ethics

A third theme that unifies the field of communication is concern with ethical dimensions of human interaction. **Ethics** is a branch of philosophy that focuses on moral principles and codes of conduct. What is right? What is wrong? What makes something right or wrong? Communication inevitably involves ethical matters because people affect each other when they interact (Makau, 2009). Therefore, it's important to think seriously about what moral guidelines we should follow in our communication and in our judgments of others' communication.

One ethical principle that is applicable to a broad range of situations is allowing others to make informed and willing choices. Adopting this principle discourages us from deceiving others by distorting evidence, withholding information, or coercing consent. Another important principle of ethical communication is respect for differences between people. Embracing this guideline deters us from imposing our ways and our values on others whose experiences and views of appropriate communication may differ from our own.

SUMMARY

Like most fields of study, communication includes many areas, which have evolved over a long and distinguished intellectual history. In this chapter we reviewed the more than 2,500-year history of the discipline of communication and noted how it has changed over time. We also discussed methods of conducting research that are used by scholars of communication.

The final section of the chapter described areas that are part of the modern field of communication, and we noted that these areas are unified by abiding interests in symbolic activities and meanings, as well as by a common interest in basic processes that form the foundations of personal, interpersonal, professional, civic, and mediated communication. The foundations established in this chapter and in Chapter 1 prepare us for chapters that focus on basic processes and skills that pertain to a wide range of communication contexts.

REVIEW, REFLECT, EXTEND

The Reflect, Discuss, and Apply Questions that follow will help you review, reflect on, and extend the information and ideas presented in this chapter. These resources, and a diverse selection of additional study tools, are also available online at the CourseMate for *Communication Mosaics*. Your CourseMate includes a student workbook, WebLinks, TED Talks hyperlinks and activities, chapter glossary and flashcards, interactive video activities, Speech Builder Express, and InfoTrac College Edition. For more information or to access this book's online resources, visit **www .cengagebrain.com.**

KEY CONCEPTS

critical research methods, 29
ethics, 39
ethos, 24
interpersonal communication, 32
intrapersonal communication, 31
logos, 24

organizational culture, 34
pathos, 24
qualitative research methods, 29
quantitative research methods, 28
triangulation, 30

Reflect, Discuss, Apply

1. Review the areas of communication discussed in the section on the breadth of the communication field. In which areas do you feel most competent as a communicator? In which areas do you feel less competent? Identify one goal for improving your communication competence that you can keep in mind as you read the rest of this book.

2. This chapter provides an overview of the field of communication and notes how it has evolved in response to social changes and issues. As a class, identify major changes you anticipate in U.S. society in the next 50 years. What kinds of changes in the field of communication might be prompted by the social changes you anticipate?

3. As a class, develop a survey to get experience with collecting data. Develop a survey with 2-3 questions to learn about attitudes held by students on your campus toward a subject your class finds interesting. For instance, you might survey student attitudes regarding the values of college education (how important is college for (a) personal growth, (b) intellectual growth, (c) career success?) or your campus's efforts to be environmentally responsible. After the class prepares the survey, each student should collect responses from 10 students. Then the class should tally all responses and discuss what the survey reveals.

Recommended Resources

1. Go to your library or an online database, such as Gale or InfoTrac College Edition, that provides full articles from academic journals. Read this article: Elise Dallimore, Julie Hertenstein, and Marjorie Platt (2004). Classroom participation and discussion effectiveness: Student-generated strategies. *Communication Education, 53,* 103–115. After reading the article, answer the following questions:

   a. What methods of research were used by the authors to conduct this study?

   b. What teacher behaviors did students identify as most helpful in enhancing the quality of classroom discussion?

   c. How might the findings of this study be applied to other contexts, such as communication in work groups and parent–child conversations?

2. Josina Makau's (2009) chapter on ethical and unethical communication is important for all students in the field. Consider how the ethical frameworks discussed in her chapter might inform volunteer civic service.

3. Go to the book's online resources for this chapter and click on WebLink 2.4 to access NCA's online magazine, *Communication Currents.* You will find articles that reflect current research and teaching in the field.

EXPERIENCE COMMUNICATION CASE STUDY

Communication Ethics

Apply what you've learned in this chapter by analyzing the following case study, using the accompanying questions as a guide. These questions and a video of the case study are also available online through your CourseMate for *Communication Mosaics.*

This case study differs from the others in this text because it is an actual interview, not an enacted fictional scenario. In the interview, Jenna Hiller asks Dr. Tim Muehlhoff some questions about communication and ethics, and Dr. Muehlhoff's responses elaborate on and clarify material covered in this chapter.

© Cengage Learning

Student: In Chapter 2, Dr. Wood states that "ethical issues infuse all forms of communication." Can you explain what she means?

Professor: Well, in Chapter 2 she defines ethics as a branch of philosophy that's concerned with moral principles and conduct—what's right and what's wrong. But can you see how much personal choice is involved in that definition? Who gets to decide what is right and what is wrong? I was in Barnes & Noble a couple of months ago and saw a book called, *What Would Machiavelli Do? The Ends Justify the Meanness.* Now, you may remember that Machiavelli was one of the most ruthless politicians, and he lived in the early 1500s. He believed that success was the goal, and you should get it however you wanted to. And in the book, this author says, "This book is for people with the courage to leave decency and kindness behind, and seize the future by the throat and have it cough up money, power, and superior office space." So if Machiavelli is your ethical guide, then, when giving a speech, make up statistics. Plagiarize part of it, and say that it's your speech. When it comes to interpersonal communication, win an argument at all costs. Manipulate a person's emotions. If they've confided information to you, go ahead and use their words against them. In small-group communication, ignore a particular person you don't agree with. Every time they start to talk, you just interrupt them. But you know, Machiavelli's not our only choice. What would our communication look like if we asked the question, "What would Gandhi do?" or "What would Martin Luther King, Jr., do?" or "What would Jesus do?" How would that change how we communicate with people? We would choose what is right for everybody. We would choose to try to respect everybody. Machiavelli or Gandhi are some of the choices we have to make in all of our communication.

Student: I'm still not sure I understand what you mean. I don't see how listening and responding to others involves ethical choices.

Professor: Well, my favorite quote about listening comes from Reuel Howe's book, *The Miracle of Dialogue.* In it, he says, "I cannot hear you because of what I expect you to say." And it's true, isn't it? We often judge people prematurely. We form unethical stereotypes of people, and then we respond to the stereotype rather than the person. For instance, when I was teaching at UNC-Chapel Hill with Julia Wood, there was a colleague of ours who was heavily criticized for using gangsta rap lyrics in a commencement address. And I was one of the critics. Even though I had not heard the speech, I thought to myself, "How can you use lyrics that are filled with anger, racism, and sexism?"—until I actually sat in on his class and listened to his rationale. I found out that this professor did not condone violence or sexism. He did argue that there's a lot we can learn about individuals by listening to their music. And I remember him saying once, "Hear the violence in those songs and condemn it. Hear the sexism, and condemn it. But also hear the pain and the hopelessness, and respond to it." You see, I had formed a caricature of this man, a stereotype— and that's unethical. Ethical communication means I allow you to speak for yourself, and then I respond to what you say—but I don't put words in your mouth and conform you to the image I want you to have.

Student: Also in Chapter 2, Dr. Wood states that a principle for ethical communication is respecting differences between people. Am I supposed to just accept everyone and every value?

Professor: There's an old Jewish proverb that says, "It is folly and shame to speak before listening." The folly part I think we can understand. It's folly for me to respond to you if I don't know what you're saying. That's uninformed communication. The second part deals with ethics. It is shameful for me to respond to you before I listen. In other words, I view you as an inferior. I don't even need to listen to your perspective before I respond to it. Ethical communication does not mean that I have to accept the views of every person. It does mean that all my communication needs to be informed, and I treat people as equals, not as people who are inferior to me. In Chapter 7 Julia talks about communication climates, which is the overall mood between two people when they communicate. Now imagine what that communication climate would be like if our communication was both informed and respectful.

1. Dr. Tim Muehlhoff quoted the following statement from *The Miracle of Dialogue:* "I cannot hear you because of what I expect you to say." Recall some instances in your own life where you have been unable to hear what someone was saying because of your expectations and stereotypes of that person.

2. Dr. Muehlhoff also noted that he had seen a book entitled, *What Would Machiavelli Do? The Ends Justify the Meanness* He then suggested that there are many people we might pick as our ethical guides. Whom would you pick as your guide for ethical communication? Fill in the blank in this sentence: What would____do? What ethical principles for communication follow from your choice of an ethical guide?

3. What ethical choices did Dr. Muehlhoff make in his conversation with Jenna Hiller about the relevance of ethics to communication?

4. Review "The New Employee," the case study for Chapter 1. What ethical choices did the senior employee make in communicating with Toya?

> *Reality is merely an illusion, albeit a persistent one.* — *Albert Einstein*

3 Perceiving and Understanding

A few years ago, Robbie and I adopted a young dog who had been abandoned. Our new family member, whom we named Cassie, seemed small to us—she was fully grown and weighed just 35 pounds. Previously, we'd owned an Irish setter and a Lab mix, each of whom weighed about 70 pounds—twice Cassie's weight. A few weeks after Cassie joined us, my 6-year-old nephew, Harrison, came to spend a week with us. I picked him up at the airport, and we drove home, chattering all the way.

When I opened the door of our home, Cassie ran to meet the new person and shower him with kisses. "She's so big!" Harrison shrieked as Cassie jumped on him, putting her paws on his shoulders so that her head was even with Harrison's. "She's a big, BIG dog," he announced. Because we were accustomed to dogs twice Cassie's size, and because Robbie and I are adults, Cassie seemed small to us. But to a boy who weighed 45 pounds and was less than 4 feet tall, she seemed large! Our perceptions reflected our different experiences and even our physical sizes. Perceptions—and differences among people's perceptions—are major influences on human communication.

This chapter focuses on perception, a basic communication process that is critical to our efforts to create meaning as we communicate with ourselves and others. Perception is the process by which we notice and make sense of phenomena. To explore the relationships between perception and communication, this chapter discusses three interrelated facets of perception and considers influences on how people perceive and why they sometimes differ in their perceptions. We'll conclude the chapter by identifying ways in which skillful perception can improve our effectiveness as communicators.

FOCUS QUESTIONS

1. What is perception?

2. What factors influence our perceptions?

3. How does the self-serving bias affect the accuracy of our perceptions?

4. Does mind reading help or hinder communication?

5. How can we use language to enhance skill in perceiving?

The Perception Process

Perception is the active process of selecting, organizing, and interpreting people, objects, events, situations, and activities. The first thing to notice in this definition is that perception is an active process. We are not passive receivers of what is "out there" in the external world. Instead, we select certain things to notice, and then we organize and interpret what we have selectively noticed. What anything means to us depends on which aspects of it we attend to and how we organize and interpret what we notice.

Perception and communication influence each other. Perception shapes our understanding of others' communication and the choices we make in our own communication. For example, if you perceive a co-worker as hostile, you are likely to notice only his or her unfriendly behaviors and to communicate defensively or to minimize interaction. Communication also influences our perceptions of people and situations. The language and nonverbal behaviors that other people use affect our perceptions of their intelligence, honesty, and so forth.

The second important aspect of the definition is that perception consists of three interrelated processes: selection, organization, and interpretation (Figure 3.1). These processes blend into one another. We organize perceptions even as we select what to perceive, and we interpret in an ongoing manner. Each process affects the other two. What we notice about people and situations influences how we interpret them. Also, our interpretation of a person or situation directs us to selectively notice certain, and not other, aspects of the person or setting.

Selection

Stop for a moment and notice what is going on around you right now. Is music playing in the background? Or do you perhaps hear several different kinds of music from different places? Is the room warm or cold, messy or clean, large or small, light or dark? Is laundry piled in the corner waiting to be washed?

Can you smell anything: food cooking, traces of cologne? Who else is in the room and nearby? Do you hear other conversations? Is a window open? Can you hear sounds of activities outside? Is it raining? Now, think about what's happening inside you. Are you tired or hungry? Do you have a headache or an itch anywhere? On what kind of paper is your book printed? Is the type large, small, easy to read?

Chances are that you weren't conscious of most of these phenomena when you began reading this chapter. Instead, you focused on reading and understanding the material in the chapter. You selectively attended to what you defined as important in this moment, and you were unaware of many other things going on around you. This is typical of how we live our lives. We can't attend to everything in our environment, because far too much is there, and most of it isn't relevant to us at any given time.

A number of factors influence which stimuli we notice. First, some qualities of external phenomena draw our attention. For instance, we notice things that **STAND OUT** because they are larger more **intense**, or unusual. We're more likely to hear a loud voice than a soft one and to notice a bright shirt more than a drab one. We also pay attention to what matters to us, so out of the 18 messages that appear when you check for text messages, you're likely to first notice those from people you want to hear from. Change also compels attention, which is why we

Figure 3.1 **The Perception Process**

become more attentive when a speaker shows a slide to enliven a speech or when a new person joins a dialogue in a chat room.

Sometimes, we deliberately influence what we notice by talking to ourselves. We tell ourselves to be alert if we have to drive when we're tired. We remind ourselves to speak loudly when we are addressing a large group without a microphone. We prompt ourselves not to interrupt during team discussions. We warn ourselves to stay in character when we have claimed an alternate identity in online chat rooms. These are examples of intrapersonal communication that helps us attend selectively to specific behaviors.

Our self-concepts may also influence our perceptions. People who consider themselves attractive and desirable may perceive other attractive people as more available than do people with lower self-concepts. Researchers (Tsai & Reis, 2009) showed that lonely people tend to perceive others more negatively than people who are not lonely. It may be the case that lonely people are lonely because they see others as unattractive or unapproachable.

Our needs, interests, and motives influence what we choose to notice. If you're bored in your job, you're likely to notice ads for other jobs. If you are interested in politics, you're likely to pay attention to political stories in the news. If you've just broken up with a partner, you're more likely to notice attractive and available people than if you are in a satisfying relationship. Motives also explain the oasis phenomenon, in which thirsty people in a desert see an oasis although none is present. If we really want something, we may perceive it when it doesn't exist.

People tend to perceive things they desire as closer or more accessible than they really are. In one study, the researchers (Balcetis & Dunning, 2010) had people sit across the table from a full bottle of water and then had them either eat pretzels or drink water from an eight-ounce glass. The participants were then asked to estimate how many inches separated them from the bottle of water. Consistently, the participants who were thirsty from eating pretzels perceived the water bottle as being closer than the other participants. In another experiment, participants were given the chance to win a $25 gift card or a $0 gift card by tossing beanbags at it. The person whose beanbag landed closest won the gift card. Once again, the researchers found that people underestimated the distance between themselves and the desirable object.

Organization

We don't perceive randomly; instead, we organize our perceptions in meaningful ways. **Constructivism** is a theory that states that we organize and interpret experience by applying cognitive structures called **cognitive schemata**, or just **schemata** (the singular noun is *schema*). We rely on four schemata to make sense of phenomena: prototypes, personal constructs, stereotypes, and scripts (Burleson & Rack, 2008) (see Figure 3.2).

Prototypes

Prototypes are knowledge structures that define the clearest or ideal examples of some category (Fehr, 1993). For example, you probably have a prototype of a teacher, a friend, and a team leader. You may also have prototypes of people in India or Afghanistan that are based on what you have witnessed in mass media. A prototype is an ideal, or best example, of a category. We

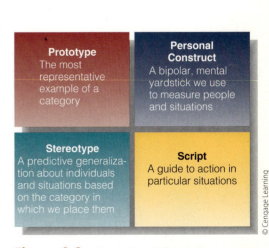

Prototype
The most representative example of a category

Personal Construct
A bipolar, mental yardstick we use to measure people and situations

Stereotype
A predictive generalization about individuals and situations based on the category in which we place them

Script
A guide to action in particular situations

© Cengage Learning

Figure 3.2 **Cognitive Schemata**

use prototypes to define exemplars: Jane is a model leader; Burt exemplifies a good friend; Ned is an ideal co-worker. The person who exemplifies a whole group, or category, is the category's prototype. We classify people by asking which of our prototypes they most closely resemble. Damion explains his prototype of a good friend.

 Damion

My ideal of a friend is my buddy Jackson. He stood by me when I got into a lot of trouble a couple of years ago. I got mixed up with some guys who used drugs, and I started using them. Pretty soon, the coach caught on to me, and he suspended me from the team. That made me feel like a total loser, and I got deeper into drugs. Jackson didn't give up on me, and he wouldn't let me give up either. He took me to a drug center and went with me every day for three weeks. He never turned away when I was sick or even when I cried most of one night when I was getting off the drugs. He just stood by me. Once I was straight, Jackson went with me to ask the coach about getting back on the team.

Prototypes are useful to us because they allow us to group people, events, and situations into broad categories. However, when our prototypes don't match those of others, we may run into problems. For example, if your prototype of an ideal team member is a jokester, and the team leader's prototype of an ideal member is an efficient worker, you may find your job on the line!

Personal Constructs

A **personal construct** is a mental yardstick that allows us to measure a person or situation along a bipolar dimension of judgment (Kelly, 1955). Examples of personal constructs are *intelligent–not intelligent*, *kind–not kind*, and *trustworthy–not trustworthy*. How intelligent, kind, and trustworthy is a speaker, journalist, friend, or co-worker? Whereas prototypes help us decide into which broad category a person, situation, or event fits, personal constructs allow us to make more detailed assessments of particular qualities of phenomena we perceive. Nai Lee's commentary offers an example of a personal construct.

 Nai Lee

One of the ways I look at people is by whether they are individualistic or related to others. In Korea, we think of ourselves as members of families and communities. The emphasis on individuals was the first thing I noticed when I came to this country, and it is still an important way I look at people.

Context influences which personal constructs are prominent in our assessments of others. If you are thinking about a person as a date, you're likely to rely on constructs such as *fun–not fun*, *intelligent–not intelligent*, and *attractive–not attractive*. When perceiving a co-worker, you're more likely to rely on constructs such as *reliable–not reliable*, *cooperative–not cooperative*, *experienced–not experienced*, and *motivated–not motivated*. Constructs such as *fair–not fair*, *knowledgeable–not knowledgeable*, and *interesting–not interesting* may guide your perceptions of teachers. We assess people according to the constructs we use, not according to all the constructs that *could* be used. Thus, we may not perceive qualities that are not highlighted by the constructs we apply. This reminds us that the processes of selecting and organizing interact to affect our perceptions.

Stereotypes

A **stereotype** is a predictive generalization about a person or situation. Based on the category (established by prototypes) in which we place something and how it measures up against personal constructs we apply, we predict what it will do. For instance, if you place someone in the category of "liberal people," you might stereotype the person as likely to vote Democratic, to support social services, and to oppose the death penalty. You may have stereotypes of fraternity and sorority members, professors, athletes, and people from other cultures.

What personal constructs do you rely on when perceiving the people in this photo?

 Winowa

> *People have a stereotype of Native Americans. People who are not Native Americans think we are all alike—how we look, how we act, what we believe, what our traditions are. But that isn't true. The Crow and Cherokee are as different as people from Kenya and New York. Some tribes have a history of aggression and violence; others have traditions of peace and harmony. We worship different spirits and have different tribal customs. All these differences are lost when people stereotype us all as Native Americans.*

Stereotypes don't necessarily reflect actual similarities among phenomena that you group into a single category, as Winowa's commentary illustrates. Our stereotypes may keep us from seeing differences between people we have grouped into a category, as the FYI box on the next page demonstrates.

Stereotypes may be accurate or inaccurate. In some cases, we have incorrect understandings of a group, and in other cases some members of a group don't conform to what is typical of the group as a whole. Although we need stereotypes in order to predict what will happen, we should remember that they are selective, subjective, and not necessarily accurate. In her commentary, Phyllis describes how a stereotype affects her.

Phyllis

> *I'll tell you what stereotype really gets to me: the older student. I'm 38 and working on a B.A., and I'm tired of being treated like a housewife who's dabbling in courses. Some students treat me like their mother, not a peer. And some faculty are even worse. One professor told me that I shouldn't worry about grades because I didn't have to plan a career like the younger students. Well, I am planning a career, I am a student, and I am serious about my work.*

Photofusion Picture Library/Alamy

Scripts

The final cognitive schema we use to organize perceptions is the script, which is a guide to action. A **script** is a sequence of activities that spells out how we and others are expected to act in a specific situation. If you run into a friend who is with someone you don't know, and your friend says, "Hi, this is Ben," you don't have to think about what you are supposed to say; your meeting-new-person script tells you that you should say, "Hi, I'm (your name)" and perhaps smile or offer to shake hands. Although we're often unaware of them, scripts guide many of our daily activities. You have a script for greeting casual acquaintances as you walk around campus ("Hey, how ya doing?" "Fine." "See ya."). You have scripts for texting friends to check in with them (<hi. where r u?> <gotta take a call. brb.>) (Carl, 2006). You also have scripts for talking with professors, engaging in interviews, and communicating online. Scripts organize perceptions into lines of action.

Dianne Holmberg and Samantha MacKenzie (2002) studied scripts for dating relationships. They found that partners who see their relationship as consistent with their perceptions of normative scripts for dating have generally positive evaluations of their relationships. Conversely, partners who perceive inconsistency between most people's perceptions of how dating relationships progress and what is happening in their own relationship tend to have less positive assessments of their relationship. Similarly, Sandra Metts (2006) has identified consistent scripts for heterosexual flirting.

Prototypes, personal constructs, stereotypes, and scripts are cognitive schemata that organize our thinking about people and situations. We use them to make sense of experience and to predict how we and others will act. The Sharpen Your Skill box on page 49 invites you to reflect on how your cognitive schemata affect your perceptions of others.

DIVERSITY

The Census Bureau's Dilemma

Systems of organizing or classifying are arbitrary constructions invented by humans. Yet we sometimes act as if our classifications are objectively true. Consider the dilemma of the U.S. Census Bureau, which found that its method of classifying races no longer works. The mushrooming diversity of Americans has created problems for the Bureau. The racial categories created in 1978 are no longer adequate to classify people with diverse languages, cultures, and ethnic heritages.

Lumping diverse groups into single categories such as Asian (which includes Japanese, Chinese, Taiwanese, Nepalese, etc.) or Native American (which includes Crow, Lumbee, Paiute, etc.) is inappropriate. The traditional classifications count Middle Easterners as White, and Alaskans as Alaskan Natives rather than as people born in the United States. Another deficiency of the standard categories is that they don't acknowledge multiracial identities, which many citizens have.

Interpretation

To interpret experiences, we ask why something happens or why someone says, does, or doesn't do a particular thing. **Interpretation** is the subjective process of creating explanations for what we observe and experience. If you have ever been around a young child, then you know that "Why?" is an incessant question: Why is the sky blue? Why are you angry with me? Why do teachers have to give tests? Why can't I have the toy I want? Children's interest in *why* is a search to figure out what causes things to happen and people to act as they do. Although adults are perhaps more sophisticated than children, we are no less interested in figuring out why things happen and why people behave as they do.

Attributions

Our quest to figure out the why of things brings us to the concept of **attribution**, which is the act of explaining why something happens or why a person acts a particular way (Manusov & Spitzberg, 2008; for the classic research in this area, see Heider, 1958; Kelley, 1967). We *attribute* our own and others' behaviors to causes.

Attributions have four dimensions. The first is the *internal–external* locus: the attribution of a person's behavior to internal factors ("He's short tempered") or external factors ("The traffic jam frustrated him"). The second dimension is *stability,* the explanation of actions as the result of stable, enduring factors that won't change over time ("She's a nervous person"; "This job is always stressful") or variable (unstable) temporary factors ("She's nervous right now because of a big deal she's closing"; "This is a stressful period at work"). The third dimension is *specificity,* the explanation of actions as the result of global factors ("She's intelligent") or specific factors ("She's gifted at math"). Finally, the dimension of *control* is the ascribing of responsibility for actions either to people themselves ("She doesn't try to control her temper") or to factors beyond their personal control ("She has a chemical imbalance"). In a recent study (Nagourney, 2008), volunteers were given a mild electric shock to their wrists. Some volunteers were told that another person chose to administer the shock. Other volunteers were told the shock was randomly selected by a computer. The volunteers who believed another person chose to shock them reported greater pain. Figure 3.3 illustrates the three dimensions of attribution.

SHARPEN YOUR SKILL

Sizing Up Others

Pay attention to the cognitive schemata you use the next time you meet a new person. First, notice how you classify the person. Do you categorize her or him as a potential friend, date, co-worker, and so on? Identify your prototype of the category into which you place the person.

Next, identify the constructs you use to assess the person. Do you focus on physical constructs (*attractive–not attractive*), mental constructs (*intelligent–not intelligent*), psychological constructs (*secure–not secure*), or interpersonal constructs (*available–not available*)? Would different constructs be prominent if you used a different prototype to classify the person?

Third, note how you stereotype the person. According to the prototype and constructs you've applied, what do you expect him or her to do? Would your expectations differ if you had placed him or her in a different category?

Finally, identify your script, or how you expect interaction to unfold between you according to the prototype, personal constructs, stereotypes, and scripts that you applied.

The Self-Serving Bias

Although we need explanations of our own and others' behaviors, the explanations, or attributions, we develop aren't necessarily accurate. Research shows that we tend to construct attributions that serve our personal interests (Hamachek, 1992; Manusov & Spitzberg, 2008; Sypher, 1984). This phenomenon is known as the **self-serving bias.** Thus, we are inclined to attribute our positive actions and our successes to internal and stable factors. We're also likely to claim that good results come about because of the personal control we exerted. You might attribute making an *A* on a test to being a smart

Dimension

1. Locus	Internal	External
2. Stability	Stable	Unstable
3. Specificity	Specific	Global
4. Responsibility	Within personal control	Beyond personal control

© Cengage Learning

Figure 3.3   **The Dimensions of of Attribution**

person (internal, stable, global) who studies hard (personal control). In her commentary, Chandra reflects on a self-serving attribution.

 Chandra

I wait tables to make money for school. It used to be that when I didn't make good tips, I would say that the customers were cheap or in bad moods or my manager assigned me to a slow station. When I made good tips, I always thought that it was because I am such a considerate server. Then we got a new manager, who told me that I made better tips when I was feeling good. He pointed out that I was really friendly and attentive to customers when I was in a good mood but that I could be careless when I felt down.

Conversely, we tend to avoid taking responsibility for negative actions and failures and instead attribute them to external and unstable events that are beyond personal control. To explain a failing grade on a test, you might say that you did poorly because the professor (external) put a lot of tricky questions on that particular test (unstable, specific) so that regardless of how hard you studied, you couldn't do well (outside personal control). The self-serving bias can distort our perceptions, leading us to take excessive credit for what we do well and to deny responsibility for our failings. It can also lead us to judge others less kindly than ourselves (Manusov, 2006; Schutz, 1999; Sedikides et al., 1998). The FYI box on page 51 shows how taking responsibility for problems may affect perceptions and loyalty to companies.

In summary, perception involves three interrelated processes. The first—selection—involves noticing certain things and ignoring others within the total context. The second process is organization, wherein we use prototypes, personal constructs, stereotypes, and scripts to order what we have selectively perceived. Finally, we engage in interpretation to make sense of the perceptions we have gathered and organized. Attributions are a primary way that we explain what we and others do. And although we've discussed each process separately, they interact continually. Thus, our interpretations shape the knowledge schemata we use to organize experiences, and how we organize perceptions affects what we notice and interpret. We're now ready to consider some factors that influence what and how we perceive.

Influences on Perception

A few years ago, I went to a neighborhood cookout, at which a neighbor who did not attend was discussed. The absent person had been behaving oddly ever since he moved into our neighborhood. He had thrown a rock at one person's dog, had been seen going into another neighbor's house when the owners weren't home, had been verbally abusive to several members of the community, and had shot squirrels and birds, which nobody else in the neighborhood did.

At the picnic, neighbors were sharing stories of what he had done and what it meant. A woman who is a psychologist ventured the opinion that he was suffering from depression and needed help. The legal aspects of his behavior were the focus of an attorney's comments, who observed that the man could be arrested for breaking and entering and verbal harassment. A third person, who had recently left an abusive partner, was afraid that our neighbor posed a threat to all of us. Those of us who have dogs and cats in our families were concerned that the neighbor might shoot our pets. As this example illustrates, people don't always perceive situations in the same ways. How each of us perceived our neighbor was shaped by many factors in our backgrounds, our training, and our individual interests.

Physiological Factors

The most obvious reason perceptions vary among people is that we differ in our sensory abilities and physiologies. The five senses are not the same for all of us. Music that one person finds deafening is barely audible to another. On a given day on my campus, students wear everything from shorts and sandals to heavy jackets, a sign that they have different sensitivities to cold.

Our physiological states also influence perception. If you are tired, stressed, or sick, you're likely to perceive things more negatively than when you are well and rested. For instance, a playful insult from a friend might anger you if you were feeling down but might not bother you if you felt good. Each of us has biorhythms, which influences how alert we are at different times of day.

Expectations

Imagine that a friend tells you she wants you to meet a person whom she describes as "one of the coolest people I've ever met: He's funny and considerate and so interested in other people. You'll find him really easy to talk to and lots of fun." Chances are you would expect to like the new person and would in fact perceive the good qualities your friend led you to expect. If instead your friend had said, "This guy is a real drag. He's always cracking bad jokes, and he's self-centered," you might expect not to like the man, and you might see only his shortcomings.

Based on a series of studies, John Bargh (1997, 1999) reports that how we act may be affected by subliminal priming of expectations. In one study, participants were told that they would be taking two tests. The researcher told each participant to go into a room and take a test and then to come out of the room and find the researcher to progress to the second test. One-half of the participants then took a test that presented them with a group of terms related to politeness. The other half of the participants took a test that presented them with a group of terms related to rudeness. When participants finished the test and went to look for the researcher, they found the researcher talking with another person. Of the participants who had worked with the terms related to rudeness, 63 percent interrupted the researcher's conversation, but only 17 percent of the participants who had worked with politeness terms interrupted the conversation. Apparently, their perceptions of appropriate behavior were affected by exposure to words that made rudeness or politeness salient to them.

Expectations affect our perceptions in a variety of communication situations. If we are told in advance that a new person on the job is "a real team player," we're likely to notice the new employee's cooperative behaviors and not likely to see competitive or self-serving behaviors that the new person may also present. If we're forewarned that a speaker tends to distort facts, we're likely to perceive misrepresentations in the speech. On the other hand, if we're told that the speaker is trustworthy, we may listen less critically and not perceive any slanting or distortions. Our sense of time has been radically reshaped by communication technologies that lead us to expect extremely quick exchanges. Just a decade ago, most people expected replies to business correspondence within a week to 10 days. Now, many people expect nearly instant responses, and we grumble if a friend isn't online when we IM her or him or if a text message isn't answered for several hours.

The influence of expectations on communication is the basis of **positive visualization,** which is a technique used to enhance success in a variety of situations by teaching people to visualize themselves positively. According to psychologists, positive visualization works because we act as we see ourselves. Businesses coach managers to visualize successful negotiations and meetings (Lau, 1989). Athletes learn to imagine playing well, and those who engage in positive visualization often improve their athletic performance (Porter & Foster, 1986).

Positive visualization is also used to reduce speaking anxiety by guiding apprehensive speakers through imagined positive speaking experiences. This technique allows people to form a mental picture of themselves as effective speakers and to then enact that mental picture in actual speaking situations (Hamilton, 1996). Researchers report that positive visualization is especially effective in reducing chronic communication apprehension (Ayres & Hopf, 1990; Bourhis & Allen, 1992). The goal of

One gift of growing older is enriched perspective. What might these people be able to share that two 20-year-olds cannot?

positive visualization in this context is to create detailed positive images of yourself in communication situations. Such visualizations encourage positive expectations of your actual communication.

What happens when our expectations are violated? That's the question asked by **expectancy violation theory.** Research shows that when our expectations are violated, we become more cognitively alert as we struggle to understand and cope with unexpected behaviors or events (Afifi & Metts, 1998; Bevan, 2003; Burgoon, 1993).

Three aspects of a violation of expectations influence how we will interpret it (Afifi & Metts, 1998). First, our interpretations are affected by whether the violation is positive (someone gives you a gift that you had not anticipated) or negative (your supervisor criticizes you). Second, our interpretations are influenced by the extent to which the behavior deviates from expected behavior. If your supervisor has never criticized you before, criticizing you now would be a significant deviation from expectations. Third, our interpretations are affected by the impact of the violation on a relationship. Think about the different impacts on a dating relationship if the person you are dating doesn't call when she or he promises and if she or he dates your best friend.

Cognitive Abilities

In addition to physiological, cultural, and social influences, perception is shaped by our cognitive abilities. How elaborately we think about situations and people, and the extent of our knowledge of others, affect how we select, organize, and interpret experiences.

Cognitive Complexity

People differ in the number and types of knowledge schemata they use to organize and interpret people and situations. **Cognitive complexity** is the number of personal constructs used (remember, personal constructs are bipolar dimensions of judgment), how

© James Shaffer/PhotoEdit

Before games, coaches often prime players to see themselves beating the opposition.

abstract they are, and how elaborately they interact to shape perceptions. Most children have fairly simple cognitive systems. They rely on few schemata, focus more on concrete constructs (*tall–not tall*) than abstract psychological ones (*secure–not secure*), and often don't perceive relationships between different perceptions (How is security related to extroversion?).

Many adults have greater cognitive complexity, which affects the accuracy of perceptions. The older we get, the richer is our perspective for perceiving situations and people. Thus, compared with a person of 20, someone who is 60 has a more complex fund of experiences on which to draw. Throughout my 20s, I was easily upset when a class didn't go well or when a friend and I argued. Often, I became disheartened because I perceived these as significant problems. In my mid-30s, my father died. After his death, a less-than-perfect class or a minor argument with a friend didn't acutely distress me, because I had a very different perspective on what a serious problem was.

The extent of discrimination that is still experienced by women, minorities, and gays and lesbians understandably discourages many college students. I am more hopeful than some because I have seen significant changes in my lifetime. When I attended college, women and minorities were not admitted on an equal basis with Caucasian men, and almost all gays and lesbians concealed their sexual orientations. When I entered the job market, there were few laws to protect women, minorities, and gays and lesbians against discrimination in hiring, pay, and advancement. The substantial progress made during my life leads me to hold optimistic perceptions about society's ability to alleviate the inequities that still exist.

Cognitive complexity influences our perceptions of others. If you can think of people only as good or bad, you have limited ways of perceiving others. Similarly, people who focus on concrete data tend to have less sophisticated understandings than people who also perceive psychological data. For example, you might notice that a person is attractive, tells jokes, and talks a lot. At a more abstract psychological level, you might infer that the behaviors you observe reflect a secure, self-confident personality. This is a more sophisticated explanation because it includes perceptions of why the person acts as she or he does.

What if you later find out that the person is quiet in classes? Someone with low cognitive complexity would have difficulty integrating the new information with earlier observations, would likely either dismiss the new information because it doesn't fit, or replace the former perception with the more recent data and redefine the person as shy. A more cognitively complex person would integrate all the information into a coherent account. Perhaps a cognitively complex person would interpret the person as more confident in social situations than in academic ones. Research shows that cognitively complex people are flexible in interpreting complicated phenomena and are able to integrate new information into their thinking about people and situations. People who are less cognitively complex tend to ignore information that doesn't fit their impressions or to throw out old ideas and replace them with new impressions (Crockett, 1965; Delia, Clark, & Switzer, 1974). Either way, they screen out some of the nuances and inconsistencies that are part of human nature.

Person-Centeredness

Person-centeredness is the ability to perceive another as a unique individual. When we perceive distinctions between people, we can adapt our communication to particular individuals. Person-centeredness is linked to cognitive complexity. People who are cognitively complex are able to perceive others and situations in more comprehensive and integrated ways than are less cognitively complex people. This allows them to adapt their communication to particular listeners (Zorn, 1991). Thus, an effective politician may adopt a different speaking style and emphasize different topics when talking with elderly citizens, elementary school children, members of unions, and business executives. Skillful group leaders recognize and adapt their communication to differences in members' abilities, needs, and so forth. When texting or chatting online, we use common shorthand (for instance, *brb, lol*) with people we know understand it, as Emma points out.

 Emma

> I talk differently when I'm e-mailing my parents and aunt than when I'm chatting online with friends. My parents and aunt don't know a lot of standard online lingo like myob [mind your own business], OMG [oh my gosh] or abbreviations like r for are and u for you. It takes more time to explain them to the family than it takes to just spell everything out.

To adapt communication to others, we must understand something about them. In relationships that aren't highly personal, communicators sometimes tailor messages to the general characteristics of groups. For example, more educated people tend to be more critical and better informed, so effective speakers include strong evidence and show respect for listeners' knowledge when addressing people with high levels of education. Because uncertainty and change foster anxiety, effective managers communicate reassurance and provide maximum information to subordinates during times of organizational change. To be effective in a job interview, an interviewee should research the history and image of the company to find out what the company looks for in new employees.

We have different degrees of insight into people with whom we interact. You need to know your intimates well to create satisfying relationships; you need to know professors and co-workers less well but well enough to work with them; you need to know clerks only well enough to transact business. As we get to know someone better, we gain insight into how he or she differs from others in their group ("Rob's not like other political activists"; "Ellen's more interested in people than most computer science majors are"). The more we interact with someone and the greater the variety of experiences we have together, the more knowledge we gain about their motives, feelings, and behaviors. As we come to understand others as individuals, we fine tune our perceptions of them. Consequently, we rely less on stereotypes to perceive them.

Person-centeredness is not the same as empathy. **Empathy** is the ability to feel *with* another person—to feel what he or she feels in a situation. Feeling with another is an emotional response that some scholars believe is not really possible. Our feelings tend to be guided by our emotional tendencies and experiences, so it may be impossible to feel precisely what another person feels. However, it is possible to recognize others as unique persons, to identify connections between us and them, and to adapt our communication to their frames of reference (Muehlhoff, 2006). In his commentary, Steve explains how he developed person-centeredness with his girlfriend, Sherry.

You really have to know somebody on an individual basis to know what they like and want. When I first started dating Sherry, I sent her red roses to let her know I thought she was special. That's the "lovers' flower," right? It turns out there were zillions of red roses at her father's funeral. Now, they make Sherry sad because they remind her he's dead. I also took her chocolates once, before I found out that she's allergic to chocolate. By now I know what she likes, but my experience shows that the general rules don't always apply to individuals.

When we take the perspective of another person, we try to grasp his or her perceptions and meanings. To do this, we have to suspend our own perspective long enough to enter the world of another person. This allows us to gain some insight into that person's point of view so we can communicate more effectively with him or her. At a later point in interaction, we may choose to express our perspective or disagree with the other person's views. This is appropriate and important in honest communication, but voicing our views is not a substitute for the equally important skill of attempting to understand another's perspective.

SHARPEN YOUR SKILL

Appreciating Multiple Perspectives

Select a controversial issue that's in the news. Find two Web sites or blogs that have dramatically different, even opposing, perspectives on the issue. Monitor these for two weeks and report to class on differences in how the issue is discussed on the different sites or blogs.

Social Roles

Our social roles also shape our perceptions and our communication. Both the training we receive to fulfill a role and the actual demands of the role affect what we notice and how we interpret, evaluate, and respond to it. Because I'm a teacher, my perceptions of classes focus on how interested students seem, whether they appear to have read assigned material, and whether what they're learning is useful in their lives. Students have told me that they think about classes in terms of number and difficulty of tests, whether papers are required, and whether the professor is interesting. We have different ways of perceiving classes. When I am consulting with attorneys, I am more careful to state evidence for the ideas and suggestions I offer than I am in casual conversations with friends.

People's professions influence what they notice and how they think and act. In the earlier example, members of my community perceived our neighbor differently because of our distinct professional roles, as well as other factors. The attorney in the group focused on the legal—or illegal—nature of the neighbor's behavior, and the psychologist's training led her to perceive his behaviors as evidence of emotional problems.

Membership in Cultures and Social Communities

Membership in a culture influences perceptions. A **culture** consists of beliefs, values, understandings, practices, and ways of interpreting experience that a number of people share (Klopf, 1991). In addition to an overall culture, people may belong to social communities that shape their experiences, perspectives, and knowledge. A **social community** is a group of people who are part of an overall society (for example, America) but also distinct from the overall society in that they hold values, understandings, and practices that are not shared by people outside the group. Gender, race, religion, and sexual orientation are examples of criteria that may indicate the existence of a social community and may affect how members of the community act—including how they communicate.

The overall culture to which we belong also influences our perceptions. Western culture's emphasis on technology and its offspring, speed, lead us to expect things to happen fast—almost instantly. We fax memos, IM friends, jet across the country, and microwave meals. In countries such as Nepal, Belize, and Mexico, life proceeds at a more leisurely pace, and people spend more time talking, relaxing, and engaging in low-key activities. The Sharpen Your Skill box on this page invites you to trace how one American value, individualism, is reflected in cultural practices and everyday behaviors.

SHARPEN YOUR SKILL

Noticing Individualism

The United States is a highly individualistic country that expects and rewards personal initiative and regards each person as unique and important. How do the individualistic values of our culture influence our perceptions and activities? Check it out by observing the following:

◆ How is seating arranged in restaurants? Are there large communal eating areas or private tables and booths for individuals or small groups?

◆ How are living spaces arranged? How many people live in the average house? Do families share homes? Does each member of the family have his or her own bedroom and/or other space?

◆ How many people share a car in your family? How many cars are there in the United States?

Other cultures, including Hispanic and Asian ones, are more collectivist and define identity in terms of membership in family and community rather than individuality. Because families are more valued in collectivist cultures, elders are given great respect and care. Rather than perceiving themselves as autonomous, as is typical in cultures that value **individualism**, people in communal cultures tend to think of themselves as members of and accountable to groups.

Differences between collectivist and individualistic cultures are also evident in child-care policies. More communal countries have policies that reflect the value they place on families. In every developed country except the United States, new parents, including adoptive parents, receive a period of paid parental leave, and some countries provide nearly a year's paid leave (Douglas, 2004; Wood, 2013).

In summary, differences based on physiology, expectations, cognitive abilities, social roles, and membership in cultures and social communities affect how we perceive others and experiences. By extension, all these influences on perception affect how we communicate.

Guidelines for Improving Skill in Perceiving

In the final pages of this chapter, we identify four guidelines for enhancing skills in perceiving people and situations in ways that enhance your understanding of them and facilitate effective communication.

Avoid Mind Reading

Because perception is subjective, people differ in what they notice and in the meaning they attribute to it. One of the most common problems in communication is **mind reading**, which in this sense means assuming we understand what another person thinks or feels. When we mind read, we act as if we know what's on someone else's mind, and this can get us into trouble. For example, we can misinterpret a co-worker's absence from meetings if we assume that it signals disinterest instead of competing commitments. Mind reading is also a common cause of tension between spouses (Dickson, 1995; Gottman, 1993).

Consider a few examples of the problems mind reading can cause. One person might assume a friend is angry because the friend hasn't responded to a text message in 24 hours. This guess could well be wrong—the friend might be preoccupied or might have a dead phone battery. Mind reading also occurs when we say or think, "I know he's upset" (Has he said he is upset?) or "She doesn't care about me anymore" (maybe she is too preoccupied or worried to be attentive). In actuality, we seldom really know what others think, feel, or perceive. When we mind read, we impose our perspectives on others instead of allowing them to say what they think. This can cause misunderstandings and resentment because most of us prefer to speak for ourselves.

Check Perceptions with Others

The second guideline follows directly from our insight about the inadvisability of mind reading. Because perceptions are subjective, checking our perceptions with others is a good idea. In the earlier example, we could ask, "Why didn't you respond?" Rather than assuming a friend is angry, it might be valuable to ask, "Are you angry with me?" It's especially important to check perceptions when communicating online, because we don't have access to many of the nonverbal cues that help us interpret face-to-face communication. Sarcasm, irony, and other forms of communication may not be obvious online. Checking perceptions enhances clarity between people and invites productive dialogue, not blame and defensiveness.

Perception checking is an important communication skill because it helps people arrive at mutual understandings of each other and their interaction. To check perceptions, first state what you have noticed. For example, you might say, "Lately, you've given me less feedback on my work than in the past." Then, you check whether the other perceives the same thing: "Would you agree?" Finally, it's appropriate to invite the other person to help you understand her or his behavior. So in the example, if the other person agrees that he or she is less pleased with your work, you could say, "Can you give me some insight into why you're giving me less feedback?" If the other person doesn't agree that she or he is giving less feedback, a useful question might be, "Could you remind me of the feedback you've given me on the last few reports?"

When checking perceptions, it's important to use a tentative tone rather than a dogmatic or accusatory one. This minimizes defensiveness and encourages good discussion. Just let the other person know that you are perceiving something and would like that person to clarify his or her perceptions of what is happening and what it means. The Sharpen Your Skill feature on this page provides guidance for developing skill in checking perceptions.

Distinguish Facts from Inferences and Judgments

Effective communicators recognize the difference between factual statements and nonfactual statements such as inferences and judgments. A fact is based on observation or proof. For instance, "The student, Taylor, is late to class most days" is a factual statement. An **inference** is a deduction that goes beyond what you know or assume to be a fact. For instance, if Taylor's teacher has known other students who were late to class because they didn't care about the class, the teacher might generalize from them to infer, "Taylor doesn't care about this class." Note that the inference goes beyond facts that the teacher knows about Taylor as an individual.

A **judgment** is a belief or opinion that is based on observations, feelings, assumptions, or other phenomena that are not facts. In our example, the teacher might judge that "Taylor is an irresponsible student." But judging Taylor as irresponsible goes beyond the facts. Taylor's lateness to class may be due to a work shift that ends right before the class. The teacher might treat Taylor differently if

SW Productions/Jupiter Images

Checking perceptions is critical to effective parent-child communication.

SHARPEN YOUR SKILL

Perception Checking

To gain skill in perception checking (and all communication behaviors), you need to practice. Try this:

1. Monitor your tendencies to mind read, especially in established relationships in which you feel you know your partners well.

2. The next time you catch yourself mind reading, stop. Instead, tell the other person what you are noticing and invite her or him to explain how she or he perceives what's happening. First, find out whether your partner agrees with you about what you noticed. Second, if you agree, find out how your partner interprets and evaluates what is happening.

3. Engage in perception checking for two or three days so that you have lots of chances to see what happens. When you've done that, reflect on the number of times your mind reading was inaccurate.

4. Think about how your perception checking affected interaction with your friends and romantic partners.

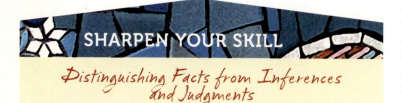

SHARPEN YOUR SKILL

Distinguishing Facts from Inferences and Judgments

Which of the following are factual statements?

1. There are 50 states in the United States.

2. People from small towns are friendly.

3. Actors are egotistical.

4. German shepherds tend to suffer from hip dysplasia.

5. Students who come to class late are disrespectful.

6. Acid rain can destroy trees.

7. College students take jobs to earn money for dating and clothes.

8. Older students aren't career oriented.

9. Evelyn made a total score of 690 on her SAT.

10. Evelyn would not do well in college.

Statements 1, 4, 6, and 9 are facts; statements 2, 3, 5, 7, 8, and 10 are inferences.

a work schedule, rather than laziness, explained the tardiness. To communicate effectively, we need to avoid mistaking nonfactual statements for factual ones. The Sharpen Your Skill box to the left allows you to check your ability to distinguish facts from inferences and judgments.

It's easy to confuse inferences with facts when we use language that makes inferences and judgments appear to be factual. When we say, "This person is rude," we've made a statement that sounds factual, and we may then perceive it as factual when it really isn't. To avoid this tendency, substitute a more tentative word for *is*. For instance, "This person seems rude" and "This person may be rude" are more tentative statements that keep us from treating an inference or judgment as a fact. The Sharpen Your Skill box that appears below allows you to develop your skill in using tentative language.

Monitor the Self-Serving Bias

We discussed the self-serving bias earlier in this chapter. You'll recall that it involves attributing our successes and nice behaviors to internal, stable qualities that we control and attributing our failures and bad behaviors to external, unstable factors beyond our control. Because this bias can distort perceptions, we need to monitor it carefully. **Monitoring** is the process of calling behaviors or other phenomena to our attention so that we can observe and regulate them. Try to monitor the tendency to explain away your failures or adverse behaviors as not your fault and to take personal credit for accomplishments that were helped along by luck or situational factors.

Monitoring the self-serving bias also has implications for how we perceive others. Just as we tend to judge ourselves generously, we may judge others harshly.

SHARPEN YOUR SKILL

Using Tentative Language

To become more sensitive to the tendency to confuse facts with inferences and judgments, pay attention to the language you use for the next 24 hours when you describe people and interactions. Listen for words such as *is* and *are*, which imply factual knowledge. Do you notice instances in which tentative language would be more accurate?

Now, extend your observations to other people and the language they use. When you hear others say "She is," "They are," or "He is," are they really making factual statements, or are they making inferences or judgments?

Monitor your perceptions to see whether you attribute others' successes and admirable actions to external factors beyond their control and their shortcomings and blunders to internal factors they can (should) control. If you do this, substitute more generous explanations for others' behaviors, and notice how that affects your perceptions of them. The FYI box on this page discusses research that links different attributional tendencies to different levels of satisfaction with personal relationships. Words crystallize perceptions. Until we label an experience, it remains nebulous and less than fully formed in our thinking. Only when we name our feelings and thoughts do we have a clear way to describe and think about them. But just as words crystallize experiences, they can freeze thought. Once we label our perceptions, we may respond to our labels rather than to the actual phenomena.

Attribution Patterns and Relationship Satisfaction

Investigations have shown that happy and unhappy couples have distinct attribution styles (Bradbury & Fincham, 1990; Fletcher & Fincham, 1991; Graham & Conoley, 2006; McNulty & Karney, 2001; Segrin, Hanzal, & Domschke, 2009). Happy couples make relationship-enhancing attributions. Such people attribute nice things a partner does to internal, stable, and global reasons. "She got the film for us because she is a good person who always does sweet things for us." They attribute unpleasant actions by a partner to external, unstable, and specific factors. "He yelled at me because all the stress of the past few days made him short with everyone."

Unhappy couples use reverse attribution patterns. They explain nice actions as resulting from external, unstable, and specific factors. "She got the tape because she had some extra time today." They see negative actions as stemming from internal, stable, and global factors. "He yelled at me because he is a nasty person who never shows any consideration to anybody else." Negative attributions encourage pessimistic views and sap motivation to improve a relationship. Whether positive or negative, attributions may be self-fulfilling prophecies.

SUMMARY

In this chapter, we've discussed perception, which is a basic communication process. It involves selecting, organizing, and interpreting experiences. These three facets of the perception process are not separate in practice; instead, they interact such that each affects the others.

What we selectively notice affects how we organize and interpret phenomena. At the same time, our interpretations influence what we notice in the world around us. Selection, organization, and interpretation interact continually in the process of perception. Our sensory capacities and physiological conditions affect what we perceive. In addition, expectations, cognitive abilities, social roles, and cultural context influence how we perceive experiences and how we communicate with ourselves and others.

Skillful perception enhances communication. We discussed four guidelines for enhancing skills in perceiving. First, because people perceive differently, we should avoid mind reading. Extending this, we discussed the importance of checking perceptions, which involves stating how we perceive something and asking how another person perceives it. A third guideline is to distinguish facts from inferences in our perceptions and the symbols we use to label them. Finally, monitoring self-serving bias helps us perceive ourselves more accurately. We need to know when we are making factual descriptions and when we are making inferences that we should check.

REVIEW, REFLECT, EXTEND

The Reflect, Discuss, and Apply Questions that follow will help you review, reflect on, and extend the information and ideas presented in this chapter. These resources, and a diverse selection of additional study tools, are also available online at the CourseMate for *Communication Mosaics*. Your CourseMate includes a student workbook, WebLinks, TED Talks hyperlinks and activities, chapter glossary and flashcards, interactive video activities, Speech Builder Express, and InfoTrac College Edition. For more information or to access this book's online resources, visit **www.cengagebrain.com.**

KEY CONCEPTS

attribution, 49
cognitive complexity, 53
cognitive schemata, 45
constructivism, 45
culture, 57
empathy, 56
expectancy violation theory, 53
individualism, 57
inference, 59
interpretation, 48
judgment, 59
mind reading, 58

monitoring, 60
perception, 44
personal construct, 46
person-centeredness, 55
positive visualization, 52
prototype, 45
schemata, 45
script, 48
self-serving bias, 49
social community, 57
stereotype, 47

Reflect, Discuss, Apply

1. As a class, discuss how you communicate with people both online and face to face. What differences can you identify in how you communicate in each medium? What differences can you identify in how others communicate with you online and in person?

2. How do physiological factors affect your perceptions? How do your biorhythms affect your daily schedules?

3. Read a local paper and pay attention to how the language in stories shapes your perceptions of events and people. Identify examples of how language shapes perceptions.

4. Think of someone you know who is person-centered. Describe the specific skills this person uses and how they affect his or her communication.

5. Go to a grocery store and notice how products are placed on shelves (at eye level, lower, or higher) and the colors and designs on product packaging. Identify factors discussed in this chapter that are used to make products stand out and gain shoppers' attention.

6. Volunteer to work in a context that allows you to interact with people you have not spent time with—for example, volunteer at a homeless shelter. At the start of your work, make a list of schemata (prototypes, personal constructs, stereotypes, and scripts) you have about these people before you interact with them. After spending time interacting with them, review your list of schemata and evaluate how accurate they were.

Recommended Resources

1. Learn more about fact–inference confusion and other ways in which language and perception affect our thinking by visiting the website of the Institute of General Semantics. You can access it by going to the book's online resources for this chapter and clicking on WebLink 3.1.

2. Paul Watzlawick (1984). *The invented reality: How do we know what we believe we know?* Don't let the publication date of this book fool you. It is as useful today as when it was published in raising awareness of how our perceptions shape our sense of reality.

EXPERIENCE COMMUNICATION CASE STUDY

College Success

Apply what you've learned in this chapter by analyzing the following case study, using the accompanying questions as a guide. These questions and a video of the case study are also available online at your CourseMate for *Communication Mosaics*.

Your friend Jim tells you about a problem he's having with his parents. According to Jim, his parents have unrealistic expectations of him. He tends to be an average student, usually making *C*'s, a few *B*'s, and an occasional *D* in his courses. His parents are angry that his grades aren't better. Jim tells you that when he went home last month, his father said this:

Jim's father: I'm not paying for you to go to school so you can party with your friends. I paid my own way and still made Phi Beta Kappa. You have a free ride, and you're still just pulling *C*'s. You just have to study harder.

Jim [to you]: I mean, I like to hang out with my friends, but that's got nothing to do with my grades. My dad's this brilliant guy, I mean, he just cruised through college; he thinks it's easy. I don't know how it was back then, but all my classes are *hard*. I mean, no matter how much studying I do, I'm *not* gonna get all A's. What should I do? I mean, how do I convince them that I'm doing everything I can?

© Cengage Learning

1. Both Jim and his parents make attributions to explain his grades. Describe the dimensions of Jim's attributions and those of his parents.

2. How might you assess the accuracy of Jim's attributions? What questions could you ask him to help you decide whether his perceptions are well founded or biased?

3. What constructs, prototypes, and scripts seem to operate in how Jim and his parents think about college life and being a student?

4. What could you say to Jim to help him and his parents reach a shared perspective on his academic work?

A different language is a different vision of life.   Federico Fellini

4 Engaging in Verbal Communication

Funerals are sad occasions, so why did hundreds of onlookers cheer as horses slowly pulled the pine coffin through downtown Detroit? Why did Julian Bond tell the onlookers, "The entity in this casket deserves to be dead" (Krolicki, 2007)? Who deserves to be dead? Who was in the casket?

Actually, nobody was in the casket; no person was being buried. This funeral was for the *N*-word. On Monday, July 9, 2007 the National Association for the Advancement of Colored People (NAACP) held a public burial for the *N*-word. This word had hurt many who attended its funeral. It was a mean, hateful word that "deserved to be dead."

Perhaps, as a child, you heard the nursery rhyme, "Sticks and stones can break my bones, but words can never hurt me." By now, most of us have figured out that the nursery rhyme would be more accurate if it were revised to say, "Sticks and stones can break my bones, but words can *really* hurt me." Words can harm us, sometimes terribly. Children often bully each other with name calling. As children get older, the verbal bullying continues, with some of the cruelest verbal attacks hurled at people who do not conform to conventional social identities and rules. If you've ever been called hurtful names, you know how deeply words can wound.

Words can also enchant, comfort, teach, amuse, and inspire us. Have you ever read a poem or heard a song that captivated you? Have you ever swelled with pride at a supervisor's praise? Have you ever felt bad and talked to a friend who said just the right thing—healing words? Have you ever been inspired to change something about yourself because of a great speech you heard?

FOCUS QUESTIONS

1. How are language and thought related?

2. What abilities are possible because humans use symbols?

3. What are the practical implications of recognizing that language is a process?

4. How do rules guide verbal communication?

65

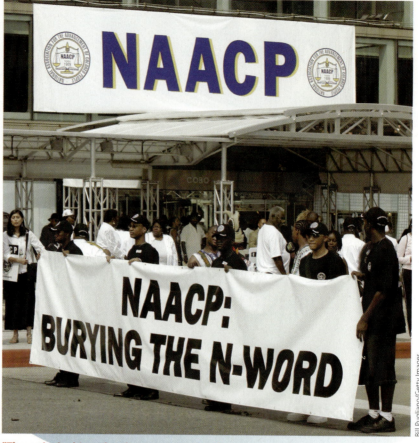

Bill Pugliano/Getty Images

"The entity in this casket deserves to be dead."

Language is our most powerful tool. It allows us to plan, dream, remember, evaluate, reflect on ourselves and the world around us, and define who we are and want to be. Because language is so powerful, we need to understand it and use it in responsible, ethical ways. This chapter will enhance your understanding of human language and your ability to use it effectively. The FYI box on page 67 shows how language creates reality.

In this chapter, we take a close look at verbal communication and explore its power. We begin by defining symbols and discussing principles of verbal communication. Next, we'll examine how language enables us to create meanings for ourselves, others, and our experiences. Finally, we'll identify guidelines for effective verbal communication. In Chapter 5, we'll explore the companion system: nonverbal communication.

Language and Meaning

Language consists of **symbols**, which are representations of people, events, and all that goes on around us and in us. All language is symbolic, yet not all symbols are linguistic. **Nonverbal communication** includes symbols that aren't words, such as facial expressions, posture, and tone of voice. Art and music are also symbolic.

Features of Language

According to Harvard psychologist Steven Pinker (2000, 2008), humans are "verbivores"—a species that lives on words. **Verbal communication,** or language, consists of symbols in the form of spoken or written words. For instance, your name is a symbol that represents you. *Dormitory* is a symbol for a particular kind of building. *Credit hour* is a term that refers to one unit in the total number of units required to graduate. *Love* represents an intense feeling. In combination with nonverbal symbols, verbal symbols form the core of the human world of meaning. As a first step in understanding the power of language, we'll examine three characteristics of symbols: arbitrariness, ambiguity, and abstraction.

Arbitrariness

Language is **arbitrary,** which means that verbal symbols are not intrinsically connected to what they represent. For instance, the term *chat room* has no natural relationship to virtual spaces for online interaction. Certain words and terms seem right because as a society we agree to use them in particular ways, but they have no inherent correspondence to their referents.

Because meanings are arbitrary instead of necessary, language changes as we invent new words or imbue existing words with new meanings. The English language now has 500 times the number of words that it had only 400 years ago (Wurman, 1989). Through mass communication, commentators have enlarged the political vocabulary with such terms as *Obamamania, gender gap,* and *political correctness. Cyberspace, hyperlink, buddy list, instant messaging,* and *World Wide Web* are terms we've created to refer to computer-mediated communication. To express feelings in online communication, people have invented *emoticons* (also a newly coined word) such as :) for "smile," :(for "frown," :D for "grin," :/ for "frustrated," and ;) for "wink."

CAREER
Talking a Union into Existence

In Poland in the 1980s, the trade union Solidarity was born. The birth was not a dramatic event. There were no fireworks. There was no grand announcement of a powerful new union. Instead, the union grew out of words. It began with simple, face-to-face conversations among 10 or so workers in a Gdansk shipyard. They talked with each other about wanting freedom from oppressive conditions, about the need for change. Then, this handful of individuals talked with other workers who talked with others and so on. Within just a few months, the Solidarity trade union had more than 9 million members.

DIGITAL MEDIA
LOL dotcom BFF

Don't accuse the *Oxford English Dictionary* of being stuffy or old fashioned. Regarded by many as the standard for English usage, the *OED* has a new word team whose job is to consider which new words should be added to formal dictionaries. In the 2009 edition of the *OED,* words added included *ego-surfing* (searching the Internet for references to your name), *irritainment* (programming that irritates viewers but that viewers feel compelled to watch), and *fashionista* (a devotee of cutting-edge fashions). The most recent edition, published in 2011, included these new words: *smack talk* (banter), *muffin top* (a new meaning was added that refers to flesh at the waistline), and *couch surfer* (someone who sleeps on friends' sofas rather than getting her or his own place) (http://www.oed.com/public/latest/latest-update, 2011).

The 2011 edition also includes symbols that arise from technologies and our use of them. In 2011, the *OED* added the following symbols: OMG, wiki, Google, dotcom, LOL, BFF, IMHO, TMI, and the heart symbol (OMG, 2011).

Because language is dynamic, it changes as the people who use it change. In America, language continually incorporates words from people of diverse cultures and social communities. For example, terms from the hip-hop subculture such as *dis* (to disrespect) have entered into mainstream English. Words such as *machismo* and *karma* come from other languages and have been incorporated into English relatively recently. The English language includes many older words that originated in other cultures (Carnes, 1994): *Chocolate* comes from the language of the Nahuatl Native American tribe, *cotton* comes from Arabic, *klutz* comes from Yiddish, *khaki* comes from Hindi, and *zombie* comes from language used by the Kongo group.

Ambiguity

Language is **ambiguous,** which means it doesn't have clear-cut, precise meanings. The term *good friend* means "someone to hang out with" to one person and "someone to confide in" to another. The words *Christmas, Kwanzaa,* and *Hanukkah* have distinct connotations for people with different religious and cultural backgrounds, and *Thanksgiving* may mean different things to Native Americans and European Americans. The meanings of these words vary according to cultural contexts and individuals' experiences. The language is the same, but what it means varies in relation to personal experiences, interests, identities, and backgrounds.

Although language doesn't mean exactly the same thing to everyone, within a culture many words have an agreed-upon range of meanings. In learning to communicate, we learn not only words but also the meanings and values of our society. Thus, all of us know that the word *dogs* refers to four-footed creatures, but each of us also

Language Creates Reality

In naming things, language brings them into human consciousness. Here are a few examples of phenomena that all of us are aware of but which became social realities only when they were given names:

◆ *Blog* entered the language only in recent years. First there was the Web, and then there were *weblogs,* soon shortened to *blogs.* You can read more about "net language" by going to the book's online resources for this chapter and clicking on WebLink 4.1.

◆ *Domestic partners* refers to cohabiting, unmarried people who are gay, lesbian, or heterosexual.

◆ *Birth mother* designates a woman who gives birth but does not keep the child.

◆ *Date rape* is a term created to define as criminal an activity that for a long time took place without being named.

◆ *Environmental justice* refers to a movement to ensure that environmental dangers such as sites for storing toxic wastes are distributed fairly instead of being the burden of poor communities (Cox, 2008, 2010; Pezzullo, 2007).

◆ *Blended family* refers to a family that includes children from one or both partners' previous relationships. Although such families have long existed, only in recent years were they named.

What terms can you add to illustrate how naming things gives them a social reality that they cannot otherwise have?

Doonesbury   BY GARRY TRUDEAU

attributes personal meanings based on dogs we have known and how our families and cultures regard dogs. In some cultures, dogs are food for human consumption—not a meaning of *dogs* in the United States! Conversely, many Westerners eat beef, whereas in Hindu cultures cows are sacred.

The ambiguity of language can lead to misunderstandings. A friend recently told me of misunderstandings that arose when he tried to negotiate a contract with a Japanese firm. My friend, Erik, said that when he made his initial proposal, O-Young, who represented the Japanese company, nodded his head and said, "This is very good." Encouraged, Erik made additional suggestions, and O-Young smiled and responded, "This is a fine idea," and "I admire your work on the project." Yet O-Young consistently refused to sign the contract that contained Erik's proposals. Finally, another American businessperson explained to Erik that Japanese culture regards it as rude to refuse another person directly. To someone socialized in Japanese society, outright disagreement or rejection causes another person to lose face, and that is to be avoided at all costs. Once Erik understood that apparently favorable responses did not mean O-Young agreed with him, their negotiations became much more productive.

Consider other misunderstandings that are fueled by the ambiguity of language. A supervisor criticizes a new employee for "inadequate quality of work." The employee assumes the supervisor wants more productivity; the supervisor means that the employee should be more careful in proofing material to catch errors. Spouses often have different meanings for "doing their share" of home chores. To many women, it means doing half the work, but to men it tends to mean doing more than their fathers did, which is still less than their wives do (Hochschild & Machung, 2003; Wood, 2011).

 Ron

A while ago, I told my girlfriend I needed more independence. She got all upset because she thought I didn't love her anymore and was pulling away. All I meant was that I need some time with the guys and some for just myself. She said that the last time a guy said he wanted more independence, she found out he was dating out on her.

Abstraction

Finally, language is **abstract,** which means that words are not the concrete or tangible phenomena to which they refer. They stand for those phenomena—ideas, people, events, objects, feelings, and so forth, but they are not the things they represent. According to Steven Pinker (2008), who sees language as a window to human nature, the words we use say far more about us than the world outside of us. Pinker believes that words reflect our attitudes, values, and sense of relationship with others. In using language, we engage in a process of abstraction in which we move further and further away from external or objective phenomena. Words vary in their degree of abstractness. *Reading matter* is an abstract term that includes everything from philosophy books to the list of ingredients on a cereal package. *Book* is a less abstract word. *Textbook* is even less abstract. And *Communication Mosaics* is the most concrete term because it refers to a specific textbook.

Our perceptions are one step away from the phenomena because perceptions are selective and subjective, as we learned in Chapter 3. We move a second step away from phenomena when we label a perception with language that is value laden. We abstract even further when we respond, not to behaviors or our perceptions of them, but to the labels we impose. This process can be illustrated as a ladder of abstraction (Figure 4.1), a concept developed by two early scholars of communication, Alfred Korzybski (1948) and S. I. Hayakawa (1962, 1964).

As language becomes increasingly abstract, the potential for confusion mushrooms. One way this happens is by overgeneralization. Mass communication often relies on highly general, abstract language to describe groups of people. Terms such as *inner-city youth, immigrant,* and *senior citizen* encourage us to notice distinctions between young people who live in the hearts of cities and young people who live elsewhere, between people who immigrate to the United States and those who were born here, between people who are elderly and people who are not. At the same time, highly general terms for social groups, such as Asian American, Hispanic American, or African American, incline us to see commonalities among people within the categories but not to recognize distinctions among them. The FYI box on page 72 shows how labels for racial and ethnic groups have changed and how, with these changes, our perceptions of groups have evolved.

Overly general language can distort how partners think about a relationship. They may make broad, negative statements, such as, "You never go along with my preferences" or "You always interrupt me." In most cases, highly abstract communication involves overgeneralizations that are inaccurate. Yet by symbolizing experience this way, partners frame how they think about each other. Researchers have shown that we are more likely to recall behaviors that are consistent with how we've labeled people than to recall behaviors that are inconsistent (Fincham &

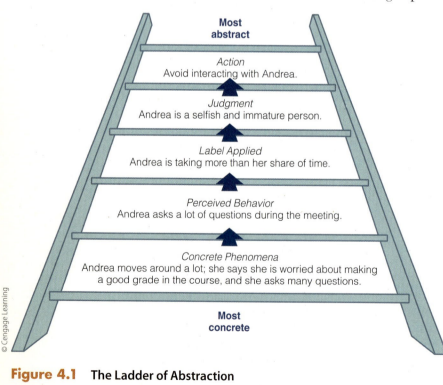

Figure 4.1   **The Ladder of Abstraction**

Bradbury, 1987). When we say a friend is *insensitive,* we're likely to notice instances in which he is insensitive and to overlook times when he is sensitive. Similarly, if we label a co-worker *lazy,* we predispose ourselves to notice her lazy behaviors and not to perceive behaviors that show she is conscientious.

We can minimize misunderstandings by using specific language instead of abstract terms. Saying, "You interrupted me a moment ago" is clearer than saying, "You're so dominating." It's clearer to say, "I would like you to look at me when I'm talking" than to say, "I wish you'd be more attentive." The Sharpen Your Skill box on this page provides an opportunity for you to develop skill in reducing the confusion caused by ambiguous language.

SHARPEN YOUR SKILL

Communicating Clearly

To express yourself clearly, it's important to translate ambiguous words into concrete language. Practice translating with these examples:

Ambiguous Language	**Concrete Language**
You are rude.	I don't like it when you interrupt me.
We need more team spirit.	_____
I want more freedom.	_____
Let's watch a good program.	_____
Your work is sloppy.	_____
That speaker is unprofessional.	_____

Principles of Communication

Now that we understand that language is arbitrary, ambiguous, and abstract, we're ready to consider three principles of communication. These principles help us understand how we create meaning for our interactions.

Interpretation Creates Meaning

Because language is abstract, ambiguous, and arbitrary, we have to interpret it to determine what it means. Interpretation is an active, creative process we use to make sense of experiences. Although we're usually not conscious of the effort we invest in interpreting words, we continually engage in the process of constructing meanings.

John Searle (1976, 1995) distinguishes between **brute facts** and **institutional facts.** Brute facts are objective, concrete phenomena and activities. Institutional facts are the meanings of brute facts based on human interpretation. Borrowing an example from Searle (1976), during a football game one brute fact is that periodically people gather into roughly circular clusters. We name that activity the *huddle,* or *huddling,* and the institutional fact is that the players are planning their next play. Searle's point is that we create meaning with language that represents institutional facts, or the social meanings we attribute to brute facts.

If someone says to you, "Get lost," you have to think about the context and the person who made it to decide whether it's an insult, friendly needling, or a colloquial way of saying you are out of line. People for whom English is a second language find idioms such as "get lost" even more difficult to interpret than native speakers of English do (Lee, 2000). Go to the book's online resources for this chapter and click on WebLink 4.2 to learn more about idioms that can be confusing to people for whom English is a second language. What the words mean depends on the relationship between communicators as well as the self-esteem and previous experiences of the person who is told to get lost.

fyi

DIVERSITY

The Languages of Race and Ethnicity

Our labels for races and ethnicities have changed over time (Davis, 1997; Delgado, 1998; Johnson, 1999; Martin et al., 1996; Orbe & Harris, 2001; Tanno, 1997).

◆ In America's early years, Irish Catholic and Eastern European immigrants were not defined as *white*. Today they are.

◆ Historic and current labels for African Americans include *Negroes, coloreds, African Americans, people of color, blacks,* and *Afro-Americans.*

◆ Historic and current labels for indigenous people of Alaska include *Eskimo* and *Inuk.*

◆ Historic and current labels for Asians and Asian Americans include *Asians, Asian nationals,* and *Orientals,* as well as more-specific ethnic labels such as *Japanese, Korean Americans,* and *Vietnamese Americans.*

◆ Native Americans may be called *Indians* or *Native Americans* or by labels that reference their specific nations, such as *Oneida* and *Sioux.*

◆ European Americans may be called *whites, Caucasians, European Americans,* or just plain *Americans,* which reflects the naive presumption that, in America, white is the "normal" race.

◆ Labels for South Americans include *Hispanics, Latinos* and *Latinas, Chicanos* and *Chicanas,* and more-specific labels, such as *Cubanos* and *Mexicans.*

Communication Is Guided by Rules

Although each of us draws on his or her individual experiences to interpret language, the process of interpretation is not entirely personal. Without realizing it, we learn rules in the process of being socialized into a particular culture, and these rules guide our communication and how we interpret the communication of others (Argyle & Henderson, 1985; Shimanoff, 1980). **Communication rules** are shared understandings among members of a particular culture or social group about what communication means and what behaviors are appropriate in various situations. Children often are taught that *please* and *thank you* are magic words that they should use. We learn that *sir* and *ma'am* are polite words to use when addressing our elders or people who have authority over us. In the course of interacting with our families and others, we unconsciously absorb rules that guide how we communicate and how we interpret others' communication. Research shows that children begin to understand and follow communication rules by the time they are one or two years old (Miller, 1993).

Two kinds of rules guide our communication (Cronen, Pearce, & Snavely, 1979; Pearce, Cronen, & Conklin, 1979). **Regulative rules** regulate interaction by specifying when, how, where, and with whom to communicate about certain things. For instance, European Americans generally don't interrupt when someone is making a formal presentation, but in more-informal settings interruptions may be appropriate. Some African Americans follow a different rule; it specifies that audience members should participate in public speeches by calling out responses. Thus, for some African American audiences at speaking events, the call–response pattern is an appropriate form of communication. The rules of some cultures say that interrupting in any context is impolite.

Some families have a rule that people cannot argue at the dinner table, whereas other families regard arguments as a normal accompaniment to meals. Families also teach us rules about how to communicate in conflict situations (Honeycutt, Woods, & Fontenot, 1993; Jones & Gallois, 1989; Yerby, Buerkel-Rothfuss, & Bochner, 1990). Regulative rules also define when, where, and with whom it's appropriate to show affection and disclose private information. Regulative rules vary across cultures; what is considered appropriate in one society may be regarded as impolite or offensive elsewhere.

Constitutive rules define what a particular communication means or stands for. We learn that most people regard specific kinds of communication as showing respect (listening attentively, not correcting) and rudeness (talking over others). We also learn what communication is counted as friendship (sharing confidences, defending our friends when others criticize them), professionalism (making good contributions in group meetings, creating supportive climates), and intimacy (offering support, expressing affection). Like regulative rules, constitutive rules are shaped by cultures. The Sharpen Your Skill box on page 74 allows you to reflect on rules that you follow in your communication.

Rules guide our everyday interactions by telling us when to communicate, what to communicate, and how to interpret others' verbal and nonverbal communication. Casual social interactions tend to adhere to rules that are widely shared in a society. Interaction between intimates also follows rules, but these are private rules that reflect special meanings partners have created (Duck, 2006; Wood, 2006). Television networks follow rules for what can and cannot be said and shown during specific times and rules for how often they insert commercials. Online chat rooms and forums develop specific and often unique rules for how people express themselves and respond to one another. Every organization develops a distinctive culture, which includes rules about how members interact.

Few rules are rigidly fixed. Like communication itself, most rules are subject to change. When we decide that a rule is not functional, we negotiate changes in it. A company may find that its rule for making decisions by consensus no longer works once the company triples in size, so voting becomes a constitutive rule to define decision making. When we don't have a rule for a particular kind of interaction, we invent one and often negotiate and refine it until it provides the assistance we want in structuring communication. When couples have a child, they often find that they don't have any guidelines for new communication situations, so they develop rules: "It is appropriate to tend to the baby while talking with each other," "We take turns eating so one of us is free to hold the baby," or "Interrupting our conversation when the baby cries does not count as rudeness."

It's important to understand that we don't have to be aware of communication rules in order to follow them. For the most part, we're really not conscious of the rules that guide how, when, where, and with whom we communicate about various things. We may not realize we have rules until one is broken, and we become aware that we had an expectation. Becoming aware of communication rules empowers you to change those that do not promote good interaction, as Emily's commentary illustrates.

Emily

My boyfriend and I had this really frustrating pattern about planning what to do. He'd say, "What do you want to do this weekend?" And I'd say, "I don't know. What do you want to do?" Then he'd suggest two or three things and ask me which of them sounded good. I would say they were all fine with me, even if they weren't. And this would keep on forever. Both of us had a rule not to impose on the other, and it kept us from stating our preferences, so we just went in circles about any decision. Well, two weekends ago I talked to him about rules, and he agreed we had one that was frustrating. So we invented a new rule that says each of us has to state what we want to do, but the other has to say if that is not okay. It's a lot less frustrating to figure out what we want to do since we agreed on this rule.

Punctuation Affects Meaning

We punctuate communication to interpret meaning. Like the punctuation you studied in grammar classes, **punctuation** of verbal communication is a way to mark a flow of activity into meaningful units. Punctuation is our perception of when interaction begins and ends (Watzlawick, Beavin, & Jackson, 1967).

Before we can attribute meaning to communication, we must establish its boundaries. Usually this involves deciding who initiated communication and when the interaction began. If a co-worker suggests going out to lunch together, you might regard the invitation as marking the start of the interaction. If you return another person's phone call, you might perceive the original call as the beginning of the episode. If someone insults you, you might regard the insult as the act that marks the start of a quarrel.

When we don't agree on punctuation, problems may arise. If you've ever heard children arguing about who started a fight, you understand the importance of punctuation. Communication on the Internet often is punctuated differently by participants who join the dialogue at different times. Because people enter online discussions at different times, it's difficult to know who launched a particular topic or which messages initiate ideas and which are responses to earlier messages. Similarly, new members of organizations may not understand relationships (allies and enemies) or the histories behind policies.

SHARPEN YOUR SKILL

Communication Rules

Think about the regulative and constitutive rules you follow in your verbal communication. For each item listed here, identify two rules that guide your verbal behavior.

Regulative Rules

List rules that regulate your verbal communication when

1. Talking with elders
2. Interacting at dinnertime
3. Having first exchanges in the morning
4. Greeting casual friends on campus
5. Talking with professors

Constitutive Rules

How do you use verbal communication to show

1. Trustworthiness
2. Ambition
3. Disrespect
4. Support
5. Anger

After you've identified your rules, talk with others about their rules. Are there commonalities among your rules that reflect broad cultural norms? What explains differences in individuals' rules?

In personal relationships, a common instance of conflicting punctuation is the demand–withdraw pattern (Figure 4.2; Bergner & Bergner, 1990; Caughlin & Vangelisti, 2000; Christensen & Heavey, 1990; Wegner, 2005). In this pattern, one person demands something such as disclosure or help with a task, and the other pulls away to avoid disclosing or helping. The more the first person demands ("Tell me what's going on in your life"), the more the second person withdraws ("There's nothing to tell"). The people involved may be coworkers, friends, romantic partners, or a parent and an adolescent-child (Caughlin & Ramey, 2005). Each person punctuates the interaction as having started with the other: The demander thinks, "I demand because you withdraw," and the withdrawer thinks, "I withdraw because you demand." There is no objectively correct punctuation, because it depends on subjective perceptions.

When people don't agree on punctuation, they don't share meanings for what is happening between them. Recent research (Siffert & Schwartz, 2011) shows that men's, but not women's, sense of their own well-being is lowered when either they make demands of their spouses or their spouses make demands of them. To break out of unconstructive cycles such as demand–withdraw, people need to realize that they may punctuate differently and should discuss how each of them experiences the pattern. The Sharpen Your Skill box on this page encourages you to check perceptions to see if you and another person are punctuating congruently.

Interpretation, communication rules, and punctuation influence the meaning we assign to language. These three principles highlight the creativity involved in constructing meaning to make sense of communication. We're now ready to explore the power of symbols by discussing uniquely symbolic abilities.

Figure 4.2 **The Demand-Withdraw Pattern**

© Cengage Learning

Symbolic Abilities

The ability to use language allows humans to live in a world of ideas and meanings. Instead of reacting without reflection to our concrete environments and experiences, we think about them and sometimes transform what they mean. Philosophers of language have identified six ways in which symbolic capacities affect our lives (Cassirer, 1944; Langer, 1953, 1979). As we discuss each, we'll consider how to recognize the constructive power of language and minimize the problems it can cause (Figure 4.3).

Language Defines Phenomena

As we noted earlier in this chapter, the most basic symbolic ability is definition. We use words to define ourselves, others, experiences, relationships, feelings,

SHARPEN YOUR SKILL

Punctuating Interaction

The next time you and another person enter an unproductive cycle, stop the conversation and discuss how each of you punctuates interaction.

1. What do you define as the start of interaction?
2. What does the other person define as the beginning?
3. What happens when you learn about each other's punctuation? How does this affect understanding between you?

© Cengage Learning

1. Symbols define phenomena.

2. Symbols evaluate phenomena.

3. Symbols allow us to organize experiences.

4. Symbols allow us to think hypothetically.

5. Symbols allow self-reflection.

6. Symbols define relationships and interactions.

Figure 4.3   **Symbolic Abilities**

and thoughts (Monastersky, 2002). In turn, the labels we use affect how we perceive what we have labeled. You see a car on the lot at a dealership and it is "a car." You test drive it, decide to buy it, and it becomes "my car," and you perceive it differently than when it was "a car." What has changed is not the car, but the meaning you attach to it and symbolize with the possessive label.

A friend of mine puts his savings into separate accounts designated for travel, retirement, and emergencies. Last spring, he told me he couldn't afford a summer vacation because he'd used up his travel fund. I pointed out that he had extra money in his emergency fund that he could use for a vacation. "No," he replied, "that account isn't for vacations." He had defined the accounts in specific ways that shaped his view of the money available for travel. The symbols we use define what things mean to us.

The labels we use to define others affect how we perceive them. When we label someone, we focus attention on particular aspects of that person and her or his activities. At the same time, we necessarily obscure other aspects of that person's identity. A person might be a loving father, a conservative, a concerned citizen, and a demanding supervisor, but we are unlikely to use all of those labels to define him. Each label directs our attention to certain aspects of the person and away from others. This implies that we have an ethical responsibility to consider how our language shapes our perceptions of others. Orest's reflection makes this point clearly.

 Orest

A lot of people relate to me as Asian, like that's all I am. Sometimes in classes, teachers ask me to explain the "Asian point of view," but they do not ask me to explain my perspective as a pre-med major or a working student. I am an Asian, but that is not all that I am.

Totalizing is responding to a person as if one label totally represents that person. We fix on one symbol to define someone and fail to recognize many other aspects of the person. Some people totalize gay men and lesbians by noticing only their sexual orientation. Interestingly, we don't totalize heterosexuals on the basis of *their* sexual orientation. Totalizing also occurs when we dismiss people by saying, "She's old," "He's just a jock," or "She's an illegal alien." Totalizing is not the same as stereotyping. When we stereotype someone, we define the person in terms of the characteristics of a group. When we totalize someone, we negate most of that person by spotlighting a single aspect of his or her identity. Reneé points out a form of totalizing that really bothers her.

 Renée

Okay, here's my issue. I love fashion—I mean I really love great clothes, jewelry, shoes, makeup—all of it! I'm always the first to wear a cool new style. So a lot of people brand me ditsy or silly. But I'm also Phi Beta Kappa and I've been accepted to law school. Why do people think that if you're into fashion, you can't also be smart and serious?

The symbols we use affect how we think and feel. If we describe our work in terms of frustrations, problems, and disappointments, we're likely to feel negative about it.

On the other hand, if we describe rewards, challenges, and successes, we're likely to feel more positive about our work. The way we define experiences in relationships also affects how we feel about them. My colleagues and I asked romantically involved couples how they defined differences between them (Wood, Dendy, Dordek, Germany, & Varallo, 1994). We found that some people defined differences as positive forces that energize a relationship and keep it interesting. Others defined differences as problems or barriers to closeness. We noted a direct connection between how partners defined differences and how they acted. Partners who viewed differences as constructive approached their disagreements with curiosity, interest, and an expectation of growth through discussion. In contrast, partners who labeled differences as problems dreaded disagreements and tried to avoid talking about them.

People who consistently use negative labels to describe their relationships heighten their awareness of aspects of the relationships that they don't like and diminish their awareness of aspects that they do like (Cloven & Roloff, 1991). In contrast, partners who focus on good facets of relationships are more conscious of virtues in partners and relationships and are less bothered by flaws (Bradbury & Fincham, 1990; Fletcher & Fincham, 1991).

Mass communication also defines people and events in ways that can shape our perceptions. Conservative commentators sometimes refer to "knee-jerk liberals" and "tree huggers," whereas the same groups of people are called "progressives" and "environmentalists" by liberal commentators. Depending on which commentators you listen to, you might have different perceptions of people in these groups.

Language Evaluates Phenomena

As we noted when we discussed the ladder of abstraction, language is not neutral; it is laden with values. We describe people we like with language that accents their good qualities and downplays their flaws ("My friend is self-confident"). The reverse is true of our language for people we don't like ("My enemy is arrogant"). We might describe people who speak their minds as honest, assertive, outspoken, courageous, or authoritarian. Each word has a distinct connotation. Restaurants deliberately use words that enhance the attractiveness of menu entries. A dish described as "tender, milk-fed veal sautéed in natural juices and topped with succulent chunks of lobster" sounds more appetizing than one described as "meat from a baby calf that was kept anemic to make it tender, then slaughtered, cooked in blood, and topped with the flesh of a crustacean that was boiled to death."

The language we use also has ethical implications in terms of how it affects others. Most people with disabilities prefer not to be called "disabled," because that totalizes them in terms of a disability. The term *African American* emphasizes cultural heritage, whereas *black* focuses on skin color. *Hispanic* defines people by the Spanish language spoken in countries of origin, whereas *Latina* and *Latino* highlight the geographic origin of women and men, respectively.

Loaded language is words that slant perceptions, and thus meanings, exceedingly. Loaded language encourages extreme perceptions. Terms such as *geezer* and *old fogey* incline us to regard older people with contempt or pity. Alternatives such as *senior citizen* and *elder* reflect more respectful attitudes.

An interesting communication phenomenon is the **reappropriation** of language. This happens when a group reclaims a term used by others to degrade its members, and treats that term as a positive self-description. Reappropriation aims to remove the stigma from term that others use pejoratively. For instance, some women and feminist musicians have reappropriated the term *girl* to resist the connotations of childishness. One collective of punk rock female bands calls itself Riot Grrrls. Some gay men and lesbians have reappropriated the term *queer* and use it as a positive statement about their identity. Southern writer Reynolds Price developed cancer of the spine that left him paraplegic. He scoffed at terms such as *differently abled* and *physically challenged;* he referred to himself as a *cripple* and to others who do not have disabilities as *temporarily able-bodied.* Perhaps the most controversial example of reappropriation is some African Americans' use of a word that was a racial epithet for years. In his book *Nigger: The Strange Career of a Troublesome Word* (2002), Harvard law professor Randall Kennedy traces the word's history and found that the word *nigger* is derived from *niger,* which is the Latin word for the color black. By the 18th century in America, it had become a particularly offensive racial slur. Today, Kennedy notes, the word is still a vile slur when used by non-blacks, but some blacks have reappropriated the term and use it as a positive term among themselves.

I'm as sensitive as the next guy, but I just can't keep up with what language offends what people anymore. When I was young, Negro *was an accepted term, then it was* black, *and now it's* African American. *Sometimes I forget and say* black *or even* Negro, *and I get accused of being racist. It used to be polite to say* girls, *but now that offends a lot of the women I work with. Just this year, I heard that we aren't supposed to say* blind *anymore, and we're supposed to say* visually impaired. *I just can't keep up.*

Probably many of us sympathize with Maynard, who was 54 when he took a course with me. Keeping up with changes in language is difficult, and occasionally we may offend someone unintentionally. Nonetheless, we should try to learn what terms hurt or insult others and avoid using them. We also should tell others when they've referred to us in ways we dislike. As long as you speak assertively but not confrontationally, others are likely to respect your ideas.

Language Organizes Experiences

Words organize our perceptions of events and experiences. As we learned in Chapter 3, the categories into which we place people influence how we interpret them and their communication. A criticism may be viewed as constructive if made by someone we categorize as a friend but insulting if made by someone we classify as an enemy. The words don't change, but their meaning varies depending on the category into which we place the person speaking those words. Because symbols organize our perceptions into broad categories, we don't have to consider each object and experience individually. This allows us to think about abstract concepts such as justice, integrity, and good family life. Our capacity to use broad concepts enables us to transcend specific concrete activities and enter the world of conceptual thought and ideals.

Our ability to abstract can also distort thinking. A primary way this occurs is by stereotyping, which is thinking unreflectively in broad generalizations about a whole class of people or experiences. Examples of stereotypes are "Management doesn't care about labor," "Teachers are smart," "Jocks are dumb," "Feminists hate men," "Religious people are good," and "Conflict is bad." Notice that stereotypes can be positive or negative generalizations.

Common to all stereotypes is the classification of a phenomenon into a category based on general knowledge of that category. When we use terms such as *Native American, lesbian, white male,* and *white collar workers,* we may see only what members of each group have in common and not perceive differences among individuals in the group. Clearly, we have to generalize; we simply cannot think about each and every thing in our lives as a specific instance. However, stereotypes can blind us to important differences among phenomena we lump together. Therefore, we have an ethical responsibility to monitor stereotypes and to stay alert to differences between things we place in any category.

Language Allows Hypothetical Thought

Where do you hope to be five years from now? What is your fondest childhood memory? What would you do if you won the lottery next week? To answer these questions, you must engage in **hypothetical thought**, which is thinking about experiences and ideas that are not part of your concrete, daily reality. Because we can think hypothetically, we can plan, dream, remember, set goals, consider alternative courses of action, and imagine possibilities.

Language allows us to name and imagine possibilities beyond what currently exists. Technology experts have conceived of many possibilities, such as implantable memory chips that will allow us to speak another language without having learned it. This kind of memory chip is still on the drawing boards of technology innovators, but we can think about it now because we have the term *implantable memory chip.* Not too many years ago, technology innovators imagined worldwide networks that connected people through computers; today that is a reality.

Hypothetical thought is possible because we are symbol users. Words give form to ideas so that we can hold them in our minds and reflect on them. We can contemplate things that have no real existence, and we can remember ourselves in the past and project ourselves into the future. Our ability to inhabit past, present, and future explains why we can set goals and work toward them, even though we do not realize the goal immediately (Dixson & Duck, 1993). For example, you've invested many hours in attending classes, studying, and writing papers because you have the idea of yourself as someone with a college degree. The degree is not real now, nor is the self that you will become once you have the degree. Yet the idea is sufficiently real to motivate you to work hard for many years. You can

Alexander Raths/Shutterstock.com

Imagining the possibility of cures for disease inspires scientists.

imagine yourself wearing academic regalia at your graduation, think of yourself as having a degree, and visualize yourself working in the career you plan to enter.

Hypothetical thought can enrich personal relationships by allowing intimates to remember shared moments. One of the strongest glues for intimacy is the ability to remember a history of shared experiences (Bruess, 2011; Bruess & Hoefs, 2006; Cockburn-Wootten & Zorn, 2006; Wood, 2006). Because they can remember rough times they have weathered, intimates can often get through trials in the present. Language that refers to a shared future ("When we're rocking on the porch at 80") also fuels intimacy. We interact differently with people we don't expect to see again and with those who are ongoing parts of our lives. Talking about future plans and dreams, another use of hypothetical thought, knits intimates together because it makes real the idea that more is yet to come (Acitelli, 1993; Wood, 2006).

Hypothetical thought also allows us to imagine being in places we have never visited. Television programs and websites show us faraway countries and expose us to people with different values, traditions, and ways of living. When we listen to or see programs or visit sites to learn about other cultures, we can think about these cultures and imagine visiting them.

Thinking hypothetically helps us improve who we are. We notice progress we have made when we can remember earlier versions of ourselves, and we motivate further self-growth when we envision additional improvements in ourselves. Your ability to think hypothetically enables you to chart a path of continuous growth. As Duk-Kyong points out, remembering ourselves at earlier times also allows us to notice progress we make toward achieving our goals.

Sometimes I get very discouraged that I do not yet know English perfectly and that there is much I still do not understand about customs in this country. It helps me to remember that when I came here 2 years ago I did not speak English at all, and I knew nothing about how people act here. Seeing how much progress I have made helps me to not be discouraged with what I do not yet know.

Language Allows Self-Reflection

Just as we use language to think about times in the past and future and to shape our perceptions of others, we use it to reflect on ourselves. We think about our existence and reflect on our actions. In his classic work in this area, George Herbert Mead (1934) noted that self-reflection is the foundation of human identity. Since Mead's original work, other scholars have developed his ideas and reaffirmed their importance (Atkinson & Housley, 2003; Leeds-Hurwitz, 2006; Sandstrom, Martin, & Fine, 2001).

According to Mead, the self has two aspects: the **I** and the ***me***. The *I* is the spontaneous, creative self. The *I* acts impulsively in response to inner needs and desires, regardless of social norms. The *I* is the part of you that wants to send a really nasty e-mail message to a chat room visitor whom you find offensive.

The *me* is the socially conscious part of self that monitors and moderates the *I*'s impulses. The *me* reflects on the *I* from the social perspectives of others. The *me* is the part of you that says, "Hey, don't send that email when you're so angry." The *I* is impervious to social conventions, but the *me* is keenly aware of them. If your supervisor criticizes your work, your *I* may want to tell that boss off, but your *me* censors that impulse and reminds you that subordinates have to defer to their bosses.

Because we have both spontaneous and reflective parts of ourselves, we can think about who we want to be and set goals for becoming the self we desire. We can feel shame, pride, and regret for our actions—emotions that are possible because we self-reflect. We can control what we do now by casting ourselves forward to consider how we might feel about our actions later—a point that Tiffany makes in her commentary.

When my niece Michelle told me she had learned to read, she was bursting with pride. How might reflecting on this accomplishment affect how Michelle thinks about herself?

My mother-in-law thinks it's wrong that I go to school instead of being a full-time homemaker and mother. She constantly criticizes me for neglecting my children and home. So many times I have wanted to tell her to butt out of my family, but I stop myself by reminding myself that in the long term it's important to me and my husband and the kids to maintain decent relations.

As Tiffany's commentary points out, self-reflection also empowers us to monitor ourselves. When we monitor ourselves, the *me* notices and evaluates the *I*'s impulses and may modify them based on the *me*'s awareness of social norms. For instance, during a discussion with a co-worker you might say to yourself, "I'm just sitting here like a lump on a log. I need to show that I'm interested in what he's saying." Based on your monitoring, you might listen more carefully, give feedback, and ask questions to show interest. Effective public speakers monitor audiences. If members of the audience start looking bored, speakers adapt by changing speaking pace or volume or by introducing a visual aid to add interest. When interacting with people from different cultures, we monitor by reminding ourselves that they may not operate by the same values and communication rules that we do. Self-reflection allows us to monitor our communication and adjust it to be effective and ethical.

Self-reflection also allows us to manage the image we present to others. When talking with teachers and supervisors, you may consciously use language that represents you as respectful, attentive, and responsible. When interacting with parents, you may repress some language that surfaces in discussions with your friends. When communicating with someone you'd like to date, you may use language that is personal and conveys friendliness. We continually use language to manage the images we project in particular situations and with specific people.

Language Defines Relationships and Interaction

A sixth way in which language creates meaning in our lives is by defining relationships and interaction. Our verbal communication conveys messages about how we perceive ourselves and others. "Mr. Buster" symbolizes a more formal relationship than "Phil." We also use language to regulate interaction. We signal that we want to speak by saying, "Excuse me" or "Let me jump in here." We invite others to speak by saying, "Do you have an opinion about this?" or "I'd like to hear what you think about the issue." You'll recall that in Chapter 1 we discussed two levels of meaning: the content level and the relationship level. Verbal communication, as well as nonverbal communication, conveys three dimensions of relationship-level meanings (Mehrabian, 1981).

Responsiveness

One facet of relationship-level meaning is *responsiveness*. Through questions and statements of agreement or disagreement, we show our interest in others' communication. When we give thoughtful feedback to a colleague, we show responsiveness. When we ask an interviewee to elaborate ideas, we demonstrate interest in him or her. Different social and cultural groups learn distinct rules for showing responsiveness. For instance, women generally display greater verbal responsiveness than men do (Montgomery, 1988; Ueland, 1992), and Koreans tend to limit verbal responses more than Americans typically do.

Liking

A second dimension of relationship-level meaning is *liking*. We express liking verbally when we say, "I really enjoy being with you," "I'm glad we're working on the same team," and so forth. Conversely, we verbally communicate dislike by saying, "I don't have time for you right now," or "I don't want to work on your team." In addition to these general rules shared in Western society, particular social groups instill more-specific rules. Masculine socialization emphasizes emotional control and independence, so men are less likely than women to verbalize their feelings of affection for most other people. Feminine socialization encourages many women to verbalize inner feelings.

Power

The third aspect of relationship-level meaning is *power*. We use verbal communication to define dominance and to negotiate status and influence. Men typically exceed women in efforts to establish control over others. Research has shown that men are more likely than women to exert control verbally by controlling conversations, having the last word, interrupting, and correcting others (DeFrancisco, 1991). People in positions of power in organizations often express control with authoritative statements such as, "That's how it's going to be" and "I've heard all I want to hear."

Like many aspects of communication, the power dimension of relationship meaning is influenced by culture. Western cultures tend to favor competitiveness and overt displays of power more than many other cultures. For example, in negotiations Japanese tend to understate their initial position, stress areas of agreement with other negotiators, and work to avoid failure, or loss of face, for any of the negotiators. This is quite different from American negotiating tendencies, such as overstating initial positions to appear strong, being adversarial, and trying to make sure they win and other negotiators lose.

Summing up, we use language to define and evaluate phenomena, organize experiences, think hypothetically, self-reflect, and define relationships and interaction. Each of these abilities helps us create meaning in our personal, professional, and social relationships.

Guidelines for Effective Verbal Communication

Because language is arbitrary, abstract, and ambiguous, the potential for misunderstanding always exists. In addition, individual and cultural differences foster varying interpretations of language. Although we can't completely eliminate misunderstandings, we can minimize them by following four guidelines for using verbal communication effectively.

Engage in Person-Centered Communication

The single most important guideline for using language effectively is to be person-centered in your communication. Recall from Chapters 1 and 3 that person-centered communication is adapted to specific, unique individuals with whom we interact. Effective communicators are aware of other people and their perspectives, and this awareness is reflected in the talk of effective communicators (Muehlhoff, 2006). When I talk with colleagues about communication theories, I use language that is specialized and incomprehensible to people who aren't specialists. When I talk with undergraduate students about the same theories, I adapt my language to students' experiences and knowledge. Medical doctors need highly specialized vocabularies to discuss medical problems with other doctors, but they should translate that vocabulary into ordinary language when talking with patients. In public presentations, speakers adapt their language to the knowledge and attitudes of listeners. If listeners already favor what a speaker advocates, the speaker can use more impassioned language than if listeners are opposed to what he or she advocates. Person-centered communicators try to understand and adapt to the perspectives of listeners.

Be Aware of Levels of Abstraction

We can reduce the likelihood of misunderstandings by being conscious of levels of abstraction. Much confusion results from language that is excessively abstract. For instance, a professor says, "Your papers should demonstrate a sophisticated conceptual grasp of material and its pragmatic implications." Would you know how to write a paper to satisfy the professor? The language is so abstract that it is hard to figure out what the professor wants. Here's a more concrete description: "Your papers should include definitions of the concepts and specific examples that show how they apply to your personal life." This second statement offers a clearer explanation of what the professor expects.

Abstract language is not always inadvisable. The goal is to use a level of abstraction that suits particular communication objectives and situations. Abstract words are appropriate when speakers and listeners have similar knowledge about what is being discussed. For example, long-term friends can say, "Let's just hang out" and understand the activities implied by the abstract term *hang out*. More-concrete language is useful when communicators don't have shared experiences and interpretations. For example, early in a friendship the suggestion to hang out would be more effective if it included specifics: "Let's hang out today—maybe watch the game and go out for pizza." Abstract language may also be useful when a communicator wants to create *strategic ambiguity,* in which meaning is *not* crystal clear. Politicians routinely use abstract language because it allows them to claim later that what they are saying is consistent with the strategically ambiguous statements made earlier.

Although abstract language is appropriate in some situations, it often contributes to misunderstandings. For example, online communication is easily misunderstood because it lacks many of the nonverbal cues that clarify meaning, and it is often condensed into phrases and incomplete thoughts. Abstract language may also promote misunderstandings when people talk about changes they want in one another. For example, "I want you to show more initiative in your work" could mean that the person who is speaking wants the other person to work more hours, take on new projects, or seek less direction from supervisors. Vague abstractions promote misunderstanding when people don't share concrete referents for the abstract terms they use.

Qualify Language

Another strategy for increasing the clarity of communication is to qualify language. Two types of language require qualification. First, we should qualify generalizations so that we don't mislead ourselves or others into mistaking a general statement for an absolute one. "Politicians are crooked" is a false statement because it is overly general. A more accurate statement would be, "A number of politicians have been shown to be dishonest." Qualifying reminds us that our perceptions are tied to specific times, places, and circumstances.

We should also qualify language when describing and evaluating people. A **static evaluation** is an assessment that suggests that something is unchanging. Static evaluations are particularly troublesome when applied to people: "Ann is selfish," "Don is irresponsible," "Vy is rude." Whenever we use the word *is*, we suggest that something is fixed. In reality, we aren't static but continually changing. A person who is selfish at one time may be generous at other times. A person who is irresponsible on one occasion may be responsible in different situations. Ken's commentary illustrates that static evaluations can be both inaccurate and irritating.

 Ken

> *Parents are the worst for static evaluations. When I first got my license seven years ago, I had a fender bender and then got a speeding ticket. Since then, I've had a perfect record, but you'd never know it from what they say. Dad's always calling me "hot rodder," and Mom goes through this safety spiel every time I get ready to drive somewhere. You'd think I was the same now as when I was 16.*

One technique for qualifying language is to index words. **Indexing** is a technique to remind us that our evaluations apply only to specific times and circumstances (Korzybski, 1948). To index, we would say "Ann $_{June\ 6,\ 2008}$ acted selfishly," "Don $_{on\ the\ task\ committee}$ was irresponsible," and "Vy $_{in\ college}$ was rude." See how indexing ties description to a specific time and circumstance? Mental indexing reminds us that we and others are able to change in remarkable ways.

Own Your Feelings and Thoughts

We often use verbal language in ways that obscure our responsibility for how we feel, think, and act. For instance, people say, "You made me mad," "You hurt me," or "You made me do that," as if what they felt or did were caused by someone else. When a person says, "You're so demanding," the person really means that she or he feels pressured by what someone else wants or expects. Feeling pressured is that person's response. Although others can influence us, they seldom actually determine how we feel. Our feelings and thoughts result from how we interpret others' communication. Although how we interpret what others say may lead us to feel certain ways, it is *our* interpretation more than others' communication that guides our responses.

You-Language	I-Language
You hurt me.	I feel hurt when you ignore what I say.
You're really domineering.	When you shout, I feel dominated.
You humiliated me.	I felt humiliated when you mentioned my problems in front of your friends.

© Cengage Learning

Figure 4.4   *I*- and *You*-Language

In certain contexts, such as abusive relationships, others may powerfully shape how we think and feel. Yet even in these extreme situations, we need to remember that we, not others, are responsible for our feelings. We can disapprove of what others do without surrendering control of our thoughts, feelings, and actions. Telling others they make you feel some way is also likely to arouse defensiveness, which doesn't facilitate healthy personal or professional relationships. Effective communicators take responsibility for themselves by using language that owns their thoughts and feelings. They claim their feelings and do not blame others for what happens within themselves.

To take responsibility for your feelings, rely on **I-language**, not **you-language**. *I*-language identifies the speaker's or perceiver's thoughts and feelings, whereas *you*-language attributes intentions and motives onto another person. Figure 4.4 gives examples of *I*- and *you*-language.

There are two differences between *I*-language and *you*-language. First, *I*-statements own responsibility, whereas *you*-statements project it onto another person. Second, *I*-statements are more descriptive than *you*-statements. *You*-statements tend to be accusations that are abstract and unspecific. This is one reason that *you*-language is ineffective in promoting change. *I*-statements provide concrete descriptions of behaviors without holding the other person responsible for how we feel.

Some people feel awkward when they first start using *I*-language. This is natural because most of us have learned to rely on *you*-language. With commitment and practice, however, you can learn to communicate using *I*-language. Once you feel comfortable using it, you will find *I*-language has many advantages. First, it is less likely than *you*-language to make others defensive, so *I*-language opens the doors for dialogue. Second, *I*-language is more honest. We deceive ourselves when we say, "You make me feel…" because others don't control how we feel. Finally, *I*-language is more empowering than *you*-language. When we say, "You did this" or "You made me feel that," we give control of our emotions, thoughts, and actions to others. This reduces our personal power and our motivation to change what is happening. Using *I*-language allows you to own your feelings while also explaining to others how you interpret their behaviors.

SHARPEN YOUR SKILL

Learning to Use I-Language

For the next 24 hours, pay attention to instances in which you use *you*-language. Catch yourself saying, "You made me angry," "You're being pushy," or engaging in other uses of *you*-language. Whenever you do so, change your language to *I*-language: "I feel angry when you…" or "I feel pressured when you…"

Do your thoughts and feelings about what is happening change when you substitute *I*-language for *you*-language?

SUMMARY

In this chapter, we've explored the nature and power of verbal communication. Verbal symbols shape who we are, what we do, and what our experiences mean. Because they are arbitrary, ambiguous, and abstract, words do not have objective concrete meanings. Instead, their significance reflects our life experiences and the views of the culture and the social groups to which we belong.

To create meaning with language and to interact with others, we follow rules of communication, and we punctuate interaction. As we have seen, regulative rules specify when, where, with whom, and how we communicate verbally. In addition, we follow constitutive rules, which define the meanings of specific forms of verbal communication within particular social groups. A final aspect of

creating the meaning of communication is punctuation of the beginnings and endings of interactions.

The ability to use language allows us to create meaning. By defining, evaluating, and classifying phenomena, language allows us to order our experiences and feelings. In addition, we use language to think hypothetically, to self-reflect, and to define relationships and interactions. Our ability to use symbols is a key part of the foundation of communication and human life. We increase the effectiveness of our verbal communication when we are person-centered and conscious of levels of abstraction, as well as own our thoughts and feelings, and when we qualify language appropriately. In Chapter 5, we'll see how nonverbal communication complements and extends verbal communication by allowing us to create meaning.

REVIEW, REFLECT, EXTEND

The Reflect, Discuss, and Apply Questions that follow will help you review, reflect on, and extend the information and ideas presented in this chapter. These resources, and a diverse selection of additional study tools, are also available online at the CourseMate for *Communication Mosaics*. Your CourseMate includes a student workbook, WebLinks, TED Talks hyperlinks and activities, chapter glossary and flashcards, interactive video activities, Speech Builder Express, and InfoTrac College Edition. For more information or to access this book's online resources, visit **www .cengagebrain.com.**

KEY CONCEPTS

abstract, 69
ambiguous, 68
arbitrary, 67
brute facts, 71
communication rules, 72
constitutive rules, 73
hypothetical thought, 79
I, 80
I-language, 85
indexing, 84
institutional facts, 71

loaded language, 77
me, 80
nonverbal communication, 66
punctuation, 74
reappropriation, 77
regulative rules, 72
static evaluation, 84
symbol, 66
totalizing, 76
verbal communication, 67
you-language, 85

Reflect, Discuss, Apply

1. To appreciate the importance of symbolic capacities, imagine the following: living only in the present without memories or hopes and plans; thinking only in terms of literal reality, not what might be; and having no broad classifications to organize experience. With others in the class, discuss how your life would be different without the symbolic abilities discussed in this chapter.

2. In the chapter, we learned that language names experiences and that language is continuously evolving. As a class, identify experiences, feelings, or other phenomena for which we don't yet have names? What is a good term to describe someone with whom you have a serious romance? *Boyfriend* and *girlfriend* no longer work for many people. Do members of your class prefer *significant other, romantic partner, special friend,* or another term?

3. Visit chat rooms and online forums and notice the screen names that people use. How do the names people create for themselves shape perceptions of their identities? What screen names do you use? Why did you choose them?

4. The national Student Voices Project was created in 2000 by the Annenberg Public Policy Center. Over the years, it has been launched in multiple cities. Learn more about this project by going to the book's online resources for this chapter and clicking on WebLink 4.3. See if there are contributors from your state or even your school.

Recommended Resources

1. Visit the Institute of General Semantics website by going to the book's online resources for this chapter and clicking on WebLink 4.4.

2. Pinker, S. (1994). *The language instinct: How mind creates language.* New York: HarperPerennial; Pinker, S. (2008). *The stuff of thought: Language as a window to human nature.* New York: Penguin. These books provide accessible discussions of how language works. Unlike some books on the subject of language, Pinker's are written with clarity and a sharp sense of humor. Be warned that Pinker's ideas are controversial—some scientists do not agree with his theories of language and mind.

EXPERIENCE COMMUNICATION CASE STUDY

The Roommates

Apply what you've learned in this chapter by analyzing the following case study, using the accompanying questions as a guide. These questions and a video of the case study are also available online at your CourseMate for *Communication Mosaics.*

Bernadette and Celia were assigned to be roommates a month ago when the school year began. Both were initially pleased with the match because they discovered commonalities in their interests and backgrounds. They are both sophomores from small towns, they have similar tastes in music and television programs, and they both like to stay up late and sleep in. Lately, however, Bernadette has been irritated by Celia's housekeeping—or lack of it!

Celia leaves her clothes lying all over the room. When they cook, Celia often leaves the pans and dishes for hours, and then it's usually Bernadette who cleans them. Bernadette feels she has to talk to Celia about this problem, but she hasn't figured out how or when to talk. When Celia gets in from classes, Bernadette is sitting on her bed, reading a textbook.

Celia: Hey, Bernie, how's it going?

[Celia drops her book bag in the middle of the floor, flops on the bed, and kicks her shoes off onto the floor. As Bernadette watches, she feels her frustration peaking and decides now is the time to talk to Celia about the problem.]

Bernadette: You shouldn't do that. You make me nuts the way you just throw your stuff all over the room.

Celia: I don't "throw my stuff all over the room." I just took off my shoes and put my books down, like I do every day.

Bernadette: No, you didn't. You dropped your bag right in the middle of the room, and you kicked your shoes where they happen to fall without ever noticing how messy they look. And you're right—that *is* what you do every day.

© Cengage Learning

Celia: There's nothing wrong with wanting to be comfortable in my own room. Are we suddenly going for the Good Housekeeping Seal of approval?

Bernadette: Comfortable is one thing. But you're so messy. Your mess makes me really miserable.

Celia: Since when? This is the first I've heard about it.

Bernadette: Since we started rooming together, but I didn't want to say anything about how angry you make me. I just can't stand it anymore. You shouldn't be so messy.

Celia: Sounds to me like you've got a problem—you, not me.

Bernadette: Well it's you and your mess that are my problem. Do you have to be such a slob?

1. Identify examples of *you*-language in this conversation. How would you change it to *I*-language?

2. Identify examples of loaded language and ambiguous language.

3. Do you agree with Celia that the problem is Bernadette's, not hers? Explain your answer.

4. To what extent do Celia and Bernadette engage in dual perspective to understand each other?

What you do speaks so loud that I cannot hear what you say.   Ralph Waldo Emerson

5 Engaging in Nonverbal Communication

▶ Ben Thompson has traveled to Japan to negotiate a joint business venture with Haru Watanabe. They both seem to see the mutual benefit of the project, yet Thompson feels something is wrong in their negotiations. Every time they talk, Thompson perceives Watanabe as untrustworthy because he does not hold eye contact. Thompson wonders whether Watanabe is trying to hide something. Meanwhile, Watanabe wonders why Thompson is behaving so rudely if he wants to work together.

▶ In the library, Maria notices a nice-looking guy two tables away. When he looks up at her, she lowers her eyes. After a moment, she looks back at him just for a second. A few minutes later, he comes over, sits down beside her, and introduces himself.

▶ Liz Fitzgerald gives a final glance to be sure the dining room table is just right for dinner: The placemats and blue linen napkins are out, and the silver and glasses sparkle; the bowl of flowers in the middle of the table adds color, and the serving dishes are warmed and ready to be filled with roast beef, buttered new potatoes, and fresh rolls. Liz whisks balsamic vinegar and olive oil together, adds a trace of fresh basil, and sprinkles it on the spinach salad just before calling the family to dinner.

▶ Across town, Benita Bradsher is also preparing dinner for her family. She puts a big spoon in the pot of mashed potatoes and transfers it from the stove to the kitchen table. Next, she piles plates, paper napkins, knives, spoons, and forks in the middle of the table. She takes the ground beef casserole from the oven, puts it on a potholder on the table, and calls her family to dinner.

FOCUS QUESTIONS

1. What is nonverbal communication?

2. What types of nonverbal behavior have scholars identified?

3. How does nonverbal communication express cultural values?

4. How can you improve your effectiveness in using and interpreting nonverbal communication?

Many of us grew up hearing "actions speak louder than words." The wisdom of this axiom is that nonverbal communication can be as powerful as or more powerful than words. Facial expressions can express love, suspicion, competitiveness, sorrow, interest, anger, and hatred. Body postures can convey relaxation, nervousness, boredom, and power. Physical objects can symbolize professional identity (stethoscope, briefcase), personal commitments (wedding band, school sweatshirt), and lifestyle (comfortable furniture casually arranged, stiff furniture in formal rooms).

In this chapter, we explore the fascinating realm of nonverbal interaction. We will identify principles of nonverbal communication and then discuss types of nonverbal behavior and guidelines for effectiveness.

The examples that opened this chapter illustrate the power of nonverbal communication. In the first case, Thompson and Watanabe have difficulty because of different nonverbal communication norms in Japan and the United States. Ben Thompson has learned that eye contact is a sign of honesty and respect, so he looks directly at Haru Watanabe when they talk. In Watanabe's culture, however, direct eye contact is considered rude and intrusive, so he doesn't meet Thompson's gaze and feels uncomfortable when Thompson looks directly at him.

In the library, we see a clear example of gendered patterns of nonverbal communication. Maria follows feminine communication norms by indirectly signaling her interest and waiting for the man to initiate contact directly. He in turn enacts the rules of masculine communication culture by gazing directly at her and moving to her table.

In the final example, nonverbal communication reflects differences in social backgrounds. Whereas Liz Fitzgerald sets her table with cloth napkins, placemats, silver, crystal, and a vase of flowers, Benita Bradsher sets her table with pans off the stove and a casual pile of utensils and paper napkins that people can take. What each woman serves and how she sets her table reflects the teachings of social groups to which she belongs and the time she has in which to prepare a meal.

Gender, ethnicity, sexual orientation, socioeconomic status, and membership in social groups are aspects of our identities that we communicate day in and day out. Recognizing this, Candice West and Don Zimmerman (1987) and Judith Butler (1990, 1993) observe that we "do gender" or "perform gender" continually by behaving in ways that symbolize femininity or masculinity according to our culture's views. We also "do" race, class, and sexual orientation by nonverbally expressing those facets of identity. Nonverbal communication, like its verbal cousin, allows us to establish identity, express thoughts and feelings, reflect on ourselves, define and regulate relationships, and create interaction climates. Like words, nonverbal communication powerfully shapes meaning in our lives.

Principles of Nonverbal Communication

Nonverbal communication includes all aspects of communication other than words. In addition to gestures and body language, nonverbal communication includes *how* we utter words (inflection, volume), features of environments that affect meaning (temperature, lighting), and objects that affect personal images and interaction patterns (dress, furniture). Nonverbal communication accounts for 65 to 93 percent of the total meaning of communication (Birdwhistell, 1970; Hickson, Stacks, & Moore, 2004; Mehrabian, 1981). Five principles of nonverbal communication clarify its importance in human interaction.

Nonverbal Communication Is Ambiguous

Like verbal communication, nonverbal behavior is ambiguous. We can never be sure that others understand the meanings we intend to express with our nonverbal behavior. Conversely, we can't know whether they read meanings into our behaviors that we do not intend. The ambiguity of nonverbal communication also arises because meanings change over time. Spreading apart the first two fingers meant victory during the World Wars and came to stand for peace during the 1960s. Both victory and peace are arbitrary meanings of this particular nonverbal behavior.

Nonverbal behaviors also reflect and perpetuate distinct organizational identities: Bankers, attorneys, and many other professionals are expected to wear business suits or dresses to work, whereas employees at many high-tech companies wear jeans and other informal attire. Each way of dressing reflects a particular organizational ethos. George W. Bush insisted on formal dress—coat and tie—at all times in the Oval Office. He once chewed out a staff person who dared to wear khakis and a buttoned-down shirt on a Saturday, and the staff person was not allowed to enter the Oval Office (Stolberg, 2009). When he became President, Barack Obama created a less formal working culture in the White House. He sometimes takes off his jacket while working in the Oval Office, and he often skips the tie on weekends.

Like verbal communication, nonverbal communication is learned and guided by rules. These rules reduce the ambiguity of nonverbal communication by telling us what certain behaviors are understood to count as (constitutive rules) and when and where certain behaviors are appropriate and inappropriate (regulative rules). For example, most of us understand that people take turns speaking, and that we should whisper in libraries but it's appropriate to yell at ball games. We know that we are supposed to raise our hands if we want to ask a question during a lecture but don't need to raise our hands to speak when interacting with friends. We dress differently for religious services, classes, dates, and job interviews. Insignia that nonverbally communicate rank define people in the military, and salutes are the standard way to acknowledge other military people. These agreed-upon rules reduce but don't completely eliminate the ambiguity of nonverbal communication.

Nonverbal Behaviors Interact with Verbal Communication

Communication researchers have identified five ways in which nonverbal behaviors interact with verbal communication (Andersen, 1999; Guerrero & Floyd, 2006). First, nonverbal behaviors may repeat verbal messages. For example, you might say "yes" while nodding your head. In making a public presentation, a speaker might hold up one, two, and three fingers when saying "first," "second," and "third," to let listeners know she or he is moving from the first to the second to the third point of a speech.

Second, nonverbal behaviors may highlight verbal communication, as when you use inflection to emphasize certain words: "This is the *most* serious problem with the business plan." Third, nonverbal communication may complement, or add to, words. Speakers often emphasize verbal statements with forceful gestures and increases in volume and inflection; capital or boldfaced letters are used to symbolize the same emphasis in online communication.

Fourth, nonverbal behaviors may contradict verbal messages (Knapp & Hall, 2006). For instance, a group member says, "Nothing's wrong" in a hostile tone of voice.

Finally, we sometimes substitute nonverbal behaviors for verbal ones. You might roll your eyes to show that you disapprove of something or shrug your shoulders instead of saying "I don't know." In all these ways, nonverbal behaviors interact with verbal communication.

Nonverbal Communication Regulates Interaction

Nonverbal communication can organize interaction between people (Guerrero & Floyd, 2006). You generally know when someone else has finished speaking, when a professor welcomes discussion from students, and when a co-worker expects you to speak. Nonverbal cues, more than verbal ones, tell us when to speak and keep silent. By averting our eyes or by increasing our speaking volume and rate, we signal that we don't want to be interrupted. When we're finished talking, we look at others to signal, "Okay, now someone else can speak." Most Westerners invite specific people to speak by looking directly at them (Drummond & Hopper, 1993; Knapp & Hall, 2006), yet eye contact is used less to regulate interaction in many Asian cultures. Although we're usually unaware of how nonverbal actions regulate interaction, we rely on them to know when to speak and when to remain silent.

Nonverbal Communication Establishes Relationship-Level Meanings

You'll recall that the relationship level of meaning defines relationships between communicators. Nonverbal communication can be powerful in expressing relationship-level meanings (Keeley & Hart, 1994). In fact, some communication scholars call nonverbal communication "the relationship language" because it so often expresses how people feel about one another (Richmond & McCroskey, 1995; Sallinen-Kuparinen, 1992). We use nonverbal communication to convey the three dimensions of relationship-level meaning that we discussed in Chapter 4: responsiveness, liking, and power. Yet *how* people communicate responsiveness, liking and disliking, and power depends on the rules of their cultures.

Responsiveness

We use eye contact, inflections, facial expressions, and body posture to show interest in others, as Maria did in one of the examples that opened this chapter. In formal presentations and casual conversations, we signal interest by holding eye contact and assuming an attentive posture. As the example with Haru Watanabe and Ben Thompson reveals, however, all cultures do not have the same rules for eye contact. To express lack of interest, Westerners tend to avoid or decrease visual contact and adopt a passive body position or turn away from the other person. Members of Asian cultures are less likely to overtly express lack of interest.

 Maryam

Americans do more than one thing at a time. In Nepal, when we talk with someone, we are with that person. We do not also write on paper or have television on. We talk with the person. It is hard for me to accept the custom of giving only some attention to each other in conversation.

Harmony in people's postures and facial expressions may reflect how comfortable they are with each other (Guerrero & Floyd, 2006) and how much they support each other (Trees, 2000). In a cohesive team, many nonverbal behaviors typically signal that members are responsive to one another. In less cohesive groups, nonverbal behavior shows less responsiveness. Happy couples sit closer to one another and engage in more eye contact than unhappy couples do (Noller, 1986, 1987). Similarly, in work settings people who like one another often sit together and exchange eye contact.

Liking

Nonverbal behaviors are keen indicators of whether we feel positive or negative about others. Smiles and friendly touching among Westerners usually are signs of positive feelings, whereas frowns and belligerent postures express antagonism (Keeley & Hart, 1994). Political candidates shake hands, slap backs, and otherwise touch people whose votes they want. These are general rules of Western society; particular social groups instill more specific rules. For example, women generally sit closer together and engage in more eye contact and more friendly touching than men do (Atsuko, 2003; Knapp & Hall, 2006).

Power

We use nonverbal behaviors to assert dominance and to negotiate status (Andersen, 1999; Remland, 2000). Compared with women, men generally assume more space and use greater volume and more forceful gestures to assert their ideas (Hall, 1987; Major, Schmidlin, & Williams, 1990). Men are also more likely to move into others' spaces, as the man in the library moved to Maria's table in one of the examples that opened this chapter.

Space also expresses power. The connection between power and space is evident in the fact that CEOs usually have large, spacious offices, entry-level and midlevel professionals have smaller offices, and secretaries often have minuscule workstations, even though secretaries often store and manage more material than executives. A widely understood regulative communication rule is that people with status or power have the right to enter the space of people with less power, but the converse is not true. Similarly, more-powerful people are more likely to touch others, interrupt, and approach more closely than less-powerful people (Hall, Coats, & Smith-LeBeau, 2004). In families, adults usually have more space than children, and men are more likely than women

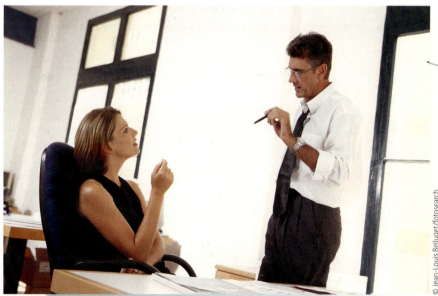

Which person in this photo has greater power? How is it expressed?

© Jean-Louis Belluget/fotosearch

to have their own rooms and to sit at heads of tables. The Sharpen Your Skill exercise on this page will help you become more attentive to nonverbal modes of expressing power.

 Ellen

Secretaries are the best decoders. They can read their bosses' moods in a heartbeat. I am a secretary, part-time now that I'm taking courses, and I can tell exactly what my boss is thinking. Sometimes, I know what he feels or will do before he does. I have to know when he can be interrupted, when he feels generous, and when not to cross his path.

Silence, a powerful form of nonverbal communication, can also be a means of exerting control. We sometimes use silence to stifle others' conversation in meetings. Silence accompanied by a glare is doubly powerful in conveying disapproval. Interviewers sometimes use silence to let interviewees know that they are not satisfied with answers given and to prompt interviewees to elaborate. In a number of Native American cultures and some Asian cultures, silence signals mindful attentiveness.

Nonverbal Communication Reflects Cultural Values

Like verbal communication, nonverbal patterns reflect rules of specific cultures (Andersen et al. 2002; Guerrero & Farinelli, 2009). This implies that most nonverbal communication isn't instinctual but is learned in the process of socialization. For instance, most Westerners consider it inappropriate to touch or hold hands with same-sex friends, but this is an acceptable way of showing closeness in many Asian cultures (Orbe & Harris, 2001).

The United States is a highly individualist culture in which people want private spaces, and we resent and sometimes fight anyone who trespasses on what we consider our territory. We want private homes, and our own rooms. In more collectivist cultures, people tend to be less territorial. For instance, Brazilians routinely stand close to one another in shops, buses, and elevators, and when they bump into each other, they don't apologize or draw back, as U.S. citizens do. In other countries, such as Hong Kong, people are used to living and working in very close quarters (Chan, 1999).

Western culture prizes time, and that is evident in the presence of clocks in most or all rooms of homes and public spaces and in the nearly universal use of wristwatches, which are not worn by people in many other cultures. Westerners' time consciousness is also reflected in the technological devices that are now part of many people's daily attire. We carry pagers and iPods, cell phones, and BlackBerrys to maintain nearly instant

SHARPEN YOUR SKILL

Noticing Spatial Clues to Power Relations

Observe a business setting—an office or other work context. To sharpen your insight into spatial indicators of power, answer the following questions:

1. Who has more space? Who has less?
2. Who enters the space of others? Who does not?
3. Who touches others?
4. Who uses commanding gestures? Who does not?

contact with others. Orientations toward time are less rigid among other cultural groups, such as Hispanics.

Yumiko

I try to teach my daughter to follow the customs of my native Japan, but she is learning to be American. I scold her for talking loud and speaking when she has not been addressed, but she tells me all the other kids talk loud and talk when they wish. I tell her it is not polite to look directly at others, but she says everyone looks at others here. She communicates as an American, not a Japanese.

Patterns of eye contact also reflect cultural values. U.S. society values frankness and assertion, so meeting another's eyes is considered appropriate and a demonstration of personal honesty. Yet in many Asian and northern European countries, direct eye contact is considered abrasive and disrespectful (Hall, 1969). Many Latinos and Latinas express attentiveness and respect by avoiding direct eye contact, whereas European Americans express attentiveness and respect by maintaining it (Orbe & Harris, 2001). In Brazil, eye contact often is so intense that many Northern Europeans consider it staring, which they find rude.

The five principles of nonverbal communication we have discussed provide a foundation for a closer look at specific kinds of nonverbal communication.

Types of Nonverbal Behaviors

Because so much of our interaction is nonverbal, this symbol system includes many kinds of communication. In this section, we will consider ten forms of nonverbal behavior, noticing how we use each to create and interpret meanings:

▶ Kinesics (face and body motion)

▶ Haptics (touch)

▶ Physical appearance

▶ Olfactics (smell)

▶ Artifacts (personal objects)

▶ Proxemics (personal space)

▶ Environmental factors

▶ Chronemics (perception and use of time)

▶ Paralanguage (vocal qualities)

▶ Silence

Kinesics

Kinesics refers to body position and body motions, including those of the face. Our bodies communicate a great deal about how we see ourselves. A speaker who stands erect and appears confident announces self-assurance, whereas someone who slouches and shuffles may seem to say, "I'm not very sure of myself." We also communicate moods with body posture and motion. For example, someone who walks quickly with a resolute facial expression appears more determined than someone who saunters along with an unfocused gaze. Similarly, people whose nonverbal behaviors indicate they have sufficient vigor to take care of themselves and move quickly are less likely to be attacked than people whose posture and movements indicate less vitality (Gunns, Johnston, & Hudson, 2002). We sit rigidly when we are nervous and adopt a relaxed posture when we feel at ease. Audiences show interest by alert body posture.

Body postures and gestures may signal whether we are open to interaction. Speakers who stay behind podiums and read notes often are perceived as less open than speakers who interact more actively with audiences. Someone who sits with arms crossed and looks downward may be perceived as saying, "Don't bother me." That's also a nonverbal strategy students sometimes use to dissuade teachers from calling on them in class. To signal that we'd like to interact, we look at others and sometimes smile. We use gestures to express how we feel about others and situations. We use one hand gesture to say "okay" and a different hand gesture to communicate contempt.

Our faces are intricate messengers. Our eyes can shoot daggers of anger, issue challenges, express skepticism, or radiate love. The face is particularly powerful in conveying liking and responsiveness (Keeley & Hart, 1994; Patterson, 1992). Many speakers smile to suggest that they are open and friendly. Smiles and warm gazes signal that we like others and are happy being around them (Gueguen & De Gail, 2003). Americans often cross their legs while seated, but this is highly offensive according to cultural rules in Ghana and Turkey (Samovar, Porter, & McDaniel 2009).

Poets call the eyes the "windows to the soul" for good reason. Our eyes communicate important and complex messages about how we feel, and we often look at others' eyes to judge their emotions, honesty, and self-confidence. This explains why strong eye contact tends to heighten the credibility of public speakers in Western societies. It may also be why customers leave larger tips to servers who maintain eye contact while serving them (Davis & Kieffer, 1998). Yet eye contact is not universally regarded as positive. Among traditional Hasidic Jews, for example, boys are taught not to look into women's eyes.

Haptics

Haptics is a term for nonverbal communication involving physical touch. Many communication scholars believe that touching and being touched are essential to healthy life (Ackerman, 1990; Whitman et al., 1999). In disturbed families,

I THINK YOU NEED TO WORK ON YOUR BODY LANGUAGE, DEAR...

wiley@non-sequitur.com   Dist. by Universal Press Syndicate   www.non-sequitur.com   8-12

fyi CAREER

Weighty Matters

Getting a job is a weighty matter. Literally. Researchers have conducted experiments on the impact of touch on decisions we make (Schmid, 2010). In one experiment, people were asked to evaluate a job candidate's résumé. For half of the people, the resume was attached to a lightweight clipboard that weighed three-fourths of a pound. The other half of the people read the résumé attached to a four and one-half pound clipboard. People holding the heavy clipboard evaluated the job candidate more highly.

Interested in how the sense of touch affected judgments of the job candidate, the researchers devised another experiment. They told 86 people who were trying to buy a car that their first offer had been rejected and they should make a second offer. Some of the would-be car buyers were seated on stiff, hard chairs whereas others were seated on comfortable, cushioned chairs. The people seated in the hard chairs raised their offer by an average of $896.50 whereas the people in the more comfortable chairs raised their offer by an average $1,243.60.

parents sometimes push children away and handle them harshly, nonverbally signaling rejection. Conversely, researchers have learned that babies who are massaged thrive more than babies who are touched less (Miller, 2009; Mwakalye & DeAngelis, 1995).

Research suggests some general sex differences in touching behavior. Compared to men, women are more likely to engage in touch to show liking and intimacy (Andersen, 1999), whereas men are more likely than women to use touch to assert power and control (Jhally & Katz, 2001).

fyi Kissing: Two Weeks of a Lifetime

Kissing is usually not considered a science, but hold on! Sheril Kirshenbaum's (2011) new book, *The Science of Kissing*, provides some facts about kissing.

◆ About 2/3 of people tilt their head to the right when kissing.

◆ The racing heart and elevated blood pressure that often accompany kissing are caused by the neurotransmitter dopamine, which is related to pleasure and emotional responses.

◆ Passionate, smoldering kissing burns 6.4 calories a minute.

◆ Over a lifetime, the average person spends approximately 2 weeks kissing.

◆ Men tend to like sloppy, wet kisses more than women, perhaps because those kisses transfer men's saliva, which contains testosterone and may enhance women's interest in further intimacy.

◆ Closed-lip kisses require only two facial muscles whereas French kisses involve all 34 facial muscles.

◆ How many bacteria are exchanged in kissing? You don't want to know: millions—yes, millions!

Physical Appearance

Western culture places an extremely high value on **physical appearance** and on specific aspects of appearance. We first notice obvious physical qualities such as sex, skin color, and size. Based on physical qualities, we may make inferences about others' personalities. Although these associations may have no factual basis, they can affect personal and social relationships as well as decisions about hiring, placement, and promotion.

Cultures prescribe ideals for physical form, and these vary across cultures and over time. Currently, Western cultural ideals emphasize thinness in women and muscularity and height in men (Davison & Birch, 2001; Lamb & Brown, 2006; Levin & Kilbourne, 2008). For most people, these body ideals can be achieved only with extreme dieting or exercise and usually cosmetic surgery. Appearance is a more significant concern for girls and women than boys and men because it is more central to how women are judged. Three out of four women say their appearance is a main factor affecting their self-image, and a third of women rank appearance as more important to self-image than job performance or intelligence (Rhode, 2010). As a result, many women to become preoccupied with dieting and other means of weight control (Buss,

Stefano Guindani/AP Photo

Pictorial Press Ltd/Alamy

Cultural views of body ideals change over time. Notice the difference between the body sizes of Marilyn Monroe on the right and Allegra Versace, an Italian heiress, on the left.

2001; Davies-Popelka, 2011). If you'd like to learn more about eating disorders and help for people who have them, go to the book's online resources for this chapter and click on WebLink 5.1. In her commentary, Cass makes a point that will be familiar to many women.

 Cass

> *I've been dieting since I was in grammar school. I'm 5' 5" and weigh 102 pounds, but I want to weigh less. I look at the models in magazines and the women in films, and they are so much slimmer than I am. I have to watch everything I eat and exercise all the time, and I'm still too fat.*

This general cultural standard for attractiveness is modified by ethnicity and socio-economic class. Traditional African societies perceive full-figured bodies as symbols of health, prosperity, and wealth, all of which are desirable (Bocella, 2001). African Americans who embrace this value accept or prefer women who weigh more than the ideal for European American women (Mernissi, 2004; Schooler et al., 2004; Walker, 2007). But ethnicity doesn't operate in isolation. Socioeconomic class modifies ethnic views about weight. Research shows that African American women who identify strongly with their ethnic cultures tend to resist Caucasian preoccupations with thinness. Conversely, middle-income African American women who are upwardly mobile may deemphasize their ethnic identities, and they are more susceptible to anxiety about weight and to eating disorders (Bocella, 2001).

Physical appearance includes physiological characteristics, such as eye color and height, as well as ways in which we manage, or even alter, our physical appearance. For instance, many people control their physical appearance by dieting, using steroids and other drugs, coloring their hair, having cosmetic surgery, wearing colored contact lenses, and using makeup. Cosmetic surgeries of many types are on the rise for both men and women. Women most often have facial surgeries, fat-reduction operations, and breast augmentation or lifting (Barrett & Springen, 2007). The most popular surgeries for men are liposuction, eyelid surgery, and nose reshaping (Mishori, 2005).

Olfactics

Olfactics (from the word *olfactory*, which refers to the sense of smell) is a term for odors and scents—or, more precisely, our perception of them. Mark Knapp and Judith Hall (2006), who study nonverbal behavior,

Kangaroo Care

Kangaroo Care is the title of Susan Ludington-Hoe's 1993 book. In it, she tells the story of an accidental discovery about the importance of touch to human survival. Until recently, it was typical for Western hospital workers to take newborn babies to nurseries where sophisticated monitoring devices could be used to ensure the babies' health.

The wisdom of separating newborns from mothers was challenged by an accidental finding from a hospital in Bogotá, Colombia. In the 1980s, the hospital experienced a serious lack of resources, including blankets used to wrap newborns. To keep the babies warm, hospital workers placed the naked babies on their mothers' naked chests. The babies thrived—more than they had when wrapped in blankets (Miller, 2006). Because the skin-to-skin contact between mothers and babies is similar to that of kangaroo moms and babies, the technique was dubbed "kangaroo care." Since the accidental discovery in Bogotá, hospitals in the United States have reported that premature babies who experience skin-to-skin contact with their moms are less fussy and calmer than babies who do not (Miller, 2006).

note that the "scientific study of the human olfactory system is in its infancy" (p. 196). Even so, we know that smell is a form of communication. The smell of freshly baked bread or cookies often makes us feel happy (and hungry!). Also, as Andy notes, scents we choose to wear can be personal signatures.

 Andy

I dated this one girl for two years, and then we broke up last year. By now, I pretty much don't think about her unless I pass somebody who is wearing the cologne she wore. One sniff of that transports me back to when she and I were together.

Andy is not alone in responding strongly to smells. Natalie Angier (2008), Pulitzer-prize-winning science columnist and science reporter, points out that olfaction is the first of our senses to develop and that it remains the quickest—we register and respond to smells faster than to sights or sounds. Further, smells are processed in the brain's ancient limbic system where emotional memories are stored. That's why the smell of cinnamon takes me back to baking cookies with Mom when I was six years old. Body odors produced by pheromones, the sex-specific chemicals our bodies produce, may affect sexual attraction. Male sweat contains a pheromone derived from progesterone, whereas female sweat contains a pheromone linked to estrogen (Bakalar, 2006). Heterosexual men and women respond to the pheromones of the opposite sex with increased activity in the hypothalamus, which is linked to sexual behavior. Interestingly, lesbians respond with elevated hypothalamic activity to the estrogen-like pheromone of other women (Bakalar, 2006).

Artifacts

Artifacts are personal objects we use to announce our identities and to personalize our environments. More women than men wear makeup and jewelry. Women are also more likely than men to wear form-fitting clothes and high-heeled shoes. Typically, men wear less jewelry, clothes with less adornment, and functional shoes (Klein, 2001; Johnson, Roberts, & Warell, 2002). Men's clothing is looser and less binding, and it includes pockets for wallets, change, keys, and so forth. In contrast, women's clothing often doesn't include pockets, so women need purses to hold personal items.

We also use artifacts to express cultural and ethnic identities. Indians may wear saris, Native Americans may wear jewelry with tribal symbols, and African Americans may wear clothes and jewelry of traditional African design. Further, as any college student knows, school symbols adorn everything from T-shirts and sweatshirts to car bumpers and notebooks. Wearing something with a symbol of your school on it declares your membership in or loyalty to that campus community.

Artifacts may also be used to announce professional identity. Nurses and doctors usually wear white and often drape stethoscopes around their necks; many executives carry briefcases, whereas students more often tote backpacks. White-collar professionals tend to wear tailored outfits and dress shoes, whereas blue-collar workers often dress in jeans or uniforms and boots. The military requires uniforms that define individuals as members of the group. In addition, stripes, medals, and insignia signify rank and accomplishments.

We also use artifacts to define settings and personal territories (Bateson, 1990; Wood, 2006). When the President of the United States speaks, the setting usually is decked with symbols of national identity and pride, such as the American flag. At annual meetings of companies, the chair usually speaks from a podium that bears the company logo. In much the same manner, we claim our private spaces by filling them with objects that matter to us and that reflect our experiences and values. Lovers of art adorn their homes and offices with paintings and sculptures that reflect their interests. Religious families often express their commitments by displaying pictures of holy scenes and the Bible, the Koran, or another sacred text. Professionals may decorate their offices with expensive furniture and framed awards to announce their status or with pictures of family to remind them of people they cherish. MySpace and Facebook pages include songs, photos, and images aimed at conveying specific personalities. Like other kinds of nonverbal communication, artifacts' meanings vary across cultures, as the FYI below illustrates.

Sam Gosling (2008) recently published an interesting book on artifacts: *Snoop: What Your Stuff Says About You*. Gosling refers to bumper stickers, tattoos, posters, and so forth as "identity claims," which give signals about how we want others to perceive us and also remind ourselves of who we are. For instance, when moving out of her home state, one woman Gosling studied tattooed the outline of her state on her inside forearm. It was intended for her eyes to remind her of her home state.

Proxemics and Personal Space

Proxemics refers to space and how we use it. The classic research on proxemics was done by Edward Hall in 1968. At the time, Hall reported that every culture has norms for using space and for how close people should be to one another. In the United States, we interact with social acquaintances from a distance of 4 to 12 feet but are comfortable with 18 inches or less between us and friends or romantic partners (Hall, 1968). Most people who were born and raised in the United States consider it normal for individuals to have separate spaces or rooms. As Sucheng points out, however, what is considered a normal amount of individual space varies from culture to culture.

Branded

The artifacts we choose increasingly announce political commitments. A baseball hat says, "End Sweatshop Labor"; a T-shirt proclaims, "Save the Planet"; a bumper sticker reads, "Biodiesel is the future"; a button says, "Free Choice" and another declares, "Pro Life." More and more people seem to want their clothes, cars, coffee mugs, and other objects to send messages about their political values. To learn more about this, go to the book's online resources for this chapter and click on WebLink 5.2 to read an article prepared for the Center for Communication and Civic Engagement.

DIVERSITY

Cultural Rules about Artifacts

Giving gifts can lead to misunderstandings when giver and recipient are from different cultures (Axtell, 2007).

◆ A Chinese person might not appreciate the gift of a clock, because clocks symbolize death in China.

◆ Giving a gift to an Arab person on first meeting would likely be interpreted as a bribe.

◆ Bringing flowers to a dinner hosted by a person from Kenya would cause confusion because in Kenya flowers express sympathy for a loss.

◆ In Switzerland, giving red roses is interpreted as a signal of romantic interest. Also, the Swiss consider even numbers of flowers bad luck, so never give a dozen.

In the United States, each person has so much room! Every individual has a separate room to sleep and sometimes another separate room to work. Also, I see that each family here lives in a separate house. People have much less space in China. Families live together, with sons bringing their families into their parents' home and all sharing the same space. At first, when I came here, it felt strange to have so much space, but now I sometimes feel very crowded when I go home.

Space also announces status, with greater space and more desirable space assumed by those with higher status in a culture. Research shows that women and minorities generally have less space than European American men in the United States (Andersen, 1999). It's no coincidence that industries expose our most vulnerable communities to pollutants and carcinogens that they seldom foist on middle- and upper-class people. The meaning of this pattern is very clear: "The space of minorities and poor people is often invaded and contaminated, but the territory of more affluent citizens is respected" (Cox, 2011).

How people arrange space may reflect closeness and desire, or lack of desire, for interaction. Highly formal businesses often have private offices with doors that are usually closed and little common space. Couples who are highly interdependent tend to have more common space and less individual space in their homes than do couples who are more independent (Fitzpatrick, 1988; Werner, Altman, & Oxley, 1985). Similarly, families who enjoy interaction arrange furniture to invite conversation and eye contact. In families who seek less interaction, chairs may be far apart and may face televisions instead of each other (Burgoon, Buller, & Woodhall, 1989; Keeley & Hart, 1994).

The ways that offices are arranged may invite or discourage interaction and may foster equal or unequal power relationships. Some professors and executives have desks that face their office doors and a chair beside the desk to promote open communication with people who come to their offices. Other professors and executives turn their desks away from the door and place chairs opposite their desks, which configures the space hierarchically. Whether office doors are open or shut may also indicate willingness to interact.

Environmental Factors

Environmental factors are elements of settings that affect how we feel, think, and act. We feel more relaxed in rooms with comfortable chairs than in rooms with stiff, formal furniture. Candlelit dining tables may promote romantic feelings; and churches, synagogues, and temples use candles to foster respect. A recent study found that color affects cognitive functions. Red stimulates accuracy, recall, and attention to detail whereas blue stimulates creativity (Belluck, 2009). Perhaps we should have blue computer screens when doing creative writing and red screens when working on math problems.

Restaurants use environmental features to control how long people spend eating. For example, low lights, comfortable chairs or booths, and soft music often are part of the environment in upscale restaurants. On the other hand, fast-food eateries have hard plastic booths and bright lights, which encourage diners to eat and move on. To maximize profit, restaurants want to get people in and out as quickly as possible. Studies show that fast music in restaurants speeds up the pace of eating; on average, people eat 3.2 mouthfuls a minute when the background music is slow and 5.1 mouthfuls a minute when music with a faster tempo is played ("Did You Know?" 1998). Restaurants use a variety of environmental cues to create the atmosphere they want—to encourage customers to linger, or to encourage them to eat and run. You can identify some of the environmental features that affect a restaurant's atmosphere by completing the Sharpen Your Skill feature on this page.

In the same way that restaurants and other public places use environmental factors to influence mood and behavior, we choose colors, furniture arrangements, lighting, and other objects to create the atmosphere we desire in our home.

Chronemics

Chronemics refer to how we perceive and use time to define identities and interaction. We use time to negotiate and convey status (Levine & Norenzayan, 1999). In Western societies, there seems to be an unwritten but widely understood cultural rule stipulating that people with high status can keep people with less status waiting. Conversely, people with low status are expected to be punctual. Subordinates are expected to report punctually to meetings, but bosses are allowed to be tardy.

Chronemics express cultural attitudes toward time. In some cultures, people saunter whereas in others they dash from place to place. In some cultures business is conducted quickly by staying on task whereas in other cultures it is conducted more slowly by intermingling task and social interaction. According to a study of pace of life (Levine & Norenzayan, 1999), the countries with the fastest pace of life are Switzerland (#1), Ireland, Germany, and Japan. The countries with the slowest pace of life are Mexico (#31), Indonesia, Brazil, and El Salvador. The United States was 16th—right in the middle of the list. Notice that the slowest pace of life is in countries that have warm climates while the fastest pace of life is in countries with colder climates.

Western societies value time and its cousin, speed (Bertman, 1998; Calero, 2005; Honoré, 2005; Keyes, 1992; Schwartz, 1989). We want computers, not

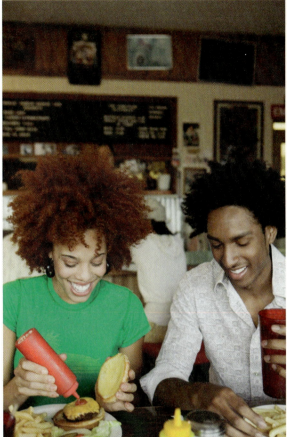

How are environmental features in the restaurant likely to shape patrons' behaviour?

SHARPEN YOUR SKILL

Increasing Awareness of Environmental Factors

Observe a restaurant in which you feel rushed and another restaurant in which you feel like taking your time. Describe the following for each restaurant:

1. How much space is there between tables?
2. What kind of lighting is used?
3. What sort of music and sound are in the place?
4. How comfortable are the chairs?
5. What colors and art do you see?

Can you make any generalizations about environmental features that promote relaxation and those that do not?

typewriters, and many of us replace our computers and software as soon as faster versions become available. We often try to do several things at once to get more done, rely on the microwave to cook faster, and take for granted speed systems such as instant copying and photos (McGee-Cooper, Trammel, & Lau, 1992). The value that Westerners place on time is evident in everyday expressions (Lakoff & Johnson, 1980): "You're *wasting* my time," "This new software program will *save* time," "That mistake *cost* me three hours," "I've *invested* a lot of time in this class," "I can't *afford* to go out tonight," "I can make up for *lost* time by using a shortcut," and "I'm *running out* of time."

Many other cultures have far more relaxed attitudes toward time and punctuality. In many South American countries, it's normal to come to meetings or classes after the announced time of starting, and it's not assumed that people will leave when the scheduled time for ending arrives. In the Philippines, punctuality has never been particularly valued, but that may be changing. The Philippine Department of Education just launched a 10-year campaign to instill in students the value of being on time (Overland, 2009).

The length of time we spend with different people reflects the extent of our interest in them and affection for them. A manager is inclined to spend more time with a new employee who seems to have executive potential than with one who seems less impressive. A speaker usually gives a fuller answer to a question from a high-status member of the audience than to one from a person with less status. In general, we spend more time with people we like than with those we don't like or who bore us. Researchers report that increased contact among college students is a clear sign that a relationship is intensifying, and reduced time together signals decreasing interest (Baxter, 1985; Dindia, 1994; Tolhuizen, 1989).

Chronemics also involves expectations of time, which are influenced by social norms. For example, you expect a class to last 50 or 75 minutes. Several minutes before the end of a class period, students often close their notebooks and start gathering their belongings, signaling the teacher that time is up. A similar pattern often is evident in business meetings. We expect religious services to last approximately an hour, and we might be upset if a rabbi or minister talked for two hours.

Paralanguage

Paralanguage is communication that is vocal but not actual words. Paralanguage includes sounds, such as murmurs and gasps, and vocal qualities, such as volume, rhythm, pitch, and inflection. Vocal cues signal others to interpret what we say as a joke, a threat, a statement of fact, a question, and so forth. Effective public speakers modulate inflection, volume, and rhythm to enhance their presentations.

We use vocal cues to communicate feelings to friends and romantic partners. Whispering, for instance, signals confidentiality or intimacy, whereas shouting conveys anger or excitement. Depending on the context, sighing may communicate empathy, boredom, or contentment. Research shows that tone of voice is a powerful clue to feelings between marital partners. Negative vocal tones often reveal marital dissatisfaction (Noller, 1987). Negative intonation may also signal dissatisfaction or disapproval in work settings. A derisive or sarcastic tone can communicate scorn clearly, whereas a warm voice conveys friendliness.

Our voices affect how others perceive us. To some extent, we control vocal cues that influence image. For instance, we can deliberately sound confident in job interviews or when asking for a raise. The president adopts a solemn voice when announcing military actions. Most of us know how to make ourselves sound apologetic, seductive, or angry when those images suit our purposes. In addition to the ways we intentionally use our voices, natural and habitual vocal qualities affect how others perceive us. For instance, people who speak at slow to moderate rates are perceived as having greater control over interaction than people who speak more rapidly (Tusing & Dillard, 2000).

 Leah

> Everyone in my family knew that when Mother raised her voice we were in trouble, but when our father lowered his, we were in trouble. His voice would drop to this low volume and get very slow and deep. It was a signal to take cover FAST!

Our ethnic heritage and identification influence how we use our voices. In general, African American speech has more vocal range, inflection, and tonal quality than European American speech (Garner, 1994). In general, African Americans are also more likely than European Americans to signal interest in what another person is saying by making listening sounds ("um hmm," "yeah, yeah") (Brilhart & Galanes, 1995). Paralanguage also reflects gender. Men's voices tend to have louder volume, lower pitch, and less inflection, features that conform to cultural views of men as assertive and emotionally controlled. Women's voices typically have higher pitch, softer volume, and more inflection, features consistent with cultural views of women as emotional and deferential. Socioeconomic level influences pronunciation, rate of speech, and accent.

Silence

A final type of nonverbal behavior is **silence,** which is a lack of communicated sound. Although silence is quiet, it can communicate powerful messages. "I'm not speaking to you" speaks volumes. Silence can convey contentment when intimates are so comfortable they don't need to talk. Silence can also communicate awkwardness, as you know if you've ever had trouble making conversation on a first date. Yet the awkwardness that many Westerners feel when silence falls is not felt by people from some other cultures, as Jin Lee explains.

 Jin Lee

> In the United States, people feel it is necessary to talk all of the time, to fill in any silence with words and more words. I was not brought up that way. In my country, it is good to be silent some of the time. It shows you are listening to another, you are thinking about what the other says, you are respectful and do not need to put in your words.

Some parents discipline children by ignoring them. No matter what the child says or does, the parents refuse to acknowledge the child's existence. The silencing strategy may also surface later in life. We sometimes deliberately freeze out others when we're angry with them (Williams, 2001). In some military academies, such as West Point, silence is a method of stripping a cadet of personhood if the cadet is perceived as having broken the academy's honor code. On the job, silence may signal disapproval, as peers often ostracize whistle-blowers and union-busters. People who violate the rules of chat rooms may be silenced by getting no responses to their messages.

Audiences sometimes shout down speakers they dislike; when angry, romantic partners may refuse to speak; and the Catholic Church excommunicates people who violate its canons. Like other forms of communication, silence—and what it means—is linked to culture. European Americans tend to be talkative; they are inclined to fill in silence with words. Among Native Americans, however, historically silence conveys respect, active listening, and thought about what others are saying (Braithwaite, 1990; Carbaugh, 1998).

We've seen that nonverbal communication includes kinesics, haptics, physical appearance, olfactics, artifacts, proxemics, environmental factors, chronemics, paralanguage, and silence. The final section of this chapter gives guidelines for improving nonverbal communication.

Guidelines for Effective Nonverbal Communication

Nonverbal communication, like verbal communication, can be misinterpreted. Following these two guidelines should reduce nonverbal misunderstandings in your interactions.

Monitor Your Nonverbal Communication

Think about the preceding discussion of ways we use nonverbal behaviors to announce our identities. Are you projecting the image you desire? Do others interpret your facial and body movements in ways consistent with the image you want to project? Do friends ever tell you that you seem uninterested when really you *are* interested? If so, you can monitor your nonverbal actions to more clearly communicate your involvement and interest in conversations. To reduce the chance that work associates will think you're uninterested in meetings, use what you've learned in this chapter to engage in nonverbal behaviors that others associate with responsiveness and attention.

Think also about how you arrange your personal spaces. Have you set up your room, office, apartment, or home to invite the kind of interaction you prefer, or are they arranged in ways that undercut your goals as a communicator? Paying attention to the nonverbal dimensions of your world can empower you to use them more effectively to achieve your interpersonal goals.

Interpret Others' Nonverbal Communication Tentatively

Although popular advice books promise to show you how to read nonverbal communications, no surefire formula exists. It's naive to think we can decode something so complex and ambiguous.

In this chapter, we've discussed findings about the meanings people attach to nonverbal behaviors. We can never be sure what a particular behavior means to specific people in a particular context (Manusov, 2004). For instance, we've said that sitting close together indicates liking. As a general rule, this is true. However, sometimes contented friends and couples like to have physical distance between them. Partners may also avoid physical closeness when one has a cold or flu.

People socialized in non-Western cultures learn distinct rules for proxemics. Because nonverbal communication is ambiguous and personal, we should not assume we can interpret it with precision. An ethical principle of communication is to qualify interpretations of nonverbal behavior with awareness of personal and contextual considerations.

Personal Qualifications

Generalizations about nonverbal behavior state what is generally the case. They don't tell us about the exceptions to the rule. For instance, although eye contact generally is a sign of responsiveness, some people close their eyes to concentrate when listening. Sometimes people who cross their arms and condense into a tight posture are expressing hostility or lack of interest in interaction. However, the same behaviors might mean that a person is cold and trying to conserve body heat. Most people use less inflection and adopt a slack posture when they're not really interested in what they're talking about. However, the same behaviors may mean merely that we're tired.

Because nonverbal behaviors are ambiguous and vary between people, we need to be cautious about how we interpret these behaviors. A key principle is that we construct the meanings we attach to nonverbal communication. A good way to keep this in mind is to rely on *I*-language, not *you*-language, which we discussed earlier. *You*-language might lead us to inaccurately say of someone who doesn't look at us, "You're communicating lack of interest." A more responsible statement would use *I*-language to say, "When you don't look at me, I feel you're not interested in what I'm saying." Using *I*-language reminds us to take responsibility for our judgments and feelings. In addition, we become less likely to make others defensive by inaccurately interpreting their nonverbal behavior.

Contextual Qualifications

Like the meaning of verbal communication, the significance of nonverbal behaviors depends on the contexts in which they occur. Our nonverbal communication reflects the various settings we inhabit. We are more or less formal, relaxed, and open depending on context. Most people are more at ease and confident in their own territories than in someone else's, so we tend to be more relaxed in our homes and offices than in business places; teams often win games when they have the "home turf" advantage. We also dress according to context—a suit for a job interview, jeans or casual slacks and a shirt for a game.

Immediate physical settings are not the only factor that affects nonverbal communication. As we have seen, all communication reflects the values and understandings of particular cultures. We are likely to misinterpret people from

SHARPEN YOUR SKILL

Using I-Language about Nonverbal Behaviors

This exercise extends principles of *I*-language we discussed in Chapter 4 to the context of nonverbal communication. Practice translating *you*-language into *I*-language to describe nonverbal behaviors.

Example	*You*-language	You're staring at me.
	I-language	When you look at me so intensely, I feel uncomfortable.

You-Language	*I*-Language
You're lying—I can tell because you won't look me in the eye.	_____
Your perfume stinks.	_____
Don't you smirk when I'm talking.	_____
You look lazy when you slouch.	_____

other cultures when we impose the norms and rules of our culture on them (Emmons, 1998). This suggests that we have an ethical responsibility not to assume that our rules and norms apply to the behaviors of others.

Even within the United States, we have diverse communication cultures, and each has its rules for nonverbal behavior. Ethical communicators try to adopt dual perspective when interpreting others, especially when they and we belong to different cultures. To enhance your awareness of cultural influences on communication, Chapter 8 deals with that topic in detail.

SUMMARY

In this chapter, we've explored the fascinating world of nonverbal communication. We learned that nonverbal communication is symbolic and functions to supplement or replace verbal messages, regulate interaction, reflect and establish relationship-level meanings, and express cultural membership. These five principles of nonverbal behavior help us understand the complex ways in which nonverbal communication operates and what it may mean.

We discussed ten types of nonverbal communication, each of which reflects cultural rules and expresses our personal identities and feelings toward others. We use nonverbal behaviors to announce and perform our identities, relying on actions, artifacts, and contextual features to embody what our culture has taught us is appropriate for our gender, race, class, sexuality, and ethnicity. Because nonverbal communication is ambiguous, we construct its meaning as we notice, organize, and interpret nonverbal behaviors that we and others enact. Effectiveness requires that we learn to monitor our nonverbal communication and to exercise caution in interpreting that of others.

REVIEW, REFLECT, EXTEND

The Reflect, Discuss, and Apply Questions that follow will help you review, reflect on, and extend the information and ideas presented in this chapter. These resources, and a diverse selection of additional study tools, are also available online at the CourseMate for *Communication Mosaics.* Your CourseMate includes a student workbook, WebLinks, TED Talks hyperlinks and activities, chapter glossary and flashcards, interactive video activities, Speech Builder Express, and InfoTrac College Edition. For more information or to access this book's online resources, visit **www. cengagebrain.com.**

KEY CONCEPTS

artifacts, 100
chronemics, 103
environmental factors, 102
haptics, 96
kinesics, 95
nonverbal communication, 90

olfactics, 99
paralanguage, 104
physical appearance, 98
proxemics, 101
silence, 105

Reflect, Discuss, Apply

1. Attend a gathering of people from a culture different from yours. It might be a meeting at a Jewish temple if you're Christian, an African-American church if you are white, or a meeting of Asian students if you are Western. Observe nonverbal behaviors of the people there: How do they greet one another? How much eye contact accompanies interaction? How close to one another do people sit?

2. Describe the spatial arrangements in the home of your family of origin. Was there a room in which family members interacted a good deal? How was furniture arranged in that room? Who had separate space and personal chairs in your family? What do the nonverbal patterns reflect about your family's communication style?

3. As a class, discuss current gender prescriptions in the United States. How are men and women "supposed" to look? How are these cultural expectations communicated? How might you resist and alter unhealthy cultural gender prescriptions?

4. Attend a public hearing at your school or in the nearby community. It could be a meeting about zoning, placement of a public facility, etc. Observe nonverbal communication such as where public officials and citizens are located (which locations suggest greater power?), timing of the meeting (who might be unable to attend?), artifacts (clothing; who has official files?). How do nonverbal factors reflect and shape what happens in the meeting?

Recommended Resources

1. R. E. Axtell. (1998). *Gestures: The do's and taboos of body language around the world.* New York: John Wiley. This is a very readable book that provides fascinating examples of how different cultures interpret gestures.

2. *Tootsie* remains one of the best films ever made depicting gendered nonverbal communication.

View the film, and notice how lead actor Dustin Hoffman changes his nonverbal behaviors when he is portraying Michael Dorsey, a male, and Dorothy Michaels, a female.

EXPERIENCE COMMUNICATION CASE STUDY

Teamwork

Apply what you've learned in this chapter by analyzing the following case study, using the accompanying questions as a guide. These questions and a video of the case study are also available online at your CourseMate for *Communication Mosaics.*

A project team is meeting to discuss the most effective way to present its recommendations for implementing a flextime policy on a trial basis. Members of the team are Jason (the team leader), Erika, Victoria, Bill, and Jensen. They are seated around a rectangular table with Jason at the head.

Jason: So we've decided to recommend trying flextime for a two-month period and with a number of procedures to make sure that people's new schedules don't interfere with productivity. There's a lot of information to communicate to employees, so how can we do that best?

Victoria: I think it would be good to use PowerPoint to highlight the key aspects of the new procedures. People always seem to remember better if they see something.

Bill: Oh, come on. PowerPoint is so overused. Everyone is tired of it by now. Can't we do something more creative?

© Cengage Learning

Victoria: Well I like it. It's a good teaching tool.

Bill: I didn't know we were teaching. I thought our job was to report recommendations.

Victoria: So what do you suggest, Bill? [She nervously pulls on her bracelet as she speaks.]

Bill: I don't have a suggestion. I'm just against PowerPoint. [He doesn't look up as he speaks.]

Jason: Okay, let's not bicker among ourselves. [He pauses, gazes directly at Bill, then continues.] Lots of people like PowerPoint, lots don't. Instead of arguing about its value, let's ask what it is we want to communicate to the employees here. Maybe talking about our goal first will help us decide on the best means of achieving it.

Erika: Good idea. I'd like for us to focus first on getting everyone excited about the benefits of flextime. If they understand those, they'll be motivated to learn the procedures, even if there are a lot of them.

Jensen: Erika is right. That's a good way to start. Maybe we could create a handout or PowerPoint slide—either would work—to summarize the benefits of flextime that we've identified in our research.

Jason: Good, okay now we're cooking. Victoria, will you make notes on the ideas as we discuss them?

Victoria opens a notebook and begins writing notes.

Noticing that Bill is typing into his personal digital assistant (PDA), Jason looks directly at Bill and says, "Are you with us on how we lead off in our presentation?"

Bill: Sure, fine with me. [He puts the PDA aside but keeps his eyes on it.]

Erika: So maybe then we should say that the only way flextime can work is if we make sure that everyone agrees on procedures so that no division is ever missing more than one person during key production hours.

Jensen: Very good. That would add to people's motivation to learn and follow the procedures we've found are effective in other companies like ours. I think it would be great if Erika could present that topic because she did most of the research on it.

He smiles at Erika, and she pantomimes tipping her hat to him.

Jason: [He looks at Erika with a raised brow, and she nods.] Good. Okay, Erika's in charge of that. What's next?

Victoria: Then it's time to spell out the procedures and…

Bill: You can't just spell them out. You have to explain each one—give people a rationale for them or they won't follow them.

Victoria glares at Bill, then looks across the table at Erika, who shrugs as if to say, "I don't know what's bothering Bill today."

Jason: Bill, why don't you lead off, then, and tell us the first procedure we should mention and the rationale we should provide for it.

Bill looks up from his PDA, which he's been using again. He shrugs and says harshly, "Just spell out the rules, that's all."

Victoria: Would it be too much trouble for you to cut off your gadget and join us in this meeting, Bill?

Bill: Would it be too much trouble for you to quit hassling me?

Jason: [He turns his chair to face Bill squarely.] Look, I don't know what's eating you, but you're really being a jerk. If you've got a problem with this meeting or someone here, put it on the table. Otherwise, be a team player.

1. Identify nonverbal behaviors that regulate turn taking within the team.

2. Identify nonverbal behaviors that express relationship-level meanings of communication. What aspects of team members' nonverbal communication express liking or disliking, responsiveness or lack of responsiveness, and power?

3. How do artifacts affect interaction between members of the team?

4. If you were the sixth member of this team, what kinds of communication might you enact to help relieve tension in the group?

6 Listening and Responding to Others

"Got a minute?" Stan asks as he enters Suzanne's office. "Sure," Suzanne agrees, without looking up from the report she is reading for a meeting later today. Lately, her supervisor has criticized her for being unprepared for meetings, and she wants to be on top of information today.

"I'm concerned about Frank. He's missed several days lately, and he's late half the time when he does come into work," Stan begins. "He hasn't given me any explanation for his absences and tardiness, and I can't keep overlooking it."

"Yeah, I know that routine," Suzanne says with irritation. "Last month, Barton missed two days in a row and left early several other days."

"That's exactly what I'm talking about," Stan agrees. "I can't let Frank disregard rules that everyone else follows, but I don't want to come down too hard on him, especially when I don't know why he's missing so much time."

"I told Barton that from now on he could either be at work when he should be or give me a darned good reason for why he wasn't," Suzanne says forcefully. Her mind wanders back to relive the confrontation with Barton.

"I wonder if the two situations are really similar," Stan says.

Suzanne realizes she was lost in her own thoughts. "Sorry, I didn't catch what you said," she says.

"I was wondering if you're saying that I should handle Frank like you handled Barton," Stan says.

"You have to enforce the rules, or he'll walk all over you." Suzanne's eyes drift back to the report she was reading when Stan dropped by.

"I hate to be so hard on Frank," Stan says.

"Remember last year when Cheryl kept missing work? Well, I tried to be subtle and hint that she couldn't skip work. In one ear and out the other. You have to be firm."

"But Frank's not like Barton or Cheryl," Stan says. "He's never tried to run over me or shirk his work. I have a hunch something is going on that's interfering with his work. Cheryl and Barton both had patterns of irresponsibility."

"I don't think my staff is any less responsible than yours. I'm a good supervisor, you know," Suzanne snaps.

"That's not what I meant. I just don't think I need to hit Frank over the head with a two-by-four," Stan says.

"And I suppose you think that's what I did?"

"I don't know. I wasn't there. I'm just thinking that maybe our situations are different," says Stan.

When we think about communication, we usually focus on talking. Yet, in the communication process, listening is at least as important as talking. As obvious as this seems, few of us devote as much energy to listening as we do to talking.

In the conversation between Stan and Suzanne, poor listening is evident in several ways. First, Suzanne is preoccupied with a report she is reading. If she really wants to listen to Stan, she should put the report aside. A second problem is Suzanne's tendency to monopolize the conversation, turning it into an occasion to discuss *her* supervisory problems instead of Stan's concerns about Frank's behavior. Third, Suzanne listens defensively, interpreting Stan as criticizing her when he suggests that his situation might call for different action than hers. Like Suzanne, most of us don't listen as well as we could much of the time. When we listen poorly, we communicate ineffectively.

Studies of people ranging from college students to professionals show that the average person spends 45 to 55 percent of waking time listening to others; that's more time than we spend in any other communication activity (Buckley, 1992; Nichols, 1996; Weaver, 1972; Wolvin, 2009). We listen in classes, at public lectures, to television and radio, in conversations, during interviews, on webcam conversations and to videos on YouTube, on the job, and when participating in teamwork. If we add the time we listen while doing other things, the total listening time is even greater.

When people don't listen well on the job, they may miss information that can affect their professional effectiveness and advancement (Darling & Dannels, 2003; Deal & Kennedy, 1999; Gabric & McFadden, 2001; Landrum & Harrold, 2003). Skill in listening is also linked to resolving workplace conflicts (Van Styke, 1999). Doctors who don't listen fully to patients may misdiagnose or mistreat medical problems (Christensen, 2004; Scholz, 2005; Underwood & Adler, 2005). Ineffective listening in the classroom diminishes learning and performance on tests. In personal relationships, poor listening can hinder understanding of others, and not listening well to public communication leaves us uninformed about civic issues. Learning to listen well enhances personal, academic, social, civic, and professional effectiveness.

Who Listens?

We might do well to heed wisdom offered by Mother Teresa. Here's an excerpt from Dan Rather's interview with Mother Teresa shortly before her death in 1997 (Bailey, 1998).

Rather: What do you say to God when you pray?

Mother Teresa: I listen.

Rather: Well, what does God say?

Mother Teresa: He listens.

Figure 6.1   **The Listening Process**
Source: Adapted from Wood, 1997, p. 21.

This chapter explores listening, which is the fourth basic communication process. First, we'll consider what's involved in listening and discuss obstacles to effective listening. Next, we'll examine common forms of ineffective listening. Then, we'll look at skills needed for good listening in various situations. Finally, we'll identify ways to improve listening.

The Listening Process

Although we often use the words listening and hearing as if they were synonyms, actually they're not. **Hearing** is a physiological activity that occurs when sound waves hit functioning eardrums. Hearing is not the only way we receive messages. We also receive them through sight, as when we notice nonverbal behaviors, read lips, or interpret American Sign Language (ASL).

Listening is more complex than hearing. The International Listening Association (http://www.listen.org, 2011) defines listening as the "process of receiving, constructing meaning from, and responding to spoken and/or nonverbal messages." This means that, in addition to hearing, or physically receiving messages, listening involves being mindful, selecting and organizing information, interpreting communication, responding, physically receiving messages, and remembering (Figure 6.1).

Being Mindful

Mindfulness is focusing on what is happening in the moment (Wood, 1997, 2004a). When you are mindful, you don't think about what you did yesterday or the paper you need to write or a problem at work or your response to what someone is saying. Instead, mindful listeners focus on the people with whom they are interacting.

One reason that many people have difficulty focusing mindfully on what another is saying is that we listen at a faster rate than we talk. The average person can understand approximately 300 words a minute, yet the average person speaks at a rate of approximately 100 words a minute. This leaves a lot of free time for listeners' minds to drift if they aren't committed to being mindful.

Mindfulness enhances communication in two ways. First, attending mindfully to others increases our understanding of their thoughts and feelings. Second, mindfulness promotes more complete communication by others. When we really listen to others, they tend to elaborate their ideas and express their feelings in greater depth. Simone's commentary highlights the impact of mindfulness on communication.

 Simone

The best listener I've ever met was Nate, a guy I worked with on the campus newspaper. He wrote the best stories on special speakers who came to campus. At first, I thought he just got more interesting personalities to interview than I did. But then he and I had a couple of joint interviews, and I saw how he listened. When an interviewee was talking, Nate gave the person his undivided attention—like there was nobody else and nothing else around. People really open up when you treat them like the most interesting person in the world.

The Power of Responsive Listening

To test the effect of responsive listening, researchers taught students in a college psychology course to give different responses to their professor. The professor was a boring lecturer who read his notes in a monotone, seldom gestured, and did little to engage students. After the first few minutes of class, the students changed their postures, kept greater eye contact, nodded, and so forth. Shortly after the students began responding, the lecturer started using gestures, increased his speaking rate and inflection, and began to interact with students visually and verbally. Then, at a prearranged signal, the students stopped showing interest. Within a few minutes, the lecturer returned to his old lecture style. The students' responses affected the professor's communication (Bolton, 1986).

Obviously, mindfulness is important in personal relationships. It is equally important in professional life. Pamela Kruger (1999) talked with business executives and concluded that "leaders must know how to listen…. But first, and just as important, leaders must *want* to listen" (p. 134).

Mindfulness isn't a talent that some people naturally have and others don't. It's an ethical commitment to attend fully to others in particular moments. No techniques will make you a good listener if you don't choose to be mindful. Thus, your choice of whether to be mindful is the foundation of how you listen—or fail to. The Sharpen Your Skill activity on this page provides guidelines for developing mindfulness.

Physically Receiving Communication

In addition to mindfulness, listening involves physically receiving communication. We might receive it by hearing sounds, interpreting nonverbal behaviors, reading lips or ASL.

Most of us take hearing for granted. However, people who do not hear well may have difficulty receiving oral messages (Carl, 1998). When we speak with someone who has a hearing impairment, we should face the person and verify that we are coming across clearly. Our ability to receive messages also declines if we are tired or stressed. You may have noticed that it's hard to sustain attention in long classes. Physical reception of messages is also hampered if others are talking around us, if TVs or radios are on, and if there are competing visual cues.

Women and men seem to differ somewhat in how they listen. As a rule, women are more attuned than men to all that

SHARPEN YOUR SKILL

Developing Mindfulness

Mindfulness develops with commitment and practice. Four guidelines will help you develop mindfulness.

1. Empty your mind of thoughts, ideas, and plans so that you are open to listening to another.

2. Concentrate on the person with whom you are communicating. Say to yourself, "I want to focus on this person and what she or he is saying and feeling."

3. Don't be surprised if distracting thoughts come up or you find yourself thinking about your responses instead of what the other person is saying. This is natural. Just push away diverting thoughts and refocus on the person with whom you are talking.

4. Evaluate how well you listened when you were focusing on being mindful. If you aren't as fully engaged as you want to be, remind yourself that mindfulness is a habit of mind and a way of living. Developing your ability to be mindful is a process that requires time and practice.

DIGITAL MEDIA

Videoconferencing for Deaf Education

At the Delaware School for the Deaf, high school students have regular tutoring sessions with students in deaf education at Valdosta State University in Georgia. To bridge the distance between students and tutors, both schools have computer labs equipped with webcams. It's a win–win situation: The students at Valdosta get valuable hands-on experience to refine their skills, and the students at Delaware get individual attention and help (Kiernan, 2006).

is going on around them. Men tend to focus, shape, and direct their hearing in specific ways, whereas women are more likely to notice contexts, details, and tangents, as well as major themes in interaction ("Men Use," 2000; Weaver, 1972).

Selecting and Organizing Communication

The third element of listening is selecting and organizing material. As we noted in Chapter 3, we don't perceive everything around us. Instead, we selectively attend to some aspects of communication and disregard others. What we attend to depends on many factors, including physiological influences, expectations, cognitive structures, social roles, and membership in cultures and social communities. If we are preoccupied, we may not notice, select, and organize material effectively. In the example that opened this chapter, Suzanne's involvement with her report impeded her ability to listen to Stan. If you want to communicate effectively, you should take responsibility for controlling thoughts and concerns that can interfere with listening. Once again, mindfulness comes into play. Choosing to be mindful doesn't guarantee that our minds won't stray, but it does mean that we will bring ourselves back to the moment.

As you'll recall from Chapter 3, we use cognitive schemata to organize our perceptions. As you listen to other people, you decide how to categorize them by deciding which of your prototypes they most closely resemble: friend with a problem, professional rival, colleague, supervisor, and so forth. You then apply personal constructs to assess whether they are smart or not smart, honest or not honest, reasonable or not reasonable, open to advice or not open, and so on. Next, you apply stereotypes to predict what they will do. Finally, you choose a script that seems appropriate to follow in interacting.

Listeners actively define the listening situation and construct its meaning. When we define someone as emotionally upset, we're likely to rely on a script that tells us to back off and let him air his feelings. On the other hand, when a co-worker comes to you with a problem that must be solved quickly, you assume she might welcome concrete advice or collaboration. It's important to realize that *we construct others and their communication* by the schemata we use to organize our perceptions of them. Because our perceptions can be wrong, we should be ready to revise them in the course of interacting.

Interpreting Communication

The fourth aspect of listening is **interpretation**. When we interpret, we put together all that we have selected and organized to make sense of communication. Effective interpretation depends on your ability to understand others on their terms. Certainly, you won't always agree with other people's feelings and thoughts. Recognizing others' viewpoints doesn't mean you agree with them, but it does mean you make an earnest effort to grasp what they think and feel. This is an ethical responsibility of listening.

Maggie

> *Don and I didn't understand each other's perspective, and we didn't even understand that we didn't understand. Once, I told him I was really upset about a friend of mine who needed money for an emergency. Don told me she had no right to expect me to bail her out, but that had nothing to do with what I was feeling. He would have seen the situation in terms of rights, but I didn't, and he didn't grasp my take. Only after we got counseling did we learn to listen to each other instead of listening through ourselves.*

As Maggie notes in her commentary, to respect another person's perspective is to give a special gift. What we give is regard for the other person and a willingness to open ourselves to that person's way of looking at the world. Too often, we impose our meanings on others, we try to correct or argue with them about what they feel, or we crowd out their words with ours. To listen effectively, we need to focus on understanding others on their own terms.

Responding

Effective listening involves **responding**, which includes expressing interest, asking questions, voicing our own ideas on a topic, and otherwise communicating attentiveness. As we noted in Chapter 1, communication is a transactional process in which we simultaneously receive and send messages. Skillful listeners give signs that they are involved in interaction, even though they are not speaking at the moment (Barker & Watson, 2000; Hutchby, 2005; ILA, 2008; Purdy & Borisoff, 1997). We respond not only when others finish speaking but also throughout interaction. At public presentations, audience members show interest by looking at speakers, nodding their heads, and adopting attentive postures. Nonverbal behaviors, such as looking out a window and slouching, signal that you aren't involved. We also show lack of involvement or interest by yawning, looking bored, or staring blankly (Deal & Kennedy, 1999).

Good listeners show that they're engaged. The only way that others know we are listening is through our feedback. Indicators of engagement include attentive posture, head nods, eye contact, and vocal responses such as "Mmhmm" and "Go on." When we demonstrate involvement, we communicate interest in the other person's ideas and they are likely to offer more details and information (Beukeboom, 2009).

Remembering

Many listening experts regard **remembering** as the final aspect of the listening process. We forget a lot of what we hear. Eight hours after receiving a message, we recall only about 35 percent of our interpretations of the message. Because we forget about two-thirds of the meanings we construct from others' communication, it's important to

Listening As an Act of Love

Perhaps you sometimes listen to *The Story*, a regular program on National Public Radio. Each story is part of a large project called StoryCorps. Dave Isay set out to make an oral history of America by listening to the stories of everyday people—not politicians, celebrities, or CEOs, but regular people. By January of 2009, StoryCorps had recorded more than 40,000 stories of ordinary Americans—what they value, how they understand life. Dave Isay gathered a number of these stories into a book, which he titled *Listening as an Act of Love* (2008). To learn more about StoryCorps, go to the book's online resources for this chapter and click on WebLink 6.1 to visit the StoryCorps site.

make sure we hang on to the most important third (Cooper, Seibold, & Suchner, 1997). Selectively focusing our attention is particularly important when we listen to presentations that contain a great deal of information. Later in this chapter, we'll discuss strategies for improving retention.

In summary, listening is a complex process that involves being mindful, physically receiving messages, selecting and organizing information, interpreting communication, responding, and remembering. We're now ready to consider hindrances to the listening process so we can recognize and manage them.

Obstacles to Effective Listening

There are two broad types of obstacles to listening well: situational obstacles that are in communication contexts, and internal obstacles that are within communicators.

Situational Obstacles

Incomprehensibility

In the summer of 2008, I traveled to Pennsylvania to attend a week-long teaching by the Dalai Lama. For eight hours each day, I sat trying to learn from this wise Tibetan monk. He always began by speaking in English, but it was heavily accented English that I had difficulty understanding. As he went into greater depth on a topic, he switched to Tibetan, which I did not understand at all. The Dalai Lama would speak for one to five minutes, then his translator would convey the gist of the message in English.

Incomprehensibility exists when a message is not clearly understandable because of language or transmission problems. In my case, the lack of clarity resulted from an accent and use of a language that I didn't know. Other causes for unclear messages may be use of jargon that listeners don't understand, lack of a microphone when one is needed for audibility, fading in and out on cell calls, mumbling by a speaker, and syntax or grammar that makes it difficult to grasp what a communicator means to say.

Message Overload

The sheer amount of communication in our lives makes it difficult to listen fully to all of it. **Message overload** occurs when we receive more messages than we can effectively process. For good reason, our era has been dubbed "the information age." Each day, we are inundated by messages—face-to-face and mediated. We simply can't attend mindfully to all the messages that come our way (Jackson, 2008; Klingberg, 2008).

Message overload often occurs in educational contexts. Students who take four or five classes each term deal with four or five sets of readings, class lectures, and discussions—a load that can overwhelm even the most conscientious student. Message overload may also happen when communication occurs simultaneously in multiple channels. For instance, you might suffer information overload if a speaker is presenting information orally while showing a slide with complex statistical data. In such a situation, it's difficult to decide whether to focus on the visual message or the oral one.

Message Complexity

Listening may also be impeded by **message complexity**, which exists when a message we are trying to understand is highly complex, is packed with detailed information, or involves intricate reasoning. The more detailed and complicated the ideas, the more difficult they are to follow and retain. Many jobs today are so specialized that communication between co-workers involves highly complex messages. Short-term memory can be taxed when trying to understand and retain multiple pieces of information (Janusik, 2007). Effective speakers make an effort to reduce the complexity of their messages. In addition, good listeners try to break down complex information or invest extra effort to understand complicated messages.

Environmental Distractions

Environmental distractions are a fourth impediment to effective listening. These are occurrences in the communication setting that interfere with effective listening (Keizer, 2010). Distractions exist in all communication situations. It might be a television in the background, side comments during a conference, or muffled traffic sounds from outside. Increasingly, we are interrupted by the buzzes of pagers and the ring tones of cell phones and BlackBerrys.

Cognitive psychologists have found that e-mail alerts, IMs, and notifications of text messages distract people and undermine their ability to give full attention to any task (Begley, 2009). Interruptions fragment concentration so we have trouble resituating ourselves in whatever we were doing before the interruption. We may miss something, particularly if we were interrupted while performing a sequential task. In the summer of 2008 an airliner taking off from Madrid crashed and killed 153 people. Post-crash investigations revealed the error resulted from interruption in the preflight check (Begley, 2009).

If you want to listen effectively, reduce environmental distractions. Turn off notifications for e-mail, text, and other applications and lower the volume of music if someone wants to talk with you. Shut your laptop to attend more fully to a conversation. Professionals often hold phone calls when they are talking with clients or business associates. Even when we can't eliminate distractions, we can usually reduce them or move to a location that is more conducive to good listening.

DIGITAL MEDIA
Supersaturation

Continuous advances in technology mean we have greater access to information and people than was possible in any previous era. Cell phones, televisions, radios, PDAs, laptops, tablets, BlackBerrys…there's no end to the information that comes our way throughout the day.

Media scholar Todd Gitlin (2005) refers to the never-ending flow of information as a "media torrent" that leads to supersaturation, or being constantly in touch, constantly informed, and constantly overloaded with information, whether we want it or not. Two other media scholars, Jane Brown and Joanne Cantor (2000), use the term *perpetual linkage* to refer to always being connected to others.

Internal Obstacles

In addition to situational impediments to effective listening, five internal obstacles hinder our efforts to listen well.

Preoccupation

One of the most common hindrances to listening is **preoccupation**. When we are absorbed in our thoughts and concerns, we can't focus on what someone else is saying. Perhaps you've attended a class right before taking a test in another class and later realized you got almost nothing out of the first class. That's because you were preoccupied with the upcoming test. If you turn on your phone and find 20 text messages, you may be preoccupied by a sense of obligation to read and respond to all of them, so you are not fully, mindfully focused on reading and responding to each one as you open it. In the example that opened this chapter, Suzanne's preoccupation with a report impeded her ability to listen to her colleague. When we are preoccupied with our thoughts, we aren't mindful.

© Frances M. Roberts/Alamy

Environmental distractions can interfere with both hearing and listening.

Prejudgment

A second internal obstacle to good listening is **prejudgment**—the tendency to judge others or their ideas before we've heard them. Sometimes we think we already know what someone will say, so we don't listen carefully. In other cases, we decide in advance that others have nothing to offer us, so we tune them out. A study of doctor–patient communication found that, on average, doctors interrupted patients 23 seconds into patients' explanations of medical problems (Levine, 2004). Doctors who assume they already know what a patient has to say are likely to miss information that is needed to understand a patient's concerns. Keeping an open mind when listening to speakers with whom you disagree is also advisable. Keith's commentary provides an example of the negative impact of prejudgments on listening.

 Keith

My parents are so quick to tell me what I think and feel or should think and feel that they never listen to what I do feel or think. Last year, I told them I was thinking about taking a year off from school. Before I could explain why I wanted to do this, Dad was all over me about the need to get ahead in a career. Mom said I was looking for an easy out from my studies. What I wanted to do was work as an intern to get some hands-on experience in media production, which is my major. I wasn't after an easy out, and I do want to get ahead, but they couldn't even hear me through their own ideas about what I felt.

When we prejudge, we mind read. As we noted in Chapter 3, mind reading is assuming we know what others feel, think, and are going to say, and we may then fit their messages into our preconceptions. This can lead us to misunderstand what they mean because we haven't really listened to them on their terms. When we impose our prejudgments on others' words, at the relationship level of meaning we express a disregard for them and what they say. Prejudgments also affect the content level of meaning because we may not grasp important content when we decide in advance that someone has nothing of value to say. This can be costly on the job, where we are expected to pay attention and understand information even if we don't like it or the person expressing it.

Lack of Effort

Listening is hard work: We have to be mindful, focus on what others say, interpret and organize messages, remember, and respond. We also have to control distractions inside ourselves and in situations. Sometimes we aren't willing to invest the effort to listen well. In other instances, we want to listen, but we're tired, ill, hungry, or unable to focus for other reasons (Isaacs, 1999). When this happens, it's effective to postpone interaction until you can listen mindfully. If you explain that you want to listen well, the other person is likely to appreciate your honesty and your commitment to listening.

Reacting to Emotionally Loaded Language

A fourth internal obstacle to effective listening is the tendency to react to emotionally loaded language—words that evoke very strong positive or negative responses.

You may find some words and phrases very soothing or pleasant. Certain other words and phrases may summon up negative feelings and images for you. When we react to words that are emotionally loaded for us, we may fail to grasp another person's meaning (Wagner, 2001).

When we react to emotionally loaded language, we don't learn what another person has to say. We give up our responsibility to think critically about what others say, to consider their words carefully instead of reacting unthinkingly to particular words. One way to guard against this is to be aware of words and phrases that tend to trigger strong emotional reactions in us. If we bring these to a conscious level, then we can monitor our tendencies to respond unthinkingly.

Not Recognizing Diverse Listening Styles

A final hindrance to effective listening is not recognizing and adjusting to different listening styles that reflect diverse cultures and social communities (Brownell, 2002). For example, in general, women are more active than men in giving verbal and non-verbal feedback, using head nods, facial expressions, and responsive questions to show interest (Wood, 2013). Some African Americans call out responses to a speaker or preacher as a way to show interest in what the speaker is saying. A speaker who doesn't understand this pattern is likely to misinterpret the responses as interruptions. Conversely, some African Americans may perceive European American listeners as uninterested because they don't participate by calling out during a speech or sermon. Nancy's reflections on her perceptions as a white person at a black church illustrate the importance of recognizing and respecting diverse listening styles.

 Nancy

I was amazed the first time I went to a black church. Members of the congregation kept speaking back to the minister and exclaiming over what they liked. At first, I was alienated, but after a while I got into the spirit, and I felt a whole lot more involved in the service than I ever had in my own church.

Forms of Ineffective Listening

Now that we've discussed obstacles to effective listening, let's identify six common forms of ineffective listening. Some may seem familiar because you and people you know probably engage in them at times.

Pseudolistening

Pseudolistening is pretending to listen. When we pseudolisten, we appear attentive, but our minds are really elsewhere. We pseudolisten when communication bores us but we feel it is important to appear attentive. Superficial social interaction and boring lectures are communication situations in which we may consciously choose to pseudolisten so that we seem polite even though we really aren't involved. On the job, we may need to appear interested in what others say because of their positions. Pseudolistening is inadvisable, however, when we really want to understand another's communication.

Monopolizing

Monopolizing is hogging the stage by continually focusing communication on ourselves instead of on the person who is talking. Two tactics are typical of monopolizing.

One is *conversational rerouting,* in which a person shifts the topic of talk to himself or herself. For example, if Ellen tells her friend Marla that she's having trouble with her roommate, Marla might reroute the conversation by saying, "I know what you mean. My roommate is a real slob." And then Marla launches into an extended description of her roommate problems. In the workplace, people may shift conversations to their accomplishments and concerns. In both personal and work relationships, rerouting takes the conversation away from the person who is talking and focuses it on oneself.

A second monopolizing tactic, *interrupting,* can occur in combination with rerouting: A person interrupts and then introduces a new topic. In other cases, diversionary interrupting involves questions and challenges that disrupt or challenge the person who is speaking. Monopolizers may fire questions that express doubt about what a speaker says ("What makes you think that?" "How can you be sure?" "Did anyone else see what you did?") or prematurely offer advice to establish their command of the situation and perhaps to put down the other person ("What you should do is …"; "You really blew that. What I would have done is …"). Both rerouting and diversionary interrupting monopolize conversations. They are the antithesis of good listening.

It's important to realize that not all interruptions are attempts to monopolize communication (Goldsmith & Fulfs, 1999). In some situations, we interrupt the flow of others' talk to show interest, to voice support, and to ask for elaboration. Interrupting for these reasons doesn't divert attention from the person speaking; instead, it affirms that person and keeps the focus on her or him.

Selective Listening

A third form of ineffective listening is **selective listening**, which involves focusing only on particular parts of communication. One form of selective listening is focusing only on communication that interests us or corresponds to our opinions and feelings. If you are worried about a storm, you may listen selectively to weather reports and disregard news. Students often become highly attentive in classes when teachers say, "This will be on the test." In the workplace, we may become more attentive when communication addresses topics such as raises, layoffs, and other matters that may affect us directly.

Selective listening also occurs when we reject communication that bores us or is inconsistent with our values, opinions, or choices. We may selectively filter out a co-worker's criticisms of our work.

Defensive Listening

Defensive listening involves perceiving a personal attack, criticism, or hostile undertone in communication when none is intended. When we listen defensively, we assume others don't like, trust, or respect us, and we read these motives into whatever they say, regardless of how innocent their communication actually is. Some people are generally defensive, expecting insults and criticism from all quarters. They hear threats and negative judgments in almost anything said to them. Thus, an innocent remark such as, "Have you finished the report yet?" may be perceived as criticism that the report hasn't been turned in yet.

In other instances, defensive listening is confined to areas where we judge ourselves inadequate or to times when we feel negative about ourselves. A woman who fears she is not valued in her job may interpret committee assignments as signs that she is not well regarded. Someone who has been laid off may perceive work-related comments as personal criticism of his or her unemployment.

Ambushing

Ambushing is listening carefully for the purpose of gathering ammunition to use in attacking a speaker. Ambushing often relies on an extreme form of monopolizing in which interruptions are constant and intentionally disruptive. Political candidates routinely listen carefully to their opponents in order to undercut them.

Ambushing may also plague work life, especially in organizations that encourage employees to compete with one another in order to stand out. These employees display no openness, make no effort to understand the other's meaning, take no interest in recognizing value in what another says, and do not want genuine dialogue. Eric provides another example of ambushing.

 Eric

> One brother at my [fraternity] house is a real ambusher. He's a pre-law-major, and he loves to debate and win arguments. No matter what somebody talks about, this guy just listens long enough to mount a counterattack. He doesn't care about understanding anybody else, just about beating them. I've quit talking when he's around.

Literal Listening

Literal listening involves listening only to the content level of meaning and ignoring the relationship level of meaning. When we listen literally, we do not listen to what's being communicated about the other person or about our relationship with that person. For example, one member of a work team might avoid eye contact, shrug his shoulders, and say in a flat voice, "I guess I can go along with this decision." If other group members listen only to his literal message, they will assume the group has reached a decision. However, the relational level of meaning, conveyed nonverbally, suggests the member is not happy with the decision. It's likely that this member will not be fully committed to the decision and will not be enthusiastic about implementing it. Literal listening neglects others' feelings and our relationship with them.

Guidelines for Effective Listening

Our discussion of listening and the obstacles to it provides a foundation for improving our effectiveness as listeners. The key guideline is to adapt listening to specific communication goals and situations. Two kinds of listening, **informational and critical listening** and **relationship listening**, require specific skills and attitudes. We'll discuss how to be effective when engaging in these two kinds of listening and briefly discuss other types of listening.

Develop Skills for Informational and Critical Listening

Much of our listening is to gain and evaluate information. We listen for information in classes and professional meetings, when we are learning a new job, during important news stories, when we need to understand a medical treatment, and when we are getting directions. In all these cases, the primary purpose of listening is to gain and understand information.

Closely related to informational listening is critical listening: We listen to make judgments about people and ideas. Like informational listening, critical listening requires attending closely to the content of communication. Yet critical listening goes beyond gaining information to analyze and evaluate it and the people who express it. We decide whether a speaker is credible and ethical by judging the thoroughness of a presentation, the accuracy of evidence, the carefulness of reasoning, and personal confidence and trustworthiness. Informational and critical listening call for skills that help us gain and retain information. Critical listening also calls for skill in evaluating information.

Be Mindful

The first step in listening to information critically is to make a decision to attend carefully, even if the material is complex and difficult. This may mean that you time your conversations, whether phone, online, or face to face, so that you have the mental energy to be mindful. Don't let your mind wander if information gets complicated or confusing. Avoid daydreaming, and stay focused on learning as much as you can. Later, you may want to ask questions if material isn't clear or if you have reservations about evidence or logic.

Control Obstacles

You can also minimize distractions. You might shut a window to block out traffic noises or adjust a thermostat so that the room's temperature is comfortable. In addition, you should minimize psychological distractions by emptying your mind of the many concerns, ideas, and prejudgments that can interfere with attending to the communication at hand.

Ask Questions

Asking speakers to clarify their messages or to elaborate allows you to understand information you didn't grasp at first and to deepen your insight into content you did comprehend. Recently, I listened to a fairly technical talk on national economic issues. After the speech, audience members asked these questions: "Could you explain what you meant by the M2 money supply?" "How does inflation affect wages?" and "Can you clarify the distinction between the national debt and the deficit?" These questions showed that the listeners had paid attention and were interested in further information. Questions compliment a speaker because they show that you are interested and want to know more.

Critical listening often calls for asking probing questions. "What is the source of your statistics on the rate of unemployment?" "Is a seven-year-old statistic on

Welfare current enough to tell us anything about Welfare issues today?" "Have you met with any policy makers who hold a point of view contrary to yours? What is their response to your proposals?" "All the sources you quoted in your presentation are fiscal conservatives. Does this mean your presentation and your conclusions are biased?"

Use Aids to Recall

To remember important information, we can apply principles of perception we discussed in Chapter 3. For instance, we learned that we tend to notice and recall stimuli that are repeated. To use this principle to increase your retention, repeat important ideas to yourself

This park official is teaching visitors how to protect themselves from Lyme disease. Do the visitors seem to be using good listening skills?

immediately after hearing them. This moves new information from short-term to long-term memory (Estes, 1989). Repeating the names of people when you meet them can save you the embarrassment of having to ask them to repeat their names.

Another way to increase retention is to use mnemonic (pronounced *"knee monic"*) devices, which are memory aids that create patterns that help you remember what you've heard. For instance, ROB is a mnemonic for remembering that Robert from Ohio, is studying Business. Perhaps the best known mnemonic is HOMES for the Great Lakes: Lakes Huron, Ontario, Michigan, Erie, and Superior.

Organize Information

Another technique for increasing your retention is to organize what you hear. When communicating informally, most people don't order their ideas carefully. The result is a flow of information that isn't coherently organized and so is hard to retain. We can impose order by regrouping what we hear. For example, suppose a friend tells you that he's confused about long-range goals, doesn't know what he can do with a math major, wants to locate in the Midwest, wonders whether graduate school is necessary, likes small towns, needs some internships to try out different options, and wants a family eventually. You could organize this stream of concerns into two categories: academic issues (careers for math majors, graduate school, internship opportunities) and lifestyle

DIVERSITY

Listening to a Second Language

Asking questions is especially important and appropriate for non-native speakers of the speaker's language. People who have learned English as a second language may not understand idioms such as *in a heartbeat* (fast), *not on your life* (very unlikely), or *off the wall* (wacky) (Lee, 1994, 2000). Another listening difficulty for non-native speakers of a language is the ability to distinguish between sounds. Research shows that this ability is learned, not innate. By the age of one, if not sooner, babies can distinguish between sounds of languages they hear spoken (Monastersky, 2001). Non-Chinese people have difficulty distinguishing between two distinct sounds in Mandarin Chinese: *qi,* which is approximately like the English *ch* sound, and *xi,* which is approximately like the English *sh* sound. People who are native to Japan have a hard time distinguishing between the English sounds *ra* and *la*. To read more about learning English as a second language, go to the book's online resources for this chapter and click on WebLink 6.2.

SHARPEN YOUR SKILL

Improving Recall

Apply the principles we've discussed to enhance what you remember.

1. The next time you meet someone, repeat his or her name to yourself three times after you are introduced. Do you find that the name sticks better?

2. After your next communication class, take 15 minutes to review your notes in a quiet place. Read them aloud so you hear as well as see the main ideas. Does this increase your retention of the material?

3. Invent mnemonics that help you remember basic information from messages.

4. Organize complex ideas by grouping them into categories. To remember the main ideas of this chapter, you might use major subheadings to form categories: listening process, obstacles to listening, and listening goals. Creating the mnemonic POG (process, obstacles, goals) could help you remember those topics.

preferences (Midwest, small town, family). Remembering these two categories allows you to retain the essence of your friend's concerns, even if you forget many of the specifics.

Develop Skills for Relationship Listening

Listening for information focuses on the content level of meaning in communication. Yet, often we are as concerned or even more concerned with the relationship level of meaning, which has to do with feelings and relationships between communicators. We engage in relationship listening when we listen to a friend's worries, let a romantic partner tell us about problems, counsel a co-worker, or talk with a parent about health concerns. Specific listening attitudes and skills enhance our ability to listen supportively (Nichols, 1996).

Be Mindful

The first requirement for effective relationship listening is mindfulness, which is also the first step in informational listening. When we're listening to give support, however, we focus on feelings that may not be communicated explicitly. Thus, mindful relationship listening involves looking for feelings and perceptions that are "between the words." As listening scholar Gerald Egan notes, "Total listening is more than attending to another person's words. It is also listening to the meanings that are buried in the words and between the words and in the silences in communication" (1973, p. 228).

Suspend Judgment

When listening to provide support, it's important to avoid judgmental responses. When we judge, we add our evaluations to other people's experiences, and this moves us away from them and their feelings. Our judgments may also lead others to become defensive and unwilling to talk further with us. To curb judgment, we can ask whether we really need to evaluate right now. Even positive evaluations ("That's a good way to approach the problem") can make others uneasy and less willing to communicate openly with us. The other person may reason that if we make positive judgments, we could also make negative ones. José's commentary illustrates the value of suspending judgment when listening relationally.

 José

My best friend makes it so easy for me to tell whatever is on my mind. She never puts me down or makes me feel stupid or weird. Sometimes, I ask her what she thinks, and she has this

way of telling me without making me feel wrong if I think differently. What it boils down to is
respect. She respects me and herself, and so she doesn't have to prove anything by acting better
than me.

Only if someone asks for our evaluation should we offer it when we are listening to offer support. Even if our opinion is sought, we should express it in a way that doesn't devalue others. Sometimes people excuse strongly judgmental comments by saying, "You asked me to be honest" or "I mean this as constructive criticism." Too often, however, the judgments are not constructive and are harsher than candor requires. Good relationship listening includes responses that communicate respect and support.

Strive to Understand the Other's Perspective

One of the most important principles for effective relationship listening is to concentrate on grasping the other person's perspective by being person-centered (Nichols, 1996). This means we have to step outside of our point of view at least long enough to understand another's perceptions. We can't respond sensitively to others until we understand their perspective and meanings. To do this, we must put aside our views and focus on their words and nonverbal behaviors for clues to others feelings and thoughts.

One communication skill that helps us gain insight into others is the use of **minimal encouragers**. These are responses that gently invite another person to elaborate. Examples of minimal encouragers are "Tell me more," "Really?" "Go on," "I'm with you," "Then what happened?" "Yeah?" and "I see." We can also use nonverbal minimal encouragers, such as a raised eyebrow to show that we're involved, a nod to signal that we understand, or widened eyes to demonstrate that we're fascinated. Minimal encouragers say we are listening and interested. They encourage others to keep talking so we can grasp what they mean. Keep in mind that these are *minimal* encouragers; they shouldn't take the focus away from the other person. Effective minimal encouragers are brief interjections that prompt, rather than interfere with, the flow of another's talk.

Paraphrasing is a second way to gain insight into others' perspectives. To paraphrase, we reflect our interpretations of others' communication back to them. For example, a friend might confide, "With all the news on teenagers and drugs, I wonder if my kid brother is messing around with drugs." You could paraphrase this way: "It sounds as if you may suspect your brother may be taking drugs." This paraphrase allows us to clarify whether the friend has any evidence of the brother's drug involvement. The response might be, "No, I don't have any reason to suspect him, but I just worry because drugs are so pervasive in high schools now." This tells us that the friend's worry is about general trends, not about evidence that her brother is using drugs. Paraphrasing can also be a way to check perceptions to see whether we understand another person's meaning: "Let me see if I followed you. What you're saying is that…"

 Lynette

I discovered something really interesting when I practiced paraphrasing for class. I found out
that knowing I needed to rephrase what someone else was saying forced me to listen more
carefully to what they were saying. I understood people better than I usually do when I'm not so
focused on what they are saying. I hadn't even realized that I wasn't listening well before.

A third way to enhance understanding of others is to ask questions. For instance, we might ask, "How do you feel about that?" or "What do you plan to do?" Another reason we ask questions is to find out what a person wants from us. Sometimes it isn't clear whether someone wants advice, a shoulder to cry on, or a safe place to vent feelings. If we can't figure out what's wanted, it's appropriate to ask, "Are you looking for advice or a sounding board?" Asking directly signals that we really want to help and allows others to tell us how we can best do that. The Sharpen Your Skill feature on the next page will help you develop your skills in paraphrasing.

Express Support

Once you have understood another's meanings and perspective, relationship listening should focus on communicating support. This doesn't necessarily require us to agree with another's perspective or ideas. It does call upon us to communicate support for the person. To illustrate how we can support someone even if we don't agree with his or her position, consider the following exchange between a son and his father:

Son: Dad, I'm changing my major to acting.

Father: Oh.

Son: Yeah, I've wanted to do it for some time, but I hesitated because acting isn't as safe as accounting.

Father: That's certainly true.

Son: Yeah, but I've decided to do it anyway. I'd like to know what you think about the idea.

Father: The idea worries me. Starving actors are a dime a dozen. It just won't provide you with any economic future or security.

Son: I understand acting isn't as secure as business, but it is what I really want to do.

Father: Tell me what you feel about acting—why it matters so much to you.

Son: It's the most creative, totally fulfilling thing I do. I've tried to get interested in business, but I just don't love that like I do acting. I feel like I have to give this a try, or I'll always wonder if I could have made it. If I don't get somewhere in 5 or 6 years, I'll rethink career options.

Father: Couldn't you finish your business degree and get a job and act on the side?

Son: No. I've got to give acting a full shot—give it everything I have to see if I can make it.

Father: Well, I still have reservations, but I guess I can understand having to try something that matters this much to you. I'm just concerned that you'll lose years of your life to something that doesn't work out.

Son: Well, I'm kind of concerned about that too, but I'm more worried about wasting years of my life in a career that doesn't excite me than about trying to make a go of the one that does.

Father: That makes sense. I wouldn't make the choice you're making, but I respect your decision and your guts for taking a big gamble.

This dialogue illustrates several principles of effective relationship listening. First, note that the father's first two comments are minimal encouragers that invite his son to elaborate on his thoughts and feelings. The father also encourages his son to explain how he feels. Later, the father suggests a compromise solution, but his son rejects that, and the father respects the son's position. It is important that the father makes his position clear, but he separates his personal stance from his respect for his son's right to make his own choices. In this way, the father disagrees without negatively evaluating his son.

Develop Skills for Other Listening Goals

In addition to listening for information, to make critical evaluations, and to provide support, we listen for pleasure and to discriminate.

SHARPEN YOUR SKILL

Practice Paraphrasing

Learning to paraphrase enhances communication. You can develop skill in paraphrasing by creating paraphrases of the following comments:

◆ "I don't know how they expect me to get my work done when they don't give me any training on how to use this new software program."

◆ "I've got three midterms and a paper due next week, and I'm behind in my reading."

◆ "My parents don't understand why I need to go to summer school, and they won't pay my expenses."

◆ "My son wants to go to summer school and expects us to come up with the money. Doesn't he understand what we're already paying for the regular school year?"

Listening for Pleasure

Sometimes we listen for pleasure, as when we attend concerts or comedy shows or listen to friends tell jokes. When listening for pleasure, we don't need to concentrate on organizing and remembering as much as we do when we listen for information, although retention is important if you want to tell the joke to someone else later. Yet listening for pleasure does require mindfulness, hearing, and interpretation.

Listening to Discriminate

In some situations, we listen to make fine discriminations in sounds in order to draw accurate conclusions and act appropriately in response. For example, doctors listen to discriminate when they use stethoscopes to assess heart function or chest congestion. Parents listen to discriminate a baby's cries for attention, food, reassurance, or a diaper change. Skilled mechanics can distinguish engine sounds far more keenly than most other people. Mindfulness and keen hearing abilities are skills that assist listening to discriminate.

Mindfulness is a prerequisite for effective listening of all types. With the exception of mindfulness, each listening purpose tends to emphasize particular aspects of the listening process and to put less weight on others. Whereas evaluating content is especially important in listening critically, it is less crucial when listening for pleasure. Hearing acoustic nuances is important when listening to discriminate but not vital to listening for information. Selecting, organizing, and retaining information matter more when we are listening for information than when we are listening for pleasure. Deciding on your purpose for listening allows you to use the most pertinent communication skills.

SUMMARY

Listening is a major and vital part of communication, yet too often we don't consider it as important as talking. In this chapter, we've explored the complex and demanding process of listening. We began by distinguishing between hearing and listening. The former is a straightforward physiological process that doesn't take effort on our part. Listening, in contrast, is a complicated process involving being mindful, hearing, selecting and organizing, interpreting, responding, and remembering. Listening well takes commitment and skill.

Obstacles in ourselves as well as in situations and messages jeopardize effective listening. Incomprehensibility, message overload, complexity of material, and environmental distractions are external obstacles to listening. In addition, preoccupations, prejudgments, reacting to emotional language, lack of effort, and not recognizing differences in listening styles can hamper listening. The obstacles to listening often lead to various forms of ineffective listening, including pseudolistening, monopolizing, selective listening, defensive listening, ambushing, and literal listening. Each form of ineffective listening prevents us from being fully engaged in communication.

We also discussed different purposes for listening and identified the skills and attitudes that advance each purpose. Informational and critical listening require us to adopt a mindful attitude and to think critically, to organize and evaluate information, to clarify understanding by asking questions, and to develop aids to retention of complex material. Relationship listening also requires mindfulness, but it calls for other distinct listening skills. Suspending judgment, paraphrasing, giving minimal encouragers, and expressing support enhance the effectiveness of relationship listening.

REVIEW, REFLECT, EXTEND

The Reflect, Discuss, and Apply Questions that follow will help you review, reflect on, and extend the information and ideas presented in this chapter. These resources, and a diverse selection of additional study tools, are also available online at the CourseMate for *Communication Mosaics.* Your CourseMate includes a student workbook, WebLinks, TED Talks hyperlinks and activities, chapter glossary and flashcards, interactive video activities, Speech Builder Express, and InfoTrac College Edition. For more information or to access this book's online resources, visit **www .cengagebrain.com.**

KEY CONCEPTS

ambushing, 123
defensive listening, 122
environmental distractions, 119
hearing, 114
incomprehensibility, 118
informational and critical listening, 123
interpretation, 116
listening, 114
literal listening, 123
message complexity, 118
message overload, 118

mindfulness, 114
minimal encouragers, 127
monopolizing, 121
paraphrasing, 127
prejudgment, 120
preoccupation, 119
pseudolistening, 121
relationship listening, 123
remembering, 117
responding, 117
selective listening, 122

Reflect, Discuss, Apply

Review the types of ineffective listening discussed in this chapter. Do any describe ways in which you attend (or don't attend) to others? Select one type of ineffective listening in which you engage and work to minimize it in your interactions.

1. As a class, identify ethical principles that guide different listening purposes. What different moral goals and responsibilities accompany informational and critical listening and relationship listening?

2. Spend time with people you do not usually interact with. If you are engaged in a service learning project, your community partners would be a good choice. Practice using minimal encouragers and paraphrasing to increase the depth of your understanding of their perspectives.

Recommended Resources

1. The film *Erin Brockovich* dramatically illustrates the power of listening. Watch the film, and pay attention to how Julia Roberts, in the role of Erin Brockovich, shows she is listening carefully to people who have been harmed by toxic chemicals.

2. To learn more about taking good notes to improve recall, go to the book's online resources for this chapter and click on WebLink 6.3 to visit the Web page created by the Office of Academic Advising at the College of St. Benedict/St. John's University. To develop skill in creating and using mnemonics and other techniques for improving recall, click on WebLink 6.4.

EXPERIENCE COMMUNICATION CASE STUDY

Family Hour

Apply what you've learned in this chapter by analyzing the following case study, using the accompanying questions as a guide. These questions and a video of the case study are also available online at your CourseMate for *Communication Mosaics*.

Over spring break, 20-year-old Josh visits his father. He wants to convince his family to support him in joining a fraternity that has given him a bid. On his second day home, after dinner, Josh decides to broach the topic. His dad is watching the evening news on television when Josh walks into the living room. Josh sits down and opens the conversation.

Josh: Well, something pretty interesting has happened at school this semester.

Dad: I'll bet you found a girlfriend, right? I was about your age when your mother and I started dating, and that was the best part of college. I still remember how she looked on our first date. She was young then, and she was very slender and pretty. I saw her and thought she was the loveliest thing I'd ever seen. Before long, we were a regular item. Yep, it was about when I was 20, like you are now.

Josh: Well, I haven't found a girlfriend, but I did get a bid from Sigma Chi.

Dad: Sigma Chi. What is that—a fraternity?

Josh: Yeah, it's probably the coolest fraternity on campus. I attended some rush parties this semester—mainly out of curiosity, just to see what they were like.

Dad: Why'd you do that? Before you ever went to college, I told you to steer clear of fraternities. They cost a lot of money, and they distract you from your studies.

Josh: Well, I know you told me to steer clear of fraternities, but I did check a few out. I'd be willing to take a job to help pay the membership fee and monthly dues. Besides, it's not that much more expensive when you figure I'd be eating at the house.

© Cengage Learning

Dad: Do you realize how much it costs just for you to go to that school? I'm paying $14,000 a year! When I went to school, I had to go to state college because my parents couldn't afford to send me to the school of my choice. You have no idea how lucky you are to be going to the school you wanted to go to and have me footing all of the bills

Josh: But we could work it out so that a fraternity wouldn't cost you anything. Like I said, I…

Dad: If you want to take a job, fine. I could use some help paying your tuition and fees. But you're not taking a job just so you can belong to a party house.

Josh: I thought they were just party houses too, until I attended rush. Now, I went to several houses that were that way, but Sigma Chi isn't. I really liked the brothers at Sigma Chi. They're interesting and friendly and fun, so I was thrilled when…

Dad: I don't want to hear about it. You're not joining a fraternity. I told you what happened when I was in college. I joined one, and pretty soon my Dean's List grades dropped to Cs and Ds. When you live in a fraternity house, you can't study like you can in your dorm room or the library. I should know. I tried it and found out the hard way. There's no need for you to repeat my mistake.

Josh: But, Dad, I'm not you. Joining a fraternity wouldn't necessarily mean that my grades…

Dad: What do you mean, you're not me? You think I wasn't a good student before I joined the fraternity? You think you're so smart that you can party all the time and still make good grades? Let me tell you something, I thought that too, and, boy! Was I ever wrong. As soon as I joined the house, it was party time all the time. There was always music blaring and girls in the house and poker games—anything but studying. I wasn't stupid. It's just not an atmosphere that encourages academic work.

Josh: I'd like to give it a try. I really like these guys, and I think I can handle being in Sigma Chi and still…

Dad: Well, you think wrong!

1. What examples of ineffective listening are evident in this dialogue?

2. If you could advise Josh's father on listening effectively, what would you tell him to do differently?

3. What advice would you offer Josh on listening more effectively to his father?

Kind words may be short … but their echoes are endless. Mother Teresa

7
Creating Communication Climates

▶ You have scheduled a performance review with an employee, who began working for you six months ago. You need to call his attention to some problems in his work while also showing that you value him and believe he can improve his performance.

▶ You know your friend Lauren is worried about not having gotten any offers after interviewing with 16 companies. You want to let her know it's okay for her to talk with you about her concerns.

▶ You're concerned that your younger brother's friends may be using drugs. You want to find a way to talk openly with your brother and to warn him about using drugs without making him feel like you are judging him or his friends

I n each of these situations, achieving your goals depends on your ability to create an effective **communication climate**, which is the emotional tone of a relationship between people. Perhaps you feel foggy-headed when the sky is overcast or stormy and feel upbeat when it's sunny. Do you respond differently to the various seasons? In much the same way that physical climate influences mood, communication climate affects how people feel and inter-act with one another. We feel defensive when a supervisor blames us, angry when someone flames us on the Internet, or hurt when a friend criticizes us. In each case, the communication climate is overcast.

FOCUS QUESTIONS

1. What kinds of communication foster defensive and supportive communication climates?

2. In what ways can conflict enrich relationships?

3. How can we confirm both ourselves and others?

4. When is it appropriate to show grace toward others?

Creating constructive climates is a basic skill that influences the effectiveness of communication in all contexts. Work teams with supportive climates foster good professional relationships and productivity. In social relationships, healthy climates allow people to feel at ease. In personal relationships, trusting, affirming climates allow us to disclose private feelings and thoughts without fear of criticism or ridicule. Effective climates for public speaking situations foster trust and respect between speakers and listeners. Thus, communication climates are basic to all settings and forms of interaction.

This chapter focuses on communication climate. We'll begin by discussing *interpersonal confirmation* as a keystone of positive communication climates. Next, we'll identify specific kinds of communication that foster defensive and supportive communication climates. In the third section of the chapter, we'll consider the role of conflict in relationships, and we'll see that creating healthy communication climates helps us manage conflict constructively. Finally, we'll discuss guidelines for creating and sustaining healthy communication climates.

Levels of Confirmation and Disconfirmation

Philosopher Martin Buber (1957, 1970) believed that each of us needs interpersonal *confirmation* to be healthy and to grow. Communication scholars (Anderson, Baxter, & Cissna, 2004; Arnett, 2004; Barge, 2009; MacGeorge, 2009; Stewart, Zediker, & Black, 2004) have drawn on Buber's work to develop philosophies of communication that emphasize interpersonal confirmation as a basis of meaningful dialogue. The essence of **interpersonal confirmation** is the expressed valuing of another person. We all want to feel we are valued by colleagues in our workplace, by audiences in public speaking settings, and by intimates in personal relationships. When others confirm us, we feel appreciated and respected. When they disconfirm us, we feel discounted and devalued.

Few climates are purely confirming or purely disconfirming. Most relationships include a mix of the two climate types or, over time, the relationship cycles between feeling confirming and feeling disconfirming (Figure 7.1). Yet in healthy, positive relationships, confirming communication outweighs disconfirming communication. Communication scholars (Cissna & Sieburg, 1986) have identified three levels of confirmation that affect communication climates: recognition, acknowledgment, and endorsement.

Recognition

The most basic form of interpersonal confirmation is **recognition**, the expression of awareness of another person's existence. We recognize others by nonverbal behaviors (a smile, a handshake, looking up when someone enters your room) and by verbal communication ("Hello," "Good to meet you," "Welcome home"). We disconfirm others at a fundamental level when we don't recognize their existence. For example, you might not speak to a person when you enter a

Figure 7.1   **The Continuum of Communication Climates**

room, or you might not look at a teammate who comes late to a meeting. Not responding to another's comments is also a failure to give recognition. As we noted in Chapter 5, silence is sometimes used to disconfirm another's existence.

Erika

Last year I was diagnosed with cancer and had to go through chemotherapy. I lost my hair and a huge amount of weight so I looked like a skeleton. It was amazing how people treated me like I was invisible. Even people who knew me would look away and not talk to me like I wasn't there.

Dr. Michael Kahn (2008) points out that doctors need to recognize patients as human beings. Kahn notes that doctors often enter patients' rooms without knocking, don't introduce themselves, and don't greet patients. Such actions fail to recognize patients, which is highly disconfirming.

Nikki

I work at a fast-food restaurant, and I'm often assigned to the drive-through window. On my last shift, four drivers were talking on their cells when they got to the window. They made gestures to order their food and never said a word to me—not "hello," not "I'd like the chicken melt," not "thank you." Nothing. They acted like a person was not there, like I was just a machine.

Acknowledgment

A second, more powerful level of interpersonal confirmation is **acknowledgment**: attentiveness to what a person feels, thinks, or says. Nonverbally, we acknowledge others by nodding our heads or by making eye contact to show we are listening. Verbal acknowledgments are direct responses to others' communication. If a friend says, "I'm really worried that I blew the LSAT exam," you could acknowledge that by responding, "So the exam made you anxious, huh?" This paraphrasing response acknowledges the thoughts and feelings of the other person. If a co-worker tells you, "I'm not sure I have the experience to handle this assignment," you could acknowledge that comment by saying, "Sounds as if you're feeling more challenged than you'd like." Communication researcher René Dailey (2006) found that adolescents talk more openly with parents if they perceive that the parents acknowledge their feelings.

We disconfirm others when we don't acknowledge their feelings, thoughts, or words. For instance, if you responded to your friend's statement about the LSAT by saying, "Want to go out and catch a film tonight?" your response would be an irrelevancy that ignored what your friend said. We also fail to acknowledge others if we deny the feelings they communicate: "You did fine on the LSAT," "There's no need to worry about handling this assignment." Lack of acknowledgment may also take the form of nonresponse to a friend's comment or nonresponse to ideas expressed in meetings or memos (Conrad & Poole, 2004). Lisa explains how she feels when others refuse to acknowledge her statements about her needs.

DIVERSITY

Disconfirming Others

People often ignore homeless individuals or others whom they perceive as "different" from them. Notice how often drivers and passers-by refuse to make eye contact with people holding signs that say, "Homeless. Please help." Failing to give even basic eye contact says, "You don't exist." Observe this phenomenon in your community; you might even notice whether you do it yourself.

Lisa

I'm amazed by how often people won't acknowledge what I tell them. A hundred times, I've been walking across campus, and someone's come up and offered to guide me. I tell them I don't need help, but they put an arm under my elbow to guide me. I am blind, but I can think just fine. I know if I need help. Why can't they acknowledge that?

Endorsement

The highest level of interpersonal confirmation is **endorsement**—accepting a person's feelings or thoughts as valid. This doesn't necessarily mean agreeing with the person's thoughts or feelings, but it does mean accepting them as real for that person. You could endorse the friend who is worried about the LSAT by saying, "It's natural to be worried about the LSAT when you have so much riding on it." You could endorse your colleague at work by saying, "Anyone would be uneasy about taking on such a big new responsibility." We fail to endorse others when we reject their thoughts and feelings. For example, it would be disconfirming to say, "How can you complain about a new responsibility when so many people are being laid off? You should be glad to have a job." This response rejects the validity of the other person's expressed feelings and may close the lines of communication between the two of you. In her commentary, Jennie provides an example of how hurtful it can be not to feel endorsed by friends.

Jennie

My father died two years ago. We were very close, so I was upset and sad for a long time. After a couple of months, some of my friends said things like, "You need to move on," or "It's time to quit mourning for your father." Those comments made me feel like I was crazy to still be grieving. I felt like they were saying what I was feeling wasn't right or something.

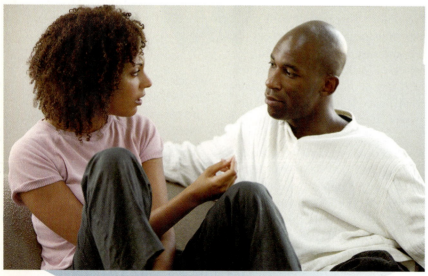

Interpersonal confirmation is a key to building supportive, trusting communication climates.

It's important to realize that disconfirmation is not mere disagreement. After all, disagreements can be productive and healthy. What is disconfirming is to be told that we don't exist or matter or that our feelings and thoughts are crazy, wrong, stupid, or deviant. The Sharpen Your Skill feature on the next page encourages you to notice confirming and disconfirming communication in online conversations.

If you think about what we've discussed, you'll probably find that the relationships in which you feel most valued and comfortable are those with high degrees of recognition, acknowledgment, and endorsement. We'll now consider other forms of communication that affect climates.

Defensive and Supportive Climates

Communication researcher Jack Gibb (1961, 1964, 1970) studied the relationship between communication and climate. He began by noting that in some climates we feel defensive whereas in

SHARPEN YOUR SKILL

Confirmation and Disconfirmation in Online Communication

Confirming and disconfirming communication is not limited to face-to-face interactions. It also establishes climates in online communication.

To gain insight into the particular forms of communication that create confirming and disconfirming climates, visit a chat room, forum, or blog of your choosing. Take notes on communication that expresses or denies recognition, acknowledgment, and endorsement of others. What differences can you identify between confirming and disconfirming communication in online interactions?

others we feel supported. Gibb identified six types of communication that promote defensive climates and six contrasting types of communication that foster supportive climates. Since Gibb published his findings, other communication scholars have confirmed them (Barge, 2009).

Evaluation versus Description

As we noted in Chapter 4's discussion of the evaluative nature of language, we tend to feel defensive when others evaluate us, particularly when they evaluate us negatively (Caughlin, Afifi, Carpenter-Theune, & Miller, 2005; Conrad & Poole, 2004; Reis et al., 2004). Examples of evaluative statements are "You have no discipline," "It's dumb to feel that way," and "That's a stupid idea."

	Confirming Messages	*Disconfirming Messages*
Recognition	You exist.	You don't exist.
	Hello.	Silence
Acknowledgment	Listening	Not listening
	I'm sorry you're hurt.	You'll get over it.
	I know you're worried.	Let's drop the subject.
Endorsement	What you think is true.	You are wrong.
	What you feel is okay.	You shouldn't feel what you do.
	I feel the same way.	Your feeling doesn't make sense.
	What you feel is normal.	It's stupid to feel that way.

© Cengage Learning

Figure 7.2 **Levels of Confirmation and Disconfirmation**

SHARPEN YOUR SKILL

Using Descriptive Language

To develop skill in supportive communication, translate the following evaluative statements into descriptive ones:

Evaluative	Descriptive
This report is poorly done.	This report doesn't include background information.
You're lazy.	_____
You are such a know it all.	_____
You're obsessing about the problem.	_____
You're too involved.	_____
You're dominating the team.	_____

Descriptive communication doesn't evaluate what others think and feel. Instead, it describes behaviors without passing judgment. In Chapter 4, we discussed *I*-language, in which a speaker takes responsibility for what she or he feels and avoids judging others. For example, "I feel upset when you scream" describes what the person speaking feels or thinks, but it doesn't evaluate another. On the other hand, "You upset me" evaluates the other person and holds her or him responsible for what you feel. "I felt hurt when you said that" describes your feelings, whereas "You hurt me" blames another for your feelings.

Descriptive language may refer to others, but it does so by describing, not evaluating, their behavior (for example, "You seem to be less involved in team meetings lately" versus "You're not involved enough in our team"). Nonverbal communication can also convey evaluation—a raised eyebrow expresses skepticism, shaking your head communicates disapproval. Therefore, it's important not to express evaluation nonverbally. The Sharpen Your Skill feature on this page gives you an opportunity to practice using descriptive language.

Certainty versus Provisionalism

The language of certainty is absolute and often dogmatic. It suggests there is only one valid answer, point of view, or course of action. Because certainty proclaims an absolutely correct position, it slams the door on further discussion. Leaders can stifle creativity if they dogmatically state what the team should do (Fisher, 1998). There's no point in talking with people who demean any point of view but their own. Certainty is also communicated when we repeat our positions instead of considering others' ideas. Monika provides an example of certainty and its impact on her relationship with her father.

 Monika

My father is totally closed-minded. He has his ideas, and everything else is crazy. I told him I was majoring in communication studies, and he said I'd never get a job as a speechwriter. He never asked what communication studies is, or I would have told him it's a lot more than speechwriting. He always assumes that he knows everything about whatever is being discussed. He has no interest in information or other points of view. I've learned to keep my ideas to myself around him—there's no communication.

One form of certainty communication is **ethnocentrism**. Ethnocentrism is a perspective based on the assumption that our culture and its norms are the only right ones. For instance, someone who says, "It's always disrespectful to be late" reveals insensitivity to societies that are less time conscious than the United States. Certainty is also evident when we say, "My mind can't be changed because I'm right," "Only a fool would think that," or "There's no point in further discussion."

An alternative to certainty is *provisionalism,* which relies on tentative language to signal openness to other points of view. Provisional language indicates that we are willing to consider alternative positions, and this encourages others to voice their ideas. Provisional language lessens the chance that others will feel they have lost face in the interaction. Provisional communication includes such statements as, "The way I tend to see the issue is …," and "One way to look at this is …." Note that each comment shows that the speaker realizes that other positions also could be reasonable. Tentative communication reflects an open mind, which is why it invites continued conversation. Yong Park and Brian Kim (2008) compared European Americans' and Asian Americans' communication styles. Park and Kim found that European Americans tend to engage in more open communication than Asian Americans.

Strategy versus Spontaneity

Strategic communication aims at manipulating a person or group for the benefit of the person manipulating. In work situations, employees may become defensive if they feel management is trying to trick them into thinking their jobs are more important than they are (Conrad & Poole, 2004). We may also feel that someone is trying to manipulate us with a comment such as, "Remember how I helped you with that project you were behind on last month?" After a preamble like that, we suspect a trap of some sort. Nonverbal behaviors may also convey strategy, as when a speaker pauses a long time before answering a question or refuses to look at listeners. A sense of deception pollutes the communication climate.

Spontaneity stands in contrast to strategy. Spontaneous communication is open, honest, and not manipulative. To be ethical, spontaneous communication must not be used against others. For instance, it may be spontaneous to be verbally abusive, but it is not ethical because it does not reflect respect for the other communicator. "I really need your help with my computer" is more spontaneous than "Would you do something for me if I told you it really mattered?" Likewise, it is more spontaneous to ask for a favor in a straightforward way ("Would you help me?") than to preface a request by reciting everything you've done for someone else.

Control versus Problem Orientation

Controlling communication attempts to coerce others. In response, others often feel defensive, and they may respond with resentment or even rebellion (Stone et al., 1999). For example, a wife who earns a higher salary than her husband might say to him, "Well, I like the Honda more than the Ford you want, and it's my money that's going to pay for it." The speaker not only pushes her preference but also implies that her salary gives her greater power. Whether the issue is trivial (which movie to see) or serious (which policy a group will recommend), controllers try to impose their points of view on others. Winning an argument or having the last word is more important than finding the best solution. Controlling communication prompts defensiveness because the relationship-level meaning is that the person exerting control thinks she or he has greater power, rights, or intelligence than others.

Rather than imposing a preference, problem-oriented communication focuses on resolving tensions and problems. The goal is to work collaboratively to come up with something that everyone finds acceptable. Here's an example of problem-oriented communication: "It seems that we have really different ideas about how to get started on this task. Let's talk through what each of us wants and see if we can find a way for all of us to achieve what we need." Note how this statement invites collaboration and confirms the other people and a team focus by expressing a desire to meet all members' needs.

Problem-oriented communication tends to reduce conflict and foster an open interaction climate (McKinney, Kelly, & Duran, 1997; McNutt, 1997). The relationship level of meaning in problem-oriented interaction emphasizes that the communicators care about and respect each other. In contrast, controlling behaviors aim for one person to triumph over others, an outcome that undercuts harmony.

Neutrality versus Empathy

We tend to become defensive when others act in a neutral manner, especially if we are talking about something we feel strongly about. Neutral communication implies indifference to others and what they say. Consequently, others may feel hurt or defensive.

In contrast to neutrality, expressed empathy confirms the worth of others and shows concern for their thoughts and feelings. We communicate empathy when we say, "I can understand why you feel that way," "It sounds like you feel uncomfortable with your job," or "I don't blame you for being worried about the situation." Gibb stressed that empathy doesn't necessarily mean agreement; instead, it conveys respect for others and what they think and feel. Especially when we don't agree with others, it's important to show that we respect them as people. Doing so fosters a supportive climate and keeps lines of communication open, even if differences continue to exist.

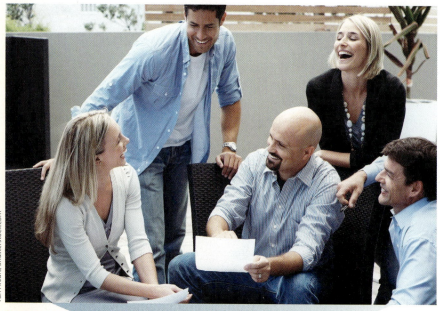

Yuri Arcurs/Shutterstock.com

Spontaneous communication tends to build team cohesion.

Superiority versus Equality

Most of us resent people who act as if they are better than we are. Consider several messages that convey superiority: "I know a lot more about this than you"; "You don't have my experience"; "Is this the best you could do?"; "You really should go to my hairdresser." Each of these messages says loudly and clearly, "You aren't as good (smart, competent, attractive) as I am." Predictably, the frequent result is that we try to save face by shutting out the people and messages that belittle us. Carl's experience in his job provides an example of the impact of communication that conveys superiority.

 Carl

I am really uncomfortable with one of the guys on my team at work. He always acts like he knows best and that nobody else is as smart or experienced. The other day, I suggested a way we might improve our team's productivity, and he said, "I remember when I used to think that." What a put-down! You can bet I won't go to him with another idea.

We feel more relaxed and comfortable communicating with people who treat us as equals. At the relationship level of meaning, expressed equality communicates respect. This promotes an open, unguarded climate for interaction. We can have special expertise in certain areas and still show regard for others and what they think, feel, and say. Creating a climate of equality allows everyone to be involved without fear of being judged inadequate.

We've seen that confirmation, which may include recognizing, acknowledging, and endorsing others, is the basis of healthy communication climates. Our discussion of defensive and supportive communication enlightens us about specific kinds of communication that express confirmation or disconfirmation. The Sharpen Your Skill activity on this page invites you to apply what you've learned about communication that fosters defensiveness and supportiveness. Our discussion of communication climates is a good foundation for considering the role of conflict in human relationships and how building and sustaining affirming communication climates allows us to manage conflict productively.

Conflict and Communication

Conflict exists when people who depend on each other have different views, interests, values, responsibilities, or objectives and perceive their differences as incompatible. The presence of conflict doesn't mean a relationship is in trouble, although how people manage conflict does affect relationship health. Typically, conflict is a sign that people are involved with each other. If they weren't, differences wouldn't matter and wouldn't need to be resolved. Co-workers argue because they care about issues that affect all of them; roommates experience conflict if they disagree about noise levels in their room; romantic partners engage in conflict when they face tensions and disagreements that jeopardize their relationship. When tensions arise, it's good to remember that

SHARPEN YOUR SKILL

Assessing Communication Climates

Use the behaviors we've discussed as a checklist for assessing communication climates. The next time you feel defensive, ask yourself whether others are communicating superiority, control, strategy, certainty, neutrality, or evaluation. In a communication climate that you find supportive and open, ask yourself whether the following behaviors are present: spontaneity, equality, provisionalism, problem orientation, empathy, and description.

engaging in conflict is a signal that we have to work something out in order to keep a relationship on course.

Conflict Can Be Overt or Covert

Conflict can be overt or covert. **Overt conflict** exists when people express differences in a straightforward manner. They might discuss a disagreement, honestly express different points of view, or argue heatedly about ideas. In each case, differences are out in the open.

 Carlotta

My roommate doesn't tell me when she's mad or hurt or whatever. Instead, she plays these games that drive me crazy. Sometimes, she refuses to talk to me and denies that anything is wrong. Other times, she "forgets" some of my stuff when she gets our groceries. I have to guess what is wrong because she won't tell me. It strains our friendship.

Yet, as Carla points out, not all conflict is overt. **Covert conflict** exists when people express disagreement or difference only indirectly. For instance, if you're annoyed that your roommate left the kitchen a mess, you might play the stereo when she or he is sleeping. It's almost impossible to resolve conflicts when we don't communicate openly about our differences.

Components in the Conflict Process

Because conflict is inevitable and can be productive, we need to understand how to manage conflict so that it is healthy for us, for our relationships, and for decision making. Clyde Feldman and Carl Ridley (2000) identify four key components of the conflict process. Their four-component model breaks down the complex process of conflict so that we can think about it and our options for managing it:

▶ Conflicts of interest: Goals, interests, or opinions that seem incompatible

▶ Conflict orientations: Individuals' attitudes toward conflict

▶ Conflict responses: Overt behavioral responses to conflict

▶ Conflict outcomes: How conflict is resolved and how the process of conflict affects relationships between people

Conflicts of Interest

The first component of conflict is goals, interests, or views that are perceived as incompatible. You want to set up a time each day when you and a co-worker will both be online to instant message, but

 fyi

DIVERSITY

Crisis = Danger + Opportunity

The Chinese word for *crisis* is made up of two characters. The character on the left means "danger." The character on the right means "opportunity." Like the Chinese word for *crisis*, we should remember that conflict can be both dangerous and an opportunity.

your co-worker doesn't want to do that. You believe money should be enjoyed, and your partner believes in saving for a rainy day. You want your team to meet weekly, and another member of the team wants to meet only monthly. When we find our interests at odds with people who matter to us, we need to resolve conflicts of interest, preferably in a way that doesn't harm the relationship.

Conflict Orientations

The second component is how we perceive conflict. Do you view conflict as negative? Do you assume that everyone is bound to lose in conflict situations? Your answers to these questions shape your orientation toward conflict and thus how you approach it. One of the greatest influences on orientations toward conflict is cultural background. Societies such as the United States accept conflict and assertive competition. Other societies teach people to avoid conflict and to seek harmony with others.

The three basic conflict orientations are *lose–lose*, *win–lose*, and *win–win*. Each of these is appropriate in some situations; the challenge is to know when each view is constructive.

The **lose–lose** approach to conflict assumes that conflict results in losses for everyone. One of my colleagues avoids conflict whenever possible because he feels that everyone loses when there is disagreement. The lose–lose view presumes that conflict cannot produce positive outcomes. Although the lose–lose perspective usually is not beneficial, it has merit in specific circumstances. Some issues aren't worth the effort of conflict. For instance, my father-in-law and I disagreed strongly about political matters. We decided not to talk about politics, because inevitably we both lose in such conversations. Similarly, in order to maintain a positive working relationship, co-workers may avoid discussing issues on which they disagree strongly, as long as resolving their differences is not relevant to job performance.

The **win–lose** orientation to conflict assumes that one person wins at the expense of the other. A person who perceives conflict as a win–lose matter thinks that whatever one person gains is at the other's expense and that what one person loses benefits the other. Partners who disagree about whether to move to a new location that provides better job prospects for only one of them might lock into a yes–no mode in which they can see only two alternatives: move or don't move. They are unlikely to make an effort to find a mutually acceptable solution, such as moving to a third place that meets both partners' needs adequately, or temporarily having a long-distance relationship so each person can maximize professional opportunities. The more person A argues for moving, the more B argues for not moving. Eventually, one of them "wins," but at the cost of the other and the relationship.

A win–lose orientation tends to undermine relationships because someone has to lose. There is no possibility that both can win, much less that the relationship can. For this reason, win–lose orientations should really be called win–lose–lose because when one person wins, both the other person and the relationship can lose.

Before you dismiss win–lose as a totally unconstructive orientation to conflict, let's consider when it might be effective. Win–lose can be an appropriate orientation when we have low commitment to a relationship and little desire to take care of the person with whom we disagree. When you're buying a car, for instance, you want the best deal you can get, and you have little concern for the dealer's profit. I adopted a win–lose approach to conflict with doctors when my father was dying. The doctors weren't doing all they could to help him, because they saw little value in investing time in a dying patient, but I wanted everything possible done to comfort my father. We had opposing views, and I cared less about whether the doctors were happy and liked me than about "winning" the best medical care for my father.

The **win–win** view of conflict assumes that there are usually ways to resolve differences so that everyone gains. For people who view conflict as interactions in which all parties can win, the goal is to come up with a resolution that is acceptable to everyone. A person is willing to make some accommodations in order to build a solution that lets others win, too. When partners adopt win–win views of conflict, they often find solutions that neither had thought of previously. This happens because they are committed to their own and the other's satisfaction. Sometimes win–win attitudes result in compromises that satisfy enough of each person's needs to provide confirmation and to protect the health of the relationship. Tess describes a situation in which she and her partner worked to find a way for both of them (and their relationship) to win.

 Tess

One of the roughest issues for Jerry and me was when he started working most nights. The time after dinner had always been "our time." When Jerry took the new job, he had to stay in constant contact with the California office. Because of the time difference, at 6 p.m., when Jerry and I used to do something together, it's only 3 p.m. on the West Coast, and the business day is still going. I was hurt that he no longer had time for us, and he was angry that I wanted time he needed for business. We kept talking and came up with the idea of spending a day together each weekend, which we'd never done. Although my ideal would still be to share evenings, this solution keeps us in touch with each other.

What we learned about perception in Chapter 3 reminds us that how we perceive and label conflict powerfully affects what it means to us and how we craft resolutions. We're unlikely to find a win–win solution when we conceive conflict as win–lose or lose–lose.

Conflict Responses

The third component of conflict is how we respond to it. A series of studies identified four responses to conflict (Rusbult, 1987; Rusbult, Johnson, & Morrow, 1986; Rusbult & Zembrodt, 1983; Rusbult, Zembrodt, & Iwaniszek, 1986). Figure 7.3 summarizes these responses to conflict, which are active or passive, depending on whether they address problems. Responses are also constructive or destructive in their effect on relationships.

The *exit response* involves leaving a relationship, either by walking out or by psychologically withdrawing. "I don't want to talk about it" is a vocal exit response. Because exit is forceful, it is active; because it fails to resolve tension, it can be destructive. However, there are situations in which exit can be a positive response, especially if it is only temporary. For instance, if you know that you will say or do something you will regret if you don't walk away from an argument, exiting may be a wise short-term response.

The *neglect response* occurs when a person denies or minimizes problems. "You're making a mountain out of a molehill" is a neglect response that denies that a serious issue exists. The neglect response is also disconfirming because it fails to acknowledge and respect how another feels. Neglect can be destructive because it evades difficulties, and it is passive because it doesn't actively promote discussion.

The *loyalty response* is staying committed to a relationship despite differences. Loyalty involves hoping that things will get better on their own. Loyalty is silent allegiance, so it is passive. Because loyalty doesn't end a relationship and preserves the option of addressing tension later, loyalty can be constructive. However, recent research (Overall, Sibley, & Travaglia, 2010) suggests that loyalty often results in the partner who expresses it feeling ignored and unappreciated.

Finally, *voice* is potentially the most active, constructive response to conflict because it focuses on dealing directly with problems and helps the relationship by managing differences (Overall, et al., 2010). A person who says to a co-worker, "I want to talk about the tension between us" exemplifies the voice response to conflict.

You may have noticed that I wrote voice is *potentially* the most active, constructive response to conflict. To achieve that potential, the voice response needs to embody good communication skills. For instance, it's important to confirm others and to rely on communication that cultivates supportive climates. It's also wise to consider others' perspectives, rely on *I*-language, and listen mindfully. Perhaps most important in conflict communication is to make sure it is truly transactional—that is, both we and others are given equal attention. When conflict arises, it is easy to become self-centered—to focus on your feelings, ideas, and goals, and to want to express your needs and emotions (Lewis, Haviland-Jones, & Barrett, 2008). Yet, if you are so busy expressing yourself that you do not recognize and acknowledge others, interaction is unlikely to be productive for the issues or the relationship. As Buddhist teacher Thubten Chodron (2001) notes, "Good communication involves expressing ourselves in a way that the other person understands. It is not simply dumping our feelings on the other" (p. 23).

Although most of us have one or two customary responses to conflict, we can develop skill in other responses. Once you understand your current ways of responding to conflict, you can consider whether you want to develop skill in additional styles.

Figure 7.3   Responses to Conflict
Source: Adapted from Wood, 1997, p. 21.

Conflict Outcomes

The final component of conflict is the outcome. When most people think of conflict outcomes, they think of the decision that has resulted. Although this is indeed an outcome of conflict, it isn't the only one nor necessarily the most important outcome.

A conflict's impact on a relationship may be a more significant and enduring outcome than the actual decision. Relationship outcomes are influenced more by how we manage conflict than by the resolution itself. Conflicts can strengthen relationships when people build a supportive interpersonal climate and work to sustain that climate as a part of managing conflict. Harm to relationships is most likely when people disconfirm each other and cultivate defensive communication climates. Because our choices of how to manage conflict have an impact on relationships, we need to be especially careful to communicate in respectful and affirming ways when conflicts arise.

Although many people have negative views of conflict, it can benefit both our relationships and ourselves. Managed constructively, conflict can help us grow personally and professionally, and it can strengthen our connections with others. Conflict prompts us

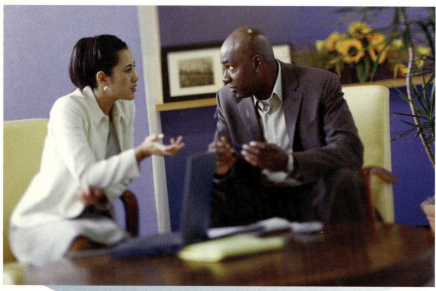

© Steve Chern/Corbis

Conflict is inevitable in relationships. Do these two co-workers seem to be managing their difference of opinion constructively?

to consider different points of view. Based on what we learn, we may change our opinions, behaviors, or goals. Conflict can also increase our insight into relationships, situations, and ourselves.

Third Party Assistance in Resolving Conflict

So far, our discussion has assumed that the people who have a conflict manage it. Yet there are times when the people having conflict cannot resolve their differences. They make lack the necessary communication skills or motivation. They may have locked themselves into opposing positions. They may have personal animosity that undermines constructive discussion. In cases such as these, it is often wise to turn to a third party.

Sometimes a co-worker or a friend can help people resolve differences. Two co-workers who are at loggerheads may gain insight and perspective from a colleague who is not invested in the positions they have staked out (Myers & Larson, 2005). A good friend who knows a couple well may be able to help one or both of the partners see a way to meet the other partner's interests.

Third parties may also be outsiders: individuals who do not have personal relationships with any of the parties who are in conflict. The most common types of third parties from the outside are mediators and arbitrators.

A **mediator** works with people who are in conflict to reach a decision but has no power to make a decision. Typically, mediators focus on helping parties in conflict communicate more productively. Mediators often begin by working with parties to create an agenda and rules for discussion: what will be covered and in what sequence, who may speak when (regulative rules), and how parties are expected to speak (constitutive rules for respect and politeness). Once an agenda and communication rules are established, mediators may clarify each party's views through paraphrasing, ask questions to make sure that all relevant information is known to all, and make direct recommendations ("You two could each take half of the royalties from the invention you each claim to have made"). Mediators also try to maintain a good communication climate by introducing humor, thanking parties for constructive participation, intervening if parties engage in behavior outside of the agreed upon rules, and helping each person recognize the other's point of view. Mediators are most advisable when the parties in conflict have relatively equal power and so feel equally able to speak up (Murphy & Rubinson, 2005). Unions often rely on mediation to resolve conflicts between union members and employers.

An **arbitrator** also facilitates discussion of conflict issues. Unlike mediators, however, arbitrators have the authority to make decisions. After gathering information from all parties and listening carefully to evidence, argument, and proposals, an arbitrator makes a decision that is typically binding on participants. Sports teams often submit disputes to arbitrators.

My brother-in-law is an attorney who frequently engages in mediation and arbitration between parties who have legal disputes. He thinks the mediation can be very helpful in helping people in conflict find equitable solutions because the mediator can help them listen mindfully to each other, which often they have lost the ability to do on their own. He also engages in arbitration, but says that it is not as satisfying to him because it gives less control to the parties involved in conflict. He offers his thoughts about arbitration and mediation as alternatives to trials in the FYI on this page.

fyi

WORK

An Attorney's Perspective

Leigh Wilco is an attorney who works in Atlanta, where he has been named one of the city's top litigators. Although he's a skilled trial lawyer, Mr. Wilco often encourages his clients to try mediation or arbitration as alternatives to trial. Following are his thoughts on the values of these third-party modes of resolving conflict.

"While jury trials are the foundation of our legal system, there are problems with them. First, because of the number of cases filed, it can often take years to get to trial. Second, even after a trial, the appeals process can take a year or more. Third, jury trials have become increasingly expensive and time consuming. Finally, while we still claim everyone has a right to trial by a "jury of your peers," it is rare that the actual jury has the same life experiences as the parties.

"The advantages of mediation are that it can be done at any time during the conflict process, it is much quicker and less expensive than trial, and, if an agreement is reached, it is final and binding. The most important advantage, however, is that the parties have control over the decision. With a jury trial one side (or sometimes both sides) might be grossly unhappy with the verdict. In mediation, if you think what is offered by the other side is not fair, you can refuse it and go to trial. Mediation empowers the parties with decision-making ability that is absent from a trial.

"Arbitration, like a trial, does not allow the parties to be the decision makers, but it can have some advantages over a jury trial. The two main advantages are speed and expertise. An arbitration should take less time than a trial. Second, an arbitration is usually conducted by an individual with expertise in the area of the dispute that most jurors don't have. This makes it particularly suitable for complex cases.

"A possible disadvantage of arbitrations is that they are usually conducted by either one or three arbitrators. This gives more control and power to a single person than a 12-person jury does.

"My experience is that most people do not enjoy the cost, time, and stress of a jury trial, even if they win. Mediation and arbitration allow the parties to have more control over the process, resolve the dispute sooner, and get on with their lives."

Guidelines for Creating and Sustaining Healthy Communication Climates

To translate what we've covered in this chapter into practical information, we'll discuss five guidelines for building and sustaining healthy climates.

Communicate in Ways That Confirm Others

We've seen that interpersonal confirmation is a cornerstone of healthy communication climates. Although interpersonal confirmation is important, it isn't always easy to give. When we disagree with what others think or do, it may be difficult to confirm them. However, we've emphasized that interpersonal confirmation is not the same as agreement. You can confirm someone as a person even if you don't admire the person's ideas or actions. Interpersonal confirmation occurs when we recognize others, acknowledge or attend to them, and endorse what they feel, think, say, and do as understandable. We can communicate interpersonal confirmation even if we do not agree with others' feelings, beliefs, or actions.

 Dean

> *My supervisor did an excellent job of letting me know I was valued when I got passed over for a promotion last year. He came to my office to talk to me before the promotion was announced. He told me both I and the other guy were qualified but that he had seniority and also field experience I didn't have. Then he assigned me to a field position for six months so I could get the experience I needed to get promoted. His talk made all the difference in how I felt about staying with the company.*

Communication can express both confirmation of another person and disagreement with that person. In fact, research tells us that people expect real friends to give honest feedback, even if it isn't always pleasant to hear (Rawlins, 1994). Similarly, in the workplace, managers who give honest feedback, including criticism, are more likely to build strong working relationships with subordinates than are managers who avoid criticism and conflict (Fisher, 1998). This implies that we have an ethical responsibility to be honest in our communication. It is false friends who tell us only what we want to hear. We can offer honest feedback within a context that assures others we value and respect them, as Dan's commentary illustrates.

 Dan

> *When I first came to school here, I got in with a crowd that drank a lot. At first, I drank only on weekends, but pretty soon I was drinking every night and drinking more and more. My grades were suffering, but I didn't stop. Then my friend Betsy told me she wanted to help me stop drinking. The way she talked to me, I knew that she was being honest because she cared. She was a better friend than all my drinking buddies because she cared enough not to let me hurt myself. All my buddies just stood by and said nothing.*

Communicate in Ways That Confirm Yourself

It is just as important to confirm yourself as others. You are no less valuable than others, your needs are no less important, and your preferences are no less valid. It is a misunderstanding to think that the interpersonal communication principles we've discussed concern only how we behave toward others. They pertain equally to how we should treat ourselves. Thus, it is ethical to confirm others and ourselves equally.

You confirm yourself when you express your thoughts and feelings honestly. By doing that, you show that you respect yourself. You also give others a chance to understand who you are. You communicate ethically when you assert your feelings, ideas, and preferences while honoring those of others. If you don't assert yourself in the workplace, you give up the possibility of influencing the quality of work produced and how it is organized. If you don't assert yourself in personal relationships, you undercut your own and your partner's respect for your ideas, feelings, and needs, as Maria points out in her commentary.

Maria

Ever since I was a kid, I have muffled my own needs and tried to please others. I thought I was taking care of relationships, but actually I was hurting them, because I felt neglected. My resentment poisoned relationships in subtle but potent ways. Now, I'm learning to tell others what I want and need, and that's improving my relationships.

Assertive communication is not aggressive. Aggressive communication occurs when one person puts herself or himself ahead of others or derides others' thoughts, feelings, goals, or actions. In contrast, assertive communication simply expresses the speaker's thoughts, feelings, preferences, and goals without disparaging anyone else. You communicate assertively when you express yourself firmly and unapologetically.

Assertive communication is also not deferential. Unlike deference, assertion doesn't subordinate your needs to those of others. Assertion also differs from passive aggression, in which a person blocks or resists while denying that she or he is doing so. Assertion is a matter of clearly stating what you feel, think, or want. This should be done without disparaging others and what they feel, think, or want. You should simply state your feelings in an open, descriptive manner. Figure 7.4 illustrates how aggression, assertion, and deference differ. Even when people disagree or have conflicting needs, each person can state her or his feelings and confirm the other's perspective. Usually, there are ways to acknowledge multiple viewpoints.

Aggressive	*Assertive*	*Deferential*
I demand that we spend time together.	I'd like to create more time for us.	If you don't want us to spend time with each other, that's okay with me.
Get this report done today. I need it.	I 'd like to get this report today. Can you manage that?	I need this report today, but if you can't get it done, that's all right.
Tell me what you're feeling; I insist.	I would like to understand more how you feel.	If you don't want to talk about how you feel, okay.

© Cengage Learning

Figure 7.4   **Aggression, Assertion, and Deference**

SHARPEN YOUR SKILL

Communicating Assertively

The following statements are deferential or aggressive. Revise each one so that it is assertive.

1. I'm going to the party regardless of what you want.
2. I'll lend you the money, even though I may have to work an extra shift to get it.
3. We're getting the car that I like, and that's it!
4. They don't have vegetarian entrees at the restaurant you want to go to, but I can just eat a salad.

Respect Diversity among People

Just as individuals differ, so do relationships in personal and professional life. There is tremendous variety in what people find comfortable, affirming, and satisfying. For this reason, it's counterproductive to try to force all people and relationships to fit into a single mode. For example, you might know one co-worker who enjoys a lot of verbal banter and another who is offended by it. There's no need to try to persuade the second co-worker to engage in verbal teasing or the first one to stop doing so. To build and sustain supportive, confirming climates, we need to adapt our communication to people's differences.

Because people and relationships are diverse, we should respect a range of communication choices and relationship patterns. In addition, we should be cautious about imposing our meaning on others' communication. People from different social groups, including distinct groups in the United States, have learned different communication styles. What Westerners consider to be open, healthy self-disclosure may feel offensively intrusive to people from some Asian societies. European Americans can misinterpret the dramatic, assertive speaking style of some African Americans. Especially in the workplace, it's important to understand that people vary widely in communication styles. To communicate effectively, we need to respect diversity among people. Valaya makes this point in her commentary.

One of the most hard adjustments for me has been how Americans assert themselves. I was very surprised that students argue with their teachers. We would never do that in Taiwan. It would be extremely disrespectful. I also see friends argue, sometimes very much. I understand this is a cultural difference, but I have trouble accepting it. I learned that disagreements very much hurt relationships.

It's also appropriate to ask others to explain behaviors that are not familiar to you. For instance, Valaya might ask other students what it means to them when they argue with teachers, and other students might ask Valaya what it means to her not to argue with teachers. Asking others what their communication means lets them know that they matter to you, and it allows us to gain insight into perspectives other than our own.

Time Conflict Effectively

A fourth guideline for creating effective communication climates is to time them so that each person can be mindful and so that the context and available time allow for constructive discussion. Most of us are irritable when we are sick, tired, or stressed, so conflict is unlikely to be managed well. It's also generally more productive to discuss problems in private rather than in public settings. It takes time to manage conflict constructively, so it's wise not to engage in conflict when we have limited time. It's impossible to express ourselves clearly, to listen well, to be confirming, and to respond sensitively when a stopwatch is ticking in our minds.

Be flexible about when you engage in conflict. Some people prefer to tackle problems as soon as they come up, whereas other people need time to reflect before interacting. If one person feels ready to talk about a problem but the other doesn't, it's wise to delay discussion if possible. Of course, this works only if the person who is ready agrees to talk about the issue at a later time. In his book *Anger at Work* (1996), Dr. Hendrie Weisinger recommends taking a "time out" if emotions are raw or tempers are flaring. For instance, suppose someone says something to you that makes you very angry. What would you do? Dr. Weisinger suggests you tell the other person that you want to discuss the issue but you need 10 minutes. You might say you have to make a phone call first or explain that you'd prefer to cool down.

A third way to use timing to promote positive conflict is **bracketing**, which marks off (or brackets) peripheral issues for later discussion. In the course of conflict, multiple issues often surface. If we try to deal with each one as it arises, we get sidetracked from the immediate or main issue. Bracketing other concerns for later discussion lets us keep conflict focused productively. Keep in mind, however, that bracketing works only if people actually do return to the issues they set aside.

Show Grace When Appropriate

Finally, an important principle to keep in mind during conflict is that **grace** is sometimes appropriate. Although the idea of grace has not traditionally been discussed in communication texts, it is an important part of spiritual and philosophical thinking about ethical communication. You don't have to be religious or know philosophy to show grace. All that's needed is a willingness to sometimes excuse someone who has no right to expect your compassion or forgiveness. Showing grace when appropriate is equally important in personal and professional relationships.

Grace is granting forgiveness, putting aside our needs, or helping another save face when no standard says we should or must do so. Rather than being prompted by rules or expectations, grace springs from a generosity of spirit. Grace isn't forgiving when we *should* do so (for instance, excusing people who aren't responsible for their actions). Nor is grace allowing others to have their way when we have no choice (deferring when our supervisor insists, for example). Instead, grace is kindness that is neither earned nor required. For instance, two roommates agree to split chores, and one doesn't do her share during a week when she has three tests. Her roommate might do all the chores even though there is no expectation of this generosity. It's also an act of grace to defer to another person's preference when you could impose yours. Similarly, when someone hurts you and has no right to expect forgiveness, you may choose to forgive anyway. We do so not because we have to, but because we want to.

Grace is given without strings. We show kindness, defer our needs, or forgive a wrong *without any expectation of reward or reciprocity*. Grace isn't doing something nice to make a co-worker feel grateful or indebted to us. Nor is it grace when we do something with the expectation of a payback. For an act to be one of grace, it must be done without conditions or expectation of return.

Grace is not always appropriate. Generosity of spirit can be exploited by people who take advantage of kindness. Some people repeatedly abuse and hurt others, confident that pardons will be granted. When grace is extended and then exploited, extending it again may be unwise. However, if you show grace in good faith and another takes advantage, you should not fault yourself. Kindness and a willingness to forgive are worthy moral precepts. Those who abuse grace, not those who offer it, are blameworthy.

Because Western culture emphasizes the assertion and protection of self-interest, grace is not widely practiced or esteemed. We are told to stand up for ourselves, to not let others walk on us, and to refuse to tolerate transgressions. It is important to honor and assert ourselves, as we've emphasized throughout this book. Yet self-assertion can work in tandem with generosity toward others.

None of us is perfect. We all make mistakes, hurt others with thoughtless acts, fail to meet responsibilities, and occasionally do things we know are wrong. Sometimes there is no reason others should forgive us when we wrong them; we have no right to expect exoneration. Yet human relations must have some room for redemption, for the extension of grace when it is not required or earned.

The guidelines we've discussed combine respect for self, others, relationships, and communication. Using these guidelines should enhance your ability to foster healthy, affirming climates in your relationships with others.

SUMMARY

In this chapter, we've explored communication climate as a foundation of interaction with others. A basic requirement for healthy communication climates is interpersonal confirmation. Each of us wants to feel valued, especially by those for whom we care most deeply. When communicators recognize, acknowledge, and endorse each other, they give the important gift of interpersonal confirmation. They say, "You matter to me." We discussed particular kinds of communication that foster supportive and defensive climates in relationships.

Communication that fosters supportive climates also helps us manage conflict constructively. We discussed lose–lose, win–lose, and win–win approaches to conflict and explored how each affects interaction. In addition, conflict patterns are influenced by whether people respond by exiting, neglecting, being loyal, or giving voice to tensions. In most cases, voice is the preferred response because it is the only response that allows people to deal with conflict actively and constructively.

To close the chapter, we considered five guidelines for building healthy communication climates. The first one is to accept and affirm others, communicating that we respect them even though we may not always agree with them or share their feelings. A companion guideline is to accept and assert ourselves. Each of us is entitled to voice our thoughts, feelings, and needs. Doing so honors ourselves and helps others understand us. A third guideline is to respect diversity. Humans vary widely, as do their preferred styles of communicating. When we respect differences between people, we gain insight into the fascinating array of human interactions.

The fourth and fifth guidelines concern communicating when conflicts arise. We learned that we can make choices about timing that increase the likelihood of constructive climate. In addition, we discussed the value of showing grace—unearned, unrequired compassion—when that is appropriate.

REVIEW, REFLECT, EXTEND

The Reflect, Discuss, and Apply Questions that follow will help you review, reflect on, and extend the information and ideas presented in this chapter. These resources, and a diverse selection of additional study tools, are also available online at the CourseMate for *Communication Mosaics*. Your CourseMate includes a student workbook, WebLinks, TED Talks hyperlinks and activities, chapter glossary and flashcards, interactive video activities, Speech Builder Express, and InfoTrac College Edition. For more information or to access this book's online resources, visit **www .cengagebrain.com.**

KEY CONCEPTS

acknowledgment, 135
arbitrator, 147
bracketing, 151
communication climate, 133
conflict, 141
covert conflict, 142
endorsement, 136
ethnocentrism, 138

grace, 151
interpersonal confirmation, 134
lose–lose, 143
mediator, 146
overt conflict, 142
recognition, 134
win–lose, 143
win–win, 144

Reflect, Discuss, Apply

1. Think about the most effective work climate you've ever experienced. Describe the communication in that climate. How does the communication in that situation reflect the skills and principles discussed in this chapter?

2. As a class, discuss the ethical principles reflected in the communication behaviors discussed in this chapter. What ethical principles underlie confirming communication and disconfirming communication?

3. Interview a professional in the field you plan to enter or return to after completing college. Ask your interviewee to describe the kind of climate that is most effective in his or her work situation. Ask what specific kinds of communication foster and impede a good working climate. How do your interviewee's perceptions relate to the material covered in this chapter?

4. How often do you use exit, voice, loyalty, and neglect responses to conflict? What are the effects?

5. When do you find it most difficult to confirm others? Is it hard for you to be confirming when you disagree with another person? After reading this chapter, can you distinguish disagreement from disconfirmation?

6. As a class, identify ways in which faculty at your school confirm and disconfirm students. Be specific in naming particular types of communication (and examples) that are confirming and disconfirming.

Recommended Resources

1. Redford Williams, M.D., and Virginia Williams, Ph.D. (1993). *Anger kills: Seventeen strategies for controlling the hostility that can harm your health.* New York: HarperPerennial. This is very-readable book details the harm that anger and hostility cause us and provides practical advice on ways to own and manage your anger to interact more effectively with others.

2. To read Jack Gibb's original paper on defensive and supportive communication, go to the book's online resources for this chapter and click on WebLink 7.1.

3. To learn how gender and other facets of identity affect communication, including listening, go to the book's online resources for this chapter and click on WebLink 7.2.

4. Clicking on WebLink 7.3 will take you to the Powerful Non-Defensive Communication site, which offers exercises to assess and improve your skill in creating supportive communication climates.

EXPERIENCE COMMUNICATION CASE STUDY

Cloudy Climate

Apply what you've learned in this chapter by analyzing the following case study, using the accompanying questions as a guide. These questions and a video of the case study are also available online at your CouresMate for *Communication Mosaics*.

Andy and Martha married five years ago when they completed graduate school. Last week, Andy got the job offer of his dreams—with one problem: He would have to move 1,500 miles away. Martha loves her current job and has no interest in moving or in living apart. Andy sees this job as one that could really advance his career. For the past week, they have talked and argued continually about the job offer. Tonight, while they are preparing dinner in their kitchen, they have returned to the topic once again. We join them midway in their discussion, just as it is heating up.

Andy: So, today I was checking on the costs for flights from here to Seattle. If we plan ahead for visits, we can get round-trip flights for around $300. That's not too bad.

Martha: While you're thinking about finances, you might consider the cost of renting a second apartment out there. We agreed last night that it would be too expensive to live apart.

Andy: I never agreed to that. Martha, can't you understand how important this job is to my career?

Martha: And what about our marriage? I suppose that's not important?

Andy: [He grabs a knife and begins cutting an onion.] I never said that! If you'd pull with me on this, our marriage would be fine. You're just not …

Martha: [She slams a pot on the stove.] Not what? Not willing to be the traditional supportive wife, I assume.

Andy: [He grimaces, puts down the knife, and turns to face Martha.] That isn't what I was going to say. I never asked you to be a traditional wife or to be anything other than who you are, but I want you to let me be myself, too.

© Cengage Learning

Martha: If you want to be yourself, then why did you get married? Marriage is about more than just yourself—it's about both of us and what's good for the two of us. You're not thinking of us at all.

Andy: And I suppose you are? You're only thinking about what you want. You don't seem to give a darn what I want. You're being incredibly selfish.

Martha: [She slams her hand against the counter and shouts.] Selfish! I'm selfish to care about our marriage?

Andy: You're using that to manipulate me, as if I don't care about the marriage and you do. If you really cared about it, maybe you'd consider moving to Seattle so we could be together.

Martha: [She raises her eyebrows and speaks in a sarcastic tone.] And just a minute ago, you said you weren't asking me to be a traditional wife. Now you want me to be the trailing spouse so you can do what you please. Dandy!

Andy: I didn't say that. You're putting words in my mouth. What I said was—

Martha: What you said was I should move to Seattle and support whatever it is you want to do.

Andy: [He slams the knife into the cutting board.] I did not say that. Quit telling me what I said!

[He takes a deep breath, lowers his voice, then continues.] Look, Martha, can we just step back from this argument and try to look at the options with a fresh eye?

Martha: I've looked all I want to look. I've heard all I want to hear. You know where I stand on this, and you know I'm right even if you don't want to admit it.

1. Identify examples of mind reading, and describe their impact on Martha's and Andy's discussion.

2. Identify communication that fosters a defensive interpersonal climate.

3. To what extent do you think Andy and Martha feel listened to by the other?

4. Do you perceive any relationship-level meanings that aren't being addressed in this conversation?

"All human activity takes place within a culture and interacts with culture." Pope John Paul II

8 Adapting Communication to Cultures and Social Communities

▶ Is it more important for society to be well-ordered or to provide personal freedom to its members?

▶ Does winning an honor reflect more on the person who receives it or the person's family?

▶ Have people who have high power in society earned their power?

FOCUS QUESTIONS

1. How do cultures and social communities shape communication?

2. How does communication shape cultures and social communities?

3. What is ethnocentric bias?

4. How do people respond to cultural differences in communication?

How you answer those questions is influenced by the culture to which you belong. If you identify with a culture that emphasizes individualism, you probably rank personal freedom as more important than social order and think an honor reflects primarily on the individual who wins it. However, if you identify with a culture that emphasizes collective well-being, you probably think an orderly society is more important than personal freedom and believe an honor reflects primarily on the family of the individual who receives it (Hofstede, 1991, 2001; Hofstede, Hofstede, & Minkov, 2010; Jandt, 2009; Simons & Zielenziger, 1996). Likewise, in cultures that emphasize collective life, people tend to think any honor an individual receives reflects on that person's family and community.

Cultures also differ in the extent to which they view power differences among people as normal and right. In cultures that have relatively low power differences among people, it's generally assumed that people with more power earned it and others who work hard can also earn power. Conversely, in cultures where there are larger gaps between people with and without power, there is a tendency to see the differences as stable and one's own position as unlikely to change.

The value people assign to individualism and collectivism and how they view power differences influence how they communicate. For instance, in cultures that emphasize collective goals and harmony, people generally do not state their positions directly or strongly and do not promote themselves. In cultures where power is very uneven, those with less power tend not to challenge the existing hierarchy and to speak respectfully to those with power. This is only one of many ways in which communication and culture are linked.

We live in a diverse world in which people increasingly move in and out of cultures. The number of students who travel abroad to study increases each year. In 2010, the number of U.S. students who studied abroad totaled 260,327; conversely, 690,923 students came from other countries to study in the United States. (IIE, 2011). Immigration to the United States adds to the diversity of life within the borders of this country. In fact, demographers predict that by 2050 Caucasians will no longer be the majority of Americans.

To participate effectively in today's world, all of us need to understand and respect cultural differences and the ways they affect communication. Effectiveness in social and professional life demands that you understand and adapt your communication to people of varied cultural backgrounds. The competitive style of negotiation customary among Americans may offend Taiwanese businesspeople. Friendly touches that are comfortable to most Americans may be perceived as rude and intrusive by Germans. Americans typically form lines to enter buildings and rooms, but in India people don't form lines; instead they push and shove to get a place, and that's not perceived as impolite (Spano, 2003). In some cultures, direct eye contact is interpreted as indicative of honesty. In other cultures, however, it is interpreted as disrespect. These examples highlight the importance of adapting communication to various cultures and social communities.

In this chapter, we discuss the sixth and final basic communication process: adapting communication to cultures and social communities. We first discuss dimensions of cultures and social communities. Next, we explore four important relationships between culture and communication. The final section of the chapter discusses guidelines for adapting communication effectively to diverse cultures and social groups.

Understanding Cultures and Social Communities

Although the word *culture* is part of our everyday vocabulary, it's difficult to define. Culture is part of everything we think, do, feel, and believe, yet we can't point to a thing that is culture. Most simply defined, **culture** is a way of life—a system of ideas, values, beliefs, customs, and language that is passed from one generation to the next and that reflects and sustains a particular way of life (Spencer, 1982).

In Chapter 1, we discussed systems, which are made up of interacting, interrelated parts. Because cultures are systems, the interconnected parts of any culture affect one another and the whole. For example, the technological revolution has had multiple and far-reaching implications for cultural life. Computer-mediated communication

© Ron Chapple/Taxi/Getty Images

What would be different in this photo if the two people were both Americans or if one was a woman?

allows us to interact with people who are not geographically close. Today many people form and sustain online friendships and romantic relationships. Telecommuting allows people who previously worked in offices to do their jobs in their homes or while traveling. Multinational organizations can hold virtual conferences that allow employees around the world to communicate in real time and with full audio and visual contact. The one factor of technology affects other factors, such as how, where, and with whom we communicate, as well as the boundaries of work and personal life. Because cultures are holistic, no change is isolated from the overall system.

Multiple Social Communities May Coexist in a Single Culture

National borders are not the only lines that mark different groups of people. Groups with distinct ways of life can coexist in a single society or geographic territory. Individuals are affected not only by the culture as a whole, but also by membership in groups outside of mainstream culture, which are called **social communities** (Harding, 2004; Healey & O'Brien, 2004; Winters & DeBose, 2004).

Most societies have a dominant, or mainstream, way of life with which most members of a culture identify. European, heterosexual, landowning, able-bodied men who were Christian (at least in heritage, if not always in actual practice) developed mainstream Western culture. Yet, Western society includes many groups that are outside of, or are not exclusively identified with, this mainstream culture. Gay men, lesbians, bisexuals, and transgendered people experience difficulty in a society that does not grant them the social standing and legal rights given to heterosexuals (Glover & Kaplan, 2009; Jagger, 2008). Mainstream customs in America often ignore or marginalize American citizens who are Muslim, Buddhist, or Hindu. The Sharpen Your Skill feature on this page encourages you to notice that many American calendars recognize Christian holidays but not holidays important to non-Christians.

SHARPEN YOUR SKILL

Communicating Culture

Locate a standard calendar and an academic calendar for your campus. Which of the following holidays of different cultural groups are recognized and treated as holidays by suspension of normal campus and community operations?

Christmas	Passover	Saka
Yom Kippur	Kwanzaa	Hegira
Elderly Day	Seleicodae	Martin Luther King, Jr. Day
Hanukkah	Easter	

What do calendars communicate about the place of different groups in a culture?

DIVERSITY

Racial Bias Starts Early

Is racial bias still a problem in America? According to an ABC News and *Washington Post* poll reported in January 2009, that depends on whom you ask. Twice as many blacks as whites think racism is still a problem, whereas twice as many whites as blacks think racial equality has been achieved (Blow, 2009).

What can explain the major discrepancy between blacks' and whites' views? One explanation is that most whites believe they are not racially biased but still hold implicit biases. That's the idea behind Project Implicit, a virtual lab managed by scholars at Harvard, the University of Virginia, and the University of Washington. After six years of testing people's biases, the findings are clear: 75% of whites have an implicit pro-white/anti-black bias. While some blacks also harbor implicit racial biases—some pro-black and some pro-white—blacks are the least likely of all races to have any racial bias (Blow, 2009).

Another question studied by scientists at Project Implicit is when racial prejudice starts. According to Mahzarin Banaji, a professor at Harvard, it starts at much earlier ages than most of us think. She has devoted her career to studying hidden and often subtle biases and attitudes. According to Banaji's research, children as young as 3 years old have the same level of bias as adults (Fogg, 2008). If you'd like to learn more about Project Implicit or take tests to determine if you harbor implicit racial biases, go to the book's online resources for this chapter and click on WebLink 8.1.

Standpoint theory illuminates the importance of social communities. **Standpoint theory** claims that social groups within a culture distinctively shape members' perspectives—their perceptions, identities, expectations, and so forth. However, belonging to a particular social community does not necessarily lead to a **standpoint**, which is political awareness of the social, symbolic, and material circumstances of the community and the larger power dynamics that hold those circum- stances in place (McClish & Bacon, 2002; Wood, 2009). One can be a mem- ber of a social community and have per- spective and experience shaped by that community without becoming conscious of the social structures and practices that define the community as outside of the mainstream. When a member of a social community develops political aware- ness of the forces that create inequity, then that person has a standpoint. Race, gender, class, and sexual orientation are primary social communities in Western culture.

In an early discussion of standpoint, philosopher Georg Wilhelm Friedrich Hegel (1807) pointed out that stand- points reflect power positions in society. To illustrate, he noted that masters and

DIVERSITY

If You Woke Up Tomorrow

How would your life change if you woke up tomorrow and discovered you were of a different race or sex or gender identity or sexual orientation than you were went you went to sleep?

That's pretty much what happened to Gregory Howard Williams. Until age 10, Gregory lived in Virginia with his white middle-class family. At age 10, however, he learned he was black—his father was a light-skinned man of African descent, which was why Gregory also appeared white. When Gregory learned he was black and began living as a black man, his whole life changed.

Read his stirring account of the changes in his life in his autobiography, *Life on the Color Line: The True Story of a White Boy Who Discovered He Was Black*. Go to the book's online resources for this chapter and click on WebLink 8.2 to learn more about Gregory Williams' life.

slaves perceive slavery very differently. Extending Hegel's point, we can see that those in positions of power have a vested interest in preserving the system that gives them privileges. Therefore, they are unlikely to perceive its flaws and inequities. On the other hand, those who are disadvantaged by a system are able to see inequities and discrimination (Wood, 1993a, 1993d, 2013).

Nonverbal communication often reflects the perspective of dominant groups. For example, the dominance of people without disabilities is reflected in the number of buildings that do not have ramps or bathroom facilities for people who use wheelchairs, and public presentations that do not include signers for people with hearing limitations. Many campus and business buildings feature portraits of white men but few of women or people of color. Mostafa's commentary illustrates how his standpoint affects his perceptions of his school.

 Mostafa

I went to a black college for two years before transferring here, and it's like two different worlds. There, I saw a lot of brothers and sisters all the time, and I had black teachers. There were portraits of black leaders in buildings and black magazines in the bookstore. Here, I've had only one black teacher, and I see 50 whites for every one black on campus. I've yet to see a black person's portrait hung in any campus building, and I have to go to specialty stores to buy black magazines. The whole atmosphere on this campus communicates, "White is right."

Of the many social communities, gendered communities have been most extensively studied. Because we know more about gender than about other social communities, we'll explore gender as a particular example of a social community. However, the principles and patterns that characterize gendered social communities also apply to other social communities.

Scholars have investigated the communication of people socialized in different gender communities. One of the earliest studies reported that children's play is sex segregated, that boys and girls tend to play different kinds of games (Maltz & Borker, 1982). Games that girls favor, such as house and school, involve few players, require talk to negotiate how to play because there aren't clear-cut guidelines, and depend on cooperation, sensitivity, and communication among players (Goodwin, 2006). Baseball, soccer, and war, which are typical boys' games, require more players and have clear goals and rules, so less talk is needed to play. Most boys' games are competitive, both between teams and for individual status within teams (Pollack, 2000; Rudman & Glick, 2008). Interaction in games teaches boys and girls distinct understandings of why, when, and how to use talk.

Research on gendered patterns of communication reveals that the rules we learn through play remain with many of us as we grow older. For instance, women's talk generally is more expressive and focused on feelings and relationships, whereas men's talk tends to be more instrumental, assertive, and competitive (Guerrero, Jones, & Boburka, 2006; Leaper & Ayres, 2007; McGuffey & Rich, 2004; Mulac, 2006; Wood, 2001b, 2001c, 2013). Many women favor management styles that are more collaborative than those typical of men (Eagly, Johannesen-Schmidt, & van Engen, 2003). In personal relationships, women tend to be more interested in talking about relationship issues than men are.

Another general gender difference is what each gender tends to perceive as the center of a relationship. For many men who were socialized in masculine communities, activities tend to be a key foundation of friendships and romantic relationships (Inman, 1996; Swain, 1989; Wood & Inman, 1993). Thus, men who are socialized in masculine communities typically build and sustain friendships by doing things together (playing soccer, watching sports) and doing things for one another. For many women who are socialized in feminine communities, communication is the crux of relationships. Communication is not only a means to other ends but also an end in itself (Acitelli, 1993; Duck & Wood, 2006; Riessman, 1990).

Although we have focused on gender to illustrate how social communities shape communication, gender isn't the only social community that affects how people communicate. Research finds that communication patterns vary between social classes. For example, lower income people tend to live closer to and rely more on extended families than middle- and upper-income people do (Acker, 2005; Cancian, 1989). Different racial and ethnic groups also teach their members distinctive ways of interacting. Communication scholar Mark Orbe (1994) describes United States society as still, in many ways, divided by race. Research also suggests that African Americans generally communicate more assertively than European Americans (Johnson, 2000; Orbe & Harris, 2001). What some African Americans perceive as authentic, powerful exchanges may be viewed as confrontational by people from different social communities because the latter learned different rules for what counts as wit and what counts as antagonism. Keep in mind that these are generalizations; they do not describe the communication of all blacks or all whites.

 Michelle

> I'm offended when I read that blacks communicate differently from whites. I don't, and neither do a lot of my black friends. Both of my parents were professionals, and I attended good schools, including a private one for two years. I speak the same way whites do. When the author of our book says blacks engage in call and response or talk differently from whites, it makes it sound like blacks are different from whites—like we don't know how to communicate like they do. If the author isn't black, how does she know how we communicate?

Michelle wrote her comment after reading a previous edition of this book. She's correct that not all blacks communicate the same way and not all blacks communicate differently from whites, who also don't communicate in a uniform way. What you've read about the communication patterns of African Americans or other social groups is based on research, much of which was conducted by scholars who are members of the groups described. I include this research because many minority students have complained to me about textbooks that present only middle-class white communication patterns and present those as standard or correct. This point of view is reflected in Jason's comment, which he wrote after reading the same book Michelle criticized.

 Jason

> This is the first time since being at this school that I've seen blacks really included in a textbook or a class, other than my Af-Am classes. I think that's good, like it affirms my identity as a black. If I have to study how whites communicate, why shouldn't they learn how I communicate and why I communicate that way? I think we're all broadened if we know more about more kinds of people and how they think and act and talk.

In this book, I include credible research on a variety of social groups so that we understand a range of ways in which people communicate. Yet it's critical to remember that statements about any group's communication are generalizations, not universal truths. Each of us communicates in some ways that are consistent with the patterns of particular social communities to which we belong, and in other ways our communication departs from norms for those communities. In part, that is because we belong to many groups. Michelle is not only black (a racial–ethnic group) but also upper-middle class (a socioeconomic group). Jason is also black, and he is from a working-class family. This may shed light on why Jason identifies with what African American scholars report as traditional black communication patterns and why Michelle does not. Similarly, descriptions of European American communication are not equally true of European Americans who belong to the upper class and the lower class.

Dimensions of Cultures and Social Communities

Geert Hofstede (1991, 2001; Hofstede et al., 2010), a Dutch anthropologist and social psychologist, provided insight into the perspectives, attitudes, and behavioral patterns that distinguish cultures. Before becoming a faculty member, Hofstede worked at IBM where he trained managers and supervised personnel research. In this role, he conducted more than 100,000 employee opinion surveys at IBM branches in countries all over the world. Hofstede noticed that there were clear differences among IBM employees in different cultures. He left IBM to study the data and was able to identify five key dimensions that vary among cultures.

Individualism/Collectivism

The dimension of **individualism/collectivism** refers to the extent to which members of a culture understand themselves as part of and connected to their families, groups, and cultures. In cultures high in collectivism (Pakistan, China), people's identity is deeply tied to their groups, families, and clans. In cultures high in individualism (United States, Australia), people tend to think of themselves as individuals who act relatively independently.

Communication scholar, Stella Ting-Toomey has studied cultural differences in what she calls face, which includes individual and cultural facets of identity. For instance, individual facets of your identity include your major or profession and your tastes in music whereas cultural facets of identity include whether you see yourself more as an individual or a member of families, groups, and your culture. Ting-Toomey (2005) reports that in collectivist cultures, the face of the group is more important than the face any individual in that culture or other group. In individualist cultures, the face of the individual is more important than the face of the group.

Uncertainty Avoidance

Uncertainty avoidance refers to the extent to which people want to avoid ambiguity and vagueness. In some cultures (Poland, South Korea), people like to have everything spelled out very explicitly in order to avoid misunderstandings. Yet, in other cultures (Hong Kong, Sweden), uncertainty is more tolerated and expectations are less set since surprises may happen.

Power Distance

The third dimension of culture is **power distance**, which refers to the size of the gap between people with high and low power and the extent to which that is regarded as normal. Social hierarchies exist in all cultures, but how they are understood and whether they are accepted varies widely. In some cultures (India, China), the distance between high and low power is wider than others, making for a society in which people respect the powerful, and there is lower expectation of movement between classes, castes, or levels. In cultures where power distance is low (New Zealand, Norway), people tend to expect that those in power will have earned it, rather than simply gaining power by virtue of position.

Masculinity/Femininity

The fourt*h dimension of cultural is* **masculinity/femininity** (sometimes called aggressiveness). This dimension refers to the extent to which a culture values aggressiveness, competitiveness, looking out for yourself, and dominating others and nature, (which are typically associated with men) versus gentleness, cooperation, and taking care of others and living in harmony with the natural world, which tend to be associated with women. In cultures that are higher in femininity (Netherlands, Norway), men and women are more gentle, cooperative, and caring. In cultures that are higher in masculinity (Japan, Germany), however, men are more aggressive and competitive. In highly masculine cultures, women may also be competitive and assertive, but generally they are less so than men.

Long Term/Short Term Orientation

The final dimension was not included in Hofstede's original work, but he added it later when it became clear to him that cultures varied how long term their orientations are. **Long term/short term orientation** refers to the extent to which members of a culture think about long term (history and future) versus short term (present). Long-term planning, thrift, and industriousness and respect for elders and ancestors are valued in cultures with a long term orientation (most Asian countries). In contrast, living for the moment, not saving for a rainy day, and not having as much respect for elders and ancestors are more likely to be found in cultures with a short term orientation (Australia, Germany). The Long Term end of the continuum is associated with what are sometimes called Confucian values, although cultures not historically connected with this influence can also have a Long Term orientation. This value is not just about future—it is also about respect for one's ancestors and plans and hopes for those who follow.

These five dimensions help us understand key differences among cultures and social communities.

Relationships between Culture and Communication

Communication is closely linked to culture because communication expresses, sustains, and alters culture (Healey & O'Brien, 2004; Jandt, 2009; Schaller & Crandall, 2004). Your culture directly shapes how you communicate, teaching you whether and when interrupting is appropriate, how much eye contact is polite, and how much distance should be kept between people. We are not born knowing how, when, and to whom to speak, just as we are not born with attitudes about cooperating or competing. We acquire attitudes as we interact with others, and we then reflect cultural teachings in the way we communicate.

To gain a deeper understanding of how culture and communication influence each other, we will discuss four central relationships between culture and communication.

We Learn Culture in the Process of Communicating

We don't study our native culture to learn how to behave appropriately. Instead, we learn a culture's perspectives and rules during the process of communicating. By observing and interacting with others and being exposed to mass communication, we learn language (the word *dog*) and what it means (a pet to love, a working animal, or food to eat). In other words, in learning language we learn the values of our culture. Children aren't born knowing that they should respect their elders or worship youth; they aren't born thinking that people should wear dresses and suits or saris; at birth, they don't perceive piercing or tattoos as attractive or ugly; they don't enter the world thinking of themselves as individuals or members of groups. We learn cultural values and norms in the process of communicating with others.

From the moment of birth, we begin to learn the beliefs, values, and norms of our society (Cummings, 2009; Schaller & Crandall, 2004). You learn to respect your elders or to devalue them by how you see others communicate with older people, how you hear others refer to older people, and how the media portray older citizens. We learn what ideal bodies are from media and from others' talk about people of various physical proportions. As Intan points out, we also learn nonverbal communication from the culture into which we are socialized.

 Intan

> *Eye contact is the hardest part of learning American culture. In my home, it would be very rude to do that. We look away or down when talking so as not to give insult. In America, if I look down, it is thought I am hiding something or am dishonest. So I am learning to look at others when we talk, but it feels very disrespectful still to me.*

Both conscious and unconscious learning are continuous processes through which we learn language and internalize culture so that it is seamlessly part of who we are and how we see the world. As we learn language, we learn cultural values that are encoded in language.

Communication Is a Primary Indicator of Culture

One of the best indicators that a culture or social community exists is communication (Hecht, Collier, & Ribeau, 1993). Because we learn to communicate in the process of interacting with others, people from different cultures use communication in different ways and attach different meanings to communicative acts.

To illustrate how communication reflects and expresses culture, we'll discuss the individualism/collectivism dimension of culture. Communication reflects and expresses the individualistic or collectivist values of cultures. For example, many Asian languages include numerous words to describe particular relationships: my grandmother's brother, my father's uncle, my youngest son, my oldest daughter. This linguistic focus reflects the cultural emphasis on collective life and family relationships (Triandis, 1990). Reflecting the Western emphasis on individualism, the English language has fewer words to describe the range of kinship bonds. As Maria points out in her commentary, people from individualistic cultures often misunderstand the values and choices of people from collectivist cultures.

Maria

I get hassled by a lot of girls on campus about being dependent on my family. They say I'm too close to my folks and my grandparents and aunts and uncles and cousins. But what they mean by "too close" is I'm closer with my family than most whites are. It's a white standard they're using, and it doesn't fit me. Strong ties with family and the community are important, good values we learn in Mexico.

Individualistic and collectivist cultures tend to cultivate distinct communication styles (Hall, 1981; Jandt, 2009; Samovar, Porter, & McDaniel, 2009, 2011). Individualistic cultures generally rely on a **low-context communication style**, which is very direct, explicit, and detailed. Because people are regarded as distinct individuals, communicators do not assume that others will share their meanings or values. Instead, everything must be spelled out carefully and clearly. Because self-expression and personal initiative are valued in individualistic cultures, argument and persuasion are perceived as appropriate (Chen & Starosta, 1998).

Collectivist cultures typically rely on a **high-context communication style**, which is indirect and undetailed and which conveys meanings more implicitly than explicitly. Because people are regarded as interconnected, it is assumed they are alike in terms of their values and understandings. Thus, there is no need to spell everything out. Instead, communicators assume that others will understand what isn't stated and will be able to use shared knowledge of situations and relationships to interpret vague statements. Also, in high-context cultures, a person's history (family, status in community) forms a context for understanding what a person says. This context is generally considered more important than the message itself (Duck & McMahon, 2009).

Consider a concrete example of the difference between high-context and low-context communication styles. A man using low-context communication style might invite friends to dinner this way: "Come to our home at 7 P.M. tomorrow, and we'll eat around 8:30. Feel free to bring your baby with you. When he gets tired, you can put him to bed in the guest room." A woman using a high-context communication style might invite the same friends to dinner this way: "Please come to our home tomorrow evening." The speaker using low-context spelled out everything—when to arrive, when to expect a meal, that the baby is invited, that there is a place for the baby to sleep, even that the invitation is for dinner. By contrast, the high-context

DIVERSITY

Proverbs Express Cultural Values

Every culture has proverbs that express its values and pass them from one generation to the next. Following are some proverbs that reflect values in particular cultures (Samovar & Porter, 2004).

◆ "A zebra does not despise its stripes." Among the Masai of Africa, this saying encourages acceptance of things and oneself as they are.

◆ "Know the family and you will know the child." This Chinese proverb reflects the belief that individuals are less important than families.

◆ "The child has no owner." "It takes a whole village to raise a child." These African adages express the idea that children belong to whole communities, not just to biological parents.

◆ "Better to be a fool with the crowd than wise by oneself." "A solitary soul neither sings nor cries." These Mexican proverbs reflect a strong commitment to collectivism.

To learn about proverbs in other cultures, including Turkey and Palestine, go to the book's online resources for this chapter and click on WebLinks 8.3 and 8.4.

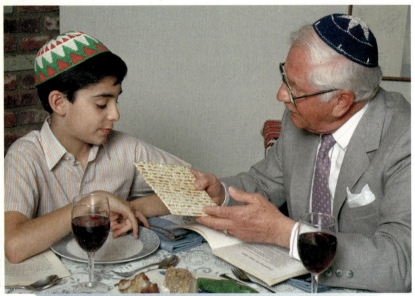

Passing tradition from one generation to the next is how cultures sustain themselves. In this photo, a Jewish elder instructs a young boy in Jewish traditions.

speaker assumed that the guests would share her understandings—being invited into a home in the evening implies that dinner will be served, that 7 P.M. is an appropriate time to arrive, that 8:30 is a typical time to eat dinner, that the baby is welcome, and that there will be a place for the baby to sleep. For people who have learned a high-context communication style, the low-context style seems overly literal and seems to belabor the obvious. (Who wouldn't serve dinner to guests in the evening? Guests' families are always included in invitations.)

Communication Expresses and Sustains Cultures

Communication simultaneously reflects and sustains cultural values. Each time we express cultural values, we also perpetuate them. When some Asian Americans avoid displaying emotions, they fortify and express the value of self-restraint and the priority of reason over emotion. When some Westerners argue, speak up for their ideas, and compete in conversations, they uphold the values of individuality and assertiveness. Communication, then, is a mirror of a culture's values and a primary means of keeping them woven into the fabric of everyday life.

The Western preoccupation with time and efficiency is evident in the abundance of words that refer to time (*hours, minutes, seconds, days, weeks*) and in common phrases such as "Let's not waste time." The value Westerners place on productivity may explain why Americans average only 13 days of vacation yearly while Italians average 42, British average 28, and Japanese average 25 (Love, 2011). In the United States, "The early bird gets the worm" implies that initiative is valuable, and "Nice guys finish last" suggests that winning is important and that it's more important to be aggressive than nice.

Communication Is a Source of Cultural Change

In addition to reflecting culture, communication is a source of change in cultures and social communities. Within in the United States, social communities have used communication to resist the mainstream's efforts to define their identity. Whenever a group says, "No, the way you describe me is wrong," that group initiates change in the cultural understandings.

Communication helps propel change by naming things in ways that shape how we understand them. For instance, the terms *environmental racism* and *environmental justice* were coined to name the practice of locating toxic waste dumps and other environmental hazards in communities where people tend to be poor and non-white. The verbal use of *google* was invented to refer to using a particular online search engine, Google. The term *sexual harassment* names a practice that certainly is not new, but for many years it was not labeled and not given social reality. Mary's commentary explains how important the label is.

Mary

It was 15 years ago, when I was just starting college, that a professor sexually harassed me, only I didn't know to call it that then. I felt guilty, like maybe I'd done something to encourage him, or I felt maybe I was overreacting to his kissing me and touching me. But I later learned the term. Now I have a name for what happened—a name that said he was wrong, not me. It was only then that I could let go of that whole business.

As a primary tool of social movements, communication prompts changes in cultural life. The Civil Rights and Black Power movements motivated black Americans to assert the value and beauty of black culture. Simultaneously, African Americans used communication to persuade non-black citizens to rethink their attitudes and practices. Marches for gay pride and AIDS awareness challenge social attitudes about gay men and lesbians just as demonstrations for immigrants' rights challenge attitudes toward immigrants.

In addition to instigating change directly, communication accompanies other kinds of cultural change. Antibiotics had to be explained to medical practitioners and to a general public that believed infections were caused by fate, not by viruses and bacteria. Ideas and practices borrowed from one culture must be translated into other cultures; for example, the Japanese system of management has been adapted to fit the culture of many U.S. companies. Calamities also must be defined and explained: Are increasing natural disasters such as tsunamis and flooding the result of global climate change or the anger of the gods? Did we lose the war because we had a weak military or because our cause was wrong? Do technologies enrich cultural life or diminish it? Cultures use communication to define what change means and implies for social life.

Both an overall culture and particular social communities shape our perceptions and ways of communicating. Yet we can learn to appreciate different cultural systems and the diverse forms of communication they foster, as well as the ways in which multiple social identities shape our communication. Doing so enables us to adapt our communication effectively in response to the diverse people with whom we interact.

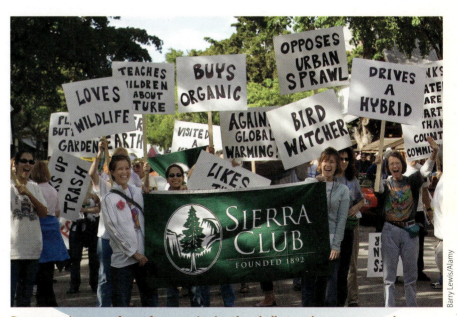

Barry Lewis/Alamy

Demonstrations are a form of communication that challenges the status quo and promotes change in cultural life.

Guidelines for Adapting Communication to Diverse Cultures and Social Communities

To participate effectively in a culturally diverse world, we must adapt our communication to different contexts and people. Effective adaptation occurs when we tailor our verbal and nonverbal symbols and our ways of perceiving, creating climates, listening, and responding. We'll consider four guidelines for adapting communication in ways that are sensitive to different cultures and communities.

Engage in Person-Centered Communication

When we encounter unfamiliar customs, we experience uncertainty—what does this behavior mean? What's going to happen next? What should I do in response? **Uncertainty reduction theory** explains that because we find uncertainty uncomfortable, we try to reduce it. To do this, we seek information—we ask questions, we listen and observe others, we look for patterns in interaction. As we learn more about values and norms in a culture or social community, we become more comfortable interacting with members of that culture or community. In turn, as we interact more, we learn more about what members of a culture believe and value and the kind of behaviors that are appropriate in the context.

Reducing uncertainty by learning about other people and cultures allows us to engage in person-centered communication. From our discussion in Chapter 3, you'll recall that person-centeredness involves recognizing another person's perspective and taking that into account as you communicate. For instance, it's advisable to refrain from using idioms when talking with someone for whom English is a second language. Competent communicators adapt to the perspectives of those with whom they interact.

Person-centeredness requires us to negotiate between awareness of group tendencies and equal awareness of individual differences. For example, we should realize that Asian Americans generally are less assertive than European Americans, yet we shouldn't assume that every Asian American will be deferential or that every European American will be assertive. What describes a group accurately may not apply equally to every member of the group. A good guideline is to assume that each person with whom you communicate fits some, but not other, generalizations about his or her social communities.

Respect Others' Feelings and Ideas

Has anyone ever said to you, "You shouldn't feel that way"? If so, you know how infuriating it can be to be told that your feelings aren't valid, appropriate, or acceptable. Equally destructive is to be told our thoughts are wrong. When someone says, "How can you think something so stupid?" we feel disconfirmed.

One of the most disconfirming forms of communication is speaking for others when they are able to speak for themselves (Alcoff, 1991; Wood, 1998). Marsha Houston (2004, p. 124), an accomplished communication scholar, explains how claiming understanding can diminish a person. She writes that white women should never tell African

American women that they understand their experiences as black women. Here's Houston's explanation:

> I have heard this sentence completed in numerous, sometimes bizarre, ways, from "because sexism is just as bad as racism," to "because I watch *The Cosby Show*," to "because I'm also a member of a minority group. I'm Jewish... Italian... overweight...." Similar experiences should not be confused with the same experience; my experience of prejudice is erased when you identify it as "the same" as yours.

Generally, it's rude and disempowering to speak for others. Just as we should not speak for others, we should not assume we understand how they feel or think. As we have seen, distinct experiences and cultural backgrounds make each of us unique. We seldom completely grasp what another person feels or thinks. Although it is supportive to make an effort to understand others, it isn't supportive to presume that we understand experiences we haven't had, as Susan's commentary points out.

 Susan

I hate it when people tell me they understand what it's like to have a learning disability. For one thing, there are a lot of learning disabilities, and I resent being lumped in a broad category. For another thing, if someone doesn't have dyslexia, which is my problem, they don't know what it means. They have no idea what it's like to see letters scrambled or wonder if you are seeing words right. People shouldn't say "I understand" what they haven't experienced.

Respecting what others say about their thoughts and feelings is a cornerstone of effective communication. Ethical communicators do not attempt to speak for others and do not assume they fully understand others' experiences. If you don't understand what others say or do, ask them to explain. This shows that you are interested and respect their experience. It also paves the way for greater understanding between people of different backgrounds.

Resist Ethnocentric Bias

Without thinking, most of us rely on our home culture and social communities as the standards for judging others. This can interfere with good communication. **Ethnocentrism** is the tendency to regard ourselves and our way of life as normal and superior to other people and other ways of life. Literally, ethnocentrism means to put our ethnicity (*ethno*) at the center (*centrism*) of the universe.

Ethnocentrism encourages negative judgments of anything that differs from our ways. In extreme form, ethnocentrism can lead one group of people to feel it has the right to dominate other groups and suppress other cultures. An abhorrent example of ethnocentrism was Nazi Germany's declaration that Aryans were the "master race," followed by the systematic genocide of Jewish people. Yet we need not look to such dramatic examples as Nazi Germany to find ethnocentrism. It occurs whenever we judge someone from a different culture as less sensitive, honest, ambitious, good, or civilized than people from our culture.

To reduce ethnocentrism, we should remember that what is considered normal and right varies between cultures. **Cultural relativism** recognizes that cultures vary in how they think and behave as well as in what they believe and value. Cultural relativism is not the same as moral relativism. We can acknowledge that a particular practice makes sense in its cultural context without approving of it. Cultural relativism reminds us that something that appears odd or even wrong to us may seem natural and right from the point of view of a different culture. This facilitates respect, even when differences exist.

Recognize That Adapting to Cultural Diversity Is a Process

Developing skill in intercultural communication takes time. We don't move suddenly from being unaware of how people in other cultures interact to being totally comfortable and competent in communication with them. Adapting to cultural diversity is a gradual process that takes time, experience with a variety of people, and a genuine desire to know and appreciate cultural differences.

SHARPEN YOUR SKILL

Becoming Self-Reflective about Your Culture

We can't resist ethnocentric bias unless we understand our own culture and social communities and the values that they attempt to instill in us. Earlier in this chapter, we identified proverbs that express values in non-Western cultures. Now, we'll do the reverse by looking at common sayings and proverbs in the United States. Read the adages below, and identify what they reflect about cultural values in the United States.

◆ "You can't be too rich or too thin."

◆ "A stitch in time saves nine."

◆ "A watched pot never boils."

◆ "It's the squeaky wheel that gets the grease."

◆ "You've made your bed, now lie in it."

What other sayings can you think of that express key United States values?

Responses to diversity range from total rejection and disapproval to full participation in a different culture's communication styles. At particular times in our lives, we may find ourselves adopting different responses to diversity or to specific forms of diversity. We may also find that our responses to people with different cultural backgrounds evolve over the course of our relationships with them. That's natural in the overall process of recognizing and responding to diversity in life.

Resistance

A common response to diversity is **resistance**, which occurs when we reject the beliefs of particular cultures or social communities. Without reflection, many people evaluate others based on the standards of their own culture. Some people, including Maggie (see her commentary), think their judgments reflect universal truths. They aren't aware that they are imposing the arbitrary yardstick of their particular culture and ignoring the yardsticks of other cultures. Devaluing whatever differs from our ways limits human experience and diminishes cultural life.

Maggie

I'm tired of being told I should "appreciate" difference. In most cases, I don't. If people from other countries want to live in America, they should act and talk like Americans. They should adapt, not me.

Resistance may be expressed in many ways. Hate crimes pollute campuses and the broader society. Denial of other cultures leads to racial slurs, anti-Semitic messages, and homophobic attacks. Resistance may also motivate members of a culture or social community to associate only with each other and to remain unaware of commonalities among people with diverse backgrounds. Insulation within a single culture occurs in both majority and minority groups.

Members of social groups may also resist and deny their group identities in an effort to fit into the mainstream. **Assimilation** occurs when people give up their ways and adopt the ways of the dominant culture. Philosopher Peter Berger (1969) calls this *surrendering* because it involves giving up an original cultural identity for a new one. For many years, assimilation was the dominant response of immigrants to the United States. The idea of America as a "melting pot" encouraged newcomers to melt into the mainstream by surrendering whatever made them different from native-born citizens.

More recently, the melting pot metaphor has been criticized as undesirable because it erases the unique heritages of people who come to America. Jesse Jackson proposed the alternative metaphor of the family quilt. This metaphor portrays the United States as a country in which diverse groups' values and customs are visible, as are the individual squares in a quilt, and at the same time each group contributes to a larger whole, just as each square contributes to a quilt's overall beauty.

Some people use another form of resistance to provoke change in cultural practices and viewpoints. For example, heterosexuals who refuse to refer to their partners as "spouses" are resisting mainstream culture's refusal to grant legal status to gay and lesbian commitments. When culturally advantaged people resist and challenge the devaluation of disadvantaged groups, they can be powerful agents of change.

Tolerance

A second response to diversity is **tolerance**, which is an acceptance of differences whether or not one approves of or even understands them. Tolerance involves

DIVERSITY

World Traveling

María Lugones is a professor of philosophy at the State University of New York's Binghamton campus. Throughout her career, she has emphasized the value of what she calls "world travelling" (1992). By this, she means traveling to worlds other than our own. Lugones (2006) notes that many people are "border dwellers." They live in the borderlands in between cultures. For instance, Hispanics, Latinas, and Latinos who have moved to the United States often live between the culture in which they were born and raised and the culture where they now live. Students who study abroad are border dwellers for a short period of time. Lugones emphasizes the importance of world traveling, or "border crossing," as a way to experience diversity in values, material conditions, people, and so forth. She believes that we are all enriched by traveling to others' worlds.

respecting others' rights to their ways even though we may think their ways are wrong, bad, or offensive. Judgment still exists, but it's not actively imposed on others. Tolerance is open-mindedness in accepting the existence of differences, yet it is less open-minded in perceiving the value of alternative lifestyles and values. Although tolerance is not as divisive as resistance, it does not actively foster a community in which people appreciate diversity and learn to grow from encountering differences.

Understanding

Actor Matt Damon recently commented, "I think many of our problems as a country would be solved if people had thick passports." Currently approximately 20% of Americans have passports (Overheard, 2008, p. 3E). What Damon meant is that traveling to other cultures and experiencing different perspectives would give us greater understanding of differences. Damon's comment reflects a third response to diversity, which is **understanding** that differences are rooted in cultural teachings and that no cultural teachings are intrinsically best or right. This response builds on the idea of cultural relativism, which we discussed earlier. Rather than assuming that whatever differs from our ways is a deviation from a universal standard (ours), a person who understands realizes that diverse values, beliefs, norms, and communication styles are rooted in distinct cultural perspectives.

People who respond to diversity with understanding might notice that a Japanese person doesn't hold eye contact but would not assume that the Japanese person was devious. Instead, an understanding person would try to learn what eye contact means in Japanese society in order to understand the behavior in its native cultural context. Curiosity, rather than judgment, dominates in this stage, as we make active efforts to understand others in terms of the values and traditions of their cultures.

Respect

Once we move beyond judgment and begin to understand the cultural basis for ways that differ from ours, we may come to **respect** differences. We can appreciate the distinct validity and value of placing family above self, of arranged marriage, and of feminine and masculine communication styles. We don't have to adopt others' ways in order to respect them on their terms.

Respect allows us to acknowledge genuine differences between groups yet remain anchored in the values and customs of our culture (Simons, Vázquez, & Harris, 1993). Learning about people who differ from us increases our understanding of them and thus our ability to communicate effectively with them. What is needed to respect others is the ability to see them and what they do on their terms, not ours. In other words, respect avoids ethnocentrism.

Participation

A final response to diversity is **participation**, in which we incorporate some practices and values of other groups into our own lives. More than other responses, participation encourages us to develop skills for participating in a multicultural world in which all of us can take part in some of each other's customs. Harvard professor Henry Louis Gates (1992) believes that the ideal society is one in which we build a common civic culture that celebrates both differences and commonalities.

People who respond to diversity by participating learn to be **multilingual**, which means they are able to speak and understand more than one language or more than one group's ways of using language. Many people are already at least bilingual (also termed *code switching*). Many African Americans know how to operate in mainstream Caucasian society and in their distinct ethnic communities (Orbe, 1994). Bilingualism, or code switching, is also practiced by many Asian Americans, Mexican Americans, lesbians, gay men, and members of other groups that are simultaneously part of a dominant and a minority culture (Gaines, 1995).

My partner, Robbie, and I have learned how to use both feminine and masculine communication styles. He was socialized to be assertive, competitive, and analytical in conversation, whereas I learned to be more expressive, cooperative, and relationship oriented. When we were first a couple, we were often frustrated by differences in our communication styles. I perceived him as insensitive to feelings and overly linear in his conversational style. He perceived me as being too focused on relationship issues and inefficient in moving from problems to solutions. Gradually, each of us learned to understand and then respect the other's ways of communicating. Still later, we came to participate in each other's styles, and now both of us are fluent in both languages. Not only has this improved communication between us, but it has made us more competent communicators in general.

People reach different stages in their abilities to respond to particular cultures and social communities. The different responses to cultural diversity that we've discussed represent parts of a process of learning to understand and adapt to diverse cultural groups. In the courses of our lives, many of us will move in and out of various responses as we interact with people from multiple cultures. At specific times, we may find we are tolerant of one cultural group, respectful of another, and able to participate in yet others.

SUMMARY

In Chapter 1, we learned that communication is systemic. Because it is systemic, it must be understood as existing within and influenced by multiple contexts. In this chapter, we've focused on cultures and social communities as particularly important systems that shape and are shaped by communication.

Five principles summarize the relationships between culture and communication. First, we learn a culture in the process of communicating with others. Second, language is a primary indicator that a culture exists. Third, multiple social communities may coexist within a single culture, and people may belong to multiple cultures and social communities. Fourth, communication both reflects and sustains cultures. Fifth, communication is a potent force for changing cultural life.

The final section of this chapter identified four guidelines for communicating effectively in a socially diverse world. The most fundamental guideline is to engage in person-centered communication, which enables us to adapt to the perspectives and communication styles of others. Extending this, the second guideline is to respect what others present as their feelings and ideas. In most situations, speaking for others is presumptuous, and disregarding what they express is rude. The third guideline is to resist ethnocentrism, which is the greatest threat to effective cross-cultural communication. Finally, we learned that adapting to diversity is a process. We may find that our response to diversity changes as we grow personally and as we develop relationships with people who differ from us. Moving beyond the belief that our ways are the only right ways allows us to understand, respect, and sometimes participate in a diverse world and to enlarge ourselves in the process.

Although this chapter has focused on differences between people, it would be a mistake to be so aware of differences that we overlook our commonalities. No matter what culture we belong to, we all have feelings, dreams, ideas, hopes, fears, and values. Our common humanity transcends many of our differences.

REVIEW, REFLECT, EXTEND

The Reflect, Discuss, and Apply Questions that follow will help you review, reflect on, and extend the information and ideas presented in this chapter. These resources, and a diverse selection of additional study tools, are also available online at the CourseMate for *Communication Mosaics*. Your CourseMate includes a student workbook, WebLinks, TED Talks hyperlinks and activities, chapter glossary and flashcards, interactive video activities, Speech Builder Express, and InfoTrac College Edition. For more information or to access this book's online resources, visit **www.cengagebrain.com**.

KEY CONCEPTS

assimilation, 171
cultural relativism, 170
culture, 157
ethnocentrism, 169
high-context communication style, 165
individualism/collectivism, 162
long term/short term orientation, 163
low-context communication style, 165
masculinity/femininity, 163
multilingual, 173
participation, 173

power distance, 162
resistance, 171
respect, 172
social community, 158
standpoint, 159
standpoint theory, 159
tolerance, 171
uncertainty avoidance, 162
uncertainty reduction theory, 168
understanding, 172

For Further Reflection And Discussion

1. Identify ways that you do and do not fit generalizations for communication by members of your sex that were discussed in this chapter. What about you—race, ethnicity, sexual orientation, etc.—might explain the ways in which you depart from general tendencies identified by researchers?

2. Continue the exercise started on page 170 by listing common sayings or adages in your culture. Decide what each saying reflects about the beliefs, values, and concerns of your culture.

3. As a class, discuss the tension between recognizing individuality and noting patterns common in specific social groups. Is it possible to recognize both that people have standpoints in social groups and that members of any group vary? You might recall the concept of totalizing from Chapter 4 to assist your consideration of this issue.

Recommended Resources

1. Fern Johnson. (2000). *Speaking culturally: Language diversity in the United States.* Thousand Oaks, CA: Sage. This book provides excellent historical information about different groups in the United States and the different ways in which they understand and use language.

2. Lena Williams. (2002). *It's the little things: Everyday interactions that anger, annoy, and divide the races.* New York: Harvest/

Harcourt. This book offers clear examples of communication misunderstandings between blacks and whites.

3. Edward Schieffelin and Robert Crittenden's *Like People in a Dream* is a richly told account of first contact between two cultures. In 1935 white explorers went into interior parts of New Guinea where the indigenous people still used Stone Age tools.

EXPERIENCE COMMUNICATION CASE STUDY

The Job Interview

Apply what you've learned in this chapter by analyzing the following case study, using the accompanying questions as a guide. These questions and a video of the case study are also available online at your CourseMate for *Communication Mosaics.*

Mei-ying Yung is a graduating senior. Like many college students, Mei-ying loves technologies. Unlike many of her peers, however, she is particularly fascinated by programming. In her senior year, she developed and installed complex new programs to make advising more efficient and to reduce the frustration and errors in registration for courses. Although she has been in the United States for six years, in many ways Mei-ying reflects the Chinese culture where she was born and where she spent the first 15 years of her life. Today, Mei-ying is interviewing for a position at New Thinking, a fast-growing tech company that specializes in developing programs tailored to the needs of individual companies. The interviewer, Barton Hingham, is 32 years old and a native of California, where New Thinking is based. As the scenario opens, Ms. Yung walks into the small room in which Mr. Hingham is seated behind a desk. He rises to greet her and walks over with his hand outstretched to shake hers.

© Cengage Learning

Hingham: Good morning, Ms. Yung. I've been looking forward to meeting you. Your résumé is most impressive.

[Ms. Yung looks downward, smiles, and limply shakes Mr. Hingham's hand. He gestures to a chair, and she sits down in it.]

Hingham: I hope this interview will allow us to get to know each other a bit and decide whether there is a good fit between you and New Thinking. I'll be asking you some questions about your background and interests. And you should feel free to ask me any questions that you have. Okay?

Yung: Yes.

Hingham: I see from your transcript that you majored in computer programming and did very well. I certainly didn't have this many *A*s on *my* college transcript!

Yung: Thank you. I am very fortunate to have good teachers.

Hingham: Tell me a little about your experience in writing original programs for business applications.

Yung: I do not have great experience, but I have been grateful to help the college with some of its work.

Hingham: Tell me about how you've helped the college. I see you designed a program for advising. Can you explain to me what you did to develop that program?

Yung: Not really so much. I could see that much of advising is based on rules, so I only need to write the rules into a program so advisers could do their jobs more better.

Hingham: Perhaps you're being too modest. I've done enough programming myself to know how difficult it is to develop a program for something with as many details as advising. There are so many majors, each with different requirements and regulations. How did you program all of that variation?

Yung: I read the handbook on advising and the regulations on each major, and then programmed decision trees into an advising template. Not so hard.

Hingham: Well, that's exactly the kind of project we do at New Thinking. People come to us with problems in their jobs, and we write programs to solve them. Does that sound like the kind of thing you would enjoy doing?

Yung: Yes. I very much like to solve problems to help others.

Hingham: What was your favorite course during college?

Yung: They are all very valuable. I enjoy all.

Hingham: Did you have one course in which you did especially well?

Yung: [blushing, looking down] I would not say that. I try to do well in all my courses, to learn from them.

Later Barton Hingham and Molly Cannett, another interviewer for New Thinking, are discussing the day's interviews over dinner.

Cannett: Did you find any good prospects today?

Hingham: Not really. I thought I was going to be bowled over by this one woman—name's Mei-ying Yung—who has done some incredibly intricate programming on her own while in college.

Cannett: Sounds like just the kind of person we're looking for.

Hingham: I thought so, too, until the interview. She just didn't seem to have the gusto we want. She showed no confidence or initiative in the interview. It was like the transcript and the person were totally different.

Cannett: Hmmm, that's odd. Usually when we see someone who looks that good on paper, the interview is just a formality.

Hingham: Yeah, but I guess the formality is more important than we realized: Yung was a real dud in the interview. I still don't know what to make of it.

1. How does Mei-ying Yung's communication reflect her socialization in Chinese culture?

2. How could Mei-ying be more effective without abandoning the values of her native culture?

3. What could enhance Barton Hingham's ability to communicate effectively with people who were raised in non-Western cultures?

The true voyage of self-discovery lies not in seeking new landscapes but in having new eyes. Marcel Proust

9 Communication and Personal Identity

When I was eight years old, I thought I would grow up to be a novelist. By age 12, my parents had taught me to cook and bake, and it become clear to me that I would be a pastry chef. When I was 20 and in love with my college sweetheart, I realized I would be a stay-at-home wife and mother. When I was 22 years old and had parted ways with my college sweetheart, I was sure that I would be single and a teacher. Then I began graduate school and met Robbie, and I started to define myself as a scholar and teacher and a partner to Robbie. Today, I am not single, not a novelist, not a stay-at-home wife and mother, and not a pastry chef, although I do bake bread every week. My sense of who I am has changed as a result of experiences and people that have affected how I define myself.

How did you define yourself when you were 8, 12, and 20 years old? It's likely that your definition of yourself today is different from your definition of yourself at earlier times in your life. Our understanding of who we are changes as we experience new relationships, situations, and people. How you define yourself today is shaped by your interactions with others throughout your life. Similarly, the self you become in the future will change in response to people and experiences that lie ahead.

In this chapter, we will explore how the self is formed and how it changes in the process of communicating with others. First, we will define the self and discuss how interaction with others shapes who we are and how we see ourselves. Second, we will examine particular types of communication that influence our identities. The final section of the chapter discusses guidelines for continuing to enrich who you are.

FOCUS QUESTIONS

1. What role does communication play in developing personal identity?

2. How do others shape personal identity?

3. What types of communication affect your understanding of who you are?

4. How can you create a supportive context for your personal growth?

Understanding the Self

The **self** is an ever-changing system of perspectives that is formed and sustained in communication with others and ourselves. This definition highlights several important aspects of personal identity. First, it points out that the self consists of perspectives: views about ourselves, others, and social life that arise out of our experiences and interactions with others. Second, this definition emphasizes that the self is not static or fixed, but dynamic. Each of us evolves and changes throughout our lives. Third, the definition calls attention to the idea that perspectives on the self are a system, which, you will recall, means that all parts are interrelated. If one perspective on yourself—for instance, your religious perspective—changes, then other perspectives will also change—for instance, how you understand your role as a parent or woman or man. Finally, the definition highlights communication as a critically important influence on who we are and how we see ourselves.

 Tim

> *When I became a Christian, everything about me changed. I realized I had not been as Jesus would want in my relationships with my parents or my girlfriend. I also saw that I had not chosen a profession that served Christ, so I changed my major from business to education. I gave up some of the friends I had and made some new friends who share my beliefs.*

The Self is Multidimensional

The term *self* is a singular noun, which implies it is a single entity. Yet, there are many facets to the self. You have a physical self that includes your height, weight, body type, abilities and disabilities, and the color of your skin, hair, and eyes. You also have an emotional self that reflects how sensitive you are, whether you have a temper, and so forth. Your cognitive self includes your intelligence and intellectual aptitudes. Roles such as son, daughter, brother, sister, friend, aunt, parent and neighbor are part of your social self.

The distinguished theorist George Herbert Mead observed that the self is not innate but is acquired in the process of communicating with others. We aren't born with clear understandings of who we are and what our value is. Instead, we develop these understandings in the process of communicating with others who tell us who we are, what we should and should not do, how valuable we are, and what is expected of us. As we internalize others' perspectives, we come to perceive ourselves through their eyes.

Mead identified two kinds of others whose perspectives influence how we see ourselves and what we believe is possible and desirable for us. The first perspective is that of society, as a whole (Mead called this the **"generalized other"**). The second perspective is that of particular individuals who are significant in our lives.

Society Shapes the Self

All societies have ways of classifying people, but the particular ways differ across cultures. In America, we do not categorize people into castes, although some cultures do. Westerners recognize only two sexes and genders, but there are cultures that acknowledge multiple genders (Gilley, 2006) and other societies that regard sex as changeable so a man can become a woman and vice versa (Bilefsky, 2008). Four key social categories recognized and considered important to identity in America today are race, gender, sexual orientation, and socio-economic class.

Race

In North America, race is considered a primary aspect of personal identity (González, Houston, & Chen, 2012). It is one of the first aspects of a person that we notice, and it is an aspect of identity that is shaped by broad cultural views. The race that has been privileged historically in the United States is Caucasian. In the early years of this country's life, some people considered it normal and right for white men to own black women, men, and children and to require them to work for no wages and in poor conditions. At that time, people also considered it natural that white men could vote but women and black men and women could not.

Although discrimination against people of color has declined since America's early days, Caucasian privilege continues. White children often have access to better schools with more resources than do children of African American or Hispanic/Latino/a heritage. The upper levels of government, education, and business are dominated by white men, whereas people of color and white women continue to fight for equal rights in admission, hiring, and advancement.

One key indication of white privilege is the assumption that white is the standard or normal race. People who are not white are often identified by their race (black congressman, Indian student), but whites seldom are (Baum, 2008; Roediger, 2006). A relatively new area of scholarship and teaching is Critical Whiteness Studies, which aims to make whiteness as visible and as open to analysis as any other race.

Race is one of the categories considered important in western culture.

Comstock (RF)/Jupiterimages

It's important to understand that race is socially constructed. What counts as "black" or "white" or any other racial category does not depend exclusively on genes or skin color. Instead, society defines the meaning of race (Morning, 2011). The word *white* wasn't used to describe race or identity until Europeans colonized the United States. They invented the label *white* as a way to increase solidarity among European settlers, who actually had varied ethnic backgrounds. By calling themselves white, these diverse people could gloss over differences among themselves and distinguish themselves from people they defined as non-whites. The first generations of Irish immigrants were not considered white (Negra, 2006).

Growing numbers of people have multiple racial and ethnic identities. More and more, multiracial individuals are challenging current categories of race and changing the cultural fabric of the nation ("Quick Facts," 2011; Brunsma, 2006). After a number of applicants to colleges complained about having to check a single category of race, the Common Application for colleges began allowing students to check all racial categories with which they identify (Schwartz & Dash, 2011).

DIVERSITY

Multiracialism

For many people, the question is not "What race or ethnicity are you?" but "What races or ethnicities are you?" Below are a few well-known Americans with multiracial heritage. You can probably add other names to the list.

Jennifer Beals – Actress, her father is black; her mother is white.

Mariah Carey – Singer/actress, her father is Venezuelan/African American; her mother is Irish.

Naomi Campbell – Model, her mother is Jamaican; her father is multiracial, at least partly Chinese.

Johnny Depp – Actor, he has acknowledged German, Irish, and Cherokee lineage.

Soledad O'Brien – Reporter/news anchor, her father is Australian (his parents are Irish, hence the surname O'Brien); her mother is a black Cuban.

Barack Obama – U.S. President, his father was Kenyan; his mother was white American.

Alicia Keys – Singer, her father is black; her mother is Italian.

Derek Jeter – Baseball player, his father is black; his mother is white.

Gender

Gender, which is the meaning society attaches to sex, is another category that is important in Western culture. Historically, Western society valued men more than women and considered men more rational, competent, and entitled to various social advantages and opportunities. In the 1800s, women in the United States as well as other Western cultures were not allowed to own property, enter professions, or vote.

Western society's gender prescriptions are less rigid today than they were in the past. Many men wear jewelry, tweeze their eyebrows, and use gels and spray to style their hair; many women wear work-out clothes and don't use makeup; and members of both sexes pursue high power careers and child rearing. Despite relaxation in social views, many gender prescriptions persist (Holmes, 2008; Wood, 2013). Girls and women are expected to be more caring, deferential, and cooperative than males, whereas boys and men are supposed to be more independent, assertive, and competitive than females. Beth's commentary indicates how others respond to her refusal to conform to social expectations for women. Men who refuse to conform to social views of masculinity and who are gentle and caring risk being called wimps or gay.

 Beth

I get along with kids, but I don't want to have any of my own. I don't really like kids. Everyone—my parents, my friends, my boyfriend—thinks that is so weird. But I know a lot of guys who don't like kids, and nobody thinks they're weird or anything.

Sexual Orientation

A third aspect of identity that is salient in Western culture is sexual orientation. Historically and today, heterosexuals are viewed as normal, and people who have other sexual orientations are often regarded as abnormal. Society communicates this viewpoint not only directly but also through privileges given to heterosexuals but denied to gay men, lesbians, bisexuals, and transgendered people. Most of us don't have to worry about where we go to the bathroom, but transsexualls often experience anger or resistance if they enter men's or women's bathrooms. Until recently, marriage was not an option between two men or two women who wanted to be life partners.

As with race and gender, social views of sexual orientation and gender identity and expression are not fixed but evolving. Society is also becoming more aware of a range of sexual orientations and gender identities. By 2010, nearly 300 colleges had added gender identity and expression to their nondiscrimination policies, many have designated some bathrooms as available to everyone, and many have passed gender-neutral housing policies so that transgender students are not forced to live with people with whom they don't identify (Tilsley, 2010).

A transgendered woman whom I know wrote the following reflection on what it felt like growing up biologically male when she felt female and how she feels now that she lives as a woman.

 Christine

> Being accepted as the girl I am has been my dream from age 4 or 5. Becoming a woman among women has been my dream for over 30 years. I was brought up in the Roman Catholic Church. From a very early age I disliked the Church. I'm sure a large part of my rejection was also due to "God" never answering my prayers to have me wake up as a girl. I cried so many nights as a child.
>
> Never did I appreciate how so quickly life-changing living as an integrated, authentic self would be. Never in my wildest dreams did I believe that "genetic" women ("gg's" as the community calls them—genetic girls) would so quickly embrace me, invite me into their private world, and want to help me find my place among them.

Socioeconomic Class

Socioeconomic class is a fourth facet of identity that Western society considers important. Socioeconomic class is difficult to pinpoint because it is not straightforwardly visible, as sex and race usually are. Even though we can't see or point to socioeconomic class, it profoundly shapes how we see ourselves and the lives we live. It affects the kinds of schools, jobs, friends, and lifestyle choices we see as possibilities for ourselves.

Socioeconomic class isn't just the amount of money a person has. It's a basic part of how we understand our place in the world and how we think, feel, and act (Acker, 2005; Lawless, 2012). Socioeconomic level affects which stores we shop in, the restaurants we patronize, the neighborhoods in which we live, and the schools we attend. It influences how we dress, including our views of what it means to be well dressed. It also influences who our friends are, what forms of recreation we enjoy, where we live and work, and what kind of vehicles we drive.

 Geneva

> I don't fit in at this college. That hits me in the face every day. I walk across campus and see girls wearing shoes that cost more than all four pairs I own. I hear students talking about restaurants and trips that I can't afford. Last week, I heard a guy complaining about being too broke to get a CD player for his car. I don't own a car. I don't know how to relate to these people who have so much money. Without my scholarship, I could never have come here. I know students here see the world differently than I do, and they see themselves as entitled to a lot more than I think I'm entitled to.

As Geneva's commentary indicates, socioeconomic class affects our ideas about what we need and what we are entitled to. For example, people with economic security have the resources and leisure time for therapy, yoga, retreats for spiritual development, and elite spas to condition their bodies. These are not feasible for people who are a step away from poverty. People in the middle and upper socioeconomic levels assume they will attend college and enter good professions, yet these often are not realistic options for working-class individuals. Guidance counselors may encourage academically gifted lower-income students to go to work or pursue vocational education after high school, whereas they routinely steer middle-income students of average ability toward colleges and professional careers. In such patterns, we see how social views shape our sense of who we are and the concrete realities of our lives.

Race, gender, sexual preference, and socioeconomic class are not independent of one another. Race interacts with gender, so Hispanic and black men face barriers not faced by white men, and women of color often experience double oppression and devaluation in our culture (Anzaldúa, 1999; Hernández & Rheman, 2002; Shenoy, 2012). Gays and lesbians are regarded differently by different races so being gay or lesbian may result in greater disadvantage for some races than others. Socioeconomic class and gender are also interlinked, with women far more likely than men to live at the poverty level (Engen, 2012; Hendrix, 2012; Wong, 2012).

In addition to race, gender, sexual preference, and socioeconomic level, society communicates other views that we may internalize. For instance, Western societies clearly value intelligence, competitiveness, individualism, and success. People, especially men, who conform to these social values receive more respect than those who don't. Mainstream Western societies also value slimness, particularly in Caucasian women and ambition and sexual prowess in men.

Broadly shared social perspectives are communicated by other people who have internalized those views and also by social institutions such as schools and media. For example, when we read popular magazines and watch television and films, we are inundated with messages about how we are supposed to look and act. Communication from media infuses our lives, repeatedly telling us how we are supposed to be, think, act, and feel. Access to the Web and the Internet expands the perspectives we encounter, which may become part of how we view the world and our place in it.

Individuals Shape the Self

In addition to the perspective of society as a whole, the self is shaped by the perspectives of individuals who matter to us. These people, called **particular others**, are especially significant to us and shape how we see ourselves. Mothers, fathers, siblings, peers, and, often, day-care providers are others who are significant to us in our early years. For some of us, particular others also include aunts, uncles, grandparents, and friends. In general, Hispanics, Latinas and Latinos, Asians and Asian Americans, and African Americans often have closer and larger extended families than European Americans. As Eugenio points out in his commentary, people other than parents can affect how children see themselves, others, and the social world.

 Eugenio

My father was not at home much when I was growing up. He worked in Merida, where the tourists go and spend money. My grandfather lived with us, and he raised me. He taught me to read and to count, and he showed me how to care for our livestock and repair the roof on our house after the rains each year. He is the one who talked to me about life and what matters. He is the one who taught me how to be a man.

Attachment Styles

One way that particular others shape our understanding of ourselves is through their **attachment styles**, patterns of care giving that teach us how to view ourselves and personal relationships. From his studies of interaction between parents and children, John Bowlby (1973, 1988) concluded that we learn attachment styles in our earliest relationships. These early relationships are especially important because they form expectations for later relationships (Bartholomew & Horowitz, 1991; Miller, 1993; Trees, 2006). Four distinct attachment styles have been identified (see Figure 9.1).

A **secure attachment style** develops when a child's primary caregiver responds in a consistently attentive and loving way to a child. In response, the child develops a positive sense of self-worth ("I am lovable") and a positive view of others ("People are loving and can be trusted"). People with secure attachment styles tend to be outgoing, affectionate, and able to handle the challenges and disappointments of close relationships without losing self-esteem. A majority of middle-class children in the United States are securely attached, but fewer children in lower economic classes are (Domingue & Mollen, 2009; Greenberg, 1997).

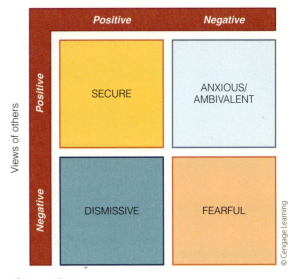

Figure 9.1   **Attachment Styles**

A **fearful attachment style** is cultivated when the primary caregiver communicates in negative, rejecting, or even abusive ways to a child. Children who are treated this way often infer that they are unworthy of love and that others are not loving. Thus, they learn to see themselves as unlovable and others as rejecting. Not surprisingly, this leads them to be apprehensive about relationships. Although they often want close bonds with others, they fear others will not love them and that they are not lovable. Thus, as adults they may avoid others or feel insecure in relationships. In some societies, members of certain groups learn early that they are less valuable than members of other groups. Zondi makes this point in her commentary.

 Zondi

> In South Africa, where I was born, I learned that I was not important. Most daughters learn this. My name is Zondomini, which means between happiness and sadness. The happiness is because a child was born. The sadness is because I am a girl, not a boy. I am struggling now to see myself as worthy as a woman.

A **dismissive attachment style** is also promoted by caregivers who are uninterested in, rejecting of, or abusive toward children. People who develop this style do not accept the caregiver's view of them as unlovable. Instead, they dismiss others as unworthy. Consequently, children develop a positive view of themselves and a low regard for others and relationships. This prompts a defensive tendency to view relationships as unnecessary and undesirable.

The final pattern is the **anxious/ambivalent attachment style**, which is the most complex of the four. Each of the other three styles results from some consistent pattern of treatment by a caregiver. The anxious/ambivalent style, however, is fostered by inconsistent treatment from the caregiver. Sometimes the adult is loving and attentive, yet at other times she or he is indifferent or rejecting. The caregiver's communication is not only inconsistent but also unpredictable. He or she may respond positively to something a child does on Monday and react negatively to the same behavior on Tuesday. Naturally, this unpredictability creates great anxiety in a child (Miller, 1993). Because children tend to assume that adults are right, children often assume that they themselves are the source of any problem. In her commentary, Noreen explains how inconsistent behaviors from her father confused and harmed her as a child.

 Noreen

When I was little, my father was an alcoholic, but I didn't know that then. All I knew was that sometimes he was nice to me, and sometimes he was really nasty. Once, he told me I was his sunshine, but later that same day he said he wished I'd never been born. Even though now I know the alcohol made him mean, it's still hard to feel I'm okay.

In adult life, people who have anxious/ambivalent attachment styles tend to be preoccupied with relationships. On one hand, they know that others can be loving, so they're drawn to relationships. On the other hand, they realize that others can hurt them and be unloving, so they are uneasy with closeness. Reproducing what the caregiver did, people with anxious/ambivalent attachment styles may act inconsistently. One day they invite affection, the next day they rebuff it and deny needing closeness.

The attachment style learned in a child's first close relationship tends to persist (Bartholomew & Horowitz, 1991; Belsky & Pensky, 1988; Bowlby, 1988; Guerrero, 1996). However, this is not inevitable. We can modify our attachment styles by challenging the unconstructive views of us that were communicated in our early years and by forming relationships, particularly romantic ones, that foster secure connections today (Banse, 2004; Neyer, 2002).

Life Scripts

Family members also shape our self-concepts by communicating **life scripts**, which are rules for living and identity (Berne, 1964; Harris, 1969, Steiner, 1994). Like scripts for plays, life scripts define our roles, how we are to play them, and the basic elements of what our families see as the right plot for our lives. Think back to your childhood to recall some of the identity scripts that your family communicated to you. Were you told, "Save your money for a rainy day," "Always help others," "Look out for yourself," or "Don't live on credit"? These are examples of identity scripts people learn in families.

Our basic identity scripts are formed early, probably by age five. This means that fundamental understandings of who

SHARPEN YOUR SKILL

Reflecting on Your Life Scripts

To take control of our lives, we must first understand influences that shape it currently. Identify the life scripts your parents taught you.

1. First, recall explicit messages your parents gave you about "who we are" and "who you are." Can you hear their voices telling you codes you were expected to follow?

2. Next, write down the scripts. Try to capture the language your parents used in teaching the scripts.

3. Now review each script. Which ones make sense to you today? Are you still following any that have become irrelevant or nonfunctional for you? Do you disagree with any of them?

4. Commit to changing scripts that aren't productive for you or that conflict with values you now hold.

In some cases, we can rewrite scripts. To do so, we must become aware of the scripts we were taught and take responsibility for scripting our lives.

we are and how we are supposed to live are forged when we have almost no control. We aren't allowed to coauthor or even edit our initial life scripts, because adults have power. As children, we aren't even conscious of learning scripts. It is largely an unconscious process by which we internalize scripts that others write and assign to us, and we absorb them with little if any awareness. As adults, however, we are no longer passive recipients of others' scripts. We have the capacity to review the life scripts that were given to us and to challenge and change those that do not fit the selves we now choose to be. The Sharpen Your Skill feature on page 184 invites you to review your life scripts and challenge those that no longer work for you.

From the moment we enter the world, we interact with others. As we do, we learn how they see us, and we take many of their perspectives inside ourselves and use them to appraise ourselves and to guide how we think and act.

The Self Arises in Communication with Others

We've seen that our understanding of who we are is shaped by the perspectives of particular others and the society in which we live. But how do we learn those perspectives? How are they imparted to us? We learn them in the process of communicating with others—both individuals who matter to us (particular others) and society as a whole (generalized other). Scholars have identified four communication processes that explain how we come to know the perspectives of others and how those shape our understandings of who we are and can be.

Reflected Appraisal

The process of seeing ourselves through the eyes of others is called **reflected apprasal**, or the "looking-glass self" (Cooley, 1912). As infants interact with others, they learn how others see them—they see themselves in the looking glass, or mirror, of others' eyes. This is the beginning of a self-concept. Note that the self starts outside of us with others' views of who we are.

In other words, we first see ourselves from the perspectives of others. If parents communicate to children that they are special and cherished, the children will probably see themselves as worthy of love. On the other hand, children whose parents communicate that they are not wanted or loved may come to think of themselves as unlovable.

Reflected appraisals are not confined to childhood but continue throughout our lives. Sometimes, a teacher is the first to see potential in a student that the student has not recognized in herself or himself. Peers also provide reflected appraisals, telling us if we are good at sports, attractive, and so forth. Later, in professional life we encounter co-workers and bosses who reflect their

Who are the people who are your looking glass? For whom are you a looking glass?

© Leigh M. Wilco

appraisals of us (we're on the fast track, average, or not suited to our positions). The friends and romantic partners we choose throughout life become primary looking glasses for us.

Direct Definition

As the term implies, **direct definition** is communication that explicitly tells us who we are by labeling us and our behaviors. Parents and other family members are usually the first people to offer direct definitions to us. They define us by the symbols they use to describe us. For instance, parents might say, "You're my sweet little girl" or "You're a big, strong boy" and thus communicate to the child what sex s/he is and what the sexual assignment means (girls are sweet, boys are big and strong). Children who hear such messages may internalize their parents' views of the sexes and use those as models for themselves.

Family members provide direct communication about many aspects of who we are. Positive labels enhance our self-esteem (Brooks & Goldstein, 2001): "You're so smart," "You're sweet," "You're great at soccer." Negative labels can damage children's self-esteem: "You're a troublemaker," "You're stupid," and "You're impossible" are messages that can demolish a child's sense of self-worth. Direct definition also takes place as family members respond to children's behaviors. If children clown around and parents respond by saying, "What a cut-up; you really are funny," the children are likely to perceive themselves as funny. From direct definition, children learn how others see them and what others value and expect of them, and this influences how they regard themselves and what they expect of themselves.

Peers also offer direct definitions of us: "You're smart," "You're clumsy," "You don't belong in our group." The ways that peers define us often have pivotal impact on how we perceive ourselves and our worth. Peers are particularly strong in commenting directly on conformity to expectations of gender. Men who are not interested in drinking and hooking up may be ridiculed and excluded for not being real men (Cross, 2008; Kimmel, 2008). Women who don't wear popular brands of clothing or who weigh more than what is considered ideal may be ridiculed as unfeminine (Adler, 2007; Barash, 2006; McRobbie, 2009).

One particularly powerful way in which reflected appraisals and direct definitions affect the self is through **self-fulfilling prophecies**—expectations or judgments of ourselves that we bring about through our own actions. If you have done poorly in classes where teachers didn't seem to respect you and have done well with teachers who thought you were smart, you know what a self-fulfilling prophecy is. Because we internalize others' perspectives, we may label ourselves as they do and then act to fulfill the labels we have internalized. We may try to live up or down to the ways we and others define us.

When I was seven years old, I took a swimming class. No matter how hard I tried to follow the teacher's directions, I sank in the pool. I couldn't swim; I couldn't even float. After three weeks, the teacher told me that I would never learn to swim and I should stay away from water. For the next 43 years, I accepted the teacher's label of *nonswimmer*. When I was 50, Robbie challenged my view of myself as a nonswimmer. He said I could learn to swim if I wanted to, and he volunteered to coach me. After just a few days of one-on-one coaching, I was swimming and floating.

Like me, many of us believe inaccurate things about ourselves. In some cases, the labels were once true but aren't any longer, yet we continue to apply them to ourselves

A Positive Prophecy

For years, Georgia Tech ran a program called Challenge, a course designed to help disadvantaged students succeed academically. Yet when administrators reviewed the records, they found that students enrolled in Challenge did no better than disadvantaged students who were not enrolled. Norman Johnson, a special assistant to the president of Georgia Tech, explained the reason for the dismal results of Challenge. He said, "We were starting off with the idea the kids were dumb. We didn't say that, of course, but the program was set up on a deficit model." Then Johnson suggested a new strategy: "Suppose we started with the idea that these youngsters were unusually bright, that we had very high expectations of them?" (Raspberry, 1994, p. 9A).

Challenge teachers were then trained to expect success from their students and to communicate their expectations through how they treated students. The results were impressive: In 1992, 10% of the first-year Challenge students had perfect 4.0 grade point averages for the academic year. That 10% was more than all the minority students who had achieved 4.0 averages in the entire decade of 1980–1990. By comparison, only 5% of the students who didn't participate in Challenge had perfect averages. When teachers expected Challenge students to do well and communicated those expectations, the students in fact did do well—a case of a positive self-fulfilling prophecy.

(remember indexing, which we discussed in Chapter 4). In other cases, the labels were never valid, but we believed them anyway. Sometimes, children are mislabeled as slow when the real problem is that they have physiological difficulties such as impaired vision or they are struggling with a second language. Even when the true source of difficulty is discovered, the children already may have adopted a destructive self-fulfilling prophecy. If we accept others' judgments, we may fulfill their prophecies. The FYI feature on this page illustrates the power of positive (and negative) prophecies.

Social Comparison

Communication with others also affects self-concept through **social comparison**, rating of ourselves relative to others with respect to our talents, abilities, qualities, and so forth. Whereas reflected appraisals are based on how we think others view us, in social comparisons we use others to evaluate ourselves.

We gauge ourselves in relation to others in two ways. First, we compare ourselves with others to decide whether we are like them or different from them. Are we the same age, color, or religion? Do we

Parents' communication is a key influence on self-concept.

DIGITAL MEDIA
Virtual Identity Development

Having make-believe friends is common among children. With technology, today's children are creating their own make-believe friends and even their own identities. One popular game, The Sims, allows players to create families and living spaces and then to direct interactions among family members. Marjorie Taylor (1999), a psychologist who has studied imaginary playmates, says that children create Sims characters who are just like themselves or characters who allow them to experiment with different identities. Researchers who study both children and technology think such games are great resources that help children learn to think about relationships and ways of interacting with others (Schiesel, 2006).

have similar backgrounds, interests, political beliefs, and social commitments? Assessing similarity and difference allows us to decide with whom we fit. However, this can deprive us of diverse perspectives of people whose experiences and beliefs differ from ours. When we limit ourselves only to people like us, we impoverish the social perspectives that form our understandings of the world.

Second, we engage in social comparisons to assess specific aspects of ourselves. Because there are no absolute standards of beauty, intelligence, musical talent, athletic ability, and so forth, we measure ourselves in relation to others. Am I as good a goalie as Hendrick? Am I as smart as Maya? Through comparing ourselves to others, we decide how we measure up on various criteria. This is normal and necessary if we are to develop realistic self-concepts. However, we should be wary of what psychologists call upward comparison, which is the tendency to compare ourselves to people who exceed us in what they have or can do (Luttmer, 2005; Tugend, 2011). It isn't realistic to judge our attractiveness in relation to stars and models, or our athletic ability in relation to professional players. Likewise, we won't have valid assessments of ourselves if we compare ourselves to people who are clearly less attractive, athletic and so forth (Buunk, Groothof, & Siero, 2007; Suls, Martin, & Wheeler, 2002).

Social comparison can lead us to be dissatisfied if we compare ourselves to others who are doing better or have more. Would you feel better about yourself if you made $100,000 a year in a community where most people make $75,000 or made $150,000 in a community where most people make $200,000? Research (Halvorson, 2010; Luttmer, 2005; Tugend, 2011) shows that most people prefer the former—they feel better about themselves if they are making more than their neighbors. In other words, we tend to feel better about ourselves if we are doing better than those around us, regardless of how well we are doing in absolute terms.

Self-Disclosure

Finally, our self-concepts are also affected—challenged, changed, reinforced, enlarged—by our self-disclosures and others' responses to them. **Self-disclosure** is the revelation of personal information about ourselves that others are unlikely to learn on their own. We self-disclose when we express private hopes and fears, intimate feelings, and personal experiences, perceptions, and goals.

Self-disclosures vary in how personal they are. To a co-worker who is upset about not receiving a promotion, you might disclose your experience in not getting a promotion some years ago. To your best friend, you might disclose more intimate feelings and experiences. Although we don't reveal our private selves to everyone and don't do it a great deal of the time even with intimates, self-disclosure is an important kind of communication. How others respond to our self-disclosures can profoundly affect how we see and accept ourselves, as Seth's commentary shows. Self-disclosure is most likely to take place when the communication climate is affirming, accepting, and supportive.

 Seth

Ever since I was a kid, my dad told me I was going to be a doctor like him and join his practice after medical school. I never really thought about it until I got to college and found I didn't like the pre-med classes. Then I took an introductory sociology class and loved it. I took more classes and decided to major in soc. I was so scared to tell my dad, but I finally did the fall of my junior year. I was afraid he would be disappointed in me and he was—at first. But as I told him more about why I loved sociology, he became more accepting, and that made me feel better about myself.

A number of years ago, Joseph Luft and Harry Ingham created a model that describes different kinds of knowledge and perceptions that are related to self-concept and personal growth (Luft, 1969). They called the model the Johari Window, which is a combination of their first names, Joe and Harry (Figure 9.2). The panes, or areas, in the Johari Window refer to four types of information and perceptions that are relevant to the self:

▶ The open, or free, area contains information that is known both to ourselves and to others. Your name, your major, and your tastes in music are probably information that you share easily with others. Our co-workers and casual acquaintances often know information about us that is in our open area.

▶ The blind area contains perceptions of us that others have but we don't. For example, others may perceive us as leaders, even though we don't see ourselves that way. Co-workers and supervisors may recognize strengths, weaknesses, and potentials of which we are unaware. Friends may see us as more or less generous than we perceive ourselves.

▶ The hidden area contains information and perceptions that we have about ourselves but choose not to reveal to others. You might not tell most people about your vulnerabilities or about traumas you've experienced. You might conceal self-doubts when interviewing for a job. Even with our closest intimates, we may choose to preserve some areas of privacy.

▶ The unknown area is made up of information about ourselves that neither we nor others know. The unknown area is the most difficult to understand because, as the area's name implies, it contains information and perceptions that are not known. We cannot know how we will handle a job layoff unless we experience one; we cannot know if we're good at bridge unless we try playing it. The unknown area includes your untapped resources, untried talents, and unknown reactions to experiences you've never had. David, who started college after serving in the Army, provides an example of what had been an unknown to him.

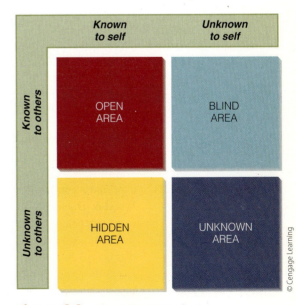

Figure 9.2 **The Johari Window**

David

I was shipped out to Iraq shortly after American troops were assigned there. Talk about scared—I was terrified. I was also really unsure of how I would do. Could I stand up to the physical challenges? Would I freeze up in battle? Could I kill someone if I had to? Being a soldier in Iraq taught me some things about myself I don't think I could have learned any other way.

Because a healthy self-concept requires knowledge of yourself, it's important to gain access to information in our blind and unknown areas. To reduce your unknown area, you might enter unfamiliar situations. You might also try novel activities, interact with people whose cultural backgrounds differ from yours, and experiment with new ways of communicating. To decrease your blind area, you could ask others how they perceive you, or you could pay attention to how they act toward you. To diminish your hidden area, in carefully chosen relationships you might disclose information that you do not share with most people.

Uncertainty reduction theory, which we mentioned in Chapter 8, asserts that people find uncertainty uncomfortable and so are motivated to use communication to reduce uncertainty. Uncertainty is very high during initial encounters. Because we find uncertainty uncomfortable, we use both indirect and direct strategies to reduce it (Berger, 1977, 1988; Gudykunst, 1995; Kim, 1995). We gain information indirectly by observing the person: How does Chris react to various people and situations? Does Chris like spicy foods? How flexible is Chris in adapting when there is a change in plans? We also use direct communication to gain information and reduce our uncertainty about a new acquaintance: Where are you from? What's your major? Do you follow politics?

Self-disclosure is another way to reduce uncertainty early in relationships. We want to share our private selves and see how others respond to our disclosures. We may also hope that if we disclose something personal, others will reciprocate by disclosing to us, which would reduce our uncertainty. Because there are risks in self-disclosing, it's wise not to disclose too much too quickly. Initial self-disclosures should involve limited risk to the discloser: I'm afraid of heights; I hope I get accepted to law school. If low-level disclosures are met with respect and affirmation, higher-level disclosures may follow: I have a difficult relationship with my father; I was seriously depressed a few years ago.

According to researchers, careful self-disclosure not only fosters personal growth but also tends to increase closeness, at least among Westerners (Derlega & Berg, 1987; Greene, Derlega, & Mathews, 2006). Yet people vary in their perceptions of the link between disclosure and intimacy. For some people, talk is a primary way of developing intimacy, whereas other people regard sharing experiences and being together as more conducive to closeness than talking intimately.

Although self-disclosure is important in the early stages of a relationship, it is not a primary communication dynamic in most enduring relationships (Dindia, 2000; Wood & Duck, 2006b). When we're first getting to know colleagues, friends, or intimate partners, we have to reveal parts of ourselves and learn about them, so disclosures are necessary and desirable. However, in relationships that endure over time, disclosures make up little of the total communication. Once co-workers and friends have established relationships, the bulk of their communication focuses on task issues, not further personal disclosures. In intimate relationships, frequency of disclosure also tends to decline over time, yet partners continue to reap the benefits of the trust and depth of personal knowledge created by early disclosures. Also, partners do continue to disclose new experiences and insights to one another; it's just that mature relationships usually see less disclosure than embryonic ones.

Although infrequent self-disclosures do not necessarily indicate a lack of closeness, a noticeable decline in the level of disclosure that has become standard in a relationship may be a sign that intimacy is waning. When a friendship, a romance, or a close working relationship wanes, typically the depth of disclosure decreases (Baxter, 1987; Duck & Wood, 2006).

Researchers have investigated online self-disclosure. Some people invent online personalities that don't match them—different races, sexes, sexual orientations, physical appearances, and so forth. Experimenting with identity can be helpful to adolescents as they try out different versions of themselves, a process that is critical to personal development. A shy teen may create an extroverted online identity that allows her or him to test how it feels to be more sociable (Turkle, 2004). Other research shows that people who are successful at online dating tend to engage in substantial positive self-disclosure and are honest about their intentions (Gibbs, Ellison, & Heino, 2006).

The human self originates in communication. From interaction with family members, peers, and society as a whole, we learn the prevailing values of our culture and of particular people who are significant to us. What we learn guides how we perceive ourselves and how we communicate. We're now ready to discuss three challenges related to personal growth.

Guidelines for Communicating with Ourselves

Throughout this chapter, we've drawn on the basic communication processes covered in Part I of this book. For example, we've noted that others are an especially important influence on the process of perceiving ourselves. Our sense of identity evolves as we listen to others and interpret their verbal and nonverbal communication with us. To demonstrate further how basic communication processes apply to interaction with ourselves, we will discuss three guidelines for communicating with ourselves in ways that foster personal growth and a healthy society.

Reflect Critically on Social Perspectives

We've seen that people tend to internalize the perspectives of their society. In many ways this is useful, even essential, for collective life. If we all made up our own rules about when to stop and go at traffic intersections, wrecks would proliferate. If each of us operated by our own inclinations, we would have no shared standards regarding tax payment, robbery, and so forth. Life would be chaotic.

Yet not all social views are as constructive as traffic regulations and criminal law. Each of us has an ethical responsibility to exercise critical judgment about which social views we personally accept and which ones we will allow to guide our behaviors, attitudes, and values. In addition, we have an ethical obligation to use our communication to contribute to constructive change in our society.

Society's perspectives are not fixed, nor are they based on objective, absolute truths. Instead, the values and views endorsed by a society at any given time are arbitrary and subject to change. The fluidity of social values becomes especially obvious when we consider how widely values differ between cultures. For example, the Agta people in the Philippines and the Tini Aborigines in Australia view hunting skill as a feminine

SHARPEN YOUR SKILL

Identifying Social Values in Media

Select four popular magazines, and read the articles and advertisements in them.

◆ What do the articles and ads convey about what and who is valued in the United States?

◆ What do articles convey about how women or men are regarded and what they are expected to be and do?

◆ How many ads aimed at women focus on beauty, looking young, losing weight, taking care of others, and attracting men?

◆ How many ads aimed at men emphasize strength, virility, success, and independence?

To extend this exercise, note the cultural values conveyed by television, films, billboards, and news stories. Pay attention to who is highlighted and how different genders, races, and professions are represented.

ideal (Estioko-Griffin & Griffin, 1997). A group in French Polynesia recognizes three sexes (Glenn, 2002), and some groups in India have a category of identity for female men (Nanda, 2004).

Social views also change over time in a single society. For instance, in the early 20th century many people with disabilities were kept in their homes or put in institutions. Today, many schools place students who have physical or mental disabilities in regular classes. Also, as we have seen, Western society's perspectives on race, gender, sexual orientation, and gender identity are not what they were 50 or even 10 years ago.

Social perspectives change in response to individual and collective efforts to revise social meanings. Each of us has an ethical responsibility to speak out against social perspectives that we perceive as wrong or harmful. By doing so, we participate in the ongoing process of refining who we are as a society.

Commit to Personal Growth

Most of us perceive ways we could improve as communicators. Maybe we want to be more assertive, more mindful when listening, or more confident as public speakers. Following three suggestions will help you nurture your own personal growth.

Set Realistic Goals

Although willpower can do marvelous things, it has limits. We need to recognize that trying to change how we see ourselves works only if our goals are realistic. It's not realistic and usually not effective to expect dramatic growth immediately. If you are shy and want to be more extroverted, it's realistic to decide that you will speak up more often and attend more social functions. On the other hand, setting the goal of being the life of the party may not be reasonable.

Realistic goals require realistic standards. In a culture that emphasizes perfectionism, it's easy to be trapped into expecting more than is humanly possible. If your goal is to be a totally perfect communicator in all situations, you set yourself up for failure. More reasonable and more constructive is to establish a series of small goals that you can meet. You might focus on improving one communication skill. When you are satisfied with your ability at that skill, you can focus on a second one.

Assess Yourself Fairly

Being realistic also involves making fair assessments of ourselves. This requires us to make reasonable social comparisons, place judgments of ourselves in context, realize that we are always in process, and assess ourselves in the perspective of time. Remembering our discussion of social comparison, we know that selecting reasonable yardsticks for ourselves is important. Comparing your academic work with that of a certified genius is not appropriate. It is reasonable to measure your academic performance against others who have intellectual abilities and life situations similar to yours. Setting realistic goals and selecting appropriate standards of comparison are important guidelines when you want to bring about change in yourself.

To assess ourselves effectively, we also should appreciate how our individual qualities and abilities fit together to form the whole self. Recall systems theory, which we discussed in Chapter 1. It reminds us that we treat ourselves unfairly if we judge specific aspects of our communication outside their overall context. Most often, we do this by highlighting our shortcomings and overlooking what we do well. This leads to a distorted self-perception.

It's more realistic to judge yourself from an overall perspective. Babe Ruth hit 714 home runs, and he also struck out 1,330 times. If he had defined himself only in terms of his strikeouts, he probably would never have become a world-renowned baseball player. One of my colleagues faults himself for being slow to grade and return students' papers. He compares himself with others in my department who return students' work more quickly. However, this man has twice as many office hours as any of his colleagues. His judgment that he is slow in returning papers is based on comparing himself with colleagues who spend less time talking with their students than he does. However, he doesn't compare himself with them when thinking about his office hours. In our efforts to improve self-concept, then, we should acknowledge our strengths and virtues as well as parts of ourselves we want to change.

To create and sustain a healthy self-concept, we also need to be attentive to unfair assessments of us that others may make. Others, including parents and bosses, sometimes have unreasonable expectations. If we measure our abilities by their unreasonable standards, we may underestimate our effectiveness. We should consider others' views of us, but we should not accept them uncritically.

A key foundation for improving self-concept is to accept yourself as someone in process. The human self is continuously in process, always changing, always becoming. This implies several things. First, it means that it's healthy to accept who you are now as a starting point. You don't have to like or admire everything about yourself, but accepting who you are today allows you to move forward. The person you are today has been shaped by all the experiences, interactions, reflected appraisals, and social comparisons during your life. You cannot change your past, but you do not have to be bound by it forever. Only by realizing and accepting who you are now can you grow in new ways.

Accepting yourself as in process also implies that you realize you can change. Who you are today is not who you will be in 5 or 10 years. Because you are in process, you are always changing and growing. Don't let yourself be hindered by negative self-fulfilling prophecies or by the belief that you cannot change (Rusk & Rusk, 1988). You can change if you set realistic goals, make a genuine commitment, and work for the changes you want. Just remember that you are not fixed as you are but always in the process of becoming.

Create a Supportive Context for the Change You Seek

Just as it is easier to swim with the tide than against it, it is easier to promote changes in ourselves in contexts that support our efforts. You can do a lot to create a climate that nurtures your personal growth by choosing contexts and people who help you become who you want to be.

First, think about settings. If you want to improve your physical condition, it makes more sense to participate in intramural sports than to hang out in bars. If you want to lose weight, it's better to go to restaurants that serve healthful foods and offer light choices than to go to cholesterol castles. If you want to become more outgoing, you need to put yourself in social situations rather than in libraries. But libraries are a better context than parties if your goal is to improve academic performance. Bob's commentary illustrates the influence of setting on personal behavior.

I never drank much until I got into this one group at school. All of them drank all the time. It was easy to join them. In fact, it was pretty hard not to drink and still be one of the guys. A while ago, I decided I was drinking too much. It was hard enough not to drink, because the guys were always doing it, but what really made it hard was the ways the guys got on me for abstaining. They let me know I was being uncool and made me feel like a jerk. Finally, I had to get a different apartment to stop drinking.

Second, the people we are with have a great deal to do with how we see ourselves and how worthy we feel we are. This means you can create a supportive context by consciously choosing to be around people who believe in you and encourage your personal growth. It's equally important to steer clear of people who pull you down or say you can't change. In other words, people who reflect positive appraisals of us enhance our ability to improve. One way to think about how others' communication affects how we feel about ourselves is to recognize that people can be uppers, downers, or vultures (Simon, 1977). The FYI feature on page 195 explains uppers, downers, and vultures.

Other people are not the only ones who can be uppers, downers, and vultures. We also communicate with ourselves, and our messages influence our self-esteem. One of the most crippling kinds of self-talk in which we can engage is **self-sabotage**. This involves telling ourselves we are no good, we can't do something, there's no point in trying to change, and so forth. We may be repeating judgments others made of us or inventing negative self-fulfilling prophecies. Either way, self-sabotage defeats us because it undermines our belief in ourselves. Self-sabotage is poisonous; it destroys our motivation to grow.

We can be downers or even vultures to ourselves, just as others can be. In fact, we can probably do more damage to our self-concept than others can because we are most aware of our vulnerabilities and fears. This may explain why vultures were originally described as people who put themselves down (Simon, 1977). We can also be uppers for ourselves. We can affirm our worth, encourage our growth, and fortify our sense of self-worth. Positive self-talk is a useful way to interrupt and challenge negative messages from yourself and others. The next time you hear yourself saying, "I can't do this," or someone else says, "You'll never change," challenge the self-defeating message by saying out loud to yourself, "I can do it. I will change." Use positive self-talk to resist counterproductive communication about yourself.

Before leaving this discussion, we should make it clear that improving your self-concept is not facilitated by uncritical positive communication. None of us grows and improves when we listen only to praise, particularly if it is less than honest. The true uppers in our lives offer constructive criticism to encourage us to reach for better versions of ourselves.

Uppers, Downers, and Vultures

Uppers are people who communicate positively about us and who reflect positive appraisals of our self-worth. They notice our strengths, see our progress, and accept our weaknesses and problems without discounting us. When we're around uppers, we feel more upbeat and positive about ourselves. Uppers aren't necessarily unconditionally positive in their communication. A true friend can be an upper by recognizing our weaknesses and helping us work on them. Instead of putting us down, an upper believes in us and helps us believe in our capacity to change.

Downers are people who communicate negatively about us and our worth. They call attention to our flaws, emphasize our problems, and put down our dreams and goals. When we're around downers, we tend to feel down about ourselves. Reflecting their perspectives, we're more aware of our weaknesses and less confident of what we can accomplish. Downers discourage belief in ourselves.

Vultures are extreme downers. They attack our self-concepts. Sometimes vultures initiate harsh criticism of us. In other cases vultures discover our weak spots and exploit them, picking us apart by focusing on sensitive areas in our self-concept. By telling us we are inadequate, vultures demolish our self-esteem.

SUMMARY

In this chapter, we explored the self as a process that evolves over the course of our lives. We saw that the self is not present at birth but develops as we interact with others. Through communication, we learn the perspectives of particular others and the broad social community. Reflected appraisals, direct definitions, and social comparisons further shape how we see ourselves and how we change over time. By interacting with society overall, we also learn society's views of aspects of identity, including race, gender, sexual preference, and income level. However, these are arbitrary views that

we can challenge if we find them unethical. In doing so, we participate in the continuous evolution of our collective world.

The last part of the chapter focused on concrete ways we can apply basic communication processes to facilitate our personal growth and our participation in society. You can foster your personal growth by setting realistic goals and assessing yourself fairly. Creating contexts that support the changes you seek makes it easier to promote those changes. Transforming how we see ourselves is not easy, but it is possible. We can make amazing changes in who we are and who we will become when we embrace our human capacity to make choices.

REVIEW, REFLECT, EXTEND

The Reflect, Discuss, and Apply Questions that follow will help you review, reflect on, and extend the information and ideas presented in this chapter. These resources, and a diverse selection of additional study tools, are also available online at the CourseMate for *Communication Mosaics*. Your CourseMate includes a student workbook, WebLinks, TED Talks hyperlinks and activities, chapter glossary and flashcards, interactive video activities, Speech Builder Express, and InfoTrac College Edition. For more information or to access this book's online resources, visit **www .cengagebrain.com.**

KEY CONCEPTS

anxious/ambivalent attachment style, 183
attachment style, 183
direct definition, 186
dismissive attachment style, 183
downer, 195
fearful attachment style, 183
generalized other, 178
life script, 184
particular others, 182
reflected appraisal, 185

secure attachment style, 183
self, 178
self-disclosure, 188
self-fulfilling prophecy, 186
self-sabotage, 194
social comparison, 187
uncertainty reduction theory, 190
upper, 195
vulture, 195

Reflect, Discuss, Apply

As a class, discuss society's views (the generalized other) of women and men. What are current social expectations for each sex? What behaviors, appearances, and attitudes violate social prescriptions for gender? Do you agree or disagree with these social expectations?

1. If you could revise the generalized other, how would you do it? Would race/ethnicity, gender, sexual orientation, and socioeconomic class be important aspects of self in your revision?

2. Write 1-2 paragraph descriptions of how you defined yourself when you were 6, 10, and 16. How is your current self different from and an extension of those earlier views of yourself? Now, write a 1-2 paragraph description of how who you think you will be in 10 years. Tuck it away and re-read it a decade from now.

Recommended Resources

If you would like to learn more about how the attachment styles discussed in this chapter affect romantic relationships, go to the book's online resources for this chapter and click on WebLink 9.1.

1. The film *Nell* dramatizes the impact of communication with others on self-concept. View the film, and notice how Nell's world changes as she begins to communicate with others.

2. Some societies have more rigid lines for class membership than the United States does. One of the most rigid systems is the caste system in India. To learn about how a person's caste affects his or her opportunities in life, go to the book's online resources for this chapter and click on WebLink 9.2.

EXPERIENCE COMMUNICATION CASE STUDY

Parental Teachings

Apply what you've learned in this chapter by analyzing the following case study, using the accompanying questions as a guide. These questions and a video of the case study are also available online at your CourseMate for *Communication Mosaics*.

Kate McDonald is in the neighborhood park with her two children, seven-year-old Emma and five-year-old Jeremy. The three of them walk into the park and approach the swing set.

Kate: Jeremy, why don't you push Emma so she can swing? Emma, you hang on tight.

Jeremy begins pushing his sister, who squeals with delight. Jeremy gives an extra-hard push that lands him in the dirt in front of the swing set. Laughing, Emma jumps off, falling in the dirt beside her brother.

Kate: Come here, sweetie. You've got dirt all over your knees and your pretty new dress.

Kate brushes the dirt off Emma, who then runs over to the jungle gym set that Jeremy is now climbing. Kate smiles as she watches Jeremy climb fearlessly on the bars.

Kate: You're a brave little man, aren't you? How high can you go?

Encouraged by his mother, Jeremy climbs to the top bars and holds up a fist, screaming, "Look at me, Mom! I'm king of the hill. I climbed to the very top!"

Kate laughs and claps her hands to applaud him. Jealous of the attention Jeremy is getting, Emma runs over to the jungle gym and starts climbing. Kate calls out, "Careful, honey. Don't go any higher. You could fall and hurt yourself." When Emma

© Cengage Learning

ignores her mother and reaches for a higher bar, Kate walks over and pulls her off, saying, "Emma, I told you that is dangerous. Time to get down. Why don't you play on the swings some more?"

Once Kate puts Emma on the ground, the girl walks over to the swings and begins swaying.

---

1. Identify examples of direct definition in this scenario. How does Kate define Emma and Jeremy?

2. Identify examples of reflected appraisal in this scenario. What appraisals of her son and daughter does Kate reflect to them?

3. What do Emma's and Jeremy's responses to Kate suggest about their acceptance of her views of them?

4. To what extent does Kate's communication with her children reflect normative gender expectations in Western culture?

10 Communication in Personal Relationships

FOCUS QUESTIONS

1. What are turning points and how do they affect relationships?

2. What kinds of communication help sustain long-distance romances?

3. How important is equity to the health of long-term romantic relationships?

4. What is the cycle of intimate partner abuse?

When my mother could no longer live alone, Robbie (my partner) and I invited her into our home where she lived for the final 14 months of her life. As you might imagine, during this period I felt much sadness. What you might not realize is that I also experienced a great deal of joy and personal growth as important relationships in my life gained greater depth. Mother and I grew close in new ways, and my ties with Robbie, my sister Carolyn, and close friends were deepened as I shared with them the fears and feelings that accompany losing a parent.

My experience is not unusual. All of us count on family, close friends, and romantic partners in bad times as well as good. Our intimates help us get through sorrows and disappointments, and they celebrate our joys and victories. Try to imagine that suddenly you have no close friends or family and no romantic partner. How would your life be different? What would be missing? If you're like most people, a great deal would be missing. Personal relationships are important sources of growth, pleasure, comfort, and fulfillment.

Healthy, effective communication is the heartbeat of strong personal relationships. In previous chapters, we've discussed basic communication processes. In this chapter, we focus on how those apply to personal relationships. The first section of the chapter defines personal relationships and explores how friendships and romances evolve. In the second section, we'll examine four guidelines for sustaining healthy personal relationships in our era.

Understanding Personal Relationships

A **personal relationship** is a voluntary commitment between irreplaceable individuals who are influenced by rules, relationship dialectics, and surrounding contexts. This definition highlights important features that distinguish personal relationships from other kinds of human connections. We'll discuss each of these features and then explore typical evolutionary paths of friendships and romantic relationships.

Features of Personal Relationships

Personal relationships are unique: Each one is distinct as a result of commitment, rules, surrounding contexts, and relationship dialectics.

Uniqueness

Most of our relationships are social, not personal. A **social relationship** is one in which participants interact according to general social roles rather than unique individual identities. For instance, you might exchange lecture notes with a classmate and talk about politics with a co-worker. In each case, the person could be replaced by someone else who took the same role. You could find other people with whom to swap class notes and discuss politics. In social relationships, the individual people are less important than the roles they fulfill. The value of social relationships lies more in what participants do than in their unique identities.

In personal relationships, however, the particular people and what they create between them define the connection. Many people are committed not to marriage in the abstract but to living their lives with a particular person. Friendships also involve unique and voluntary bonds (Norwood & Duck, 2009). Others cannot replace intimate partners, best friends, siblings, or parents. When one person in a personal relationship leaves or dies, that relationship ends, although it may remain strong in memory. We may later have other intimates, but a new partner or best friend will not be a duplicate of the former one.

Commitment

The sparks and the emotional high of being in love or discovering a new friend stem from **passion,** an intense feeling based on the rewards of involvement with another person. Passion is why we have the sensations of butterflies in the stomach and giddiness. As exciting as passion is, it isn't the basis of enduring relationships.

Commitment is the decision to remain with a relationship. The hallmark of commitment is the intention to share the future (Beck, 1988; Ragan, 2003). Committed friends and romantic partners assume they will stay together. Because commitment assumes a shared future, partners are unlikely to bail out if the going gets rough. Instead, they weather bad times (Le & Agnew, 2003; Lund, 1985). Unlike passion, commitment is a decision to stay together despite trouble, disappointments, sporadic restlessness, and lulls in emotional depth.

Commitment grows out of **investment:** what we put into a relationship that we could not retrieve if the relationship were to end (Rusbult, Drigotas, & Verette, 1994). When we care about another person, we invest time, energy, thought, and feelings in interaction. In doing this, we invest *ourselves* in others. We also make material investments

Warren Goldswain/Shutterstock

Shared time and experiences are important investments that fuel commitment.

that can't be recovered if a relationship ends. Gifts, money spent on dates, and so forth cannot be recovered fully if the relationship ends. Investments are powerful because they are personal choices to give things that can't be recovered. We can't get back the feelings and energy we invest in a relationship. We can't recover history shared with another. The more we invest in a relationship, the more difficult it is to end it (Dainton, 2006; Guerrero, Andersen, & Afifi, 2008). Sarah points out that investing heavily in a relationship can sometimes trap a person.

When Sean and I were first married, I was so happy I didn't care about anything else. My friends tried to talk me out of quitting school, but I wanted to work to put Sean through medical school. Then, we had one baby and another and a third, and I was a stay-at-home mom who was totally involved in family. Then things started unraveling between Sean and me. I thought about a divorce. But then I thought, "Where could I go? How could I support myself and the kids?" I hadn't finished college, so I couldn't earn a decent income. My job skills were rusty because I'd been out of the job market for 10 years. It was like I was trapped because I'd put too much in the marriage to leave.

Relationship Rules

All relationships have **rules** that guide how partners communicate and interpret each other's communication (Argyle & Henderson, 1984). Typically, relationship rules are unspoken understandings between partners. Although friends and romantic partners may never explicitly discuss rules, they learn how important rules are if they violate one that a partner perceives, as Miguel's commentary illustrates.

Sherry and I had been dating for about six months when some of my friends from another school came to visit on their spring break. We decided to go out on Saturday night to hear a local band. It never occurred to me to check with Sherry, because we hadn't made plans for that night. But she was so mad at me. She said, "We always go out on Fridays and Saturdays"—like it was written in stone or something.

As we noted in Chapter 4, two kinds of rules guide our communication. *Constitutive rules* define how to interpret communication. For instance, some people count listening to problems as caring, whereas others count engaging in activities to divert attention from problems as caring (Tavris, 1992; Wood, 2001c). Families often have constitutive rules that define what kinds of communication symbolize love and commitment (visiting at least three times a year, remembering birthdays). Constitutive rules are worked out over time as people in personal relationships learn what things mean to each other and what each of them needs and wants.

Regulative rules govern interaction by specifying when and with whom to engage in various kinds of communication. For example, many people operate according to a regulative rule that says it's okay to criticize a personal friend in private but to do so in front of others is not acceptable. Some romantic partners limit physical displays of affection to private settings.

Equally important are "shalt not" rules that define what each won't tolerate. For example, most Westerners would consider it a betrayal if a friend became sexually involved with their romantic partner. Some families have strong "shalt not" rules that members cannot marry outside their race, religion, or ethnic group. Rules regulate both trivial and important aspects of interaction. Not interrupting may be a rule, but breaking it probably won't wreck a good friendship. On the other hand, deceitful communication or divulging confidences may sound the death knell of a friendship.

 Kiran

Nobody in my family has ever married a non-Indian, and I am expected to follow this tradition. If my parents find out I even dated someone who is not Indian, they get very upset. My father has told me that if I marry outside of our ethnicity, he will disown me.

Because rules reflect our cultures and social communities, friends and romantic partners from different racial and ethnic backgrounds may not understand each other's relationship rules. Communication scholar Mary Jane Collier (1996) found that Latinas and Latinos regard supportive communication and respect as key norms in friendship whereas African Americans place more priority on showing respect and consideration, Asian-Americans emphasize exchanging ideas, and European Americans place highest priority on honesty, disclosure, and advice.

Affected by Contexts

Personal relationships are not isolated from the social world. Instead, the surroundings of relationships influence interaction between people (Dainton, 2006; Felmlee, 2001; Klein & Milardo, 2000). Our families of origin influence what we look for in people with whom we want close relationships. Our social circles establish norms for such activities as religious involvement, drinking, political activism, participation in community groups, studying, working, and socializing. Circumstances in the larger society may also influence interaction between intimates. For instance, during deep recessions people who are laid off may experience a diminished sense of self-worth. Because personal relationships are systems, shifts in one partner's earning power and self-worth reverberate throughout relationships, causing ripples of change throughout the systems. The many social contexts of our lives affect what we expect of relationships and how we communicate in them.

Speed dating and online dating sites such as eHarmony maximize the number of potential dates you can screen in a short time (Samp & Palevitz, 2009). The growing number of dual-career couples is revising traditional expectations about how much each partner participates in earning income, homemaking, and child care

DIGITAL MEDIA
Staying in Touch

Today's college students tend to stay in touch with their parents. On average, college students call, e-mail, skype, or send text messages to their parents 13 times a week (Lourgos, 2010)—up from 10.4 times a week in 2006 (Setoodeh, 2006). Not surprisingly, the main topic of communication is finances (30.6 percent of students), but that's not the only topic. College students also talk with parents about career planning (19.9 percent), academics (12.6 percent), health and safety (7.7 percent), and personal relationships (7.2 percent) (Setoodeh, 2006).

(Galvin, 2006; Wood, 2010). As our society becomes more culturally diverse, interracial, interreligious, and interethnic personal relationships become more common and more socially accepted. The number of interracial marriages tripled between 1970 and 2002, and interracial dating grew at an even higher rate (Troy & Laurenceau, 2006). Thus, our social circles and the larger society as well are contexts that influence the relationships we form and the ways we communicate within them.

Relationship Dialectics

A final quality of personal relationships is the presence of **relationship dialectics.** These are opposing and continuous tensions that are normal in all close relationships. Communication scholar Leslie Baxter and her colleagues have led the way in studying the many dialectics that affect relationships (Anderson, Baxter, & Cissna, 2004; Baxter, 1990, 1993, 2010; Baxter & Montgomery, 1996). Of the many possible dialectics, we will discuss three that are particularly prominent in close relationships.

The **autonomy/connection** dialectic involves the desires to be separate, on the one hand, and to be connected, on the other. Opposition between these two desires sometimes generates tension in relationships. Because we want to be deeply linked to others, we cherish spending time with our intimates, sharing experiences, and feeling connected. At the same time, we don't want relationships to swallow our individuality, so we seek some distance and time apart, even from our intimates.

Most people in personal relationships experience a continuous friction as a result of the contradictory desires for autonomy and connection (Erbert, 2000). Friends and romantic partners may vacation together and be with each other constantly for a week or more. They're often surprised when they return home and crave time apart. Intense immersion in togetherness prompts us to reestablish independent identity. When we get together with our families during holidays, we're often excited about catching up and talking intensely. Yet we often feel glad when the visit is over and we can part from families for a time. Both autonomy and closeness are natural human needs. The challenge is to nurture both individuality and intimacy.

The dialectic of **novelty/predictability** is the opposition of the desire for familiar routines and the desire for novelty. We like a certain amount of routine to provide security and predictability in our lives. Friends often have standard times to get together, families develop rituals for holidays and birthdays, and romantic couples settle on preferred times and places for going out (Bruess & Hoefs, 2006; Duck, 2006; Wood, 2006a). Yet too much routine is boring, so we seek novel experiences. Friends may take up a new sport together, families may plan unusual vacations, and romantic partners might explore a new hobby or do something spontaneous and different to introduce variety into their customary routine.

MEG

Craig and I have been together for ten years, so it's no surprise that we've settled into a lot of routines—too many! Last summer, I started biking to get some exercise. After a while, Craig decided to join me, and that's led to so many new experiences for us—places we go for great rides, mishaps we've had with flat tires and the like. These new experiences are a booster shot for our relationship.

The third dialectic, **openness/closedness,** involves the desire for openness in tension with the desire for privacy. Although intimate relationships sometimes are idealized as totally open and honest, complete openness would be intolerable (Baxter, 1993, 2006; Petronio, 1991; Petronio & Caughlin, 2006). Most of us want to share our inner selves with our intimates, yet there are times when we don't feel like disclosing and topics we don't want to discuss with anyone. Families often share deep feelings and thoughts but don't discuss sexual activities and attitudes. Friends and romantic partners, on the other hand, may talk about sex and other personal topics but may not share family secrets.

Researchers have identified four ways in which friends and romantic partners deal with dialectical tensions (Baxter, 1990; Baxter & Simon, 1993). One response, called **neutralization,** negotiates a balance between the opposing dialectical forces. This involves striking a compromise in which both needs are met to an extent, but neither is fully satisfied. A couple might agree to be generally open but not highly disclosive.

Separation addresses one need in a dialectic and ignores the other. For example, friends might agree to make novelty a priority and suppress their needs for routine. Research suggests that separation, which denies one natural, human need, is generally the least satisfying response (Baxter, 1990).

There is a form of separation that doesn't require denying either need in a dialectic. Cyclic alteration occurs when partners cycle between dialectical poles to favor each pole alternately. Couples involved in long-distance relationships often spend weekends in close contact and don't see each other during the week.

A third way to manage dialectics is **segmentation,** in which partners assign each pole to certain spheres, issues, activities, or times. For instance, friends might be open about many topics but respect each other's privacy and refrain from prying in one or two areas. Romantic partners might be autonomous in their professional activities yet connected in their interaction in the home and in their involvement with children. Jessica's commentary explains how segmentation surfaces in her relationship with her father.

 Jessica

I can talk about anything with my mom. She's like my best friend. She knows all about every part of my life. With my dad, it's a different story. We can talk about my classes and my job and cars and stuff like that. What we never, never talk about is dating and my boyfriends. Mom says he doesn't like to think about his "little girl" being romantically involved. Maybe that's it. All I know is that we don't ever talk about boys in my life.

The final method of managing dialectics is **reframing.** This is a complex strategy that redefines apparently contradictory needs as not really in opposition. My colleagues and I found clear examples of reframing in a study of intimate partners (Wood et al., 1994).

Some couples said that their autonomy enhances closeness because knowing they are separate in some ways allows them to feel safer about being deeply connected in other ways. Instead of viewing autonomy and closeness as opposing, these partners transcended the apparent tension between the two to define the needs as mutually enhancing.

The Evolutionary Course of Personal Relationships

Every personal relationship develops at its own pace and in unique ways. Yet a majority of friendships and romances have some common patterns of growth and, sometimes, decline. Scholars who study relationships have developed models that describe typical growth and decline trajectories for friendships and romantic relationships.

As we discuss relationship evolution, keep in mind that changes in relationships do not just happen automatically. Rather, particular experiences and events cause relationships to become more or less intimate. These events and experiences are called turning points. A **turning point** moves a relationship toward or away from intimacy. In romantic relationships, turning points that propel a relationship toward intimacy might include first kiss, first "I love you," and meeting parents. Turning points that move a relationship away from closeness might include learning a person has a drug problem or discovering infidelity (Baxter & Bullis, 1986). Turning points that move friendships toward increased closeness include taking a trip together, participating in a common activity, and sharing personal information. Turning points that decrease closeness between friends include moving apart and conflict (Johnson et al., 2004). As you read about friendship and romantic relationship development, think about turning points that might propel movement.

Friendships

Although friendships sometimes jump to life quickly, usually they unfold through a series of fairly predictable stages. Based on extensive study of friendships, Bill Rawlins (1981, 1994) developed a model of how friendships develop. His model broke friendships into six distinct stages. Rather than enumerating specific stages, however, our discussion will highlight the general flow of friendship as people move from being strangers to friends and—sometimes—back to less personal relationships.

Most friendships begin with interactions based on social roles. We meet potential friends in classes, at work, through membership in teams or clubs, or in an airport, a store, or public event. We might also meet a new person online. In initial interactions, we tend to rely on standard social rules. Generally, we stick with safe topics and exercise care in making disclosures. Disclosures sometimes are made more quickly online than in person because people seem willing to take more risks when not interacting face to face.

If we enjoy initial interactions, we're likely to try to get to know them better, so we see if there are sufficient common ground and interests to develop a friendship (Weinstock & Bond, 2000). According to communication scholar Michael Monsour (2002, 2006), most people seek friends who are like them in many ways, including age, background, interests, and status. A businessperson mentions aspects of family life to see whether an associate wants to get more personal. People on social networking sites often talk about experiences, books, and ideas. Although friendly exchanges are not dramatic, they allow us to explore the potential for a deeper relationship.

If both people enjoy interacting, they may begin to move outside of conventional social roles. Two co-workers might schedule a dinner after work. People who have gotten to know each other over the Internet sometimes develop enough interest to meet

DIGITAL MEDIA

Meeting New People through Facebook

With 250 million photos uploaded daily, Facebook is one of most trafficked sites in the United States **(http://www.zdnet.com/blog/facebook/facebooks-ipo-by-the-numbers/8329?tag= content;siu-container)**. Users create personal profiles, typically containing photos and lists of interests, exchange private or public messages, and join groups of friends. The viewing of detailed profile data is restricted to users from the same school or confirmed friends.

Facebook began as a local effort at Harvard. Within a few weeks of its launch by Mark Zuckerberg in February 2004, more than half the undergraduate population at Harvard had registered. Just two months later, Facebook expanded to the rest of the Ivy League. By December 2004, Facebook had become a network phenomenon across the country. By October 2005, Facebook had expanded to universities outside the United States. To learn more about the history of Facebook, go to the book's online resources for this chapter and click on WebLink 10.1.

in person. As people interact more personally, they begin to talk about feelings, values, goals, and attitudes (Yost, 2004). This personal knowledge forms the initial foundation of friendship.

Friendship grows as people show increased involvement and caring. At this point, friends often begin to work out their private ways of relating. When my friend Sue and I were in graduate school, we developed the ritual of calling each day between 6 and 7 P.M. to catch up while we were each fixing dinner. Some friends settle into patterns of getting together for specific things (watching games, shopping, racquetball, Saturday brunch, walking).

The benchmark of an established friendship is the assumption of continuity. Whereas earlier in the relationship people didn't count on getting together unless they made a specific plan, established friends don't have to ask whether they'll get together.

Trust is another criterion of established friendship. Through disclosing private information and responding with acceptance, friends earn each other's trust. In turn, they feel safe sharing even more intimate information and revealing vulnerabilities that they conceal from most people (Monsour, 2002; Taylor, 2002). Good friendships may continue indefinitely, in some cases for a lifetime.

Friendships wane when one or both people cease to be committed to them. Sometimes friends drift apart because each is pulled in a different direction by career demands or personal circumstances (Guerrero et al., 2008). This reminds us of the influence of surrounding contexts on relationships. The common interests and experiences that once fueled the friendship begin to dissolve. Casey's commentary illustrates how changes can cause friendships to wither.

Molly and I became friends our first day in middle school. We were best friends through high school and for our first year at college when we roomed together. Then she got really into the social scene—parties, hookups—and I got into campus-community partnerships. After a while, we were just into such different things that we didn't share any interests and didn't have anything to talk about.

Friends of the Heart and Friends of the Road

Lillian Rubin (1985) has made a career of studying close relationships, particularly friendships. One of her more interesting findings is that there are two basic kinds of friends: friends of the heart and friends of the road.

Friends of the heart are people we meet who become part of us in enduring ways. They are soul mates with whom we feel deeply and permanently connected. If friends of the heart move far away from each other, they often stay in touch and visit. Even if they don't maintain regular contact, they feel deeply woven into each other's lives.

Friends of the road are friends we make and from whom we part as we travel the road of life. We make friends wherever we are, and we provide support, companionship, fun, and so forth. When they or we move, we make no effort to stay in touch or maintain any continuing sense of connection. Friends of the road are people we enjoy for a time, then leave behind.

Friendships may also deteriorate because they've run their natural course and become boring or are no longer enriching (Norwood & Duck, 2009). The fact that some friendships don't last a lifetime doesn't mean that they aren't special and important. The FYI box on this page points out that friends at a particular time and place in our lives are important to us, even though they aren't forever friends. A third reason friendships end is the violation of rules. Telling a friend's secrets to a third person is a violation if you and your friend had an agreement to keep confidences. Deterioration doesn't always lead to the end of the friendship. Even when serious violations occur between friends, relationships can sometimes be repaired. For this to happen, both friends must be committed to rebuilding the relationship.

Romantic Relationships

Like friendships, many romantic relationships follow a similar evolutionary path. Researchers have identified as many as 12 specific stages, but we don't need to know all of these. It's more useful to think of romantic relationships as including three broad stages: escalating, navigating, and deteriorating.

Before forming romantic relationships, each of us has figured out some things about who we are and what qualities we look for in romantic partners. The self that we have developed influences our choice of romantic partners.

The earliest interaction in romantic relationships involves expressing interest (Metts, 2006). This stage involves both taking the initiative with others and responding to invitations they make to us. "I love this kind of music" is an example of an invitation to interact. We may also signal interest nonverbally by smiling or holding

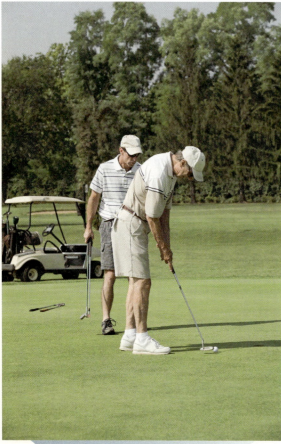

Sonya Etchison/Shutterstock

Friends share activities that allow them to get together regularly.

eye contact. The meaning of invitational communication is found on the relationship level, not the content level. "I love this kind of music" literally means that a person loves the music. On the relationship level of meaning, however, the message is "I'm interested in talking with you."

The two greatest influences on initial attraction are proximity and similarity. Proximity, or physical nearness, influences initial attraction. We can interact only with people we meet, whether in person or online. Consequently, where we live, work, and socialize and our online social communities constrain the possibilities for relationships. This reminds us that communication is systemic. From our discussion in Chapter 1, recall that the systemic character of communication means that context affects what happens when people transact. Some contexts, such as college campuses, promote meeting potential romantic partners, whereas other contexts are less conducive to meeting and dating.

Similarity is also important in romantic relationships. In the realm of romance, "birds of a feather flock together" seems truer than "opposites attract" (Levin, Taylor & Caudle, 2007; Samp & Palevitz, 2009). The **matching hypothesis** predicts that people will seek relationships with others who closely match their own values, attitudes, social background, and physical attractiveness (Kurt & Sherker, 2003). We may fantasize about relationships with stunning people, but in reality we're likely to pass them by for someone at our level of attractiveness. We also tend to be attracted to people whose values, attitudes, interests, and lifestyles are similar to ours.

As we continue to interact with others, both breadth and depth of disclosure increase. People may talk about difficulties in their lives, reasons for ending previous relationships, dreams for the future, and so forth. Increasingly, couples who are developing intimacy email, text, and IM to share private information and get to know each other (Samp & Palevitz, 2009).

If increased interaction intensifies attraction, the relationship may escalate. A turning point that signals greater intimacy is that two people begin to spend more and more time together and to rely less on external structures such as movies or parties. During this phase, some couples are almost inseparable. They immerse themselves in the budding relationship and may feel they can't be together enough.

As a romantic relationship heats up, partners often idealize each other. Idealizing occurs when we see a relationship and partner as more wonderful, exciting, and perfect than they really are (Guerrero et al., 2008; Hendrick & Hendrick, 1988, 1996). Yet not everyone idealizes a new romantic partner. A person who is calm and prefers to get to know someone gradually and as a friend first will not experience relationship escalation in the same way as a person who is impulsive and likes to move quickly in relationships. The FYI box on page 208 elaborates different styles of loving.

As a relationship escalates, partners also begin to develop relationship vocabularies that include nicknames and private codes. Private language heightens partners' sense of being a special couple. Partners invent words and nicknames for each other, and they develop ways to send private messages in public settings. Private language both reflects and enhances intimacy (Wood, 2006a).

Although online romantic relationships and face-to-face romantic relationships are alike in many respects, they also differ in some ways. Compared to face-to-face relationships, online ones tend to form more rapidly, and they tend to involve more deliberate and sometimes deceptive attempts to control self-presentation (Lengel, 2009). Also, online relationships foster idealized perceptions, so people involved in them may be more likely than partners in face-to-face relationships to see each other in terms of

DIVERSITY

Styles of Loving

Just as people differ in their tastes in food and dress, so do we differ in how we love. Researchers have identified six different styles of loving, each of which is valid, although not all styles are compatible with one another (Hendrick & Hendrick, 1996; Hendrick et al., 1984; Lee, 1973, 1988). Although these researchers refer to styles of "love," you will notice that both love and commitment characterize the styles. See whether you can identify your style of loving in the descriptions that follow:

Eros is a style of loving that is passionate, intense, and fast moving. Not confined to sexual passion, eros may be expressed in spiritual, intellectual, or emotional ways.

Storge (pronounced "store-gay") is a comfortable, "best friends" kind of love that grows gradually to create a stable, even-keeled companionship.

Ludus is a playful, sometimes manipulative style of loving. For ludic lovers, love is a challenge, a puzzle, a game to be relished but not to lead to commitment.

Mania is an unsettling style of loving marked by emotional extremes. Manic lovers often are insecure about their value and their partners' commitment.

Agape is a selfless kind of love in which a beloved's happiness is more important than one's own. Agapic lovers are generous, unselfish, and devoted.

Pragma is a pragmatic and goal-oriented style of loving. Pragmas rely on reason and practical considerations when initially selecting people to love.

what they want or need. Third, because physical presence is not part of online relationships, partners cannot experience the kind of closeness that is fueled by touch, smell and taste.

Some couples move onto commitment. Others discover that the magic fades quickly and they part ways. A third option is for couples to reflect and perhaps discuss their relationship's strengths, problems, and potential for the future. After the exhilaration of falling in love is over, partners consider whether they want to transform love into commitment. If so, they work through problems and obstacles to long-term viability. Some gay and lesbian partners have to resolve differences in openness about their sexual orientations. Couples may need to work out differences in religions and conflicts of location and career goals.

As you might expect, working through problems often involves negotiation and even conflict. Many couples are able to revise their relationships in ways that make them stronger and more able to endure. Other couples cannot resolve problems. Thus, people often fall in love and move through the intensifying stage yet choose not to stay together. As the FYI box on the next page points out, some couples have additional issues to work through in forming a long-term relationship.

If partners decide to make a long-term commitment, they transform their relationship into a given around which they arrange other aspects of their lives. Long-term commitments take many forms. The most common forms are marriage and cohabitation. Historically, marriage was available only to heterosexuals, but that is changing. Many more same-sex couples cohabit without being married, and a good number of both married and cohabiting same-sex couples have children. Increased social acceptance of same-sex couples has allowed more to adopt. Approximately 19 percent of same-sex couples raising children have adopted a child, more than double the number in 2008 (Tavernise, 2011).

Yet, not everyone marries, and not everyone who marries stays married. Currently, 25 percent of households in the United States consist of one person—the greatest number of people living alone in this country's history (Olds & Schwartz, 2010). Marriage is also occurring later than it once did—today, half of Americans in the 25- to 29-year-old age range are unmarried (Coontz, 2007; Parker-Pope, 2010). By the age of 35, 10 percent of American women have lived with three or more husbands or domestic partners, showing that commitments don't necessarily last (Cherlin, 2010).

Not being married doesn't necessarily mean not having a family. Increasing numbers of people are creating social networks that function as families (Braithwaite, Bach, Baxter, Diverniero, Hammonds, Hosek, Willer, & Wolf, 2010). People also have children without being married. Nearly 40 percent of births in America are to unmarried parents (Coontz, 2007). Single women and single men who adopt children increase the number of single-parent families. Also adding to the number of single-parent families are divorced parents who have custody of children.

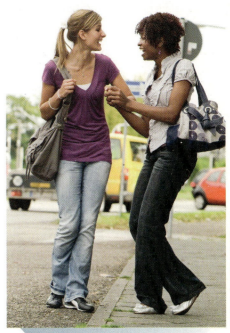

Trust and comfort characterize established friendships.

Stephanie Coontz (2005), who studies the history of marriage, thinks the mushrooming variety of family forms makes it possible for more people to have fulfilling family lives. Because we don't all have to try to fit into one form or one model of a family, we are able to create families that suit our values and needs.

DIVERSITY

Stages in the Escalation of Interracial Relationships

In addition to the stages generally followed in developing intimacy, partners in interracial relationships often deal simultaneously with relationship stages prompted by external pressures, such as bias against interracial dating and disapproval by friends and family. The following model (Foeman & Nance, 1999) describes four stages experienced by many interracial romantic partners.

1. Racial awareness: Each partner becomes conscious of his or her racial identity and views of the partner's racial identity. In addition, partners heighten awareness of broad social perspectives on their own and the other's racial groups.

2. Coping: The couple struggles with external pressures, including families' and friends' disapproval, and develops strategies to protect their relationship from external damage.

3. Identity emergence: Partners reject external definitions of who they are and declare their couple identity to others. Partners also develop a definition of the relationship for themselves.

4. Relationship maintenance: The couple works to preserve the relationship as it incorporates new challenges, such as having children, moving to new areas, and entering new social circles.

For many committed romantic relationships, the longest stage involves maintaining intimacy over time and in the face of changes in partners, the relationship, and surrounding contexts. Couples continuously work through new problems, revisit old ones, and accommodate changes in their individual and joint lives. To use an automotive analogy, maintaining a relationship involves both preventive maintenance and periodic repairs (Canary & Stafford, 1994; Stafford, 2009). In her study of older couples who have stayed together, therapist Maggie Scarf (2008) found that the later years in very long-term marriages can be the happiest, in part because couples have learned to focus on what matters and not to sweat the small stuff. Other research (Parker-Pope, 2009) confirms the finding that many couples find the "empty nest years" the happiest because there is less stress and more couple time.

The nucleus of an established intimate relationship is its **relationship culture,** which is the private world of rules, understandings, meanings, and patterns of interacting that partners create (Wood, 1982). By the time a couple commits to an intimate relationship, there is a well-established relationship culture, but it is not static. Instead, it continues to evolve throughout the life of the relationship. Especially important in navigating is ongoing small talk, through which partners weave the fabric of their history and their current lives, experiences, and dreams.

The concept of the relationship culture includes how a couple manages relationship dialectics. Chris and Jimmy may do a great many things together, whereas Lana and Kaya emphasize autonomy. Brent and Carmella may be open and expressive, whereas Marion and Paige prefer more privacy in their marriage. There aren't right and wrong ways to manage dialectics, because individuals and couples differ in their needs and in their preferences for managing tensions between autonomy and connection, openness and privacy, and novelty and routine.

Not all committed relationships endure. Tensions within a relationship as well as pressures and problems in surrounding contexts may contribute to the ending of the intimate bond (Duck & Wood, 2006).

Often the first sign that a relationship is in trouble is that one or both partners individually dwells on problems in the relationship and dissatisfactions with the partner. It's easy for focusing on problems to become a self-fulfilling prophecy: As gloomy thoughts snowball and awareness of positive features of the relationship ebbs, partners may actually bring about the failure of their relationship.

There are some general sex and gender differences in what partners brood about during intrapsychic processes (Duck & Wood, 2006; Wood, 1993c, 1993d, 2013). For women, unhappiness with a relationship most often arises when communication declines in quality or quantity. Men are more likely to be dissatisfied by specific behaviors or the lack of valued behaviors. In other words, many women feel a relationship is breaking down if "we don't really communicate with each other anymore," whereas men are more likely to feel dissatisfied if "we don't do fun things together anymore."

Our era is witnessing increasing variety in long-term romantic relationships.

There are also sex differences in sources of jealousy. In general, women are more jealous of emotional commitments and men are more jealous of sexual involvements. These gender differences also show up in reactions to online relationships. Women are more jealous of a partner's emotional investment in another relationship whereas men are more jealous of a partner's sexual infidelity (cybersex) (Groothof, Dijkstra, & Bareids, 2009).

Deteriorating relationships often experience the breakdown of established patterns, understandings, and rules. Partners may stop talking during dinner, no longer bother to call when they are running late, and in other ways depart

SHARPEN YOUR SKILL

Good Endings

We've all been through bad breakups. Anger, frustration, confusion, and a sense of betrayal are feelings that can prompt us to behave less well than we should when ending a relationship. But what would a good breakup look like? As a class, create a script for effective and ethical communication during the breakup of a serious romantic relationship.

I am indebted to Emily Brooke Anzicek, who is on the faculty at Bowling Green State University, for developing this exercise and allowing me to include it in this chapter.

from rules and patterns in their relational culture. As the fabric of intimacy weakens, dissatisfaction mounts. Because many women are socialized to be sensitive to interpersonal nuances, they are generally more likely than men to notice tensions and early symptoms of relationship distress (Wood, 2013). Whether a troubled relationship ends depends on how committed partners are, whether they perceive attractive alternatives to the relationship, and whether they have the communication skills to resolve problems.

If partners lack commitment or the communication skills they need to restore intimacy, they often begin to tell others about problems in the relationship. They look to friends and family members to listen and provide support. Partners may give self-serving accounts of the breakup to save face and secure sympathy from others. Thus, Vera may tell her friends all the ways in which Frank was at fault and portray herself as the innocent party. Each partner may criticize the other and expect friends to take sides (Duck & Wood, 2006). Although self-serving explanations of breakups are common, they aren't necessarily constructive.

If partners decide to part ways, they decide, either separately or in collaboration, how to explain their problems to friends, co-workers, children, in-laws, and social acquaintances. In addition, each partner must individually make sense of the relationship: what it meant, why it failed, and how it affected them. Typically, we mourn a relationship that has died. Even the person who initiates a breakup often is sad about the failure to realize what seemed possible at one time. Yet sadness may be accompanied by other, more positive outcomes from breakups. Ty Tashiro and Patricia Frazier (2003) surveyed undergraduates who had recently broken up with a romantic partner. They found that breakups generate not only distress but also personal growth. People reported that breaking up gave them new insights into themselves, improved family relationships, and clarified their ideas about future partners.

Our discussion describes how many people experience the evolution of romantic relationships. However, not everyone follows the pattern presented here. Some long-term partners experience falling in love again or experience problems that lead to brooding and dissatisfaction. Couples may slide into deterioration and then invest to revive intimacy.

Guidelines for Communicating in Personal Relationships

To sustain fulfilling personal relationships, partners rely on communication to deal with internal tensions and external pressures. We'll consider four specific guidelines to help friends and romantic partners sustain satisfying relationships.

Adapt Communication to Manage Distance

Geographic separation can be difficult for friends and romantic couples. Two of the greatest problems for long-distance commitments are the lack of daily communication about small events and issues, and unrealistic expectations about interaction when partners are geographically together (Stafford, 2005). Greg's commentary offers an example of both of these problems.

 Greg

When Annie and I first moved to different cities, I don't know whether it was harder being apart or together. I missed her so much when we were apart for weeks at a time, and I really missed just being together in a laid-back kind of way. But whenever we were together, we both felt really pressured to be together every minute and not to have any disagreements or bad times. That's just not possible, and expecting it really caused us a lot of grief. Now, we are careful to call and stay in touch with email so that we feel part of each other's regular lives. And we've learned that it's okay to have some private time even when we're together for only a few days.

The first problem—not being able to share small talk and daily routines—is a major loss, especially for people who don't have access to cell phones and email. As we have seen, communication about ordinary topics weaves partners' lives together. Mundane conversations between friends and romantic partners are the foundation of relationships.

A second common problem is unrealistic expectations for time together. Because partners have so little time when they are physically together, they often believe that every moment must be perfect. They feel there should be no conflict and that they should spend every minute together. Yet this is an unrealistic expectation. The need for autonomy may even be greater for long-distance couples because partners are used to living alone and have established independent rhythms that may not mesh well.

The good news is that these problems don't necessarily sabotage long-distance romance. Many couples maintain satisfying commitments despite geographic separation (Rohlfing, 1995; Stafford, 2005). Developments in communication technologies have increased the ways in which people can stay in touch.

SHARPEN YOUR SKILL

Connect with Others in Long-Distance Relationships

If you are in a long-distance relationship, you can learn a lot from others who are or have been in one. There are Web sites and online communities devoted to long-distance relationships. Most of them offer advice, and some feature stories in which people who are in or have been in long-distance relationships share experiences and ideas about what worked and didn't work. Clicking on WebLinks 10.2, 10.3, and 10.4 in the book's online resources for this chapter will take you to three sites that focus on managing long-distance relationships.

Coping with Geographic Separation

Following are some strategies that people report are helpful in sustaining long-distance love (Franklin & Ramage, 1999; Justice, 1999; Stafford, 2005):

1. Recognize that long-distance relationships are common; you're not alone.

2. Create more social support systems (friends) while separated from a romantic partner.

3. Communicate creatively; send video- and audiotapes.

4. Before separating, work out ground rules for going out with friends, phoning, visiting, and writing.

5. Use time together wisely: Be affectionate and have fun. Being serious all the time isn't smart.

6. Maintain honesty. Especially when partners live apart, they need to be straight with each other.

7. Build an open, supportive communication climate so you can talk about issues and feelings.

8. Maintain trust by abiding by ground rules that were agreed on, phoning when you say you will, and keeping lines of communication open.

9. Focus on the positive aspects of separation, such as career advancement or ability to concentrate on work.

10. Set a time limit for how long you'll be apart.

To discover additional ways of managing long-distance relationships, go to the book's online resources for this chapter and click on WebLink 10.5.

Ensure Equity in Family Relationships

Today, most adults work outside the home. Therefore, partners in a relationship must balance investments in two careers with investments in maintaining the relationship. According to **equity theory,** people are happier and more satisfied with equitable relationships than with inequitable ones. In equitable relationships, partners perceive that the benefits and costs of being in the relationship are about equal for each of them. When we think we are investing more than our partner is, we tend to be resentful and angry; when it seems our partner is investing more than we are, we're likely to feel guilty (Guerrero, La Valley, & Farinelli, 2008).

Although few partners demand moment-to-moment equality, most of us want our relationships to be equitable over time (Dainton & Zelley, 2006; Wood, 2011). Equity has multiple dimensions. We may evaluate the fairness of financial, emotional, physical, and other contributions to a relationship. One area that strongly affects satisfaction of spouses and cohabiting partners is equity in housework and child care. Inequitable division of domestic obligations fuels dissatisfaction and resentment, both of which harm intimacy (Chethik, 2008; DeMaris, 2007).

Traditionally, women were assigned care of the home and family because men were more likely to be the primary or only wage earners. That is no longer true. Today, most adults of both sexes work outside the home. Unfortunately, divisions of family and home responsibilities inadequately reflect changes in employment. Even when both partners in heterosexual relationships work outside the home, in most dual-career families women do most of the child care and homemaking (Canary & Wahba, 2006;

Gerson, 2004; Guldner, 2003; Hochschild with Machung, 2003). In her commentary, Molly gives us insight into the resentment that can grow when both partners work outside the home but one does most of the work in and for the home.

Molly

It really isn't fair when both spouses work outside the home but only one of them takes care of the home and kids. For years, that was how Jake's and my marriage worked, no matter how much I tried to talk with him about a fairer arrangement. Finally, I had just had it, so I quit doing everything. Groceries didn't get bought, laundry piled up, and he didn't have clean shirts, he didn't remember his mother's birthday (and for the first time ever, I didn't remind him), bills didn't get paid. After a while, he suggested we talk about a system we could both live with.

How do gay and lesbian partners manage domestic responsibilities? According to existing research, lesbian couples generally create more egalitarian relationships than either heterosexuals or gay men do. More than any other type of couple, lesbians are likely to communicate collaboratively to make decisions about domestic work and parenting (Huston & Schwartz, 1995; Peplau & Beals, 2003). Consequently, lesbians are least likely to have negative feelings involving inequity (Kurdek, 1993). Gay men, like heterosexual men, tend to use the power derived from income to authorize inequitable contributions to domestic life. In gay couples, the man who makes more money tends to have and use more power, both in making decisions that affect the relationship and in avoiding housework (Huston & Schwartz, 1995).

Not only do women usually do more of the actual labor of maintaining a home and caring for children, they also tend to assume a greater portion of **psychological responsibility,** which involves remembering, planning, and coordinating domestic activities (Wood, 2006b). Parents may alternate taking children to the doctor, but it is usually the mother who remembers when the kids need checkups, makes the appointments, and reminds the father to take the children. Both partners sign cards and give gifts, but in many families it is women who assume responsibility for remembering the birthdays and buying the cards and gifts. Successful long-term relationships in our era require partners to communicate collaboratively to design equitable divisions of responsibility.

The consequences of inequity are substantial. Women who do most of the homemaking and child-care tasks are often stressed, fatigued, and susceptible to illness (Hochschild with Machung, 2003), and they are at a disadvantage in their paid work because they have such heavy responsibilities at home (McDonald, Phipps, & Lethbridge, 2005). In addition, the inequity of the arrangement is a primary source of relationship dissatisfaction and instability (Chethik, 2008; DeMaris, 2007).

To work out an equitable division of domestic labor requires more than agreeing that each partner will do a fair share. Partners must also agree on a standard of housekeeping. Many couples argue because one person wants floors vacuumed and beds changed more often than the other person. The person with the higher standard may feel frustrated that her or his partner doesn't do more while the person with the lower standard resents being nagged to do work he or she considers unimportant (Wood, 2011). There's no right or wrong standard for domestic labor, but family members need to agree on one.

Avoid Intimate Partner Violence

Intimate partner violence cuts across lines of socioeconomic status, race, and ethnicity (Johnson, 2008; Spitzack & Cupach, 2009). Violence is high not only in marriages but also in dating and cohabiting relationships (Johnson, 2006, 2008). In addition to physical abuse, verbal and emotional brutality poison altogether too many relationships.

CAREER
A New Job for Dad

The recession that began in 2008 has propelled changes in men's involvement in home life. Between 2008 and 2010, millions of Americans lost jobs, and the majority of them were men. Currently, nearly 20 percent of men between 25 and 54 do not hold jobs. This is the highest percentage of unemployed men during earning years since 1948 when the labor bureau began keeping track (Brooks, 2010; Yen, 2011). As a consequence, many men who are out of work have become stay-at-home dads while their partners have become sole breadwinners. Laid off after 20 years in a Fortune 500 company, Andrew Emery says, "It was a big part of my identity; it's who you are. It took me a long time to fill in the blank when people asked me what I do" (Kershaw, 2009, p. E6). Yet, after the initial adjustment, many men discover opportunities and satisfaction in being full-time fathers. In fact, many of them are hoping to find reemployment in careers that enable them to spend more time with their children (Kershaw, 2009).

Among heterosexuals, intimate partner violence is inflicted primarily by men against women. In fact, intimate partner violence is the most common form of violence committed against women in the United States (Haynes, 2009). Men make up an estimated 15 percent of all victims of intimate partner violence (France, 2006). Although a majority of perpetrators of intimate partner violence are men, we need to remember that the vast majority of men do not inflict violence on girlfriends and wives, and they would not consider doing so.

A rising form of intimate partner violence is stalking, which is repeated, intrusive behavior that is uninvited and unwanted, that seems obsessive, and that makes the target afraid or concerned for her or his safety. In studies conducted on college campuses (Bazar, 2007, Spitzack & Cupach, 2009), 13 to 21 percent of students report having been stalked—approximately the same percentage of the general population that reports being stalked (Spitzack & Cupach, 2009). About half of female victims are stalked by ex-partners and another 25 percent by men they have dated at least once (Meloy, 2006). Stalking is particularly easy on campuses because it isn't difficult to learn others' routines. IMing and social networking sites such as MySpace and Facebook give stalkers more ways to learn about (potential) victims' habits and patterns.

Violence seldom stops without intervention. Instead, in most cases it follows a predictable cycle: Tension mounts in the abuser; the abuser explodes, becoming violent; the abuser then is remorseful and loving; the victim feels loved and reassured that the relationship is working; then tension mounts anew, and the cycle begins again (Figure 10.1).

Communication and violence are related in two ways. Most obviously, patterns of communication between couples, and abusers' patterns of intrapersonal

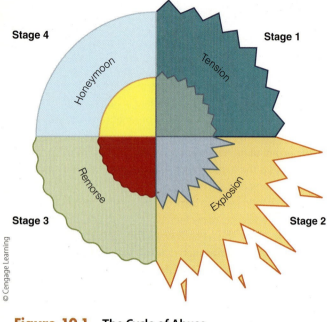

Stage 4

Stage 1

Stage 3

Stage 2

© Cengage Learning

Figure 10.1   **The Cycle of Abuse**

communication, can fuel tendencies toward violence. Some partners deliberately annoy and taunt each other, a pattern that can lead to extreme violence. Also, the language that abusers use to describe physical assaults on partners includes denial, trivializing the harm done, and blaming the partner or circumstances for "making me do it" (Johnson, 2006; Wood, 2004b). These intrapersonal communication patterns allow abusers to deny their offenses, justify unjustifiable actions, and cast responsibility outside themselves.

Violent relationships are *not* the fault of victims. A person cannot earn battering, and nobody deserves violence. If you know or suspect that someone you care about is a victim of abuse, don't ignore the situation, and don't assume it's none of your business. It is an act of friendship to notice and offer to help. Victims of violence must make the ultimate decision about what to do, but the support and concern of friends can help them.

Insist on Safer Sex

In the HIV/AIDS era, sexual activities pose serious, even deadly, threats. To date, 617,000 people in the United States have died of AIDS (Notable Numbers, 2011), and more than one and a quarter million people in the United States are living with HIV (Altman, 2008). Many of them contracted the virus through sex with a hookup, casual date, or serious romantic partner. New HIV and AIDS cases have actually increased since 1999 (Altman, 2008). Every single day, an estimated 7,000 people are infected with HIV (Notable Numbers, 2011).

In 2009, 1,244,180 Chlamydial infections were reported, and between 1990 and 2009, the rate of reported Chlamydial infection increased from 160.2 to 409.2 cases per 100,000 (2009).

Despite these dangers, a great many people still don't practice safer sex, which includes abstinence, restricting sexual activity to a single partner who has been tested and found to be free of HIV and other STDs, and using latex condoms.

Communication scholars have found two primary reasons why people don't practice safer sex. First, ironically, many people find it more embarrassing to talk about sex than to engage in it. They find it awkward to ask direct questions of partners ("Have you been tested for HIV?" "Are you having sex with anyone else?") or to make direct requests of partners ("I want you to wear a condom," "I would like you to be tested for HIV before we have sex"). Because about 25 percent of people who are HIV positive are not aware of their medical infection, tests are imperative before having sexual relationships (Centers for Disease Control and Prevention, 2011). Naturally, it's difficult to talk explicitly about sex and the dangers of STDs. However, it is far more difficult to live with HIV or another disease or the knowledge that you infected another person.

A second reason people sometimes fail to negotiate safer sex is that alcohol or other drugs have diminished their rational thought and control. Alcohol and other drugs loosen inhibitions, including appropriate concerns about personal safety.

SHARPEN YOUR SKILL

Test Your Knowledge about Sexually Transmitted Diseases

Many people hold dangerous misunderstandings about sexually transmitted diseases (STDs). Here's a chance for you to test your knowledge against the facts (American Social Health Association, 2005; Cates et al., 2004; Centers for Disease Control and Prevention, 2011; "Notable Numbers," 2011;"One in Four," 2008; Weinstock, Berman, & Cates, 2004).

Misconception: If I'm tested for HIV and make sure any sexual partner is, I'm safe.

Get the Facts: HIV is not the only STD, and it's not the most common. Other STDs are genital warts, genital herpes, hepatitis B, chlamydia, gonorrhea, human papillomavirus (HPV), syphilis, and trichomoniasis. One in 20 people will get hepatitis B in his or her lifetime, and 15 to 25 percent of those who do will die from liver disease.

Misconception: I'm not taking much of a chance because few people have STDs.

Get the Facts: By age 25, 1 of 2 sexually active youths will contract an STD. More than 65 million Americans are currently living with an STD, and 15 million new cases are diagnosed each year.

Misconception: STDs affect older people.

Get the Facts: Half of all new STDs occur in people 15 to 24 years old. Each year, one in four teens contracts an STD. Among blacks, 50 percent of 14- to 19-year-olds contract an STD.

Misconception: The incidence of STDs is declining.

Get the Facts: Some STDs, such as genital warts, are actually increasing.

Misconception: I can't catch an STD if I have only oral sex.

Get the Facts: Think again. You can catch STDs from oral, anal, or vaginal sexual activity.

Misconception: I could tell if someone had an STD because there are symptoms.

Get the Facts: Many STDs have no symptoms or no early ones. For instance, HPV, which 50 percent of sexually active people will contract at some point, often has no symptoms.

Misconception: STDs can be treated, so there aren't serious consequences even if I do get one.

Get the Facts: Some can be treated. Some are resistant to treatment. And because some have no symptoms, people may not seek treatment until it's too late.

Misconception: I see a doctor regularly, so I am tested for STDs.

Get the Facts: Most doctors do not routinely test for STDs.

Misconception: Other than HIV, STDs don't have major consequences.

Get the Facts: Because STDs often have no symptoms, they may go untreated for some time. Effects of STDs include infertility, blindness, liver cancer, increased vulnerability to HIV, and death.

Learn more about STDs by going to the book's online resources for this chapter and clicking on WebLink 10.6.

Good communication skills facilitate negotiating safer sex. It is more constructive to say, "I feel unsafe having unprotected sex" than "Without a condom, you could give me an STD" (note that the first statement uses *I*-language, whereas the second one uses *you*-language). Relationship language fosters a positive communication climate; for example, talk about *our safety* and *our relationship* when negotiating sexual activity. People who care about themselves and their partners are honest about their sexual histories and assertive about safer sex practices.

SUMMARY

In this chapter, we've explored communication in personal relationships, which are defined by commitment, uniqueness, relationship dialectics, relationship rules, and interaction with surrounding contexts. We traced the typical evolutionary paths of friendships and romances by noting how partners communicate during escalating, stabilizing, and declining trajectories of personal relationships.

In the final section of the chapter, we considered four guidelines for friends and romantic partners.

The communication principles and skills we have discussed in this and previous chapters can help us meet the challenges of sustaining intimacy across geographic distance, creating equitable relationships, resisting violence, and negotiating safer sex. Good communication skills are essential to managing these challenges so that we, our intimates, and the relationships we create survive and thrive over time.

REVIEW, REFLECT, EXTEND

The Reflect, Discuss, and Apply Questions that follow will help you review, reflect on, and extend the information and ideas presented in this chapter. These resources, and a diverse selection of additional study tools, are also available online at the CourseMate for *Communication Mosaics*. Your CourseMate includes a student workbook, WebLinks, TED Talks hyperlinks and activities, chapter glossary and flashcards, interactive video activities, Speech Builder Express, and InfoTrac College Edition. For more information or to access this book's online resources, visit **www .cengagebrain.com**.

KEY CONCEPTS

agape, 208
autonomy/connection, 202
commitment, 199
equity theory, 213
eros, 208
investment, 199
ludus, 208
mania, 208
matching hypothesis, 207
neutralization, 203
novelty/predictability, 202
openness/closedness, 203
passion, 199

personal relationship, 199
pragma, 208
psychological responsibility, 214
reframing, 203
relationship culture, 210
relationship dialectics, 202
rules, 200
segmentation, 203
separation, 203
social relationship, 199
storge, 208
turning point, 204

Reflect, Discuss, Apply

1. Think about the distinction between love and commitment and the role each plays in personal relationships. Describe relationships in which commitment is present but love is not. Describe relationships in which love exists but not commitment. What can you conclude about the impact of each?

2. As a class, discuss differences in the goals and rules for friendships and romantic relationships.

Does comparing the two kinds of relationships give you any insight into the difficulties that commonly arise when two people who have been friends become romantically involved? What are the difficulties of trying to be friends with someone with whom you've been romantically involved?

Recommended Resources

1. Visit an online dating service. Identify qualities men and women claim they have and qualities men and women are looking for in romantic partners. What similarities and differences can you identify?

2. Many men as well as women are committed to ending violence against women. To learn more about men who are committed to stopping

violence, go to the book's online resources for this chapter and click on WebLink 10.7.

3. View the film, *About a Boy* (2002), directed by Paul and Chris Weitz. The story is about a surprising and unusual friendship between a selfish single man and a lonely boy. The central themes are friendship and support.

EXPERIENCE COMMUNICATION CASE STUDY

Abuse

Apply what you've learned in this chapter by analyzing the following case study, using the accompanying questions as a guide. These questions and a video of the case study are also available online at your CourseMate for *Communication Mosaics*.

Amy met Hailley at the beginning of the school year. Amy was drawn to Hailley because she seemed confident and positive. Over several months, the two of them became good friends, sharing high and low points about school, family, and dates.

Two months ago, Hailley started dating Dan, a man who dropped out of college after two years and who now works as a waiter. At first, Hailley seemed happy with Dan, but then she started changing. She's become less extroverted and a lot less positive.

Often, when Amy suggests doing something together, Hailley says she can't because Dan might come over or call, and he doesn't like her not to be available to him. When Amy sees them together, she notices that he doesn't treat her with respect and often criticizes her harshly. For example, when

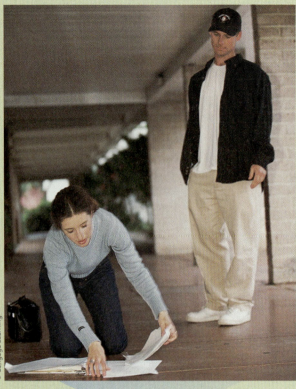

© Cengage Learning

Hailley said something to Dan when he was on his cell phone, he shouted, "Don't talk to me. I'm on the phone." Later, when Hailey dropped some papers, Dan said harshly, "You are so clumsy!"

Amy is concerned that Hailley may be in a relationship that is verbally and physically abusive. Amy thinks that Dan is damaging Hailley's self-concept, and she wants to help.

Amy: I'm just worried about you. I don't like the way he treats you.

Hailley: Because he called me clumsy? I am clumsy, and besides, if I do something stupid, I can't expect him not to notice.

Amy: But he doesn't show any respect for you at all.

Hailley: Well, he's a guy. He says what he's thinking. I know a lot of people's boyfriends like that. Besides, I don't think there's anything wrong with Dan. I think I just have to stop doing things that make him mad.

1. If you were Hailley's friend, what responsibilities would you have, if any, for helping her?

2. If you were Dan's friend, what might you say to alter his behaviors?

3. How does the concept of reflected appraisal, discussed in Chapter 9, apply to this case?

Never doubt that a small group of thoughtful, committed people can change the world. Indeed, it is the only thing that ever has. *Margaret Mead*

11

Communication in Groups and Teams

▶ If a patient wants to die when medical procedures could save him, should his doctors follow his wishes?

▶ A woman whose health makes carrying a fetus dangerous to her nonetheless wants to become pregnant, and she asks doctors for fertility treatment. Should doctors provide the treatment?

Imagine trying to answer these questions. Imagine that you have only two minutes to consider each question and come up with an opinion about it. And imagine that how you handle these questions determines whether you get into medical school. For many people aspiring to attend medical school, this is reality, not imagination. A number of medical schools, including those at Stanford, Los Angeles, and Cincinnati, have decided that the standard criteria for admissions decisions to med school—grades, test scores, and the traditional interview—are ineffective in screening out applicants who lack the communication skills to be good doctors (Harris, 2011). No longer is a doctor the sole and unquestioned expert. Instead, most doctors today are members of health care teams, so the ability to work collaboratively is critical. Doctors who bully nurses, don't listen to patients, and are too dogmatic to consider other points of view are poor team members. In fact, as many as 98,000 preventable deaths each year have been traced to poor communication among doctors, nurses, patients, and other members of health-care teams (Harris, 2011).

FOCUS QUESTIONS

1. Why are groups and teams becoming increasingly popular in professional life?

2. What are the potential strengths of group discussion?

3. What are the potential limitations of group discussion?

4. To what extent should leadership be assigned to a single group member?

To assess communication skills for teamwork, applicants have nine eight-minute interviews in which they discuss specific situations with interviewers. There are no right or wrong answers to the questions. Rather, applicants are assessed on how well they communicate with interviewers. Are they overly opinionated? Do they listen well to others? Are they comfortable working collaboratively? Do they encourage others to offer ideas? How do they handle disagreement, which is common among members of health-care teams? Teamwork is so critical to effective patient-care today that a number of medical schools not only base admissions on the ability to collaborate, but also require students to take courses in teamwork.

Have you had experiences in groups and teams where everyone participated and had a strong sense of commitment? Have you had other experiences with groups and teams that were neither cohesive nor productive? Based on all your experiences, do you enjoy working on groups and teams? If so, you have lots of company. If not, you also have lots of company. For every person who is enthusiastic about group work, there is another person who dreads or merely tolerates it. There are sound reasons for both points of view. Groups generally take more time to reach decisions than individuals do, yet group decisions often are superior to those made by a single person. Although group interaction can heighten creativity and commitment, it may also suppress individuals and their ideas.

Whether your experiences in groups have been positive, negative, or a mix of the two, groups are an inescapable part of life. Pick up any newspaper, and you will see announcements for social groups, volunteer service committees, personal support groups, health teams, focus groups run by companies trying out new products, and political action coalitions. If you go online, you'll encounter a range of virtual groups that you can join to give and get personal support, exchange information, and share interests. It is a rare person who doesn't participate in groups.

In this chapter, we'll see how basic communication skills covered in Part II apply to interaction in groups and teams. We begin by defining groups and teams and tracing their rising popularity. Second, we identify potential strengths and weaknesses of groups and teams. Third, we consider aspects of groups that affect communication. Fourth, we identify two effective methods of group decision making. Finally, we discuss guidelines for effective participation in groups.

Understanding Communication in Groups and Teams

There are many kinds of groups, each with distinctive goals and communication patterns. Social groups provide us with conversation and recreation with people we enjoy. Communication in social groups tends to be relaxed, informal, and more focused on the interpersonal climate than on a task (Barge, 2009). Personal growth groups enable people to deal with significant issues and problems in a supportive context. In personal growth groups, communication aims to help members clarify and address issues in their lives. Task groups exist to solve problems, develop policies, or achieve other substantive goals. The communication of task groups concentrates on evidence, reasoning, and decision making, as well as on organizing, discussing, and maintaining a healthy climate for interaction.

Although different types of groups have distinct primary purposes, most groups include three kinds of communication: *climate communication, procedural communication*, and *task communication*. For example, social groups devote the bulk of their talk to climate communication, yet they often move into task discussion, as when one friend asks another for help in solving a problem. Task groups typically include some climate communication and a good deal of procedural communication, and personal growth groups include task communication to deal with members' issues, climate communication to create and sustain support and trust, and procedural communication to manage time and move conversation along.

Groups and teams are central to work life in our era.

Mark Edward Atkinson/Jupiter Images

Communication in groups and teams involves the basic processes we discussed in earlier chapters. For example, constructive group communication requires that members use effective verbal and nonverbal communication, check perceptions with one another, listen mindfully, build good climates, and adapt communication to each other and various group goals and situations.

Defining Groups and Teams

What is a group? Are six people standing in line to buy tickets a group? Are four businesspeople in an airport lounge a group? Unless people are interacting and involved in collective endeavors, a group does not exist. The foregoing examples describe collections of individuals but not groups.

For a group to exist, the people must interact, be interdependent, have a common goal, and share some rules of conduct (Harris & Sherblom, 2010; Lumsden & Lumsden, 2009; Rothwell, 2009). Thus, we can define a **group** as three or more people who interact over time, depend on one another, and follow shared rules of conduct to reach a common goal. Individual members' goals may differ from or be in tension with the collective goal, but a common goal still exists. Group members perceive themselves as interdependent—as needing one another to achieve something, such as developing a policy for the workplace, playing a sport, or promoting personal growth.

A **team** is a special kind of group characterized by different, complementary resources of members and by a strong sense of collective identity (Rothwell, 2009). Like all groups, teams involve interaction,

DIGITAL MEDIA

Virtual Teams

Increasingly, teams do their work virtually. Communication researchers Erik Timmerman and Craig Scott (2006) point out that the degree of virtualness varies. Some teams work face-to-face part of the time and online part of the time. Some teams rely entirely on videoconferencing, whereas other teams never even see each other but communicate via e-mail and groupware. Across teams with different degrees of virtualness, those that communicate effectively, especially in terms of members' responsiveness to one another, have the highest cohesiveness and greatest member satisfaction.

interdependence, shared rules, and common goals. Yet teams are distinct from groups in two respects. First, teams consist of people who bring different and specialized resources to a common project. Second, teams develop greater interdependence and a stronger sense of collective identity than some groups (Lumsden & Lumsden, 2009).

Groups and teams develop rules that members understand and follow. You will recall from Chapter 4 that constitutive rules state what counts as what. For example, in some groups disagreement counts as a positive sign of involvement and critical thinking, whereas other groups regard disagreement as negative. Regulative rules regulate how, when, and with whom we interact. For instance, a group might have the regulative rules that members do not interrupt each other and that disagreements within the group are not discussed with outsiders.

Shared goals also characterize groups and teams. Citizens form groups to accomplish political goals, establish community programs, influence zoning decisions, support and raise money for political candidates, and provide neighborhood security. Workers form groups to safeguard benefits and job security, and they work in teams to evaluate, make, and implement policies and to improve productivity. Other groups, both face-to-face and online, promote personal growth (therapy and support groups), nourish shared interests (backpacking groups, gardening clubs), socialize (fraternities and sororities), engage in service work (Lions Club, Kiwanis Club), and participate in sports and games (intramural teams, bridge clubs). As Mieko's account shows, when a common goal dissolves, the group disbands or redefines its purpose.

 Mieko

When I first came here to go to school, I felt very alone. I met some other students from Japan, and we formed a group to help us feel at home in America. For the first year, that group was most important to us because we felt uprooted. The second year, it was not so important, because we'd all started finding ways to fit in here, and we felt more at home. The third year, we decided not to be a group anymore. The reason we wanted a group no longer existed.

The Rise of Groups and Teams

Today, groups and teams are more than ever a part of work life (Barge, 2009; Harris & Sherblom, 2010). Whether you are an attorney working with a litigation team, a healthcare professional on a medical team, or a teacher on a team assigned to reduce drop outs, your professional success and advancement will be linked to how effectively you communicate in groups. Because task groups and teams are especially common, we'll concentrate on them in this chapter. Of course, much of the information we'll discuss pertains to other types of groups as well. We'll identify six kinds of task groups that are prevalent in business and civic life.

Project Teams

Many businesses and professions rely on project teams, which consist of people who have expertise related to different facets of a project and who combine their knowledge and skills to accomplish a common goal. For example, to launch a new product, pharmaceutical companies often put together product teams that include scientists and doctors who understand the technical character of the new drug, along with other personnel who have expertise in marketing, product design, advertising, and customer relations. Working together, team members develop a coherent, coordinated plan for testing, packaging, advertising, and marketing the new product.

Focus Groups

Focus groups are used to find out what people think about a specific idea, product, issue, or person. Focus groups are a mainstay of advertisers who want to understand attitudes, preferences, and responses of people whom they want to buy their product, vote for their candidate, and so forth. How do 21- to 25-year-olds respond to a name that might be given to a microbrew? How do retirees respond to a planned advertising campaign for cruises? What do middle-income women and men think of a mayoral candidate's environmental record? A focus group is guided by a leader or facilitator who develops a list of questions in advance and uses these to encourage participants to express ideas, beliefs, feelings, and perceptions relevant to the topic.

Brainstorming Groups

When idea generation is the goal, brainstorming groups or brainstorming phases in group discussion are appropriate. The goal of **brainstorming** is to come up with as many ideas as possible. Because criticism tends to stifle creativity, brainstorming groups bar criticism and encourage imaginative, even wild, thinking. (Rules for brainstorming appear in Figure 11.1.)

Perhaps you are concerned that brainstorming might produce unrealistic ideas. That's not really a problem, because evaluative discussion follows brainstorming. During evaluation, members work together to appraise the ideas generated through brainstorming. During this stage, the group discards impractical ideas, refines weak or undeveloped contributions, consolidates related suggestions, and further discusses promising ones.

To set a tone for creative communication, leaders or facilitators of brainstorming groups express energy, stoke members' imaginations, and respond enthusiastically to ideas. If the group runs out of ideas, the leader may prompt members by saying, "Let's try to combine some of the ideas we already have," or "We're being too restrained—how about some wild proposals?"

CAREER

Teamwork Lacking in the Operating Room

Reports of errors in surgery are not uncommon. Have you ever wondered how a sponge could be left inside a patient or the wrong limb operated on? One contributor to surgical errors is poor teamwork among those working in the operating room. A survey of more than 2,100 surgeons, anesthesiologists, and nurses at 60 hospitals showed that many teams suffer from weak teamwork (Nagourney, 2006). Doctors' disregard for nurses' expertise was one of the most commonly cited dynamics that undermined effective teamwork.

▶ Do not evaluate ideas in any way. Both verbal and nonverbal criticism are inappropriate.

▶ Record all ideas on a board or easel so that all members of the group can see them.

▶ Go for quantity: The more ideas, the better.

▶ Build on ideas. An idea presented by one member of the group may stimulate an extension by another member. This is desirable.

▶ Encourage creativity. Welcome wild and even preposterous ideas. An idea that seems wacky may lead to other ideas that are more workable.

© Cengage Learning

Figure 11.1 Rules for Brainstorming

CAREER

Young Presidents Organization

In 1950, Ray Hickok opened the first meeting of the Young Presidents' Organization (YPO). Today, there are more than 300 YPO chapters, which include 20,000 members in 100 countries. Members have included politicians such as Lloyd Bentsen and Bo Callaway, financial superstars such as Sir John Templeton and Steve Forbes, and U.S. Postmaster General Bob Tisch (McNees, 1999). The premise of YPO is simple: By engaging each other, peers can help each other become better leaders. In YPO meetings, members share experiences, help one another cope with the unusual pressures and pleasures of early business success, and coach one another through career stages and challenges. To learn more about YPO, go to the book's online resources for this chapter and click on WebLink 11.1.

Advisory Groups

Advisory groups develop and submit recommendations to others, who make the final decisions. The solitary manager, president, or CEO who relies only on his or her own ideas is not functional in modern life. Instead, most high-level decision makers rely on advisory groups to provide expert briefing on the range of issues relevant to decisions they must make. Advisory groups allow decision makers to benefit from other experts' information and advice pertinent to developing effective policies and making informed decisions.

Quality Improvement Teams

Quality improvement teams (also called *continuous quality improvement teams*) include three or more people who have distinct skills or knowledge and who work together to improve quality in an organization (Lumsden & Lumsden, 2009). These teams mix not only people with differing expertise but also people at different levels in an organization's hierarchy. Thus, a secretary may contribute as much as a manager to a discussion of ways to improve office productivity.

For quality improvement teams to be effective, management must support their work and recommendations. Nothing is more frustrating than to be asked to invest energy in making recommendations and then to have the recommendations ignored. When given support, quality improvement teams often generate impressive and creative solutions to organizational problems such as high costs, on-the-job accidents, and low worker morale.

Decision-Making Groups

A sixth kind of task group exists to make decisions. In some cases, decision-making groups actually make decisions: What should be the company's policy on medical leave? What benefits and personnel should be cut to achieve a 15 percent decrease in annual expenses? Other decision-making groups are ongoing; they meet on a regular basis to make decisions about training and development, public relations, budgets, and other matters. Later in this chapter, we'll discuss two methods commonly used by decision-making groups.

Potential Limitations and Strengths of Groups

A great deal of research has compared individual and group decision making. As you might expect, the research identifies potential weaknesses and potential strengths of groups.

Potential Limitations of Groups

One significant disadvantage of group discussion is the time needed for the group process. Operating solo, an individual can think through ideas efficiently. In group discussion, however, all members have an opportunity to voice ideas and respond to the ideas others put forward. It takes substantial time for each person to express thoughts, clarify misunderstandings, and respond to questions or criticisms. In addition, groups take time to deliberate about alternative courses of action. Therefore, group discussion generally isn't a wise choice for routine policy making and emergency tasks. When creativity and thoroughness are important, however, the value of groups may be more important than the time they take.

Groups also have the potential to suppress individuals and encourage conformity. This can happen in two ways. First, conformity pressures may exist when a majority has an opinion different from that of a minority or a single member. Holding out for your point of view is difficult when most or all of your peers have a different one. In effective groups, however, all members understand and resist conformity pressures. They realize that the majority is sometimes wrong and the minority, even just one person, is sometimes right. Members have an ethical responsibility to encourage expression of diverse ideas and open debate about different views.

Conformity pressures may also arise when one member is extremely charismatic or has more power or prestige than other members. Even if that person is all alone in a point of view, other members may conform to it. Sometimes a high-status member doesn't intend to influence others and may not overtly exert pressure. However, the other members still perceive the status, and it may affect their judgments. For example, President Kennedy's advisers regarded him so highly that in some cases they suspended their individual critical thinking and agreed with whatever he said (Janis, 1977). As this example illustrates, often neither the high-status person nor others are consciously aware of pressures to conform. This implies that members should be on guard against the potential to conform uncritically. Lance's commentary illustrates how a member who is perceived to have special status can suppress others' individual thought and creativity.

 Lance

> I used to belong to a creative writing group where all of us helped each other improve our writing. At first, all of us were equally vocal, and we had a lot of good discussions and even disagreements that helped us grow as writers. But then one member of the group got a story accepted by a big magazine, and all of a sudden we thought of her as a better writer than any of us. She didn't act any different, but we saw her as more accomplished, so when she said something, everybody listened and nobody disagreed. It was like a wet blanket on our creativity because her opinion just carried too much weight once she got published.

Another potential disadvantage of group work is the possibility of **social loafing**, which exists when members of a group exert less effort than they would if they worked alone (Hoon & Tan, 2008). If an individual is charged with a task and the task doesn't get done, the individual can be held accountable. When a group is charged with a task, however, members may have less of a sense of accountability for the end product. They may work less hard because each member thinks that no one will notice if she or he slacks off. Scott Snook (2000), a professor at West Point, asserts that social loafing contributed to the accidental shooting down of two U.S. Army Black Hawk helicopters in Iraq. Snook's analysis of records led him to conclude that the team that was assigned to keep track of helicopters to prevent shooting them was ineffective because no single member of the team felt compelled to take responsibility.

Potential Strengths of Groups

The primary potential strengths of groups in comparison to individuals are greater resources, more thorough thought, heightened creativity, and enhanced commitment to decisions. A group obviously exceeds any individual in the ideas, perspectives, experiences, and expertise it can bring to bear on solving a problem. One member knows the technical aspects of a product, another understands market psychology, a third is talented in advertising, and so forth. Health-care teams consist of specialists who combine their knowledge to care for a patient.

Groups also can be more thorough than individuals. Greater thoroughness by groups isn't simply the result of more people. When conformity pressures are controlled, discussion can promote critical and careful analysis because members propel each other's thinking. **Synergy** is a special kind of collaborative vitality that enhances the efforts, talents, and strengths of individual members (Lumsden & Lumsden, 2009; Rothwell, 2009).

A third value of groups is that they are generally more creative than individuals. Again, the reason seems to lie in the synergy of groups. Any individual eventually runs out of new ideas, but groups seem to have almost infinite generative ability. As members talk, they build on each other's ideas, refine proposals, and see new possibilities in each other's comments.

Finally, an important strength of groups is their ability to generate commitment to outcomes. The greater commitment fostered by group discussion arises from two sources. First, participation enhances commitment to decisions. Groups in which all members participate tend to generate greater commitment among members, which is especially important if members will be involved in implementing the decision. Second, because groups have greater resources than individual decision makers, their decisions are more likely to take into account the points of view of the various people needed to make a decision work. This is critical because a decision can be sabotaged if people dislike it or feel that their perspectives weren't considered.

Einstein's Mistakes

That's the title of a book by Hans Ohanian (2008). As brilliant as Einstein may have been, he didn't make his great discoveries alone. He is most famous for $E = mc^2$, the equation expressing the law of relativity. However, math wasn't Einstein's strong suit and his proof of the law contained a number of mathematical errors. Another physicist, Max Von Laue, worked out a complete and correct proof, at which point $E = mc^2$ was on scientifically solid ground.

The myth of the individual genius is popular in Western societies, in part because they place high value on individualism. However, great innovations, discoveries, and inventions usually reflect the work of many people (Rae-Dupree, 2008). In his book *Group Genius*, Keith Sawyer (2008) shows that most creativity is the product of groups and teams. One person may get the credit—the raise, the patent, the Nobel prize—but it took many to do the work.

Greater resources, thoroughness, creativity, and commitment to group goals are powerful values of group process. To incorporate these values, members must be willing to invest the time that discussion takes and must resist pressures to conform or engage in social loafing.

Features of Small Groups

What happens in groups and teams depends largely on members' abilities to participate effectively. If members are not skilled in basic communication processes, groups are unlikely to achieve their potential for productivity and creativity. We'll consider five features of small groups that affect and are affected by participation.

Cohesion

Have you ever felt really connected to others and excited about working to achieve a common goal? If so, then you know what **cohesion** is. Cohesion is the degree of closeness among members and the sense of group spirit. In highly cohesive groups, members see themselves as tightly linked and committed to shared goals. This heightens satisfaction with group membership. High cohesion and the satisfaction it generates tend to increase members' commitment to a group and its goals. Consequently, cohesion is important for effective and satisfying group communication. Clicking on WebLink 11.2, available among the book's online resources for this chapter, will take you to an article on team cohesion among athletes.

Cohesion is fueled by communication that builds group identity and creates a climate of inclusion for all members. Comments that stress pulling together and collective interests build cohesion by reinforcing group identity. Cohesion is also fostered by communication that highlights similarities between members—common interests, values, goals, experiences, and ways of thinking. A third way to enhance cohesion is for members to be responsive to one another so that everyone feels valued by the group.

Cohesion and participation are reciprocal in their influence. Cohesion is promoted when all members are involved and communicating in the group. At the same time, cohesiveness generates a feeling of identity and involvement; once established, it fosters participation. Thus, high levels of participation tend to build cohesion, and strong cohesion generally fosters vigorous participation. Encouraging all members to be involved and responding

© Franck Fife/AFP/Getty Images

Successful athletic teams are highly cohesive.

to each person's contributions fuels cohesion and continued participation. Although cohesion is important for effective group communication, excessive cohesion can actually undermine sound group work. When members are too close, they may be less critical of each other's ideas and less willing to engage in analysis and arguments that are necessary to develop the best outcomes.

Extreme cohesion sometimes leads to **groupthink,** in which members cease to think critically and independently. Groupthink has occurred in high-level groups such as presidential advisory boards and national decision-making bodies (Janis, 1977; Young et al., 2001). Members tend to perceive their group so positively that they assume it cannot make bad decisions. Consequently, members do not critically screen ideas generated in deliberations. The predictable result is low-quality group outcomes that often fail.

America's invasion of Iraq was based on intelligence that Iraq had weapons of mass destruction. An in-depth investigation by the Senate concluded that the decision to go to war was propelled by members of the CIA and other agencies who unintentionally engaged in groupthink (Isikoff, 2004) so that critical thinking was suspended. You can learn more about groupthink by going to the book's online resources for this chapter and clicking on WebLink 11.3.

Group Size

The number of people in a group affects the amount and quality of communication. In a group of five people, each idea must be received and interpreted by four others, each of whom may respond with comments that four others must receive and interpret. As group size increases, the contributions of each member tend to decrease. You may have experienced frustration when participating in large online chat rooms and blogs. It can be hard to get your ideas in, and the sheer number of people contributing ideas can mean that no idea receives much response.

Because participation is linked to commitment, larger groups may generate less commitment to group outcomes than smaller groups do. Because participation also affects cohesion and satisfaction, larger groups may also be less cohesive and less satisfying than smaller ones (Benenson, Gordon, & Roy, 2000; DeCremer & Leonardelli, 2003).

 Yolanda

The worst group I was ever in had three members. We were supposed to have five, but two dropped out after the first meeting, so there were three of us to come up with proposals for artistic programs for the campus. Nobody would say anything against anybody else's ideas, even if we thought they were bad. For myself, I know I held back from criticizing a lot of times because I didn't want to offend either of the other two. We came up with some really bad ideas because we were so small we couldn't risk arguing.

As Yolanda's commentary shows, groups can be too small as well as too large. With too few members, a group has limited resources, which diminishes a primary value of group decision making. Also, members of small groups may be unwilling to criticize each other's ideas, because alienating one member would dramatically weaken the group. Five to seven members is an ideal size for a group (Lumsden & Lumsden, 2009).

Power Structure

Power structure is a third feature that influences participation in small groups. **Power** is the ability to influence others (Rothwell, 2007). There are two distinct kinds of power.

Power over is the ability to help or harm others. This form of power usually is expressed in ways that emphasize and build the status of the person wielding influence. A team leader might exert positive power over a member by providing mentoring, giving strong performance reviews, and assigning the member high-status roles on the team. A leader could also exert negative power by withholding these benefits, assigning unpleasant tasks, and responding negatively to a member's contributions to meetings.

Power to is the ability to empower others to reach their goals (Boulding, 1990; Conrad & Poole, 2004). People who empower others do not emphasize their status. Instead, they act behind the scenes to enlarge others' influence and visibility and help others succeed. Power to creates opportunities for others, recognizes achievements, and helps others accomplish their goals. Go to the book's online resources for this chapter and click on WebLink 11.4 to visit a site that provides information on mediation as an example of *power to* instead of *power over.*

If all members of a group have roughly equal power, the group has a *distributed power structure.* On the other hand, if one or more members have greater power than others, the group has a *hierarchical power structure.* Hierarchy may take the form of one person who is more powerful than all the others, who are equal in power to one another. Alternatively, hierarchy may involve multiple levels of power. A leader might have the greatest power, three others might have power equal to each other's but less than the leader's, and four other members might have little power. The FYI box on this page summarizes the primary sources of power.

How is power related to participation? First, members with high power tend to be the centers of group communication; they talk more, and others talk more to them. **Social climbing** is the attempt to increase personal status in a group by winning the approval of high-status members. If social climbing doesn't increase the status of those doing it, they often become marginal participants in groups. Members with more power tend to find discussion more satisfying than members with less power (Young et al., 2001). This makes sense because those with power get to participate more and get their way more often.

Power influences communication and is influenced by it. In other words, how members communicate affects how much power they acquire. People who make good substantive comments, cultivate a healthy climate, and organize deliberations tend to earn power quickly. These are examples of earned power that is conferred because a member provides skills valued by the group. Members who demonstrate that they have done their homework and respond thoughtfully likewise gain power.

Five Bases of Power

What is power? How does a person get it? There is more than one answer to each of these questions because there are different sources of power (Arnold & Feldman, 1986).

Reward Power	The ability to give people things they value, such as attention, approval, public praise, promotions, and raises
Coercive Power	The ability to punish others through demotions, firing, and undesirable assignments
Legitimate Power	The organizational role, such as manager, supervisor, or CEO, that results in others' compliance
Expert Power	Influence derived from expert knowledge or experience
Referent Power	Influence based on personal charisma and personality

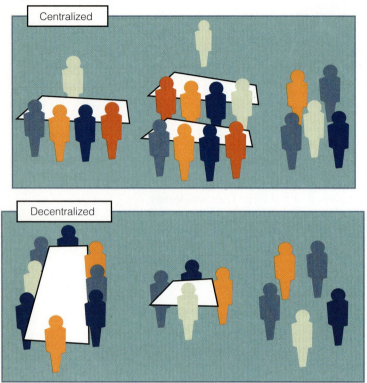

© Cengage Learning

Figure 11.2   **Patterns of interaction in groups**

Interaction Patterns

Another important influence on communication in groups is interaction patterns (Figure 11.2). In centralized patterns, one or two people hold central positions, and most or all communication goes directly to them or is funneled through them.

Decentralized patterns promote more balanced communication. As you might suspect, the power of individual members often affects interaction patterns. If one or two members have greater power, a centralized pattern of interaction is likely to emerge. Decentralized patterns are more typical when members have roughly equal power.

Group Norms

A final feature of small groups is the presence of **norms**—guidelines that regulate how members act as well as how they interact with each other. Group norms control everything from the most trivial to the most critical aspects of a group's life. Relatively inconsequential norms may regulate meeting time and whether eating is allowed during meetings. More substantive norms govern how members express and analyze ideas, listen to one another, and manage conflict.

Norms grow directly out of interaction. For example, at an initial meeting some members might check messages on their smartphones when others are speaking. If this continues, a norm of disrespect will develop, and members will form the habit of listening poorly. On the other hand, one member might say, "I think we need to put our phones away during meetings so we can attend to the discussion." If other members heed this suggestion, a norm of respectful communication may develop.

When our team first formed, everyone was pretty casual. There was a lot of kidding around before we got down to work at each meeting, and members often drifted in late. I didn't want to crack down at the beginning, because I thought that might dampen group spirit. With 20–20 hindsight, I now see I should have imposed some rules at the outset. I've tried to get members to get to meetings on time and buckle down to work, but I'm fighting against a history of being laid back.

As Baxter's commentary demonstrates, norms often become entrenched early in a group's life, so it's important to pay attention to them from the outset. By noticing patterns and tendencies, you can exert influence over the norms that govern conduct in a group. Cohesion, size, power structure, interaction patterns, and norms are features of groups that affect participation, productivity, and satisfaction.

Methods of Group Decision Making

Many groups are charged either to make decisions or to give recommendations to an individual or other group that has the authority to implement them. Because decision making is a primary goal of groups, we'll discuss two methods of group decision making.

Standard Agenda

The standard agenda is a time-tested and logical, six-step method for solving problems and making decisions. It is one of the most accepted methods for task-orientated group discussion.

1. Stage 1: Define the problem. Is the problem a matter of fact (What are the current requirements for a major in communication?) or value (What are the most useful courses to prepare communication majors for careers?) or policy (What can be done to encourage communication majors to take a broad range of courses in the major?)? Defining the problem also requires reaching agreement on what terms mean. For instance, what is meant by "a broad range of courses" or "prepare for careers"?

2. Stage 2: Gather and analyze evidence and information. Groups gather and examine information related to the defined problem. How many communication majors are there? How many majors take each of the courses offered by the department? What do communication departments at peer institutions require for majors? How do communication majors fare in the job market?

3. Stage 3: Establish criteria for a solution. Criteria are standards that the group can use to evaluate alternative solutions. Here are criteria that might be appropriate for a group deciding the policy issue of requirements for communication majors: Students must be able to complete the major in four years. Faculty must be qualified to teach the required classes. The requirements must be consistent with university requirements for all majors.

4. Stage 4: Generate and evaluate solutions. Members may brainstorm solutions and may also derive solutions from the research completed during Stage 2. Once the group has a number of solutions to consider, each one is measured against the criteria established in Stage 3.

5. Stage 5: Select and implement the best solution or decision. (Some versions of standard agenda separate this stage into two separate stages: selecting and implementing.) Ideally, a clearly preferred decision emerges when all options are tested against criteria. If no single solution is clearly best, group members must deliberate about the advantages and disadvantages of competing solutions. Once a group makes a choice by consensus or voting, then the group implements its decision. If it is a decision-making group, it authorizes the decision and personnel to implement it. If the group is advisory, it forwards its recommendation to the person or group that has the power to implement.

6. Stage 6: Monitor the decision. The final stage is critical and often overlooked by decision-making groups. The goal of this stage is to monitor the solution once it has been implemented. Too often groups end their work with implementing a decision or recommending a decision to someone who implements it. But how do you know if the solution works? How do you know if there are unintended consequences of the solution? The only way to know is to monitor the decision and, if necessary, modify it. A good monitoring plan spells out how effectiveness will be assessed: More majors will complete in four years. Majors will get more job interviews. Majors will evaluate their classes at a designated level of quality.

The standard agenda guides groups through stages that allow members to understand problems and issues and develop, implement and assess decisions to remedy the problems and respond to issues.

Nominal Group Technique

A second widely-used method of making decisions is the nominal group technique (NGT) (Delbecq & VandeVen, 1971; Potter, Gordon & Hamer, 2004). This method is appropriate when a group wants to make a decision quickly and wants every member's opinions taken into account NGT typically has a facilitator, who may or may not be a member of the group. The facilitator guides a group through five stages.

1. Stage 1: Introduction and explanation. The goals of this stage are to welcome the participants, clarify the purpose of meeting, outline the process or procedures that will be followed, and establish a healthy climate for group interaction.

2. Stage 2: Silent generation of ideas. The facilitator gives each group member a sheet of paper or an index card on which to record all of the ideas she or he has in relation to the question, problem, or topic posed by the facilitator. As the name of the stage indicates, this is a silent process; members don't discuss ideas with one another. This stage is a form of individual brainstorming.

3. Stage 3: Sharing ideas. When all members are through writing, the facilitator invites participants to share their ideas with the group. Using a flip chart, board, or computer-projected system, the facilitator lists ideas for all to see. As ideas are shared, participants write down any new ideas that are sparked by other members' contributions. A major benefit of this process is that all members have equal ability to participate, which is a corrective in groups where some members tend to be more vocal.

4. Stage 4: Group discussion. The facilitator encourages group members to elaborate on ideas and to ask questions of one another to gain clarification on what the idea is and what benefits it might have. The facilitator should also monitor group climate, making sure that all ideas are given respectful consideration. Finally, the facilitator encourages group members to think about ways that the ideas might be combined to create additional ideas.

5. Stage 5: Voting and ranking. Members individually rank each idea, giving a "1" to the most favored idea. The typical way of reaching a decision is to total all members' rankings for each item and the group's decision is the idea with the lowest total ranking. (There are variations on computing a final decision.) The group's decision is announced immediately so that members have a sense of closure when the meeting ends.

Both standard agenda and NGT provide procedural structure for moving a group through stages of discussion that encourage thoughtful analysis and careful decision making.

Guidelines for Communicating in Groups and Teams

To realize the strengths of group work and avoid its potential weaknesses, members must participate constructively, provide leadership, and manage conflict so that it benefits the group and its outcomes.

Participate Constructively

Because interaction is the heart of groups and teams, communication skills are vital to effectiveness. There are four kinds of communication in groups (Figure 11.3). The first three—task communication, procedural communication, and climate communication—are constructive because they foster healthy group climate and quality outcomes. The fourth kind of communication is egocentric communication, which detracts from a positive group climate and effective decision making.

Task Communication

Task communication provides ideas and information, clarifies members' understanding, and critically evaluates ideas. Task contributions may initiate ideas, respond to others' ideas, or provide critical evaluation of information. Task comments also include asking for ideas and feedback.

Procedural Communication

If you've ever participated in a disorganized group, you understand the importance of **procedural communication**. It helps a group get organized and stay on track. Procedural contributions establish agendas, coordinate members' comments, and

Task Communication	Initiates ideas
	Seeks information
	Gives information
	Elaborates on ideas
	Evaluates, offers critical analysis
Procedural Communication	Establishes agenda
	Provides orientation
	Curbs digressions
	Guides participation
	Coordinates ideas
	Summarizes others' contributions
	Records group progress
Climate Communication	Establishes and maintains healthy climate
	Energizes group process
	Harmonizes ideas
	Recognizes others
	Reconciles conflicts
	Builds enthusiasm for the group
Egocentric Communication	Is aggressive toward others
	Blocks ideas
	Seeks personal recognition (brags)
	Dominates interaction
	Pleads for special interests
	Confesses, self-discloses, seeks personal help
	Disrupts task
	Devalues others
	Trivializes the group and its work

© Cengage Learning

Figure 11.3 **Types of Communication in Groups**

record group progress. In addition, procedural contributions curb digressions and tangents, summarize progress, and regulate participation so that everyone has opportunities to speak and nobody dominates.

Climate Communication

A group is more than a task unit. It is also people involved in a relationship that can be more or less pleasant (Barge, 2009). **Climate communication** focuses on creating and maintaining a constructive climate that encourages members to contribute and evaluate ideas critically. Climate comments emphasize a group's strengths and progress, recognize members' contributions, reconcile conflicts, add humor, and build enthusiasm for the group's work.

Egocentric Communication

I was once on a committee that had one member who was continuously negative. If one person suggested an idea for our task, this member would say, "We've already tried that" or "That will never work." The member's negativity undermined the committee. Perhaps you've been in groups where one person was always negative, argumentative, or domineering. **Egocentric communication,** or dysfunctional communication, blocks others, sabotages a healthy climate, or is self-absorbed. It detracts from group progress because it is self-centered rather than group-centered. Examples of egocentric talk are devaluing a member's ideas, trivializing group efforts, being aggressive toward others, bragging about personal accomplishments, dominating, disrupting group work, and pleading for special causes that aren't in the group's interests.

Figure 11.4 provides a transcript of a group discussion that includes the four kinds of communication we've discussed. Notice how skillfully Ann communicates to defuse tension between Bob and Jan before it disrupts the group. You might also notice that Ed provides the primary procedural leadership for the group, and Bob is effective in interjecting humor to enhance the climate. Several members recognize contributions to the discussion. You can further improve your ability to recognize different kinds of group communication by completing the Sharpen Your Skill exercise on this page.

Provide Leadership

All groups need leadership. However, leadership is not necessarily one individual. Instead, leadership is a set of behaviors that helps a group maintain a good climate and accomplish tasks in an organized way. Sometimes one member provides guidance on task and procedures, and another member focuses on building a healthy group climate by recognizing and responding to members' ideas and feelings (Goleman, McKee, & Boyatzis, 2002) as well as by encouraging cohesion. It's also not uncommon for different people to provide leadership at different times in a group's life. The person who guides the group at the outset may not be the one who advances the group's work in later phases. Even when an official leader exists,

SHARPEN YOUR SKILL

Noticing Communication in Groups

Observe a group meeting—either a group you belong to or one you visit. For 10 minutes of group discussion, keep track of the communication, noting whether each comment is task, procedural, climate, egocentric, or a combination of two or more. Do the patterns of communication give you insight into why the group is effective or ineffective?

Ed:	Let's start by talking about our goals. [procedural]
Jan:	That's a good idea. [climate]
Bob:	I think our goal is to come up with a better meal plan for students on campus. [task]
Ed:	What do you mean by "better"? Do you mean cheaper or more variety or more tasteful? [task]
Ann:	I think it's all three. [task]
Ed:	Well, we probably do care about all three, but maybe we should talk about one at a time so we can keep our discussion focused. [procedural]
Bob:	Okay, I vote we focus first on taste—like it would be good if there were some taste to the food on campus! [task and climate (humor)]
Jan:	Do you mean taste itself or quality of food, which might also include nutrition? [task]
Bob:	Pure taste! When I'm hungry, I don't think about what's good for me, just what tastes good. [task and possibly climate (humor)]
Jan:	Well, maybe we want the food service to think about nutrition because we don't. [task]
Bob:	If you're a health food nut, that's your problem. I don't think nutrition is something that's important in the food service on campus. [task; may also be egocentric if his tone toward Jan is snide]
Ed:	Let's do this: Let's talk first about what we would like in terms of taste itself. [procedural] Before we meet next time, it might be a good idea for one of us to talk with the manager of the cafeteria to see whether they have to meet any nutritional guidelines in what they serve. [task]
Ann:	I'll volunteer to do that. [task]
Ed:	Great. Thanks, Ann. [climate]
Bob:	I'll volunteer to do taste testing! [climate (humor)]
Jan:	With your weight, you'd better not. [egocentric]
Bob:	Yeah, like you have a right to criticize me. [egocentric]
Ann:	Look, none of us is here to criticize anyone else. We're here because we want to improve the food service on campus. [climate] We've decided we want to focus first on taste, [procedural] so who has an idea of how we go about studying that? [task]

© Cengage Learning

Figure 11.4 Coding Group Communication

other members may contribute much of the communication that provides the overall leadership of a group.

Leadership is the process of establishing and maintaining a good working climate, organizing group processes, and ensuring that discussion is substantive. Effective leadership also controls disruptive members who engage in egocentric communication. Whether a group has one or multiple leaders, the primary responsibilities of leaders are to organize discussion, to ensure sound research and reasoning, to promote norms for mindful listening and clear verbal and nonverbal communication, to create a productive climate, to build group morale, and to discourage egocentric communication that detracts from group efforts. Krystal's commentary provides an example of effective shared leadership.

CAREER

Servant Leadership

We often think of leaders as individuals whom others serve, but maybe it's the reverse. For servant leaders, the decision to lead arises from a humble desire to serve others and causes bigger than themselves. Their leadership isn't an effort to increase their personal power or comfort, but rather aims to help others. As a result, servant leaders focus on the needs and aspirations of their followers, whom they serve.

Although contemporary leadership experts such as Stephen Covey (1989) extol servant leadership, esteem for servant leaders has much older roots in spiritual and religious teachings such as those of the Buddha, Lao-Tzu, Chanakya, and Jesus.

The most effective group I've ever been in had three leaders. I was the person who understood our task best, so I contributed the most to critical thinking about the issues. But Belinda was the one who kept us organized. She could get us off tangents, and she knew when it was time to move on from one stage of work to the next. She also pulled ideas together to coordinate our thinking. Kevin was the climate leader. He could always tell a joke if things got tense, and he was the best person I ever saw for recognizing others' contributions. I couldn't point to any one leader in that group, but we sure did have good leadership.

Manage Conflict Constructively

In Chapter 7, we learned that conflict is natural and can be productive. In groups and teams, conflict stimulates thinking, helps members consider diverse perspectives, and enlarges members' understanding of issues involved in making decisions and generating ideas (McClure, 2005). To achieve these goals, however, conflict must be managed skillfully. The goal is to manage conflict so that it enriches group processes and helps a group achieve collective goals. Although many of us may not enjoy conflict, we can nonetheless recognize its value—even its necessity—for effective group work. Trey's experience illustrates what can happen when a group puts conflict avoidance ahead of high-quality work.

I used to think conflict was terrible and hurt groups, but last year I was a member of a group that had no—I mean, zero—conflict. A couple of times, I tried to bring up an idea different from what had been suggested, but my idea wouldn't even get a hearing. The whole goal was not to disagree. As a result, we didn't do a very thorough job of analyzing the issues, and we didn't subject the solution we developed to critical scrutiny. When our recommendation was put into practice, it bombed. We could have foreseen and avoided the failure if we had been willing to argue and disagree in order to test our idea before we put it forward.

Disruptive Conflict

Effective members promote conflict that is constructive for the group's tasks and climate and discourage conflict that disrupts healthy discussion. Conflict is disruptive when it interferes with effective work and a healthy communication climate. Typically, **disruptive conflict** is marked by egocentric communication that is competitive as members vie with each other to wield influence and get their way. Accompanying the competitive tone of communication is a self-interested focus in which members talk about only their own ideas, solutions, and points of view. The competitive and self-centered communication in disruptive conflict fosters diminished cohesion and a win–lose orientation to conflict.

Group climate deteriorates during disruptive conflict. Members may feel unsafe volunteering ideas because others might harshly evaluate or scorn them. Personal attacks may occur as members criticize one another's motives or attack one another personally. Recall the discussion in Chapter 7 about communication that fosters defensiveness; we saw that defensive climates are promoted by communication that expresses evaluation, superiority, control orientation, neutrality, certainty, and closed-mindedness. Just as these forms of communication undermine healthy climates in personal relationships, they also interfere with group climate and productivity.

Constructive Conflict

Constructive conflict occurs when members understand that disagreements are natural and can help them achieve their shared goals. Communication that expresses respect for diverse opinions reflects this attitude. Members also emphasize shared interests and goals. The cooperative focus of communication encourages a win–win orientation. Discussion is open and supportive of differences, and disagreements focus on issues, not personalities.

To encourage constructive conflict, communication should demonstrate openness to different ideas, willingness to alter opinions when good reasons exist, and respect for the integrity of other members and the views they express. Also, keep in mind that conflict grows out of the entire system of group communication. Thus, constructive conflict is most likely to occur when members have established a supportive, open climate of communication. Group climate is built throughout the life of a group, beginning with the first meeting. It is important to communicate in ways that build a strong climate from the start so that it is already established when conflict arises.

SUMMARY

In this chapter, we've considered small groups and how they operate. We defined groups as three or more people who meet over time, share understandings of how to interact, and have a common goal. Group members must recognize and manage the potential weaknesses of group discussion such as time, conformity pressures and social loafing to realize the important advantages of group decision making.

Many factors, including cohesion, size, power, norms, and interaction patterns, influence communication in task groups and teams. Each of these features shapes the small group system within which communication transpires. Understanding and managing these influences should enable you to enhance the climate of groups, the quality of outcomes, and the efficiency of group processes. Following time-tested decision-making models, such as the standard agenda or nominal group technique, further enhances a task groups' efficiency and effectiveness.

The final part of this chapter discussed three guidelines for effective communication in groups and teams. The first one, participating effectively, requires task, climate, and procedural contributions that foster good group climate and outcomes. Developing skill in constructive types of communication and avoiding egocentric comments will make you a valuable member of any group. The second guideline for effective communication in groups and teams is to ensure leadership, which may be provided by one or more members. Good leadership exists when members communicate to organize discussion, ensure careful work on the task, and build cohesion, morale, and an effective climate for collective work. A third guideline is to manage conflict so that it enhances, rather than detracts from, group processes. Constructive conflict in groups, as we have seen, grows out of a supportive communication climate that is built over the course of a group's life.

REVIEW, REFLECT, EXTEND

The Reflect, Discuss, and Apply Questions that follow will help you review, reflect on, and extend the information and ideas presented in this chapter. These resources, and a diverse selection of additional study tools, are also available online at the CourseMate for *Communication Mosaics*. Your CourseMate includes a student workbook, WebLinks, TED Talks hyperlinks and activities, chapter glossary and flashcards, interactive video activities, Speech Builder Express, and InfoTrac College Edition. For more information or to access this book's online resources, visit **www .cengagebrain.com.**

KEY CONCEPTS

brainstorming, 225
climate communication, 236
cohesion, 229
constructive conflict, 239
disruptive conflict, 239
egocentric communication, 236
group, 223
groupthink, 230
leadership, 237
norm, 232

power, 231
power over, 231
power to, 231
procedural communication, 235
quality improvement team, 226
social climbing, 231
social loafing, 227
synergy, 228
task communication, 235
team, 223

Reflect, Discuss, Apply

1. Interview a professional in the field you hope to enter after college. Ask her or him to identify how various groups and teams discussed in this chapter are used on the job. If you are already employed in a career, reflect on your experiences with groups on the job.

2. Ask several people who have lived in non-Western cultures whether the cultural values that affect group communication in the United States are present in the countries where they lived. In your conversation, explore how differences in cultural values affect group interaction.

3. Observe a meeting of a campus governing group—for instance, the Board of Trustees. Do the communication patterns you observe explain the effectiveness or ineffectiveness of the group?

4. In your class, form groups of five to seven. Select a topic for discussion such as "What is the best method of testing in this class?" or "How can our campus be more environmentally responsible?" Have half of the groups follow standard agenda and the other half follow NGT to discuss the question. When the groups have finished the task, discuss your impression of each method of decision making.

Recommended Resources

1. Although *Twelve Angry Men* was produced many years ago, it remains an excellent film about group dynamics in a decision-making group, in this case a jury.

2. Ken Blanchard, John Carlos, and Alan Randolph wrote *Empowerment Takes More Than a Minute* (1998) to give working tools to people who want to be empowering leaders. The book is organized in story form, relying on an extended case study to provide hands-on advice, tools, and exercises for increasing employees' sense of empowerment. They emphasize the importance of personal contact, encouragement, and feedback between leaders and employees.

EXPERIENCE COMMUNICATION CASE STUDY

Group Communication

© Cengage Learning

Apply what you've learned in this chapter by analyzing the following case study, using the accompanying questions as a guide. These questions and a video of the case study are also available online at your CourseMate for *Communication Mosaics*.

As members of the Student Government Financial Committee, Davinia, Joyce, Thomas, and Pat make decisions on how much funding, if any, to give various student groups that request support from the funds collected from student fees. They are meeting for the first time in a campus cafeteria.

Thomas: Well, we've got 23 applications for funding and a total of $19,000 that we can distribute.

Davinia: Maybe we should start by listing how much each of the 23 groups wants.

Joyce: It might be better to start by determining the criteria that we'll use to decide if groups get any funding from student fees.

Davinia: Yeah, right. We should set up our criteria before we look at applications.

Thomas: Sounds good to me. Pat, what do you think?

Pat: I'm on board. Let's set up criteria first and then review the applications against those.

Joyce: Okay, we might start by looking at the criteria used last year by the Financial Committee. Does anyone have a copy of those?

Thomas: I do. [He passes out copies to the other three people.] They had three criteria: service to a significant number of students, compliance with the college's nondiscrimination policies, and educational benefit.

Davinia: What counts as "educational benefit"? Did last year's committee specify that?

Joyce: Good question. Thomas, you were on the committee last year. Do you remember what they counted as educational benefit?

Thomas: The main thing I remember is that it was distinguished from artistic benefit—like a concert or art exhibit or something like that.

Pat: But can't art be educational?

Davinia: Yeah, I think so. Thomas, Joyce, do you?

Thomas: I guess, but it's like art's primary purpose isn't to educate.

Joyce: I agree. It's kind of hard to put into words, but I think educational benefit has more to do with information and the mind, and art has more to do with the soul. Does that sound too hokey? [Laughter.]

Pat: Okay, so we want to say that we don't distribute funds to any hokey groups, right? [More laughter.]

Davinia: It's not like we're against art or anything. It's just that the funding we can distribute is for educational benefit, right? [Everyone nods.]

Joyce: Okay, let's move onto another criterion. What is a significant number of students?

Thomas: Last year, we said that the proposals for using money had to be of potential interest to at least 20 percent of students to get funding. How does that sound to you?

Pat: Sounds okay, as long as we remember that something can be of potential interest to students who aren't members of specific groups. Like, for instance, I might want to attend a program on Native American customs even though I'm not a Native American. See what I mean?

Davinia: Good point; we don't want to define student interest as student identity or anything like that. [Nods of agreement.]

Thomas: Okay, so are we agreed that 20 percent is about right, with the understanding that the 20 percent can include students who aren't in a group applying for funding? [Nods.] Okay, then do we need to discuss the criterion of compliance with the college's policies on nondiscrimination?

1. Classify each statement in this scenario as one of the forms of group communication (task, procedural, climate, egocentric). Is the balance among forms appropriate for a decision-making group?

2. Based on this discussion, does this group seem to have a single leader, or do different members provide leadership to the group?

3. How do you perceive the interaction pattern between members? Does everyone seem to be involved and participating?

4. Are any of the potential values of group versus individual decision making evident in this discussion?

> *"Like a human being, a company has to have an internal communication mechanism, a 'nervous system,' to coordinate its actions."* Bill Gates

12 Communication in Organizations

▶ Josh is a senior systems analyst at MicroLife, an innovative technology firm in Silicon Valley. Although he typically works more than 40 hours a week, his schedule varies according to his moods and his responsibilities for caring for his daughter, Marie. Some days, Josh is at his desk by 8 A.M., and on other days he gets to the office around noon. Life on the job is casual, as is dress. Sneakers, T-shirts, and jeans are standard attire for all employees at MicroLife. People drop by each other's offices without appointments and sometimes even without specific business to conduct.

When Josh first joined MicroLife, drop-by chats with longer-term employees gave him insight into the company. He can still remember hearing stories about Wayne Murray—fondly called "Wild Man Wayne"—who launched the company from a makeshift workstation in his garage. He also heard tale after tale of oddball ideas the company backed that became highly profitable. Josh really enjoys the creative freedom at MicroLife: Everyone is encouraged to think innovatively, to try new ways of doing things. Weekly softball games provide friendly competition between the Nerds (the team of systems analysts) and the Words (the team of software writers).

▶ Jacqueline slips her shoes off under her desk, hoping nobody will see, because Bankers United has a strict dress code requiring suits, heels (for women), and clean-shaven faces (for men). On her first day at work, a manager took her out to lunch and mentioned two recent hires who "just didn't work out" because they didn't dress professionally. Jacqueline got the

FOCUS QUESTIONS

1. What is organizational culture?

2. How do rituals and routines express organizational values?

3. How do today's organizations differ from those of earlier eras?

4. What are the advantages and disadvantages of personal relationships on the job?

message. From other employees, she heard about people who had been given bad performance reviews for being late more than once in a six-month period. When Jacqueline suggested a way to streamline mortgage applications, she was told, "That isn't how we do things here." She quickly figured out that at Bankers United the operating mode was rigid rules rigidly enforced. Although she sometimes feels constrained by the authoritarian atmosphere of Bankers United, Jacqueline also likes having clear-cut rules to follow. For her, rules provide a kind of security.

Would you rather work for MicroLife or Bankers United? If you're a relaxed person who enjoys informality and does well in unstructured environments, MicroLife may appeal to you. MicroLife is one of many businesses and professions that are flexible about dress and hours. As long as the work gets done—programs debugged, products developed—it doesn't matter how people dress and when they work.

On the other hand, if you like clear rules and a traditional working environment, Bankers United may be more attractive to you. Bankers United, like many organizations, must accommodate a time clock and must follow inflexible procedures to meet their objectives. Bank employees need to be in place during standard business hours to take care of customers. Likewise, hospitals must schedule operating rooms, and doctors, nurses, and anesthesiologists must be on time for surgery.

Although organizations differ in many ways, common to them is the centrality of communication. This chapter focuses on organizational communication. In the first section, we'll identify key features of organizational communication. Next, we'll discuss the overall culture of the organization, which is what creates the interpersonal and task climate for its members. As we will see, organizational culture is created and expressed through communication. Every organization has a distinct culture that consists of traditions, structures, and practices that reflect and reproduce a particular form of work life and on-the-job relationships. In the third section of the chapter, we'll discuss three guidelines for communicating in organizations in our era.

Key Features of Organizational Communication

Much of what you've learned in previous chapters applies to communication in organizations. For instance, successful communication on the job requires listening skills, care in making attributions and checking perceptions, verbal and nonverbal competence, awareness of and adaptation to differences among people, and the abilities to build supportive climates and manage conflict. In addition, organizational communication has three distinct features: structure, communication networks, and links to external environments.

Structure

Organizations are structured. As Charles Conrad and Marshall Scott Poole (2004) point out, the very word *organization* means "structure." In organizations, structure provides predictability about roles, procedures, and expectations.

Many modern organizations rely on a hierarchical structure that assigns different levels of power and status to different members and specifies the chain of command that says who is to communicate with whom about what. Although hierarchies may be more or less rigid, a loose chain of command doesn't mean there isn't one. My department, like many academic units, has a fairly loose structure in which members generally interact as equals. However, faculty are ultimately responsible to the chair of the department. He can reprimand or assign tasks to any faculty member, but we can't do the same to him.

Communication Networks

A second characteristic of organizational communication is that it occurs in **communication networks,** which are formal and informal links between members of organizations (Modaff, Butler, & DeWine, 2011). In most organizations, people belong to multiple networks. For example, in my department I belong to a social network that includes colleagues, students, and staff with whom I have personal relationships. I'm also involved in task networks made up of people concerned about teaching, research, and departmental life. I participate in ad hoc networks that arise irregularly in response to specific crises or issues. I also belong to networks outside my department yet within the university. Overlaps among networks to which we belong ensure that we will communicate in various ways with many people in any organization.

In addition to networks in physical places of work, virtual networks are becoming more common in the workplace (Rothwell, 2009). The growth in telecommuting is striking. Estimates suggest that over 50 million U.S. workers (about 40 percent of the working population) work from home at least part of the time, and 2.5 million employees (not including the self-employed) consider their home their primary place of business (Conley, 2009; Lister, 2009). In 2010, 67 percent of federal employees worked from home or other sites from 1 to 5 days a week either 1-2 days a week, or 3 or more days per week (Lister, 2009; Telework, 2010). Made possible by technologies, telecommuting allows millions of people to work from their homes or mobile offices. Using computers, e-mail, cell phones, BlackBerrys, PDAs, and faxes, telecommuters do their work and maintain contact with colleagues and clients without being at a central, physical workplace.

Links to External Environments

In Chapter 1, we discussed systems as interdependent, interacting wholes. Like other communication systems, organizations are embedded in multiple contexts that affect how they work and whether they succeed or fail. In other words, an organization's operation cannot be understood simply by looking within the organization. We must also look outside it to grasp how the organization is related to and affected by its contexts.

Consider the impact on a few U.S. businesses of the recession that began in 2008:

▶ As the housing industry slumped, construction workers were laid off, and home supply stores lost business.

▶ Legal firms laid off attorneys who specialize in closings on home sales.

▶ As the economy continued to weaken, financial institutions lowered the interest they pay on savings, giving consumers less reason to save.

▶ As people lost jobs, they had less income, forcing retailers in all spheres to lower prices, have more sales, and lure customers with special promotions.

Although internal factors may have contributed to how specific businesses fared, clearly many organizations suffered because of factors outside their organizational boundaries. When economic times are good, when war is not a threat, and when inflation is in check, even mediocre companies survive and sometimes thrive. When external conditions are bad, even good companies can be hurt or driven out of business. All organizations are linked to and influenced by the contexts in which they are embedded.

Systems in which organizations exist influence communication in organizations. Directors, CEOs, and other leaders who feel pressured by economic problems may tighten controls, demand greater efficiency and productivity, and become less willing to invest in social events for employees. They may communicate to motivate employees when raises and bonuses are not in the picture.

Organizational Culture

In Chapter 8, we noted that cultures are characterized by shared values, behaviors, practices, and communication forms. Extending the idea of culture to organizations, communication scholars focus on **organizational culture,** which consists of ways of thinking, acting, and understanding work that are shared by members of an organization and that reflect an organization's identity.

Just as ethnic cultures consist of meanings shared by members of the ethnic groups, organizational cultures consist of meanings shared by members of organizations. Just as new members of ethnic cultures are socialized into a particular culture's preexisting meanings and traditions, new members of organizations are socialized into a particular organization's preexisting meanings and traditions (Goodall & Trethewey, 2009; Miller, 2009). Just as a culture's way of life continues even though particular people leave or die, an organization's culture persists despite the comings and goings of particular workers.

Scholars have gained insight into the ways in which communication creates, sustains, and expresses the culture of organizations (Pacanowsky, 1989; Pacanowsky & O'Donnell-Trujillo, 1982, 1983; Riley, 1983; Scott & Myers, 2005; Smircich, 1983). The relationship between communication and organizational culture is reciprocal: Communication between members of organizations creates, sustains, and sometimes alters the culture. At the same time, organizational culture influences patterns of communication between members.

As employees interact, they create, sustain, and sometimes change their organization's culture (Pacanowsky, 1989; Van Maanen & Barley, 1985). Four kinds of communication that are particularly important in developing and conveying organizational culture are vocabularies, stories, rites and rituals, and structures.

Erin Siegal/REUTERS

Based on this photo, what can you infer about this organization's culture?

Vocabulary

The most obvious communication dimension of organizational culture is vocabulary. Just as the language of an ethnic culture reflects and expresses its history, norms, values, and identity, the language of an organization reflects and expresses its history, norms, values, and identity.

Hierarchical Language

Many organizations and professions have vocabularies that designate status. The military, for example, relies on language that continually acknowledges rank ("Yes, sir," "Captain," "Major," "General"), which reflects the close ties among rank, respect, and authority. Salutes, as well as stripes and medals on uniforms, are part of the nonverbal vocabulary that emphasizes rank and status.

Unequal terms of address also communicate rank. For instance, the CEO may use first names ("Good morning, Jan") when speaking to employees. Unless given permission to use the CEO's first name, however, lower-status members of an organization typically use Mr., Ms., Sir, or Ma'am in addressing the CEO. Colleges and universities use titles to designate faculty members' rank and status: instructor, assistant professor, associate professor, full professor, and distinguished (or chaired) professor. Faculty generally use students' first names, whereas students tend to use titles to address their teachers: Dr. Matthews or Professor Matthews.

Masculine Language

Because organizations historically were run by men, and men held most or all of the high-level positions, it's not surprising that many organizations have developed and continue to use language reflecting men's traditional interests and experiences (Ashcraft & Mumby, 2004; Mumby, 2007). Consider the number of phrases in the work world that are taken from sports (*home run, ballpark estimate, touchdown, develop a game plan, be a team player, take a time out, the starting lineup*), from military life (*battle plan, mount a campaign, plan of attack, under fire, get the big guns, offensive strike*), and from male sexual parts and activities (a troublesome person is a "prick"; you can "hit on" a person, "screw" someone, or "stick it" to them; bold professionals have "balls").

Less prevalent in most organizations is language that reflects traditionally feminine interests and experiences (*put something on the back burner, percolate an idea, stir the pot, give birth to a plan*). Whether intentional or not, language that reflects traditionally masculine experiences and interests can bind men together in a community in which many women may feel unwelcome or uncomfortable (Murphy & Zorn, 1996; Taylor & Conrad, 1992; Wood, 1992b, 1994c).

fyi

CAREER

Not Exactly a Slam Dunk

The prevalence of sports-related terms in U.S. business culture is not generally a problem within the United States. However, it can be baffling when used in international contexts. Consider these examples (Jones, 2007):

◆ At a global leadership meeting in Italy, the CEO of an electronics company wanted to alter the agenda, so he said, "I'm calling an audible."

◆ In a meeting with Indian executives, a U.S. CEO wanted to modify a clause in a contract, so he asked for "a jump-ball scenario."

◆ AFLAC CEO Dan Amos assured Japanese executives that using the AFLAC duck in ads in Japan would be a "slam dunk."

Stories

Scholars of organizational culture recognize that humans are storytellers by nature. We tell stories to create meaning in our lives. Furthermore, the stories we tell do some real work in establishing and sustaining organizational cultures. Three kinds of stories are important in organizational contexts.

Corporate Stories

Corporate stories convey the values, style, and history of an organization. Just as families have favorite stories about their histories and identities that they retell often, organizations have favorite stories that reflect their collective visions of themselves (Conrad & Poole, 2004; Gargiulo, 2005; Mumby, 1993, 2006).

One important function of corporate stories is to socialize new members into the culture of an organization. For example, both Levi Strauss and Microsoft are known for an informal style of operation. Veteran employees regale new employees with tales about the laid-back character of the companies: casual dress, relaxed meetings, fluid timetables, and non-bureaucratic ways of getting things done. In some workplaces, corporate stories teach employees to regard the company as a family. These stories socialize new employees into the cultures of the companies.

When told and retold among members of an organization, stories foster feelings of connection and vitalize organizational ideology. You've heard the term *war stories*, which refers to frequently retold stories about key moments such as crises, successes, and takeovers. When long-term members of organizations rehash pivotal events in their shared history, they cement the bonds between them and their involvement with the organization. Jed's commentary provides a good example of how stories express and reinforce organizational culture.

Jed

I sing with the Gospel Choir, and we have a good following in the Southeast. When I first joined the group, the other members talked to me. In our conversations, what I heard again and again was the idea that we exist to make music for God and about God, not to glorify ourselves. One of the choir members told me about a singer who had gotten on a personal ego trip because of all the bookings we were getting, and he started thinking he was more important than the music. That guy didn't last long with the group.

Every time they say they want us to think of this company as a family, I want to lock myself in my room or run away from home.

Personal Stories

Members of organizations also tell stories about themselves. Personal stories are accounts that announce how people see themselves and how they want to be seen by others (Cockburn-Wootten & Zorn, 2006). For example, if Sabra perceives herself as a supportive team player, she could simply tell new employees this by saying, "I am a supportive person who believes in teamwork." On the other hand, she could define her image by telling a story: "When I first came here, most folks were operating in isolation, and I thought a lot more could be accomplished if we learned to collaborate. Let me tell you something I did to make that happen. After I'd been on staff for three months, I was assigned to work up a plan for downsizing our manufacturing department. Instead of just developing a plan on my own, I talked with several other managers, and then I met with people who worked in manufacturing to get their ideas. The plan we came up with reflected all of our input." This narrative gives a concrete, coherent account of how Sabra sees herself and wants others to see her.

Collegial Stories

The third type of organizational story offers accounts of other members of the organization. When I first became a faculty member, a senior colleague took me out to lunch and told me anecdotes about people in the department and university. At the time, I thought he was simply sharing some interesting stories. Later, however, I realized he had told me who the players were so that I could navigate my new context.

Collegial stories told by co-workers forewarn us about what to expect from whom. "If you need help getting around the CEO, Jane's the one to see. A year ago, I couldn't finish a report by deadline, so Jane rearranged his calendar so he thought the report wasn't due for another week." "Roberts is a real stickler for rules. Once when I took an extra 20 minutes on my lunch break, he reamed me out." "Pat trades on politics, not performance. Pat took several of the higher-ups out for lunch and golfed with them for the month before bonuses were decided." Whether positive or negative, collegial stories assert identities for others in an organization. They are part of the informal network that teaches new members of an organization how to get along with various other members of the culture.

Rites and Rituals

Rites and rituals are verbal and nonverbal practices that express and reproduce organizational cultures. They do so by providing standardized ways of expressing organizational values and identity.

Rites

Rites are dramatic, planned sets of activities that bring together aspects of cultural ideology in a single event. Harrison Trice and Janice Beyer (1984) identified six kinds of organizational rites. *Rites of passage* are used to mark membership in different levels or parts of organizations. For example, a nonverbal symbol of change may be the moving of an employee's office from the second to the fourth floor after a promotion. A desk plaque with a new employee's name and title is a rite that acknowledges a change in identity. *Rites of integration* affirm and enhance the sense of community in an organization. Examples are holiday parties, annual picnics, and graduation ceremonies.

Commencement is an important rite of passage at colleges and universities.

Organizational cultures also include rites that blame or praise people. Firings, demotions, and reprimands are common *blaming rites*—the counterpart of which is *enhancement rites*, which praise individuals and teams that embody the organization's goals and self-image. Campuses bestow awards on faculty who are especially gifted teachers or outstanding scholars. Many sales companies give awards for productivity (most sales of the month, quarter, or year). Many organizations use organizational newsletters to congratulate employees on accomplishments. Audrey describes an enhancement rite in her sorority.

Audrey

In my sorority, we recognize sisters who make the dean's list each semester by putting a rose on their dinner plates. That way everyone realizes who has done well academically, and we can also remind ourselves that scholarship is one of the qualities we all aspire to.

Organizations also develop rites for managing change. *Renewal rites* aim to revitalize and update organizations. Training workshops serve this purpose, as do periodic retreats at which organizational members discuss their goals and the institution's health. Organizations also develop rituals for managing conflicts between members of the organization. *Conflict resolution rites* are standard methods of dealing with differences and discord. Examples are arbitration, collective bargaining, mediation, executive fiat, voting, and ignoring or denying problems. The conflict resolution rite that typifies an organization reflects the values of its overall culture.

Rituals

Rituals are forms of communication that occur regularly and that members of an organization perceive as familiar and routine parts of organizational life. Rituals differ from rites in that rituals don't necessarily bring together a number of aspects of organizational ideology into a single event. Rather, rituals are repeated communication performances that communicate a particular value or role definition.

Organizations have personal, task, and social rituals. *Personal rituals* are routine behaviors that individuals use to express their organizational identities. In their study of organizational cultures, Pacanowsky and O'Donnell-Trujillo (1983) noted that Lou Polito, the owner of a car company, opened all the company's mail every day. Whenever possible, Polito hand-delivered mail to the divisions of his company to communicate his openness and his involvement with the day-to-day business.

CAREER
Workplace Bullying

The term "schoolyard bully" reflects the common experience of being bullied—or being a bully—in elementary school. Most of us expect bullying to be left behind as we move into adult life. But that doesn't always happen. According to a 2010 survey (Workplacebullying. org, 2010), at least 35 percent of employees in the United States report they have experienced **workplace bullying,** which is recurring hostile behaviors used by people with greater power against people with lesser power (Keashly & Neuman, 2005; Tracy, Lutgen-Sandvik, & Alberts, 2006; Yamanda, 2010). The key is power: When a person with power devalues a person with less power, the person with lesser power lacks the authority to protect herself or himself or to make the bullying stop. Bullying includes ridicule, spreading untrue and hurtful rumors, insults, and making false accusations. Both sexes engage in workplace bullying, but men do so more frequently: 62 percent of bullies are male and 38 percent are female (Workplacebullying.org, 2010). The costs of bullying are high: decreased morale, weak or broken employee networks, increased turnover, lowered commitment, and reduced productivity (Yamanda, 2010).

Workers' rights advocates have been campaigning for years to get states to enact laws against workplace bullying, and in May 2010 they scored their biggest victory. The New York state senate passed a bill that would let workers sue for physical, psychological or economic harm due to abusive treatment on the job. However, New York state's Assembly Labor Committee put the bill on hold so it's not law . . . yet.

Social rituals are standardized performances that affirm relationships between members of organizations (Mokros, 2006; Mumby, 2006). Some organizations have a company dining room to encourage socializing among employees. In the United Kingdom and Japan, many businesses have afternoon tea breaks. E-mail chatting and forwarding jokes are additional examples of socializing rituals in the workplace. Tamar Katriel (1990) identified a social ritual of griping among Israelis. *Kiturim*, the name Israelis give to their griping, most often occurs during Friday night social events called *mesibot kiturim*, which translates as "gripe sessions." Unlike griping about personal concerns, *kiturim* typically focuses on national issues, concerns, and problems. Sharon provides an example of an office griping ritual.

 Sharon

Where I work, we have this ritual of spending the first half-hour or so at work every Monday complaining about what we have to get done that week. Even if we don't have a rough week ahead, we go through the motions of moaning and groaning. It's kind of like a bonding ceremony for us.

Task rituals are repeated activities that help members of an organization perform their jobs. Perhaps a special conference room is used for particular tasks, such as giving marketing presentations, holding performance reviews, or making sales proposals. Task rituals are also evident in forms and procedures that members of organizations are expected to use to do various things. These forms and procedures standardize

SHARPEN YOUR SKILL

Noticing Your School's Culture

Like all organizations, your school has an organizational culture. Based on material in this chapter, see if you can identify aspects of that culture. You might start by reading your college's policies governing students. From its policies concerning class attendance, drug use, and dishonorable conduct, what can you infer about the culture the college wants to promote? (Note how dishonorable conduct is defined; this differs among schools.)

Next, think about stories about campus life and people that you were told during your first weeks on campus. How did these stories shape your understandings and expectations of the school? Finally, identify rites and rituals at your school. What values do they convey and uphold?

If you belong to particular campus groups (political, athletic, social), identify policies, stories, rites, and rituals that are part of these groups.

task performance in a manner consistent with the organization's view of itself and how it operates. In their study of a police unit, Pacanowsky and O'Donnell-Trujillo (1983) identified the routine that officers are trained to follow when they stop drivers for traffic violations. The questions officers are taught to ask ("May I see your license, please?" "Do you know why I stopped you?" "Do you know how fast you were going?") allow them to size up traffic violators and decide whether to give them a break or ticket. The Sharpen Your Skill exercise on this page allows you to notice rituals in an organization to which you belong.

Structures

Organizational cultures are also represented through structural aspects of organizational life. As the name implies, **structures** organize relationships and interaction between members of an organization. We'll consider four structures that express and uphold organizational culture: roles, rules, policies, and communication networks.

Roles

Roles are responsibilities and behaviors expected of people because of their specific positions in an organization. Most organizations formally define roles in job descriptions:

▶ Training coordinator: Responsible for assessing needs and providing training to Northwest branches of the firm; supervises staff of 25 professional trainers, coordinates with director of human relations. Supervisory experience required.

▶ Assistant professor: Duties include teaching three classes per term, supervising graduate student theses, serving on departmental and university committees, and conducting research. Ph.D. and experience required.

A role is not tied to any particular person. Rather, it is a set of functions and responsibilities that could be performed by any number of people who have particular talents, experiences, and other relevant qualifications. If one person quits or is fired, another can be found as a replacement. Regardless of who is in the role, the organization will continue with its structure intact. Organizational charts portray who is responsible to whom and clarify the hierarchy of power among roles in the organization.

Rules

Rules, which we discussed in Chapters 1, 4, and 10, are patterned ways of interacting. Rules are present in organizational contexts just as they are in other settings. As in other contexts, organizational rules may be formal (in the contract or organizational chart) or informal (norms for interaction).

Within organizations, constitutive rules specify what various kinds of communication symbolize. Some firms count working late as evidence of commitment. Socializing with colleagues after work may count as showing team spirit. Taking on extra assignments, attending training sessions, and dressing like upper management may communicate ambition. Lyle's commentary points out what counted as violating the chain of command in his company.

I found out the hard way that a company I worked for was dead serious about the organizational chart. I had a problem with a co-worker, so I talked with a guy in another department I was friends with. Somehow my supervisor found out, and he blew a gasket. He was furious that I had "gone outside of the chain of command" instead of coming straight to him.

Regulative rules specify when, where, and with whom communication should occur. Organizational charts formalize regulative rules by showing who reports to whom. Other regulative rules may specify that problems should not be discussed with people outside the organization and that social conversations are (or are not) permitted during working hours. Some organizations have found that employees spend so much time online that productivity suffers, so rules regulating online time are instituted.

DIGITAL MEDIA
Keeping Track of Employees

◆ A majority of today's employers monitor their employees. Two-thirds of employers monitor their employees' Web site visits and 43 percent monitor e-mail, sometimes with dire consequences: 28 percent of employers have fired workers for e-mail misuse ("Workplace Privacy," 2011). Here are a few facts to keep in mind:

◆ In most cases, employers have the right to monitor employees' computer screens while they are working and to see what is stored in computers terminals and hard disks.

◆ Employers have the right to monitor employees' Internet usage, including email.

◆ In most cases, employers have the right to monitor employees' phone calls and to obtain records of calls made. Personal calls are an exception; employers are supposed to cease monitoring if they realize a call is personal.

◆ In most cases, employers have the right to videotape employees. Videotaping is not allowed in bathrooms, locker rooms, and other places where courts have ruled it would be intrusive.

◆ A 2010 legal ruling broadened employers' rights. This ruling states that an employer's policy regarding monitoring need not specify every means of communication subject to the policy. In other words, employees should assume they, as well as their phones and computers, are subject to monitoring.

To learn more about privacy (or lack thereof) in the workplace, visit WebLink 12. 1.

Policies

Policies are formal statements of practices that reflect and uphold the overall culture of an organization. Most organizations codify policies governing such aspects of work life as hiring, promotion, benefits, grievances, and medical leave. The content of policies in these areas differs among organizations in ways that reflect the distinct cultures of diverse work environments.

Organizational policies also reflect the larger society within which organizations are embedded. For example, as public awareness of sexual harassment has increased, most organizations have developed formal policies that define sexual harassment, state the organization's attitude toward it, and detail the procedure for making complaints. Because of the prevalence of dual-career couples, many organizations have created procedures to help place the spouses of people they want to hire.

Communication Networks

As we noted earlier in this chapter, networks link members of an organization together. These networks play key roles in expressing and reinforcing an organization's culture.

Job descriptions and organizational charts, which specify who is supposed to communicate with whom about what, are formal networks. Formal networks provide the order necessary for organizations to operate. They define lines of upward communication (subordinates to superiors; providing feedback, reporting results), downward communication (superiors to subordinates; giving orders, establishing policies), and horizontal communication (peer to peer; coordinating between departments).

Informal networks are more difficult to describe because they are neither formally defined nor based on fixed organizational roles. Friendships, alliances, carpools, and nearby offices can be informal networks through which a great deal of information flows. Communication outside the formal channels of an organization is sometimes called the *grapevine*, a term that suggests its free-flowing character. Although details often are lost or distorted as messages travel along a grapevine, the general information conveyed informally has a surprisingly high rate of accuracy: 75 to 90 percent (Hellweg, 1992). If details are important, however, the grapevine may be a poor source of information.

Guidelines for Communicating in Organizations

We'll discuss three guidelines that are particularly relevant to organizational communication in our era.

Adapt to Diverse Needs, Situations, and People

Consider the following descriptions of people who work in one company in my community:

▶ Eileen is 28, single, Jewish, fluent in English and Spanish, and the primary caregiver for her disabled mother.

▶ Frank is 37, a father of two, and a European American married to a full-time homemaker. He is especially skilled in collaborative team building.

▶ Denise is 30, single, European American, an excellent public speaker, and mother of a 4-year-old girl.

▶ Sam is 59, African American, father of two grown children, and married to an accountant. He is widely regarded as supportive and empathic.

▶ Ned is 42, divorced, European American, and recovering from a triple bypass operation.

▶ Javier is 23, a Latino, and married to a woman who works full time. They are expecting their first child in a few months.

These six people have different life situations, abilities, and goals that affect what they need and want in order to be effective on the job. Eileen and Denise need flexible working hours so they can take care of family members. Eileen may also expect her employer to respect Rosh Hashanah, Yom Kippur, Hanukkah, and other holidays of her religion. Ned may need extended disability leave and a period of part-time work while he recuperates from his heart surgery. Javier may want to take family leave when his child is born, a benefit that wouldn't be valued by Frank or Sam. These six people are typical of the workforce today. They illustrate the diversity of people, life situations, and needs that characterize the modern workplace. The variety of workers is a major change that requires organizations to adapt.

In our era, employees increasingly expect organizations to tailor conditions and benefits to their individual needs and circumstances. Many organizations have a cafeteria-style benefits package that allows employees to select benefits from a range of options that include family leave, flexible working hours, employer-paid education, telecommuting, onsite day care, dental insurance, and personal days. Someone with primary caregiving responsibilities might sacrifice vacation time for additional family leave. A person nearing retirement might want maximum insurance and medical coverage but little family leave time. Flextime, which allows people to adjust working hours to their lifestyles, would be a valuable benefit for many workers. Employer-sponsored classes would be sought by workers who want to learn new skills that might accelerate their advancement. Still another increasingly cherished option is telecommuting, which allows workers to work in their homes or other locations removed from a central office.

The organizations that survive and thrive in an era of diversity will be those that adapt effectively to meet the expectations and needs of different workers and the present era (see the FYI box on the next page). Flexible rules and policies, rather than one-size-fits-all formulas, will mark the successful workplaces of the future. By extension, the most competent, most effective professionals will be those who are comfortable with a stream of changes in people

DIVERSITY

Employee Mistreatment in Culturally Diverse Organizations

We hear a lot about the increasing diversity of the workforce in the United States and elsewhere.

What we hear less about is emerging as a serious problem that seems more prevalent in culturally diverse workplaces than in culturally homogeneous ones. The problem is employee mistreatment, particularly against minorities and women.

Mistreatment ranges from unlawful activities, such as harassment and inequitable benefits, to more subtle activities, such as stereotyping, ridicule, and exclusion from informal networks (Allen, 2006; Carter & Silva, 2010; Mumby, 2006).

Individuals who are treated unfairly in the workplace tend to withdraw, leave, become resentful, or experience anger, which may be expressed in a variety of ways. Clearly, these consequences are not limited to individual employees—they affect organizations' health and productivity. If employees are not contributing constructively on the job, the entire organization suffers.

DIGITAL MEDIA
Tomorrow's Organizations

Work groups and teams will increasingly work virtually, with people connecting from different places and even different countries (Rothwell, 2009). Technologies such as text messaging, voip, audio- and videoconferencing, and webcasts allow groups to work across time and distance. In future years, we're sure to see additional technologies that further facilitate virtual group work.

One of the best ways to learn about social and organizational trends that are reshaping the world of work is to read online magazines. *Entrepreneur* (WebLink 12.2 in the book's online resources for this chapter) discusses emerging trends and resources for entrepreneurs. Other savvy sites are an idea café created by business owners (WebLink 12.3 in the book's online resources for this chapter), where you'll find advice on starting and running a business, using technologies, and networking, and entrepreneur.org (Weblink 12.4). It's free for as many as five members.

and ways of working. You might work closely with a colleague for several years and then see little of that person if he or she modifies working hours to accommodate changes in family life. If you choose to telecommute, you will need to develop new ways of staying involved in the informal network (which may operate largely on the Internet) and having the amount of social contact you enjoy. Managers will need to find ways to lead employees who work in different locations and at different hours. Project teams may interact through e-mail bulletin boards as often as or more often than they interact face to face.

The workforce of today is different from that of yesterday, and today's workforce is not what we will see in the years ahead. Because rapid change is typical in modern work life, an adaptive orientation is one of the most important qualifications for success. Openness to change and willingness to experiment are challenges for effective participation in organizations.

Expect to Move In and Out of Teams

Effective communication in today's and tomorrow's organizations requires interacting intensely with members of teams that may form and dissolve quickly. Whereas autonomous workers—single leaders, mavericks, and independent professionals—were prized in the 1940s, the team player is most highly sought today (Rothwell, 2007). John, who returned to school in his mid-forties, describes the changes in his job over the past 13 years.

My job is entirely different today than when I started it 13 years ago. When I came aboard, each of us had his own responsibilities, and management pretty much left us alone to do our work. I found authors and helped them develop their ideas, Andy took care of all art for the books, someone else was in charge of marketing, and so forth. Each of us did our job on a book and passed the book on to the next person. Now the big buzzword is team. *Everything is done in teams. From the start of a new book project, the author and I are part of a team that includes the art editor, marketing director, manuscript designer, and so forth. Each of us has to coordinate with the others continually; nobody works as a lone operator. Although I had reservations about teams at first, by now I'm convinced that they are superior to individuals working independently. The books we're producing are more internally coherent, and they are developed far more efficiently when we collaborate.*

The skills we discussed in Part II of this book will help you perceive carefully, listen well, use verbal and nonverbal communication effectively, promote constructive climates, and adapt your style of interacting to the diverse people on your teams. The challenge is to be able to adjust your style of communicating to the expectations and interaction styles of a variety of people and to the constraints of a range of situations. The greater your repertoire of communication skills, the more effectively you will be able to move in and out of teams on the job.

Manage Personal Relationships on the Job

A third challenge of organizational life involves relationships that are simultaneously personal and professional. You probably will be involved in a number of such relationships during your life. In a 1995 study titled "Bosses and Buddies," Ted Zorn described his long friendship with a colleague who became his supervisor. Zorn described tensions that arose because of conflicts between the role of friend and those of supervisor and subordinate. Although management has traditionally discouraged personal relationships between employees, the relationships have developed anyway. The goal, then, is to understand these relationships and manage them effectively.

Friendships between co-workers or supervisors and subordinates often enhance job commitment and satisfaction (Allen, 2006; Mokros, 2006; Mumby, 2006). This is not surprising, because we're more likely to enjoy work when we work with people we like. Yet workplace friendships also have drawbacks. On-the-job friendships may involve tension between the role expectations for friends and for colleagues. A supervisor may have difficulty rendering a fair evaluation of a subordinate who is also a friend. The supervisor might err by overrating the subordinate–friend's strengths or might try to compensate for personal affection by being especially harsh in judging the friend–subordinate. Friendship may also constrain negative feedback, which is essential to effective performance on the job (Larson, 1984). Also, workplace friendships that deteriorate may create stress and job dissatisfaction (Sias et al., 2004).

SHARPEN YOUR SKILL

Get Informed about On-the-Job Relationships

Workplace relationships—whether romances or friendships—can enhance professional life and jeopardize careers. Before you get involved in a workplace romantic relationship or friendship, take the time to get informed so you can make informed choices.

Check out three online resources, all available as WebLinks within the book's online resources for this chapter. Click on WebLink 12.5 to visit About.com's human resources page, which provides information and advice on workplace dating, sex, and romance. WebLink 12.6 takes you to SelfGrowth.com, where Dr. Janet Yager discusses her research and offers sound advice about both friendships and romances in the workplace. WebLink 12.7 gives you access to AppleOne.com's summary of the upside and downside of workplace romance.

Anna

It's hard for me now that my best friend has been promoted over me. Part of it is envy, because I wanted the promotion, too. But the hardest part is that I resent her power over me. When Billie gives me an assignment, I feel like as my friend she shouldn't dump extra work on me. But I also know that as the boss she has to give extra work to all of us sometimes. It just doesn't feel right for my best friend to tell me what to do and evaluate my work.

Clerkenwell_Images/iStockphoto

The work place creates opportunities to interact with people who we may find attractive romantically.

Romantic relationships between people who work together are also increasing. Most women and men work outside the home, sometimes spending more hours on the job than in the home. In Chapter 10, we learned that proximity is a key influence on the formation of romantic relationships. It's no surprise, then, that people who see each other almost every day sometimes find themselves attracted to each other. Yet on-the-job romances pose challenges (Fox, 1998). They are likely to involve many of the same tensions that operate in friendships between supervisors and subordinates. In addition, romantic relationships are especially likely to arouse co-workers' resentment and discomfort. Romantic breakups also tend to be more dramatic than breakups between friends. As Eugene points out, when a workplace romance dies, tension and discomfort may arise.

Eugene

Once I got involved with a woman where I was working. We were assigned to the same team and really hit it off, and one thing led to another, and we were dating. I guess it affected our work some, since we spent a lot of time talking and stuff in the office. But the real problem came when we broke up. It's impossible to avoid seeing your "ex" when you work together in a small office, and everyone else acted like they were walking on eggshells around us. She finally quit, and you could just feel tension drain out of everyone else in our office.

It's probably unrealistic to assume we can avoid personal relationships with people on the job. The challenge is to manage those relationships so that the workplace doesn't interfere with the personal bond and the intimacy doesn't jeopardize professionalism. Friends and romantic partners may need to adjust their expectations and styles of interacting so that personal and work roles do not conflict. It's also advisable to make sure that on-the-job communication doesn't reflect favoritism and privileges that could cause resentment in co-workers. It's important to invest extra effort to maintain an open communication climate with other co-workers.

SUMMARY

In this chapter, we've seen that the culture of an organization is created, sustained, and altered in the process of communication between members of an organization. As they talk, interact, exchange stories, develop policies, and participate in the formal and informal networks, they continuously weave the fabric of their individual roles and collective life.

Organizations, like other contexts of communication, involve a number of challenges. To meet those challenges, we discussed three guidelines. One is to develop a large repertoire of communication skills so you can adapt effectively to diverse people, situations, and needs in the workplace. A second guideline is to be prepared to move in and out of teams rapidly, which is required in many modern organizations. Finally, we discussed ways to manage personal relationships in the workplace. It's likely that you and others will form friendships and perhaps romantic relationships with people in the workplace. The communication skills we've discussed throughout this book will help you navigate the tensions and challenges of close relationships on the job.

REVIEW, REFLECT, EXTEND

The Reflect, Discuss, and Apply Questions that follow will help you review, reflect on, and extend the information and ideas presented in this chapter. These resources, and a diverse selection of additional study tools, are also available online at the CourseMate for *Communication Mosaics*. Your CourseMate includes a student workbook, WebLinks, TED Talks hyperlinks and activities, chapter glossary and flashcards, interactive video activities, Speech Builder Express, and InfoTrac College Edition. For more information or to access this book's online resources, visit **www .cengagebrain.com**.

KEY CONCEPTS

communication network, 245
organizational culture, 246
policy, 254
rite, 249

ritual, 250
role, 252
structure, 252
workplace bullying, 251

Reflect, Discuss, Apply

1. Think about a group to which you belong. It may be a work group or a social group such as a fraternity or an interest club. Describe some common rites and rituals in your group. What do these rites and rituals communicate about the group's culture?

2. Talk with an administrator of a for-profit organization in your community. Ask the administrator what the organization does to support the community—contributions to schools, pro bono work, employee time off to volunteer, etc.

3. As a class, analyze your school's culture. Go online to find your school's policies governing matters such as class attendance, drug use, plagiarism, academic eligibility, and so forth. Based on these policies, what can you infer about the culture your school wants to promote? How successful is the school in establishing that culture?

4. Visit your school's career planning and placement office. Ask to speak with someone who is familiar with nonprofit organizations. Talk with this person to learn about opportunities for service that might appeal to you.

Recommended Resources

1. Visit the Web site of an organization you think you might like to join. Explore different links on the site to learn about the organization's policies and the image it presents. From the material on its site, what can you infer about the organization's culture?

2. The film *Remember the Titans* provides a dramatic account of a man who was assigned to coach a group of athletes in a recently integrated school. The players didn't work together well, largely because of ethnic differences and ethnocentric attitudes. This film provides rich insights into leadership and the development of a cohesive organizational culture for the team.

3. Robin Clair's book *Organizing Silence* (1998; Albany: State University of New York Press) offers an excellent analysis of ways organizations and their members silence employees who object to unfair treatment.

4. Interviews are a common form of communication in organizations. Among the types of interviews that are part of organizational life are hiring interviews, problem-solving interviews, reprimand interviews, appraisal interviews. An online chapter on interviewing is available to you at your CourseMate at **www.cengagebrain.com**.

EXPERIENCE COMMUNICATION CASE STUDY

Ed Misses the Banquet

Apply what you've learned in this chapter by analyzing the following case study, using the accompanying questions as a guide. These questions and a video of the case study are also available online at your CourseMate for *Communication Mosaics*.

Ed recently began working at a new job. Although he's been in his new job only five weeks, he likes it a lot, and he's told you that he sees a future for himself with this company. But last week, a problem arose. Along with all other employees, Ed was invited to the annual company banquet, at which everyone socializes and awards are given for outstanding performance. Ed's daughter was in a play the night of the banquet, so Ed chose to attend his daughter's play rather than the company event. The invitation to the banquet had stated only, "Hope to see you there" and had not been RSVP, so Ed didn't mention to anyone that he couldn't attend. When he arrived at work the next Monday morning, however, he discovered the case was otherwise and had the exchange that follows with his manager. Later, when Ed talked with several co-workers who had been around a few years, he discovered that top management sees the annual banquet as a "command performance" that signifies company unity and loyalty.

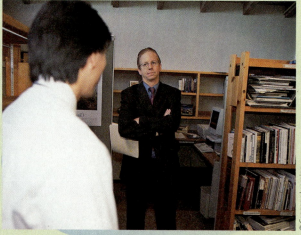

© Cengage Learning

Ed's manager: You skipped the banquet last Saturday. I had really thought you were committed to our company.

Ed: My daughter was in a play that night.

Ed's manager: I don't care *why* you didn't come. We notice who is really with us and who isn't.

1. How does the concept of constitutive rules, which we first discussed in Chapter 4, help explain the misunderstanding between Ed and his manager?

2. How might Ed use the informal network in his organization to learn the normative practices of the company and the meanings they have to others in the company?

3. How do the ambiguity and abstraction inherent in language explain the misunderstanding between Ed and his manager?

4. How would you suggest that Ed repair the damage done by his absence from the company banquet? What might he say to his manager? How could he use *I*-language, indexing, and dual perspective to guide his communication?

5. Do you think the banquet is a ritual? Why or why not?

> *Speech belongs half to the speaker, half to the listener.* — Michel de Montaigne

13 Public Communication

FOCUS QUESTIONS

1. How is public speaking similar to conversation?

2. How can speakers enhance their credibility?

3. What are the advantages and disadvantages of different styles of delivery?

4. How can speakers manage speaking anxiety?

5. How can you listen critically to others' public speeches?

When Wendy Kopp entered Princeton's first-year class in 1985, she didn't realize she was going wind up on the covers of *Time* and *U.S. News & World Report* for launching one of the most effective civic engagement programs for youth in America. Kopp was born into an affluent family that gave her every advantage possible. At Princeton, she noticed that her roommate from the South Bronx hadn't had advantages such as excellent preparatory schooling, and that put her roommate at a disadvantage at Princeton.

Kopp decided to do something about the inequities in opportunities. She wrote her senior thesis on her idea for starting a national teaching corps in which college students would spend a year or two after graduating teaching students in low-income communities. Today that organization is well known: Teach for America. It has grown from 489 teachers in its first year to 12,000 today.

To realize her dream, Kopp had to become an effective speaker. She had to persuade people to donate money to start Teach for America, she had to persuade students to give a year or more of their time to teaching students in underresourced schools, and had to inform citizens and media about her vision and, as the results came in, the impressive effectiveness of her program. You can learn more about Kopp's work by going to the book's online resources for this chapter and clicking on WebLink 13.1; you can hear an interview with her by clicking WebLink 13.2.

Good ideas like Wendy Kopp's have impact only if they are communicated effectively. Public communication allows you to be an active citizen, an effective professional, and a responsible member of your community and the groups to which you belong. It allows you to affect what others believe, think, and do. Therefore, skill in public communication is important both for individuals and for society. Equally important is skill in listening critically to the public communication of others. People who present their ideas effectively and listen critically to the ideas of others are capable of informed, vigorous participation in all spheres of life. The importance of free speech to democratic life is recognized by the First Amendment (see the FYI box on the right).

The First Amendment

"Congress shall make no law respecting an establishment of religion, or prohibiting the free exercise thereof; or abridging the freedom of speech, or of the press; or the right of people peaceably to assemble, and to petition the Government for a redress of grievances."

This chapter focuses on public communication. In the first part of the chapter, we will discuss the different purposes of public speaking and its distinctive features. The second section of the chapter provides an overview of planning and presenting public speeches. In the third section, we identify three guidelines for effective public communication: reducing speaking anxiety, adapting to audiences, and listening critically to public discourse. The complex process of public speaking cannot be taught in a single chapter. This chapter's goal is to give you a conceptual understanding of what is involved in public communication. The information we cover will be especially useful in helping you become a more critical listener when you attend to others' public communication.

Public Speaking as Enlarged Conversation

Many years ago, James Winans (1938), a distinguished professor of communication, said that effective public speaking is enlarged conversation. What Winans meant was that in many ways public speaking is similar to everyday talk. More than 50 years later, two other communication scholars, Michael Motley and Jennifer Molloy, observed that, "except for preparation time and turn-taking delay, public speaking has fundamental parallels to everyday conversation" (1994, p. 52). Whether we are talking with a couple of friends or speaking to an audience of 1,000 people, we must adapt to others' perspectives, create a good climate for interaction, use effective verbal and nonverbal communication, organize what we say so others can follow our ideas, support our claims, present our ideas in an engaging and convincing manner, and attend and respond to questions and responses from listeners.

Thinking of public speaking as enlarged conversation reminds us that most public speaking is neither stiff nor exceedingly formal. In fact, some of the most effective public speakers use an informal, personal style that invites listeners to feel that they are interacting with someone, not being lectured.

I learned that effective public speaking is much like conversation when I first taught a class with 150 students. Previously, I had taught small classes, and I relied on discussion. In the large class, I lectured in a fairly formal style because I thought that was appropriate for a class of 150 students. One day, a student asked a question, and I responded with another question. He replied, then another student added her ideas, and an open discussion was launched. Both the students and I were more engaged with one another and the course material than we had been when I lectured formally. That's when I realized that even in large classes effective classroom style is enlarged conversation.

Distinctive Features of Public Communication

Although public speaking is enlarged conversation, it differs from casual interaction in two primary ways. First, public speeches tend to involve more planning and preparation than informal conversations. Second, public speaking is less obviously interactive than much of our communication. In public speaking situations, communicators are more clearly in speaker and listener roles and the listeners' contributions are less obvious than the speakers'.

Greater Responsibility to Plan and Prepare

When a friend asks your opinion on a political candidate, you respond without conducting research, carefully organizing your ideas, or practicing your delivery. Before speaking to a group of 50 people about that candidate, however, you would likely do some research, organize your ideas, and practice delivering your speech. In public speaking situations, you have a responsibility to provide evidence and reasoning to support your beliefs, to structure your ideas clearly, and to practice your presentation so your delivery is engaging.

Listeners' expectations affect the planning and preparation needed for effective public speaking. We expect more evidence, clearer organization, and more polished delivery in public speeches than in casual conversations. Therefore, public speakers who do not prepare well are likely to disappoint listeners and to be judged inadequate. When you are giving a public speech, your responsibility is to analyze listeners, to do research, to organize ideas, and to practice and polish delivery.

Less Obviously Interactive

Public speaking also tends to be less obviously interactive than some forms of communication, such as personal conversations, interviews, and team deliberations. In most day-to-day interaction, people take turns talking, but speakers tend to do most or all of the talking in public presentations. It would be a mistake, however, to think that listeners don't participate actively in public presentations. They are sending messages even as they listen: head nods, frowns, perplexed expressions, applause, smiles, bored looks. For that reason, effective public speakers pay attention to listeners' feedback throughout their speeches.

Even though listeners participate actively, public speaking places special responsibility on speakers. To be effective, they must anticipate listeners' attitudes and knowledge and must adapt their presentation to the views of listeners. One of the first steps in planning successful public communication is to ask what listeners are likely to know about a topic and how they are likely to feel about it. Based on what you know or learn about listeners, you can make informed choices about what information to include and how to support and organize your ideas.

While actually giving a speech, you should also adapt to listeners' feedback. If some listeners look confused, you might add an example or elaborate on an idea. If listeners' nonverbal behaviors suggest that they are bored, you might alter your volume, incorporate gestures, change your speaking position, or offer a personal example to enliven your talk. Later in this chapter, we'll return to the topic of adapting to listeners. For now, you should realize that because public speaking gives the speaker primary control, the speaker has a special responsibility to be sensitive to listeners' ideas, values, interests, and experiences. With this background, we're ready to consider the purposes of public speaking.

The Purposes of Public Communication

Traditionally, three general purposes of public communication have been recognized: to entertain, to inform, and to persuade. You probably realize that these purposes often overlap. For example, persuasive communication generally includes information. Some of your professors include stories and interesting examples to enliven informational lectures (see the Sharpen Your Skill exercise on this page). Speeches to entertain may also teach listeners something new.

Sasha, a student in one of my classes, gave a speech on arranged marriages, which are still common in her native country. Her goal was to inform her classmates about the history of arranged marriages and why they work for many people. Although her primary goal was to inform, her speech had a persuasive aspect because she encouraged listeners not to impose their values on the practices of other cultures. Although purposes of speaking overlap, most speeches have one primary purpose.

Speaking to Entertain

In a **speech to entertain,** the primary objective is to engage, interest, amuse, or please listeners. You might think that only accomplished comics and performers present speeches to entertain. Actually, many of us will be involved in speaking to entertain during our lives. You might be asked to give an after-dinner speech, present a toast at a friend's wedding, or make remarks at a retirement party for a colleague.

Humor, although often part of speeches to entertain, is not the only way we engage others. We also entertain when we tell stories to share

Speaking to entertain is something most of us will do in our lives.

Fuse/Jupiter Images

experiences, build community, pass on history, or teach a lesson. Parents share with children stories of family history and mentors share stories of an organization's history with new employees.

Speaking to Inform

A **speech to inform** has the primary goal of increasing listeners' understanding, awareness, or knowledge of some topic. For example, a speaker might want listeners to understand the rights guaranteed in the Bill of Rights or to make listeners aware of recycling programs. In both cases, the primary purpose is to enrich listeners' knowledge, although each topic has persuasive implications. A speech to inform may also take the form of a demonstration, in which the speaker shows how to use a new computer program or how to distinguish between poisonous and nonpoisonous species of mushrooms. As Gladys points out, however, speaking to inform may be more successful when speakers also entertain or otherwise capture listeners' interest.

I've taught second grade for eight years, and there's one thing I've learned: If you don't get the students' interest, you can't teach them anything. My education classes taught me to focus on content when planning lessons. But working in real classrooms with real children taught me that before a teacher can get content or information across to students, she has to first capture their interest.

Speaking to Persuade

A **speech to persuade** aims to influence attitudes, change practices, or alter beliefs. Rather than primarily an entertainer or teacher, the persuasive speaker is an advocate who argues for a cause, issue, policy, attitude, or action. In one of my classes, a student named Chris gave a speech designed to persuade other students to contribute to the Red Cross blood drive. He began by telling us that he was a hemophiliac, whose life depended on blood donations. He then explained the procedures for donating blood (a subordinate informational purpose) so that listeners would not be deterred by fear of the unknown. Next, he described several cases of people who had died or had become critically ill because adequate supplies of blood weren't available. In the two weeks after his speech, more than one-third of the students who had heard his speech donated blood.

As communication scholar Cindy Griffin (2012) points out, many of the values and principles of the United States were carved out in key persuasive speeches that changed what people believed and did. Consider a few examples of speeches that contributed to changing America:

Moved to Speak

Candace Lightner had never thought of herself as a public speaker. She had never sought the limelight and had seldom been required to speak out to others. Then, in 1980, her 13-year-old daughter was killed by a teenage drunk driver. Once she recovered from the immediate grief of her daughter's untimely death, Lightner began a crusade for stricter laws against drunk driving (Lightner, 1990; Sellinger, 1994).

She founded Mothers Against Drunk Driving (MADD), which now has thousands of members. In addition, Lightner persuaded state and federal legislators to approve stiffer laws and penalties for drunk driving and to raise the age for drinking to 21. Although not an experienced speaker when she began her crusade, Lightner became a skillful speaker in order to get her message across.

▶ In 1841, Frederick Douglass spoke against slavery.

▶ In 1848, Elizabeth Cady Stanton advocated women's enfranchisement.

▶ In 1963, Martin Luther King, Jr. gave his famous "I Have a Dream" speech.

▶ In 1964, President Lyndon Johnson explained affirmative action.

▶ In 2001, President George W. Bush announced the War on Terror.

But speeches that change a country's laws and actions are not the only important forms of public speaking. Citizens' votes are affected by persuasive speeches that champion or criticize particular candidates. Likewise, students' attitudes and behaviors can be changed by classroom speeches that advocate wearing seat belts, giving blood, spaying and neutering pets, and engaging in community service. The FYI box on page 266 provides an example of how one average citizen became a persuasive advocate for stronger laws against drunk driving.

Planning and Presenting Public Speeches

Effective public speaking is a process, not a static event. The process begins with understanding credibility and ways to earn it. The next steps are to define the purpose of speaking, develop a strong thesis statement, and decide how to organize the speech. Next, speakers conduct research to identify evidence that can be used to support their ideas. Finally, speakers select delivery styles and practice the presentation. We will discuss each step.

Earning Credibility

Effective public speaking (and, indeed, communication in all contexts) requires credibility. **Credibility** exists when listeners believe in a speaker and trust what the speaker says. Credibility is based on listeners' perceptions of a speaker's position, authority, knowledge (also called expertise), dynamism, and trustworthiness (also called character). Therefore, to earn credibility, speakers should demonstrate that they are informed about their topics, that they are dynamic communicators, and that they are ethical in using evidence and reasoning.

A speaker's credibility is not necessarily static. Some speakers have high **initial credibility,** which is the expertise, dynamism, and character that listeners attribute to them before they begin to speak. Initial credibility is based on titles, experiences, and achievements that are known to listeners before they hear the speech. For example, Al Gore has high initial credibility on environmental issues.

 Ricardo

Last month, I went to a lecture about getting started in financial planning. I figured the speaker just wanted to sell me something, so I didn't have too high a regard for him. But during his talk, he quoted lots of information from unbiased sources, so I saw that he really knew his stuff. He also didn't try to sell us anything, so I began to trust what he said. And he made the ideas really easy to follow with charts and handouts. By the time he was through, I thought he was excellent.

As Ricardo points out, a speaker without much initial credibility may gain strong credibility in the process of presenting a speech. Speakers may gain **derived credibility,** which listeners grant as a result of how speakers communicate during presentations. Speakers may earn derived credibility by providing clear, well-organized information and convincing evidence, and by an engaging delivery style. Speakers may also increase credibility during a presentation if listeners regard them as likable and as having goodwill toward the listeners (McCroskey & Teven, 1999).

Terminal credibility is a cumulative combination of initial and derived credibility. Terminal credibility may be greater or less than initial credibility, depending on how effectively a speaker has communicated.

Planning Public Speeches

A well-crafted speech begins with careful planning. Speakers should select a limited topic, define a clear purpose, and develop a concise thesis statement.

Select a Topic

Speakers should select topics that they know and care about. When you choose a topic that matters to you, you have a head start in both knowledge and dynamism, two bases of credibility.

Speakers should also choose topics that are appropriate to listeners. It's important to consider listeners' values, backgrounds, attitudes, knowledge, and interests so that you can select topics and adapt how you address them in ways that respect the perspectives and interests of listeners.

Speech topics should be appropriate to the situation. If you are asked to speak at a professional meeting, your speech should address issues relevant to that profession. If you are speaking about someone who has won an award or who is retiring, the situation calls for a speech that praises the person.

Finally, effective topics are limited in scope. You may be concerned about education, but that topic is too broad for a single speech. You might narrow it to a speech on funding for education or training of teachers or some other specific aspect of your general area of interest.

Define the Speaking Purpose

The second step in planning a speech is to define your general and specific purposes. The general purpose is to entertain, inform, or persuade. The **specific purpose** is exactly what you hope to accomplish. For example, specific purposes could be to get 25 percent of the audience to sign up to work on a Habitat house, to have listeners give correct answers to a quiz about the spread of HIV, or to get listeners to laugh at your jokes. The specific purpose of a speech states the behavioral response the speaker seeks: "I want listeners to agree to donate blood"; "I want listeners to sign a petition in support of the War on Terror."

Develop the Thesis

The thesis statement is the single most important sentence in a speech. A clear **thesis statement,** which is the main idea of the entire speech, guides an effective speech: "Habitat volunteers build community as they build houses" or "The electoral college should be abolished because it does not represent the popular vote and does not fit the current times." Each of these thesis statements succinctly summarizes the focus of a speech (building a Habitat house; abolishing the electoral college) and the main points of the speech (building community, building a house; unrepresentative, not fitted to current time). Once a speaker has a well-formed thesis statement, he or she is ready to consider how to organize the speech.

Organizing Speeches

Organization increases speaking effectiveness in several ways (Griffin, 2012; Verderber, Verderber, & Sellnow, 2012). First, organization affects comprehension of ideas. Listeners can understand, follow, and remember a speech that is well planned and well ordered. Listeners are less likely to retain the key ideas in a poorly organized speech. Second, experimental evidence shows that listeners are better persuaded by an organized speech than by a disorganized one. Finally, organization enhances speakers' credibility, probably because a carefully structured speech reflects well on a speaker's preparation and respect for listeners. When someone gives a disorganized speech, listeners may regard the person as incompetent or unprepared, which reduces derived and terminal credibility.

Organizing an effective speech is not the same as organizing a paper. Oral communication requires more explicit organization, greater redundancy, and simpler sentence structure. Unlike readers, listeners cannot refer to an earlier passage if they become confused or forget a point already made. Providing signposts to highlight organization and repeating key ideas increase listeners' retention of a message (Coopman & Lull, 2012; Hamilton, 2012).

Consistent with the need for redundancy in oral communication, good speeches tell listeners what the speaker is going to tell them, present the message, and then remind listeners of the main points. This means preparing an introduction, a body, and a conclusion. In addition, speakers should include transitions to move listeners from point to point in the speech.

The Introduction

The introduction is the first thing an audience hears, and a good introduction does a lot of work. It should gain listeners' attention, give them a reason to listen, establish the credibility of the speaker, and state the thesis and how it will be developed.

The first objective of an introduction is to gain listeners' attention, which may also provide them with a motivation to listen. You might open with a dramatic piece of evidence, say, a startling statistic: "In the United States, four women per day are battered to death by intimates." Other ways to gain attention are to present a striking visual aid (a photo of a victim of battering) or a dramatic example (the detailed story of one battered woman).

You could pose a question that invites listeners to think actively about the topic: "Have you ever feared for your life and had no way to escape?" Speakers may also gain listeners' attention by referring to personal experience with the topic: "For the past year, I have worked as a volunteer in the local battered women's shelter." Notice that this introductory statement establishes some initial credibility for the speaker.

The introduction should also include a thesis statement, which we discussed earlier. Your thesis should be a clear, short sentence that captures the main idea of your talk and the key points supporting that idea. A good thesis statement presents the principal claim of a speech and the main points by which it will be developed: "In my talk, I will show you that vegetarianism is healthful, and I will demonstrate that a vegetarian diet is also delicious," or "To inform you about your legal rights in an interview, I will discuss laws that prohibit discrimination and protect privacy, tell you what questions are illegal, and inform you what you can do if an interviewer asks an illegal question." Crafting a strong introduction helps speakers earn credibility. In summary, a good introduction:

▶ Captures listeners' attention

▶ Motivates listeners to listen

▶ Informs listeners of the main idea (thesis) of the speech and the key points supporting that idea

▶ Enhances the speaker's credibility

The Body

The body of a speech develops the thesis by organizing content into points that are distinct yet related. In short speeches of 5 to 10 minutes, two or three points usually are all that a speaker can develop well. Longer speeches may include more points. You can organize speeches in many ways, and each organizational pattern has distinct effects on the overall meaning (see Figure 13.1).

Chronological patterns or *time patterns* organize ideas chronologically. They emphasize progression, sequences, or development. *Spatial patterns organize* ideas

---

Topic: Literacy

Speech 1: Temporal Organization

Thesis:	As America changes, so must our ways of teaching literacy.
Claim 1:	When America was founded, reading was restricted primarily to the aristocratic class.
Claim 2:	By the late 1800s more members of working class and African Americans were also taught to read.
Claim 3:	Today, America must find ways to provide literacy education to immigrants.

Speech 2: Spatial Organization

Thesis:	Teaching literacy happens in homes, schools, and volunteer-run literacy programs.
Claim 1:	The home is where many children first learn to read.
Claim 2:	Schools teach literacy to many students.
Claim 3:	When home and school don't teach literacy, volunteer-run programs can teach literacy.

Speech 3: Cause–Effects

Thesis:	Literacy programs will increase their productivity, enhance citizens' engagement with society, and reduce incarceration rates.
Claim 1:	People who can read are more economically stable and productive than people who cannot read.
Claim 2:	Citizens who can read more actively engage civic and social issues.
Claim 3:	Literate citizens are less likely to break the law and go to prison.

© Cengage Learning

Figure 13.1   **Organizing Speeches**

according to physical relationships. They are useful in explaining layouts, geographic relationships, or connections between parts of a system.

Topical patterns (also called *classification patterns*) order speech content into categories or areas. This pattern is useful for speeches in which topics break down into two or three areas that aren't related temporally, spatially, or otherwise. The *star structure*, which is a variation on the topical pattern, has several main points (as a star has five or six) that are related and work together to develop the main idea of a speech (Jaffe, 2007).

Wave patterns feature repetitions; each "wave" repeats the main theme with variations or extensions. *Comparative patterns* compare two or more phenomena (people, machines, planets, situations). This pattern demonstrates similarities between phenomena ("In many ways, public speaking is like everyday conversation") or differences between phenomena ("Public speaking requires more planning than everyday conversation").

Persuasive speeches typically rely on organizational patterns that encourage listeners to change attitudes or behaviors. *Problem–solution patterns* allow speakers to describe a problem and propose a solution. *Cause–effect* and *effect–cause patterns* order speech content into two main points: cause and effect. This structure is useful for persuasive speeches that aim to convince listeners that certain consequences will follow from particular actions.

A final way to organize a persuasive speech is the *motivated sequence pattern* (Gronbeck et al., 1994; Jaffe, 2007; Monroe, 1935). This pattern is effective in diverse communication situations, probably because it follows a natural order of human thought. The motivated sequence pattern includes five sequential steps. The *attention step* focuses listeners' attention on the topic with a strong opening ("Imagine this campus with no trees whatsoever"). The *need step* shows that a real and serious problem exists ("Acid rain is slowly but surely destroying the trees on our planet"). Next is the *satisfaction step*, in which a speaker recommends a solution to the problem described ("Stronger environmental regulations and individual efforts to use environmentally safe products can protect trees and thus the oxygen we need to live"). The *visualization step* intensifies listeners' commitment to the solution by helping them imagine the results that the recommended solution would achieve ("You will have air to breathe, and so will your children and grandchildren. Moreover, we'll have trees to add beauty to our lives."). Finally, in the *action step* the speaker appeals to listeners to take concrete action to realize the recommended solution ("Refuse to buy or use any aerosol products.").

The Conclusion

A good speech ends on a strong note. The conclusion is a speaker's last chance to emphasize ideas, increase credibility, and gain listeners' support or approval. An effective conclusion accomplishes two goals. First, it summarizes the main ideas of the speech. Second, it leaves listeners with a memorable final idea such as a dramatic quote or example, a challenge, or an unforgettable computer graphic.

Transitions

The final aspect of organizing a speech is developing **transitions,** which are words, phrases, and sentences that connect ideas in a speech. Transitions signal listeners that you have finished talking about one idea and are ready to move to the next one. Within the development of a single point, speakers usually rely on such transitional words and phrases as *therefore, and so, for this reason,* and *as the evidence suggests.* To make

Personal involvement with a topic enhances speaker credibility.

transitions from one point to another, the speaker may use phrases: "My second point is…"; "Now that we have seen how many people immigrate to the United States, let's ask what they bring to our country." Speakers typically use one or more sentences to create transitions between the major parts of a speech (introduction, body, conclusion). A student in one of my classes moved from the body to the conclusion of his speech with this transition: "I have discussed in some detail why we need protection for wetlands. Before I leave you, let me summarize the key ideas I've presented."

Researching and Supporting Public Speeches

Evidence is material used to support claims, such as those made in a public speech. In addition to supporting claims, evidence may enhance listeners' interest and emotional response to ideas. Evidence serves a number of important functions in speeches. First, it can be used to make ideas clearer, more compelling, and more dramatic. Second, evidence fortifies a speaker's opinions, which are seldom sufficient to persuade intelligent listeners. Finally, evidence heightens a speaker's credibility. A speaker who supports ideas well comes across as informed and prepared. Therefore, including strong evidence allows speakers to increase credibility during a presentation.

The effectiveness of evidence depends directly on whether listeners understand and accept it. This reinforces the importance of adapting to listeners. Even if you quote the world's leading authority, it won't be effective if your listeners don't find the authority credible (Olson & Cal, 1984). Consequently, your choices of evidence for your speech should take listeners' perspectives into account. You want to include support that they find credible, while also making sure your evidence is valid.

Four forms of support are widely respected, and each tends to be effective in specific situations and for particular goals. The kinds of evidence are **statistics**, **examples**, **comparisons**, and **quotations**. In addition, **visual aids**, which are not technically a form of evidence, allow speakers to present and enhance other forms of evidence. For instance, a graph (visual aid) of statistics (evidence) enhances the impact of a speaker's point. Figure 13.2 summarizes the types of evidence and their uses.

Before including any form of evidence, speakers have an ethical responsibility to check the accuracy of material and the credibility of sources. It is advisable to ask questions such as these:

▶ Are the statistics still valid? Population demographics, social trends, and other matters become quickly outdated, so it's important to have current statistics.

***Examples* provide concrete descriptions of situations, individuals, problems, or other phenomena.**

    Types: Short (instance)
                  Detailed
                  Hypothetical
                  Anecdotal

    Uses: To personalize information and ideas
                  To add interest to a presentation
                  To enhance dramatic effect

***Comparisons (analogies)* compare two ideas, processes, people, situations, or other phenomena.**

    Types: Literal analogy (A heart is a pump.)
                  Figurative analogy (Life is a journey.)
                  Metaphor (The company is a family.)
                  Simile (The company is like a family.)

    Uses: To show connections between phenomena
                  To relate a new idea to one that is familiar to listeners
                  To provide interest

***Statistics* summarize quantitative information.**

    Types: Percentages and ratios
                  Demographic data
                  Frequency counts
                  Correlations
                  Trends

    Uses: To summarize many instances of some phenomenon
                  To show relationships between two or more phenomena (cause or correlation)
                  To demonstrate trends or patterns

***Quotations (testimony)* restate or paraphrase the words of others, giving appropriate credit to the sources of the words.**

    Types: Short quotation
                  Extended quotation
                  Paraphrase

    Uses: To add variety and interest
                  To support a speaker's claims
                  To draw on the credibility of people whom listeners know
                  To include particularly arresting phrasings of ideas

***Visual aids* reinforce verbal communication and provide visual information and appeals.**

    Types: Handmade charts and graphs
                  Overheads/transparencies
                  Computer-created charts and graphs
                  PowerPoint slides
                  Objects, pictures, handouts, film clips

    Uses: To strengthen and underscore verbal messages
                  To translate statistics into pictures that are understandable
                  To add variety and interest
                  To give listeners a vivid appreciation of a topic, issue, or point

© Cengage Learning

Figure 13.2   **Types of Evidence and Their Uses**

Adapting to Listeners

On Saturday, January 8, 2011, Representative Gabrielle Giffords of Arizona was shot in the head when Jared Lee Loughner opened fire during Giffords' meeting with constituents. Giffords is a popular congressperson, and many people anxiously awaited news about her injury and chances of recovery. Miraculously, she survived the head wound.

Her doctors held a press conference to inform the public of her status. In that public communication, Dr. Dong Kim, the chair of neurosurgery at UT Health where Giffords was treated, demonstrated how to adapt highly technical medical information to listeners without medical expertise. He told viewers that Giffords had mild hydrocephalus. Since many in his audience wouldn't know the term *hydrocephalus*, Dr. Kim translated it by saying, it's like "water in the head." He went on to explain that patients with brain injury often have difficulty absorbing fluid in the head, which he made easily understandable by adding that it's like "having a partially clogged drain." The entire press conference is available at: http://www.youtube.com/watch?v=OuG6uV4cJ54

▶ Does the person quoted have any personal interest in endorsing a certain point of view? For example, natural gas companies' statements about the harmlessness of hydrofracking may reflect financial interests.

▶ Is the person an expert on the topic? It is inappropriate to rely on the **halo effect,** in which people who are well known in one area (sports stars, for example) are quoted in an area outside their expertise (the nutritional value of cereal).

▶ Is an example representative of the point it is used to support? Is it typical of the general case?

▶ Are comparisons fair? For instance, it might be appropriate to compare Christianity and Buddhism as spiritual paths, but it would not be appropriate to compare them as religions that believe in a single diety.

When presenting evidence to listeners, speakers have an ethical obligation to identify each source, including titles and qualifications, and to tell listeners its date, if the date matters. You can use an **oral footnote**, which acknowledges a source of evidence and sometimes explains the source's qualifications. For instance, a speaker might say, "Doctor Bingham, who won the 1988 Nobel Prize in physics, published a study in 1996 in which she reported that …" or "As Senator Bollinger remarked in 1997, …" Oral footnotes give appropriate acknowledgment to the source that initially generated the evidence, and they enable listeners to evaluate the speaker's evidence. Here's another example of an oral footnote that was presented in a persuasive speech advocating stronger gun control laws: "In the June 2006 issue of *Marie Claire*, investigator Jennifer Friedlin reported that it took her only 30 minutes to buy a gun but 4 weeks to obtain a restraining order."

Developing Effective Delivery

As we have seen, dynamism is one dimension of a speaker's credibility. Therefore, an engaging delivery is important. **Oral style**

SHARPEN YOUR SKILL

Noticing Oral Style

Attend a speech on your campus. Identify instances of oral style:

specific ideas and evidence	redundancy	short, simple sentences
rhetorical questions	interjections	personal stories and language

If you perceived the speech as ineffective, was it lacking oral style? If you perceived it as effective, was oral style featured?

generally should be personal (Wilson & Arnold, 1974). Speakers may include personal stories and personal pronouns, referring to themselves as *I* rather than *the speaker*. Also, speakers may use phrases instead of complete sentences, and contractions (*can't*) are appropriate. Speakers should also sustain eye contact with listeners and show that they are approachable. If you reflect on speakers you have found effective, you will probably realize that they seemed engaging, personal, and open to you.

Effective oral style also tends to be immediate and active (Wilson & Arnold, 1974). This is important because listeners must understand ideas immediately, as they are spoken, whereas readers can take time to comprehend ideas. Speakers foster immediacy by using short sentences instead of complex sentences. Immediacy also involves following general ideas with clear, specific evidence or elaboration. Rhetorical questions ("Would you like to know that a good job is waiting for you when you graduate?"), interjections ("Imagine that!"; "Look!"), and redundancy also enhance the immediacy of a speech (Thompson & Grundgenett, 1999). The Sharpen Your Skill box on page 274 invites you to notice oral style in a speech.

Throughout this book, we've seen that we should adapt our communication to its context. This basic communication principle guides a speaker's choice of a presentation style. The style of speaking that is effective at a political rally is different from the style that is appropriate for an attorney's closing speech in a trial; delivering a toast at a wedding requires a different style from that required for testifying before Congress. Each speaking situation suggests guidelines for presentation, so speakers must consider the context when selecting a speaking style.

Four styles of delivery are generally recognized, and each is appropriate in certain contexts. **Impromptu delivery** involves little or no preparation. It can be effective for speakers who know their material thoroughly. Many politicians speak in an impromptu fashion ["impromptu" not an adverb] when talking about their experience in public service and policies they advocate. Impromptu speaking generally is not advisable for novice speakers or for anyone who is not thoroughly familiar with a topic.

Probably the most commonly used presentational style is **extemporaneous delivery.** Extemporaneous speaking involves substantial preparation and practice, but it stops short of memorizing the exact words of a speech and relies on notes. Speakers conduct research, organize materials, and practice delivering their speeches, but they do not rehearse so much that the speeches sound canned. Attorneys, teachers, politicians, and others who engage in public speaking most often use an extemporaneous style of presentation because it allows them to prepare thoroughly and yet engage listeners when speaking.

Manuscript delivery, as the name implies, involves presenting a speech from a complete, written text. Manuscript style requires the speaker to write out the entire speech and to rely on the written document or a teleprompter projection when making the presentation. Few people can present manuscript speeches in an engaging, dynamic manner. However, manuscript delivery is appropriate, even advisable, in situations that call for precision. For instance, U.S. presidents generally use manuscripts for official presentations. In these circumstances, speakers cannot run the risk of errors or imprecise language.

Extemporaneous speaking allows speakers to be engaged with listeners.

© Chuck Savage/CORBIS

An extension of the manuscript style of speaking is **memorized delivery,** in which a speaker commits an entire speech to memory and presents it without relying on a written text or notes. This style shares the primary disadvantage of manuscript speaking: the risk of a canned delivery that lacks dynamism and immediacy. In addition, the memorized style of delivery entails a second serious danger: forgetting. If a speaker is nervous, or if something happens to disrupt a presentation, the speaker may become rattled and forget all or part of the speech. Without the written text, he or she may be unable to get back on track.

When choosing a style of delivery, speakers should consider the advantages and disadvantages of each speaking style and the constraints of particular communication situations. No single style suits all occasions. Instead, the most effective style is one that suits the particular speaker and the situation. Regardless of which delivery style they use, effective speakers devote thought and practice to their verbal and nonverbal communication. It is important to select words that convey your intended meanings and that create strong images for listeners. Equally important are effective gestures, paralanguage, and movement. Because public speaking is *enlarged* conversation, nonverbal behaviors generally should be more vigorous and commanding than in personal communication.

Guidelines for Public Speaking

In this section, we discuss three guidelines for public speaking. The first two pertain to occasions when you might present a speech. The third focuses on effective, critical listening to speeches given by others.

Understand and Manage Speaking Anxiety

One of the most common challenges for public speakers is anxiety. The communication situations that prompt apprehension vary among people, as the commentaries by Tomoko and Trish illustrate.

Talking to a big group of people is no problem for me. I like being able to prepare what I want to say in advance and to control what happens. But I get very nervous about one-on-one talking. It's too personal and spontaneous for me to feel secure about what will happen.

I can talk all day with one friend or a few of them and be totally at ease, but put me in front of a group of people, and I just freeze. I feel I'm on display or something and everything I say has to be perfect and it all depends on me. It's just a huge pressure.

Both Trish and Tomoko are normal in feeling some anxiety about specific communication situations. Almost all of us sometimes feel apprehensive about talking with others (Behnke & Sawyer, 1999; Bippus & Daly, 1999; Richmond & McCroskey, 1992). What many people don't realize is that a degree of anxiety is natural and may actually improve communication. When we are anxious, we become more alert and energetic, largely because our bodies produce adrenaline and extra blood sugar, which enhance our vigilance. The burst of adrenaline increases vitality, which can make speakers more dynamic and compelling. You can channel the extra energy that accompanies public speaking into gestures and movements that enhance your presentation.

You should also realize that anxiety is common for seasoned speakers. Many politicians feel nervous before and during a speech, even though they may have made hundreds or even thousands of speeches. Likewise, teachers who have taught for years usually feel tension before meeting a class, and such a seasoned journalist as Mike Wallace claimed to get butterflies when conducting interviews. The energy fostered by communication anxiety allows speakers to be more dynamic and more interesting.

Although a degree of anxiety about speaking is natural, too much can interfere with effectiveness. When anxiety is great enough to hinder our ability to interact with others, communication apprehension exists. **Communication apprehension** is a detrimental level of anxiety associated with real or anticipated communication encounters (McCroskey, 1977; Richmond & McCroskey, 1992). Communication apprehension exists in degrees and may occur at times other than when we're actually speaking. Many people feel anxious primarily in advance of communication situations; they worry, imagine difficulties, and dread the occasion long before the communication occurs.

Causes of Communication Apprehension

Communication apprehension may be situational or chronic (Motley & Molloy, 1994). Situational anxiety is limited to specific situations that cause apprehension: performance reviews on the job, first dates, or major social occasions. A common cause of situational apprehension is a past failure or failures in specific speaking situations. For example, my doctor called me one day to ask me to coach her for a speech she had to give to a medical society. When I asked why she thought she needed coaching, Eleanor told me that the last speech she had given was eight years earlier, in medical school. She was an intern, and it was her turn to present a case to the other interns and in front of the resident who supervised her. Just before the speech, she lost her first patient to a heart attack and was badly shaken. All her work preparing the case and rehearsing her presentation was eclipsed by the shock of losing the patient. As a result, she was disorganized, flustered, and generally ineffective. That single incident, which followed a history of successful speaking, was so traumatic that Eleanor developed acute situational speaking anxiety.

Chronic anxiety exists when we are anxious about most or all situations in which we are expected to speak. Chronic anxiety appears to be learned. In other words, we can learn to fear communication, just as some of us learn to fear dogs, heights, or lightning. One cause of learned communication apprehension is observation of other people who are anxious about communicating. If we see family members or friends perspiring heavily and feeling stressed about making presentations, we may internalize their anxiety as an appropriate response to speaking situations.

Reducing Communication Apprehension

Because communication apprehension is learned, it can also be unlearned or reduced. Communication scholars have developed several methods of reducing speaking apprehension, four of which we'll discuss.

Systematic desensitization focuses on reducing the tension that surrounds the feared event by relaxing and thereby reducing the physiological features of anxiety, such as shallow breathing and increased heart rate (Beatty & Behnke, 1991). Once people learn to control their breathing and muscle tension, counselors ask them to think about progressively more difficult speaking situations.

A second method of reducing communication apprehension is **cognitive restructuring,** a process of revising how people think about speaking situations. According to this method, speaking is not the problem; rather, the problem is irrational beliefs about speaking. A key part of cognitive restructuring is learning to identify and challenge negative self-statements. Users of this method would criticize the statement "My topic won't interest everyone" for assuming that others will not be interested and that any speaker can hold the attention of everyone. Michael Motley and Jennifer Molloy (1994) report that apprehension decreases when people read a short booklet that encourages them to develop new, rational views of communication.

A third technique for reducing communication apprehension is **positive visualization,** which aims to reduce speaking anxiety by guiding apprehensive speakers through imagined positive speaking experiences. This technique allows people to form mental pictures of themselves as effective speakers and to then enact those mental pictures in actual speaking situations. Researchers report that positive visualization is especially effective in reducing chronic communication apprehension (Ayres & Hopf, 1990; Bourhis & Allen, 1992).

Skills training assumes that lack of speaking skills causes us to be apprehensive. This method focuses on teaching people such skills as starting conversations, organizing ideas, and responding effectively to others (Phillips, 1991).

After reading about these methods of reducing communication apprehension, you may think that each seems useful. If so, your thinking coincides with research that finds that a combination of methods is more likely to relieve speaking anxiety than any single method (Allen, Hunter, & Donahue, 1989). The major conclusion is that communication apprehension is not necessarily permanent. Ways to reduce it exist. Eliminating all communication anxiety is not desirable, however, because some vigilance can enhance a speaker's dynamism and alertness. If you experience communication apprehension that interferes with your ability to express your ideas, ask your instructor to direct you to professionals who can work with you.

Adapt Speeches to Audiences

A second guideline for effective public speaking is to adapt to audiences, a topic we discussed earlier in this chapter. Listeners are the whole reason for speaking; without them, communication does not occur. Therefore, speakers should be sensitive to listeners and should adapt to listeners' perspectives and expectations (Griffin, 2012; Hamilton, 2012). You should take into account the perspectives of listeners if you want them to consider your views. We consider the views of our friends when we talk with them. We think about others' perspectives when we engage in business negotiations. We use dual perspective when communicating with children, dates, and neighbors. Thus, audience analysis is important to effectiveness in all communication encounters.

In one of my classes, a student named Odell gave a persuasive speech designed to convince listeners to support affirmative action. He was personally compelling, his delivery was dynamic, and his ideas were well organized. The only problems were that his audience had little knowledge about affirmative action, and he didn't explain exactly what the policy involves. He assumed listeners understood how affirmative action works, and he focused on its positive effects. His listeners were not persuaded, because Odell failed to give them the information necessary for their support. Odell's speech also illustrates our earlier point that speeches often combine more than one speaking purpose; in this case, giving information was essential to Odell's larger goal of persuading listeners.

The mistake that Odell made was failing to learn about his audience's knowledge of his topic. It is impossible to entertain, inform, or persuade people if we do not consider their perspectives on our topics. Speakers need to understand what listeners already know and believe and what reservations they might have about what we say (McGuire, 1989). To paraphrase the advice of an ancient Greek rhetorician, "The fool persuades me with his or her reasons, the wise person with my own." This advice—that effective speakers understand and work with listeners' reasons, values, knowledge, and concerns—is as wise today as it was more than 2,000 years ago.

Although politicians and corporations can afford to conduct sophisticated polls to find out what people know, want, think, and believe, most of us don't have the resources to do that. So how do ordinary people engage in goal-focused analysis? One answer is to be observant. Usually, a speaker has some experience in interacting with his or her listeners or people like them. Drawing on past interactions, a speaker may be able to discern a great deal about the knowledge, attitudes, and beliefs of listeners.

Gathering information about listeners through conversations or surveys is also appropriate. For example, I once was asked to speak on women leaders at a governor's leadership conference. To prepare my presentation, I asked the conference planners to send me information about the occupations and ages of people attending the conference. In addition, I asked the planners to survey the conferees about their experience as leaders and working with women leaders. The material I received informed me about the level of experience and the attitudes and bias of my listeners. Then I could adapt my speech to what they knew and believed.

By taking listeners into consideration, you build a presentation that is interactive and respectful. As we learned earlier in this chapter, listeners tend to confer credibility on speakers who show that they understand listeners and who adapt presentations to listeners' perspectives, knowledge, and expectations.

Listen Critically

A final guideline is to listen critically to speeches you hear. Because we often find ourselves in the role of listener, we should know how to listen well and critically to ideas that others present. As you will recall from Chapter 6, critical listening involves attending mindfully to communication in order to evaluate its merit. Critical listeners assess whether a speaker is informed and ethical and whether a speech is soundly reasoned and supported.

The first step in critical listening is to take in and understand what a speaker says. You cannot evaluate an argument or idea until you have grasped it and the information that supports it. Thus, effective listening requires you to concentrate on what a speaker says. You can focus your listening by asking questions such as these:

▶ What does the speaker announce as the purpose of the talk?

▶ What evidence does the speaker provide to support claims?

▶ Does the speaker have experience that qualifies him or her to speak on this topic?

▶ Does the speaker have any vested interest in what she or he advocates?

You probably noticed that these questions parallel those we identified in our earlier discussion of ways to improve your credibility when you are making speeches. The questions help you zero in on what others say so that you can make informed judgments of their credibility and the credibility of their ideas.

To listen critically, you should suspend your preconceptions about topics and speakers. You need not abandon your ideas, but you should set them aside long enough to listen openly to a speech, especially if you are predisposed to disagree with it. By granting a full and fair hearing to ideas that differ from yours, you increase the likelihood that your perspective and ideas will be well-informed and carefully reasoned.

Critical listeners recognize fallacies in reasoning and do not succumb to them. To accept a speaker's ideas, critical listeners demand that the ideas be well-supported with evidence and sound reasoning. The FYI box on this page provides examples of some of the more common fallacies in reasoning in public communication.

fyi Common Fallacies in Reasoning

Ad hominem attack	You can't believe what Jane Smith says about voting, because she doesn't vote.
After this, therefore because of this (Post hoc, ergo propter hoc)	The new flextime policy is ineffective because more people have been getting to work late since it went into effect.
Bandwagon appeal	You should be for the new campus meal plan because most students are.
Slippery slope	If we allow students to play a role in decisions about hiring and tenure of faculty, pretty soon students will be running the whole school.
Hasty generalization	People should not be allowed to own pit bulls, because there have been instances of pit bulls attacking children.
Either–or	Tenure should be either abolished or kept as it is.
Red herring argument	People who own pit bulls should switch to cats. Let me tell you why cats are the ideal pet....
Reliance on the halo effect	World-famous actor Richard Connery says that we should not restrict people's right to own firearms.

SUMMARY

In this chapter, we discussed the role of public speaking in everyday life. We began by dispelling the widely held misperception that only a few, highly visible people engage in public speaking. As we saw, most of us will communicate publicly in the normal course of professional, civic, and personal life.

In the first part of the chapter, we noted that although public speaking is similar in many ways to other kinds of communication, it is distinct in the greater planning and practice it involves and the less obvious contributions of listeners. We also identified entertaining, informing, and persuading as general purposes of public speaking, and we noted that these goals often overlap.

The second section of this chapter described how to plan, organize, research, support, and deliver public speeches. Throughout our discussion, we highlighted how each aspect of speech development influences the credibility that listeners confer on speakers. To earn credibility, speakers should demonstrate that they are knowledgeable (mentioning personal experience with the topic and including good evidence), trustworthy (making ethical choices that show respect for listeners and for the integrity of evidence), and dynamic (engaging delivery).

The third section of the chapter focused on three guidelines related to public speaking. The first guideline is to understand and manage communication apprehension, which is normal and can be helpful in energizing speakers. If speaking anxiety is strong enough to hinder effective communication, ways to reduce it exist, and we reviewed four of these. A second guideline, to adapt speeches to listeners, is critical to effective public speaking. In our discussion, we emphasized that speakers have an ethical responsibility to consider listeners' perspectives, knowledge, and expectations as they plan, prepare, and present speeches. A final guideline is to listen critically to public speeches by others. Good listeners suspend their views long enough to give a full and fair hearing to what others say. As they listen, they identify and evaluate the quality of speakers' experience, evidence, and reasoning, which allows them to make informed critical assessments of the ideas presented.

Public communication is vital to personal and professional success and to the health of our society. Not reserved for people who have high status or who are in the public limelight, public speaking is a basic skill for us all. In this chapter, we have seen what is involved in presenting and listening to public presentations, and we have identified ways to enhance our effectiveness in this vital realm of social life.

REVIEW, REFLECT, EXTEND

The Reflect, Discuss, and Apply Questions that follow will help you review, reflect on, and extend the information and ideas presented in this chapter. These resources, and a diverse selection of additional study tools, are also available online at the CourseMate for *Communication Mosaics*. Your CourseMate includes a student workbook, WebLinks, TED Talks hyperlinks and activities, chapter glossary and flashcards, interactive video activities, Speech Builder Express, and InfoTrac College Edition. For more information or to access this book's online resources, visit **www .cengagebrain.com**.

KEY CONCEPTS

cognitive restructuring, 278
communication apprehension, 277
comparison (analogy), 272
credibility, 267

derived credibility, 268
evidence, 272
example, 272
extemporaneous delivery, 275

For Further Reflection and Discussion

1. Make a point of listening to students who speak out for causes on your campus. How do the speakers' attempt to establish that they are informed, dynamic, and trustworthy (the dimensions of credibility)?

2. During the next week, pay attention to evidence cited by others in public presentations. You might note what evidence is used on news programs, by professors in classes, and by special speakers on your campus. Evaluate the effectiveness of evidence presented. Are visuals clear and uncluttered? Do speakers explain the qualifications of sources they cite, and are those sources unbiased? What examples and analogies are presented, and how effective are they?

3. Note the use of stories to add interest and effect to public presentations. Describe a speaker who uses a story effectively and one who uses a story ineffectively. What are the differences between them? What conclusions can you draw about the effective use of stories in public presentations?

4. As a class, discuss what makes professors interesting or uninteresting in their classroom communication.

Recommended Resources

1. AmericanRhetoric.com provides an online bank of speeches. You access this resource by clicking on WebLink 13.3.

2. Use an online periodicals database, such as InfoTrac College Edition, to access the journal *Vital Speeches* and read President George W. Bush's October 7, 2001, speech, "We Are at War Against Terrorism: The Attack on the Taliban." How did President Bush recognize American values in opening his speech? What evidence did he provide for declaring war?

EXPERIENCE COMMUNICATION SAMPLE SPEECH

Together, We Can Stop Cyber-Bullying

Apply what you've learned in this chapter by analyzing the following student speech, using the accompanying questions as a guide. These questions and a video of the speech are also available online at your CourseMate for *Communication Mosaics.*

Adam Parrish was an undergraduate, attending University of Kentucky, when he presented this speech. The text of the speech is printed in its entirety. As you read Adam's speech, you should critically assess the choices he made in planning, researching, developing, organizing, and presenting his ideas.

As you read the speech and view it online, consider how it could be made even more effective. Also, think about different ways you might accomplish the speaker's objectives; can you identify alternative organizational structures, kinds of evidence, transitions, and so forth? Following the speech are three questions to guide your thinking about what Adam did and might have done.

TOGETHER, WE CAN STOP CYBER-BULLYING

By Adam Parrish, University of Kentucky

"I'll miss just being around her." "I didn't want to believe it." "It's such a sad thing." These quotes are from the friends and family of 15-year-old Phoebe Prince, who, on January 14, 2010, committed suicide by hanging herself. Why did this senseless act occur? The answer is simple … Phoebe Prince was bullied to death.

Many of us know someone who has been bullied in school. Perhaps they were teased in the parking lot or in the locker room. In the past, bullying occurred primarily in school. However, with the advent of new communication technologies such as cell phones, text messaging, instant messaging, blogs, and social networking sites, bullies can now follow and terrorize their victims anywhere, even into their own bedrooms. Using electronic communications to tease, harass, threaten, and intimidate another person is called cyber-bullying.

As a tutor and mentor to young students, I have witnessed cyber-bullying first hand, and by examining current research, I believe I understand the problem, its causes, and how we can help end cyber-bullying. What I know for sure is that cyber-bullying is a devastating form of abuse that must be confronted on national, local, and personal levels.

Today, we will examine the widespread and harmful nature of cyber-bulling, uncover how and why it persists, and pinpoint some simple solutions we must begin to enact in order to thwart cyber-bullies and comfort their victims. Let's begin by tackling the problem head on.

Many of us have read rude, insensitive, or nasty statements posted about us or someone we care about on social networking sites like MySpace and Facebook. Well, whether or not those comments were actually intended to hurt another person's feelings, if they did hurt their feelings, then they are perfect examples of cyber-bullying.

Cyber-bullying is a pervasive and dangerous behavior. It takes place all over the world and through a wide array of electronic media. According to Keith and Martin's article in the winter 2005 edition of *Reclaiming Children and Youth*, 57 percent of American middle-school students had experienced instances of cyber-bullying ranging from hurtful comments to threats of physical violence. Quing Li's article published in the journal *Computers in Human Behavior* noted that cyber-bullying is not gender biased. According to Li, females are just as likely as males to engage in cyber-bullying, although women are 10 percent more likely to be victimized.

While the number of students who are targets of cyber-bullies decreases as students age, data from the *Youth Internet Safety Survey* indicates that the instances of American high school students being cyber-bullied had increased nearly 50 percent from 2000 to 2005. The problem does not exist in the United States alone.

Li noted that Internet and cell-phone technologies have been used by bullies to harass, torment, and threaten young people in North America, Europe, and Asia. However, some of the most horrific attacks happen right here at home.

According to Keith and Martin, a particularly disturbing incident occurred in Dallas, Texas, where an overweight student with multiple sclerosis was targeted on a school's social networking page. One message read, "I guess I'll have to wait until you kill yourself which I hope is not long from now, or I'll have to wait until your disease kills you." Clearly, the cyber-bullying is a worldwide and perverse phenomenon. What is most disturbing about cyber-bullying is its effects upon victims, bystanders, and perhaps even upon bullies themselves.

Cyber-bullying can lead to physical and psychological injuries upon its victims. According to a 2007 article in the *Journal of Adolescent Health*, Ybarra and colleagues noted that 36 percent of the victims of cyber-bullies are also harassed by their attackers in school. For example, the Dallas student with MS had eggs thrown at her car and a bottle of acid thrown at her house.

Ybarra et al. reported that victims of cyber-bullying experience such severe emotional distress that they often exhibit behavioral problems such as poor grades, skipping school, and receiving detentions and suspensions. Furthermore, Smith et al. suggested that even a few instances of cyber-bullying can have these long-lasting negative effects.

What is even more alarming is that, according to Ybarra and colleagues, victims of cyber-bullying are significantly more likely to carry weapons to school as a result of feeling threatened. Obviously, this could lead to violent outcomes for bullies, victims, and even bystanders.

Now that we have heard about the nature, scope, and effects of cyber-bullying, let's see if we can discover its causes. Let's think back to a time when we may have seen a friend or loved one being harassed online. Did we report the bully to the network administrator or other authorities? Did we console the victim? I know I didn't. If you are like me, we may unknowingly be enabling future instances of cyber-bullying.

Cyber-bullying occurs because of the anonymity offered to bullies by cell phone and internet technologies, as well as the failure of victims and bystanders to report incidents of cyber-bullying. You see, unlike schoolyard bullies, cyber-bullies can attack their victims anonymously.

Ybarra and colleagues discovered that 13 percent of cyber-bullying victims did not know who was tormenting them. This devastating statistic is important because, as Keith and Martin noted, traditional bullying takes place face-to-face and often ends when students leave school. However, today, students are subjected to nonstop bullying, even when they are alone in their own homes.

Perhaps the anonymous nature of cyber-attacks partially explains why Li found that nearly 76 percent of victims of cyber-bullying and 75 percent of bystanders never reported instances of bullying to adults. Victims and bystanders who do not report attacks from cyber-bullies can unintentionally enable bullies.

According to De Nies, Donaldson, and Netter of *ABCNews.com* (2010) several of Phoebe Prince's classmates were aware that she was being harassed but did not inform the school's administration. Li suggested that victims and bystanders often do not believe that adults will actually intervene to stop cyber-bullying. However, *ABCNews.com* reports that 41 states have laws against bullying in schools and 23 of those states target cyber-bullying specifically.

Now that we know that victims of cyber-bullies desperately need the help of witnesses and bystanders to report their attacks, we should arm ourselves with the information necessary to provide that assistance. Think about the next time you see a friend or loved one being tormented or harassed online. What would you be willing to do to help?

Cyber-bullying must be confronted on national, local, and personal levels. There should be a comprehensive national law confronting cyber-bullying in schools. Certain statutes currently in state laws should be amalgamated to create the strongest protections for victims and the most effective punishments for bullies as possible.

According to Limber and Small's article titled, *State Laws and Policies to Address Bullying in Schools*, Georgia law requires faculty and staff to be trained on the nature of bullying and what actions to take if they see students being bullied.

Furthermore, Connecticut law *requires* school employees to report bullying as part of their hiring contract. Washington takes this a step further by protecting employees from any legal action if a reported bully is proven to be innocent. When it comes to protecting victims, West Virginia law demands that schools must ensure that a bullied student does not receive additional abuse at the hands of his or her bully.

Legislating punishment for bullies is difficult. As Limber and Small noted, zero-tolerance polices often perpetuate violence because at-risk youth, i.e., bullies, are removed from all of the benefits of school, which might help make them less abusive. A comprehensive anti cyber-bullying law should incorporate the best aspects of these state laws and find a way to punish bullies that is both punitive and has the ability to rehabilitate abusers. However, for national laws to be effective, local communities need to be supportive.

Local communities must organize and mobilize to attack the problem of cyber-bullying. According to Greene's 2006 article published in the *Journal of Social Issues*, communities need to support bullying prevention programs by conducting a school-based bullying survey for individual school districts. We can't know how to best protect victims in our community without knowing how they are affected by the problem. It is critical to know this information as Greene noted, only three percent of teachers in the United States perceive bullying to be a problem in their schools.

Local school districts should create a Coordinating Committee made up of "administrators, teachers, students, parents, school staff, and community partners" to gather bullying data and rally support to confront the problem. Even if your local school district is unable or unwilling to mobilize behind this dire cause, there are some important actions you can take personally to safeguard those you love against cyber-bullying.

There are several warning signs that might indicate a friend or loved one is a victim of a cyber-bully. If you see a friend or loved one exhibiting these signs, the decision to get involved can be the difference between life and death.

According to Keith and Martin's article, *Cyber-Bullying: Creating a Culture of Respect in a Cyber World*, victims of cyber-bullies often use electronic communication more frequently than do people who are not being bullied. Victims of cyber-bullies have mood swings and difficulty sleeping, they seem depressed and/or become anxious; victims can also become withdrawn from social activities and fall behind in scholastic responsibilities. If you witness your friends or family members exhibiting these symptoms there are several ways you can help.

According to Raskauskas and Stoltz's 2007 article in *Developmental Psychology,* witnesses of cyber-bullying should inform victims to take the attacks seriously, especially if the bullies threaten violence. You should tell victims to report their attacks to police or other authorities, to block harmful messages by blocking email accounts and cell phone numbers, and to save copies of attacks and provide them to authorities.

If you personally know the bully and feel safe confronting him or her, do so! As Raskaukas and Stoltz noted, bullies will often back down when confronted by peers. By being a good friend and by giving good advice, you can help a victim report his or her attacks from cyber-bullies and take a major step toward eliminating this horrendous problem. So, you see, we are not helpless to stop the cyber-bulling problem as long as we make the choice NOT to ignore it.

To conclude, cyber-bullying is a devastating form of abuse that must be reported to authorities. Cyber-bullying is a worldwide problem perpetuated by the silence of both victims and bystanders. By paying attention to certain warning signs, we can empower ourselves to console victims and report their abusers.

Today, I'm imploring you to do your part to help stop cyber-bullying. I know that you agree that stopping cyber-bullying must be a priority. First, although other states have cyber-bullying laws in place, ours does not. So I'm asking you to sign this petition that I will forward to our district's State Legislators. We need to make our voices heard that we want specific laws passed to stop this horrific abuse and to punish those caught doing it.

Second, I'm also asking you to be vigilant in noticing signs of cyber-bullying and then taking action. Look for signs that your friend, brother, sister, cousin, boyfriend, girlfriend, or loved one might be a victim of cyber-bullying and then get involved to help stop it! Phoebe Prince showed the warning signs, and she did not deserve to die so senselessly. None of us would ever want to say, "I'll miss just being around her" "I didn't want to believe it," or "It's such a sad thing" about our own friends or family members. We must work to ensure that victims are supported and bullies are confronted nationally, locally, and personally.

I know that if we stand together and refuse to be silent, we can and will stop cyber-bullying.

---

1. Is Adam's speech persuasive or informative or both?

2. Describe Adam's credibility—initial, derived, and terminal.

3. What organizational pattern did Adam use and to what extent was it effective?

Whoever controls the media—the images—controls the culture.   Allen Ginsberg

14 Mass Communication

T**HE MORMON MOMENT.** This phrase with *Mormon* in red was the headline on a June 2011 issue of *Newsweek*. Accompanying the headline was a digitally manipulated image of Mitt Romney dressed as a door-to-door Mormon missionary character from the hit musical satire, "The Book of Mormon." Inside the magazine, the story titled "Mormons Rock!" told readers that "Mitt Romney and 6 million Mormons may have the secret to success" (Kirn, 2011, p. 38).

Mitt Romney holds law and M.B.A. degrees, both from Harvard. Before entering politics, he worked for a management consulting company and went on to found his own investment firm. When the committee charged to organize Salt Lake City for the 2002 Winter Olympics jeopardized the success of that venture, Romney stepped in and got the organizing effort on sound financial and logistical grounds. After that, in 2003, he was elected Governor of Massachusetts. Are any of these facts relevant to Romney's ability to serve as president? Might knowledge of law and business come in handy for our chief executive officer?

Many of us would agree that Romney's Mormon faith is less relevant to his qualifications to lead the country than other factors. However, the *Newsweek* cover and inside story made his Mormonism THE most prominent feature of Romney's identity.

Researchers who study mass communication would point out that magazines, as well as television and other mass media, routinely focus on certain aspects of people, events, and issues and deemphasize other aspects. In so doing, mass communication shapes what we think about and how we see things. After seeing

FOCUS QUESTIONS

1. How do media shape our thinking?

2. To what extent is news constructed or created?

3. What is the *mean world syndrome*?

4. To what extent is the content of media controlled by powerful corporations?

5. How can you develop media literacy?

the cover of *Newsweek* and reading the story, *Mormon* is likely to be prominent in the minds of readers when they think about Romney.

This chapter focuses on mass communication. The first section of the chapter examines mass communication and discusses features of mass communication that give insight into how it affects our thoughts, attitudes, and sense of identity. In the second section of this chapter, we consider two guidelines for interacting with mass communication.

Understanding Mass Communication

Mass communication consists of all media that address large audiences or publics: books, film, television, radio, newspapers, advertising, magazines, and other forms of visual, audio, and print communication that reach masses of people. Mass communication also includes computer technologies, such as the Web and WebTV, that reach a great number of people; but it does not include electronic communication such as e-mail messages, IMs, and texting. Chapter 15 focuses on computer-mediated communication that is not directed to large publics.

When most of us think about mass communication, we think of information and entertainment. Yet information and entertainment are not all we get from mass communication. We also get impressions of people, events, issues, and cultural life; we get images of who we are and should be; and we get lessons on what is important in the life of our society.

Despite the popularity of digital communication, Americans still engage mass communication in their daily lives. Television remains Americans' top choice for national and international news. Fully two-thirds of Americans rely on television for news, whereas 41 percent rely on the Internet, 31 percent rely on newspapers as a primary source of news, and 16 percent rely on radio (Pew Research Center, 2011). People also rely on television for local weather, traffic news, and reports of breaking news ("Pew Media Study," 2011). Other forms of mass communication also remain popular. Most books are still restricted to hard copy. Currently, there are about 130 million books in the world and only 15 million (about 12 percent) have been digitized (Darnton, 2011). And most of us continue to watch movies, read magazines, and listen to radio.

In this section, we discuss four premises that help us understand how mass communication affects our lives.

Changes in Mass Communication Change Human Life

Communication scholar Marshall McLuhan was fascinated by how mass communication evolves over time and how changes in mass communication transform other aspects of human life. He believed that the dominant media in any era strongly shape both individual and collective life. The FYI box on page 289 summarizes one of McLuhan's main ideas about the relationship between media and human consciousness.

To explain how media shape our lives, McLuhan identified the media that dominated in four distinct eras in human history

Figure 14.1   **Media Epochs in Human History**

(Figure 14.1; McLuhan, 1962, 1964; McLuhan & Fiore, 1967). During the early years of human existence, people lived in tribal communities and the oral tradition reigned. People communicated face to face, giving and getting immediate feedback. Oral cultures were knitted together by stories and rituals that passed along the history and traditions of a culture, as well as by oral transmission of information and forms of entertainment. Reliance on the spoken word fostered cohesive communities and made hearing a dominant sense (McLuhan, 1969). As Derek points out in his commentary, tribal communities and the oral tradition they foster have not disappeared altogether. Although they no longer prevail in the United States, oral cultures continue among insulated communities in regions such as Appalachia and in groups that deliberately isolate themselves from mainstream culture. Oral cultures also prevail in many undeveloped countries.

I spent two years as a Peace Corps volunteer in some of the smaller and poorer countries in Africa. It was an incredible experience to live in societies that had no mass communication. Information was passed along by visitors who traveled into villages or by villagers who traveled to one of the larger cities and returned with news. What I noticed most about these societies is that people interact with each other more and more intensely than in the United States. Talking is living, talking is information, talking is entertainment, talking is history in oral cultures.

Invention of the phonetic alphabet ushered in what McLuhan called the literate epoch in human history. Writing allowed people to communicate without face-to-face interaction. They could read when not in the presence of others in their communities. Because we can reread printed materials, reading requires less memory than oral communication. Thus hearing declined in importance and sight ascended as a primary sense.

fyi DIGITAL MEDIA

The Medium Is the Message/Massage

Marshall McLuhan probably is best known for his statement, "The medium is the message." For him, this statement had multiple meanings (McLuhan & Fiore, 1967). It implied, first, that the medium of communication is important in its own right. Before McLuhan, most media scholars focused on the content of mass communication. McLuhan, however, thought the medium by which content was disseminated makes a difference. For example, he argued that watching television shapes how we think, regardless of what we watch on television.

"The medium is the message" had other meanings for McLuhan. By changing only one letter, the statement becomes "The medium is the massage." This implies that media massage our consciousness and transform our perceptions. Finally, McLuhan sometimes made a play on words by saying, "The medium is the mass age," by which he meant that the dominant medium of the era in which he lived had become mass communication.

Writing also established a linear form for communication—letter follows letter, word follows word, sentence follows sentence. According to McLuhan, the continuous sequential order of print cultivated linear thinking and hence the development of disciplines such as mathematics that are based on linear logic.

Although the invention of the alphabet made written communication possible, print did not immediately gain prominence as the medium that reached the masses. Because there was as yet no way to mass-produce the written word, only the elite class of society had access to written media.

When Gutenberg invented the printing press in the 15th century, literacy ascended in human history. The printing press made possible the printing of thousands of copies of a single book at moderate cost. Written media were no longer limited to elite members of society. In addition, mass-produced writing cultivated homogeneity of perspectives and values because the same message could be delivered to many people.

The dominance of print as a medium and the eye as a primary sense organ diminished with the invention of the telegraph, which launched the electronic epoch in human history. According to McLuhan (1969), electronic media revived the oral tradition and made hearing and touch preeminent.

The telegraph was only the first of a long line of electronic media with the potential to revitalize a sense of community among people. The first television debuted in 1926. Today, assisted by satellite and cable transmissions, television allows us to see and hear around the world. We tune into television news programs to understand what is happening in Iraq or Afghanistan. We watch a live broadcast of a presidential speech and know what our president said and how he looked when he spoke. The increased access to information made possible by electronic communication led McLuhan to claim that electronic media created a **global village** (McLuhan & Fiore, 1967) that resembles the tribal village (Sparks, 2006).

McLuhan died in 1980. He left a partial manuscript that described the computer as a new medium that would change human beings and culture once again. As we will see in Chapter 15, McLuhan was right: Computer-mediated communication has greatly influenced our lives.

Mass Communication Serves Individuals' Needs and Desires

Think about the last time you watched a movie. Did you attend because the story mattered to you? Did you go to escape from problems and worries? Did you attend because it featured stars you like? Did you only pay attention to the parts you liked? If so, you acted as would be predicted by **uses and gratification theory.** This theory states that we use mass communication to gratify ourselves (Reinhard & Dervin, 2009).

Uses and gratification theory assumes that we select media that we think will give us something we value or want. For example, if you are interested in national affairs, you might listen to National Public Radio. If you are concerned about whether a game will be rained out, you might watch The Weather Channel. If you invest in the stock market, you might read *The Wall Street Journal*.

We also use media for pleasure. If you are bored and want excitement, you might watch an action film or read an action novel.

We might choose soft music to enhance romantic feelings, rock to generate excitement, spirituals to inspire or comfort ourselves, and ritualistic chants and folk music to foster a sense of unity among protesters at a rally.

A classic study of how people use mass communication to gratify themselves was conducted by Janice Radway (1991). She investigated what romance novels mean to Midwestern women who read these novels, sometimes as many as 12 in a week. Rather than dismissing romance novels as "mindless drivel," which is how many critics view them, Radway talked with the women who read them to find out why they did. She found that readers gained pleasure by identifying with independent heroines and escaping from the routines of their own lives. Women who frequently read romance novels also explained that to read them was to have personal time, free from the demands of families and housework.

If people use media to gratify themselves, then we might expect that people will also create media if existing media do not satisfy them and others in their communities. That's exactly what happens. Most national and regional newspapers in the United States largely reflect the interests, concerns, and biases of middle-class Caucasian heterosexuals. Typically, they don't offer many stories that speak to the particular

Many of us use mass communication for pleasure.

DIGITAL MEDIA

Romance on the Run

If you are a fan of romance novels, you no longer have to choose between reading books and being wired. Harlequin Books, the largest publisher of steamy romance novels, offers electronic books that can be read on cell phones. To fit today's reader, who often have neither long periods of time to curl up with fat novels nor room in briefcases to tote them around, Harlequin has divided books into daily installments that can be read in just a few minutes—usually fewer than 10. Installments are automatically downloaded to subscribers' cell phones for a small monthly fee (Flynn, 2006).

And then there are wireless reading devices such as the iPad and Kindle. Weighing less than a pound, these devices can store more than 1,000 books, most of which can be downloaded for under $10. If reading seems too much trouble, Kindle allows users to push a button and have the book read to them.

concerns of Hispanics, gays, Asian Americans, or other groups. To compensate for this, Spanish-language newspapers and Native American newspapers have been created. These newspapers serve the interests of specific groups that are neglected by mainstream media. Likewise, the exploding number of satellite and cable channels expands our options for choosing media that gratify us.

Mass Communication Influences Human Knowledge and Perspectives

As we saw in the *Newsweek* story that opened this chapter, mass communication spotlights some issues, events, people, and aspects of phenomena and downplays others.

Agenda Setting

You set an agenda for a meeting when you decide what issues will be discussed. In a similar fashion, mass communication sets an agenda for public consciousness when it selects particular issues to call to the public's attention (Bryant & Oliver, 2008; McCombs & Ghanem, 2001; McCombs, Ghanem, & Chernov, 2009; Robinson, 2009; Vivian, 2006). In other words, by selecting what events and issues to cover, how to present them and how much time to give each one, mass communication tells us what we should think about.

Agenda setting involves two distinct processes. First, mass media direct us to pay attention to particular topics by giving those topics coverage. For instance, during the 2008 presidential campaign, mass media devoted a great amount of space and time to coverage of Sarah Palin's wardrobe and the $150,000+ price tag for it. Media also gave substantial attention to Michelle Obama's and Hillary Clinton's fashion choices. This coverage reinforced the long-standing cultural view associating women and fashion, and it encouraged viewers and readers to see women's appearance as important.

Agenda setting also works in a second way. Mass media lead us to ignore or give minimum attention to some topics and people by covering them barely or not at all. What did Michelle Obama do in her community organizing and her work as a hospital administrator? What were Hillary Clinton's accomplishments as a senator? What fashion choices did John McCain and Barack Obama make? By giving little or no coverage to these issues, media tell us they are not important to think about.

Gatekeeping

A **gatekeeper** is a person or group that decides which messages pass through the gates that control information flow to reach consumers (Altheide, 1974; Gitlin, 1980; McCombs et al., 2009; Shaw, 1999; Shoemaker, 1991). Gatekeepers screen messages, stories, and perspectives to create messages (programs, interviews, news clips) that shape our perceptions of events and people.

Mass communication has many gatekeepers. Editors of newspapers, books, and magazines screen the information that gets to readers; owners, executives, and producers filter information for radio and television programs; advertisers and political groups may also intervene to influence which messages reach end users of mass communication. For example, radio and television stations that are owned and financed by conservatives air Rush Limbaugh's comments but not those of progressives and liberals. Radio and television stations owned and funded by more liberal groups are likely to shut the gate on Rush Limbaugh but include Rachel Maddow and Jon Stewart. As a result, people who tune into conservative and liberal stations are likely to be aware of different issues and to have different perspectives on those issues.

Cultivation of World Views

Mass communication is a cumulative process that promotes particular understandings about the world and how it operates. The word *cumulative* is important to understanding **cultivation**. Researchers don't argue that a particular television program has significant effects on viewers' beliefs or that television viewing directly determines public opinion. However, they claim that watching television over a long period of time affects viewers' basic views of the world. By extension, the more television people watch, the more distorted their ideas about life are likely to be (Gerbner, 1990; Gerbner et al., 1986; Robinson, 2009; Signorielli, 2009; Signorielli & Morgan, 1990).

The primary way that television and other forms of mass communication cultivate particular world views is by **mainstreaming.** Mainstreaming is the stabilizing and homogenizing of views within a society. For example, if commercial programming consistently portrays European Americans as upstanding citizens, and members of other races as lazy, criminal, or irresponsible, viewers may come to accept such representations as factual. If television programs, from Saturday morning cartoons to prime-time dramas, feature extensive violence, viewers may come to believe that violence is pervasive.

Media scholar Glenn Sparks (2006) reports that nearly 60 percent of all television programs include violence. This raises particular concerns about young children, for violence is common on children's TV (Ho, 2006; Parents Television Council, 2006). By age six, the average child in the United States has watched 5,000 hours of television; by age 18, the average person has watched fully 19,000 hours of television. The average 18-year-old in the United States has viewed 200,000 separate acts of violence on television, including 40,000 murders (Kirsh, 2006; Palmer & Young, 2003; Valkenburg, 2004). Given the incidence of violence on television, it's no wonder that many heavy viewers think the world is more violent than crime reports show it to be. Mike's commentary illustrates a concern of many parents. To read a 2006 study of violence on children's TV, go to the book's online resources for this chapter and click on WebLink 14.1.

 Mike

> *Adults may be able to separate fantasy from real life, but kids aren't. What they see on the TV is real life to them. My wife and I have raised our son not to be aggressive—not a sissy, but not aggressive either. But any time he watches TV, he's picking up sticks and aiming them like they were guns or imitating karate chops he saw some TV character do.*

Perhaps you are thinking that few people confuse what they see on television with real life. Research shows that this may not be the case. Watching violent media has been shown to make viewers less sensitive to actual violence (Sparks, 2006). Further, children—both male and female—who watched a great deal of television had higher measures of personal aggression as young adults than did people who watched less television (Huesmann et al., 2003)

Defining Desirability and Normalcy

Mass communication also shapes mainstream ideas of what is desirable and normal, particularly in terms of physical appearance. Reality TV is particularly strong in encouraging us to conform to traditional views of women and men. Judges on *America's Next Top Model* lavish praise on seriously underweight contestants and

SHARPEN YOUR SKILL

Testing the Mean World Syndrome

The basic worldview studied by cultivation theorists is exemplified in research on the mean world syndrome (Gerbner et al., 1986). The **mean world syndrome** is the belief that the world is a dangerous place, full of mean people who cannot be trusted and who are likely to harm us. Although less than one percent of the U.S. population is victimized by violent crime in any year, television presents the world as a dangerous place in which everyone is at risk.

To test this theory, ask 10 people whether or not they basically agree or disagree with the following five statements, which are adapted from the mean world index used in research. After respondents have answered, ask them how much television they watch on an average day. Do your results support the claim that television cultivates the mean world syndrome?

1. Most public officials are not interested in the plight of the average person.

2. Despite what some people say, the lot of the average person is getting worse, not better.

3. Most people mostly look out for themselves rather than trying to help others.

4. Most people would try to take advantage of you if they had a chance.

5. You can't be too careful in dealing with people.

Bill Aron/PhotoEdit

Media encourages us to want to buy, own, and have more, more, and more.

call normal-sized contestants (130 pounds at 5'8") "plus sized" (Pozner, 2004). Judges on *Are You Hot?* used laser pointers to spotlight parts of contestants' bodies that were "shameful" (Douglas, 2004b). E! Network's popular *Keeping Up with the Kardashians* follows the lives of young women who unabashedly use their sexuality to advance. The hypersexual identity they are urged to cultivate to is one that can be achieved only through consumption of products and services. Marketers aim to persuade girls and women to maximize their potential through consumption. The good girl or woman is a serious consumer (Gill, 2008; Kilbourne, 2007, 2010; McRobbie, 2000, 2004; Morreale, 2007). The message that much popular media sends to women is clear: Your worth is based on your sexuality; if you aren't super thin and super hot, you must transform yourself.

A number of reality TV programs also portray men in very traditional, stereotyped ways. The favored stereotype is the macho man, who proves his manliness by degrading women. For example, a man on *Joe Millionaire* was praised for ordering his dates, who were dressed to the nines, to shovel horse manure. A man on *Average Joes* was praised for calling his date a "beaver," and a contestant on *For Love or Money* forced a woman to bend over to pull off his boots while he kicked her bottom (Pozner, 2004). The guiding premise of *Who Wants to Marry a Millionaire* is that being rich makes men desirable—the most traditional of all images of men.

fyi DIVERSITY

Media-Created Body Ideals

Anthropologist and psychiatrist Anne Becker and her colleagues (Becker et al., 2002) reported research suggesting that media are very powerful in shaping—or distorting—body images.

For centuries, Fiji had been a food-loving society. Fijian people enjoyed eating and considered fleshy bodies attractive in women and men. In fact, when someone seemed to be losing weight, acquaintances chided her or him for "going thin." All of that changed in 1995, when television stations in Fiji began to broadcast American programs such as *Melrose Place, Seinfeld,* and *Beverly Hills, 90210.* Within three years, an astonishing number of Fijian women began to diet and to develop eating disorders. When asked why they were trying to lose weight, young Fijian woman cited characters such as Amanda (Heather Locklear) on *Melrose Place* as their model.

Sally Steindorf found that as televisions have become common in the quiet village of Kothariya, India, long-standing ethnic and cultural traditions have waned. In their place, villagers have adopted Western values and seek Western products that are advertised on television. Villagers see motorcycles, color TVs, and brand-name shampoo as status symbols (Overland, 2004).

Mainstreaming was also identified among female high school students in South Australia. The students who often read fashion magazines and watched soap operas on television thought it was important to be slim and that bulimia was an acceptable way to keep body weight low (Tiggemann, 2005).

Programs such as *Extreme Makeover* and *The Swan* send the message that women don't have to—and, in fact, shouldn't—settle for how they naturally look. On these shows, ordinary-looking people undergo up to 14 cosmetic surgeries to be transformed into looking like celebrities, and the message is clear: We too can look better. We should look better. It's our job to do what's necessary to make ourselves look like superstars (Harris, 2004; Morreale, 2007). Economics are deeply linked to the image of ideal femininity, because achieving that image—or even trying to—requires buying products and services (Taft, 2004). Thus, programs such as *The Swan* and the advertisers that support them encourage girls and women to believe that their only real power is purchasing power—their power is reduced to what they can buy (Seely, 2007). The FYI box on this page illustrates how mainstream body ideals have been created by what we see on television.

To earn money, I babysit two little boys four days a week. One day, they got into a fight, and I broke it up. When I told them that physical violence isn't a good way to solve problems, they reeled off a list of TV characters that beat up on each other. Another day, one of them referred to the little girl next door as a "ho." When I asked why he called her that, he started singing the lyrics from an MTV video he'd been watching. In that video, women were called "hos." It's scary what kids absorb.

Mass Communication Advances the Dominant Ideology

Mass media advance viewpoints on issues, people and events. When you read a newspaper article or watch a television news report, you do not get a set of unrelated facts.

Instead, you get a narrative—a story that first captures your interest and then shapes the information into a coherent account that predisposes you to particular conclusions and perspectives on the people and events in the story.

A good example of narrative framing was a story on the *McNeil/Lehrer NewsHour.* This segment, entitled "Focus–Logjam," reported on a protest by Earth First!, an environmental group, against logging redwood forests in northern California. Using textual analysis, communication scholar Harold Schlechtweg (1992) identified visual and verbal factors that shaped the story's frame. Although the Earth First! protesters had emphasized that their protest was nonviolent and had tried to engage in dialogue with loggers, the "Focus–Logjam" story referred to them as "radical," "terrorists," "violent," "wrong people" who were engaging in "sabotage" (p. 273). On the other hand, loggers were described as "workers," "timber people," and "regular people" who were simply trying to survive in "small-town economies" that provide limited "jobs" and sources of "livelihood" (p. 273). Schlechtweg also called attention to visual cues, such as an Earth First! protester hammering a spike into a tree, that supported the frame of the story. The framing of this story clearly presented the protesters as the antagonists, the "bad guys," and the loggers as vulnerable protagonists who merit our sympathy and support. The FYI box on the next page provides further insights into how media frame stories and attempt to influence audiences' perceptions.

Scholars of mass communication point out that gatekeepers' choices of which issues to emphasize and how to frame them are often driven by the interests of conservative capitalist values (Liu & Albarran, 2009; McChesney, 1999, 2004, 2008). Making money is the primary goal of multinational corporations such as General Electric, which owns NBC, and Westinghouse, which owns CBS (Grossberg et al., 1998). If making a profit is the key objective, then corporations that own media may not be only, or even primarily, interested in the accuracy of media or serving the general public. How seriously can *Time* magazine criticize AOL when both *Time* and AOL are owned by Time Warner? Should we be surprised that in 1995 CNN, which is owned by Time Warner (a major cable TV operation), refused to run an ad that claimed cable TV rates were likely to rise (Zuckerman, 2002)?

Mass communication depends on the revenues generated by advertising. Currently, advertising in the United States is nearly a $1 trillion business (Dowling, 2009, p. 680). And commercials aren't the only form of advertising on television and in films. **Product placement,** which is paid for by advertisers and program sponsors, is the practice of featuring products in media and ensuring that viewers recognize the product (for instance, having a character drink Coke from a Coke can) so that the products are associated with particular characters, storylines, and so forth. Because product placement inserts advertising

RD/Orchon/Retna Ltd./Corbis

Product placement associates particular products with celebrities.

Constructing the News

Many people think news programs present information and news in a factual, neutral way. However, most mass communication scholars think differently (Ghanem, McCombs, & Chernov, 2009). They assert that media construct the news, shaping what is presented and how:

◆ Selecting what gets covered: Only a minute portion of human activity is reported in the news. Gatekeepers in the media decide which people and events will be covered. By presenting stories on these events and people, the media make them newsworthy.

◆ Choosing the frame: Reporters and journalists choose how to focus a story, or how to frame it. In selecting a frame, gatekeepers choose a point of view that shapes how an audience interprets the story. The frame directs our attention to certain aspects of the story and certain ways of seeing those aspects. For example, in a story on a politician accused of sexual misconduct, the focus could be the charges made, the politician's denial, or overall sexual misconduct by public figures.

◆ Choosing how to tell the story: In the foregoing example, media might tell it in a way that fosters sympathy for the person who claims to have been the target of sexual misconduct (interviews with the victim, references to other victims of sexual misconduct), or they might tell it in a way that inclines people to be sympathetic toward the politician (shots of the politician with his or her family, interviews with colleagues who proclaim the politician's innocence).

Use the information in this box to engage media critically. Select an issue that is in the news. How do television, newspapers and online news services shape the issue? Compare coverage in conservative and progressive papers, TV stations, and online sites. What gets covered and what does not? What hook(s) is used? Who are the heroes, villains, and victims in the story told?

into programs, it blurs the traditional distinction between program content and ads (Jamieson & Campbell, 2006). For instance, Sears is the primary sponsor of the popular show *Extreme Makeover: Home Edition.* Each episode of the show features Sears' Craftsman tools and Kenmore appliances. Viewers of the program are 25 percent more likely to shop at Sears after an episode is aired than before it (Roberts, 2004).

If product placement blurs the line between advertising and content, immersive advertising completely erases the line. **Immersive advertising** incorporates a product or brand into actual storylines in books, television programs, and films (Lamb & Brown, 2006). For instance, Naomi Johnson (2007, 2011) analyzed romance novels marketed to young girls. She found that storylines in series such as *A List* and *Gossip Girl* revolved around buying products such as La Perla lingerie and Prada bags. The characters' identities were associated with particular products and services.

Because mass communication's survival depends on attracting and keeping advertisers, it is unlikely to feature criticism of advertisers' products or to cover news that is not consistent with advertisers' interests. For instance, some communication scholars assert that media provide inadequate coverage of environmental dangers and threats because they don't want to offend advertisers whose companies would be hurt by additional environmental regulations (Cox, 2009; Shabecoff, 2000).

Mass communication's alliance with capitalism also explains why it tends to represent the ideology of privileged groups as normal, right, and natural (Hall, 1986a, 1986b,

DIVERSITY

Race on Television and in Real Life

Occasionally television's gatekeepers are willing to criticize racism quite overtly. Even in the 1960s, early episodes of *Star Trek* raised questions about stereotypes and bias related to race. Other programs, such as *Sanford and Son* and *The Cosby Show,* offered alternatives to racist portrayals of blacks. A particularly interesting example of media attention to race and racism appeared in 2006 when FX aired a six-part documentary series titled *Black. White.* Professional makeup artists made a white mother, father, and son, the Wurgels, appear black and made a black mother, father, and daughter, the Sparks, appear white. For six weeks, the two families lived as members of the other race and learned, along with viewers, how much difference race still makes in America (Peyser, 2006).

1988, 1989a, 1989b; Hasinoff, 2008). Television programs, from children's shows to prime-time news, represent white, heterosexual, able-bodied males as the norm in the United States, although they are actually not the majority. Magazine covers and ads as well as billboards portray young, able-bodied, attractive white people as the norm. Despite criticism of bias in media, minorities continue to be portrayed most often as criminals, victims, subordinates, or otherwise less-than-respectable people (Dixon, 2006; Dubrofsky & Hardy, 2008; Hasinoff, 2008; Ramasubramanian, 2010; Robinson, 2009). Even scarcer in the world of television are Latinos and Latinas, the fastest growing ethnic–racial group in the United States (Robinson, 2009). Although bias continues to exist, we've also seen an increase in programs, news stories, and popular magazines about groups and lifestyles that are not mainstream. The FYI box on this page offers more information on media representation of races.

Let's summarize our discussion of mass communication by restating the four premises we have discussed:

1. Changes in mass communication change human life.

2. Mass communication serves individuals' interests and desires.

3. Mass communication influences human knowledge and perspective

4. Mass communication advances dominant ideologies.

Taken together, these four premises give us considerable insight into how mass communication affects our thoughts, attitudes, behaviors, and beliefs about ourselves and the world in which we live.

Guidelines for Engaging Mass Communication

Because mass communication surrounds and influences us, we have an ethical obligation to be responsible and thoughtful consumers. Two critical guidelines for interacting with mass communication are to develop media literacy and to respond actively.

Develop Media Literacy

The first challenge is to develop media literacy. Just as it takes work to become literate in reading, in communicating orally, and in using technologies, we need to invest effort

6 Months	3 Years	4 Years	7–8 Years	Throughout Life
Children pay attention to television.	Children engage in exploratory viewing.	Children search for preferred viewing.	Children make clear distinctions between ads and programs.	People who commit to media literacy learn to recognize puffery, hooks, and other devices for directing their attention and behavior.
	Children establish preferred patterns of viewing.	Children develop a viewing agenda.		
	Children do not distinguish between programs and ads.	Children's attention is held by a story line.	Children become skeptical of ads for products with which they are familiar; they are less skeptical of ads for products they haven't tried or don't own.	People who commit to media literacy learn to use media in sophisticated ways to meet their needs and to compensate for media bias and techniques.
		Children begin to distinguish between ads and programs.		
		Children do not realize that ads seek profits.		

© Cengage Learning

Figure 14.2 **Stages in the Development of Media Literacy**

to develop literacy in interacting with media. Instead of passively absorbing media, cultivate your ability to analyze, understand, and respond thoughtfully to media. Figure 14.2 describes key stages in developing media literacy. How literate we become, however, depends on the extent to which we commit to developing sophisticated skills in interpreting media.

Realistically Assess Media's Influence

Media literacy begins with understanding how much influence you believe mass communication has on people. One view—a rather extreme one—claims that mass communication determines individual attitudes and social perspectives. Another view—also extreme—is that mass communication doesn't affect us at all. In between those two radical views is the more reasonable belief that mass communication is one of many influences on individual attitudes and social perspectives.

This last claim represents a thoughtful assessment of the qualified influence of mass communication and our ability to exercise control over its effects. Television, individual viewers, and society interact in complex ways. The same argument can be made for the influence of other mass media, such as radio, film, billboards, books, magazines, and newspapers. If this is so, it's inaccurate to presume that a linear relationship exists between media and individuals' attitudes.

Become Aware of Patterns in Media

If you aren't aware of the patterns that make up basketball, you will not be able to understand what happens in a game. If you don't understand how church or synagogue services are organized, you won't appreciate the meaning of those services. In the same way, if you don't understand patterns in media, you can't understand fully the workings of music, advertising, programming, and so forth. Learning to recognize patterns in media empowers you to engage media in critical and sophisticated ways.

As W. James Potter (2001, 2004) points out, media use a few standard patterns repeatedly. For example, although there are various genres of music, there are a few basic chords, melody progressions, and rhythms of which all music is comprised. Even the lyrical content of songs tends to follow stock patterns, most often love and sex (Christianson & Roberts, 1998). Most stories, whether in print, film, or television, open with some problem or conflict that progresses until it climaxes in final dramatic scenes. Romance stories typically follow a pattern in which we meet a main character who has suffered a bad relationship or has not had a relationship. The romance pattern progresses through meeting Mr. or Ms. Right, encountering complications or problems, resolving the problems, and living happily ever after (Riggs, 1999).

Actively Interrogate Media Messages

When interacting with mass communication, you should use critical thought to assess what is presented. Rather than accepting news accounts unquestioningly, you should be thoughtful and skeptical. It's important to ask questions such as these:

▶ Why is this story getting so much attention? Whose interests are served, and whose are muted?

▶ What are the sources of statistics and other forms of evidence? Are the sources current? Do the sources have any interest in taking a specific position? (For example, tobacco companies have vested interest in denying or minimizing the harms of smoking.)

▶ What's the frame for the story, and what alternative frames might have been used?

▶ Are stories balanced so that a range of viewpoints are given voice? For example, does news coverage of regulations for the financial industry include statements from the representatives of banks, investors, auditors, and economists?

▶ How are different people and viewpoints framed by gatekeepers (e.g., reporters, photographers, experts)?

It's equally important to be critical in interpreting mass entertainment communication, such as music, magazines, and Web sites. When listening to popular music, ask whose views of society it portrays and who and what it represents as normal or good, and abnormal or bad. Raise the same questions about the images in magazines and on billboards. When considering an ad, ask whether it offers meaningful evidence or merely puffery (see the FYI box on the next page). Asking questions such as these allows you to be critical and careful in assessing what mass communication presents to you.

SHARPEN YOUR SKILL

Detecting Dominant Values in Media

Watch two hours of prime-time commercial television. Pay attention to the dominant ideology that is represented and normalized in the programming. Who are the good and bad characters? Which personal qualities are represented as admirable, and which are represented as objectionable? Who are the victims and victors, the heroes and villains? What goals and values are endorsed?

Expose Yourself to a Range of Media Sources

Media scholar W. James Potter (2009) regards "mindful exposures" (p. 565) as key to media literacy. Many people choose to view and listen only to what they particularly like. For instance, if you are conservative politically, you might read a conservative daily paper and listen to a conservative radio station. The problem with that is that you don't expose yourself to criticisms of conservative policies and stances, and you don't give yourself the opportunity to learn about more liberal alternatives. If you listen only to popular music, you'll never learn to understand, much less appreciate, classical music, jazz, or reggae. You cannot be informed about any issue or type of media unless you deliberately expose yourself to multiple sources of information and perspectives.

Exposing yourself to multiple media also means attending to more than entertainment. Television focuses primarily on entertainment and popular culture. Tuning into celebrity culture is not sufficient if you want to be media literate.

Puffery: The Best of Its Kind!

One of the most popular advertising strategies is **puffery**—superlative claims for a product that seem factual but are actually meaningless. For instance, what does it mean to state that a particular juice has "the most natural flavor"? Most natural in comparison to what? Other juices, other drink products, the whole fruit from which the juice is made? Who judged it to have the most natural flavor—the corporation that produces it? A random sample of juice drinkers? What is the meaning of an ad that claims a car is "the new benchmark"? Who decided this was the new benchmark? To what is this car being compared? It's not clear from the ad, which is only puffery.

Focus on Your Motivations for Engaging Media

Sophisticated media users realize that media serve many purposes, and they make deliberate choices that serve their goals and needs at particular times. For example, if you feel depressed and want to watch television, it might be better to watch a comedy or action drama than to watch a television movie about personal trauma and pain.

Respond Actively

People may respond critically or uncritically to mass communication and the world-views that it portrays, depending on how media literate they are (Fiske, 1987; S. Hall, 1982, 1989b). If we respond uncritically, we mindlessly consume messages and their ideological underpinnings. On the other hand, if we interact critically with media, we recognize that the worldviews presented in mass communication are not unvarnished truth but partial, subjective perspectives that serve the interests of some individuals and groups while disregarding the interests of others.

To assume an active role in interacting with media, you must recognize that you are an agent who can affect what happens around you. You begin to take action by noticing what media ask you to think about, believe, and do. Once you become aware of mass communication's efforts to shape perceptions and attitudes, you can then question or challenge the views of reality they advance.

 Manuel

I was really angry about a story in the local paper. It was about Mexicans who come to the U.S. The story only mentioned Mexican Americans who get in trouble with the law, are on Welfare, or are illegal residents. So I wrote a letter to the editor and said the story was biased and inaccurate. The editor invited me to write an article for the opinion page, and I did. In my article, I described many Mexican Americans who are hardworking, honest citizens who are making this country better. There were a lot of responses to my article, so I know I made a difference.

SHARPEN YOUR SKILL

Responding Actively

If you want to learn more about gender and media, or if you want to become active in working against media that foster views of violence as normal, girls and women as subordinate, and buying as the route to happiness, visit these Web sites by clicking the appropriate WebLinks, all available among the book's online resources for this chapter:

◆ Media Education Foundation: WebLink 14.2

◆ Children Now: WebLink 14.3

◆ Media Watch: WebLink 14.4

◆ National Association for Family and Community Education: WebLink 14.5

◆ TV Parental Guidelines Monitoring Board: WebLink 14.6

◆ Center for Media Literacy: WebLink 14.7

Manuel's experience demonstrates that speaking out is not just personally empowering; it also enriches cultural life. People have an ethical responsibility to resist and redefine those messages of mass communication that they consider inaccurate or harmful. The Sharpen Your Skill box on this page lists Web sites for people who are interested in taking a voice in regard to mass communication.

Speaking out can make a difference. In 1995, Calvin Klein discontinued an ad campaign because so many individuals and groups objected to the ads, which a number of people saw as mimicking scenes from vintage pornography. Other companies have withdrawn ads and even products in response to voices of resistance. Power relationships and social perspectives are never fixed in cultural life. They are always open to change and negotiation between voices that offer rival views of reality.

SUMMARY

In this chapter, we examined mass communication. We began by discussing how the different media epochs have affected individual lives and social organization. Next, we considered five theories that describe and explain the influence of mass communication. Most of these theories recognize that consumers of media are actively involved in shaping media's meanings and using media to affect emotions, moods, and pleasures. But the influence is not just one way. Mass communication supports dominant social relations, roles, and perspectives by portraying them as normal and right.

The second section of the chapter focused on two related guidelines for us as we interact with mass communication. The first is to develop media literacy. This requires, first, that we develop a realistic, balanced perspective on the power of mass communication. Media do not exist in isolation, nor do we as consumers of mass communication. Each of us participates in multiple and diverse social systems that shape our responses to mass communication and the worldviews it presents. To be responsible participants in social life, we need to question what is included—and what is made invisible—in mass communication.

A second guideline is to assume an active voice by responding to mass communication. We have an ethical responsibility to speak out against communication that we think is inaccurate, hurtful, or wrong. One means of negotiating social meanings is to respond to mass communication. Without our consent and support, mass communication cannot exist.

REVIEW, REFLECT, EXTEND

The Reflect, Discuss, and Apply Questions that follow will help you review, reflect on, and extend the information and ideas presented in this chapter. These resources, and a diverse selection of additional study tools, are also available online at the CourseMate for *Communication Mosaics*. Your CourseMate includes a student workbook, WebLinks, TED Talks hyperlinks and activities, chapter glossary and flashcards, interactive video activities, Speech Builder Express, and InfoTrac College Edition. For more information or to access this book's online resources, visit **www .cengagebrain.com.**

KEY CONCEPTS

agenda setting, 292
cultivation, 293
gatekeeper, 292
global village, 290
immersive advertising, 297
mainstreaming, 293

mass communication, 288
mean world syndrome, 294
product placement, 296
puffery, 301
uses and gratification theory, 290

Reflect, Discuss, Apply

1. To what extent, if any, should there be control over the violence presented in media? Do you think viewers, especially children, are harmed by the prevalence of violence in media? Are you concerned about the lack of correspondence between the synthetic world of television violence and the actual incidence of violence in social life? If you think there should be some controls, what groups or individuals would you trust to establish and implement them?

2. Make a list of the forms of mass communication you use most often. Include newspapers, magazines, television programs, types of films, radio stations, and so forth. How do your choices of mass communication reflect and shape your identity and your social perspectives?

3. As a class, select the current issue of two mainstream magazines. Carefully go through the magazines, both content articles and advertising. After reviewing the magazines, answer this question: If an alien had only these two magazines as evidence of American culture today, what would the alien conclude about who Americans are and what they care about?

Recommended Resources

1. Embrace the challenge advanced in this chapter by taking an active role in responding to mass communication. Write a letter to the editor of a local paper, or write to a manufacturer to support or criticize its product or the way it advertises its product. Visit the Web sites mentioned in the Sharpen Your Skill box on page 302 to learn about opportunities to become a more involved consumer and controller of mass media.

2. Robert McChesney. (1999). *Rich media, poor democracy: Communication politics in dubious times.* Urbana: University of Illinois Press. This book makes a convincing argument that the concentration of media ownership in the hands of a few corporations has undercut the democratic potential of mass communication.

EXPERIENCE COMMUNICATION CASE STUDY

The Power Zapper

Apply what you've learned in this chapter by analyzing the following case study, using the accompanying questions as a guide. These questions and a video of the case study are also available online at your CourseMate for *Communication Mosaics*.

Charles and Tina Washington are in the kitchen area of their great room working on dinner. At the other end of the room, their six-year-old son, Derek, is watching television. Tina is tearing lettuce for a salad while Charles stirs a pot on the stove.

© Cengage Learning

Tina: One of us is going to have to run by the store tomorrow. This is the last of the lettuce.

Charles: While we're at it, we'd better get more milk and cereal. We're low on those, too.

Tina: I'll flip you for who has to make the store run.

[Charles pulls a quarter out of his pocket, flips it in the air, and covers it with one hand when it lands on his other hand.] "Call it."

Tina: Heads, you have to go by the store.

Charles removes the hand covering the quarter and grins. "Tails—it's your job." She rolls her eyes and says, "Just can't win, some days."

Derek suddenly jumps up from his chair, points his finger at the chair in which he had been sitting, and shouts "Zap! You're dead! You're dead! I win!" Charles goes to Derek. An advertisement for Power Zapper is just ending on the television, and Charles turns down the volume.

Charles: What's going on, Derek? Who's dead?

Derek: The chair is. I zapped it with the Power Zapper, Mom. It's the coolest weapon.

Tina walks over to join Charles and Derek.

Tina: Power Zapper? What's a Power Zapper?

Derek: It's the most popular toy in America, Mom! It's really cool!

Tina: Oh really? Who says so?

Derek: They just said it on TV.

Tina: Does that mean it's true?

Derek points a finger at his mother and shouts, "Pow! I zapped you! You're dead!" At this point, Charles walks over and takes Derek's hand.

Charles: Hold on there, son. Don't go pointing at your mother.

Derek: I was zapping her, Dad.

Charles: I see you were, but we don't hurt people, do we?

Derek: I could if I had a Power Zapper. Can I have one for my birthday? Everybody else has one.

Charles: If everybody jumped off the roof, would you do that?

Derek: I wouldn't need to if I had a Power Zapper because I could zap anyone who bothered me. I'd be so cool.

Charles: But zapping other people would hurt them. You wouldn't want to do that, would you?

Tina [to Charles]: You're overreacting. It's just a toy.

Charles [to Tina]: Kids learn from toys. I don't want Derek to learn that violence is cool.

Tina [to Charles]: He isn't going to learn that with us as his parents. Don't get so worked up over a toy.

1. Identify an example of puffery in the advertisement for the Power Zapper.

2. Are Charles and Tina Washington teaching Derek to be a critical viewer of mass communication?

3. How does this scenario illustrate the process of mainstreaming?

4. Are you more in agreement with Charles or with Tina about whether toys teach important lessons to children?

15

The danger from computers is not that they will eventually get as smart as men, but we will meanwhile agree to meet them halfway. *Bernard Avishai*

Digital Media and the Online World

▶ *"Helicopter hovering above Abbottabad at 1AM (is a rare event)."* This tweet, sent by Sonaib Athar, an IT professional living in Abbottabad, was the first unofficial communication about the attack that resulted in the death of Osama Bin Laden (Gilsten, 2011). Shortly after Athar's tweet, others followed, telling of high activity—including explosions—in the compound in Abbottabad. As Twitter users got the tweets, they sent questions, updates, and speculations. An average of 3,000 tweets per second were sent as the story developed (Gilsten, 2011). Only hours later did President Obama come on national television to announce that he had authorized the attack and that Bin Laden was dead.

▶ In June of 2011, Anthony Weiner, a former representative of New York, was forced to resign when provocative online photos and sexually suggestive text messages he had intended to be private became public.

▶ The Initiators and Organizers of the Chinese Jasmine Revolution are a network of educated, young Chinese who use the Internet to encourage Chinese citizens to engage in peaceful protests to persuade the ruling Communist Party to move toward more democratic government. The anonymity of the Internet shields them from punishment by the government (Wong, 2011).

FOCUS QUESTIONS

1. What are digital media?

2. In what ways do digital media change how we think?

3. How can you be a critical, reflective user of digital media?

4. What are the democratic and nondemocratic potentials of digital media?

Digital media profoundly shape our lives in the 21st century. They affect who we know, how others see us, and how we interact with others. They also shape how we learn, engage in professional activities, participate in community life, and we engage with others in social, professional, and educational contexts.

Figure 15.1 **Americans' Internet Use by Generation**
Source: Pew Research Center's Internet & American Life Project (Zickhur, 2010)

Seventy-nine percent of American adults use the Internet (Rainie, Purcell, Goulet, & Hampton, 2011), and usage is high for people of all ages (see Figure 15.1). For many of them, digital media are seamlessly integrated into daily routines and identities (Bohil et al., 2009; Potter, 2009). Most contemporary students are tech-savvy. However, skill at using digital media doesn't guarantee thoughtful choices about how it does or should fit into and affect our lives. This chapter encourages you to do just that—reflect on how you use digital media in your life.

The first section of the chapter defines digital media and surveys the ways they fit into our lives. In the second section, we consider key controversies about the effects of digital media that will help you develop a more critical perspective on this form of communication. The third section of the chapter identifies two guidelines to keep in mind as we live in a technology-saturated world. Throughout the chapter, I invite you to think critically about the roles you choose to give digital media in your life.

Understanding Digital Media

Digital media are electronic modes of communication that store and manage data in digital form. When you communicate f2f (face-to-face), you don't have digital, electronic systems mediating between you and the other person or persons. But when you use your cell or smart phone or communicate online—email, IM, chat rooms, postings on Facebook, and so forth—your messages are not transmitted directly from you to another

David J. Green/Alamy

Social media are pervasive in our lives.

person. Instead, they go through computer technologies that digitize, store and send them. Video games, e-books, and most televisions are also digital media.

Features of Digital Media

Digital media are possible because of digital technologies. Older forms of electronic communication, such as the telegraph and radio, rely on analog technology, which transmits messages in continuous numerical form. In contrast, digital media rely on digital technology, which is easier to store and manage because it uses only two numerical values (0 and 1). Three key characteristics of digitization are ease of manipulation, convergence, and nearly instant speed (Steele, 2009; Turow, 2008).

Manipulation

The ability to manipulate information is not new; it was possible with analog film and video and film photography. For instance, a photo could be retouched and video could be edited. However, manipulating analog media took a high level of skill that few people had. In contrast, most people who have grown up using digital media know how to manipulate them—for instance, using Photoshop's clone stamping and Despeckle filter allows you to alter photos. The line that divided production and consumption of media in the analog era is blurred, if not erased, in the digital era. We now see home-made videos on television news programs and tweets repeated in newspapers ("Bulletins from the Future," 2011).

Convergence

Digital media also cultivate convergence. Just a few years ago, it was difficult and expensive to have a voice-over-Internet (VoIP) phone call. Today, soldiers in Iraq routinely have Skype with family members. This is possible because the technology for transmitting sound and the technology for transmitting visual images are both digital and, thus, they can be managed on a single network. When video, audio (telephone), and computer data are all stored and transmitted as digital signals, they can be managed on the same network. Thus, we can have video and sound when we Skype with someone.

Speed

The third distinguishing feature of digital media is speed. Most obviously, this means that information can travel very quickly: You send an email or text and the recipient gets it almost immediately. And IM is named *instant* messaging because it's so fast.

But the speed of digital technology does more than let us send and receive messages quickly. It also affects our expectations for the pace in general. Have you ever gotten impatient when you texted a friend and didn't get an immediate reply? Have you ever been irritated by an online site that was slow to load? If so, you understand how living with digital media affects your expectations of speed. We expect faster responses to our texts and IMs, and we may feel pressured to answer others' messages quickly.

A third implication of the increased speed of digital technology is its potential to jeopardize accuracy. Rayford Steele (2009), who studies digital media, points out that "in a world of instant access where everyone can be published or viewed, the time pressure and the volume increase make careful vetting that much harder" (p. 494). Thus, newspapers and magazines—both online and print—fearing that they will lose a scoop on a story publish what they believe to be true before all information has been gathered and evaluated.

A History of Communication Technologies

Many of my students think that communication technologies are relatively new. Actually, technologies of many types have been with us since humans first inhabited the Earth. For example, fire and the wheel are technologies that profoundly changed human life. Let's review the history of communication technologies, not merely to understand specific technologies but also to grasp the broader idea that humans continuously invent new ways to communicate and connect.

Communication technologies are means of recording, transferring, and working with information. Communication technologies include long-established devices, such as the telephone, and newer technologies, such as BlackBerrys, iPods, and iPads, for example. Figure 15.2 provides a time line so you can grasp the overall history of communication technologies and notice the speedup in the past few years.

DIGITAL MEDIA
Holder of Precious Things

Again and again we've heard that new media companies are nimble and cool, whereas old media companies are out of date, out of touch, and out of luck. So when, in 2007, NBC Universal and News Corp. decided to build their own Internet video site to rival the likes of YouTube, most people expected the NBC–News Corp. venture to fail. So much for expectations.

The NBC–News Corp free online video site was named Hulu, derived from a Chinese word that means "holder of precious things" (Lyons, 2009). Its first year out, Hulu is estimated to have racked up a $12 million gross profit, while YouTube reported no gross profit (Lyons, 2009).

What's the story behind Hulu's success? The first is that top talent was recruited to build Hulu: Jason Kilar, formerly a division chief at Amazon, is CEO, and Eric Feng, formerly a Microsoft worker, oversees development. With those two at the helm, it's no wonder that Hulu has a clean, easy user interface and a razor-sharp search engine. Second, unlike YouTube, Hulu has legal access to premier programming that is professionally produced. Would you rather watch a home video of a puppy licking a baby or episodes of *30 Rock* and *The Daily Show*? Hulu distributes shows from NBC, Fox, and others. Compare those shows to amateur videos and you begin to see why audiences like Hulu. Users have to go to other video sites to watch shows, but Hulu brings the content from multiple sites to users. And that, of course, attracts advertisers, which adds to profits.

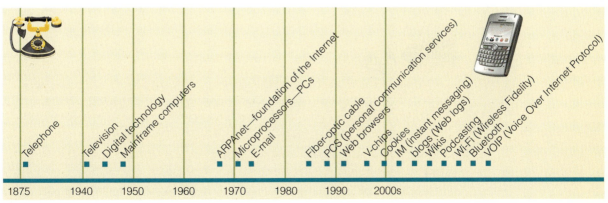

Figure 15.2 The Evolution of Communication Technologies

DIGITAL MEDIA

Time Travel

When was the microwave oven invented? How about television and the cordless phone? The PBS technology Web site (go to the book's online resources for this chapter and click on WebLink 15.1) lets you go through the 20th century to find out when everyday technologies first came on the scene.

Written Communication

Although you might not think of writing as a technology, it is. Like other technologies, writing allows us to record, transfer, and work with information by writing letters, papers, reports, legal documents, articles, books, and so forth.

Telephonic Communication

When Alexander Graham Bell invented the telephone in the mid-1870s, he made it possible for people, as the marketing slogan says, to "reach out and touch someone." Another communication technology based on the telephone is the facsimile machine, which is better known as the fax.

 Luke

I used to love e-mail, but now I communicate mainly by cell, particularly texting. It's a great way to stay in touch with people no matter where you are or what you are doing. I text or leave a message when I have time, friends text back when they have time. It's so much easier than having to be free at the same time.

Today, many people rely less on "land lines" than on cell phones and personal digital assistants (PDAs), which allow them to send and receive calls wherever they are. Cell phones were first made available in 1977, when AT&T introduced the first cellular network to serve a mere 2,000 customers in the single city of Chicago (Stone, 2004). In 2011, there were 5.3 billion cell subscribers worldwide (Global Mobile Statistics, 2011). That is 77 percent of the world's population, with the greatest proportion of people using cells in China and India.

Computers

The electronic computer was invented in 1940. In the 1970s, the Internet came on the scene, having been developed by the U.S. Department of Defense. Today, approximately 79 percent of the U.S. population uses the Internet (Zickuhr, 2010).

 Kay

Technology is turning human communication into something impersonal. Now people log on and send e-mail about what they are doing—apparently they are too busy doing all of that to pick up the telephone or write a letter. Newer technology has made us lazy. Instead of spelling out words, people write LOL and BRB. Can't we talk to each other anymore?

Wi-Fi

Wireless modes of communication greatly increase use of an unlicensed part of the spectrum previously used only to power appliances such as microwave ovens and cordless phones. Originally called 802.11, marketers later gave it the cooler name

Wi-Fi (Levy, 2004b). Once wireless technology was developed, it rapidly expanded beyond Internet connections. Today, the Global Positioning System (GPS), digital voice recorders, fourth-generation (4G) cell networks, the Bluetooth protocol, cellular cards, and satellite radio are common uses of wireless connectivity (Fitzgerald, 2006; Pogue, 2006).

Electronic Conferencing

An increasingly popular technology is **teleconferencing,** which can take several forms that vary in the extent to which they emulate face-to-face meetings. Audioconferencing allows people at different locations to participate in a discussion over the telephone. Computer conferencing allows multiple participants to send and receive e-mail in sequential exchanges. Videoconferencing is rapidly expanding in popularity, largely because it combines the advantages of other kinds of teleconferencing while avoiding many of their disadvantages. You probably have witnessed examples of videoconferencing on news programs. Using satellites to transmit visual images, people in distant locations appear on-screen with newscasters in a studio. A number of regular computer users download Skype or a similar VoIP program and use a Webcam to see a person with whom they are talking over the Internet.

DIGITAL MEDIA
Big Parent Is Watching

First, parents were offered V-chips so they could control young children's television viewing. Now, parents can use cell phones to monitor their children—did they get to school, are they really at the library as they said? The newest phones have built-in technology that can report not only our location but our speed and direction as well (Richtel, 2006). Of course, children have ways of avoiding parents' surveillance. One 16-year-old points out, "If I was going somewhere I wasn't supposed to, I'd just turn it off and say my phone died" (Richtel, 2006, p. E6).

Some companies are betting that people will want to make it easy for others to find them. In February of 2009 Google launched a locating system that allows people to keep track of each other. Another friend-finding system, Loopt, let a businessman dining in California know that his college roommate was eating at a nearby restaurant. They got together for an after-dinner drink (Markoff, 2009).

Interconnected Communication Technologies

Convergence of technologies allows **interconnectivity,** which is the connecting of various devices to each other and to the Internet so users don't have to independently configure each new system. For instance, yesterday's separate technologies of telephone and computer are combined today in cell phones that allow people to mange e-mail, text, take photos, and visit the Web.

Bill Joy, who worked as Sun Microsystems' chief scientist, believes that computers will increasingly work more like simple appliances such as toasters, alarm clocks, and electric drills (Jamieson & Campbell, 2006). Soon, he says, we will buy computerized products, plug them in, and they will work automatically. With interconnectivity, your refrigerator can text you that the milk has reached its expiration date, the mirror over the bathroom sink can show you the news headlines while you wash in the morning, and dolls will come with sensor chips that allow them to sense and respond to a child's emotions—if the child is upset, the doll may give a hug; if the child is angry, the doll will know to talk softly to calm the child down (Sennott, 2003).

Uses of Digital Media

We use digital media for many of the same reasons we use other modes of communicating. However, the features of digital media that we've discussed affect the nature

DIGITAL MEDIA
Uncle Sam Wants You, PacBot

If one of the soldiers had to be lost, the commanding officer was glad it was the one it was. His hardest job is writing letters to parents, telling them their son or daughter was killed on the battlefield. This soldier had no family—or heart or personality. It was a PacBot, a robot that takes on some of the most dangerous missions in war. PacBots made their timely debut on September 11, 2001. Their first mission was helping with the cleanup at Ground Zero. Unlike people, PacBots weren't affected by smoke or noxious chemicals, and they weren't traumatized by the sight of dead and dismembered human beings.

Soon after, iRobot, the company that makes PacBots, sent a few PacBots overseas to test how they worked. When iRobot wanted them back, the troops resisted—they didn't want to part with their PacBots, who took the most dangerous and disgusting jobs without complaint. By 2008, the Pentagon had a $286 million contract to cover the purchase of 3,000 PacBots.

PacBot is not the only technology changing war. P. W. Singer, author of *Wired for War* (2009), details how the development of new technologies changes the ways we engage in war. For instance, pilots in Nevada operate remote controls to kill terrorists in Afghanistan. These "drone pilots" engage in remote-controlled warfare for eight or more hours, then leave their offices, get in their cars, and drive home. Interestingly, Singer says that drone pilots suffer a higher rate of posttraumatic stress disorder (PTSD) than conventional pilots do. He thinks it may be because they are removed from seeing the immediate consequences of their actions and later realize those consequences.

and the possibilities of interaction (Logan, 2011). We'll look at five prominent ways we use digital media.

Creating Identity

In Chapter 9, we discussed how the self develops through interaction with others and through processes such as reflected appraisal and social comparison. Our sense of who we are and can be also develops online as we craft identities that others interact with and respond to. The most basic ways in which we craft online identities are through screen names and email addresses. You must have a screen name to participate in chat rooms and online role-playing games. The name you choose says something about who you are or who you want others to think you are. A screen name such as *dancer* announces that the person using the name is a dancer or likes dancing. *Tequilaman* and *partygirl* create different impressions of the users. As Steve Duck and David McMahan (2009) note, email addresses also communicate identities. The email address teacher@email.unc.edu tells you that (1) the user is probably a teacher who (2) works at UNC, which is (3) an educational (edu) institution. If the top-level domain in the email address were gov, you would infer that the user is connected to the government.

As I was writing this chapter in June of 2011, the Internet Corporation for Assigned Names and Numbers voted to broaden the range of domain names that will be available. The Domain Name System was created in the 1980s. Initially, it allowed only eight suffixes: .com, .edu, .gov, .int, .mil, .net, .org, and .arpa. Later, it approved 14 more, making a total of 22 domain suffixes (Sarno, 2011; Tessler, 2011). Starting in

2012, an estimated 500 more domain names may be approved. For instance, Jaguar might exchange its current jaguar.com address for drive.jaguar. This change is a response to requests from users for domain names that enhance branding for companies, bloggers, and individuals.

When we use digital media, many aspects of personal identity are not known unless we choose to disclose them. Some people adopt online identities to fit different moods and goals and even the norms of particular communities—for instance, buyers and sellers on eBay announce their identities by proclaiming their fandom and expertise regarding objects associated with their fandom (Desjardins, 2006; Hillis & Petit, 2006a). Some have extensive collections of avatars that represent different aspects of themselves or who they would like to be.

People may also create on-screen identities that help them learn social skills. Mizuko Ito (2008), who studies digital youth culture, says that participation in online communities teaches people "how to get along with others, how to manage a public identity" (Lewin, 2008, p. 10A). Online identities may also allow people to experiment with new facets of identity. As we express this aspect of identity online, feedback from other online characters may provide insight into whether we really want this to be part of us.

Another healthy use of on-screen personalities is to accept limitations or changes in ourselves. One woman lost her leg as a result of an automobile accident. After the amputation, she had difficulty accepting her disability. One way she coped was by logging into a Multi-User Dungeon (MUD) in an online game and creating a one-legged character to represent her. In the MUD, she made friends who accepted her disability, and she became romantically involved with another character in the MUD. For this woman, the virtual character she created helped her accept her real self (Turkle, 2002).

The positive possibilities of online identities are not the whole story. We also have to recognize that online identities hold the potential for hurt or serious harm. Some

DIGITAL MEDIA
Lez Get Real

Lez Get Real is a popular lesbian news site that claims to offer "a gay girl's view on the world." Readers had come to appreciate the site's author, Paula Brooks, who gave impressions and observation from a lesbian perspective. There's just one problem: Paula Brooks is a man. In 2011, readers learned that Paula is really Bill Graber, who was in the military and, after that, construction (Flock & Bell, 2011). Graber insists that he wanted to be an advocate for gay issues because he was upset when lesbian friends of his were mistreated. He invented the online persona of Paula Brooks because he thought no one would take him seriously if he were a man. The revelation about Graber came just one day after it was discovered that Amina Arraf, author of the Syrian lesbian blog *A Gay Girl in Damascus*, was exposed as Tom MacMaster, an American man.

digital media scholars question whether people who become skilled at adopting online personas have difficulty developing authentic selves and sharing real feelings and fears with others (Turkle, 2002, 2004).

Another concern is that online identities can mislead others, sometimes in dangerous ways. Predators may represent themselves as children's and teens' friends and sometimes seduce children and teens into meeting them in person, which can lead to appalling abuses.

Yet social networks are not inherently bad or unsafe. In fact, they are very much like real-world communities. For the most part, they "are comprised mostly of good people who are there for the right reasons" (Stone, 2009, p. A14). There are some people online who are mean and even dangerous, but mean and dangerous people also exist offline. This doesn't mean that online communication is without danger. Rather, the reports suggest that it is probably no more (or less) dangerous online than offline.

Connecting with Others

A primary use of digital media is social interaction and relationship development and maintenance. In the United States and Britain, nearly 50 percent of people use Facebook and seven to nine percent of people use Twitter ("Bulletins from the Future," 2011). It is increasingly common to meet people online. Perhaps you meet someone in an online chat room or on Facebook and that person becomes a friend. Or maybe you meet a romantic partner on a networking site that allows you to search for dates or marriage partners who meet criteria that you specify.

When I wake up in the morning, the first thing I do is check my messages. I respond to the important ones and then get out of bed and take my shower. While I'm fixing my hair and dressing, I update my Facebook page and see who's posted messages on my wall. On the way to classes, I text my three closest friends to see what they're doing and call Mom.

Currently, 47 percent of adult Americans use at least one social networking site (SNS) (Rainie, et al., 2011). Facebook is the most popular SNS, used by 92 percent of people who engage with any SNS. MySpace is used by 29 percent, LinkedIn by 13 percent, and Twitter by 13 percent of people who go to SNS (Rainie, et al., 2011). The youngest generations are still leaders in using SNS, but the fastest growth has come from people aged 74 and older. Social networking site usage for this age cohort has quadrupled since 2008, from four to 16 percent (Zickuhr, 2010).

For many people, online matching is easier and more productive than face-to-face dating. And don't think online romance is just for twenty-somethings: Baby boomers now represent about 20 percent of online daters (Hill, 2011). Online dating sites make it easy to find people who share our interests and values and who meet criteria that are important to us (Anderson & Emmers-Sommer, 2006). In part, this is because digital media promote getting to know others on the basis of what they say and do more than how they look. It's not uncommon for people whose relationships began online to admit that they would never have dated one another if they had met face-to-face. We may screen out people with whom we would be very compatible based on superficial qualities such as physical appearance.

Ally

Never in a million years would I have gone out with Clifford if I had met him in person first. He is totally not my type. I've always liked guys with dark hair who are tall and wiry. Clifford is blonde and medium height and muscular but a little heavy. Like I said, never in a million years would I have given him a second look. But we met online and talked a lot before we ever saw each other or even exchanged photos. By the time I actually met him, I already liked who he is and what he stands for. We just got engaged!

Communication that relies on digital media also tends to involve more disclosures at early stages of interaction than is typical in face-to-face relationships (Lengel, 2009). Sites that aim to make romantic matches generally ask new users to provide significant information about themselves to facilitate matching them with others who are similar. This information, which creates a user profile that other members of the site can view in advance of contacting a user, would typically be revealed in the course of multiple face-to-face interactions. Of course, there is no guarantee that the information people provide online is accurate. In fact, 50 percent of people in one survey of online dating acknowledged they had misrepresented themselves by providing inaccurate information about matters such as attractiveness, weight, age, and interests (Whitty, 2007).

In addition to meeting people online, many of us use digital media to maintain and develop relationships in which people also interact face-to-face. Perhaps you stay in touch with high school friends that you seldom see face-to-face through a social networking site and texting. Probably you also keep up with friends you do see through online sites as well as in-person interaction. Perhaps you have Skype visits with friends and family.

Woody

I could never stay in touch with all my old friends without Facebook. Most of them went to in-state colleges but I went across the whole country to come to this school. I get home three times a year so we couldn't make it if we had to do the retro f2f talking. We post on each other's walls weekly or even more often, and we text a lot. That keeps all of us connected and tight like we were in high school.

Digital media, especially texting, are typically brief blurbs rather than extended conversation. "where r u?" "wrk. u?" "same. ok with yr boss?" "no—bad mood again.

DIGITAL MEDIA
Job DISqualifications

Be careful what information you put on social networking sites. That's the advice of Steven Rothberg (2008), who works with employers who hire college and university students. Rothberg says a majority of employers' background checks now involve Googling candidates' names and checking social networking sites such as MySpace and Facebook. One third of the employers that Rothberg talked with said they had dismissed candidates because of information they found on social networking sites. The four types of information found on these sites most likely to result in dismissing a candidate were:

1. Information about using alcohol or other drugs

2. Sexually provocative or photographs or descriptions of inappropriate activity

3. Poor communication skills

4. Speaking negatively about employers or co-workers at previous jobs.

But social networking sites aren't the only source of potential trouble for prospective employees. Santa Barbara startup company Social Intelligence does what CEO Max Drucker calls "deep searches" of the Internet (Preston, 2011). His company searches not only major social networking sites, but also bulletin boards, YouTube, Flickr, Picasa, Yfrog, Photobucket, blogs, posts on small sites such as Tumblr, and even Craigslist. Social Intelligence gives prospective employers a dossier that includes online records of racist remarks, references to drugs, sexually explicit photos and videos, displays of weapons, and violent activity. Privacy advocates charged that Social Intelligence should not be allowed to operate because it was intrusive in people's personal lives. The Federal Trade Commission investigated Social Intelligence, but ruled that the company was compliant with the Fair Credit Reporting Act. Bottom line: Anything online is fair game for background searches (Waters, 2011).

☹" "sad 4 u. c u ltr??" "gr8." There's not a great deal going on in such messages at the content level of meaning. At the relationship level of meaning, however, they say a lot. They say "I want to stay in touch with you," "I care what is happening in your life," and "I want to see you." Digital media facilitate constant connection. It massages relationships with many small strokes instead of one extended one.

Digital media also allow us to check on people we care about in times of danger. In March 2011, Japan suffered a triple disaster: a tsunami, followed by an earthquake, followed by damage to a nuclear reactor. Immediately after the disasters, which killed more than 18,000 people, conventional communication was difficult or impossible. Phone networks, for both landlines and cells, were either not working or overloaded with traffic from people trying to find out if their loved ones had survived. Twitter bridged the communication gap: Nielsen NetRatings Japan said that millions relied on Twitter or similar sites to check on friends and family, adding 33 percent more users than in most weeks (Hosaka, 2011).

Social networking, and online communication in general, is subject to abuses. In addition to misrepresenting identity in devious and harmful ways, it can be used to attack others. When communicating online, people often feel less inhibited than when communicating face-to-face. This can lead to lessened accountability for what we say to others.

Some scholars worry that online communities have the potential to promote narrow-mindedness, because people may join only communities that share their values and views (Dreyfus, 2008). People who visit only networks, blogs, forums, and chat rooms that support their own perspectives risk being uninformed about other perspectives and not getting useful questioning about their own views. Ideas that differ from those of the majority in an online community may be ignored and the person expressing them may be ousted as members police community norms (Jarrett, 2006).

Learning

Digital media are also prevalent in education at all grade levels and all types of institutions. Students and faculty alike are relying on more and more types of technologies for teaching and learning. Many colleges and universities have course management systems such as Blackboard or Sakai that faculty are encouraged or required to use. These allow faculty to post readings and other course material, record grades, set up discussion forums, and email students. In addition, faculty often post PowerPoint and Pretzi presentations to supplement class lectures and discussions. Despite the pressure on faculty to use course management systems, the benefit to students is not clear. Only 9 percent of students say they are very positive about these systems, and another 42 percent are positive (Information Technology, 2011). A minority of students (37 percent) agree that information technologies stimulate more active student involvement in classes, and only 13 percent think information technologies improve learning (Information Technology, 2011).

Today's students are the most wired ever. In 2011, 84 percent of college and university students have laptops, 46 percent have desktops, 63 percent have internet-capable handheld devices, and 13 percent have netbooks (Information Technology, 2011). Today, 73 percent of students send text messages daily, 59 percent visit social-networking sites daily, and 24 percent send instant messages daily ("Student Use," 2011).

Although students are continuously engaged with digital media, they aren't wholly positive about it. A 2011 report (Levy, Nardick, Turner, & McWatters, 2011) noted that more than half of college students surveyed were concerned about their immersion in technology. Many students feel pressure to be connected and responsive all the time. Alexis's commentary makes this point.

DIGITAL MEDIA
Cyberbullying

Bullying used to be done in person, but today it's at least as likely to occur online. **Cyberbullying** is intentional harm that is deliberately inflicted on others through phones and computers (Cyberbullying Research Center). As far as impact on victims, cyberbullying is every bit as harmful as face-to-face bullying. Either can have devastating effects on self-esteem, and can lead to depression, responsive violence, and even suicide. Although people of any age can engage in cyberbullying, it is most common among middle-schoolers (Hinduja & Patchin, 2008; Jacobs, 2010). At that age, people are uniquely vulnerable to derision and exclusion by peers. Middle-schoolers have online discussions, often with voting, to decide if someone is ugly or stupid or promiscuous. The online group's decisions are typically sent to others, often including the victim who is then publicly humiliated.

The online environment may encourage less personal responsibility for one's actions (Freeman, 2009; Hinduja & Patchin, 2008; Jacobs, 2010). As one eighth-grade student remarked, "It's easier to fight online because you feel more brave and in control. On Facebook, you can be as mean as you want" (Hoffman, 2010, p. A12).

DIGITAL MEDIA

Digital Media on Campus

Campuses are a prime place to develop new uses for digital. Here are examples of innovative ways to enhance learning.

◆ Stanford's medical school uses iPads to train students. One application allows students to draw anatomical structures with fingers and then annotate the drawings. The iPad is also how students watch videos of medical procedures being performed. Advanced medical students who sometimes confront emergencies can pull up a video that gives them moment-by-moment visual instruction on what they need to do (Keller, 2011).

◆ At the University of Warwick in England, students use smart phones to watch videos that teach about different body organs and take quizzes on anatomy (Young, 2011).

◆ A number of colleges use the location-tracking feature of smart phones to help students, particularly new ones, find their way around campus. For students who ride busses, many campuses have developed an app that lets them know how long they have to wait for the next bus (Young, 2011).

◆ Art departments on many campuses use a Google site to allow students to visit museums around the world and see famous works of art (http//www.googleartproject.com) (Cordell, 2011).

◆ Knewton is a computerized software program that functions as a personal tutor. Knewton gives students immediate feedback on their work and adapts to individual students' learning curves, giving more advanced material to students only when they are ready for it (Fischman, 2011).

◆ Piazza is a platform designed by an enterprising student named Pooja Nath. Piazza allows students to post questions on a course page, and peers and teachers can respond. Compared to rival sites such as Blackboard, Piazza is much faster because it is supported by a system of notification alerts (Rusli, 2011).

The other day I left my phone in my apartment because I was going to be really busy all day and didn't want to be distracted. When I got home I found all of these messages, many really angry because I had not replied to texts immediately. It's like I can't have a life without being available to everyone else 24/7.

Communicating on the Job

Digital media have radically altered how we communicate in professional contexts. Many issues that used to require face-to-face meetings can now be handled by email, which remains a primary form of digital media in the workplace. It allows co-workers in different physical locations to plan, review documents, make decisions, and collaborate. Skype and other VOIP protocols allow professionals to be visually and verbally present in meetings without being physically present. And intranet systems allow posting of documents that can be accessed by members of an organization or organizational unit.

People frequently comment that digital media allow us to be more efficient and productive. Because computers manage information so quickly, it seems obvious that they have greatly boosted both individual productivity and our collective, economic productivity. But do digital media really make us more efficient or productive? If so, then we should see a noticeable spike in productivity after companies and corporations start using computers to automate record keeping and erase the need for human workers to spend hours calculating. Yet, many industries have reaped small gains from large investments in digital technology (Bucy, 2005). Thomas Landauer (2002) analyzed data on productivity before and after major investments in technology. Here are two of his surprising findings:

Computer mediated communications (CMC) is integral to professional life.

Image Source/Jupiter Images

▶ The IRS spent more than $50 million to provide agents with computer systems that were expected to find information and make calculations quickly. After the systems were installed, agents' productivity declined by 40 percent.

▶ An insurance company invested $30 million on a computer system to increase efficiency. Sure enough, a year later employees were processing 30 percent more claims than before the system was installed. The only drawback was that the cost for processing each claim jumped from $3.50 to $5.00.

A number of people say that digital media not only don't lessen work, but actually create more work and more hours on the job. One study (Madden & Jones, 2008) reported that nearly half of workers say that digital media result in more hours and greater pressure to stay engaged in work even when "off the clock."

But productivity is not the only value to be assessed. Convenience also matters. Automated teller machines (ATMs) that operate 24 hours a day may not increase banks' profits, but they make it easier for people to withdraw money when they want to. People who buy clothes and other items online may not spend more than they did in the 1980s, but online shopping saves them a lot of time. In 2011, some pilots replaced the 40+ pound flight manuals they used to carry on board with a 1.5 pound iPad that allows them to read aeronautical charts and assess other information (Murphy, 2011).

Digital media can also reduce the operating expenses of businesses and government. The small town of Cornelius, North Carolina, with a population of only 25,000, recently gave its 20 town commissioners iPads to save the cost of printing 200 page agendas for meetings—that's 4,000 pages per meeting that don't have to be printed, collated, distributed to commissioners, and then tossed in the trash or a recycling bin (Williams 2011).

Digital media also allow employers to monitor employees to ensure that they are working while on the job. Recent court rulings have made it clear that employees' communication is not necessarily private. Electronic communication on devices provided by employers are not necessarily protected by constitutional privacy rights, but may be audited by employers (Liptak, 2010). The Supreme Court has given employers wide power to search and monitor text messages that employees send on pagers.

Organizing

Digital media are also an extraordinary tool for social and political organizing. They allow contact, interaction, strategizing, and community building among people who are geographically scattered.

Barack Obama's campaign relied on social networking in unprecedented ways—from list servers and texting to blogs to YouTube videos. And President Obama is continuing to rely on new media now that he's in the White House. Instead of weekly radio addresses, used by previous presidents, each week Obama tapes a video and releases it on the White House Web site and YouTube (Rutenberg & Nagourney, 2009).

Digital media also provide a degree of anonymity that is important for political organizing that challenges powerful forces that could harm those who oppose them. The Initiators and Organizers of the Chinese Jasmine Revolution, which I mentioned in the opening of this chapter, rely on digital media to pass information, plan strategy, and mobilize support for their efforts. Fear of reprisal from the government is minimized because the dissidents' identities can be concealed online (Wong, 2011).

Digital media also feature prominently in organizing for social change in Saudi Arabia. In that country, there are strict governmental regulations that prohibit public gatherings, so Saudis cannot demonstrate in public spaces without risk of grave repercussions. When Manal al-Sharif posted a video of herself driving, which is illegal for women in Saudi Arabia, she was jailed for nine days and clerics urged the government to subject her to public flogging for her crime. Within a few days of her arrest, other Saudis posted more than 30,000 tweets in support of Ms. Sharif (MacFarquhar, 2011). Emboldened by her work and the online support, a handful of Saudi women took driving lessons and posted to Twitter. Activists have posted videos and tweets criticizing other governmental actions with increasing frequency. The greater anonymity that inheres in digital media allows Saudis to organize and build support without risking harsh punishments.

We've seen that five primary uses of digital media are to create and perform identities, connect socially, teach and learn, engage in workplace interaction, and organize for social and political purposes. We can engage in all of these activities face-to-face as well, yet each way of interacting offers particular advantages and disadvantages.

Controversies about Digital Media

How do digital media shape our lives and—perhaps more important—how do we *want* them to shape our lives? In this section, we will discuss two controversies about their impact on us. These are current debates that do not yet have clear answers. Instead, they raise important questions that each of us must consider if we are to be active, informed participants in the present era.

Who Benefits?

Many of us are aware of the ways that digital media benefit us. We appreciate the convenience, speed, and possibilities for entertainment, relating, and crafting identities. As much as digital media enrich our lives, we would be naïve to think that it exits primarily to please or help us. In Chapter 14, we noted that mass communication first and foremost benefits the people who own and invest in media companies—providing us with news and entertainment provides them with huge profits. The same is true of digital media.

Consider the case of LinkedIn. Reid Hoffman, the chair of LinkedIn, took his company public in May of 2011. The initial public offering of LinkedIn stock was priced at $65 and soared to over $100 on its first day of trading. In addition to making stock traders rich overnight, there were other beneficiaries of LinkedIn's success. The team that underwrote the stock, which included financial giants such as Bank of America, JPMorgan Chase, and Morgan Stanley, made a tidy $28.4 million in fees. LinkedIn's primary law firm made $1.5 million, and its accounting firm made $1.35 million. Venture capitalists who had provided financial support when LinkedIn was a start-up company were given stock in the $2 to $5 range that became worth $200-$500 a share after the stock went public.

LinkedIn exemplifies the commercialization of digital media. Users provide the content that makes LinkedIn valuable, and the owners and venture capitalists profit. The same is true of social networking sites such as Facebook and MySpace and the wildly popular YouTube. People like you provide the content that makes the sites profitable for others. This doesn't necessarily mean that we shouldn't use and enjoy digital media, but it does suggest that we should be aware that our online activity—such as posting YouTube videos—benefits others handsomely.

How Do Digital Media Affect Thinking?

Recall that Marshall McLuhan claimed that the media we use change how we think and experience the world. Scholars identify three ways in which use of digital media affects human thinking. Whether these changes serve us well or not is a matter of great debate.

They Encourage Multitasking

A primary way digital media affect thinking is by encouraging **multitasking,** which is engaging in multiple tasks simultaneously or in rapid sequence in overlapping and interactive ways.

Computers facilitate multitasking, but it's no longer confined to computer usage. It's become common for people to interrupt conversations to answer cell phones, make notes on PDAs, and check pagers. Students bring laptop computers to class and, when not taking notes, they IM friends, play games, surf the Internet, or work on other tasks. The buzz of call waiting prompts a person to suspend the present telephone conversation and answer the new caller.

But can humans really concentrate on more than one thing at a time? Probably not. In fact, computers can't either. Even computers can't multitask. They do one thing at a time—just very, very quickly. A slow computer running with a 100-megahertz processor can implement a million instructions in less than a second (Harmon, 2002). But it executes each operation individually in sequence. Because a computer gives its full attention to a single task at a time, it does the task with great accuracy. When we try to do several

DIGITAL MEDIA
Drvng whl txtng

Perhaps the only thing more popular than cell phones is arguments about whether using them distracts drivers. At first, those who want to talk while driving argued that talking on a cell was no different than talking to a passenger. Once evidence discredited that claim, the new defense was that it was safe to drive and talk if you used a hands free cell. Now that claim has also been disproved. Substantial research demonstrates that talking on phones—hands-free or not—while driving is dangerous. The problem isn't that "your hands aren't on the wheel. It's that your mind isn't on the road" (Parker-Pope, 2009, p. D5). Researchers tested drivers' concentration when talking on a hands-free phone, talking with other passengers, and listening to radio or audio books. The results were clear-cut: Phone conversations are more distracting than any of the other activities. Accident statistics bear this out: Drivers talking on cell phones are four times as likely to have an accident as drivers who are not talking on cell phones. That's the same level of risk as driving while legally drunk!

tasks at once, we're likely to do each one less well than if we concentrated on one thing at a time (Brooks, 2001; Jackson, 2009). Adults who shift between two tasks take longer to do both tasks, and they make more mistakes (Freeman, 2009; Guterl, 2003). The habit of shifting attention moment to moment is so pervasive that Linda Stone, former Microsoft and Apple executive, calls it Continuous Partial Attention (Levy, 2006).

They Encourage Response to Visual Stimuli

Flashy game players, bright colors for wallpaper and pictures on social network sites, and clever avatars shape neural maps so that we expect new stimulation frequently. Because Web sites are visually vibrant and interesting, we learn to respond to dazzling images more than to other stimuli such as verbal content or dull images. As a result, heavy use of computers and other digital media may teach us to hold attention for only short spans of time and to expect— perhaps need—new and visually exciting stimuli continuously (Freeman, 2009; Guterl, 2003; Lester, 2006). Research that appeared as I was writing this chapter also indicates that we are more likely to forget information that we find online (Cohen, 2011; Sparrow, Liu, & Wegner, 2011). The reason seems to be that we assume we don't need to remember information since we can easily retrieve it again from the Internet.

A second way in which visual stimulation affects thinking is that it unequally stimulates the two brain lobes. The right lobe of the brain is specialized in artistic activity, parallel processing, and visual and spatial tasks. The left lobe is specialized in sequential thought, abstraction, and analytic thinking. The highly visual nature of computer technology stimulates the right side of the brain (as does television) and cultivates its development. Conversely, because computers stimulate the left side of the brain far less, computer use doesn't foster development of the skills essential for sequential activities such as reading and math. Given this, it's not surprising that children who use computers heavily for tasks other than writing may have difficulty with academic subjects that require analytic, reflective thinking (Gross, 1996; Guterl, 2003).

They May not Facilitate Independent, Critical Thinking

There are three ways in which digital media may discourage independent, critical thinking. First, they make it easy to rely on external authorities. Do you use a program to check and correct grammar and spelling on papers you write? Such programs are useful to skilled writers because they allow them to catch typing errors or occasional mistakes in grammar, syntax, and punctuation. However, such programs are not as useful to people who do not know the rules of grammar, spelling, syntax, and punctuation. Most programs designed to check spelling note only combinations of letters that are not recognizable words—*ybgir*, for instance. But a spell-check program won't catch the six spelling errors in the following sentence: *Wee should watch hour wait because its important four us too stay healthy.* Each misspelling in the sentence is an actual word, so most spell-checking programs will not flag it. Users who don't know spelling are likely to rely on the program and wind up with error-laden prose.

Second, relying on digital media for entertainment may undermine imaginative, independent thought and sustained mental focus (Begley, 2009). Imagination is ripe to develop at about the age children learn to talk. Children build their imaginative power by using words to create make-believe situations and invisible playmates and by collaborating with other children in play. Children don't have to invent characters' personalities or create the rules for what characters can and cannot do. In short, children are required to use less imagination to participate in high-tech play than in old-fashioned, make-believe activities.

When I was a kid, I played all the time without any fancy toys, much less high-tech ones. Once, when we got a new refrigerator, my sister and I took the box it came in. We thought that box was the greatest thing ever! One day it was a house, another day it was a space ship, another day a pirate ship. Last summer, we got a new stove, and I offered the box to my 5-year-old son. He said, "What do you want me to do with this?" That made me worry that he's not learning to create fantasy worlds. But I see him doing things on his Game Boy that are more sophisticated than anything I did at his age. Some of my friends are huge fans of technology for kids; some are absolutely against it. I'm more of a middle-way person. My son benefits from technology, but he also needs to learn that a big box can be anything in the world.

Does this mean that parents should take away videogames, TV, and the Internet and tell their children to go outside and play? Not necessarily. The wisest conclusion at this time is probably what Dianna advises in her commentary—to encourage activities that allow children to derive the benefits of both technology and old-fashioned play, so that they learn to operate within preset virtual worlds and to think outside the lines and ask, "What if …?"

A third way in which digital media may discourage independent thought comes, ironically, from the democratization of the Internet. Tim Clydesdale (2009), who studies teens, claims that the access to nearly infinite information makes teens and college-age people distrustful that there is any real authority. Any opinion or claim posted online is likely to be met with a counter claim and a different opinion. Clydesdale says that "authorities can be found for every position," which makes students doubt there is any hard-and-fast truth or authority. Communication professor Rayford Steele (2009) extends this thinking one step further. He believes that newer media tempt people to rely on peer authority rather than expert authority. Many online sites allow postings by anyone; the editor may or may not be vigilant in checking the postings and their accuracy. As a result, the "information" we find online may be flawed or just plain wrong. According to Steele, "the democratization of information can quickly degenerate into an intellectually corrosive radical egalitarianism" (p. 493). Everyone may state

DIGITAL MEDIA
Falling through the Net?

When computers first gained widespread popularity, some critics and scholars worried about what they called "the digital divide," a term for the gap between people and communities that do and do not have access to technologies. As the costs of technologies and linking systems such as cable have declined, concern over the digital divide has lessened. Yet, access is still not uniform. Consider these findings from recent surveys of Americans' access to digital media:

◆   Income affects access: Internet access is available in 87 percent of households with income over $75,000 and only 40 percent of households with income under $30,000 (Wayne, 2010).

◆   (Dis)ability affects access: Approximately 80 percent of all adults in America use the Internet, but only 54 percent of Americans with disabilities do (Fox, 2011).

◆   Blacks and Hispanics are more likely than whites to use phones for email and social networking, but more whites have broadband access in homes. Cell phones don't help with tasks such as preparing and updating résumés and filling out job applications (Washington, 2011).

opinions and make claims—but not everyone is equally qualified, and not every opinion is equally well grounded.

In this section, we discussed two important controversies about digital media. In the months between my writing this chapter and your reading it, new information relevant to these issues will have appeared, perhaps changing our awareness of how social and personal media affect our lives.

Guidelines for Interacting with Digital Media

There's no chance we are going to return to land lines, typewriters, and hand-written letters. Digital media are here to stay. How they affect us individually and our society as a whole, however, is up to us. We need to think about how we want to integrate digital media into our lives. In this section, we consider two guidelines for doing that.

Consciously Manage Information Flow

More information was produced between 1970 and 2000 than in the previous 5,000 years (Potter, 2001), and the amount of information produced continues to expand. On average, Americans hear, see and read 34 gigabytes of information every day—that's 100,000 words (Read, 2010). But access to more information doesn't necessarily make us more knowledgeable. Knowledge requires more than information. It requires evaluating the credibility of sources of information, thinking about how bits of information fit together, and connecting information to understand the big picture and draw reasoned conclusions.

The sheer amount of information many people receive causes stress and confusion. The problem is so serious that the very companies that made information overload

DIVERSITY

What Kind of Person Would You Become?

That's a key question Amish people ask when considering whether to adopt technologies ranging from cars to cell phones. Although the Amish still wear homemade clothes and live in homes without electricity, some Amish people use power tools, cell phones, and computers. Although this may sound inconsistent, actually it's not ("Amish," 2009; Umble, 2000). *Wired* magazine's Howard Rheingold (2009) spent some time in an Amish settlement in Pennsylvania to learn how they made decisions about technology.

When considering whether a particular technology belongs in their community, one question the Amish pose is how it would affect them. One Amish man expresses it this way: "It's not just how you use the technology that concerns us. We're also concerned about what kind of person you become when you use it." The Amish don't allow phones in homes. Five or more families may share a phone that is housed in a small structure between homes. Why not in the home? Because people interrupt face-to-face conversations to answer phone calls. Because a ringing phone disturbs family conversation over a meal. Why are cars not allowed by Old Order Amish? Because they allow people to travel greater distances and this undermines the custom of visiting nearby families every other Sunday.

possible are now trying to help people cope with it. Tech giants such as Google, Microsoft, and Intel have formed a nonprofit group to study the problem and devise ways to help people cope with the relentless onslaught of information. In addition to concerns about the stress on people, the tech giants are concerned about the costs to business of information overload. Studies of information workers show that the continuous switching from e-mail to IM to cell to Internet fractures attention spans. RescueTime, which analyzes computer use, reports that interruptions and switching between tasks costs U.S. businesses more than $650 million a year (Parker-Pope, 2008). After each interruption or switch, a person has to remember what she or he was doing and get back into that task … just in time for the next interruption.

It is ironic that technologies designed to save time and increase efficiency often make our lives more frenetic. Cell phones and PDAs make us available all the time to everyone, but what if we don't want to be available all the time? Media scholars (Bracken & Skalski, 2009) use the term "telepresence" to refer to personal and social media's saturation of our everyday lives.

We can exercise choice over how digital media affect us. For one person, a cell phone may reduce stress, but for another it may increase stress. Each of us can make deliberate choices about which digital media enhance our lives. If certain of them better our lives and we can afford them, we may choose to have them. But if they don't fit our lives and don't help us be the people we want to be, we don't have to join the crowd.

Participate in Deciding How to Regulate Digital Media

It's important for all of us to participate in decision making about how, if at all, we should regulate digital media. What guidelines are reasonable? What guidelines infringe on freedom of speech and freedom of the press? What guidelines protect

DIGITAL MEDIA
Enduring Fame

Increasingly, we hear about people who are charged with sexting—using their cell phones to send nude photos of themselves or parts of themselves (Irving, 2009, p. 64). While some sexting is done to harass, the majority seems to be done either to get attention or to flirt. In most cases so far, the charges have been dropped or reduced, but one consequence of sexting is not going away: File endurance. Once the message is sent, it exists and may resurface at any time such as when a potential employer does an online search of an interviewee!

people, particularly minors; and what trade-offs in freedom are we willing to accept to have those safeguards?

Privacy is a key issue that regulations must address. Many online advertisers collect **cookies,** bits of data that Web sites collect and store in users' personal browsers. This gives advertisers information about you that you might not choose to release. Software manufacturers have developed programs to disable cookies, but this will help only people who buy and install the programs.

And then there is **spyware,** which allows a third party to track individuals' online activity, gain personal information, and send pop-up ads tailored to users' profiles. Spyware is often bundled without users' knowledge into software that can be downloaded for free. For instance, free software that people use to swap MP3 music files often contains spyware that monitors what users do on the Web. Because spyware implants itself in the user's computer, the monitoring can take place even when the free software isn't being used. Many people mistakenly assume that their online communication is private and cannot be released without their permission.

DIGITAL MEDIA
Cyberhate

Some online communities that specialize in hate speech are particularly adept at attracting young children. There are numerous Web sites where people can engage in hate speech, or hate mongering, and there is little regulation of these sites, which may provide instructions on how to make a bomb or engage in hate speech against particular groups. Should anyone be allowed to create a site that proclaims hate of particular groups and exhorts others to hate the groups and act against them? Should anyone be allowed to visit sites that exist to promote hate? Is this kind of communication protected by the constitutional right to freedom of speech? To learn more about this issue, go to the book's online resources for this chapter and click on WebLink 15.3, which will give you access to the First Amendment Web site and an article that summarizes issues involved in the regulation of cyberhate.

SUMMARY

In this chapter, we've considered what it means to live in an era that is saturated with digital media. After reviewing the evolution of communication technologies, we discussed features of digital media and how we use them. We then explored three important controversies about the impact of these technologies on individuals and societies.

The final section of this chapter discussed two guidelines for interacting with communication technologies. One is to make deliberate choices about how to manage the place we give digital media in our lives. Second, we need to be informed and to participate in making decisions about how, if at all, to regulate communication technologies.

REVIEW, REFLECT, EXTEND

The Reflect, Discuss, and Apply Questions that follow will help you review, reflect on, and extend the information and ideas presented in this chapter. These resources, and a diverse selection of additional study tools, are also available online at the CourseMate for *Communication Mosaics*. Your CourseMate includes a student workbook, WebLinks, TED Talks hyperlinks and activities, chapter glossary and flashcards, interactive video activities, Speech Builder Express, and InfoTrac College Edition. For more information or to access this book's online resources, visit **www .cengagebrain.com.**

KEY CONCEPTS

communication technologies, 309
cookies, 326
cyberbullying 317
digital media, 307
interconnectivity, 311

multitasking, 321
spyware, 326
teleconferencing, 311
Wi-Fi, 310

Reflect, Discuss, Apply

1. How do relationships between people who never meet face-to-face differ from relationships between people who can see each other? What are the advantages and limitations of forming and sustaining relationships each way?

2. As a class or in small groups, discuss cyberbullying and, more generally, hurtful online communication. What about the online environment facilitates mean behavior such as making insults, spreading false rumors, and ridiculing appearance, ethnicity, and other aspects of identity? Could the factors that facilitate such behaviors be altered or do you think they are inherent in digital media?

3. As a class, discuss similarities and differences between interaction with friends online and face-to-face.

Recommended Resources

1. Read the most current issue of *Wired* or a similar magazine that focuses on technologies. Identify technological products and services that are not mentioned in this book, which went to press in the spring of 2012.

2. Dalton Conley's *Elsewhere, U.S.A.* (2009) provides a lively and provocative perspective on living technology-saturated lives. Dalton doesn't argue that technologies are good or bad. Instead,

he elaborates on some of their implications for identity, work, and family.

3. Larry Browning, Alf Saetre, Keri Stephens, and Jan-Oddvar Sornes (2008) present stories of the ways personal and social media facilitate and hinder work in a range of organizations. Their book shows how theories of media work in everyday life.

EXPERIENCE COMMUNICATION CASE STUDY

Online Dating

Apply what you've learned in this chapter by analyzing the following case study, using the accompanying questions as a guide. These questions and a video of the case study are also available online at your CourseMate for *Communication Mosaics*.

Christina is visiting her family for the holidays. One evening after dinner, her mother comes into her room where Christina is typing at her computer. Her mother sits down, and the following conversation takes place.

© Cengage Learning

Mom: Am I disturbing you?

Chris: No, I'm just signing off on e-mail. [She finishes at the keyboard and turns to face her mom.]

Mom: E-mailing someone?

Chris: Just a guy.

Mom: Someone you've been seeing at school?

Chris: Not exactly.

Mom: [laughs] Well, either you are seeing him or you're not, honey. Are you two dating?

Chris: Sort of. Yeah, you could say we're dating.

Mom: [laughs] What's the mystery? What's he like?

Chris: He's funny and smart and so easy to talk to. We can talk for hours and it never gets dull. I've never met anyone who's so easy to be with. We're interested in the same things and we share so many values. Brandon's just super. I've never met anyone like him.

Mom: Sounds great. When do I get to meet this fellow?

Chris: Well, not until I do. [Laughs] We met online and we're just starting to talk about getting together in person.

Mom: Online? You met this man online? And you act as if you know him!

Chris: I do know him, Mom. We've talked a lot—we've told each other lots of stuff, and …

Mom: How do you know what he's told you is true? For all you know, he's a 50-year-old mass murderer!

Chris: You've been watching too many movies on Lifetime, Mom. Brandon's 23, he's in college, and he comes from a family a lot like ours.

Mom: How do you know that? He could be lying about every part of what he's told you.

Chris: So? A guy I meet at school could lie, too. Meeting someone in person is no guarantee of honesty.

Mom: Haven't you read about all of the weirdos that go to these online matching sites?

Chris: Mom, Brandon's not a weirdo, and we didn't meet in a matching site. We met in a chat room where people talk about politics. He's as normal as I am. After all, I was in that chat room, too!

Mom: But, Chris, you can't be serious about someone you haven't met.

Chris: I have met him, Mom, just not face to face. Actually, I know him better than lots of guys I've dated for months. You can get to know a lot about a person from talking.

Mom: This makes me really nervous, honey. Please don't meet him by yourself.

Chris: Mom, you're making me feel sorry I told you how we met. This is exactly why I didn't tell you about him before. Nothing I say is going to change your mind about dating online.

Mom: [Pauses, looks away, then looks back at Chris.] You're right. I'm not giving him—or you— a chance. Let's start over. [Smiles] Tell me what you like about him.

Chris: [Tentatively] Well, he's thoughtful.

Mom: Thoughtful? How so?

Chris: Like, if I say something one day, he'll come back to it a day or so later and I can tell he's thought about it, like he's really interested in what I say.

Mom: So he really pays attention to what you say, huh?

Chris: Exactly. So many guys I've dated don't. They never return to things I've said. Brandon does. And another thing, when I come back to things he's said with ideas I've thought about, he really listens.

Mom: Like he values what you think and say?

Chris: Exactly! That's what's so special about him.

---

1. Review Chapter 6, which focuses on listening and responding. Identify examples of ineffective and effective listening and responding on the part of Chris's mother.

2. Chapter 10 stated that proximity and similarities are the two most significant influences on initial romantic attraction. Does this statement hold true for the online relationship between Chris and Brandon?

3. If Chris and Brandon meet face-to-face, how will communication on their initial date be different from communication on first dates between people who have not met online?

4. If you were romantically attracted to a person you met online and wanted to have a face-to-face date with her or him, what would you do to maximize your safety?

Epilogue

Although this is the final page of this book, what you have learned from it and from the class you are taking will continue to serve you throughout your life. Because communication is central to everything you do, the understandings and skills you have gained will enhance the quality of your personal life, enrich your social and civic involvements, help you succeed in the world of work, and prepare you to be an informed, active user of mass communication and communication technologies.

In the years ahead, you will find that what we've discussed in this book will help you understand a range of people and communication situations. Whether you are watching television, listening to a friend, participating on a work team, working through conflict with a romantic partner, or communicating online, the ideas and skills we have explored in *Communication Mosaics* will enlarge your insight into yourself, others, and the ways in which communication operates.

I hope that the theories, concepts, processes, and skills we've discussed will increase your effectiveness and pleasure as you communicate with others in all the spheres of your life.

Julia T. Wood

Glossary

abstract Removed from concrete reality. Symbols are abstract because they refer to, but are not equivalent to, reality.

acknowledgment The second of three levels of interpersonal confirmation; communicating that you hear and understand another's expressed feelings and thoughts.

agape One of the six styles of loving; it is selfless and focused on the other's happiness.

agenda setting Media's selection of issues, events, and people to highlight for attention.

ambiguous Subject to multiple meanings. Symbols are ambiguous because their meanings vary from person to person, context to context, and so forth.

ambushing Listening carefully to a speaker in order to attack her or him.

anxious/ambivalent attachment One of the four styles of attachment; a style, characterized by preoccupation with relationships, in which intimacy is both wanted and feared. It is fostered by inconsistent treatment from a caregiver.

arbitrary Random or not necessary. Symbols are arbitrary because there is no need for any particular symbol to stand for a particular referent.

arbitrator Outside third party who has the authority to make a decision on a conflict between two or more people.

artifact Any personal object with which one announces one's identities or personalizes one's environment.

assimilation The giving up of one's native ways to take on the ways of another culture.

attachment style The pattern of interaction between child and primary caregiver that teaches the child who he or she is, who others are, and how to approach relationships. Four attachment styles have been identified: anxious/ambivalent, dismissive, fearful, and secure.

attribution An explanation of why things happen and why people act as they do; not necessarily correct interpretations of others and their motives.

authoritarian interview An interviewing style in which the interviewer has and exerts greater power than the interviewee.

autonomy/connection One of three relationship dialectics; the tension between the need for personal autonomy, or independence, and connection, or intimacy.

bracketing Identifying and setting aside for later discussion the issues peripheral to a current conflict.

brainstorming A group technique for generating potential solutions to a problem; the free flow of ideas without immediate criticism.

brute facts Objective, concrete phenomena.

chronemics Nonverbal communication involving the perception and use of time to define identities and interaction.

climate communication One of three constructive forms of participation in group decision making; the creating and sustaining of an open, engaged atmosphere for discussion.

cognitive complexity The number of mental constructs an individual uses, how abstract they are, and how elaborately they interact to create perceptions.

cognitive restructuring A method of reducing communication apprehension that involves teaching people to revise how they think about speaking situations.

cognitive schemata Mental structures people use to organize and interpret experience. Four schemata have been identified: prototypes, personal constructs, stereotypes, and scripts.

cohesion Closeness, or feeling of esprit de corps, among members of a group.

collectivist culture A culture that regards people as deeply connected to one another and to their families, groups, and communities.

commitment The decision to remain in a relationship. One of three dimensions of enduring romantic relationships, commitment has more influence on relationship continuity than does love alone. An advanced stage in the process of escalation in romantic relationships.

communication A systemic process in which people interact with and through symbols to create and interpret meanings.

communication apprehension Anxiety associated with real or anticipated communication encounters. It is common and can be constructive.

communication climate The overall feeling, or emotional mood, between people.

communication network The links among members of an organization. May be formal (e.g., as specified in an organizational chart) or informal (friendship circles).

communication rules Shared understandings of what communication means and what behaviors are appropriate in various situations.

communication technologies Means of recording, transferring, and working with information.

comparison A form of evidence associating two things that are similar or different in some important way or ways.

complaint interview An interview that allows a person to register a complaint about a product, service, person, company, etc.

computer-mediated communication is interaction between people that relies on digital, electronic management of messages. Also called CMC.

conflict The expression of different views, interests, or goals and the perception of differences as incompatible or in opposition by people who depend on each other.

constitutive rules Communication rules that specify how certain communicative acts are to be counted.

constructive conflict In groups, disagreement that is characterized by respect for diverse opinions, emphasis on shared interests and goals, and a win–win orientation.

constructivism A theory that holds that we organize and interpret experience by applying cognitive structures called schemata.

content level of meaning One of two levels of meaning; the literal information in a message.

cookies Bits of data that Web sites collect and store in users' personal browsers.

counseling interview An interview in which one person with expertise helps another to understand a problem and develop strategies to overcome or cope more effectively with the difficulty.

covert conflict Conflict that is expressed indirectly; generally more difficult to manage constructively than overt conflict.

credibility The ability of a person to engender belief in what he or she says or does. Listeners confer or refuse to confer credibility on speakers.

critical listening Listening to analyze and evaluate the content of communication or the character of the person speaking.

critical research method A type of data analysis that aims to identify, critique, or change communication practices that oppress, marginalize, or otherwise harm people.

cultivation A cumulative process by which the media foster beliefs about social reality, including the belief that the world is more dangerous and violent than it actually is.

cultural relativism The recognition that cultures vary in thought, action, and behavior as well as in beliefs and values; not the same as moral relativism.

culture The beliefs, understandings, practices, and ways of interpreting experience that are shared by a group of people.

cyberbullying Intentional harm that is deliberately inflicted on others through phones and computers.

defensive listening The perception of personal attacks, criticisms, or hostile undertones in communication when none is intended.

derived credibility The expertise and trustworthiness attributed to a speaker by listeners as a result of how the speaker communicates during a presentation.

direct definition Communication that tells us who we are by explicitly labeling us and reacting to our behaviors; usually occurs first in families and later in interaction with peers and others.

dismissive attachment One of the four attachment styles; characterized by a view of others as unworthy of love and the self as adequate yet removed from intimate relationships; fostered by disinterested, rejecting, or abusive treatment by a caregiver.

disruptive conflict In groups, disagreement characterized by competitive communication, self-interested focus on the part of members, and a win–lose orientation.

distributive interview A style of interviewing in which power is roughly equal between interviewer and interviewee.

downer A person who communicates negatively about us and our worth.

egocentric communication An unconstructive form of group contribution that is used to block others or to call attention to oneself.

electronic epoch The fourth era in McLuhan's media history of civilization; ushered in by the invention of the telegraph, which made it possible for people to communicate personally across distance.

empathy The ability to feel with another person, to feel what he or she feels in a situation.

employment interview An interview in which employers and job candidates assess each other to determine whether there is a good fit between them.

endorsement The third of three levels of interpersonal confirmation; the communication of acceptance of another's thoughts and feelings. Not the same as agreement.

environmental distraction In communication situations, any occurrence that interferes with listening.

environmental factor Any nonverbal element of a setting that affects how we think, feel, act, and communicate.

equity theory The theory that people are happier and more satisfied with equitable relationships than inequitable ones. In equitable relationships, partners perceive the benefits and costs of the relationship as about equal for each of them.

eros One of the six styles of loving; passionate, intense, and erotic.

ethics The branch of philosophy that deals with the goodness or rightness of particular actions. Ethical issues infuse all areas of the communication field.

ethnocentrism The tendency to assume that one way of life is normal and superior to other ways of life.

ethos One of three forms of proof; proof based on the speaker's credibility (trustworthiness, expertise, and goodwill).

evidence Material used to interest, move, inform, or persuade people: statistics, examples, comparisons, and quotations.

example A form of evidence in which a single instance is used to make a point, to dramatize an idea, or to personalize information. The four types of examples are undetailed, detailed, hypothetical, and anecdotal.

exit interview An interview designed to gain information, insights, and perceptions about a place of work or an educational program from a person who is leaving.

expectancy violation theory A theory claiming that when our expectations are violated, we become more cognitively alert as we struggle to understand and cope with unexpected behaviors.

extemporaneous delivery A presentational style that includes preparation and practice but not memorization of actual words and nonverbal behaviors.

fearful attachment One of the four styles of attachment; characterized by the perception of self as unworthy of love; fostered by dismissive, rejecting, or abusive treatment by a caregiver.

feedback Verbal or nonverbal response to a message. The concept of feedback as applied to human communication appeared first in interactive models of communication.

funnel sequence In interviews, a pattern of communication that begins with broad, general questions and moves to progressively narrower, more probing questions.

gatekeeper A person, group, or institution that controls the choice and presentation of topics by media.

generalized other The perspective that represents one's perception of the rules, roles, and attitudes endorsed by one's group or community.

global village The modern-day, worldwide community made possible by electronic communication that instantaneously links people all over the world.

grace Granting forgiveness, putting aside our own needs, or helping another save face when no standard says we should or must do so.

group More than two people who interact over time, who are interdependent, and who follow shared rules of conduct to reach a common goal. A team is one type of group.

groupthink The absence of critical and independent thought on the part of group members about ideas generated by the group.

halo effect The attribution of expertise to someone in areas unrelated to the person's actual expertise.

haptics Nonverbal communication involving physical touch.

hearing A physiological activity that occurs when sound waves hit our eardrums. Unlike listening, hearing is a passive process.

high-context communication style An indirect and undetailed way of speaking that conveys meanings implicitly rather than explicitly; typical of collectivist cultures.

homeostasis A state of equilibrium that systems strive for but cannot sustain.

hypothetical thought Thinking about experiences and ideas that do not exist or are not present to the senses.

I The creative, spontaneous, impulsive aspect of the self. The I is complemented by the *me*.

I-language Language that identifies the speaker's or perceiver's thoughts and feelings. (Compare with *you*-language.)

immersive advertising Incorporating a product or brand into actual storylines in books, television programs, and films.

impromptu delivery A delivery style that involves little preparation; speakers think on their feet as they talk about ideas and positions with which they are familiar.

incomprehensibility When a message is not clearly understandable due to language or transmission problems; one of four situational obstacles to listening.

indexing A technique of noting that every statement reflects a specific time and circumstance and may not apply to other times or circumstances.

individualism A predominant Western value that regards each person as unique, important, and to be recognized for her or his individual qualities and behavior.

individualism/collectivism Dimension of cultures that refers to the extent to which members of a culture understand themselves as part of and connected to their families, groups, and cultures.

individualistic culture A culture in which each person is viewed as distinct from other people, groups, and organizations.

inference An interpretation that goes beyond the facts known but is believed to logically follow from them.

informational listening Listening to understand information and ideas.

information-getting interview An interview in which one person asks questions to learn about another person's qualifications, background, experience, opinions, knowledge, attitudes, or behaviors.

information-giving interview An interview in which one person provides information to another.

initial credibility The expertise and trustworthiness listeners attribute to a speaker before a presentation begins. Initial credibility is based on the speaker's titles, positions, experiences, or achievements that are known to listeners before they hear the speech.

institutional facts Meanings people assign to brute facts (objective, concrete phenomena) that are based on human interpretation.

interconnectivity The capacity of multiple devices to be connected to each other and to the Internet so that the devices can "talk" to each other.

interpersonal communication Communication between people, usually in close relationships such as friendship and romance.

interpersonal confirmation The expressed valuing of another person.

interpretation The subjective process of organizing and making sense of perceptions.

interview A communication transaction that emphasizes questions and answers.

intrapersonal communication Communication with ourselves, or self-talk.

investment Something put into a relationship that cannot be recovered should the relationship end. Investments, more than rewards and love, increase commitment.

judgment A belief or opinion based on observations, feelings, assumptions, or other nonfactual phenomena.

kinesics Body position and body motions, including those of the face, that may be used to communicate or may be interpreted as communicating.

leadership A set of behaviors that helps a group maintain a good climate and accomplish tasks in an organized way.

life script A guide to action based on rules for living and identity. Initially communicated in families, scripts define our roles, how we are to play them, and the basic elements in the plot of our lives.

listening The process of receiving, constructing meaning from, and responding to spoken and/or nonverbal messages. The process consists of being mindful, hearing, selecting and organizing information, interpreting communication, responding, and remembering.

literal listening Listening only to the content level of meaning and ignoring the relationship level of meaning.

loaded language An extreme form of evaluative language that relies on words that strongly slant perceptions and thus meanings.

logos One of three forms of proof; proof based on logic and reasoning.

long-term/short-term orientation Dimension of culture that refers to the extent to which members of a culture think about and long-term (history and future) versus short-term (present).

lose–lose One of three orientations to conflict; assumes that everyone loses when conflict occurs.

low-context communication style Language that is very explicit, detailed, and precise; generally used in individualistic cultures.

ludus One of six styles of loving; playful and sometimes manipulative.

mainstreaming The effect of television in stabilizing and homogenizing views within a society; one of two processes used to explain television's cultivation of synthetic worldviews.

mania One of six styles of loving; an obsessive style that often reflects personal insecurity.

manuscript delivery A presentational style that involves speaking from a complete manuscript of a speech.

masculinity/femininity Dimension of culture that refers to the extent to which a culture values aggressiveness, competitiveness, looking out for yourself, and dominating others, which are typically associated with men, versus gentleness, cooperation, and taking care of others and the natural world, which tend to be associated with women. Also called aggressiveness.

mass communication All media that address mass audiences.

matching hypothesis The prediction that people will seek relationships with others who closely match their values, attitudes, social background, and physical attractiveness.

me The reflective, analytical, socially conscious aspect of self. *Me* complements the *I* aspect of self.

mean world syndrome The belief that the world is dangerous and full of mean people.

meaning The significance we attribute to a phenomenon; what it signifies to us.

mediator Outside third party who facilitates discussion between two or more parties who are in conflict but who does not have the power to make a decision.

memorized delivery A presentational style in which the speech is delivered word for word from memory.

message complexity The amount of detailed information or intricate reasoning in a message; can interfere with effective listening.

message overload The receiving of more messages than we can interpret, evaluate, and remember; can interfere with effective listening.

mindfulness From Buddhism, the concept of being fully present in the moment; the first step of listening and the foundation of all the other steps.

mind reading The assumption that we understand what another person thinks or how another person perceives something.

minimal encourager Communication that gently invites another person to elaborate by expressing interest in hearing more.

mirror interview A style of interviewing in which the interviewer's questions reflect previous responses and comments of the interviewee. Mirror interviews give substantial power to interviewees.

monitoring The observation and regulation of one's own communication.

monopolizing Hogging the stage by continuously focusing communication on oneself instead of on the person who is talking.

multilingual Able to speak and understand more than one language or communication style used in a social group or culture.

multitasking Engaging in multiple tasks simultaneously or in overlapping and interactive ways.

neutralization One of four responses to relationship dialectics; balancing or finding a compromise between two dialectical poles.

noise Anything that interferes with the intended meaning of communication; includes sounds (e.g., traffic) as well as psychological interferences (e.g., preoccupation).

nonverbal communication All forms of communication other than words themselves; includes inflection and other vocal qualities as well as several other behaviors such as shrugs, blushing, and eye movements.

norm An informal rule that guides how members of a culture or group think, feel, and act. Norms define what is normal or appropriate in various situations.

novelty/predictability One of three relationship dialectics; the tension between the desire for spontaneous, new experiences, and the desire for routines and familiar experiences.

olfactics The perception of scents and odors; one form of nonverbal communication.

openness The extent to which a system interacts with its surrounding environment.

openness/closedness One of three relationship dialectics; the tension between the desire to share private thoughts, feelings, and experiences with intimates and the desire to preserve personal privacy.

oral footnote Phrases or sentences in a speech that acknowledge a source of evidence and sometimes explain the source's qualifications.

oral style Visual, vocal, and verbal aspects of the delivery of a public speech or other communication.

organizational culture Understandings about identity and codes of thought and action that are shared by the members of an organization.

overt conflict Conflict expressed directly and in a straightforward manner.

paralanguage Communication that is vocal but not verbal. Paralanguage includes accent, inflection, volume, pitch, and sounds such as murmurs and gasps.

paraphrasing A method of clarifying another's meaning by reflecting one's interpretation of the other's communication back to that person.

participation A response to cultural diversity in which one incorporates some practices, customs, and traditions of other groups into one's life.

particular others Specific people who are significant to the self and who influence the self's values, perspectives, and esteem.

passion Intensely positive feelings and desires for another person. Passion is based on the rewards of involvement and is not equivalent to commitment.

pathos One of three forms of proof; proof based on appealing to listeners' emotions.

perception An active process of selecting, organizing, and interpreting people, objects, events, situations, and activities.

performance review A type of interview in which a supervisor comments on a subordinate's achievements and professional development, identifies weaknesses or problems, and collaborates to develop goals for future performance; also known as a *performance appraisal.*

personal construct A bipolar mental yardstick that allows us to measure people and situations along specific dimensions of judgment, such as "honest– dishonest."

personal relationship A relationship defined by uniqueness, rules, relationship dialectics, commitment, and embeddedness in contexts. Personal relationships, unlike social ones, are irreplaceable.

person-centeredness The ability to perceive another as a unique and distinct individual apart from social roles and generalizations.

persuasive interview An interview in which the interviewer aims to influence the attitudes, beliefs, values, or actions of the interviewee.

physical appearance A form of nonverbal communication; how we look, including the cultural meanings, values, and expectations associated with looks.

policy A formal statement of practice that reflects and upholds an organization's culture.

positive visualization A technique for reducing speaking anxiety, in which one visualizes oneself communicating effectively in progressively challenging speaking situations.

power The ability to influence others; a feature of small groups that affects participation.

power distance Dimension of culture that refers to the size of the gap between people with high and low power and the extent to which that is regarded as normal.

power over The ability to help or harm others. Power over others usually is communicated in ways that highlight the status and influence of the person exerting the power.

power to The ability to empower others to reach their goals. People who use power to help others generally do not highlight their own status and influence.

pragma One of six styles of loving; based on practical considerations and criteria for attachment.

prejudgment Judging others or their ideas before one has heard them.

preoccupation Absorption in our own thoughts or concerns.

problem-solving interview An interview in which people collaborate to identify sources of a mutual problem and to develop means of addressing or resolving it.

procedural communication One of three constructive ways of participating in group decision making; orders ideas and coordinates contributions of members.

process An ongoing continuity, the beginning and end of which are difficult to identify; for example, communication.

product placement A practice, paid for by advertisers and program sponsors, of featuring products in media so that the products are associated with particular characters, storylines, and so forth.

prototype A knowledge structure that defines the clearest or most representative example of some category.

proxemics A form of nonverbal communication that involves space and how we use it.

pseudolistening Pretending to listen.

psychological responsibility The obligation to remember, plan, and coordinate domestic work and child care. In general, women assume psychological responsibility for child care and housework even when both partners share in the actual doing of tasks.

puffery Exaggerated, superlative claims about a product that appear to be factually based but are actually meaningless and unverifiable.

punctuation Defining the beginning and ending of interaction or interaction episodes. Punctuation is subjective and not always agreed on by those involved in the interaction.

qualitative research methods Interpretive techniques, including textual analysis and ethnography, used to understand the character of experience, particularly how people perceive and make sense of communication.

quality improvement team A group in which people from different departments or areas in an organization collaborate to solve problems, meet needs, or increase the quality of work life. Also called *continuous quality improvement team.*

quantitative research methods Techniques such as descriptive statistics, surveys, and experiments, used to gather quantifiable data.

quotation A form of evidence that uses exact citations of others' statements. Also called *testimony.*

reappropriation A group's reclamation of a term used by others to degrade the group's members; the treatment of those terms as positive self-descriptions. Aims to remove the stigma from terms that others use pejoratively.

recognition The most basic level of interpersonal confirmation; the communication of awareness that another person exists and is present.

reflected appraisal The image and estimate of ourselves that others communicate to us.

reframing One of four responses to relationship dialectics; transcends the apparent contradiction between two dialectical poles and reinterprets them as not in tension.

regulative rules Communication rules that regulate interaction by specifying when, how, where, and with whom to talk about certain things.

relationship culture A private world of rules, understandings, and patterns of acting and interpreting that partners create to give meaning to their relationship; the nucleus of intimacy.

relationship dialectics The tensions between opposing forces or tendencies that are normal parts of all relationships: autonomy/connection, novelty/predictability, and openness/closedness.

relationship level of meaning One of two levels of meaning in communication; expresses the relationship between communicators.

relationship listening Listening to support another person or to understand how another person thinks, feels, or perceives some situation, event, or other phenomenon.

remembering The process of recalling what one has heard; the sixth element of listening.

reprimand interview An interview conducted by a supervisor to identify lapses in a subordinate's professional conduct, to determine sources of problems, and to establish a plan for improving future performance.

resistance A response to cultural diversity; attacking the cultural practices of others or proclaiming that one's own cultural traditions are superior.

respect A response to cultural diversity in which one values others' customs, traditions, and values even if one does not actively incorporate them into one's life.

responding Symbolizing interest in what is being said with observable feedback to speakers during interaction; the fifth of six elements of listening.

rite A dramatic, planned set of activities that brings together aspects of cultural ideology in a single event.

ritual A form of regularly occurring communication that members of an organization perceive as a familiar, routine part of organizational life and that communicates a particular value or role definition.

role The responsibilities and behaviors expected of a person by virtue of his or her position.

rules Patterned ways of behaving and interpreting behavior. All relationships develop rules.

schemata Cognitive structures we use to organize and interpret experiences. The four types of schemata are prototypes, personal constructs, stereotypes, and scripts. (Singular: *schema*)

script One of four cognitive schemata; scripts define expected or appropriate sequences of action in particular settings.

secure attachment One of the four styles of attachment; a style fostered by a caregiver who communicates with an infant in consistently loving and attentive ways and which inclines people to view themselves and others as worthy and to be comfortable both alone and in intimate relationships.

segmentation One of four responses to relationship dialectics; segmentation responses meet one dialectical need while ignoring or not satisfying the contradictory dialectical need.

selective listening Focusing only on selected parts of communication; e.g., screening out parts of a message that don't interest us or with which we disagree, or riveting our attention on parts of communication that interest us or with which we agree.

self A multidimensional process that involves forming and acting from social perspectives that arise and evolve in communication with others and ourselves.

self-disclosure The revelation of personal information about ourselves that others are unlikely to discover in other ways.

self-fulfilling prophecy Acting in ways that bring about others' or our own expectations or judgments of ourselves.

self-sabotage Self-talk that communicates that we are no good, that we can't do something, that we can't change, and so forth; undermines belief in ourselves and motivation to change and grow.

self-serving bias The tendency to attribute our positive actions and successes to stable, global, internal influences that we control and to attribute negative actions and failures to unstable, specific, external influences beyond our control.

separation One of four responses to relationship dialectics, in which friends or romantic partners assign one pole of a dialectic to certain spheres of activities or topics and assign the contradictory dialectical pole to distinct spheres of activities or topics.

silence Lack of sound. Silence can be a powerful form of nonverbal communication.

skills training A method of reducing communication apprehension that assumes that anxiety results from lack of speaking skills and thus can be reduced by learning skills.

social climbing The attempt to increase personal status in a group by winning the approval of high-status members.

social community A group of people who live within a dominant culture yet also belong to another social group or groups that share values, understandings, and practices distinct from those of the dominant culture.

social comparison Comparing ourselves with others to form judgments of our talents, abilities, qualities, and so forth.

social loafing Exists when members of a group exert less effort than they would if they worked alone.

social relationship Replaceable relationships that tend to follow broad social scripts and rules and in which participants tend to assume conventional social roles in relation to one another. Contrast with *personal relationship*.

specific purpose What a speaker aims to accomplish by presenting a speech; often called *behavioral objectives*.

speech to entertain A speech intended to amuse, interest, and engage listeners.

speech to inform A speech intended to increase listeners' understanding, awareness, or knowledge of some topic.

speech to persuade A speech intended to change listeners' attitudes, beliefs, or behaviors or to motivate listeners to action.

spyware Software that allows a third party to track computer users' web activity, to collect personal information about users, and to send pop-up ads tailored to users' profiles. Spyware is often bundled without users' knowledge into software that can be downloaded for free.

standpoint The social, symbolic, and material conditions common to a group of people that influence how they understand themselves, others, and society.

standpoint theory A theory that holds that a culture includes a number of social groups that differently shape the perceptions, identities, and opportunities of members of those groups.

static evaluation An assessment that suggests that something is unchanging or static; e.g., "Bob is impatient."

statistics A form of evidence that uses numbers to summarize a great many individual cases or to demonstrate relationships between phenomena.

stereotype A predictive generalization about people or situations.

storge One of six styles of loving; based on friendship; even-keeled.

stress interview A style of interviewing in which the interviewer deliberately attempts to create anxiety in the interviewee.

structure An organized relationship and interaction between members of an organization. Structures include roles, rules, policies, and communication networks.

symbols An arbitrary, ambiguous, and abstract representation of a phenomenon. Symbols are the basis of language, much nonverbal behavior, and human thought.

synergy A special kind of collaborative vitality that enhances the energies, talents, and strengths of individual members.

system A group of interrelated elements that affect one another. Communication is systemic.

systematic desensitization A method of reducing communication apprehension that first teaches people how to relax physiologically and then helps them practice feeling relaxed as they imagine themselves in progressively more difficult communication situations.

task communication One of three constructive forms of participation in group decision making; focuses on giving and analyzing information and ideas.

team A special kind of group characterized by different and complementary resources of members and by a strong sense of collective identity. All teams are groups, but not all groups are teams.

teleconferencing Meetings, formal or informal, conducted among people who are geographically separated; can take several forms that differ in the extent to which they emulate face-to-face meetings.

terminal credibility The cumulative expertise and trustworthiness listeners attribute to a speaker as a result of initial and derived credibility; may be greater or less than initial credibility, depending on how effectively a speaker has communicated.

thesis statement The main idea of an entire speech; should capture the key message in a concise sentence that listeners can remember easily.

tolerance A response to diversity in which one accepts differences, although one may not approve of or even understand them.

totalizing Responding to a person as if one aspect of that person were the total of who the person is.

transition A word, phrase, or sentence that connects ideas and main points in a speech so that listeners can follow a speaker.

triangulation Studying phenomena from multiple points of view by relying on multiple sources of data, theories, researchers, and/or methodological approaches.

turning point Particular experiences and events that cause relationships to become more or less intimate.

uncertainty avoidance Dimension of culture that refers to the extent to which people want to avoid ambiguity and vagueness.

uncertainty reduction theory The theory that people find uncertainty uncomfortable and so are motivated to use communication to reduce uncertainty.

understanding A response to cultural diversity that assumes that differences are rooted in cultural teachings and that no traditions, customs, or behaviors are intrinsically better than others.

upper A person who communicates positive messages about us and our worth.

uses and gratification theory Claims people use mass communication to gratify their interests and desires.

verbal communication Words and only words; does not include inflection, accent, volume, pitch, or other paralinguistic features of speech.

visual aid A visual image, such as a chart, graph, photograph, or physical object, that reinforces ideas presented verbally or provides information.

vulture A person who attacks a person's self-esteem; may attack others or himself or herself.

Wi-Fi A wireless means of connecting devices to the Internet and to each other.

win–lose One of three orientations toward conflict; assumes that in any conflict one person wins and the others lose.

win–win One of three orientations to conflict; assumes that everyone involved in a conflict can win and attempts to bring about a mutually satisfying solution.

workplace bullying Recurring hostile behaviors used by people with greater power against people with lesser power.

you-**language** Language that attributes intentions and motives to another person, usually the person to whom one is speaking. (Compare with *I*-language.)

References

Acitelli, L. (1993). You, me, and us: Perspectives on relationship awareness. In S. W. Duck (Ed.), *Understanding relationship processes, 1: Individuals in relationships* (pp. 144–174). Thousand Oaks, CA: Sage.

Acker, J. (2005). *Class questions: Feminist answers.* Lanham, MD: Rowman & Littlefield.

Ackerman, D. (1990). *A natural history of the senses.* New York: Random House.

Adler, J. (2007, March 12). The great sorority purge. *Newsweek*, p. 47.

Afifi, W., & Metts, S. (1998). Characteristics and consequences of expectation violations in three close relationships. *Journal of Social and Personal Relationships, 15,* 365–392.

Agyeman, J. (2007). Communicating "just sustainability." *Environmental Communication, 1,* 119–122.

Alcoff, L. (1991, Winter). The problem of speaking for others. *Cultural Critique, 5–32.*

Allen, B. (2006). Communicating race at WeighCo. In J. T. Wood & S. W. Duck (Eds.), *Composing relationships: Communication in everyday life* (pp. 146–155). Belmont, CA: Thomson Wadsworth.

Allen, M., Hunter, J., & Donahue, W. (1989). Meta-analysis of self-report data on the effectiveness of public speaking anxiety treatment techniques. *Communication Education, 38,* 54–76.

Alter, J. (2009, January 12). Don't muffle the call to serve. *Newsweek*, p. 48.

Altheide, D. (1974). *Creating reality.* Thousand Oaks, CA: Sage.

Altman, L. K. (2008, August 3). HIV estimates low, CDC study shows. *Raleigh News & Observer*, p. 4A.

American Social Health Association. (2005). *State of the nation 2005: Challenges facing STD prevention in youth.* Retrieved September 1, 2006, from http://www.ashastd.org/learn/learn_overview.cfm.

The Amish flock to small business. (2009, January 9). *New York Times*, p. A3.

Andersen, P. (1999). *Nonverbal communication: Forms and functions.* Mountain View, CA: Mayfield.

Andersen, P., Hecht, M., Hoobler, G., & Smallwood, M. (2002). Nonverbal communication across cultures. In W. Gudykunst & B. Mody (Eds.), *The handbook of international and intercultural communication* (2nd ed., pp. 89–106). Thousand Oaks, CA: Sage.

Anderson, R., Baxter, L., & Cissna, K. (Eds.). (2004). *Dialogue: Theorizing difference in communication studies.* Thousand Oaks, CA: Sage.

Anderson, R., & Killenberg, G. (1999). *Interviewing: Speaking, listening, and learning for professional life.* Mountain View, CA: Mayfield.

Anderson, T., & Emmers-Sommer, T. (2006). Predictors of relationship satisfaction in online romantic relationships. *Communication Studies, 17,* 152–172.

Angelou, M. (1991). *I shall not be moved.* New York: Random House.

Angier, N. (2008, August 5). The nose, an emotional time machine. *New York Times*, pp. D1, D4.

Anzaldúa, G. (1999). *Borderlands/la frontera: The new mestiza.* San Francisco: Spinsters/Aunt Lute.

Argyle, M., & Henderson, M. (1984). The rules of friendship. *Journal of Social and Personal Relationships, 1,* 211–237.

Argyle, M., & Henderson, M. (1985). The rules of relationships. In S. W. Duck & D. Perlman (Eds.), *Understanding personal relationships: An interdisciplinary approach* (pp. 63–84). Thousand Oaks, CA: Sage.

Arnett, R. (2004). A dialogic ethic "between" Buber and Levinas: A responsive ethical "I." In R. Anderson, L. Baxter, & K. Cissna, (Eds.), *Dialogue: Theorizing difference in communication studies* (pp. 75–90). Thousand Oaks, CA: Sage.

Arnold, H., & Feldman, D. (1986). *Organizational behavior.* New York: McGraw-Hill.

Ashcraft, K., & Mumby, D. (2004). *Reworking gender: A feminist communicology of organization.* Thousand Oaks, CA: Sage.

Atkinson, P., & Housley, W. (2003). *Interactionism: An essay in sociological amnesia.* Thousand Oaks, CA: Sage.

Atsuko, A. (2003). Gender differences in interpersonal distance: From the viewpoint of oppression hypothesis. *Japanese Journal of Experimental Social Psychology, 42,* 201–218.

Axtell, R. (1998). *Gestures: The dos and taboos of body language around the world.* New York: Wiley.

Axtell, R. (2007). *Essential do's and taboos: The complete guide to international business and leisure travel.* New York: Wiley.

Ayres, J., & Hopf, T. S. (1990). The long-term effect of visualization in the classroom: A brief research report. *Communication Education, 39,* 75–78.

Bailey, A. (1998, February 29). Daily bread. *The Durham Herald–Sun*, p. C5.

Bakalar, N. (2006, May 16). Link is cited between smell and sexuality. *New York Times*, p. D5.

Balcetis, E., & Dunning, D. (2010). Wishful seeing: Desirable objects are seen as closer. *Psychological Science, 21,* 147–152.

Banse, R. (2004). Adult attachment and marital satisfaction: Evidence for dyadic configuration effects. *Journal of Social and Personal Relationships, 21,* 273–282.

Barash, S. (2006). *Tripping the prom queen.* New York: St. Martin's Griffin.

Barge, K. (2009). Social groups, workgroups, and teams. In W. F. Eadie (Ed.), *21st century communication: A reference handbook* (pp. 340–348). Thousand Oaks, CA: Sage.

Bargh, J. (1997). *The automaticity of everyday life.* Mahwah, NJ: Erlbaum.

Bargh, J. (1999, January 29). The most powerful manipulative messages are hiding in plain sight. *Chronicle of Higher Education,* p. B6.

Barker, L., & Watson, K. (2000). *Listen up: How to improve relationships, reduce stress, and be more productive by using the power of listening.* New York: St. Martin's Press.

Barrett, J. & Springen, K. (2007, December 24). Mommy has a makeover. *Newsweek,* p. 18.

Bartholomew, K., & Horowitz, L. M. (1991). Attachment styles among young adults: A test of a four-category model. *Journal of Personality and Social Psychology, 61,* 226–244.

Bateson, M. C. (1990). *Composing a life.* New York: Penguin/Plume.

Battaglia, D., Richard, F., Datter, D., & Lord, C. (1998). Breaking up is (relatively) easy to do: A script for the dissolution of close relationships. *Journal of Social and Personal Relationships, 15,* 829–845.

Baum, B. (2008). *The rise and fall of the Caucasian race: A political history of racial identity.* New York: New York University Press.

Baxter, L. A. (1984). Trajectories of relationship disengagement. *Journal of Social and Personal Relationships, 7,* 141–178.

Baxter, L. A. (1985). Accomplishing relational disengagement. In S. Duck & D. Perlman (Eds.), *Understanding personal relationships: An interdisciplinary approach* (pp. 243–265). Thousand Oaks, CA: Sage.

Baxter, L. A. (1990). Dialectical contradictions in relational development. *Journal of Social and Personal Relationships, 7,* 69–88.

Baxter, L. A. (1993). The social side of personal relationships: A dialectical perspective. In S. Duck (Ed.), *Understanding relationship processes, 3: Social context and relationships* (pp. 139–165). Thousand Oaks, CA: Sage.

Baxter, L. A. (2006). Relational dialectics theory: Multivocal dialogues of family communication. In D. O. Braithwaite & L. A. Baxter (Eds.), *Engaging theories in family communication: Multiple perspectives* (pp. 130–145). Thousand Oaks, CA: Sage.

Baxter, L. A. (2010). *Voicing relationships.* Thousand Oaks, CA: Sage.

Baxter, L. A., & Beebe, E. (2004). *The basics of communication research.* Belmont, CA: Wadsworth.

Baxter, L. A., & Bullis, C. (1986). Turning points in developing romantic relationships. *Human Communication Research, 12,* 469–493.

Baxter, L. A., & Montgomery, B. (1996). *Relating: Dialogues and dialectics.* New York: Guilford.

Baxter, L. A., & Simon, E. P. (1993). Relationship maintenance strategies and dialectical contradictions in personal relationships. *Journal of Social and Personal Relationships, 10,* 225–242.

Bazar, E. (2007, April 24). Stalking "definitely a problem" for women at college. *USA Today,* p. 5A.

Beatty, M. J., & Behnke, R. R. (1991). Effects of public speaking trait anxiety and intensity of speaking task on heart rate during performance. *Human Communication Research, 18,* 147–176.

Becker, A., Burwell, R., Gilman, S., Herzog, D., & Hamburg, P. (2002). Eating behaviours and attitudes following prolonged exposure to television among ethnic Fijian adolescent girls. *British Journal of Psychiatry, 180,* 509–514.

Beckman, H. (2003). Difficult patients. In M. Feldman & J. Christensen (Eds.), *Behavioral medicine in primary care* (pp. 23–32). New York: McGraw-Hill.

Begley, S. (2009, February 16). Will the BlackBerry sink the presidency? *Newsweek,* pp. 36–39.

Behnke, R., & Sawyer, C. (1999). Milestones of anticipatory public speaking anxiety. *Communication Education, 48,* 164–172.

Bell, A. (1989). *The complete manager's guide to interviewing.* Homewood, IL: Dow Jones–Irwin.

Belluck, P. (2009, January 6). Creative lift? Find blue room. Better accuracy? Go with red. *New York Times,* pp. A1, A17.

Belsky, J., & Pensky, E. (1988). Developmental history, personality, and family relationships: Toward an emergent family system. In R. A. Hinde & J. Stevenson-Hinde (Eds.), *Relationships within families: Mutual influences* (pp. 193–217). Oxford, UK: Clarendon.

Benenson, J., Gordon, A., & Roy, R. (2000). Children's evaluative appraisals of competition in tetrads versus dyads. *Small Group Research, 31,* 635–652.

Bergen, K., & Braithwaite, D. O. (2009). Identity as constituted in communication. In W. F. Eadie (Ed.), *21st century communication: A reference handbook* (pp. 166–173). Thousand Oaks, CA: Sage.

Berger, C. (1988). Communicating under uncertainty. In M. Roloff & G. Miller (Eds.), *Interpersonal processes: New directions in communication research* (pp. 39–62). Newbury Park, CA: Sage.

Berger, C. K. (1977). The covering law perspective as a theoretical basis for the study of human communication. *Communication Quarterly, 25,* 7–18.

Berger, P. (1969). *A rumor of angels: Modern society and the rediscovery of the supernatural.* New York: Doubleday.

Bergner, R. M., & Bergner, L. L. (1990). Sexual misunderstanding: A descriptive and pragmatic formulation. *Psychotherapy, 27,* 464–467.

Berne, E. (1964). *Games people play.* New York: Grove Press.

Bertman, S. (1998). *Hyperculture: The human cost of speed.* Westport, CT: Praeger.

Beukeboom, C. (2009). "When words feel right: How affective expressions of listeners change a speaker's language use." *European Journal of Social Psychology, 39,* 747–756.

Bevan, J. (2003). Expectancy violation theory and sexual resistance in close, cross-sex relationships. *Communication Monographs, 70,* 68–82.

Bilefsky, D. (2008, June 25). Albanian Custom Fades: Woman as Family Man http://www.nytimes.com/ 2008/06/25/world/europe/25virgins.html?ex=1372132800&en=8668ba514ff6f5fd&ei=5124&partner=permalink&exprod=permalink accessed July 7, 2008.

Bippus, A., & Daly, J. (1999). What do people think causes stage fright? Naïve attributions about the reasons for public speaking anxiety. *Communication Education, 48,* 63–72.

Birdwhistell, R. (1970). *Kinesics and context.* Philadelphia: University of Pennsylvania Press.

Blanchard, K. (2003). *Servant leader.* Nashville, TN: Thomas Nelson.

Blow, C. M. (2009, February 21). A nation of cowards? *New York Times,* p. A17.

Bocella, K. (2001, January 31). Eating disorders spread among minority girls, women. *Raleigh News & Observer,* p. 5E.

Bodey, K. (2009). *Exploring the possibilities of self work: girls speak about their lives.* Ph.D. Dissertation. Department of Communication Studies. The University of North Carolina at Chapel Hill.

Bodey, K. R., & Wood, J. T. (2009). Whose voices count and who does the counting? *Southern Communication Journal, 74,* 325–337.

Bohill,, C., Owen, C., Jeong, E., Alicea, B., & Bocca, F. (2009). Virtual reality. In W. F. Eadie (Ed.), *21st century communication: A reference handbook* (pp. 534–542). Thousand Oaks, CA: Sage.

Bolkan, S., & Daly, J. (2009). Organizational responses to consumer complaints: An examination of effective remediation. *Journal of Applied Communication Research, 37,* 21–39.

Borchers, T. (2006). *Rhetorical theory: An introduction.* Belmont, CA: Thomson Wadsworth.

Boulding, K. (1990). *Three faces of power.* Thousand Oaks, CA: Sage.

Bourhis, J., & Allen, M. (1992). Meta-analysis of the relationship between communication apprehension and cognitive performance. *Communication Education, 41,* 68–76.

Bowlby, J. (1973). *Separation: Attachment and loss* (Vol. 2). New York: Basic Books.

Bowlby, J. (1988). *A secure base: Parent–child attachment and healthy human development.* New York: Basic Books.

Bracken, C. C., & Skalski, P. (Eds.). (2009). *Immersed in media: Telepresence in everyday life.* New York: Routledge.

Bradbury, T. N., & Fincham, F. D. (1990). Attributions in marriage: Review and critique. *Psychological Bulletin, 107,* 3–33.

Braithwaite, C. (1990). Communicative silence: A crosscultural study of Basso's hypothesis. In D. Carbaugh (Ed.), *Cultural communication and intercultural contact* (pp. 321–327). Hillsdale, NJ: Erlbaum.

Braithwaite, D. W., Bach, B. W., Baxter, L. A., Diverniero, R., Hammonds, J. R., Hosek, A. M., Willer, E. K., & Wolf, B. M. (2010). Constructing family: A typology of voluntary kin. *Journal of Social and Personal Relationships, 27,* 388–407.

Braithwaite, S. R., Delevi, R., & Fincham, F. D. (2010). Romantic relationships and the physical and mental health of college students. *Personal Relationships, 17,* 1–12.

Brilhart, J., & Galanes, G. (1995). *Effective group discussion* (8th ed.). Dubuque, IA: WCB Brown & Benchmark.

Brooks, D. (2001, April 30). Time to do everything except think. *Newsweek,* p. 71.

Brooks, D. (2010, February 16). The lean years. *New York Times,* p. A23.

Brooks, R., & Goldstein, S. (2001). *Raising resilient children.* New York: Contemporary Books.

Brown, J., & Cantor, J. (2000). An agenda for research on youth and the media. *Journal of Adolescent Health, 27,* 2–7.

Brownell, J. (2002). *Listening: Attitudes, principles, and skills* (2nd ed.). Boston: Allyn & Bacon.

Browning, L., Saetre, A., Stephens, K., & Sornes, J. (2008). *Information and communication technologies in action.* New York: Routledge.

Bruess, C. (2011). Yard sales and yellow roses: rituals in enduring relationships. In D. O. Braithwaite & J. T. Wood (Eds.), *Casing interpersonal communication* (pp. 131–138). Dubuque, IA: Kendall Hunt.

Bruess, C., & Hoefs, A. (2006). The cat puzzle recovered: Composing relationships through family ritual. In J. T. Wood & S. W. Duck (Eds.), *Composing relationships: Communication in everyday life* (pp. 65–75). Belmont, CA: Thomson Wadsworth.

Brunsma, D. L. (Ed.). (2006). *Mixed messages: Multiracial identities in the "color-blind" era.* Boulder CO: Lynne Reinner.

Bryant, J., & Oliver, M. B. (Eds.). (2008). *Media effects* (3rd ed.). New York: Routledge.

Buber, M. (1957). Distance and relation. *Psychiatry, 20,* 97–104.

Buber, M. (1970). *I and thou* (Walter Kaufmann, Trans.). New York: Scribner's.

Buckley, M. F. (1992). Focus on research: We listen a book a day; we speak a book a week: Learning from Walter Loban. *Language Arts, 69,* 622–626.

Bucy, E. (Ed.). (2005). *Living in the information age* (2nd ed.). Belmont, CA: Wadsworth.

Bulletin from the Future (2011, July 9). *The Economist,* pp. 1–16 (Special report within the July 9–15 issue).

Burgoon, J. (1993). Interpersonal expectations, expectation violations, and emotional communication. *Journal of Language and Social Psychology, 12,* 30–48.

Burgoon, J., Buller, D., & Woodhall, G. (1989). *Nonverbal communication: The unspoken dialogue.* New York: Harper & Row.

Burleson, B. R., & Rack, J. (2008). Constructivism theory. In L. A. Baxter & D. O. Braithwaite (Eds.), *Engaging theories in interpersonal communication: Multiple perspectives* (pp. 51–63). Thousand Oaks, CA: Sage.

Buss, A. H. (2001). *Psychological dimensions of the self.* Thousand Oaks, CA: Sage.

Butler, J. (1990). Performative acts and gender constitution: An essay in phenomenology and feminist theory. In S. Case (Ed.), *Performing feminisms: Feminist critical theory and theatre* (pp. 270–282). Baltimore: Johns Hopkins University Press.

Butler, J. (1993). *Bodies that matter: On the discursive limits of "sex."* New York: Routledge.

Buunk, B., Groothof, H. & Siero, F. (2007). Social comparison and satisfaction with one's social life. *Journal of Social and Personal Relationships, 24,*197–205.

Calero, H. (2005). *The power of nonverbal communication: What you do is more important than what you say.* Los Angeles: Silver Lake.

Campbell, K. (1989). *Man cannot speak for her: II. Key texts of the early feminists.* New York: Greenwood.

Campbell, R., Martin, C., & Fabos, B. (2004). *Media and culture: An introduction to mass communication.* Boston: Bedford/ St. Martin's.

Canary, D., & Stafford, L. (Eds.). (1994). *Communication and relational maintenance.* New York: Academic Press.

Canary, D., & Wahba, J. (2006). Do women work harder than men at maintaining relationships? In K. Dindia & D. Canary (Eds.), *Sex differences and similarities in communication* (2nd ed., pp. 359–377). Mahwah, NJ: Erlbaum.

Cancer. (2009, September 1). *New York Times,* p. D6.

Cancian, F. (1989). Love and the rise of capitalism. In B. Risman & P. Schwartz (Eds.), *Gender in intimate relationships* (pp. 12–25). Belmont, CA: Wadsworth.

Cannell, C., & Kahn, R. (1968). Interviewing. In G. Lindzey & E. Aronson (Eds.), *The handbook of social psychology* (Vol. 2, 2nd ed., pp. 569–584). Reading, MA: Addison-Wesley.

Carbaugh, D. (1998). "I can't do that! But I can actually see around the corners": American Indian students and the study of public communication. In J. Martin, T. Nakayama, & L. Flores (Eds.), *Readings in cultural context* (pp. 160–171). Mountain View, CA: Mayfield.

Carbaugh, D., & Buzzanell, P. M. (2009). *Distinctive qualities of communication research.* New York: Routledge.

Carl, W. (1998). A sign of the times. In J. T. Wood, *But I thought you meant…: Misunderstandings in human communication* (pp. 195–208). Mountain View, CA: Mayfield.

Carnes, J. (1994, Spring). An uncommon language. *Teaching tolerance,* pp. 56–63.

Carter, N. M., & Silva, C. (2010). *Broken promises.* New York: Catalyst.

Cassirer, E. (1944). *An essay on man.* New Haven, CT: Yale University Press.

Cates, J. R., Herndon, N. L., Schultz, S. L., & Darroch, J. E. (2004). *Our voices, our lives, our futures: Youth and sexually transmitted diseases.* Chapel Hill: University of North Carolina at Chapel Hill.

Caughlin, J., Afifi, W., Carpenter-Theune, K., & Miller, L. (2005). Reasons for, and consequences of, revealing personal secrets in close relationships: A longitudinal study. *Personal Relationships, 12,* 43–59.

Caughlin, J., & Ramey, M. (2005). The demand/withdraw pattern of communication in parent–adolescent dyads. *Personal Relationships, 12,* 337–355.

Caughlin, J., & Vangelisti, A. (2000). An individual differences explanation of why married couples engage in the demand/withdraw pattern of conflict. *Journal of Social and Personal Relationships, 17,* 523–551.

Centers for Disease Control and Prevention. (2009). *STD surveillance 2009.* Retrieved July 1, 2011 from http://www.cdc.gov/std/stats09/chlamydia.htm

Centers for Disease Control and Prevention (2011). HIV/AIDS. Retrieved June 27, 2011 from http://www.cdc.gov/hiv/default.htm

Chan, Y. (1999). Density, crowding, and factors intervening in their relationship: Evidence from a hyperdense metropolis. *Social Indicators Research, 48,* 103–134.

Chen, V., & Starosta, W. (1998). *Foundations of intercultural communication.* Boston: Allyn & Bacon.

Cherlin, A. J. (2010). *The marriage go-round: The state of marriage and the family in America today.* New York: Vintage.

Chethik, N. (2008). *VoiceMale: What husbands really think about their marriages, their wives, sex, housework and commitment.* New York: Simon & Schuster.

Chodron, T. (2001). *Working with anger.* New York: Snow Lion Publications.

Christensen, A. (2004). *Patient adherence to medical treatment regiment: Bridging the gap between behavioral science and biomedicine.* New Haven, CT: Yale University Press.

Christensen, A., & Heavey, C. (1990). Gender and social structure in the demand/withdraw pattern in marital conflict. *Journal of Personality and Social Psychology, 59,* 73–81.

Christianson, P., & Roberts, D. (1998). *It's not only rock & roll: Popular music in the lives of adolescents.* Cresskill, NJ: Hampton Press.

Cissna, K. N. L., & Sieburg, E. (1986). Patterns of interactional confirmation and disconfirmation. In J. Stewart (Ed.), *Bridges, not walls* (4th ed., pp. 230–239). New York: Random House.

Cloven, D. H., & Roloff, M. E. (1991). Sense-making activities and interpersonal conflict: Communicative cures for the mulling blues. *Western Journal of Speech Communication, 55,* 134–158.

Clydesdale, T. (2009, January 23). Wake up and smell the new epistemology. *Chronicle of Higher Education,* pp. B7–B9.

Cockburn-Wootten, C., & Zorn, T.

(2006). Cabbages and headache cures: Work stories within the family. In J. T. Wood & S. W. Duck (Eds.), *Composing relationships: Communication in everyday life* (pp. 137–145). Belmont, CA: Thomson Wadsworth.

Cohen, P. (2011, July 15). Internet use affects how we remember. *New York Times,* p. A14.

Collier, M. J. (1996). Communication problematics in ethnic friendships. *Communication Monographs, 63,* 314–336.

Conley, D. (2009). *Elsewhere, U.S.A.* New York: Pantheon.

Conrad, C., & Poole, M. (2004). *Strategic organizational communication in a global economy* (7th ed.). New York: Harcourt.

Cooley, C. H. (1912). *Human nature and the social order.* New York: Scribner's.

Coontz, S. (2005b). *Marriage, a history.* New York: Viking Adult.

Coontz, S. (2007, November 26). Taking marriage private. *New York Times,* p. A27.

Cooper, L., Seibold, D., & Suchner, R. (1997). Listening in organizations: An analysis of error structures in models of listening competency. *Communication Research Reports, 14,* 3.

Coopman, S., & Lull, J. (2012). *Public speaking: The evolving art* (2nd 3 ed.). Belmont, CA: Wadsworth/ Cengage.

Cordell, R. (2011, May 13). Resources for teaching with technology. *Chronicle of Higher Education,* p. B10.

Covey, S. (1989). *The seven habits of highly effective people.* New York: Simon and Schuster.

Covey, S. (1992). *Principle-centered leadership.* New York: Fireside Press.

Cox, J. R. (1989). The fulfillment of time: King's "I have a dream" speech (August 28, 1963). In M. C. Leff & F. J. Kaufeld (Eds.), *Texts in context: Critical dialogues on significant episodes in American*

rhetoric (pp. 181–204). Davis, CA: Hermagoras.

Cox, J. R. (2011). Personal communication.

Cox, J. R. (2010). *Environmental communication and the public sphere* (2nd ed.). Thousand Oaks, CA: Sage.

Cox, J. R., & McCloskey, M. (1996). Advocacy and the Istook amendment: Efforts to restrict the civic speech of nonprofit organizations in the 104th U.S. Congress. *Journal of Applied Communication Research, 24,* 273–291.

Crockett, W. H. (1965). Cognitive complexity and impression formation. In B. A. Maher (Ed.), *Progress in experimental personality research* (Vol. 2, pp. 47–90). New York: Academic Press.

Cronen, V., Pearce, W. B., & Snavely, L. (1979). A theory of rule-structure and types of episodes and a study of perceived enmeshment in undesired repetitive patterns ("URPs"). In D. Nimmo (Ed.), *Communication yearbook* (Vol. 3). New Brunswick, NJ: Transaction Books.

Cross, G. (2008). *Men to boys: The making of modern immaturity.* New York: Columbia University Press.

Crowley, G. (1995, March 6). Dialing the stress-meter down. *Newsweek,* p. 62.

Cubbans, L. A., & Vannoy, D. (2004). Division of household labor as a source of contention for married and cohabiting couples in Metropolitan Moscow. *Journal of Family Issues, 25,* 182–185.

Cummings, M. (2009). Ethnicity. In W. F. Eadie (Ed.), *21st century communication: A reference handbook* (pp. 380–387). Thousand Oaks, CA: Sage.

Cyberbullying Research Center. www. cyberbullying.us

Cyphert, D. (2009). Professional communication careers. In W. F. Eadie (Ed.), *21st century communication: A reference handbook* (pp. 506–515). Thousand Oaks, CA: Sage.

Dailey, R. (2006). Confirmation in parent–adolescent relationships and adolescent openness: Toward extending confirmation theory. *Communication Monographs, 73* 434–458.

Dainton, M. (2006). Cat walk conversations: Everyday communication in dating relationships. In J. T. Wood & S. W. Duck (Eds.), *Composing relationships: Communication in everyday life.* Belmont, CA: Thomson Wadsworth.

Dainton, M., & Zelley, E. (2006). Social exchange theories: Interdependence and equity. In D. O. Braithwaite & L. A. Baxter (Eds.), *Engaging theories in family communication: Multiple perspectives* (pp. 243–259). Thousand Oaks, CA: Sage.

Darling, A., & Dannels, D. (2003). Practicing engineers talk about the importance of talk: A report on the role of oral communication in the workplace. *Communication Education, 52,* 1–16.

Darnton, R. (2011, April 22). 5 myths of the 'information age.' *Chronicle of Higher Education,* pp. B9–B10.

Davies-Popelka, W. (2011). Mirror, mirror on the wall: Weight, identity, and self-talk. In D. O. Braithwaite & J. T. Wood (Eds.), *Casing interpersonal communication* (pp. 25–32). Dubuque, IA: Kendall Hunt.

Davis, R. (1997). *The myth of black ethnicity: Monophylety, diversity, and the dilemma of identity.* Greenwich, CT: Ablex.

Davis, S., & Kieffer, J. (1998). Restaurant servers influence tipping behaviors. *Psychological Reports, 83,* 223–236.

Davison, K., & Birch, L. (2001). Weight, status, parent reaction, and self-concept in five-year-old girls. *Pediatrics, 107,* 42–53.

Deal, T., & Kennedy, A. (1999). *The new corporate cultures: Revitalizing the workplace*

after downsizing, mergers, and reengineering. Reading, MA: Perseus Books.

DeCremer, D., & Leonardelli, G. J. (2003). Group dynamics. *Theory, Research, and Practice, 7,* 168–174.

DeFrancisco, V. (1991). The sounds of silence: How men silence women in marital relations. *Discourse & Society, 2,* 413–423.

Delbecq, A. L. and VandeVen, A. H, (1971). "A group process model for problem identification and program planning," *Journal of Applied Behavioral Science, 7,* 466–91.

Delgado, F. (1998). Moving beyond the screen: Hollywood and Mexican American stereotypes. In Y. Kamalipour & T. Carilli (Eds.), *Cultural diversity in the U.S. media* (pp. 169–182). Albany: State University of New York Press.

Delia, J., Clark, R. A., & Switzer, D. (1974). Cognitive complexity and impression formation in informal social interaction. *Speech Monographs, 41,* 299–308.

DeMaris, A. (2007). The role of relationship inequity in marital disruption. *Journal of Social and Personal Relationships, 24,* 177–195.

Demographics. (2009, January 26). *Newsweek,* p. 70.

Derlega, V. J., & Berg, J. H. (1987). *Self-disclosure: Research, theory, and therapy.* New York: Plenum.

Derlega, V. J., Metts, S., Petronio, S., & Margulis, S. (1993). *Self-disclosure.* Thousand Oaks, CA: Sage.

Desjardins, M. (2006). Ephemeral culture/eBay culture: Film collectibles and fan investments. In K. Hillis & M. Petit, with N. Epley (Eds.), *Everyday eBay: Culture, collecting, and desire* (pp. 31–43). New York: Routledge.

Dewey, J. (1910). *How we think.* Boston: Heath.

Dickson, F. (1995). The best is yet to be: Research on long-lasting marriages. In J. T. Wood & S. W. Duck (Eds.), *Understanding relationship processes, 6:*

Understudied relationships (pp. 22–50). Thousand Oaks, CA: Sage.

Did you know? (1998, September 30). *Raleigh News & Observer,* p. F1.

Dillard, J. P., & Pfau, M. (2002). *The persuasion handbook: Developments in theory and practice.* Thousand Oaks, CA: Sage.

Dillon, J. (1990). *The practice of questioning.* New York: Routledge.

Dindia, K. (1994). A multiphasic view of relationship maintenance strategies. In D. Canary & L. Stafford (Eds.), *Communication and relational maintenance* (pp. 91–112). New York: Academic Press.

Dindia, K. (2000). Self-disclosure, identity, and relationship development. In K. Dindia & S. W. Duck (Eds.), *Communication and personal relationships* (pp. 147–162). Chichester, UK: Wiley.

Dixson, M., & Duck, S. W. (1993). Understanding relationship processes: Uncovering the human search for meaning. In S. W. Duck (Ed.), *Understanding relationship processes, 1: Individuals in relationships* (pp. 175–206). Thousand Oaks, CA: Sage.

Domingue, R., & Mollen, D. (2009). Attachment and conflict communication in adult romantic relationships. *Journal of Social and Personal Relationships, 26,* 678–696.

Donahue, H., Leonard, J., & Williams, M. (Writers/Directors/Producers). (1999). *The Blair Witch Project* [Motion picture]. United States: Artisan Entertainment.

Douglas, S. (2004, May 10). Confronting the mommy myth. *In These Times,* pp. 28–29.

Douglas, S. (2004b, July 19). We are what we watch. *In These Times,* p. 14.

Dowling, R. (2009). The business of journalism. In W. F. Eadie (Ed.), *21st century communication: A reference handbook* (pp. 679–686). Thousand Oaks, CA: Sage.

Dreyfus, H. L. (2008). *On the Internet* (2nd ed.). New York: Routledge.

Drummond, K., & Hopper, R. (1993). Acknowledgment tokens in series. *Communication Reports, 6*, 47–53.

Dubrofsky, R. E., & Hardy, A. (2008). Performing race in Flavor of Love and The Bachelor. *Critical Studies in Media Communication, 25*, 373–392.

Duck, S. W. (1992). *Human relationships* (2nd ed.). Thousand Oaks, CA: Sage.

Duck, S. W. (2006). The play, playfulness and the players: Everyday interaction as improvised rehearsal of relationships. In J. T. Wood & S. W. Duck (Eds.), *Composing relationships: Communication in everyday life* (pp. 15–23). Belmont, CA: Wadsworth.

Duck, S. W., & McMahon, D. T. (2009). *The basics of communication: A relational perspective.* Thousand Oaks, CA: Sage.

Duck, S. W., & Wood, J. T. (Eds.). (1995). *Understanding relationship processes, 5: Confronting relationship challenges.* Thousand Oaks, CA: Sage.

Duck, S. W., & Wood, J. T. (2006). What goes up may come down: Sex and gendered patterns in relational dissolution. In M. A. Fine & J. H. Harvey (Eds.), *The handbook of divorce and relationship dissolution* (pp. 169–187). Mahwah, NJ: Erlbaum.

Eagly, A. H., Johannesen-Schmidt, & van Engen, M. L. (2003). Transformational, transactional, and laissez-faire leadership styles: A meta-analysis comparing women and men. *Psychological Bulletin, 108*, 233–256.

Eastman, S., & Billings, A. (2000). Sportscasting and news reporting: The power of gender bias. *Journal of Sport and Social Issues, 24*, 192–213.

Egan, G. (1973). Listening as empathic support. In J. Stewart (Ed.), *Bridges, not walls.* Reading, MA: Addison-Wesley.

Ellis, A., & Harper, R. (1977). *A new guide to rational living.* North Hollywood, CA: Wilshire.

Emmons, S. (1998, February 3). The look on his face: Yes, it's culture shock. *Raleigh News & Observer,* p. 5E.

Engen, D. (2012). Invisible identities: Notes on class and race. In A. González, M. Houston, & V. Chen (Eds.), *Our voices: Essays in culture, ethnicity, and communication* (pp. 233–239). New York: Oxford University Press.

Erbert, L. (2000). Conflict and dialectics: Perceptions of dialectical contradictions in marital conflict. *Journal of Social and Personal Relationships, 17,* 638–659.

Estes, W. K. (1989). Learning theory. In A. Lessold & R. Glaser (Eds.), *Foundations for a psychology of education.* Mahwah, NJ: Erlbaum.

Estioko-Griffin, A., & Griffin, P. (1997). Woman the hunter: The Agta. In C. Brettell & C. Sargent (Eds.), *Gender in cross-cultural perspectives* (pp.123–149). Englewood Cliffs, NJ: Prentice Hall.

Fackelmann, K. (2006, March 6). Arguing hurts the heart in more ways than one. *USA Today,* p. 10D.

Fehr, B. (1993). How do I love thee? Let me consult my prototype. In S. W. Duck (Ed.), *Understanding relationship processes, 1: Individuals in relationships* (pp. 87–122). Thousand Oaks, CA: Sage.

Feldman, C., & Ridley, C. (2000). The role of conflict-based responses and outcomes in male domestic violence toward female partners. *Journal of Social and Personal Relationships, 17,* 552–573.

Felmlee, D. H. (2001). No couple is an island: A social network perspective on dyadic stability. *Social Forces, 79,* 1259–1287.

Fincham, F. D., & Bradbury, T. N. (1987). The impact of attributions in marriage: A longitudinal analysis. *Journal of Personality and Social Psychology, 53,* 510–517.

Fishman, J. (2011, May 13). The rise of teaching machines. *Chronicle of Higher Education,* pp. B12, B14.

Fiske, J. (1987). *Television culture.* London: Methuen.

Fitzgerald, T. (2006, May 18). Going wireless most places you go. *New York Times,* p. C7.

Fitzpatrick, M. A. (1988). *Between husbands and wives: Communication in marriage.* Thousand Oaks, CA: Sage.

Fleishman, J., Sherbourne, C., & Crystal, S. (2000). Coping, conflictual social interactions, social support, and mood among HIV-infected persons. *American Journal of Community Psychology, 28,* 421–453.

Fletcher, G. J., & Fincham, F. D. (1991). Attribution in close relationships. In G. J. Fletcher & F. D. Fincham (Eds.), *Cognition in close relationships* (pp. 7–35). Mahwah, NJ: Erlbaum.

Flock, E., & Bell, B. (2011, June 13). 'Paula Brooks,' editor of 'Lez Get Real,' also a man. http://www.washingtonpost.com/blogs/blogpost/post/paula-brooks-editor-of-lez-get-real-also-a-man/2011/06/13/AGld2ZTH_blog.html. Accessed June 11, 2011.

Flynn, L. (2006, May 3). A romantic read between cell calls. *New York Times,* p. E3.

Foddy, W. (1993). *Constructing questions for interviews and questionnaires.* Cambridge, UK: Cambridge University Press.

Foeman, A., & Nance, T. (1999). From miscegenation to multiculturalism: Perceptions and stages of interracial relationship development. *Journal of Black Studies, 29,* 540–557.

Fogg, P. (2008, July 25). Thinking in black and white. *Chronicle of Higher Education,* p. B19.

Foss, S., Foss, K., & Trapp, R. (1991). *Contemporary perspectives on rhetoric* (2nd ed.). Prospect Heights, IL: Waveland.

Foucault, M. (1970). *The order of things: An archaeology of the human sciences.* New York: Pantheon.

Foucault, M. (1972a). The discourse on language. In *The archaeology of knowledge* (Sheridan Smith, Trans., pp. 215–237). New York: Pantheon.

Foucault, M. (1972b). In C. Gordon (Ed.), *Power/knowledge: Selected interviews and other writings 1972–1977* (C. Gordon, L. Marshall, J. Mepham, & K. Soper, Trans.). New York: Pantheon.

Foucault, M. (1978). Politics and the study of discourse (C. Gordon, Trans.). *Ideology and Consciousness, 3,* 7–26.

Fox, G. (1998). *Everyday etiquette: A guide to modern manners.* New York: Berkeley Books.

Fox, S. (2011, January 21). Americans living with disabilities and their technology profile. Pew Research Center: http://www.pewinternet .org/Reports/2011/Disability.aspx.

France, D. (2006, January & February). Domestic violence. *AARP Magazine,* pp. 84–85, 112–118.

Franklin, M., & Ramage, J. (1999). Till a long-distance job do us part. *Kiplinger's Personal Finance, 53,* p. 56.

Freeman, J. (2009). *The tyranny of e-mail.* New York: Simon & Schuster/Scribner.

Friedlin. J. (2006, June). "Is it easier to get a gun or a restraining order?" *Marie Claire,* pp. 92–100.

Gabric, D., & McFadden, K. (2001). Student and employer perceptions of desirable entry-level operations management skills. *Mid-American Journal of Business, 16,* 51–59.

Galvin, K. (2006). Gender and family interaction: Dress rehearsal for an improvisation? In B. Dow & J. T. Wood (Eds.), *Handbook of gender and communication research* (pp. 41–55). Thousand Oaks, CA: Sage.

Galvin, K., Dickson, F. & Marrow, S. (2006). Systems theory: Patterns and (w)holes in family communication. In D. O. Braithwaite & L. A. Baxter

(Eds.), *Engaging theories in family communication: Multiple perspectives* (pp. 309–324). Thousand Oaks, CA: Sage.

Gargiulo, T. (2005). *The strategic use of stories in organizational communication and learning.* New York: M. E. Sharpe.

Garner, T. (1994). Oral rhetorical practice in African American culture. In A. Gonzaléz, M. Houston, & V. Chen (Eds.), *Our voices: Essays in culture, ethnicity, and communication* (pp. 81–91). Los Angeles: Roxbury.

Gates, H. L. (1992). *Loose canons: Notes on the culture wars.* New York: Oxford University Press.

Gerbner, G. (1990). Epilogue: Advancing on the path of righteousness (maybe). In N. Signorielli & M. Morgan (Eds.), *Cultivation analysis: New directions in media effects research* (pp. 250–261). Thousand Oaks, CA: Sage.

Gerbner, G., Gross, L., Morgan, M., & Signorielli, N. (1986). Living with television: The dynamics of the cultivation process. In J. Bryant & D. Zillmann (Eds.), *Perspectives on media effects* (pp. 17–40). Mahwah, NJ: Erlbaum.

Gerson, K. (2004). Moral dilemmas, moral strategies, and the transformation of gender: Lessons from two generations of work and family change. In J. Spade & C. Valentine (Eds.), *The kaleidoscope of gender* (pp. 413–424). Belmont, CA: Wadsworth.

Ghanem, S., McCombs, M., & Chernov, G. (2009). Agenda setting and framing. In W. F. Eadie (Ed.), *21st century communication: A reference handbook* (pp. 516–524). Thousand Oaks, CA: Sage.

Gibb, J. R. (1961). Defensive communication. *Journal of Communication, 11,* 141–148.

Gibb, J. R. (1964). Climate for trust formation. In L. Bradford, J. Gibb, & K. Benne (Eds.), *T-group theory and laboratory method* (pp. 279–309). New York: Wiley.

Gibb, J. R. (1970). Sensitivity training as a medium for personal growth and improved interpersonal relationships. *Interpersonal Development, 1,* 6–31.

Gibbs, J., Ellison, N. & Heino, R. (2006). Self-presentation in online personals: The role of anticipated future interaction, self-disclosure, and perceived success in Internet dating. *Communication Research, 33,* 152.

Gill, R. (2008). Empowerment/sexism: Figuring female sexual agency in contemporary advertising. *Feminism & Psychology, 18,* 35–60.

Gilley, B. J. (2006). *Becoming two-spirit: Gay identity and social acceptance in Indian country.* Lincoln: University of Nebraska Press.

Gilster, P. (2011, May 9). Ushered in by the age of Twitter. *Raleigh News & Observer,* p. 1D.

Giroux, H. (2008). *Against the terror of neoliberalism.* Boulder, CO: Paradigm.

Gitlin, T. (1980). *The whole world is watching: Mass media in the making and unmaking of the new left.* Berkeley: University of California Press.

Gitlin, T. (2005). Supersaturation, or the media torrent and disposable feeling. In E. Bucy (Ed.), *Living in the information age: A new media reader* (2nd ed., pp. 139–146). Belmont, CA: Thomson Wadsworth.

Global Mobile Statistics (2011). http://mobithinking.com/ mobile-marketing-tools/ latest-mobile-stats.

Glover, D. & Kaplan, C. (2009). *Genders* (2nd ed.), New York: Routledge.

Goldsmith, D. & Fulfs, P. (1999). You just don't have the evidence: An analysis of claims and evidence in Deborah Tannen's *You Just Don't Understand.* In M. Roloff (Ed.), *Communication yearbook, 22* (pp. 1–49). Thousand Oaks, CA: Sage.

Goleman, D. (2007). *Social intelligence.* New York: Bantam/Dell.

Goleman, D., McKee, A., & Boyatzis, R. (2002). *Primal leadership: Realizing the power of emotional intelligence.* Cambridge, MA: Harvard Business School Press.

González, A. Houston, M., & Chen, V. (Eds.). (2012). *Our voices: Essays in culture, ethnicity, and communication.* New York: Oxford University Press.

Goodall, H., & Trethewey, A. (2009). *Organizational communication: Balancing creativity and constraint.* Boston: Bedford/St. Martin's.

Goodwin, M. H. (2006). *The hidden life of girls.* Maiden, MA: Blackwell Publishing.

Gosling, S. (2008). *Snoop: What your stuff says about you.* New York: Basic Books.

Gottman, J. M. (1993). The roles of conflict engagement, escalation or avoidance in marital interaction: A longitudinal view of five types of couples. *Journal of Consulting and Clinical Psychology, 61,* 6–15.

Gottman, J., & Carrère, S. (1994). Why can't men and women get along? Developmental roots and marital inequities. In D. Canary & J. Stafford (Eds.), *Communication and relational maintenance* (pp. 203–229). New York: Academic Press.

Gottman, J., & DeClaire, J. (2001). *The relationship cure: A five-step guide for building better connections with family, friends, and lovers.* New York: Crown Books.

Graham, J. M., & Conoley, C. (2006). The role of marital attributions in the relationship between life stressors and marital quality. *Personal Relationships, 13,* 231–241.

Greenberg, S. (1997, Spring/Summer Special Issue). The loving ties that bind. *Newsweek,* pp. 68–72.

Greene, K., Derlega, V. J., & Mathews, A. (2006). Self-disclosure in personal relationships. In A. L. Vangelisti & D. Perlman (Eds.). *Cambridge handbook of personal relationships* (pp. 89–104) Cambridge, MA: Cambridge University Press.

Greenleaf, R., Spears, L., & Covey, S. (2002). *Servant leader.* Mahwah, NJ: Paulist Press.

Griffin, C. (2012). *Invitation to public speaking* (4th ed.). Belmont, CA: Wadsworth/Cengage.

Gronbeck, B. E., McKerro, R., Ehninger, D., & Monroe, A. H. (1994). *Principles and types of speech communication* (12th ed.). Glenview, IL: Scott, Foresman.

Groothof, H. A.K, Dijkstra, P., & Bareids, D. P. H. (2009). Differences in jealousy: The case of Internet infidelity. *Journal of Social and Personal Relationships, 26,* 1119–1129.

Gross, N. (1996, December 23). Zap! Splat! Smarts? *Newsweek,* pp. 64–71.

Gudykunst, W. (1995). Anxiety uncertainty management (AUM) theory: Current status. In R. Wiseman (Ed.), *Intercultural communication theory* (pp. 33–71). Newbury Park, CA: Sage.

Gueguen, N., & De Gail, M. (2003). The effect of smiling on helping behavior: Smiling and good Samaritan behavior. *Communication Reports, 16,* 133–140.

Guerrero, L. (1996). Attachment style differences in intimacy and involvement: A test of the four-category model. *Communication Monographs, 63,* 269–292.

Guerrero, L., Andersen, P., & Afifi, W. (2008). *Close encounters: Communication in relationships* (2nd ed.). Thousand Oaks, CA: Sage.

Guerrero, L., & Farinelli, L. (2009). The interplay of verbal and nonverbal codes. In W. F. Eadie (Ed.), *21st century communication: A reference handbook* (pp. 239–248). Thousand Oaks, CA: Sage.

Guerrero, L., & Floyd, K. (2006). *Nonverbal communication in close relationships.* Mahwah, NJ: Erlbaum.

Guerrero, L., Jones, S., & Boburka, R. (2006). Sex differences in emotional communication. In K. Dindia & D. Canary (Eds.), *Sex differences and similarities in communication* (pp. 242–261). Mahwah, MJ: Erlbaum.

Guerrero, L., La Valley, A., & Farinelli, L. (2008). The experience and expression of anger, guilt, and sadness in marriage: An equity theory explanation. *Journal of Social and Personal Relationships, 25,* 699–724.

Gunns, R., Johnston, L., & Hudson, S. (2002). Victim selection and kinematics: A point-light investigation of vulnerability to attack. *Journal of Nonverbal Behavior, 26,* 129–158.

Guterl, F. (2003, September 8). Overloaded? *Newsweek,* pp. E4–E8.

Hall, E. T. (1968). Proxemics. *Current Anthropology, 9,* 83–108.

Hall, E. T. (1969). *The hidden dimension.* New York: Anchor.

Hall, E. T. (1981). *Beyond culture.* New York: Doubleday.

Hall, J. A. (1987). On explaining gender differences: The case of nonverbal communication. In P. Shaver & C. Hendricks (Eds.), *Sex and gender* (pp. 177–200). Thousand Oaks, CA: Sage.

Hall, J. A., Coats, E., & Smith-LeBeau, L. (2004). Nonverbal behavior and the vertical dimension of social relations: A meta-analysis. Cited in M. L. Knapp & J. A. Hall (2006) *Nonverbal communication in human interaction,* 6th ed. Belmont, CA: Thomson Wadsworth.

Hall, S. (1982). The rediscovery of "ideology": Return of the repressed in media studies. In M. Gurevitch, T. Bennett, J. Curran, & J. Woollacott (Eds.), *Culture, society, and the media* (pp. 56–90). London: Methuen.

Hall, S. (1986a). Cultural studies: Two paradigms. In R. Collins (Ed.), *Media, culture, and society: A critical reader.* London: Sage.

Hall, S. (1986b). The problem of ideology: Marxism without guarantees. *Journal of Communication Inquiry, 10,* 28–44.

Hall, S. (1988). *The hard road to renewal: Thatcherism and the crisis on the left.* London: Verso.

Hall, S. (1989a). Ideology. In E. Barnouw et al. (Eds.), *International encyclopedia of communication* (Vol. 2, pp. 307–311). New York: Oxford University Press.

Hall, S. (1989b). Ideology and communication theory. In B. Dervin, L. Grossberg, B. O'Keefe, & E. Wartella (Eds.), *Rethinking communication theory* (Vol. 1, pp. 40–52). Thousand Oaks, CA: Sage.

Halvorson, H. (2010). *Succeed: How we can reach our goals.* New York: Penguin/Hudson Street Press.

Hamachek, D. (1992). *Encounters with the self* (3rd ed.). New York: Harcourt, Brace, Jovanovich.

Hamilton, C. (2012). *Successful public speaking* (5th ed.). Belmont, CA: Wadsworth.

Harding, S. (Ed.). (2004). *The feminist standpoint theory reader.* New York: Routledge.

Harmon, A. (2002). Talk, type, read e-mail: The trials of multitasking. In E. Bucy (Ed.), *Living in the information age* (pp. 79–181). Belmont, CA: Wadsworth.

Harris, A. (2004). *Future girl.* London: Routledge.

Harris, G. (2011, July 11). For aspiring doctors, the people skills test. *New York Times*, pp. A1, A12.

Harris, T. J. (1969). *I'm OK, you're OK.* New York: Harper & Row.

Harris, T., & Sherblom, J. (2010). *Small group and team communication.* Boston: Allyn & Bacon.

Hasinoff, A. (2008). Fashioning race for the free market on *America's Next Top Model. Critical Studies in Media Communication, 25,* 324–343.

Hayakawa, S. I. (1962). *The use and misuse of language.* New York: Fawcett.

Hayakawa, S. I. (1964). *Language in thought and action* (2nd ed.). New York: Harcourt, Brace & World.

Haynes, J. (2009). Exposing domestic violence in country music videos. In L. Cuklanz & S. Moorti (Eds.), *Local violence, global media* (pp. 201–221). New York: Peter Lang.

Hecht, M. L., Collier, M. J., & Ribeau, S. A. (1993). *African American communication: Ethnic identity and cultural interpretation.* Thousand Oaks, CA: Sage.

Hegel, G. W. F. (1807). *Phenomenology of mind* (J. B. Baillie, Trans.). Germany: Wurzburg & Bamburg.

Heider, F. (1958). *The psychology of interpersonal relations.* New York: Wiley.

Hellweg, S. (1992). Organizational grapevines. In K. L. Hutchinson (Ed.), *Readings in organizational communication* (pp. 159–172). Dubuque, IA: Wm. C. Brown.

Hendrick, C., & Hendrick, S. (1988). Lovers wear rose-colored glasses. *Journal of Social and Personal Relationships, 5,* 161–184.

Hendrick, C., & Hendrick, S. (1996). Gender and the experience of heterosexual love. In J. T. Wood (Ed.), *Gendered relationships* (pp. 131–148). Mountain View, CA: Mayfield.

Hendrick, C., & Hendrick, S. (Eds.). (2000). *Close relationships: A sourcebook.* Thousand Oaks, CA: Sage.

Hendrick, C., Hendrick, S., Foote, F. H., & Slapion-Foote, M. J. (1984). Do men and women love differently? *Journal of Social and Personal Relationships, 2,* 177–196.

Hendrix, K. (2012). Home as respite for the working-class academic. In A. González, M. Houston, & V. Chen (Eds.), *Our voices: Essays in culture, ethnicity, and communication* (pp. 240–246). New York: Oxford University Press.

Hernández, D., & Rheman, B. (Eds.). (2002). *Colonize this! Young women of color on today's feminism.* Seattle, WA: Seal Press.

Hickson, M., Stacks, D., & Moore, N. (2004). *Nonverbal communication: Studies and applications.* Los Angeles: Roxbury.

Hillis, K., & Petit, M., with Epley, N. (2006a). *Everyday eBay: Culture, collecting, and desire.* New York: Routledge.

Hinduja, S., & Patchin, J. (2008). *Bullying beyond the schoolyard.* Thousand Oaks, CA: Corwin.

Ho, D. (2006, March 3). Study criticizes kids' TV violence. *Raleigh News & Observer*, p. 5A.

Hochschild, A., with Machung, A. (2003). *The second shift: Working parents and the revolution at home* (Rev. ed.). New York: Viking/Penguin Press.

Hoffman, J. (2010, June 28). Online bullies pull schools into the fray. *New York Times*, pp. A13, A14, A15.

Hofstede, G. (1991). *Culture and organizations: Software of the mind.* New York: McGraw-Hill.

Hofstede, G. (2001). *Cultures' consequences: Comparing values, behaviors, institutions, and organizations across nations.* Thousand Oaks, CA: Sage.

Hofstede, G., Hofstede, G. J., & Minkov, M. (2010). *Cultures and organizations: software of the mind* (3rd ed.). New York: McGraw-Hill.

Holmberg, D., & MacKenzie, S. (2002). So far, so good: Scripts for romantic relationship development as predictors of relational well-being. *Journal of Social and Personal Relationships, 19,* 777–796.

Holmes, M. (2008). *Gender and everyday life.* New York: Routledge.

Honeycutt, J. M., Woods, B., & Fontenot, K. (1993). The endorsement of communication conflict rules as a function of engagement, marriage, and marital ideology. *Journal of Social and Personal Relationships, 10,* 285–304.

Honoré, C. (2005). *In praise of slowness.* San Francisco: Harper.

Hoon, H., & Tan, M. (2008). "Organizational citizenship behavior and social loafing: The role of personality, motives, and contextual factors." *The Journal of Psychology, 142,* 89–108.

Hoover, E. (2010, January 29). An immigrant learns 2 new languages. *Chronicle of Higher Education,* p. A22.

Hosaka, T. (2011, April 4). Quake shapes social media. *Raleigh News & Observer,* pp. 2D, 2D.

Houston, M. (2004). When Black women talk with White women: Why dialogues are difficult. In A. Gonzaléz, M. Houston, & V. Chen (Eds.), *Our voices: Essays in culture, ethnicity, and communication* (4th ed., pp. 119–125). Los Angeles: Roxbury.

Huesmann, L. R., Moise-Titus, J., Podolski, C., & Eron, L. D. (2003). Longitudinal relations between children's exposure to TV violence and their aggressive and violent behavior in young adulthood: 1977–1992. *Developmental Psychology, 39,* 201–221.

Huston, M., & Schwartz, P. (1995). Relationships of lesbians and gay men. In J. T. Wood & S. W. Duck (Eds.), *Understanding relationship processes, 6: Understudied relationships: Off the beaten track* (pp. 89–121). Thousand Oaks, CA: Sage.

Hutchby, I. (2005). "Active listening": Formulations and the elicitation of feelings-talk in child counseling. *Research on Language and Social Interaction, 38,* 303–329.

Ihlen, O., Fredrikson, M., & van Ruler, B. (Eds.). (2009). *Public relations and social theory.* New York: Routledge.

IIE. (2010). *Open doors.* Washington, DC. http://opendoors.iienetwork.org/?p=131592. Accessed June 10, 011.

ILA (2008). Priorities of listening research: Four interrelated initiatives. Belle Plaine, MN: ILA.

ILA (2011). http://www.listen.org/ accessed June 6, 2011.

Information technology on campuses: By the numbers. (2011, May 13). *Chronicle of Higher Education,* pp. B22–B23.

Inman, C. C. (1996). Men's friendships: Closeness in the doing. In J. T. Wood (Ed.), *Gendered Relationships* (pp. 95–110). Mountain View, CA: Mayfield.

Internet World Stats. (2009). http://www.internetworldstats.com/stats.htm. Accessed February 6, 2009.

Irvine, M. (2009, February 5). Teens charged for "sexting" racy photos. *Raleigh News & Observer,* p. 6A.

Isaacs, W. (1999). *Dialogue and the art of thinking together.* New York: Doubleday.

Isay, D. (2008). *Listening is an act of love.* New York: Penguin.

Isikoff, M. (2004, July 19). The dots never existed. *Newsweek,* pp. 36–38.

Ito, M., Horst, H., Bittanti, M., Boyd, D., Herr-Stephenson, B., Lange, P., Poscoe, C., & Robinson, L. (2008). *Living and learning with new media: Summary of findings from the digital youth project.* The John D. and Catherine T. MacArthur Foundation Reports on Digital Media and Learning. Chicago.

Jackson, M. (2008). *Distracted: The erosion of attention and the coming dark age.* New York: Prometheus.

Jacobs, T. (2010). *Cyberbullying investigated.* Minneapolis, MN: Free Spirit Publishing.

Jaffe, C. (2007). *Public speaking: Concepts and skills for a diverse society* (5th ed.). Belmont, CA: Thomson Wadsworth.

Jagger, G. (2008). *Judith Butler: Sexual politics, social change and the power of performance.* New York: Routledge.

Jamieson, K., & Campbell, K. K. (2006). *The interplay of influence*

(6th ed.). Belmont, CA: Thomson Wadsworth.

Janis, I. L. (1977). *Victims of groupthink.* Boston: Houghton Mifflin.

Jandt, F. (2009). Culture. In W. F. Eadie (Ed.), *21st century communication: A reference handbook* (pp. 396–404). Thousand Oaks, CA: Sage.

Janusik, L. (2007). Building listening theory: The validation of the Conversational Listening Span. *Communication Studies, 58,* 139–156.

Jarrett, K. (2006). The perfect community: Disciplining the eBay user. In K. Hillis & M. Petit with N. Epley (Eds.), *Everyday eBay: Culture, collecting, and desire* (pp. 107–121). New York: Routledge.

Jhally, S., & Katz, J. (2001, Winter). Big trouble, little pond. *Umass,* pp. 26–31.

Johnson, A. J., Wittenberg, E., Haigh, M., & Wigley, S. (2004). The process of relationship development and deterioration: Turning points in friendships that have terminated. *Communication Quarterly, 52,* 54–68.

Johnson, C. B., Stockdale, M. S., & Saal, F. E. (1991). Persistence of men's misperceptions of friendly cues across a variety of interpersonal encounters. *Psychology of Women Quarterly, 15,* 463–465.

Johnson, F. L. (2000). *Speaking culturally: Language diversity in the United States.* Thousand Oaks, CA: Sage.

Johnson, M. (2006). Gendered communication and intimate partner violence. In B. Dow & J. T. Wood (Eds.), *Handbook of gender and communication research* (pp. 71–87). Thousand Oaks, CA: Sage.

Johnson, M. (2008). *A typology of domestic violence.* Boston: Northeastern University Press.

Johnson, N. (2007). *All I want is everything: A feminist analysis of consumption in bestselling teen romance novels.* Ph.D. dissertation. The University of North Carolina at Chapel Hill.

Johnson, N. (2011). The whole package. In D. O. Braithwaite & J. T. Wood (Eds.), *Casing interpersonal communication* (pp. 9–15). Belmont, CA: Wadsworth/Cengage.

Johnson, N., Roberts, M., & Warell, J. (Eds.). (2002). *Beyond appearance: A new look at adolescent girls.* Washington, DC: American Psychological Association.

Johnson, P. (1999). Reflections on critical White(ness) studies. In T. Nakayama & J. Martin (Eds.), *Whiteness: The communication of social identity* (pp. 1–12). Thousand Oaks, CA: Sage.

Jones, D. (2007, March 30). Do foreign executives balk at sports jargon? *USA Today*, pp. 1B–2B.

Jones, E., & Gallois, C. (1989). Spouses' impressions of rules for communication in public and private marital conflicts. *Journal of Marriage and the Family, 51,* 957–967.

Jones, S., & Fox, S. (2009). Generations online. http://pewinternet.org/pdfs/PIP_Generations_2009.pdf. Accessed February 10, 2009.

Justice, R. (1999). We're happily married and living apart. *Newsweek,* p. 12.

Kahn, M. (2008, December 2). The six habits of highly respectful physicians. *New York Times*, p. D6.

Kalb, C. (2003, September 8). Playing ye olde way. *Newsweek,* pp. E-26–E-28.

Katriel, T. (1990). "Griping" as a verbal ritual in some Israeli discourse. In D. Carbaugh (Ed.), *Cultural communication and intercultural contact* (pp. 99–114). Mahwah, NJ: Erlbaum.

Keashly, L., & Newman, J. H. (2005). Bullying in the workplace: Its impact and management. *Employee Rights and Employment Policy Journal, 8,* 335–373.

Keeley, M. P., & Hart, A. J. (1994). Nonverbal behavior in dyadic interaction. In S. W. Duck (Ed.), *Understanding relationship processes, 4: Dynamics of relationships* (pp. 135–162). Thousand Oaks, CA: Sage.

Keith, W. (2009). The speech tradition. In W. F. Eadie (Ed.), *21st century communication: A reference handbook* (pp. 22–30). Thousand Oaks, CA: Sage.

Keizer, G. (2010). *The unwanted sound of everything we want: A book about noise.* New York: Perseus-Public Affairs.

Keller, J. (2011, May 13). The slow-motion mobile campus. *Chronicle of Higher Education*, pp. B4–B6.

Kelley, H. H. (1967). Attribution theory in social psychology. In D. Levine (Ed.), *Nebraska symposium on motivation* (Vol. 15, pp. 192–238). Lincoln: University of Nebraska Press.

Kelly, G. A. (1955). *The psychology of personal constructs.* New York: Norton.

Kennedy, R. (2002). *Nigger: The strange career of a troublesome word.* New York: Pantheon.

Kershaw, S. (2009, April 23). Mr. Moms (by way of Fortune 500). *New York Times*, pp. E1, E6.

Keyes, R. (1992, February 22). Do you have the time? *Parade,* pp. 22–25.

Kiernan, V. (2006, May 12). Sign of the times. *Chronicle of Higher Education*, pp. A37–A38.

Kim, Y. (1995). Cross-cultural adaptation: An integrated theory. In R. Wiseman (Ed.), *Intercultural communication theory* (pp. 170–193). Newbury Park, CA: Sage.

Kimmel, M. (2008). *Guyland: The perilous world where boys become men.* New York: Macmillan.

Kirn, W. (2011, June 13 & 20). Mormons rock! *Newsweek,* pp. 38–45

Kirsh, S. J. (2006). *Children, adolescents, and media violence: A critical look at the research.* Thousand Oaks, CA: Sage.

Kirshenbaum, Sheril (2011). *The science of kissing.* New York: Grand Central Publishing.

Klein, N. (2009). *The shock doctrine.* New York: Macmillan/Picador.

Klein, R. (2001). *Jewelry talks: A novel thesis.* New York: Pantheon.

Klein, R., & Milardo, R. (2000). The social context of couple conflict: Support and criticism from informal third parties. *Journal of Social and Personal Relationships, 17,* 618–637.

Klingberg, T, (2008). *The overflowing brain: Information overload and the limits of working memory.* New York: Oxford University Press.

Klopf, D. (1991). *Intercultural encounters: The fundamentals of intercultural communication* (2nd ed.). Englewood Cliffs, NJ: Morgan.

Knapp, M. L., & Hall, J. A. (2006). *Nonverbal communication in human interaction* (6th ed.). Belmont, CA: Thomson Wadsworth.

Korzybski, A. (1948). *Science and sanity* (3rd ed.). Lakeville, CT: International Non-Aristotelian Library.

Krolicki, K. (2007, July 7). U.S. civil rights group holds funeral for "N-word." http://www.reuters.com/article/domesticNews/idUSN0929653620070709. Accessed January 10, 2009.

Kruger, P. (1999, June). A leader's journey. *Fast Company,* pp. 116–138.

Kupfer, D., First, M., & Regier, D. (2002). *A research agenda for DSM-V.* Washington, DC: American Psychiatric Press.

Kurdek, L. A. (1993). The allocation of household labor in gay, lesbian, and heterosexual married couples. *Journal of Social Issues, 49,* 127–139.

Kurt, J., & Sherker, J. (2003). Relationship quality, trait similarity, and self-other agreement on personality ratings in college roommates. *Journal of Personality, 71,* 21–40.

LaFasto, F., & Larson, C. (2001). *When teams work best: 6,000 team members and leaders tell what it takes to succeed.* Thousand Oaks, CA: Sage.

Lakoff, G., & Johnson, M. (1980). *Metaphors we live by.* Chicago: University of Chicago Press.

Lamb, S., & Brown, L. (2006). *Packaging girlhood: Rescuing our daughters from marketers' schemes.* New York: St. Martin's Press.

Landauer, T. (2002). The productivity puzzle. In E. Bucy (Ed.), *Living in the information age* (pp. 194–199). Belmont, CA: Wadsworth.

Landrum, R., & Harrold, R. (2003). What employers want from psychology graduates. *Teaching of psychology, 30,* 131–133.

Langer, S. (1953). *Feeling and form: A theory of art.* New York: Scribner's.

Langer, S. (1979). *Philosophy in a new key: A study in the symbolism of reason, rite, and art* (3rd ed.). Cambridge, MA: Harvard University Press.

Larson, J. R. (1984). The performance feedback process: A preliminary model. *Organizational Behavior and Human Performance, 33,* 42–76.

Laswell, H. D. (1948). The structure and function of communication in society. In L. Bryson (Ed.), *The communication of ideas.* New York: Harper & Row.

Lau, B. (1989). Imagining your path to success. *Management Quarterly, 30,* 30–41.

Lawless, B. (2012). More than white: Locating an invisible class identity. In A. González, M. Houston, & V. Chen (Eds.), *Our voices: Essays in culture, ethnicity, and communication* (pp. 247–253). New York: Oxford University Press.

Leaper, C., & Ayres, M. (2007). A meta-analytic review of gender variations in adults' language use: Talkativeness, affiliative speech, and assertive speech. *Personality & Social Psychology Review, 11,* 328–363.

Le, B., & Agnew, C. (2003). Commitment and its theorized determinants: A meta-analysis of the investment model. *Personal Relationships, 10,* 37–57.

Ledbetter, A., Broeckelman-Post, M., & Krawsczyn, A. (2011). Modeling everyday talk: Differences across communication media and sex composition of friendship dyads. *Journal of Social and Personal Relationships, 28,* 223–241.

Lee, J. A. (1973). *The colors of love: An exploration of the ways of loving.* Don Mills, Ontario, Canada: New Press.

Lee, J. A. (1988). Love-styles. In R. J. Sternberg & M. L. Barnes (Eds.), *The psychology of love* (pp. 38–67). New Haven, CT: Yale University Press.

Lee, W. S. (1994). On not missing the boat: A processual method for intercultural understandings of idioms and lifeworld. *Journal of Applied Communication Research, 22,* 141–161.

Lee, W. S. (2000). That's Greek to me: Between a rock and a hard place in intercultural encounters. In L. Samovar & R. Porter (Eds.), *Intercultural communication: A reader* (9th ed., pp. 217–224). Belmont, CA: Wadsworth.

Leeds-Hurwitz, W. (2006). Social theories: Social constructionism and symbolic interactionism. In D. O. Braithwaite & L. A. Baxter (Eds.), *Engaging theories in family communication: Multiple perspectives* (pp. 229–242). Thousand Oaks, CA: Sage.

Lenbgel, L. (2009). Computer-mediated communication. In W. F. Eadie (Ed.), *21st century communication: A reference handbook* (pp. 543–549). Thousand Oaks, CA: Sage.

Lester, P. M. (2006). *Visual communication: Images with messages* (4th ed.). Belmont, CA: Thomson Wadsworth.

Levi, D. (2010). *Group dynamics for teams.* Thousand Oaks, CA: Sage.

Levin, D., & Kilbourne, J. (2008). *So sexy, so soon.* New York: Ballantine.

Levin, S., Taylor, P., & Caudle, E. (2007). Interethnic and interracial dating in college: A longitudinal study. *Journal of Social and Personal Relationships, 24,* 323–341.

Levine, M. (2004, June 1). Tell the doc all your problems, but keep it to less than a minute. *New York Times,* p. D6.

Levine, R., & Norenzayan, A. (1999). The pace of life in 31 countries. *Journal of Cross-Cultural Psychology, 30,* 178–205.

Levy, D., Nardick, D., Turner, J., & McWatters, L. (2011, May 13). No cellphone? No internet? So much less stress. *Chronicle of Higher Education,* pp. B27–B28.

Levy, S. (2003, September 8). A geek bill of rights. *Newsweek,* p. E30.

Levy, S. (2004b, June 7). Something in the air. *Newsweek,* pp. 46–49.

Levy, S. (2006, March 27). (Some) attention must be paid! *Newsweek,* p. 16

Lewin, K. (1947). *Human relations.* New York: Harper & Row.

Lewin, T. (2008, November 20). Teens' Internet socializing may not be so bad. *Raleigh News & Observer,* p. 10A.

Lewis, M. (2002). *Next: The future just happened.* New York: Norton.

Lewis, M., Haviland-Jones, J. M., & Barrett, L. F. (Eds.). (2008). *Handbook of emotions.* New York: Guilford.

Lightner, C. (1990). *Giving sorrow words: How to cope with grief and get on with your life.* New York: Warner.

Liptak, A. (2011, June 18). Audit of officer's pager was reasonable, court says. *New York Times,* p. A15.

Lister, K. (2009). *Undress for success: The naked truth about making money at home.* New York: John Wiley and Sons.

Liu, F., & Albarran, A. (2009). Media economics and ownership. In W. F. Eadie (Ed.), *21st century communication: A reference handbook* (pp. 851–858). Thousand Oaks, CA: Sage.

Lloyd, S., & Emery, B. (2000). The context and dynamics of intimate aggression against women. *Journal of Social and Personal Relationships, 17,* 503–521.

Logan, R. (2010). *Understanding new media: Extending Marshall McLuhan.* New York: Peter Lang.

Lohr, S. (2002). Computer age gains respect of economics. In E. Bucy (Ed.), *Living in the information age* (pp. 181–203). Belmont, CA: Wadsworth.

Lourogos, A. (2010, August 10). Staying in touch—college students, parents stay connected via technology. *Chicago Tribune:* http://blogs.cofc. edu/parents/2010/08/24/staying-in-touch-college-students-parents-stay-connected-via-technology/.

Love, D. (2011, June 10). Americans have earned a break. *Raleigh News & Observer,* p. 11A.

Ludington-Hoe, S. (1993). *Kangaroo care: The best you can do to help your preterm infant.* New York: Bantam.

Luft, J. (1969). *Of human interaction.* Palo Alto, CA: Natural Press.

Lugones, M. (1992). On "Borderlands/ La Frontera": An interpretive essay. *Hypatia 7,* 31–37.

Lugones, M. (2006). On complex communication. *Hypatia, 21,* 75–85.

Lumsden, G., & Lumsden, D. (2009). *Communicating in groups and teams* (5th ed.). Belmont, CA: Wadsworth.

Lund, M. (1985). The development of investment and commitment scales for predicting continuity of personal relationships. *Journal of Social and Personal Relationships, 2,* 3–23.

Luttmer, E. (2005, August). Neighbors as negatives: Relative earnings and well-being. *Quarterly Journal of Economics,* 963–1002.

Lyons, D. (2009, March 2). Old media strikes back. *Newsweek,* p. 13.

MacFarquhar, N. (2011, June 16). Social media help keep the door open to sustained dissent inside Saudi Arabia. *New York Times,* p. A5.

MacGeorge, E. (2009). Social support. In W. F. Eadie (Ed.), *21st century communication: A reference handbook* (pp. 283–291). Thousand Oaks, CA: Sage.

Madden, M., & Jones, S. (2008). Networked workers. Pew Internet & American Life Project Report. www.pewinternet.org/ Reports/2008/Networked-Workers. aspx. Accessed March 30, 2009.

Major, B., Schmidlin, A. M., & Williams, L. (1990). Gender patterns in social touch: The impact of setting and age. In C. Mayo & N. M. Henley (Eds.), *Gender and nonverbal behavior* (pp. 3–37). New York: Springer-Verlag.

Makau, J. (2009). Ethical and unethical communication. In W. F. Eadie (Ed.), *21st century communication: A reference handbook* (pp.435–443). Thousand Oaks, CA: Sage.

Maltz, D. N., & Borker, R. (1982). A cultural approach to male–female miscommunication. In J. J. Gumperz (Ed.), *Language and social identity* (pp. 196–216). Cambridge, UK: Cambridge University Press.

Manusov, V. (Ed.). (2004). *The sourcebook of nonverbal measures.* Mahwah, NJ: Erlbaum.

Manusov, V. (2006). Attribution theories: Assessing causal and responsibility judgments in families. In D. O. Braithwaite & L. A. Baxter (Eds.), *Engaging theories in family communication: Multiple perspectives* (pp. 181–196). Thousand Oaks, CA: Sage.

Manusov, V., & Spitzberg, B. (2008). Attribution theory. In L. A. Baxter & D. O. Braithwaite (Eds.), *Engaging theories in interpersonal communication: Multiple perspectives* (pp. 37–49). Thousand Oaks, CA: Sage.

Markoff, J. (2009, February 17). The cellphone, navigating our lives. *New York Times,* pp. D1, D4.

Martin, J., Krizek, R., Nakayama, T., & Bradford, L. (1996). Exploring whiteness: A study of self labels for white Americans. *Communication Quarterly, 44,* 125–144.

Martin, T. (2007). Muting the voice of the local in the age of the global: How communication practices compromised public participation in India's Allain Dunhangan environmental impact assessment. *Environmental Communication, 1,* 171–193.

Mastro, D. (2003). A social identity approach to understanding the impact of television messages. *Communication Monographs, 70,* 98–113.

Maugh, T. H., II (2002, February 26). Center says AIDS virus is nearly 1 million in U.S. *Raleigh News & Observer,* p. 8B.

McChesney, R. (1999). *Rich media, poor democracy: Communication politics in dubious times.* Urbana: University of Illinois Press.

McChesney, R. (2004). *The problem of the media: U.S. communication politics in the twenty-first century.* New York: Monthly Review Press.

McChesney, R. (2008). *The political economy of media.* New York: Monthly Review Press.

McClish, G., & Bacon, J. (2002). "Telling the story her own way": The role of feminist standpoint theory in rhetorical studies. *Rhetoric Society Quarterly, 32,* 27–55.

McClure, B. (2005). *Putting a new spin on groups: The science of chaos* (2nd ed.). Mahwah, NJ: Erlbaum.

McClure, M. (1997). Mind/body medicine: Evidence of efficacy. *Health and Healing, 1,* 3.

McCombs, M., & Ghanem, S. (2001). The convergence of agenda setting and framing. In S. Reese, O. Gandy, & A. Grant (Eds.), *Framing public life: Perspectives on media and our understanding of the social world* (pp. 240–279). Mahwah, NJ: Erlbaum.

McCombs, M., Ghanem, S., & Chernov, G. (2009). Agenda setting and framing. In W. F. Eadie (Ed.), *21st century communication: A reference handbook* (pp. 516–524). Thousand Oaks, CA: Sage.

McCroskey, J., & Teven, J. (1999). Goodwill: A reexamination of the construct and its measurement. *Communication Monographs, 66,* 90–103.

McCroskey, J. C. (1977). Oral communication apprehension: A summary of recent theory and research. *Human Communication Research, 4,* 78–96.

McDonald, M., Phipps, S. & Lethbridge, L. (2005). Taking its toll: The influences of paid and unpaid work on women's well-being. *Feminist Economics, 11,* 63–94.

McGee-Cooper, A., Trammel, D., & Lau, B. (1992). *You don't have to go home from work exhausted.* New York: Bantam.

McGuffey, S., & Rich, L. (2004). Playing in the gender transgression zone: Race, class, and hegemonic masculinity in middle childhood. In J. Spade & C. Valentine (Eds.), *The kaleidoscope of gender: Prisms, patterns, and possibilities* (pp. 172–183). Belmont, CA: Wadsworth.

McGuire, W. J. (1989). Theoretical foundations of campaigns. In R. E. Rice & C. K. Atkin (Eds.), *Public communication campaigns* (2nd ed., pp. 43–65). Thousand Oaks, CA: Sage.

McKinney, B., Kelly, L., & Duran, R. (1997). The relationship between conflict message style and dimensions of communication competence. *Communication Reports, 10,* 185–196.

McKinney, M. (2006, October). Communication among top-10 fields of study. *Spectra,* p. 8.

McLuhan, M. (1962). *The Gutenberg galaxy.* Toronto, Canada: University of Toronto Press.

McLuhan, M. (1964). *Understanding Media.* New York: McGraw-Hill.

McLuhan, M. (1969, March). Interview. *Playboy,* pp. 53–54, 56, 59–62, 64–66, 68, 70.

McLuhan, M., & Fiore, Q. (1967). *The medium is the message.* New York: Random House.

McNees, P. (1999). *YPO: The first fifty years.* Wilmington, OH: Orange Frazier Press.

McNulty, J. K., & Karney, B. R. (2001). Attributions in marriage: Integrating specific and global evaluations of a relationship. *Personality and Social Psychology Bulletin, 27,* 943–955.

McNutt, P. (1997, October/November). When strategic decisions are ignored. *Fast Company,* p. 12.

McRobbie, A. (2000). *Feminism and youth culture.* New York: Routledge.

McRobbie, A. (2004). Post-feminism and popular culture. *Feminist Media Studies, 4,* 255–264.

McRobbie, A. (2009). *The aftermath of feminism: Gender, culture and social change.* Thousand Oaks, CA: Sage.

Mead, G. H. (1934). *Mind, self, and society.* Chicago: University of Chicago Press.

Medhurst, M. (2010). George W. Bush at Goree Island: American slavery and the rhetoric of redemption. *Quarterly Journal of Speech, 96,* 257–277.

Media Trends Track. (2010). http://www.tvb.org/rcentral/ mediatrendstrack/tvbasics/02_ TVHouseholds.asp. Accessed April 22, 2010.

Meeks, B., Hendrick, S., & Hendrick, C. (1998). Communication, love, and satisfaction. *Journal of Social and Personal Relationships, 15,* 755–773.

Mehrabian, A. (1981). *Silent messages: Implicit communication of emotion and attitudes* (2nd ed.). Belmont, CA: Wadsworth.

Meloy, R. (2006). *The psychology of stalking: Clinical and forensic perspectives* (2nd ed.). New York: Academic Press.

Men use half a brain to listen, study finds. (2000, November 29). *Raleigh News & Observer,* p. 8A.

Mernissi, F. (2004). Size 6: The Western woman's harem. In J. Spade & C. Valentine (Eds.), *The kaleidoscope of gender: Prisms, patterns, and possibilities.* (pp. 297–301). Belmont, CA: Thomson Wadsworth.

Metts, S. (2006). Gendered communication in dating relationships. In B. Dow & J. T. Wood (Eds.), *Handbook of gender and communication research* (pp. 25–40). Thousand Oaks, CA: Sage.

Metts, S., Cupach, W. R., & Bejlovec, R. A. (1989). "I love you too much to ever start liking you": Redefining romantic relationships. *Journal of Social and Personal Relationships, 6,* 259–274.

Milia, T. (2003). *Doctor, you're not listening.* Philadelphia: Xlibris.

Miller, C. (2009). *Organizing communication: Approaches and processes* (6th ed.). Belmont, CA: Wadsworth/Cengage.

Miller, J. (2006, May 9). Touch. *Raleigh News & Observer,* pp. 1E, 3E.

Miller, J. B. (1993). Learning from early relationship experience. In S. W. Duck (Ed.), *Understanding relationship processes, 2: Learning about relationships* pp. 1–29). Thousand Oaks, CA: Sage.

Mino, M. (1996). The relative effects of content and vocal delivery during a simulated employment interview. *Communication Research Reports, 13,* 225–238.

Mishori, R. M. D. (2005, June 10). Is cosmetic surgery right for you? *Parade,* pp. 1011.

Modaff, D., Butler, J., & DeWine, S. (2011). *Organizational communication: Foundations, challenges, and misunderstandings* (3rd ed.). Boston: Allyn & Bacon.

Moffatt, T. (1979). *Selection interviewing for managers.* New York: Harper & Row.

Mokros, H. (2006). Composing relationships at work. In J. T. Wood

& S. W. Duck (Eds.), *Composing relationships: Communication in everyday life* (pp. 175–185). Belmont, CA: Thomson Wadsworth.

Monastersky, R. (2001, July 6). Look who's listening. *Chronicle of Higher Education,* pp. A14–A16.

Monastersky, R. (2002, March 29). Speak before you think. *Chronicle of Higher Education,* pp. A17–A18.

Monroe, A. H. (1935). *Principles and types of speech.* Glenview, IL: Scott, Foresman.

Monsour, M. (2002). *Women and men as friends.* Mahwah, NJ: Erlbaum.

Monsour, M. (2006). Communication and gender among adult friends. In B. Dow & J. T. Wood (Eds.), *Handbook of gender and communication research* (pp. 57–69). Thousand Oaks, CA: Sage.

Montgomery, B. (1988). Quality communication in personal relationships. In S. W. Duck (Ed.), *Handbook of personal relationships* (pp. 343–366). New York: Wiley.

Morning, A. (2011). *The nature of race: How scientists think and teach about human difference.* Berkeley, CA: University of California Press.

Morreale, J. (2007). Faking it and the transformation of identity. In D. Heller (Ed.), *Makeover television: Realities remodeled* (pp. 6–22). New York: Palgrave Macmillan.

Motley, M., & Molloy, J. (1994). An efficacy test of a new therapy ("communication-orientation motivation") for public speaking anxiety. *Journal of Applied Communication Research, 22,* 48–58.

Muehlhoff, T. (2006). "He started it": Everyday communication in parenting. In J. T. Wood & S. W. Duck (Eds.), *Composing relationships: Communication in everyday life* (pp. 46–54). Belmont, CA: Wadsworth.

Mulac, A. (2006). The gender-linked language effect: Do language differences really make a difference? In K. Dindia & D.

Canary (Eds.), *Sex differences and similarities in communication* (pp. 219–239). Mahwah, NJ: Erlbaum.

Mumby, D. (Ed.). (1993). *Narratives and social control: Critical perspectives.* Newbury Park, CA: Sage.

Mumby, D. (2006). Constructing working-class masculinity in the workplace. In J. T. Wood & S. W. Duck (Eds.), *Composing relationships: Communication in everyday life* (pp. 166–174). Belmont, CA: Thomson Wadsworth.

Mumby, D. (2007). Introduction: Gendering organization. In B. Dow & J. T. Wood (Eds.), *Handbook of gender and communication research.* Thousand Oaks, CA: Sage.

Munter, M. (1993). Cross-cultural communication for managers. *Business Horizons, 36,* 68–77.

Murphy, J., & Rubinson, R. (2005). *Domestic violence and mediation: Responding to the challenges of crafting effective screens, Family Law Quarterly, 39,* 177–194.

Murphy, K. (2011, July 5). The paperless cockpit. *New York Times,* p. B6.

Mwakalye, N., & DeAngelis, T. (1995, October). The power of touch helps babies survive. *APA Monitor,* p. 25.

Myers, L., & Larson, R. (2005). Preparing students for early work conflict. *Business Communication Quarterly, 68,* 306–317.

Nagourney, E. (2006, May 9). Surgical teams found lacking in teamwork. *New York Times,* p. D6.

Nagourney, E. (2008, December 23). Pain is greater if harm seems intentional. *New York Times,* p. D6.

Nanda, S. (2004). Multiple genders among North American Indians. In J. Spade & C. Valentine (Eds.), *The kaleidoscope of gender* (pp. 64–70). Belmont, CA: Wadsworth.

National Telecommunications and Information Administration. *Falling through the net.* (1999). Retrieved September 25, 2004,

from http://www.ntia.doc.gov/ntiahome/fftn99/

Negra, D. (Ed.). (2006). *The Irish in us: Irishness, performativity, and popular culture.* Durham, NC: Duke University Press.

Nerone, J. (2009). Journalism. In W. F. Eadie (Ed.), *21st century communication: A reference handbook* (pp. 31–38). Thousand Oaks, CA: Sage.

Neyer, F. (2002). The dyadic interdependence of attachment security and dependency: A conceptual replication across older twin pairs and young couples. *Journal of Social and Personal Relationships, 19,* 483–503.

Nichols, M. (1996). *The lost art of listening.* New York: Guilford.

Noller, P. (1986). Sex differences in nonverbal communication: Advantage lost or supremacy regained? *Australian Journal of Psychology, 38,* 23–32.

Noller, P. (1987). Nonverbal communication in marriage. In D. Perlman & S. Duck (Eds.), *Intimate relationships: Development, dynamics, and deterioration* (pp. 149–176). Thousand Oaks, CA: Sage.

Norwood, K., & Duck, S. W. (2009). Friendship. In W. F. Eadie (Ed.), *21st century communication: A reference handbook* (pp. 313–321). Thousand Oaks, CA: Sage.

Norton, T. (2007). The structuration of public participation: Organizing environmental control. *Environmental Communication, 1,* 146–170.

Notable numbers (2011, June 11). *Raleigh News & Observer,* p. 16A.

OED. http://www.oed.com/public/latest/latest-update/ Retrieved June 4, 2011.

O'Hair, D., & Eadie, W. F. (2009). In W. F. Eadie (Ed.), *21st century communication: A reference handbook* (pp. 3–11). Thousand Oaks, CA: Sage.

Ohanian, H. (2008). *Einstein's mistakes.* New York: W. W. Norton.

Olds, J., & Schwartz, R. (2010). *The lonely American: Drifting apart in the twenty-first century.* Boston: Beacon.

Olson, J. M., & Cal, A. V. (1984). Source credibility, attitudes, and the recall of past behaviors. *European Journal of Social Psychology, 14,* 203–210.

OMG!!!!! OED ❤ LOL!!!!! (2011, April 5). *New York Times, p. A20.*

One in Four Girls. (2008, March 17). *New York Times,* p. A22.

Hill, C. (2011). Online dating. http://www.smartmoney.com/retirement/planning/online-dating-no-longer-just-for-youngsters-1308948789940/?link=SM_hp_ls4e. Accessed June 29, 2011.

Ono, K. A. (2009). Critical/cultural approaches to communication. In W. F. Eadie (Ed.), *21st century communication: A reference handbook* (pp. 74–81). Thousand Oaks, CA: Sage.

Orbe, M. P. (1994). "Remember, it's always the Whites' ball": Descriptions of African American male communication. *Communication Quarterly, 42,* 287–300.

Orbe, M. P., & Harris, T. M. (2001). *Interracial communication: Theory into practice.* Belmont, CA: Wadsworth.

Ornish, D. (1998). *Love and survival: The scientific basis for the healing power of intimacy.* New York: HarperCollins.

Overall, N., Sibley, C., & Travaglia, L. (2010). Loyal but ignored: The benefits and costs of constructive communication behavior. *Journal of Personal Relationships, 17,* 127–148.

Overheard. (2008, August 24). *Raleigh News & Observer,* p. 3E.

Overland, M. (2004, January 9). Tea, TV, and sympathy. *Chronicle of Higher Education,* p. A48.

Overland, M. (2009, January 23). A long time coming. *Chronicle of Higher Education,* p. A6.

Pacanowsky, M. (1989). Creating and narrating organizational realities. In B. Dervin, L. Grossberg, B. O'Keefe, & E. Wartella (Eds.), *Rethinking communication: Paradigm exemplars* (pp. 250–257). Thousand Oaks, CA: Sage.

Pacanowsky, M., & O'Donnell-Trujillo, N. (1982). Communication and organizational cultures. *Western Journal of Speech Communication, 46,* 115–130.

Pacanowsky, M., & O'Donnell-Trujillo, N. (1983). Organizational communication as cultural performance. *Communication Monographs, 30,*126–147.

Page, S. (2008). *The difference: How the power of diversity creates better groups, firms, schools and societies.* Princeton, NJ: Princeton University Press.

Palmer, E., & Young, B. (Eds.). (2003). *The faces of televisual media.* Mahwah, NJ: Erlbaum.

Parents Television Council (2006). [Web site]. Accessed May 20, 2006. http://www.parentstv.org/PTC/publications/reports/childrensstudy/main.asp.

Parker-Pope, T. (2009, January 13). A problem of the brain, not the hands: Group urges phone ban for drivers. *New York Times,* p. D5.

Parker-Pope, T. (2008, January 20). Your nest is empty? Enjoy each other. *New York Times,* p. D5.

Parker-Pope, T. (2010, April 6). Surprisingly, family time has grown. *New York Times,* p. D5.

Park, Y. S., & Kim, B. (2008). Asian and European American cultural values and communication styles among Asian American and European American college students. *Cultural Diversity and Ethnic Minority Psychology, 14,* 47–56.

Patterson, M. L. (1992). A functional approach to nonverbal exchange. In R. S. Feldman & B. Rime (Eds.), *Fundamentals of nonverbal behavior* (pp. 458–495). New York: Cambridge University Press.

Pearce, W. B., Cronen, V. E., & Conklin, F. (1979). On what to look at when analyzing communication: A hierarchical model of actors' meanings. *Communication, 4,* 195–220.

Peplau, L. A., & Beals, K. B. (2003). The family lives of lesbians and gay men. In A. Vangelisti (Ed.), *Handbook of family communication* (pp. 233–248). Mahwah, NJ: Erlbaum.

Petronio, S. (1991). Communication boundary management: A theoretical model of managing disclosure of private information between married couples. *Communication Theory, 1,* 311–335.

Petronio, S., & Caughlin, J. (2006). Communication privacy management theory: Understanding families. In D. O. Braithwaite & L. A. Baxter (Eds.), *Engaging theories in family communication: Multiple perspectives* (pp. 35–49). Thousand Oaks, CA: Sage.

Pew media study shows reliance on many outlets (2011, September 26). *New York Times,* p. B6.

Pew Research Center (2011, June 4). http://people-press.org/2011/01/04/internet-gains-on-television-as-publics-main-news-source/ Accessed June 17, 2011.

Peyser, M. (2006, March 6). Color us impressed. *Newsweek,* p. 59.

Pezzullo, P. (2007). *Toxic tourism: Rhetorics of travel, pollution, and environmental justice.* Tuscaloosa: University of Alabama Press.

Pezzullo, P. (2008). Overture: The most complicated world. *Cultural Studies, 22,* 3–4.

Pfanner, E. (2011, June 20). A universe of new web suffixes could be coming. *New York Times,* p. B9.

Phillips, G. M. (1991). *Communication incompetencies.* Carbondale: Southern Illinois University Press.

Pinker, S. (2000). *Words and rules.* New York: HarperPerennial.

Pinker, S. (2008). *The stuff of thought: Language as a window to human nature.* New York: Penguin.

Pogue, D. (2006, May 3). Going online on the go: Options. *New York Times,* pp. E1, E5.

Pollack, W. (2000). *Real boys: Rescuing ourselves from the myths of boyhood.* New York: Owl Books.

Porter, K., & Foster, J. (1986). *The mental athlete: Inner training for peak performance.* New York: Ballantine.

Potter, M., Gordon, S., & Hamer, P. (2004). The Nominal Group Technique: A useful consensus methodology in physiotherapy research. *New Zealand Journal of Physiotherapy, 32,* 126–130.

Potter, W. J. (2001). *Media literacy* (2nd ed.). Thousand Oaks, CA: Sage.

Potter, W. J. (2004). *Theory of media literacy: A cognitive approach.* Thousand Oaks, CA: Sage.

Potter, W. J. (2009). Media literacy. In W. F. Eadie (Ed.), *21st century communication: A reference handbook* (pp. 558–567). Thousand Oaks, CA:Sage.

Pozner, J. (2004, Fall). The unreal world. *Ms.,* pp. 50–53.

Preston, J. (2011, July 21). Social media history becomes a new job hurdle. *New York Times,* pp. B1, B4.

Purdy, M., & Borisoff, D. (Eds.). (1997). *Listening in everyday life: A personal and professional approach* (2nd ed.). Lanham, MD: University of America Press.

Putnam, R. (2000). *Bowling alone.* New York: Simon & Schuster.

Putnam, R., & Feldstein, L. (2003). *Better together.* New York: Simon & Schuster.

Quick Facts. (2011). U.S. Bureau of the Census. http://quickfacts .census.gov/qfd/states/00000.html. Accessed July 5, 2011.

Radway, J. (1991). *Reading the romance.* Chapel Hill: University of North Carolina Press.

Rae-Dupree, J. (2008, December 7). Teamwork, the true mother of invention. *New York Times,* p. B3.

Rainy, L., Purcell, K., Goulet, L., & Hampton, L. (2011). Social networking sites and our lives. Pew Internet Project: http:// pewresearch.org/pubs/2025/ social-impactsocial-networking-sites-technology-facebook-twitter-linkedin-myspace

Ragan, P. (2003). *The mating game: A primer on love, sex and marriage.* Thousand Oaks, CA: Sage.

Ramasubramanian, S. (2010). Television viewing, racial attitudes, and policy preferences: Exploring the role of social identity and intergroup emotions in influencing support for affirmative action. *Communication Monographs, 77,* 102–120.

Raspberry, W. (1994, July 5). Major gains in minorities' grades at Tech. *Raleigh News & Observer,* p. 9A.

Rawlins, W. K. (1981). *Friendship as a communicative achievement: A theory and an interpretive analysis of verbal reports.* Doctoral dissertation, Temple University, Philadelphia.

Rawlins, W. K. (1994). Being there and growing apart: Sustaining friendships during adulthood. In D. Canary & L. Stafford (Eds.), *Communication and relational maintenance* (pp. 275–294). New York: Academic Press.

Read, K. (2010, July & August). May I please have my attention back. *AARPORG Magazine,* pp. 28–31.

Reeder, H. (2000). "I like you … as a friend": The role of attraction in cross-sex friendship. *Journal of Social and Personal Relationships, 17,* 329–348.

Reinhard, C. D., & Dervin, B. J. (2009). Media uses and gratifications. In W. F. Eadie (Ed.), *21st century communication: A reference handbook* (pp. 506–515). Thousand Oaks, CA: Sage.

Reinhard, J. (2007). *Introduction to communication research.* New York: McGraw-Hill.

Reis, H. T., Clark, M. S., & Holmes, J. G. (2004). Perceived partner responsiveness as an organizing construct in the study of intimacy and closeness. In D. J. Mashek & A. P. Aron (Eds.), *Handbook of closeness and intimacy* (pp. 201–225). Mahwah, NJ: Erlbaum.

Remland, M. (2000). *Nonverbal communication in everyday life.* Boston: Houghton Mifflin.

Renegar, V., & Malkowski, J. (2009). Rhetorical and textual approaches to communication. In W. F. Eadie (Ed.), *21st century communication: A reference handbook* (pp. 49–56). Thousand Oaks, CA: Sage.

Rheingold, H. (2009, January 9). Look who's talking. *Wired.* http://www .wired.com/wired/archive/7.01/ amish_pr.html. Accessed July 25, 2009.

Rhode, D. (2011). *The beauty bias: The injustice of appearances in life and law.* New York: Oxford University Press.

Rhodes, T. (2010, November). Learning across the curriculum. *Spectra,* pp. 12–15.

Richmond, V. P., & McCroskey, J. C. (1992). *Communication: Apprehension, avoidance, and effectiveness* (3rd ed.). Scottsdale, AZ: Gorsuch Scarisbrick.

Richmond, V. P., & McCroskey, J. C. (1995). *Nonverbal communication in interpersonal relations* (3rd ed.). Boston: Allyn & Bacon.

Richtel, M. (2006, May 3). Selling surveillance to anxious parents. *New York Times,* p. E6.

Riessman, C. (1990). *Divorce talk: Women and men make sense of personal relationships.* New Brunswick, NJ: Rutgers University Press.

Riggs, D. (1999, February 28). True love is alive and well, say romance book writers. *Tallahassee Democrat,* p. 3D.

Riley, P. (1983). A structurationist account of political culture. *Administrative Science Quarterly, 28,* 414–437.

Roberts, J. (2004, November 22). TV's new brand of stars. *Newsweek,* pp. 62–64.

Roberts, S. (2008, August 14). A generation away, minorities may be the majority. *New York Times,* pp. A1, A18.

Robinson, J. D. (2009). Media portrayals and representations. In W. F. Eadie (Ed.), *21st century communication: A reference handbook* (pp. 497–505). Thousand Oaks, CA: Sage.

Roediger, D. (2006. May 14). Whiteness and its complications. *Chronicle of Higher Education*, pp. B6–B8.

Rohlfing, M. (1995). "Doesn't anybody stay in one place anymore?": An exploration of the understudied phenomenon of long-distance relationships. In J. T. Wood & S. W. Duck (Eds.), *Understanding relationship processes, 6: Understudied relationships: Off the beaten track* (pp. 173–196). Thousand Oaks, CA: Sage.

Rothberg, S. (2008, September 26). CollegeRecruiter.com. Posted on job board. Cited in Alberts, J., Nakayama, T., & Martin, J. (2010). *Communication in society*. Boston: Allyn & Bacon.

Rothenberg, D. (1999, July 16). Use the Web to connect with "ideas in motion." *Chronicle of Higher Education*, p. B8.

Rothwell, J. D. (2009). *In mixed company: Small group communication* (7th ed.). Belmont, CA: Thomson Wadsworth.

Rubin, L. (1985). *Just friends: The role of friendship in our lives.* New York: Harper & Row.

Rudman, L. A., & Glick, P. (2008). *The social psychology of gender.* New York: Guilford Press.

Rusbult, C. E. (1987). Responses to dissatisfaction in close relationships: The exit–voice–loyalty–neglect model. In D. Perlman & S. W. Duck (Eds.), *Intimate relationships: Development, dynamics, and deterioration* (pp. 109–238). London: Sage.

Rusbult, C. E., Drigotas, S. M., & Verette, J. (1994). The investment model: An interdependence analysis of commitment processes and relationship maintenance phenomena. In D. J. Canary and L. Stafford (Eds.), *Communication and relational maintenance* (pp. 115–140). New York: Academic Press.

Rusbult, C. E., Johnson, D. J., & Morrow, G. D. (1986). Impact of couple patterns of problem solving on distress and nondistress in dating relationships. *Journal of Personality and Social Psychology, 50,* 744–753.

Rusbult, C. E., & Zembrodt, I. M. (1983). Responses to dissatisfaction in romantic involvement: A multidimensional scaling analysis. *Journal of Experimental Social Psychology, 19,* 274–293.

Rusbult, C. E., Zembrodt, I. M., & Iwaniszek, J. (1986). The impact of gender and sex-role orientation on responses to dissatisfaction in close relationships. *Sex Roles, 15,* 1–20.

Rusk, T., & Rusk, N. (1988). *Mind traps: Change your mind, change your life.* Los Angeles: Price Stern Sloan.

Rusli, E. (2011, July 4). Homework help site has a social networking twist. *New York Times*, pp. B1, B4.

Rutenberg, J., & Nagouney, A. (2009, January 26). Retooling a grass-roots network to serve a YouTube presidency. *New York Times,* pp. A1, A12.

Sabourin, T., & Stamp, G. (1995). Communication and the experience of dialectical tensions in family life: An examination of abusive and nonabusive families. *Communication Monographs, 62,* 213–242.

Sahlstein, E. (2006a). Relational life in the 21st century: Managing people, time, and distance. In J. T. Wood & S. W. Duck (Eds.), *Composing relationships: Communication in everyday life* (pp. 110–118). Belmont, CA: Thomson Wadsworth.

Sahlstein, E. (2006b). The trouble with distance. In C. Kirpatrick, S. W. Duck, & M. Foley (Eds.), *Relating difficulty* (pp.118–140). Mahwah, NJ: Erlbaum.

Sallinen-Kuparinen, A. (1992). Teacher communicator style. *Communication Education, 41,* 153–166.

Samp, J., & Palevitz, C. (2009). Dating and romantic relationships. In W. F. Eadie (Ed.), *21st century communication: A reference handbook* (pp. 322–329). Thousand Oaks, CA: Sage.

Samovar, L., & Porter, R. (Eds.). (2004). *Intercultural communication: A reader* (10th ed.). Belmont, CA: Wadsworth.

Samovar, L., Porter, R., & McDaniel, E. R. (2009). *Communication between cultures* (12th ed.). Belmont, CA: Wadsworth-Cengage.

Samovar, L., Porter, R., & McDaniel, E. (Eds.). (2011). *Intercultural communication: A reader.* Belmont, CA: Wadsworth.

Samp, J., & Palevitz, C. (2009). Dating and romantic partners. In W. F. Eadie (Ed.), *21st century communication: A reference handbook* (pp. 322–330). Thousand Oaks, CA: Sage.

Sandler, R., & Pezzullo, P. (Eds.). (2007). *Environmental justice and environmentalism: The social justice challenge to the environmental movement.* Cambridge, MA: MIT Press.

Sandstrom, K. L., Martin, D. D., & Fine, G. A. (2001). Symbolic interactionism and the end of the century. In G. Ritzer & B. Smart (Eds.), *Handbook of social theory* (pp. 217–231). Thousand Oaks, CA: Sage.

Sarno, D. (2011, June 21). Internet minders approve big increase in domain names. *Raleigh News & Observer*, p. 4A.

Sawyer, K. (2008). *Group genius: The power of creative collaboration.* New York: Basic.

Scarf, M. (2008). *September song: The good news about marriage in the later years.* New York: Riverhead.

Schaller, M., & Crandall, C. (2004). *The psychological foundations of culture.* Mahwah, NJ: Erlbaum.

Schiebel, D. (2009). Qualitative, ethnographic and performative approaches to communication. In W. F. Eadie (Ed.), *21st century communication: A reference handbook* (pp. 65–73). Thousand Oaks, CA: Sage.

Schieffelin, E., & Crittenden, R. (1991). *Like people you see in a dream.* Palo Alto, CA: Stanford University Press.

Schiesel, S. (2006, May 9). The Sims' stimulate kids who play. *Raleigh News & Observer,* p. 8E.

Schlechtweg, H. (1992). Framing Earth First!: *The McNeil/Lehrer NewsHour* and Redwood summer. In C. Oravec & J. Cantrill (Eds.), *The conference on the discourse of environmental advocacy* (pp. 262–287). Salt Lake City: University of Utah Humanities Center.

Schmid, R. (2010, July 5). Sense of touch affects behavior in startling ways. *Raleigh News & Observer,* p. 4B

Schmidt, J., & Uecker, D. (2007). Increasing understanding of routine/everyday interaction in relationships. *Communication Teacher, 21,* 111–116.

Schneider, C., & Kenny, D. (2000). Cross-sex friends who were once romantic partners: Are they platonic friends now? *Journal of Social and Personal Relationships, 17,* 451–466.

Scholz, M. (2005, June). A "simple" way to improve adherence. *RN, 68,* 82.

Schooler, D., Ward, M., Merriwether, A., & Caruthers, A. (2004). Who's that girl: Television's role in the body image of young white and black women. *Psychology of Women Quarterly, 28,* 38–47.

Schott, B. (2008, May 16). Minute waltz. *New York Times,* p. A23.

Schramm, W. (1955). *The process and effects of mass communication.* Urbana: University of Illinois Press.

Schwartz, N., & Dash, E. (2011, June 14). On college forms, a question of race or races, can perplex. *New York Times,* pp. A1, A12.

Schwartz, T. (1989, January–February).

Acceleration syndrome: Does everyone live in the fast lane nowadays? *Utne Reader,* pp. 36–43.

Scott, C., & Myers, K. (2005). The socialization of emotion: Learning emotion management at the fire station. *Journal of Applied Communication Research, 33,* 67–92.

Searle, J. (1976). *Speech acts: An essay in the philosophy of language.* London: Cambridge University Press.

Searle, J. (1995). *The construction of social reality.* New York: Free Press.

Sedikides, C., Campbell, W., Reeder, G., & Elliot, A. (1998). The self-serving bias in relational context. *Journal of Personality and Social Psychology, 74,* 3763–3864.

Seely, Megan (2007). *Fight like a girl: How to be a fearless feminist.* New York: New York University Press.

Segrin, C., Hanzal, A., & Domschke, T. (2009). Accuracy and bias in newlywed couples' perceptions of conflict styles and the association with marital satisfaction. *Communication Monographs, 76,* 107–233.

Setoodeh, R. (2006, May 22). The long goodbye. *Newsweek,* pp. 60–61.

Seligman, M. E. P. (1990). *Learned optimism.* New York: Simon & Schuster/Pocket Books.

Seligman, M. E. P. (2002). *Authentic happiness: Using the new positive psychology to realize your potential for lasting fulfillment.* New York: Free Press.

Sellinger, M. B. (1994, July 9). Candy Lightner prods Congress. *People,* pp. 102, 105.

Sennott, S. (2003, September 8). Next in toyland. *Newsweek,* p. E29.

Shabecoff, P. (2000). *Earth rising: American environmentalism in the 21st century.* Washington, DC: Island Press.

Shannon, C., & Weaver, W. (1949). *The mathematical theory of communication.* Urbana: University of Illinois Press.

Shattuck, T. R. (1980). *The forbidden experiment: The story of the wild boy of Aveyron.* New York: Farrar, Straus & Giroux.

Shaw, C. (1999). *Deciding what we watch: Taste, decency, and media ethics in the UK and the USA.* Oxford, UK: Oxford University Press.

Shenk, D. (1997). *Data smog: Surviving the information glut.* San Francisco: HarperEdge.

Shenoy, S. (2012). Navigating the third space with double consciousness: South Asian Indian women in the American workplace. In A. González, M. Houston, & V. Chen (Eds.), *Our voices: Essays in culture, ethnicity, and communication* (pp. 71–76). New York: Oxford University Press.

Shiffert, A., & Schwarz, B. (2011). Spouses' demand and withdrawal during marital conflict in relation to their subjective well-being. *Journal of Social and Personal Relationships, 28,* 262–277.

Shimanoff, S. B. (1980). *Communication rules: Theory and research.* Thousand Oaks, CA: Sage.

Shoemaker, P. (1991). *Gatekeeping.* Thousand Oaks, CA: Sage.

Sias, P., Heath, R., Perry, T., Silva, D., & Fix, B. (2004). Narratives of workplace friendship deterioration. *Journal of Social and Personal Relationships, 21,* 321–340.

Signorielli, N. (1990). Television's mean and dangerous world: A continuation of the cultural indicators perspective. In N. Signorielli & M. Morgan (Eds.), *Cultivation analysis: New directions in media effects research* (pp. 85–106). Thousand Oaks, CA: Sage.

Signorelli, N. (2009). Cultivation and media exposure. In W. F. Eadie (Ed.), *21st century communication: A reference handbook* (pp. 525–567). Thousand Oaks, CA: Sage.

Signorielli, N., & Morgan, M. (Eds.). (1990). *Cultivation analysis: New directions in media research.* Thousand Oaks, CA: Sage.

Simon, S. B. (1977). *Vulture: A modern allegory on the art of putting oneself down.* Niles, IL: Argus Communications.

Simons, G. F., Vázquez, C., & Harris, P. R. (1993). *Transcultural leadership: Empowering the diverse workforce.* Houston, TX: Gulf.

Simons, H., Morreale, J., Gronbeck, B. (2001). *Persuasion in society.* Thousand Oaks, CA: Sage.

Simons, L. I., & Zielenziger, M. (1996, March 3). Culture clash dims U.S. future in Asia. *San Jose Mercury News,* pp. A1, A22.

Singer, D. & Singer, J. (2002). *Make-believe: Games and activities for imaginative play.* Washington, DC: Magination.

Singer, P. W. (2009). *Wired for war.* New York: Penguin.

Smircich, L. (1983). Concepts of culture and organizational analysis. *Administrative Quarterly, 28,* 339–358.

Smith, R. (2009). *Strategic planning for public relations* (3rd ed.). New York: Routledge.

Snook, Scott A. (2000). *Friendly fire: The accidental shootdown of U.S. black hawks over northern Iraq.* Princeton, NJ: Princeton University Press.

Spano, S. (2003, June 1). Rude encounters versus cultural differences. *Raleigh News & Observer,* pp. 1H, 5H.

Sparks, G. (2006). *Media effects research: A basic overview* (2nd ed). Belmont, CA: Thomson Wadsworth.

Sparrow, B., Liu, J., & Wegner, D. 2011. Google effects on memory: cognitive consequences of having information at our fingertips. *Science.* http://dx.doi.org/10.1126/science.1207745

Spencer, M. (1982). *Foundations of modern sociology.* Englewood Cliffs, NJ: Prentice Hall.

Spitzack, B., & Cupach, W. (2009). Unwanted communication,

aggression, and abuse. In W. F. Eadie (Ed.), *21st century communication: A reference handbook* (pp. 444–462). Thousand Oaks, CA: Sage.

Stafford, L. (2005). *Maintaining long-distance and cross-residential relationships.* Mahwah, NJ: Erlbaum.

Stafford, L. (2009). Spouses and other intimate partnerships. In W. F. Eadie (Ed.), *21st century communication: A reference handbook* (pp. 295–302). Thousand Oaks, CA: Sage.

Stamp, G., & Sabourin, T. (1995). Accounting for violence: An analysis of male spousal abuse narratives. *Journal of Applied Communication Research, 23,* 284–307.

Steele, R. (2009). Traditional and new media. In W. F. Eadie (Ed.), *21st century communication: A reference handbook* (pp. 489–496). Thousand Oaks, CA: Sage.

Steiner, C. (1994). Scripts people live: Transactional analysis of life scripts. New York: Grove Press.

Sterling, C. H. (Ed.). (2009). *Encyclopedia of journalism.* Thousand Oaks, CA: Sage.

Stewart, C., & Cash, W. (1991). *Interviewing: Principles and practices* (6th ed.). Dubuque, IA: Wm. C. Brown.

Stewart, J., Zediker, K., & Black, L. (2004). Relationships among philosophies of dialogue. In R. Anderson, L. Baxter, & K. Cissna (Eds.), *Dialogue: Theorizing difference in communication studies* (pp. 21–38). Thousand Oaks, CA: Sage.

Stolberg, S. (2009, January 29). From the top, the White House unbuttons formal dress code. *New York Times,* pp. A1, A14.

Stone, B. (2004, June 7). Your next computer. *Newsweek,* pp. 51–54.

Stone, B. (2009, January 14). Despite news reports, task force finds online threat to children overblown. *New York Times,* p. A14.

Stroman, C. A., & Dates, J. L. (2008). African Americans, Latinos, Asians, and Native Americans in the media. In P. E. Jamieson & D. Romer (Eds.), *The changing portrayal of adolescents in the media since 1950.* (pp. 198–219). New York: Oxford.

Student Use. (2011, August 26). *Chronicle of Higher Education, Almanac Issue 2011–2012,* p. 51.

Suls, J., Martin, R., & Wheeler, L. (2002). Social comparison: Why, with whom and with what effect? *Current Directions in Psychological Science, 11,* 159–163.

Swain, S. (1989). Covert intimacy: Closeness in men's friendships. In B. Risman & P. Schwartz (Eds.), *Gender and intimate relationships* (pp. 71–86). Belmont, CA: Wadsworth.

Sypher, B. (1984). Seeing ourselves as others see us. *Communication Research, 11,* 97–115.

Taft, J. (2004). Girl power politics: Pop-culture barriers and organizational resistance. In A. Harris (Ed.), *All about the girl* (pp. 69–78). London: Routledge.

Tanno, D. (1997). Names, narratives, and the evolution of ethnic identity. In A. González, M. Houston, & V. Chen (Eds.), *Our voices: Essays in culture, ethnicity, and communication* (pp. 28–34). Los Angeles: Roxbury.

Tashiro, T., & Frazier, P. (2003). "I'll never be in a relationship like that again": Personal growth following romantic relationship breakup. *Personal Relationships, 10,* 113–128.

Tavernise, S. (2011, June 14). Adoptions rise by same-sex couples, despite legal barriers. *New York Times,* pp. A10, A15.

Tavris, C. (1992). *The mismeasure of woman.* New York: Simon & Schuster.

Taylor, M. (1999). *Imaginary companions and the children who create them.* New York: Oxford University Press.

Telework. (2010). http://www.telework .gov/Reports_and_Studies/Annual_ Reports/2010teleworkreport.pdf

Thompson, F., & Grundgenett, D. (1999). Helping disadvantaged learners build effective learning skills. *Education, 120,* 130–135.

Tiggemann, M. (2005). Television and adolescent body image: The role of content and viewing motivation. *Journal of Social and Clinical Psychology, 24,* 361–381.

Tilsley, A. (2010, July 2). New policies accommodate transgender students. *Chronicle of Higher Education,* pp. A19–A20.

Timmerman, C., & Scott, C. (2006). Virtually working: Communicative and structural predictors of media use and key outcomes in virtual work teams. *Communication Monographs, 73,* 108–136.

Ting-Toomey, S. (2005) The matrix of face: An updated Face-Negotiation Theory. In W.B. Gudykunst (Ed.), *Theorizing about intercultural communication* (pp. 71–92). Thousand Oaks, CA: Sage.

Tolhuizen, J. H. (1989). Communication strategies for intensifying dating relationships: Identification, use, and structure. *Journal of Social and Personal Relationships, 6,* 413–434.

Tracy, S. J., Lutgen-Sandvik, P., & Albrets, J. (2006). Nightmares, demons, and slaves: Exploring painful metaphors of workplace bullying. *Management Communication Quarterly, 20,* 1–38.

Trees, A. (2006). Attachment theory: The reciprocal relationship between family communication and attachment patterns. In D. O. Braithwaite & L. A. Baxter (Eds.), *Engaging theories in family communication: Multiple perspectives* (pp. 165–180). Thousand Oaks, CA: Sage.

Trees, A. R. (2000). Nonverbal communication and the support process: International sensitivity in interactions between mothers and young adult children. *Communication Monographs, 67,* 239–261.

Triandis, H. C. (1990). Cross-cultural studies of individualism and collectivism. In J. J. Berman (Ed.), *Cross-cultural perspectives* (pp. 41–133). Lincoln: University of Nebraska Press.

Trice, H., & Beyer, J. (1984). Studying organizational cultures through rites and ceremonials. *Academy of Management Review, 9,* 653–669.

Troy, A., & Laurenceau, J. (2006). Interracial and intraracial romantic relationships: The search for differences in satisfaction, conflict, and attachment style. *Journal of Social and Personal Relationships, 23,* 65–80.

Tsai, F., & Reis, H. (2009). Perceptions by and of lonely people in social networks. *Personal Reltionships, 16,* 221–238.

Tugend, A. (2011, July 2). Comparing yourself to others: It's not all bad. *New York Times,* p. B6.

Turkle, S. (2002). Identity crisis. In E. Bucy (Ed.), *Living in the information age* (pp. 155–161). Belmont, CA: Wadsworth.

Turow, J. (2008). *Media today* (3rd ed.). New York: Routledge.

Turow, J., & McAllilster, M. (Eds.). (2009). *The advertising and consumer culture reader.* New York: Routledge.

Tusing, K., & Dillard, J. (2000). The sounds of dominance: Vocal precursors of perceived dominance during interpersonal influence. *Human Communication Research, 26,* 148–171.

Ueland, B. (1992, November–December). Tell me more: On the fine art of listening. *Utne Reader,* pp. 104–109.

Umble, D. (2000). *Holding the line: The telephone in Old Order Mennonite and Amish life.* Baltimore, MD: Johns Hopkins University Press.

Underwood, A., & Adler, J. (2005, April 25). When cultures clash. *Newsweek,* pp. 68–72.

Valkenburg, P. (2004). *Children's responses to the screen.* Mahwah, NJ: Erlbaum.

Van Maanen, J., & Barley, S. (1985). Cultural organization: Fragments of a theory. In P. J. Frost et al. (Eds.), *Organizational culture* (pp. 31–54). Thousand Oaks, CA: Sage.

Van Styke, E. (1999). *Listening to conflict: Finding constructive solutions to workplace disputes.* New York: AMA Communications.

Verderber, R., Verderber, K., & Sellnow, D. (2012). *The challenge of effective speaking* (15th ed.). Belmont, CA: Wadsworth/ Cengage.

Vivian, J. (2006). *The media of mass communication* (8th ed.). Boston: Allyn & Bacon.

Vocate, D. (Ed.). (1994). *Intrapersonal communication: Different voices, different minds.* Mahwah, NJ: Erlbaum.

Wagner, E. (2001, May 11). Listening: Hear today, probably gone tomorrow. *Business Journal,* p. 25.

Walker, S. (2007). *Style and status: Selling beauty to African American women.* Lexington: University of Kentucky Press.

Washington, J. (2011, January 10) For minorities, new 'digital divide' seen. Pew Research Center: http:// www.pewinternet.org/Media-Mentions/2011/For-minorities-new-digital-divide-seen.aspx

Waters, J. (2011, July 24). Facebook is fun for recruiters, too. *Raleigh News & Observer,* p. 5E.

Watzlawick, P., Beavin, J., & Jackson, D. D. (1967). *Pragmatics of human communication.* New York: Norton.

Wayne, T. (2010, December 12). Digital divide is a matter of income. Pew Center for Research: http://www .nytimes.com/2010/12/13/business/ media/13drill.html

Weaver, C. (1972). *Human listening: Processes and behavior.* Indianapolis, IN: Bobbs-Merrill.

Wegner, H., Jr. (2005). Disconfirming communication and self-verification in marriage: Associations among the demand/withdraw interaction pattern, feeling understood, and marital satisfaction. *Journal of Social and Personal Relationships, 22,* 19–31.

Weinstock, H., Berman, S., & Cates, W., Jr. (2004). Sexually transmitted diseases among American youth: Incidence and prevalence estimates, 2000. *Perspectives on Sexual and Reproductive Health, 36,* 6–10.

Weinstock, J., & Bond, L. (2000). Conceptions of conflict in close friendships and ways of knowing among young college women: A developmental framework. *Journal of Social and Personal Relationships, 17,* 687–696.

Weisinger, H. (1996). *Anger at work.* New York: William Morrow.

Weiss, K. (1999, January 25). *Los Angeles Times* [Online]. Retrieved from http://www.latimes.com/home/news/asection/t000007602.html.

Weiss, S. E. (1987). The changing logic of a former minor power. In H. Binnendijk (Ed.), *National negotiating styles* (pp. 44–74). Washington, DC: Department of State.

Weitz, P., & Weitz, C. (Directors). 2002. *About a boy* [Motion picture]. USA: Universal Studios.

Werner, C., Altman, I., & Oxley, D. (1985). Temporal aspects of homes: A transactional perspective. In I. Altman & C. M. Werner (Eds.), *Home environments: Vol. 8: Human behavior and environment: Advances in theory and research* (pp. 1–32). Thousand Oaks, CA: Sage.

West, C., & Zimmerman, D. H. (1987). Doing gender. *Gender and Society, 1,* 125–151.

Whitman, T., White, R., O'Mara, K., & Goeke-Morey, M. (1999). Environmental aspects of infant health and illness. In T. Whitman & T. Merluzzi (Eds.), *Life-span perspectives on health and illness* (pp. 105–124). Mahwah, NJ: Erlbaum.

Whitty, M. (2007). Revealing the "real" me, searching for the "actual" you:

Presentations of self on an Internet dating site. *Computers in Human Behavior, 24,* 1707–1723.

Wilco, L. (June 15, 2011). Personal communication.

Williams, K. D. (2001). *Ostracism: The power of silence.* New York: Guilford.

Williams, G. (1995). *Life on the color line: The true story of a white boy who discovered he was black.* New York: Dutton.

Williams, T. (2011, July 23). Town turns to iPads in cost-cutting move. *New York Times,* p. A13.

Wilson, G., & Goodall, H., Jr. (1991). *Interviewing in context.* New York: McGraw-Hill.

Wilson, J. F., & Arnold, C. C. (1974). *Public speaking as a liberal art* (4th ed.). Boston: Allyn & Bacon.

Winans, J. A. (1938). *Speechmaking.* New York: Appleton-Century-Crofts.

Winters, L., & DeBose, H. (Eds.). (2004). *New faces in a changing America.* Thousand Oaks, CA: Sage.

Wolvin, A. (2009). Listening, understanding and misunderstanding. In W. F. Eadie (Ed.), *21st century communication: A reference handbook* (pp. 137–146). Thousand Oaks, CA: Sage.

Wong, G. (2011, April 7). China's Internet protestors. *Raleigh News & Observer,* p. 3A.

Wong, K. (2012). Working through identity: Understanding class in the context of race, ethnicity, and gender. In A. González, M. Houston, & V. Chen (Eds.), *Our voices: Essays in culture, ethnicity, and communication* (pp. 254–260). New York: Oxford University Press.

Wong, N., & Cappella, J. (2009). Antismoking threat and efficacy appeals: Effects on smoking cessation intentions for smokers with low and high readiness to quit. *Journal of Applied Communication Research, 37,* 1–20.

Wood, J. T. (1982). Communication and relational culture: Bases for

the study of human relationships. *Communication Quarterly, 30,* 75–84.

Wood, J. T. (1992a). *Spinning the symbolic web: Human communication as symbolic interaction.* Norwood, NJ: Ablex.

Wood, J. T. (1992b). Telling our stories: Narratives as a basis for theorizing sexual harassment. *Journal of Applied Communication Research, 4,* 349–363.

Wood, J. T. (1993a). Diversity and commonality: Sustaining their tension in communication courses. *Western Journal of Communication, 57,* 367–380.

Wood, J. T. (1993c). Enlarging conceptual boundaries: A critique of research on interpersonal communication. In S. P. Bowen & N. J. Wyatt (Eds.), *Transforming visions: Feminist critiques in communication studies* (pp. 19–49). Cresskill, NJ: Hampton.

Wood, J. T. (1993d). Gender and moral voice: From woman's nature to standpoint theory. *Women's Studies in Communication, 15,* 1–24.

Wood, J. T. (1994c). Saying it makes it so: The discursive construction of sexual harassment. In S. Bingham (Ed.), *Conceptualizing sexual harassment as discursive practice* (pp. 17–30). Westport, CT: Praeger.

Wood, J. T. (1997). Diversity in dialogue: Communication between friends. In J. Makau and R. Arnett (Eds.), *Ethics of communication in an age of diversity* (pp. 5–26). Urbana: University of Illinois Press.

Wood, J. T. (1998). *But I thought you meant …: Misunderstandings in human communication.* Mountain View, CA: Mayfield.

Wood, J. T. (2001a). *Communication theories in action* (2nd ed.). Belmont, CA: Wadsworth.

Wood, J. T. (2001b). The normalization of violence in heterosexual relationships: Women's narratives of love and violence. *Journal of Social and Personal Relationships, 18,* 239–261.

Wood, J. T. (2001c). He says/she says: Misunderstandings between men and women. In D. Braithwaite & J. T. Wood (Eds.), *Case studies in interpersonal communication: Processes and problems* (pp. 93–100). Belmont, CA: Wadsworth.

Wood, J. T. (2004a). Buddhist influences on scholarship and teaching. *Journal of Communication and Religion*, pp. 32–39.

Wood, J. T. (2004b). Monsters and victims: Male felons' accounts of intimate partner violence. *Journal of Social and Personal Relationships, 21*, 555–576.

Wood, J. T. (2006). Critical feminist theories of interpersonal communication: Voice and visibility in cultural life. In D. O. Braithwaite & L. A. Baxter (Eds.), *Engaging theories of interpersonal communication: Multiple perspectives* (pp. 197–212). Thousand Oaks, CA: Sage.

Wood, J. T. (2006a). Chopping the carrots: Creating intimacy, moment by moment. In J. T. Wood & S. W. Duck (Eds.), *Composing relationships: Communication in everyday life* (pp. 24–35). Belmont, CA: Thomson Wadsworth.

Wood, J. T. (2006b). Critical feminist theories: A provocative perspective on families. In D. O. Braithwaite & L. A. Baxter (Eds.), *Engaging theories in family communication: Multiple perspectives* (pp. 197–242). Thousand Oaks, CA: Sage.

Wood, J.T. (2010). The can-do discourse and young women's anticipations of future. *Women & Language, 33*, 103–107.

Wood, J.T. (2011). Which ruler? What are we measuring?: Thoughts on theorizing the division of domestic labor. *Journal of Family Communication, 11*, 39–49.

Wood, J. T. (2013). *Gendered lives: Communication, gender and culture* (10th ed.). Belmont, CA: Wadsworth.

Wood, J. T., Dendy, L., Dordek, E., Germany, M., & Varallo, S. (1994). Dialectic of difference: A thematic analysis of intimates' meanings for differences. In K. Carter & M. Presnell (Eds.), *Interpretive approaches to interpersonal communication* (pp. 115–136). New York: State University of New York Press.

Wood, J. T., & Duck, S. W. (Eds.) (2006a). *Composing relationships: Communication in everyday life*. Belmont, CA: Thomson Wadsworth.

Wood, J. T., & Duck, S. W. (2006b). Composing relationships: Communication in everyday life (Introduction). In J. T. Wood & S. W. Duck (Eds.), *Composing relationships: Communication in everyday life* (pp. 1–13). Belmont, CA: Thomson Wadsworth.

Wood, J. T., & Inman, C. C. (1993). In a different mode: Masculine styles of communicating closeness. *Journal of Applied Communication Research, 21*, 279–295.

Workplacebullying.org. (2010).

Workplace Privacy (2011). Fact Sheet 7. http://management.about .com/gi/o.htm?zi=1/XJ&zTi=1& sdn=management&cdn=mone y&tm=53&gps=464_1035_100 1_592&f=00&su=p560.11.336. ip_&tt=2&bt=0&bts=0&zu=http% 3A//www.privacyrights.org/fs/fs7- work.htm. Accessed July 5, 2011.

Yakin, B. (Director). 2000. *Remember the Titans* [Motion picture]. USA: Buena Vista Pictures.

Yamada, D. (2010). Workplace bullying and American employment law: A ten-year progress report and assessment *Comparative Labor Law & Policy Journal, 32*, 251–268.

Yen, H. (2011, April 27). As more women earn degrees, more men stay home. *Raleigh News & Observer*, pp. 1A, 6A.

Yerby, J., Buerkel-Rothfuss, N., & Bochner, A. (1990). *Understanding family communication*. Scottsdale, AZ: Gorsuch Scarisbrick.

Yost, B. (2004). We all need someone to lean on. Online edition of *IndyStar*. Retrieved May 21, 2004, from http://www.indystar.com/ articles/2/148176-9362-052.html.

Young, J. (2006, June 2). The fight for classroom attention: Professor vs. laptop. *Chronicle of Higher Education*, pp. A27–A29.

Young, J. (2011, May 13). Smartphones on campus: The search for 'killer' apps. *Chronicle of Higher Education*, pp. B6–B7.

Young, S., Wood, J. T., Phillips, G. M., & Pedersen, D. (2001). *Group discussion: A practical guide to participation and leadership* (3rd ed.). Prospect Heights, IL: Waveland.

Zeleny, J. (2008, November 16). Life without beloved BlackBerry awaits. *Raleigh News & Observer*, p. 4A.

Zichuhr, K. (2010, December). Generations online in 2010. Pew Internet & American Life Project: http://pewresearch.org/pubs/1831/ generations-online-2010.

Zorn, T. (1991). Construct system development, transformational leadership, and leadership messages. *Southern Communication Journal, 56*, 178–193.

Zuckerman, L. (2002). Questions abound as media influence grows for a handful. In E. Bucy (Ed.), *Living in the information age* (pp. 139–142). Belmont, CA: Wadsworth.

Index

Note: Boldfaced page numbers refer to definitions of terms. Page numbers followed by the *italicized* letter *f* refer to figures.